MEAT DISHES IN THE INTERNATIONAL CUISINE

Meat dishes

in the international cuisine

Conceived and created by
René Kramer

Editor: Professor John Fuller

VIRTUE & COMPANY LIMITED
London, Dublin and Coulsdon

British Library Cataloguing in Publication Data
.Meat dishes in the international cuisine.
  1. Cookery (Meat)
  I. Kramer, Rene   II. Fuller, John
  III. Fleischgereichte in der Internationale
  küche. *English*
  641.6'6   TX749

  ISBN 0-900778-21-0

Copyright © 1983 Zomer & Keuning Boeken B.V., Ede, the Netherlands.
English edition copyright © 1984 Virtue & Company Ltd., 25 Breakfield,
Coulsdon, Surrey CR3 2UE.

Printed in Great Britain for Virtue & Company Ltd.,
by Ebenezer Baylis & Son Ltd, The Trinity Press, Worcester and London.
Colour plates printed in the Netherlands.

iv

Foreword

At one time people used the word meat as a synonym for food. The term 'meat and drink' embraced in common parlance everything ingested by man. Yet despite the dominant part meat played, and still fulfills, in human diet, or perhaps because of it, opinions about its role have been strong and varied. Dr. Buchanan, the author of popular medical works of the 18th century, believed that the 'choleric disposition of the English is almost proverbial, and if he were to assign a cause of it, it would be their living so much on animal food'. He concluded that 'there is no doubt but this induces a ferocity of temper unknown to man whose food is chiefly taken from the vegetable kingdom'. There were, however, many other more balanced and temperate appraisals of flesh foods and even in 1799 another medical man, Dr. A. F. M. Willich, was endorsing the virtues of a mixed diet. He advocated that 'in general, two-thirds or three-fourths of vegetables, to one half or fourth part of meat, appears to be the most proper. By this judicious mixture, we may avoid diseases arising from a too copious use of either'.

Today, most nutritionists would advocate a similar approach to a balanced and varied diet in which meat should feature. Dietetic opinion is now shaded by a more sophisticated appreciation than in the eighteenth century of the benefits and drawbacks in meat eating; for example of the effects of cholesterol in animal fat. There remains virtually universal acceptance that meat is, and will continue to be, a prime element in mankind's meals in the western world. This applies particularly to those main meals of the day to which we attach such importance.

However much medical opinion about diet may be affected by research, meat seems destined to retain its place, gained over many centuries of dining, as the principal element in most western main meals. What *has* changed are the economics of catering. This change affects feeding families at home, and catering by professional restaurateurs and hoteliers for those eating out.

A quarter of a century ago meat was cheaper, for example, than chicken. The fowl was so expensive as to make a roast chicken a luxury. Today, intensive farming methods make this bird a relatively cheap item. Its cheapness serves to promote further the idea of meat, especially

v

prime cuts, as the pre-eminent feature of a fine meal. At the same time, catering economics prompt all of us to consider even more carefully how best to exploit the cheaper cuts. Not only are those less costly parts of beef, lamb, pork and veal highly acceptable when intelligently incorporated into dishes, but there is growing interest in how offal, like feet, tail and head from the outside of the animal and interior offals such as heart, liver, kidneys may be used both at home and by restaurants. This book is timely because there is great need to make the best use of what is a dietetically important, relatively costly but much demanded element in domestic and professional dining.

When teaching basic catering economics to those entering our industry, I often refer to the significance of the letter 'P', especially for protein, price and profit. Meat is first class protein. Because it is more expensive than all but the most rare vegetables, it is a price determinant in menu and dish costing. In the old days, caterers used to work for profit by food cost percentage. Today, with labour so costly and with the protein element in meals similarly dear, new approaches to catering pricing are applied. A low percentage on a high cost item can still yield a satisfactory margin of profit. Hence high quality cuts like rib roast from carveries, steaks in grill room and steak houses, and escalopes from the guéridon, may be high cost items but they are ones on which a lower percentage can still yield a satisfactory profit margin.

When dealing with cheaper cuts, caterers have always had to be mindful of the cost of human time and skill when these have to be applied in creating acceptable dishes. It is no wonder that epigrammes made from a breast of lamb are less commonly seen on menus than they were pre-war when labour costs remained static for many years. Dishes like these are, however, still attractive in cost-conscious feeding. Many dishes in this book require time, trouble and labour for their production. They will need careful costing for professionals, and even amateurs in domestic kitchens must judge how much time, as well as food cost, to allocate to meal creation.

However, both professional and amateur alike will, I am sure, agree upon one thing. It is that the ideas in this book that have emanated from many chefs from all over the world, offer dishes with great visual appeal and which not only will be tried themselves in our own kitchens, but will stimulate an adventurous spirit in further exploiting meat for public and private catering.

Except that this volume is a most substantial one, there is a case for launching it with Robert Louis Stevenson's godspeed:

'Go little book, and wish to all
Flowers in the garden, meat in the hall
A bin of wine, a spice of wit
A house with lawns enclosing it'

if only because 'meat in the hall' is enhanced or otherwise by the ambience in which it is eaten. Contributors here cover other aspects relevant to meat presentation. I have never much cared for the jargon expression 'meal experience' but it does remind us of elements other than commodities and cooking which are required to provide satisfaction to diners. The 'bin of wine', elements of service, dish decor and service factors are all touched upon in the pages which follow and complement the treatment of meat.

vi

Above all, this book like so many of the other fine books in this series, conveys much of its message visually. Its pictures both instruct in techniques like carving and dish assembly and will inspire cooks through their impact.

John Fuller

Publisher's Preface

During the past decade Virtue & Company have been proud to produce the English language versions of an incomparable series of colourful and authoritative books for the professional chef: MODERN FRENCH CULINARY ART, FISH & SHELL-FISH, THE NEW INTERNATIONAL CONFECTIONER, BUFFETS & RECEPTIONS—taken together there are now nearly 150,000 copies in print in the English language alone, with many foreign editions available. These superb books are now joined by a further title, MEAT DISHES IN THE INTERNATIONAL CUISINE, and we are confident that it will prove just as successful as the others and establish itself as an indispensable recipe book for every chef and restaurateur.

As before, the book was conceived by René Kramer of Switzerland who is also responsible for the beautiful colour plates which have done much to establish the popularity of this series. We have also been very fortunate to have secured the editorial services of Professor John Fuller who has provided expert help and guidance.

The layout of the book follows the pattern established by Buffets & Receptions, providing both metric and imperial measures for the ingredients. The title of each dish is usually presented with the English translation first followed by the French version and then the national name. In some cases this means a degree of repetition but we feel that this is better than a lack of information.

At the end of the recipe we give the country of origin of the dish and the chef who contributed it. Observant readers will note that there are a number of gentlemen who appear to be multinational, but the country of origin applies only to the dish!

Contents

ACKNOWLEDGEMENTS

The publishers wish to express their gratitude to all the organisations and individuals from the world of gastronomy who have contributed to this book, making their comprehensive professional knowledge and practical experience available for this purpose.

We would like to make special mention of the following experts for their contributions: –

Karl Brunnengräber
Gottfried Albert
Werner Dabernig
Maximilian Dick
Ernst Faseth
Josef Haueis
Erich Istvan
Johann Kögl
Uwe Kohl
Alfred Lengheim
Eduard Mayer
Adolf Meindl
Erich Muskovich
Ewald Plachutta
Franz Sailer
Siegfried Seelos
Helmuth Stadlbauer
Franz Zodl
André Béghin
Roger J. Souvereyns-Verbrugghe
Silvio Ballinari
Edward Mathis
Kenneth H.C. Lo
Vilém Vrabec
Eric Cederholm
Jens Peter Kolbeck
Karl-Otto Schmidt
Jean-Paul Bossée-Francois
Jean Esslinger
Marcel François
Pierre Gleize
Emile Jung
François Kiener
Patrick Klipfel
Wladimir Levyckyi
Armand Roth
Jean Schillinger
Rudolf Achenbach
Otto Brust
Erwin Frohmann

Gerhard Gartner
Susanne Gartner
Walter Haas
Michael König
Bernd Moos
Werner Schall
Samuel J. Chalmers
Anton Mosimann
Victor Sassie
Willy Bode
Patricia Scobie
Emil Wälti
Julius Bandl
Józszf Csanyi
László Csizmadia
Gyula Gullner
Attila Kondorosi
Zsolt Körmendy
Egon Lontai
Dénes Nemeskövi
Percy Sullivan
Hermann Wohl
Guido Belotti
Franco Boffetti
Francesco Borari
Fiorenzo Boroni
Carlo Calvetti
Ambrogio Cella
Sergio Chiesa
Franco Colombani
Mario De Filippis
Daniel Drouadaine
Attilio Gatti
Marco Guarnori
Franco Mamoli
Luigi Mamoli
Gualtiero Marchesi
Eugenio Medagliani
Gigi Milesi
Dino Oberti

Enzo Ronzoni
Mario Saporito
Salvatore Schifano
Alfredo Sonzogni
Maurizio Tassi
Paolo Teverini
Giovanni Maria Tobia
Nico Donato
Franco Vurro
T. Nakanishi
Felix Real
Germain Gretsch-Rösner
Bernard van Beurten
Paul Fagel
Alexander Koene
Hroar Dege
Rolf Froshaug
Otto Ramsbacher
Günther Rett
Arvid Skogseth
Josep Lladonosa
Eric Carlström

Giovanni Albisetti
Josef Ammann
Ivo Balestra
Willi Bartenbach
Paola Bianchi
Giulio Casazza
Gérard van Dijk
Robert Haupt-Felber
Roger Fernand Hoffmann
Kurt Jordi
Otto Ledermann
Otto Franz Müller
Roger Parrot
François Perret
Hermann Rieger
Rudolf Roth
Vito Vanini
Sandro Volonté
Manfred Wyler
Otto Ledermann
Hermann G. Rusch

The general and technical chapters were written by Otto Ledermann and Emil Wälti, technical teachers, Basel, Switzerland.

The chapter on *Meat Dishes and Wines* was written by
Alberto Gozzi, technical teacher, Stresa, Italy;
Georg Guth, retired restaurant manager, Karben, Germany;
Christoph von Ritter-Záhony, Ing. agr., Lausanne, Switzerland;
Vito Vanini, restaurant owner, Agno, Switzerland.

The original book was edited by Mrs. Helene von Ritter and Mr. René Kramer of René Kramer AG, publishers, Lugano, Switzerland.

The English edition was translated by Mrs. A. Jackson and edited by Prof. John Fuller.

Photographs of dishes and interiors were taken in the following establishments: –

Restaurants
K & K Restaurant am Waagplatz, Salzburg, Austria
Peterskeller, Salzburg, Austria
Zu den 3 Husaren, Vienna, Austria
Salons van dijck, Kermt, Belgium
Ken Lo's Memories of China, London, England
Le Talboth, Dedham, Colchester, Essex, England

The Gay Hussar, London, England
Au Nid de Cigognes, Mutzig, France
Du Kochersberg, Landersheim, France
Au Crocodile, Strasbourg, France
La Bonne Etape, Château Arnoux, France
Gala, Aachen, Germany
Del Sole, Maleo, Italy
Gualtiero Marchesi, Milan, Italy
La Taverna, Campione d'Italia, Italy
Real, Vaduz, Liechtenstein
Handelsstand, Trondheim, Norway
Alpe Vicania, Vico Morcote, Switzerland
Bianchi-Biassi, Lugano, Switzerland
Gambrinus, Lugano, Switzerland
Da Ivo, Ascona, Switzerland

Hotels
Goldener Hirsch, Salzburg, Austria
Schlosshotel Klessheim, Salzburg, Austria
The Dorchester, London, England
La Chenaudière, Colroy-la-Roche, France
Duna-Intercontinental, Budapest, Hungary
Okura Inter-Continental, Amsterdam, Netherlands
International, Oerlikon, Switzerland

Delicatessen suppliers
Rudolf Achenbach, Sulzbach, Germany
Pannonia, Budapest, Hungary

Test kitchens
G. & W. Faseth, Vienna, Austria
Karl Brunnengräber, Ruhpolding (Obb.), Germany

We thank the following professional associations, schools and firms: –

Gastgewerbefachschule der Wiener Gastwirte, Vienna, Austria
Hotelfachschule Wien, Vienna, Austria
Landesberufsschule für das Gastgewerbe, Absam, Tyrol, Austria
Verband der Köche Deutschlands e.V., Frankfurt am Main, Germany
Hungarian Chefs' Association, Budapest, Hungary
Associazione Cuochi Agrigento, Agrigento, Italy
Associazione Italia Settentrionale Cuochi Bergamo, Bergamo, Italy
Federazione Italiana Cuochi, Milan, Italy
Hotel School Maggia, Stresa, Italy
Firma Forenede Margarinenfabrikker, Oslo, Norway
Haco-Service-Culinaire, Gümlingen, Switzerland

We would also like to thank the photographers: –

Ferdinand Schreiber, Hof bei Salzburg, Austria
de Schutter, Antwerp, Belgium – Walter Jouret, Ludo van Mechelen
John Lee, London, England
Marcel Ehrhard, Strasbourg, France
Johannes Wanke, Ruhpolding (Obb.), Germany
Karoly Szelényi, Budapest, Hungary
Francesco Brotto, Brescia, Italy
Massimo Listri, Florence, Italy
Enzo Minnino, Milan, Italy
Pierluigi Portner, Milan, Italy
Martino Schiera, Milan, Italy
Mario Toffolatti, Milan, Italy
Ed Suister, Amsterdam, Netherlands
Roberto Paltrinieri, Breganzona, Switzerland

The line drawings in the various chapters are by Miss Annemarie Kuriger, Bern, Switzerland.

Part 1:

General

1 Meat for Nutrition and Enjoyment

Meat in the diet

Meat is defined as any part of an animal that is fit for human consumption. In Britain this is normally confined to the muscular parts and offal of beef cattle, pigs, sheep and rabbits. There is also an increasing use of deer and hare which is adding a variety of flavours and textures to our menus.

Meat forms an important part of the daily diet, for it is a valuable source of good quality protein which is essential to the body. It is also important as a source of energy, particularly if it contains large amounts of fat. It is one of the major sources of B vitamins in our diet and is rich in iron and phosphorus.

Chemical composition of meat

Even though it may be surprising to learn that meat contains 70% water, its high economic value is justified for it is one of the main sources of dietary protein from which our bodies obtain the amino acids required for cell repair. The following table clearly shows the differences between the various types of lean meat, particularly the fat content, which is not usually visible.

Table to show the average contents of lean meat
(Source: The Composition of Foods, Paul & Southgate)

	Beef %	Veal %	Pork %	Lamb %	Rabbit %	Calf's Liver %
Water	74	75	72	70	25	70
Protein	20	21	21	21	22	20
Fat	5	3	7	8	4	7
Carbohydrate	—	—	—	—	—	2
Minerals	1	1	2	1	1	1

Muscular structure

Microscopic examination shows bundles of small muscular fibres held together by a sheath of connective tissue (sarcolemma). The length and thickness of these bundles varies in every animal according to the natural function of the muscle concerned. The fibres are also visible to the naked eye; the shorter they are, the softer the connective tissue and the more tender and digestible is the meat.

Depending on the animal's condition and the way it has been fattened, fatty tissue develops between the muscle fibres. Meat containing such tissue is called 'marbled' by butchers, for whom this is a sign of quality. Although the uninformed customer tends to reject meat containing such threads of fat, it is much esteemed by the expert and by all those – chefs, for example – who constantly handle meat in the kitchen. Marbling makes meat tender and succulent, brings out its flavour and facilitates its preparation.

Nutritive value

Meat contains the following nutrients: protein, fat, mineral salts, and vitamins; liver contains small amounts of carbohydrate. Its energy value may be expressed in terms of calories (1g fat = 9 calories, 1g protein = 4 calories). On the assumption that an adult male needs 2,500-3,500 calories per day, depending on his size, age and occupation, with a protein requirement of 63-84 g a large part of his protein requirement and approximately one third of his energy needs can be supplied by one meat meal per day.

Animal fats

All good cooks and every true gourmet appreciate the quality of fat meat, yet at the present time the value of good marbling is not generally recognised by the consumer. The fat content of meat determines not only its calorific value, but also its flavour, succulence and tenderness. Since the diet should be as varied as possible it is understandable that too much fat cannot be beneficial. Yet fat has the highest calorie content of all nutrients and can easily be used if there is an increased requirement for energy. This can be met by choosing a piece of meat with a higher fat content, combining additional nutritive value with an excellent flavour.

Fats are composed of glycerol and fatty acids. The latter, which are required by the body, are subdivided into saturated and unsaturated fatty acids. Like our diet as a whole our intake of fatty acids should be as varied and balanced as possible.

The quality of meat

In any one animal there are no primary differences in quality between the various pieces of meat as far as the actual muscular flesh is concerned. There are, however, differences in the shape and length of the muscular fibres and therefore in the tenderness of the meat, for instance between a muscle which has been subject to a great deal of activity and one which has not (leg of beef as against fillet). These differences are even more marked than those found between young and old animals. This is why some pieces of meat are more sought after than others and hence more expensive.

Meat is therefore classified on a quality basis, both for sale as butcher's meat and for manufacturing. The quality is considered good if the following criteria are met.

If the animal has firm flesh, has been well fed and is of the right age.

If the animal has been well rested before slaughter.

If the animal has been properly slaughtered.

If the rules of hygiene and cleanliness have been observed.

If the carcase has been transported under optimum conditions.

If provision has been made for rapid refrigeration and the appropriate hanging time.

If dissection and cleaning of the carcase satisfy optimum requirements.

If the meat to be displayed for sale looks as attractive and appetising as the customer has a right to expect.

Animals for the meat market

The main types of animals for the meat market are beef cattle, pigs and sheep. Beef cattle are divided into several categories:

Calf – young ox up to 6 months old.

Heifer – young female up to about 18 months, i.e. before calving.

Bull calf – young male up to 18 months old.

Steer – castrated male particularly suitable for fattening for the meat market. In general the meat is leaner than that of a cow or heifer. These animals provide plentiful amounts of meat with good display features, but the quality does not bear comparison with other, fatter types of meat which the knowledgeable buyer will prefer.

Cow – adult female after calving, up to five years old. A well fattened cow provides excellent butcher's meat. Beyond this age cows are used for milking or manufacturing.

Bull – entire adult male used for breeding. Its muscles are very well developed and the coarse-fibred meat is mostly used for manufacturing.

Butcher's meat

This is meat from young animals especially suitable for retail sale and immediate use in the kitchen and it includes the flesh of heifers, bull calves, young pigs up to 100 kg live weight, and lambs. Apart from being young, the animals should be well-fed, with well developed muscles containing a marbling of fat, if prime quality is to be guaranteed.

Meat for sausage making and other manufacturing

Sausages are made with meat unsuitable for use as fresh meat for the table but suitable for making various meat products. It is mostly the flesh of older animals – cows, steers and sheep, as well as heavy pigs, i.e. animals with leaner and more strongly developed muscles. Its inferior quality limits its use to sausage making, canning and other forms of processing.

Sausages in Britain are generally divided into three main types. (1) Fresh sausages made from raw meat and fat with a rusk filler, the common ones being beef, pork or chipolata. They are purchased raw and need to be grilled or fried. Unlike other sausages, they are perishable and should be eaten within a few days of manufacture.

(2) Cooked sausages which are made from raw meats but cooked before sale. Luncheon meats, liver sausage, black puddings and frankfurters come into this category. They can be eaten cold or warmed through before serving.

(3) Dried sausages are the larger cured sausages imported from Europe and are normally sliced and served cold. Salamis and cervalat sausages are the most common ones of this type to be found in our shops.

The colour of meat

The colour of meat depends on its myoglobin content, i.e. on the pigment in the muscular tissue. Colour is an aid in identifying the type of meat, the category, age and quality of the animal. Where beef is concerned, good quality ox meat is bright pink, reddish or tinged with light violet in the case of a bull calf (Italian 'vittelone'). As already mentioned, there should be a marbling of fat, which gives the meat a lighter appearance. Other types of beef from young, well-fed animals are of a deeper red colour and also contain marbling.

The fat cover is another sign of quality. It takes the form of a thin white layer in the bull calf or adult; in the heifer it is light yellow, and in the cow a greyish yellow. This cover is found over certain parts such as the ribs or fillet.

If veal is quite white, the calf has been entirely milk fed, whereas pink or red meat comes from a grass fed calf. The colour differences are due to pigmentation, however, not to the quality of the meat, nor to its flavour which may be more pronounced in darker meat. It is also wrong to think that white meat originates from sickly calves, or that darker veal is less valuable or less tender.

Some calves fall into a lower category and are unsuitable for fattening. They are killed and used in making fine sausages. Animals of this kind are recognised, not so much by the colour of their flesh, as by their conformation, which shows much poorer development than in calves suitable for butcher's meat.

The colour of pork also depends a great deal on feeding. There may even be differences between cuts from the same animal. Nevertheless older, well-fattened pigs have somewhat darker flesh, which may vary from light pink to rose-red, or even greyish-red. They are fatter, but their flesh is firmer and for this reason they are used in the manufacture of sausages as well as various types of charcuterie. Unfortunately the tendency to avoid excessive fat formation in pigs has resulted in the breeding of leaner and leaner animals with a detrimental effect on the quality of the meat, which has become leaner and lighter, but also more watery and less nutritious. In general, firm, dry, opaque, compact meat is preferable to moist, glistening meat. The former denotes freshness and correct conditioning and storage.

STORING MEAT

Proper storage of meat means prevention of spoilage and control of bacterial growth in order to avoid decomposition and prolong the time during which the meat can be used fresh. In discussing the chemical composition of meat we have seen that its main constituents are water and protein, which may be regarded as a particularly favourable medium for the growth of bacteria. For this reason meat is particularly perishable.

Safe storage times for meat depend largely on the type of animal. Extreme care should be taken to avoid exciting or frightening an animal intended for slaughter, for this would cause the blood to be retained in the muscular parts of the carcase, with a very detrimental effect on the keeping properties of the meat. During slaughter excessive washing should be avoided. Pigs' carcases in particular should not be wetted.

As soon as *rigor mortis* has set in, the flesh undergoes a biochemical process which alters the muscular fibres. The first stage, maturing, makes the meat tender and tasty. If this process is prolonged, the meat soon reaches the point when it is over mature and after only a short time traces of putrefaction can be detected. To prevent decomposition and ensure that the meat can be kept fresh for as long as possible, appropriate treatment must be applied immediately.

Treatment

Anyone who handles meat, whether as a professional or a layman, should always realise that it is a delicate commodity to be treated with the utmost care. Meat spoils quickly if its surface becomes moist either from within, through external circumstances, or if it cannot dry properly. Care must be taken to avoid placing too many pieces of meat close together or stacking them one on another in more than one layer. It is also important to protect the meat against other conditions which might give rise to unnecessary moisture, such as activities that produce steam or heat, open refrigerator doors, wet hands or utensils, or leaving the meat wrapped in polythene.

The simplest method of treating meat in the absence of appropriate modern facilities is to hang it in a sufficiently cold and dry place. If it still becomes necessary to dry the surface, disposable paper napkins should be used.

PROFESSIONAL METHODS OF KEEPING AND PRESERVING MEAT

1 *Refrigeration or cold storage*

Temperature is one of the most critical factors for the growth of micro-organisms. By reducing the temperature the safe storage time is increased. Meat must always be chilled as soon as the animal has been killed, with the aid of vigorous air circulation and rapid cooling. It is essential to avoid any subsequent rise in temperature and the meat must be stored at a constant temperature of 0 to 1°C (32–34°F) and a relative humidity of 80–85%. The air should not be too dry in order to prevent desiccation (loss of weight) but excessive humidity makes meat too slimy and consequently increases waste. Ventilation should not be excessive as this would cause the meat to dry out and possibly to discolour. Meat stores should therefore be checked several times a day.

As meat rapidly takes on extraneous smells, no other foods should be kept in the same store. Pickling brines and similar liquids should also be excluded. There must be adequate circulation of air between the pieces of meat, which should not under any circumstances be in contact with one another. For obvious reasons cut meat should be handled as little as possible. The more carefully meat is stored, the less waste occurs. It goes without saying that the stores must be scrupulously clean.

When storing meat in a refrigerator it may be kept wrapped for a day. If it is to be kept longer, the paper must be removed and the meat placed in the refrigerator after oiling it well on both sides.

Storage times in a chill room

To reduce loss of weight meat should be stored in large pieces bone-in or in vacuum packs after boning. The storage times are as follows:

beef for quick frying and grilling	14–21 days
beef cuts requiring prolonged cooking	3–14 days
veal	5–10 days
mutton and lamb	5–10 days
pork	3–8 days

During this time the meat already loses 3–7% of its weight. A biochemical process alters the intramuscular connective tissue, making the meat tender.

2 *Deep freezing*

This is a term used to describe the rapid reduction of temperature to well below freezing point. The process must be very quick, as it is in the commercial production of quick-frozen foods. Here a special freezing tunnel is used at temperatures below – 40°C (– 40°F); as a result the temperature of the food very quickly falls to – 18°C (0°F). If the freezing process is too slow, it results in the formation of ice crystals which damage the cell structure of the meat, causing greater loss of the natural juices on thawing. Care should be taken to avoid placing too many pieces of meat close together or on top of one another, even if the freezer is on the small side. A constant temperature of – 18°–20°C (0–4°F) should be maintained. At this temperature meat will remain fresh for several months without losing its nutritive value. Storage times are 12–14 months for beef, 12 months for lamb, about 10 months for veal, 6 months for cooked meats, 4 months for pork and sausages, 3 months for minced meat. These figures apply only to meat that was originally in perfect condition and has been correctly treated in every way.

The most critical stage in preparing frozen meat for the table is always the thawing process, for freezing does not destroy the viability of micro-organisms, but merely inhibits their multiplication. Thawing allows the bacteria to return to full activity under temperature and moisture conditions favourable to their growth. Consequently, meat should be thawed as slowly as possible, ideally over a period of 24 hours or more, in a refrigerator or chill store. Defrosted meat of any type should never be refrozen. Individual portions such as steaks may be fried at once, with an appropriate adjustment of the frying time to the initial temperature.

3 *Sterilisation*

Sterilising (cooking under pressure at more than 100°C (212°F)) or ordinary boiling kills micro-organisms, but some spore formation is still possible. As soon as temperature and humidity reach levels at which bacteria are active they begin to multiply again. This means that heat treated food must be cooled as quickly as possible, for example under cold running water. The most dangerous temperatures are between 30 and 50°C (86–122°F).

4 *Vacuum packing*

Another critical factor for the growth of micro-organisms is the presence of oxygen. Vacuum packing involves placing meat that is as germ free as possible in a plastic bag, extracting all the air at the same time and sealing the bag to exclude all external influences, including oxygen. This process prolongs safe storage time and also prevents surface drying, which would have a disagreeable effect on appearance and flavour. The necessary maturing process, however, is not interrupted.

In contrast to frozen meat, the maturing process continues inside a vacuum pack so this method of keeping meat is by no means free from problems. It is easy to be misled into believing that the elegant plastic packaging fully protects the contents against any deterioration, but this is not the case. Vacuum packed meat has to be treated in the same manner as fresh meat. In addition, it is essential for the pack to be absolutely seamless and airtight; an air bubble inside could destroy the contents and make them unfit for consumption.

Meat in vacuum packs is stored for the following periods of time: –
   Small cuts of beef or veal, 4 to 7 days, and of pork, 3 to 5 days.
   Large joints of beef or veal, 3 weeks, and of pork 1 week.
The packs are refrigerated at a temperature between 0 and 4°C (32 and 40°F). As far as possible they should not be stacked. Damaged packs must be opened at once and their contents either used or preserved by one of the other methods described. The meat should be stored with the fatty side up to avoid discoloration of the fat. Packs must be opened at least six hours before use. After removal from the pack, the meat slowly recovers its original colour due to the presence of oxygen. Meat in vacuum packs is particularly suitable for deep freezing, for the packaging prevents the 'burning' or drying which takes place in the presence of air, even in a freezer.

5 *Salting*
Salt inactivates proteolytic enzymes and has a toxic action on certain groups of bacteria. In addition, it almost totally removes moisture from meat. Salt is also an indispensable factor in enhancing the flavour of meat products and prolonging their storage life.

(a) DRY SALTING The meat is repeatedly rubbed with salt until well salted. The length of time needed depends primarily on the diameter of the piece of meat.
(b) WET SALTING OR PICKLING This is the most common process. Depending on their nature and size, the pieces of meat are left for 8–30 days in a brine consisting of water, salt and saltpetre; the strength of the solution varies between 11 and 18° Baumé.
(c) QUICK SALTING When meat is subjected to dry or wet salting, the salt has to penetrate the flesh from outside. A relatively long period of time is required until the meat is salted right through. To speed up the process, the brine may be injected into the meat with the aid of a hollow needle.

6 *Smoking*
This is often combined with salting. Its purpose is to preserve the meat by removing a large proportion of the moisture. In addition, chemical substances are deposited on the surface which have an antiseptic effect and are derived from the slow combustion of wood in combination with sawdust. These substances are creosote, phenol and formalin and they give the product its distinctive flavour.

SMOKE PRODUCTION Beech, oak, hickory and juniper sawdust or oak wood may be used to produce smoke; conifers are unsuitable because they leave behind an odour of turpentine. Shrinkage may amount to 25%.

Meat and sausages to be smoked are hung in a place where the smoke can circulate more or less slowly. This may be an ordinary farmhouse chimney, where the meat is traditionally hung for up to three months; alternatively, a large specially constructed wood or gas fired chimney may be used, or a modern electrically heated smokehouse. In the smokehouse system the sawdust is burned in a separate combustion chamber on a red-hot plate. The smoke produced is channelled into the smokehouse where temperature and humidity can be regulated at will. The advantage of this system is that the unpleasant heavy 'drops of pitch', the tar distillates, do not come into contact with the meat, but are collected and removed beforehand.

The air temperature in the smokehouse has to be kept between 60 and 80°C (140–176°F) for 30 to 90 minutes. As a rule, cooked products or those intended for cooking are smoked hot (e.g. boiling sausages or ham). Hot smoking is also used for the so-called 'German' sausages, which are mostly cooked soon after smoking and then put on sale.

Cold smoking, at a maximum temperature of 25°C (77°F) is used for raw items intended for prolonged storage (raw ham, fat pork, sausages). Smoked meat and sausages should be stored in a cold, dry, dark place; relatively cool storage rooms are also suitable, but may give rise to a slight change in the colour and flavour of the products. The invention of vacuum packs has provided a very convenient way of keeping smoked and matured meat.

Storage of salted meat products (especially salami)
The salted meat is hung for a relatively long period of time at the appropriate temperature. It now acquires its final appearance and distinctive flavour. After a curing period of about three weeks for sausages, three to seven days' drying is required. The temperature should rise to 20°C (68°F); the products gradually lose surface moisture and take on a reddish colour. After the second period of drying, they are transferred to cooler storage conditions (about 15°C (59°F) with a relative humidity of 75%). The meat slowly but steadily loses up to 30% of its weight in moisture loss. A thin film of mould starts to form on the surface; it may be white, grey or green depending on the bacterial flora. This fungus or 'bloom', which must be dry and clear, gives salami its particular appearance and aroma.

Certain products, such as dried meats or ham, are pressed while maturing to give them the desired shape and assist the drying process. Ham is matured for one to three months, depending on size. Raw ham on the bone, however, requires up to twelve months.

Types of sausage
Sausages are made of a mixture of finely or coarsely chopped beef, pork or veal, seasoned with salt and spices and packed into natural or synthetic casings. They may be divided into three types according to composition and method of preservation.

> Boiling, frying or grilling sausages (such as cervelat, Viennas, Lyons sausages, veal frying sausages).
> Raw sausages (such as salami, salametti, salsiz).
> Boiled sausages (liver sausage, blood sausage or black pudding).

Mortadella, liver sausage and polony do not belong specifically to any one of the above categories as they are sold to be eaten as they are not further cooked.

Frying, grilling and boiling sausages: these are the so-called 'German' sausages and English varieties such as Oxford and Cambridge sausage; they are made by thoroughly blending together the binding constituents of meat, i.e. protein and fat. As a result these ingredients hold the mixture together well after cooking and give the sausages the necessary keeping qualities. To make this smooth, homogeneous mixture the beef, veal or pork is worked in a special cutter with the addition of pork fat and, in many cases, bacon rinds, ice and water.

Like the professional chef the expert sausage maker, on the basis of experience, can interpret the various recipes according to the facilities available; he can vary not only the seasonings, but also the temperatures and the duration and order of the different procedures, to produce a first-class sausage. The quality of the sausage meat and the smoking process are the main factors that determine the colour and final appearance of a sausage. Perfection is only achieved if the sausage is rapidly cooled under cold running water as soon as it has been boiled or steamed.

The main factor in making raw sausages is the selection of the basic ingredients (meat and fat). They must originate from healthy, well-fed, mature, dry animals. The meat must be well chilled, lean and free from sinews. The pork fat must be very firm and dry; it should be lightly chilled before use. The meat and fat are minced together, coarsely or finely according to the type of sausage, then well mixed with the addition of salt and spices until the meat begins to hold together.

Natural casings (made from horse, pig or cattle intestines) are preserved in salt. Before use they are rinsed for some time in cold water, then in warm water, and finally wine vinegar is poured through them. They are only ready for use once this procedure has been completed.

The process of pulling the casing off the filling machine while the meat mixture is pushed into it is a very delicate operation. Care must be taken to avoid gaps or air bubbles, as the filling must remain compact and evenly distributed; it should not move or twist inside the casing during insertion and subsequent tying off of the finished sausage. This work requires a certain amount of caution and skill to avoid damage to the casing. The mixture must be handled carefully to ensure that there are no hollows, bulges or other irregularities in the shape of the sausage. Synthetic casings are convenient to use and easy to fill but they have disadvantages as the contents dry more rapidly and have limited storage life.

Salami derives its name, not only from its origin, but also from the special meat mixture it contains (a fine one, or a somewhat coarser one for the 'nostrano' type) and the nature of its casing (e.g. bindone – horse intestine or casings with special names such as 'gentile', 'filzette', 'crespone', salsiz – fat intestine or casing). The raw sausage meat has to remain in a cool temperature of 12–14°C (53–57°F) on the first day to allow the salt to start its action. As already mentioned, the drying process is complete when the casing has lost its bright colour and the pinkish tinge of the filling can be seen through it. While drying the sausage has to be checked constantly. Ventilation and temperature are adjusted to the external weather conditions which have a considerable effect on the treatment of the product. It is not by chance that the dry, cold winter months are preferred for slaughtering, since at this time of year it is easier to begin drying salami. It will virtually have finished drying by the beginning of the warm, damp season, when it will be ready for use and also easier to store.

Boiled sausages include liver sausage, mettwurst, collared pork and black pudding or blood sausage, the main ingredients of which, milk and blood, are filled into the casings hot after being more or less half cooked.

7 *Air drying*

Good quality leg cuts are used (silverside or topside) from well-fed but not excessively fat cattle. The meat is cut in pieces, trimmed, salted by a special process and air dried (Bündnerfleisch, raw ham, 'coppa'). For dry salting 25 g (1 oz) salt and ½ g (a pinch) saltpetre is used per kilogram (2¼ lb) of meat.

Duration of drying process

Bündner raw ham	about 6 months
Bündnerfleisch (type of Swiss salted dried beef joints eaten as hors d'oeuvre or snack)	about 4–5 months (including salting)
Salami	about 2–3 months
Salsiz	about 6 weeks
Shrinkage	about 30%. Salami up to 35%.

8 *Marinating* (short-term pickling)

The marinade, consisting of red wine and vinegar, must have a pH of 3–8% to exclude pathogens and toxins. The meat is marinated for about 8–10 days. If it is left in the marinade beyond this time, it takes on a strong acid taste and decomposes. In quick marinating the marinade is brought to the boil, poured over the meat while hot and left overnight.

9 *Canning, bottling, sterilising*

This method was invented at the beginning of the nineteenth century by the French chemist Nicolas Appert. Meat to be canned must be heated to between 110 and 130°C (230–265°F) and subsequently stored in a cool place. It is a method of preserving meat only suitable for skilled and well equipped manufacturers.

2   Buying Meat

When buying meat the first requirement is to know for what purpose it is intended. There is no point in buying whole carcases, sides or quarters if the various cuts from these cannot be used at the same time. This will be dependent on the menu being offered. Once its use has been determined and appropriate cold storage facilities provided, the purchase of the meat can be planned.

For meat purchase to be economic, attention must be paid to quality, cut and yield when buying. Quality is largely dependent on the way in which the animal has been fattened. The fat should be light in colour, the meat fine-grained; marbling should be present in red meat and pork. The age of the animal is crucial, which means that the appearance of the bones and gristle is very important. Attention should also be paid to the proportion of bone and fat to flesh. In general there should be less than 25% bone. If the proportions are right then the yield may be expected to be good.

4 *Portion weights* (quantities of meat per person)
The table of raw weights that follows is based on experience of present-day eating habits in restaurants. The figures are intended only for guidance.

Average weight per person

Cut	à la carte	as part of a menu with several courses
Beef		
Entrecôte	150–175 g	125 g
Rump steak	150–175 g	125 g
Viennese fried steak	150 g	100 g
Fillet steak	150–175 g	125 g
Tournedos	125–150 g	100 g
Roast beef	175–200 g	150 g
Double entrecôte (for 2)	300–350 g	
Châteaubriand (for 2)	300–350 g	
Porterhouse steak (for 3)	500–750 g	
T-bone steak (for 2)	450–500 g	
Roast ribs		150 g
Boiled beef		125 g
Braised or pot-roasted beef		125 g
Stew		125 g
Ox tongue, pickled		125 g
Tripe	180 g	125 g
Veal		
Escalope, plain	150 g	125 g
Escalope, breaded	125 g	100 g
Cutlet	175 g	150 g
Steak	150 g	100 g
Roast best end		125 g
Ragoût (stewing) or fricassée, boneless	125–150g	125 g
Calf's head, boneless	250 g	150 g
Knuckle or ossobuco	300–350 g	200 g
Roast leg or shoulder, boned	125–150 g	125 g
Liver or kidneys	125–150 g	125 g
Fillet	125–150 g	125 g
Pork		
Cutlet	175 g	150 g
Ham on the bone	200 g	175 g
Ham, boneless	150 g	100 g
Roast spare rib		120 g
Fillet (slices, medallions – two)	150 g	100 g
Ragoût, boneless	200 g	150 g
Knuckle	300–350 g	200 g
Belly	180 g	125 g
Sucking pig	350 g	250 g

Cut	à la carte	as part of a menu with several courses
Mutton, lamb		
Mutton cutlet, crown	200 g	125 g
Loin chops	175 g	100 g
Mutton stew, with bone	200 g	150 g
Mutton stew, boneless	150 g	120 g
Roast saddle and roast baron	250 g	180 g
Tame rabbit		
Saddle, whole	250 g	175 g
Leg, whole	250 g	175 g
Ragoût (stewing)	150–250 g	150 g

3 Preparing Meat for Cooking

The proper use of a joint of meat requires expert knowledge, including the ability to assess the nature of the meat and the condition of the animal shortly before and during slaughter, which are decisive factors. The utmost care is necessary in storing meat, whether it has been purchased by the piece or by sides or quarters. The correct temperature and relative humidity must be maintained.

When dissecting a side or quarter or other large piece, the first step is to look for the connective tissue between the muscles and to make sure that this remains undamaged while jointing proceeds. There will then be no unnecessary waste if the joints are kept in storage for a time, as the cut surfaces will remain in good condition. This method also facilitates removal of sinews and subcutaneous fat.

Boning and dissection require both impeccable equipment, and a clean, dry work surface. After appropriate storage of the various cuts, work can commence on preparing the smaller cuts required. The sinews and membranes must first be carefully removed with a very sharp knife; they may be used in making stock. Meat should be cut across the grain to avoid shrinkage while cooking. In the interests of customer satisfaction and good management, the correct cuts must be used for the items listed on the menu. Only experience and expertise can ensure good results.

It is sometimes necessary to cut certain quantities in advance ('mise en place'). The ready trimmed pieces of meat may conveniently be laid on a tray until required, and then they can be quickly cut into individual portions. Experience will show the quantities of each menu item that are needed to meet likely demand. Cutting the meat in advance once a day has the advantage of making bones, trimmings etc. available for immediate use in stocks, soups, minced meat or other suitable dishes. This also contributes to profitability.

PREPARING MEAT FOR RITUAL KOSHER COOKING

Any meat used in Jewish cooking must originate from animals that have been killed according to Jewish rites. Blood is strictly prohibited in the diet of persons of the Jewish faith.

The animal to be killed is tied and laid on the ground. A specially trained butcher cuts through the carotid artery, using a sharp knife which must be absolutely free from nicks or other defects; all the blood then drains out of the carcase. The latter is carefully examined (including the offal) for malformations or disease. Even a deformed lung makes the meat unusable. In some orthodox Jewish communities only the forequarters are used but in Israel it is not unknown for hindquarters to be used. They are dissected and all sinews and membranes containing blood are removed by experts familiar with the blood vessels and skilled in the delicate work of cutting them out.

Koshering meat
The boned meat and any bones required for cooking must be koshered within three days. First the meat is placed in a bowl kept for this purpose and soaked in water for half an hour. Next it is removed, well drained, and carefully sprinkled all over with a generous amount of coarse salt. It is then left on wooden racks for an hour to drain off any remaining blood, and finally very carefully washed. Once the meat has been prepared in this way, it may be used for any purpose in kosher cooking. Meat and poultry are preserved by freezing.

Koshering liver
The liver is thoroughly washed and the whole surface is pricked with a coarse needle. It is placed on an iron grill over an open flame and left there until no blood remains, then carefully washed again. It may now be used in cooking.

In Jewish kosher cooking any contact between dairy produce and meat is strictly prohibited and no dairy foods may be eaten or drunk until four hours after a meat meal. Separate kitchen utensils and tableware have to be used for meat and dairy foods. This dietary law is based on the biblical precept, 'Thou shalt not seethe a kid in its mother's milk'.

4 Cooking Methods

Apart from sausage and certain specialities, meat is seldom eaten raw. Cooking and the addition of the customary seasonings make meat more palatable and bring out its qualities to the full. It becomes more digestible and will keep better since pathogenic micro-organisms are destroyed. The information below is intended to supplement the table 'Technology of Meat Cookery' (see p 24).

Blanching
This may be carried out in different ways. (1) To clean bones and meat or to remove fat (e.g. when preparing beef or veal stock), place in cold water and bring to the boil, strain and refresh. (2) If meat is to retain its juices it should be blanched in boiling water (e.g. when preparing boiled beef, blanquette of veal, boiled mutton or lamb). Once again it should be strained and refreshed before continuing the cooking process.

Boiling
To ensure that the cooked meat is succulent and tasty, all the pores must be closed at the beginning of the cooking process so that the flavouring substances and meat juices cannot escape. The meat should therefore be immersed in boiling water. To produce good, strong beef broth, however, the process must be reversed: meat and bones are placed in cold water which is then brought to the boil. A temperature of 70–80°C (158–176°F) alters the meat pigment. This explains why some boiled meats appear grey but with added garnishes or sauces this is acceptable. In other cases, as with English boiled beef and carrots or brisket, the meat is brined (penetrated with salt and nitrate) which enhances the colour and makes it more acceptable to the eye.

Temperature is also important when boiling sausages. It should lie between 72 and 75°C (162–167°F). At 72°C a sausage is cooked right through; above 75°C the casing tends to split open. Sausages for boiling have, in most cases, been cooked before they are sold. To heat them for the table they must be allowed to reach the temperatures mentioned above. In the absence of a special thermometer, the water may be brought to the boil, the heat turned off and the sausages immersed in the water for about ten minutes. This procedure is suitable for medium-size and small sausages.

Boiling a ham
In the industry the cured hams are kept in special cabinets at a constant temperature of 70–72°C (158–162°F) which is sufficient to ensure that the required internal temperature has been reached overnight. Alternatively, a ham may be left to simmer in water at 78–80°C (172–176°F) allowing one hour per kg (2¼ lb).

Cooking under pressure
This is a satisfactory method of minimising nutritive loss and saving time and energy. Meats to be stewed or braised, either diced or in joints, are particularly suitable for this process. To cook ox tongues in this way, the autoclave should be half or three quarters full with water, depending on the number of tongues and type of vessel. The thermostat is set at 95–100°C (203–212°F). The tongues are placed in the boiling water and the vessel tightly covered. For small quantities the heat may be turned off; for larger amounts it should be left on a low setting with the thermostat at 75°C (167°F). With careful regulation, there is no danger of the contents boiling away, even if left overnight.

Boiled beef can also be prepared in the same way, but should be checked after an hour to make sure that the temperature does not exceed 85°C (185°F). Braised beef and pork or veal ragoût may also be cooked under pressure. The cooking time will be only one third as long as by the conventional method.

Roasting in a forced convection oven
When using a forced convection oven various items can be cooked at the same time without the flavours intermingling, which is one of the substantial advantages of this method. The roasting process is simplified as the oven is heated evenly throughout and there is no need to turn or baste the meat, which acquires an enhanced flavour and remains juicier. Joints will roast evenly with less browning and shrinkage.

The disadvantages are that gravy has to be prepared separately and that this type of oven is not very suitable for glazing meat. It is advisable to allow the cooked meat to rest in a moderate heat for 20–30 minutes before serving in order to minimise waste when carving.

To obtain satisfactory results the manufacturer's instructions must be followed carefully. Examples:
(a) Roast beef – the meat is lightly fried to seal and colour it, then roasted in a forced convection oven at 100°C (212°F), for about one hour, depending on thickness and quality. Shrinkage is 10–13%. Meat thermometer reading should be 50–55°C (122–131°F).
(b) Kasseler smoked ribs of pork – at 100°C (212°F) for about 1¼–1½ hours. Shrinkage 10–12%.

(c) Roast veal or pork – at 100°C (212°F) for about 1¾–2 hours. Shrinkage 18–20%.

Stewing
Traditionally this method involves the use of a casserole or braising pan with a heavy lid. Some steam will escape and it is therefore necessary to add liquid during the cooking. The pieces of meat should all be of the same size and quality and be fried off prior to being covered in the cooking liquid.

Braising
This means cooking in stock or sauces and is usually applied to the coarser cuts of meat which can either be braised in portions (e.g. braising steaks, beef olives) or as whole joints. Two distinctions are made when talking about braising: (1) a brown braise: usually dark meat; (2) a white braise: usually white meats.

For the brown meat, portions or joints are seasoned, floured, sealed and browned in a pan, then transferred to a braisiere, covered with stock or sauce, given a flavouring agent (e.g. mirepoix) and a bouquet garni. In the second method, the white meat is set and sealed, but not browned, covered with white stock or sauce and a flavouring agent and bouquet garni are added.

After braising gently on the stove (or more often in the oven) for 60–80 minutes for small pieces and 80–120 minutes per kg for larger joints, the meat is lifted into a clean pan, the sauce is strained, corrected for consistency and flavour and then poured over the meat.

In both cases the use of wine is recommended – red wine for dark meat and white for white meat. Meat is often marinated before braising and the marinade becomes part of the cooking liquor.

Glazing
There are several types of glazing. The processes for sweet items differ from those for vegetables. Glazing meat also differs from these other methods. Meat stock may, for example, be continuously reduced by simmering to create first a half glaze (demi-glace) or a meat glaze (glace de viande). Glazing is also a method of putting a shine on a finished dish of meat. It can be achieved by continuous basting of roasts or braising joints and then placing them under the salamander for a good colour and shine just prior to service. Cold meats are glazed for buffet purposes by the use of aspics or chaud-froid sauces.

Poêler
This is used for dark or white meat but requires great care. In contrast to ordinary oven roasting the meat is placed on a bed of fried vegetables and herbs (matignon) with fat and then put in a fairly cool oven – about 150–160°C (302–320°F) – in a covered casserole. The temperature may later be increased to 175°C (347°F). The meat is basted frequently to colour lightly and the lid can be removed in the last half hour of cooking to brown the surface of the joint. This method is suitable for tender cuts only.

Deep frying
Deep frying in oil or any suitable fat is used for food first prepared in various ways. The meat is often pre-cooked, e.g. chickens, young lamb, kid (speciality), calf's brains. Made-up dishes

containing chopped or minced meat, such as croquettes, crepinettes etc., may also be deep fried. A protective coating of flour and bread crumbs may be used to prevent excessive fat absorption.

Grilling

Grilling requires a spotlessly clean grill to avoid transferring unpleasant smells to the food. The oil with which the meat is brushed must be stable at the high temperature needed for meat grilling. The heat should preferably be adjustable; this is an easy procedure in the case of a charcoal grill and ensures that thicker cuts such as Châteaubriand or rib steaks are protected from excessive browning. To grill white meat the temperature must be reduced if at all possible. Grilling time depends on the thickness and quality of the meat and, in the case of red meat, the degree of cooking desired.

Sauter

This is a process only suitable for prime cuts, which are the most expensive ones – fillet or entrecôte steak, escalopes, medallions, lamb cutlets or chops, chicken supremes, calf's liver, etc. Items to be cooked this way should be seasoned and sometimes floured. A special sauté pan is generally used. Unless the frying medium is butter, it should be poured off before adding liquid (wine, cream or basic entrée sauces) to the pan to make sauce, so that the latter is not excessively fatty.

Spit roasting

This has become popular in the home as well as in catering establishments. It does not require much work apart from occasional basting and always produces good results. The spit roasted meat is succulent and an attractive golden brown. Both white and red meats are suitable, e.g. leg of lamb, sucking pig, young lamb, loin of veal, larded or plain fillet of beef, veal or pork, etc. The degree of cooking may easily be tested by pricking, or with the aid of a meat thermometer.

MICROWAVE COOKING

This rapid cooking process was one of the most revolutionary innovations for the caterer. The microwave oven is very simple to operate, even for unskilled staff, since it incorporates a timer for automatic heating and cooking and now fully automated programmable microwaves are available. Ordinary electric current charges the magnetron which generates electro-magnetic waves.

Behaviour of microwaves

This differs according to the substances they encounter.
(1) They are reflected by metal. Consequently food should not be placed in metal containers.
(2) They have no effect on inorganic substances such as glass, china, paper or plastics.
(3) They are absorbed by any substance containing water and so food is heated by this means.

Action of microwaves on food

Only foods containing water absorb microwaves. Each tiny part contains millions of molecules of cell and tissue water. The microwaves penetrate the food and cause the water molecules to rotate extremely fast, generating energy in the form of frictional heat which spreads very rapidly through the food and cooks it. Thus the heat is generated inside the food itself, which cooks from the inside and on the surface simultaneously.

As they penetrate a piece of meat the microwaves lose their intensity; their maximum depth of penetration is approximately 2½–3 cm. This means that meat of a greater thickness than this will not cook in the centre which is a particular disadvantage with rounded joints such as poultry. The colour and appearance of food is unaffected by microwaves and therefore no browning occurs. Since the water content, which actually determines the structure of foods including meat, varies from one type to another, there is a difference in the absorption of microwaves according to the surface of the joints as the areas with a higher water content cook more slowly. There are also certain very vulnerable areas which have to be protected by a piece of aluminium foil which will reflect the microwaves.

Advantages
(1) Contact media such as pans, fat or water are no longer required, since the food is heated from within.
(2) If meat is roasted in a microwave oven it does not become as crisp or brown as in a conventional one, but if the cut is large enough and requires more than 15 minutes' cooking the end result is very satisfactory, at least to the eye. There is little water loss, therefore less shrinkage than in a conventional oven. To make microwave roasted meat look really attractive, however, it can either be coated with a mixture of melted butter, meat stock and finely chopped herbs before the end of the cooking process, or shallow fried to brown first.
(3) Very tender meat cooks much more quickly although time is lost in pre-preparation.
(4) Another real advantage is that slices of rare or medium-done meat can be reheated without losing their colour or being cooked again.
(5) A long thin piece of meat takes a shorter time to cook than a compact one of the same weight.
(6) Microwaves are very useful for defrosting frozen meat portions.

Applications (examples)
    Small meat pies or patties
    Boiling sausages
    Soups
    Ragoûts (stews) and fricassées
    Sautés such as escalope in cream sauce
    Meat balls in sauce

To keep food succulent it should be covered with foil. Larger cuts for braising or roasting are tougher and should be cooked by the conventional method.

TECHNOLOGY OF MEAT COOKERY

Cooking methods:	Boiling/ Simmering	Stewing	*Steaming in moist air	Poêler
Definition	Cooking in water or stock at simmering point at atmospheric pressure	Cooking in liquid at simmering point	Cooking in circulated moist air	Cooking in fat, steam and meat juices
Heat transfer medium	Water/stock	Liquid	Circulating steam	Fat, air
Type of heat transfer	Convection	Convection	Convection, condensation	Conduction, condensation
Cooking temperature	up to 100°C (212°F)	100–140°C (212–284°F)	75–100°C (167–212°F)	140–160°C (284–320°F)
Types of meat (examples)	Beef, veal, mutton, ham, bacon	Cuts for slow cooking	Ham, pickled meat	Veal, small cuts for slow cooking
Conventional cooking equipment:	Boiling table, boiling or stew pan	Boiling table, stew pan, tilting 'brat' pan	Steamer	Boiling table, oven, tilting 'brat' pan
Modern cooking equipment	Automatic cooker, high pressure steamer	To a limited extent automatic cooker, forced convection oven	Automatic cooker, high pressure steamer	

*This cooking process is not widely used.

Cooking methods:	Roasting or baking	Shallow frying	Deep frying	Sauter (sauté)	Grilling
Definition	Cooking in an oven or on a spit	Cooking in shallow fat	Cooking submerged in hot deep fat	Cooking by tossing in shallow fat	Cooking by radiant or infra-red heat
Heat transfer medium	Air, fat used in basting	Fat	Fat	Fat	Fat, air

Cooking methods:	Roasting or baking	Shallow frying	Deep frying	Sauter (sauté)	Grilling
Type of heat transfer	Radiation, conduction, convection	Conduction	Convection	Conduction	Conduction, radiation
Cooking temperature	140–250°C (284–482°F)	160–240°C (320–464°F)	140–190°C (284–374°F)	160–240°C (320–464°F)	220–280°C (428–536°F)
Types of meat (examples)	Joints, meat pies	Steaks, chops, veal escalopes	Veal, mutton	Small cuts of beef, veal, lamb, pork, offal	Small tender cuts, chops, cutlets
Conventional cooking equipment	Roasting/ baking oven	Frying pan, 'brat' pan, griddle	Deep fryer	Sauté pan, 'brat' pan	Grill, contact grill, salamander
Modern cooking equipment	Forced convection oven, continuous baking oven		Continuous deep fryer	Forced convection oven, continuous automatic cooker	Forced convection oven

Cooking methods:	Gratiner (au gratin)	Glazing	Braising	Regenerating
Definition	Browning under a salamander with fierce top heat	Frying lightly, then cooking in mixture of fat and liquid	Browning quickly in fat, then cooking slowly with a little added liquid	Heating pre-cooked chilled or frozen food
Heat transfer medium	Fat, air	Fat, liquid	Fat, liquid	
Type of heat transfer	Radiation	Conduction, condensation	Conduction, condensation, convection	High frequency radiation waves

N.B. The fat used in frying or grilling must be stable at the high temperatures required for these processes.

Cooking methods:	Gratiner (au gratin)	Glazing	Braising	Regenerating
Cooking temperature	250–300°C (482–572°F)	200–160°C (392–320°F)	220–180°C (428–356°F)	max 100°C (212°F)
Types of meat (examples)	Saddle of veal, veal or mutton cutlets	White meat	Red meat	Cooked meat
Conventional cooking equipment	Salamander, oven top heat	Boiling table, stew pan, braising pan, tilting 'brat' pan	Boiling table, oven, tilting 'brat' pan, braising pan	Microwave oven, convection oven
Modern cooking equipment	Forced convection oven		Forced convection oven	Continuous microwave tunnel

5 Cooking Times for Boiling, Roasting and Frying

Boiling meat

To ensure that the meat remains succulent, it must be cooked in boiling water or bouillon to reduce leaching of soluble constituents, which lowers the nutritive value of the meat while somewhat improving the flavour of the bouillon. To obtain both well flavoured bouillon and juicy meat, a good bone broth should first be prepared and brought to the boil; the meat is then placed in it and simmered at a temperature below boiling point.

COOKING TIME

Boiled beef French style	50–80 mins per kg according to quality
Salt beef, brisket, after pre-blanching	50–60 mins per kg according to quality
Ham, gentle simmering	40–60 mins per kg
Pig's head	2– 3 hours.

Roasting meat

COOKING TIME

Ribs, very thick cut	30–35 min per kg
Sirloin I (cut thicker than 8 cm (3 in)	20–30 min per kg
Sirloin II (cut about 6 cm (2 in) thick)	20 min per kg
Leg of mutton, medium done	25–30 min per kg (for large joints)

Saddle of mutton   20 min per kg
Loin of pork   25 min per kg

Shallow frying meat

COOKING TIME
Fillet steak   3–6 min
Châteaubriand steak   5–12 min
Tournedos   3–5 min
Veal escalope   5–10 min
Veal chop   12–15 min
Calf's liver   3– 6 min
Pork chop   12–18 min

Meat should not be overcooked, for it may quickly become too dry. The times set out above are not absolute, but are merely intended for general guidance, since there are many factors involved in determining exactly how long any particular piece of meat will take to cook. Quality, age, length of fibres, structure, size and thickness of a piece of meat are all decisive influences. (See also 'Technology of Meat Cookery', page 24)

DEGREES OF COOKING

It is not easy to determine the time required to cook meat. This depends mainly on the quality and conditioning of the meat, the age of the animal, the amount of fat present and the firmness of the flesh. The size of the cut and the fineness of the grain are also important, as well as the wishes of the guests.

A meat thermometer is an excellent aid. It can even be of service to the experienced rôtisseur (roast cook). He will be able to tell whether a cut of meat is cooked to the desired degree by pressing it with his finger, but for a larger cut (such as sirloin ribs or saddle) a meat thermometer will provide reliable readings.

The degrees of cooking which the waiter has to specify when ordering are as follows:—

(a) bleu – very rare

For red meat only. The interior meat is dark red (blueish), i.e. the meat is charred on the outside but raw in the middle.
Temperature of meat approx. 42–46°C (108–115°F).

(b) saignant – underdone or rare

For red meat only. The interior meat juice is red.
Temperature of meat approx. 47–52°C (117–126°F).

(c) à point – medium or just cooked

For meat and game. The meat juice is pink.
Temperature of meat 57–62°C (135–144°F).

(d) bien cuit – well done

For roasts or grills, especially pork.
Temperature of meat approx. 80°C (176°F);
red meat approx. 67–72°C (153–162°F).

These terms above are commonly applied to degrees of cooking for cuts of meat such as châteaubriands, fillets, tournedos, cutlets, chops, medallions, etc.

MEAT SHRINKAGE DURING COOKING

The amount of weight lost by a piece of meat during cooking varies according to quality, type of meat, and also the cooking method used. Weight loss is highest for boiled meat and lowest for grilled, fried and sautéd dishes.

Grills, sauté and shallow fried meat
Entrecôte, rump and fillet steak, cutlets and chops, veal and pork escalopes, saumé veal, liver, kidneys, etc.

about 5–7%

Roasts
(a) Leg of mutton   about 14–17%
(b) Roast beef   about 15–18%

Pot-roasted joints
(a) Best end or loin of veal   about 23–26%
(b) Pork from young animals   about 23–26%

Larded braised beef
(a) Flank, topside, etc.   about 32–35%
(b) Meat from old animals (cow beef)   up to 40%

Boiled meat
(a) Beef (ribs, brisket)   about 32–35%
(b) Mutton (leg, shoulder)   about 30–33%
(c) Meat from old animals   up to 40%

6 Rules for Dressing Hot and Cold Dishes

Economic considerations and the amount of time required to prepare a dish must be borne in mind. Food must please the eye if it is to please the palate. Untidily dished food loses its appeal however well it has been cooked. Dishes and plates containing a neat arrangement of food, without being overloaded, are attractive to look at and stimulate the appetite.

Plated service
Where this system is in use care must be taken to present the food to its best possible advantage. For reasons of hygiene and neat appearance the rim of the plate should never be covered with food, with the exception of a sprig of watercress or parsley as a garnish. Hot plates should be used for hot food and cold dry plates for cold food. Before assembly a good mise en place of all additions and garnishes to the main item should be ready and easily available.

In many hotels and restaurants plates are decorated with a crest and this should always face the guest at twelve o'clock, therefore when assembling food on a plate this should be the first consideration. Where a crest is not part of the plate an imaginary crest or a piece of garnish may start off the assembly. Meat portions should always be placed at the front of the plate at six o'clock, or alternatively from twelve to six, allowing space for vegetables or salad to be added.

After placing the meat on the plate together with the vegetables any gravy or sauce may be added, taking care not to dirty the rim. Care should be taken that this is not too thin. Lastly any garnishes required by the dish (lemon, tomato, parsley etc.) should be added. These points also apply to service of meat on flats.

A dish should not be dressed until just before serving and should be brought to the table covered. Plates should always be warmed before serving. These points are all essential for first-class service.

Guidelines for dressing food for the table have been laid down for international culinary exhibitions. They may be exemplified by the rules governing the international competition, Salon Culinaire Mondial 1977, held in Basel. These are given below.

Example – Salon Culinaire Mondial 1977, Basel
Guidance for Exhibitors (Participants) and Judges

International Culinary Competition – Category A

Category B

Category C   Confectioners

---

1. The standard for every dish is set by the recipe. Ingredients and method in telegraphic style.
2. Garnishes and accompaniments should be in harmony with the main dish as regards amount, flavour and colour and in keeping with modern tastes.
3. The dishes should be correctly prepared, wholesome and free from any unnecessary ingredients.
4. It is unhygienic to place food on the rim of a plate or dish.
5. Meat should be cleanly and properly cut. To ensure that no juices can escape when it is glazed, it should be medium done.
6. The dish on which the food is presented should not be made unsightly by meat juices or vegetable liquor.
7. To make it keep better the garnish should be left fairly firm when cooking and then glazed with aspic jelly.
8. Failure to trim vegetables neatly will incur penalties.
9. Artificial binding agents may be used for whipped and other creams.
10. More gelatine than usual may be used in preparing aspic jelly.
11. The food should be dished in an appropriate, attractive manner conducive to efficient service.
12. Inedible ornamental items should be avoided (these do not include croûtons).
13. Only deep-fried food may be dished on paper napkins; no paper frills should be used.
14. Food that is meant to be eaten hot should not be dressed on buffet dishes.
15. Eggs should be dressed only on glass, china or a bed of aspic jelly.
16. For food that is meant to be eaten hot, plates or dishes should not be lined with aspic jelly.
17. Hot dishes exhibited cold may be glazed with aspic jelly to keep them fresh.
18. Dishes should not be overfilled; the accompaniments may be dished separately.
19. Serving dishes should be of suitable size for the food being presented and the number of portions.
20. Sauce-boats should be half full only.
21. Clear fish aspic should be used for fish, meat aspic for meat, game and poultry.

22. Portion weights should generally correspond with accepted practice.
23. Slices of meat should not be left as carved, but arranged in front of the joint with the cut side facing outwards to facilitate self-service.
24. Any fruit used to garnish a meat dish should be small or thinly sliced.
25. Drops of aspic jelly on meat or accompaniments should be carefully removed.

7   Carving at Table

The skills that every experienced waiter and chef ought to possess include carving and cooking at table. These procedures, which are greatly appreciated, require a great deal of practice and impeccable preparation.

'Mise en place' (preparation) for carving
A meat fork and four different knives should be ready for use. The knives are:
(1) A 'tranchelard' about 32 cm (14 in) long, with a thin flexible blade. This is used for ham, smoked salmon, roast sirloin of beef, etc.
(2) A broad knife about 24 cm (10 in) long. This broad knife is used for saddle of veal, lamb or venison.
(3) A smaller knife, about 18 cm (7 in) long, with a strong blade. This is mainly required for carving game and also Châteaubriand and double entrecôte steak.
(4) A fish knife.
(5) In addition, there should be a *clean* carving board with a groove to collect meat juices. For hot dishes the board is pre-heated on an electric hot-plate.
(6) It is advisable to have a chafing-dish to hand in case any guest finds the meat too rare.

Carving
When carving, light pressure only should be exerted on the knife, which should therefore be very sharp; if it is not, the slices will be unevenly shaped and the cut surface will be jagged. Each slice should be smoothly cut and be of uniform thickness throughout. The following are particularly suitable for carving at table:

BEEF Porterhouse, T-bone, entrecôte, sirloin, fillet and Châteaubriand steaks, sirloin and rib roasts.

LAMB Saddle, best end, leg.

VEAL Leg, best end, loin.

PORK Loin, roast leg, fillet, ham.

BEEF

Small cuts such as double entrecôte, Châteaubriand, etc. may be carved on a plate, but never on a silver or chrome steel dish. A carving board is essential, however, for larger items.

Double sirloin or entrecôte
This is always cut into oblique slices, holding the meat with the back of the fork but not piercing it. The tip is first cut off, then the steak is carved into slices about 1 to 2 cm (⅜ to ¾ in) thick. These are replaced in position on a plate or dish and served with the juices from the steak, maître d'hôtel or another savoury butter, and the garnish.

Double sirloin or entrecôte steak.

Carve with the knife at an oblique angle, if possible on a board with a groove to catch the meat juices.

Châteaubriand
This steak is usually grilled and served with maître d'hôtel or Colbert butter or sauce, Béarnaise sauce or similar. It is cut from right to left, holding the knife at a slightly oblique angle, into 2 cm (¾ in) thick slices which should be placed immediately on well warmed plates with pats of the accompanying savoury butter.

Rib steak (côte de boeuf)
This steak, sufficient for four portions, is always grilled. At table the meat is cut cleanly off the bone while holding the trimmed end of the bone with a cloth or paper napkin. The meat is then carved in the same way as a double entrecôte, i.e. from right to left into slices about 2 cm (¾ in) thick and dressed immediately on well warmed plates together with the garnish.

Porterhouse steak
This is cut across the prepared but unboned sirloin and fillet, and both parts are first cut away from the bone. The fillet is cut into somewhat thinner slices and, as far as possible, each guest receives the same number of slices from both parts of the steak. A smaller sirloin can be used to cut individual porterhouse or T-bone steaks, one per person (American).

Boned sirloin (contrefilet)
This joint is carved from left to right into very thin, straight slices, using a 'tranchelard'. The joint is held with the back of a fork to ensure that slices of uniform size and shape are cut, an operation that requires practice and dexterity.

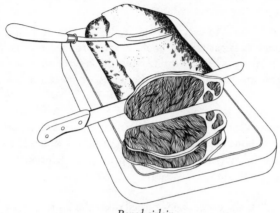

Boned sirloin

Roast fillet (filet de boeuf)
On account of its shape, fillet of beef is always more completely cooked at the thin end than in the middle or at the thick end. It is therefore advisable to cut about 10 cm (4 in) off the thin end first and to set this aside for guests preferring well-done meat. As this joint is almost always larded, it is cut into straight slices about 1 cm (⅜ in) thick. The carver starts at the thick end, steadying the joint with the back of a two-pronged fork. Oblique slices are unattractive as the lardoons may be pulled out while cutting at an angle.

VEAL

Whole legs of veal are scarcely ever roasted nowadays unless they are from very young milk-fed calves. In that case they are carved in the same way as leg of mutton or lamb (see page 39).

Saddle of veal (selle de veau)
The back comprises the best end and the saddle. To obtain the saddle for roasting, the kidneys with their fat are removed and the best end is cleanly cut away. The small fillets under the bones are usually left in place, but the backbone is straightened a little underneath to provide a firm base. The thin flanks are folded under and the saddle is tied round with string. The large saddle fillets are usually skinned and larded on the upper side before roasting. A good-sized saddle of veal weighs 3–4 kg (6½–8¾ lb). A good saddle of lamb weighs 1½–3 kg.

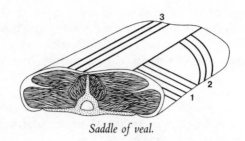

Saddle of veal.

(1) Oblique cut. (2) Cross cut. (3) Lengthwise (English) cut.

A board should always be used to carve this joint. Using a sharp knife, a lengthwise cut is made along the backbone as far as the rib bone. A two-pronged fork is inserted close to the backbone to hold the joint firmly in position. Now the carver works across the width of the loin along the ribs towards the backbone; the slices of meat can be lifted out without difficulty.

Once the first half has been carved, the same procedure is used for the other. The two saddle fillets are now cut into oblique slices about 1½ cm (½ in) thick. To keep them hot the slices should be transferred immediately to well warmed plates, a little gravy poured on the side and the garnish added.

For access to the small fillets the backbone is turned over; the knife is run along it to detach the fillets and these are cut obliquely into three or four slices, depending on size. When carving a joint of this size, speed and expertise are essential to minimise heat loss. Another prerequisite is very hot plates.

Roast loin of veal with kidneys (rognonade de veau)
This joint is carefully carved straight downwards into slices about 1½ cm (½ in) thick, while avoiding excessive piercing of the thick meat by the fork. A small palette knife is very useful for transferring the slices to the plates without detaching the slices of kidney from their covering. The plates should be very hot.

Best end of veal (carré de veau)
Roast best end of veal is relatively easy to carve. A sharp knife is run along the rib bone and the cutlets are cut off one by one. The joint is held in position either with the back of the carving fork or with the help of a table fork inserted into the meat at the side of the rib bone. Often the joint is carved in such a way that alternate slices contain a rib bone while the ones between them are boneless.

MUTTON OR LAMB

Leg of mutton or lamb (gigot de mouton)
For roasting, the chump end bone is always removed and the knuckle end is shortened and trimmed. If a fairly large number of guests is to be served, the best procedure is as follows: (1) Hold the shank in a napkin unless it has been provided with a holder (there are special

screw-in holders for the purpose). (2) Stand the leg on the board with the thick part downwards, holding it very firmly. (3) Using a long, sharp knife, make an incision behind the knuckle and remove the first very small slices. (4) The cushion can be cut into fair-sized, uniform slices while holding the knuckle bone firmly and working from left to right, i.e. towards the carver. This makes it easier to guide the knife; the cut is more uniform and across the grain. (5) After the cushion has been carved, the leg is turned over and the underside is evenly sliced in the same manner, starting at the thickest part and now working from right to left.

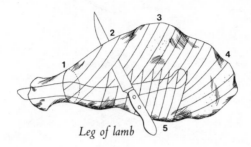

Leg of lamb

At position 1 cut the meat away right round the bone. At position 2 cut off four slices. Stand the leg up with position 3 uppermost and carve with the knife towards the carver. Turn the leg at position 4 and carve the rest of the meat in position 4 and 5.

Saddle of lamb or mutton (selle d'agneau ou de mouton)
The procedure is the same as for saddle of veal, the meat being carved into oblique slices about 1 cm (⅜ in) thick. English method – each saddle fillet is cut vertically into 4 cm (1½ in) slices. This is always done with saddle of lamb, but only on request in the case of saddle of mutton or venison.

Best end of lamb or mutton (carré d'agneau ou de mouton)
The procedure is the same as for best end of veal. As best end of lamb is considerably smaller than best end of veal, a portion consists of two cutlets.

PORK

Pork is unlikely to be carved at table, with the exception of ham, leg loin, saddle from a young animal and, at banquets, sucking pig.

Leg (cuisse de porc)
The roast leg of pork is presented as follows. First the crackling is cut away, then the leg is carved in the same way as ham, but into thicker slices. Finally the crackling is cut into smaller pieces, a few of which are added to the meat on each plate.

Saddle and fore loin (selle du jeune porc et carré de porc)
These are carved in the same way as veal.

Sucking pig (cochon de lait)
See *Techniques* page 102.

Ham (jambon)
Ham is served raw, boiled (hot or cold), braised or 'en croûte' (in a pastry crust).

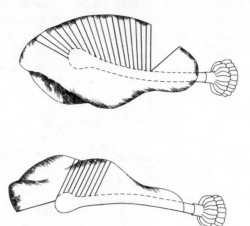

Carving a ham

Very thin, almost vertical slices are cut across the grain. A board is used when carving warm ham or ham in a crust. The knuckle bone is held in a napkin. Close behind it an incision is made down to the bone. The ham is then carved into thin vertical slices (the thickness will depend on whether it is hot or cold) working downwards and turning the knife slightly to the left each time it reaches the bone to release the slices. Once the part lying uppermost has been carved, the ham should then be turned over and the underside carved; the carver works from left to right as for leg of lamb.

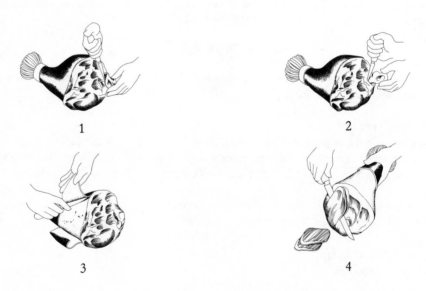

5

6

CARVING A BOILED HAM

(1) Place the ham while still warm on a carving board with the fat side underneath. Slip a paper frill over the end of the knuckle bone. (No sketch).

(2) Using a small, sharp knife, make an incision to expose the chump end bone, sever the tendon at the joint and remove the chump end bone. (Sketch 1 and 2).

(3) About 10 cm (4 in) from the end of the shank, make an incision in the skin with a sharp knife right round the bone. Make a second incision lengthwise, then peel off the skin.

(4) Make a quarter turn to place the ham on its narrow side. Carve down to the bone.

(5) Make a quarter turn to replace the ham; holding the knife at an oblique angle and working downwards, cut this side into even slices.

(6) Make a quarter turn back and slice the meat remaining on the bone.

8   Meat and Wine

The link between meat and wine deserves to be considered in a book dealing with meat dishes. First, wine, and the spirits distilled from wine, together with other alcoholic liquors, are extensively used in meat cookery. Bourgeois dishes, like carbonnade of beef, have beer as an ingredient, whereas the more sophisticated steak Diane may be flambéed with cognac in the restaurant itself. Additionally, there is a vast selection of wines or other alcoholic drinks to go with the kind of dishes discussed in this book. Hence an appreciation of wine and its partnership at table with meat is desirable.

Wine in cookery

Gourmets often contend that any dish prepared with wine should be served with the same wine. Certainly, the use of inferior 'cooking' wines should be rejected. However, the use of the 'same' wine in the cooking of a food and in service with it must in the present period be interpreted with common sense. Fine burgundies and clarets which are frequently selected to accompany meat dishes are today extremely costly. It is hardly practicable to use a first, or indeed any good growth, claret as a cooking wine. Many chefs would settle for a respectable ordinary burgundy or red bordeaux in cooking a dish that might be partnered by their more costly wine relatives. This would apply both to dishes cooked in wine and also to those in which wine is used to deglaze the sauté pan or otherwise to dilute cooking juices. Hence, a good cook seeking to satisfy the gourmet by achieving the best flavour in practice uses as good a wine as can be cost effective to achieve his finished dish.

Wine with food

At simple meals one wine at table normally suffices. Where a menu consists of several courses at more elaborate luncheons and evening dinners and banquets, different wines are selected to accompany different courses. As a general rule in such cases, white wines are drunk before red, younger before older wines and lighter wines before those of fuller body.

It was once thought mandatory to select white wine with white meat and red wine with red meat. Today many discriminating diners would not hesitate to take a red bordeaux, a beaujolais or a rosé wine with white meat such as veal particularly when that meat has not been cooked, say, in blanquette style.

The fact is that wine selection is an intensely personal matter. Any general 'rules' enunciated in this section are useful for guidance, but they should never be regarded as hard and fast regulations which prevent a diner from selecting the wines that please him. Moreover, it is well known that in particular areas of France associations of wine growers demonstrate at promotional dinners the versatility of a regional wine. For example, champagne may frequently be drunk throughout a meal of different courses. Even relatively 'unlikely' wine such as sauternes have even been promoted by the sauternes viticulturists in a similar way. That is an extreme example but certainly those who love claret may seldom select a burgundy and vice versa.

Nowadays, wine is demanded by an increasingly wide range of customer both in their homes and in restaurants. There is greater familiarity with wine even among those of modest income. Many will happily drink less expensive wine from parts of France such as the Loire and the Roussillion areas which only seldom appeared on pre-war wine lists. Additionally, wines from countries other than France and Germany are increasingly in demand, particularly those from Italy, Spain, Portugal, Yugoslavia and Hungary; and from the New World (North and South America, South Africa and Australia). Many of these wines are made from the grapes of the same varieties used in the longer-known French and German types and thus have something of their characteristics.

Whether relatively inexpensive or rare and costly, a discriminating diner seeks to select a wine which harmoniously complements a dish, enhancing its flavour. When several wines are to be served, the aim will be to provide a variety of wines similarly suitable for the course. As indicated earlier, the sequence of wines builds forward from the lesser, lighter and younger wines to reach a climax of excellence.

When encountering regional wines, the wine traveller will consult an expert such as a sommellier in the restaurant or a reliable vintner in a retail outlet. Certainly, local wine should be sampled. Many will provide excellent mates for local meat dishes.

Other beverages
In the United Kingdom only a small amount of white wine is produced, the rest is imported. A considerable range of beer is brewed. The full flavoured stouts to the lighter lagers, with ale and bitters in between, also provide opportunity for matching a beer with some of the simpler dishes. Sausage dishes, for example, such as with sauerkraut are admirably partnered with beer. For highly flavoured food such as curry, wine is seldom selected (though the less expensive and slightly sweeter white wines are often thought suitable) but generally with such dishes beer or cider is the choice.

Meat dishes and wine partners
As the foregoing indicates, general rules can thus only be applied most loosely. The following merely broadly indicates what may frequently be chosen by many diners or recommended by sommeliers.

SUGGESTED WINE PARTNERS FOR MEAT DISHES

SOUPS	Table wines are not always chosen to accompany soups, but for meat broths a claret or Beaujolais might be selected. Stronger meat consommés are usually accompanied by a fortified wine such as a dry sherry, Sercial Madeira or even a dry port.
COLD HORS D'OEUVRES & RAW MEAT DISHES Canapés	When hors d'oeuvres are varied and include fish, poultry and other items beside meat, the choice of wine is equally wide but is usually of younger, lighter and less expensive wines, often white, and rosé. When meat predominates, Beaujolais or a red Bordeaux may be appropriate.
Meat salads with or without vegetables	Macon or other white Burgundy, a rosé or lighter red wine.

Raw ham:
     Air dried (Parma)
     Smoked (Ardennes, Westphalia)
	An Italian white (e.g. Orvieto), or an Alsatian or German white or Meursault.

Ham with melon	Frascati or other white Italian wine, white Graves, Riesling or Burgundy.
Sausages	Flavoury German or Alsace whites, such as Traminer, Gerwurtztraminer or other dry whites (e.g. Pouilly fumé).
Mousse (ham, calf's liver) Stuffed breast of veal	Traminer, Gewurtztraminer, Beaujolais, rosé.
Sandwiches (as a snack)	With meat fillings, the choice is determined by the nature of the filling but generally as for canapés above.

Raw meat dishes
     Steak tartare
     Sliced raw beef Alba
	Lighter red wine: Beaujolais, red Bordeaux.
	 Vouvray, Loire white.

HOT HORS D'OEUVRES OR
PRELIMINARY COURSES

Pastry savouries (at receptions or
as hors d'oeuvres)
    Puff pastry – bouchées, vol au
    vent, sausage rolls, ham,
    croissants
    Short pastry – barquettes, tartlets

As for cold hors d'oeuvres, a wide range of choice from white, rosé to red and may include Pouilly fumé, Muscadet, Macon white, Riesling, Côtes de Provence, Tavel, red Bordeaux, Chianti and many others.

Toasts
    Cassolettes, croquettes, fricadelles,
    fritters, Rissoles

Eggs
    Poached au plat etc with meat
    Omelettes, pancakes (meat filled)
    Soufflés (brain, ham)

The sulphorous element in eggs prompts choice of simpler wines, red or white.

PIES, PATES & TERRINES

The Comité National des Vins de France recommend rosés (Anjou, Jura or Côtes de Provence) for hors d'oeuvres in general. For delicatessen, they suggest a dry, light white claret such as a Medoc, St. Julien, Margaux or St. Estephe.
For stronger flavoured pâtés etc, a red Burgundy, Rhone or Italian red may be selected.

MAIN DISHES (HOT)

Beef
    Grills
    Roast
    Sautés (shallow fried dishes)

Red wines are chosen to accompany beef dishes. For plain roasts, grills and even simple shallow fried ones: Beaujolais, Loire red, Macon red, Claret, (Médoc, St. Julien, Château Margaux, St. Estephe) Côtes de Beaune, Côtes du Rhone red, Pauillac, Pomerol, Corbière and Minervois, Bergerac red.

    Braised dishes, stews
    Oxtail
    Ragoûts, with wine or without
    wine
    Tongue
    Tripe

For dishes cooked in wine, accompany with wine of the same or similar origin, e.g. Boeuf à la Bordelaise, a Médoc; à la Bourguignon, a Chambertin. For red meat in sauce, the French Wine Committee recommendations embrace: Côtes de Nuits, St. Emilion, Pomerol, Hermitage red, Châteauneuf du Pape, Côtes de Beaune such as Pommard or Corton, Jura red, Provence red, Côte Rotie, Fitou and Cahors.

Veal
  Sautés
  Shallow fried dishes
  Roasts, e.g. fillet, cushion, loin
  Ragoûts, with or without wine
  Blanquettes
  Liver
  Sweetbreads
  Kidneys
  Tongue
  Heart
  Head
  Brains
  Feet

Lighter wines including German and Alsatian wines and white Burgundies. For breaded veal sautés, e.g. escalopes or cutlets a Hock (e.g. Niersteiner) or a Moselle. For an escalope such as Escalope de Veau Jardinière, a Médoc. For a blanquette a white Burgundy such as Clos Blanc Vougeot. For veal offals similar wines especially the flavoury Rieslings and Traminers from Alsace and Germany.

Mutton & Lamb
  Roast, leg, shoulder, saddle,
    best end, loin
  Grills, e.g. chops, cutlets
  Kebabs
  Pilaffs
  Braised
  Shallow fried, e.g. cutlets
  Ragoût
  Feet
  Offal: kidneys, liver, tongue, brain

On the continent where lamb is cooked 'pink', grills and roasts especially may be thought of almost as red meat and wine choice is not dissimilar from that for beef. Examples are: roast loin, a Pomerol; roast shoulder, a St. Emillion; a roast leg, a Médoc; a lamb chop, a Beaune; a lamb cutlet, a red Graves. For lamb in sauces or sautés or blanquettes follow the guidance as for beef and veal above.

Pork
  Roast
  Grills
  Braised
  Pot roast
  Shallow fried
  Ragoûts

Pork's rich, white meat is admirably partnered by flavoury white wines for example: pork chops, an Alsace Riesling; a roast of pork, a fine Hock, but many will choose a light red wine to accompany roasts and grills of pork or a Bordeaux (an inexpensive Côtes de Bourg) for a sucking pig. Otherwise, for dishes in sauce follow the guidelines for the other meats above.

Ham
  Boiled
  Braised
  En croûte
  Bacon, pickled
  Sausages
  Trotters

Similar considerations apply to ham but when braised, say, au Madère, the red wines of the Rhone, e.g. Châteauneuf du Pape may be chosen. A wide range of light, red and white wines are suitable with ham and bacon dishes.

Rabbit (farmed)

Fillets

Ragoûts

Fricassée

If cooked in a more strongly flavoured ragoût, a Beaujolais, red Bordeaux or even Macon might be chosen. Otherwise, in simply prepared fillets or in fricassées or blanquettes, a white wine, e.g. Pouilly fuissé.

9 Techniques

IN THE KITCHEN

Eminçé of veal
(Recipe page 544)

The ingredients ready
for use.

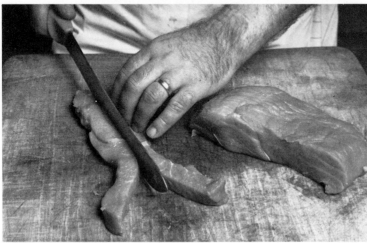

Cut the cushion of veal into
slices 2–3 cm (about 1 in)
thick. Cut each slice in half
lengthwise.

Thinly slice each half with
a sharp knife.

Place the sliced meat in
hot butter.

Fry the meat lightly, separating the slices with a fork. Shake the pan well to prevent sticking.

Add the shallots which have been finely chopped. Often the shallots are lightly fried in butter without colouring before the meat is added.

Add the mushrooms which have been very thinly sliced.

Moisten with a good white wine and allow to cook for a short time.

Add the cream, stir, bring
to the boil, dish and
sprinkle with chopped
parsley.

Stuffed breast of veal

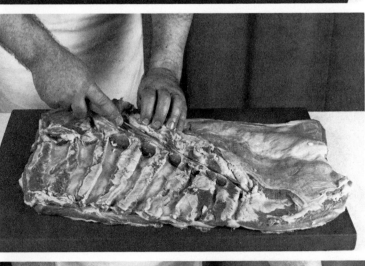

Insert the knife at the
breastbone...

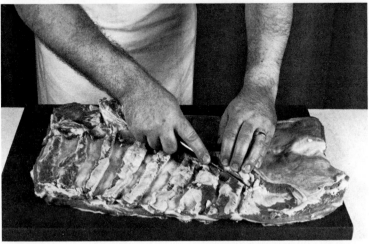

...and run it along the
cartilage.

Turn the breast over.

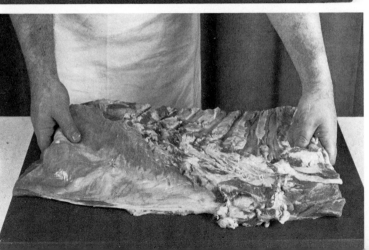

Insert the knife again to detach the rib bones and expose the flanks.

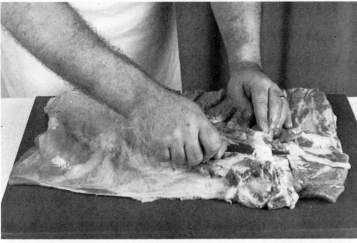

Exposing the breastbone and cartilage.

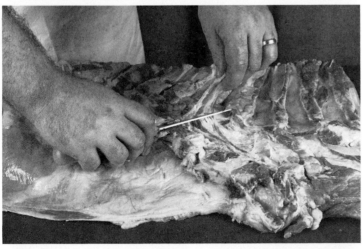

Trim the breastbone neatly, removing the periosteum and fat; all bones should be trimmed in this way. Cut away the breastbone.

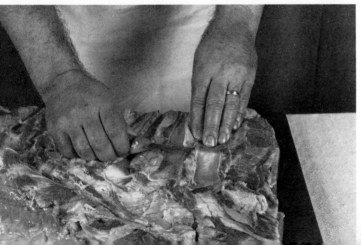

Inserting the stuffing.

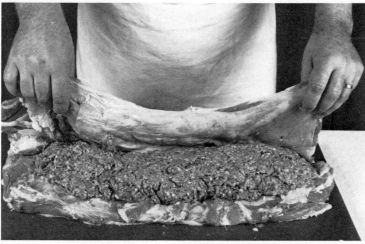

Folding the breast over to enclose the stuffing.

The opening is sewn up at the ends...

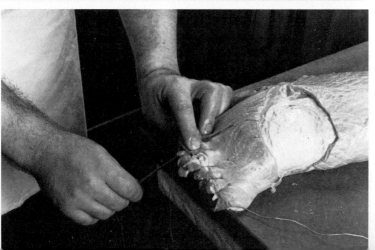

... and along the side. The stuffed breast is now ready for roasting in a pre-heated oven.

Best end of veal

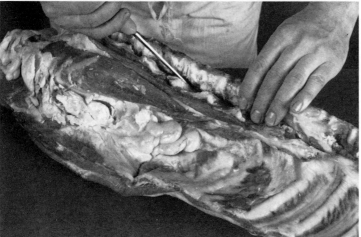

Insert the knife and run it along the vertebrae to loosen the fillets.

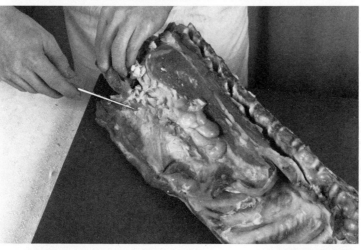

Then insert the knife at the end near the small rib bone...

...and make an incision along the small rib bone...

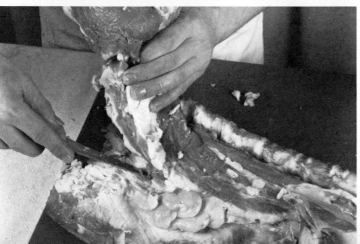

...to cut away the fillets.

Remove the cartilage from the spinous process.

Detaching the spinous process.

Trimming – remove any remaining flesh and cut away the periosteum from the small ribs.

Chining up to the large rib bone.

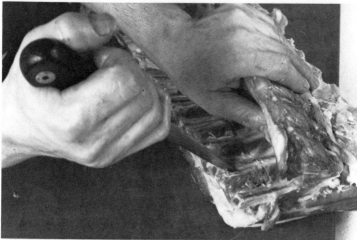

For crown of veal, the ribs are cut away from the periosteum halfway along their length.

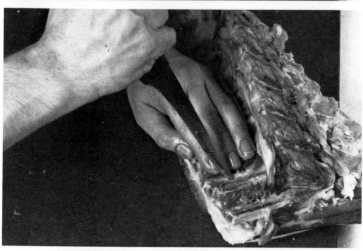

Spread out and hold down so that the best end...

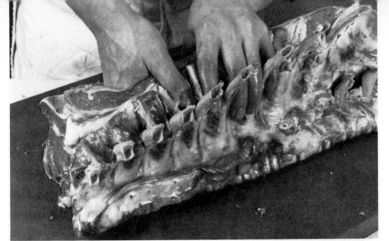

...can be flattened halfway.

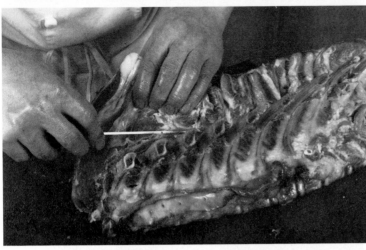

Start cutting to uncover the loin.

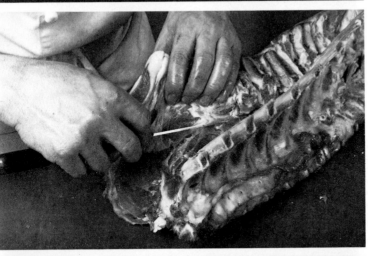

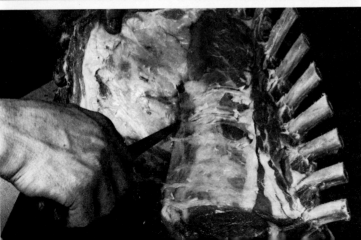

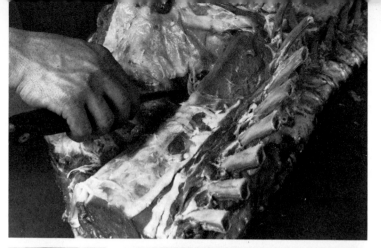

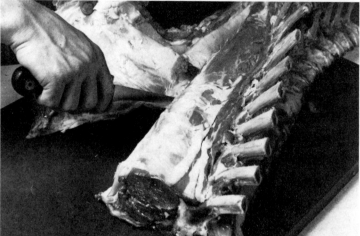

Continue cutting...

...until the covering over the loin has been detached.

Now turn the loin over and start cutting at the large rib end.

Cutting into the spinous process up to the chine.

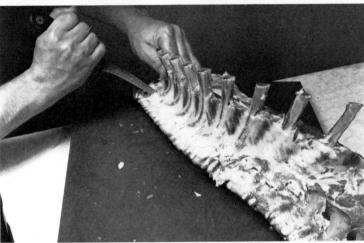

Chining – detaching each rib bone.

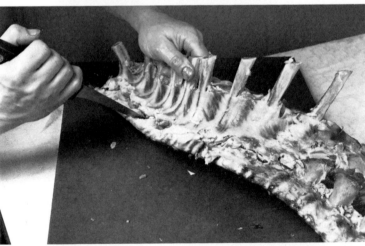

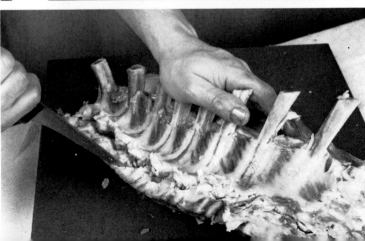

Detaching the rest of the backbone.

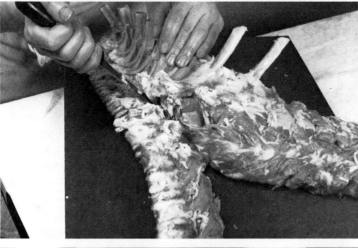

Cutting away the rest of the backbone.

Trimming off the layer of fat.

An incision is made to expose the dorsal tendon, which must be removed as it is much too hard.

The tendon is removed.

The joint is trimmed flat, the periosteum and excess fat have to be removed.

The trimmed best end.
Important – the rib bones
must be carefully scraped
quite clean.

For crown roast, see **Crown
of lamb,** illustrations
following.

Crown of lamb
Crown of lamb is prepared for
roasting in the same way.

The best end which has
been carefully trimmed
(illustration page 57) is
placed round an empty
can...

...and tied to make a
crown.

The twine is securely
knotted. The crown is
ready for roasting.

Calf's sweetbreads

Before use, sweetbreads require prolonged soaking under cold running water to whiten them. They are then blanched for three or four minutes.

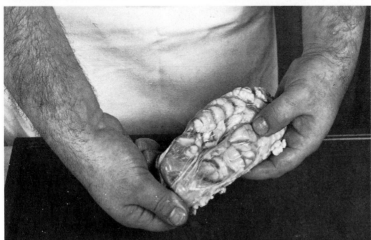

Pull off the skin.

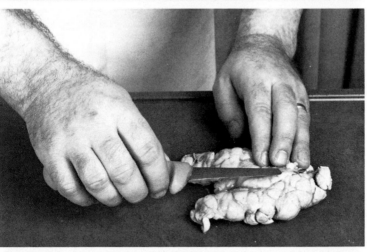

Cut off the blood clots and any inedible portions.

Above: untrimmed sweetbreads.
Below: sweetbreads ready for use.

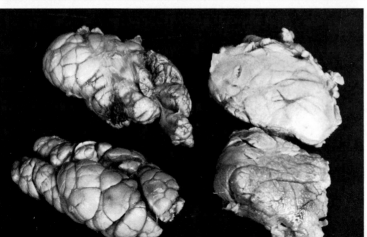

To use in fillings (e.g. for bouchées) divide the sweetbread into segments and carefully break up each one.

Saddle of veal

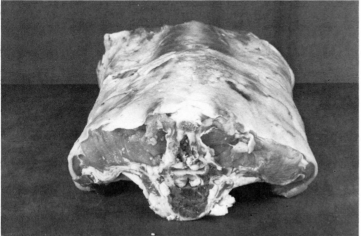

Removing the fillets
The whole untrimmed saddle of veal.

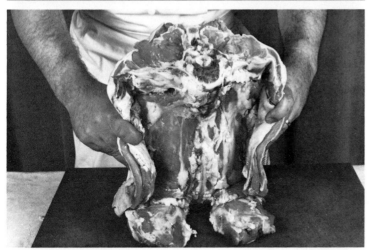

The two fillets can be seen on the inside.

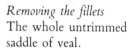

Start removing the fillets by making an incision with a sharp knife...

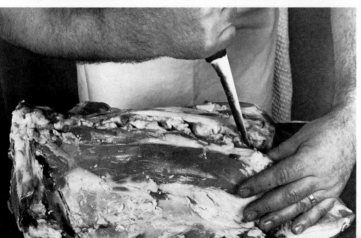

...and running it along the bone.

Insert the knife at the small rib bone.

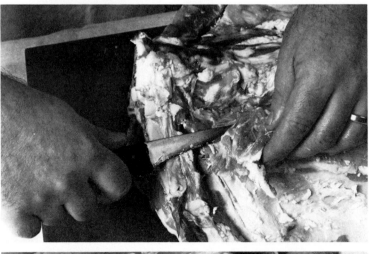

Run the knife along the small rib bone to cut away the fillet.

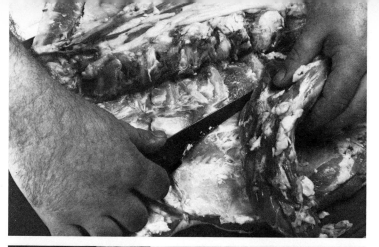

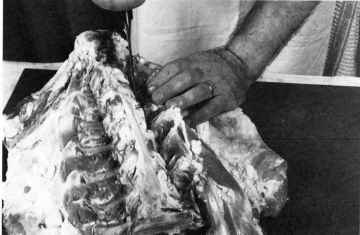

Cutting away the fillet on the opposite side.

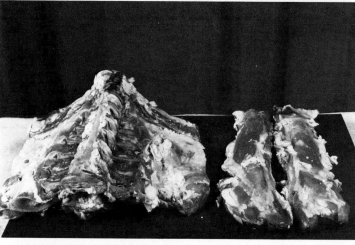

The two fillets after removal.

Removing the loin
Trim the short ribs, removing the periosteum and any scraps of flesh.

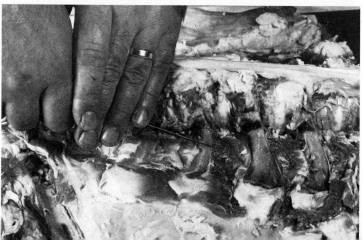

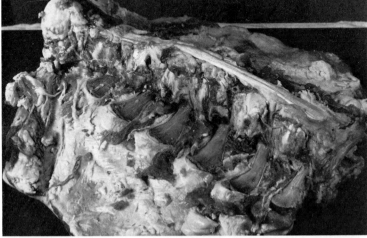

The trimmed ribs.

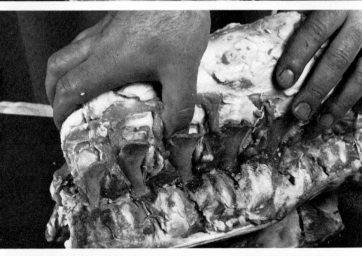

Detaching the short ribs. Push the thumb between the vertebrae and the meat.

The rib bones are freed in this way.

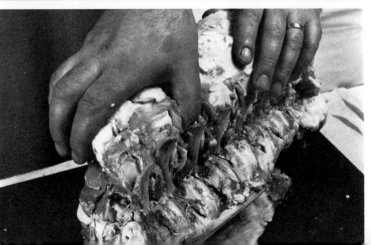

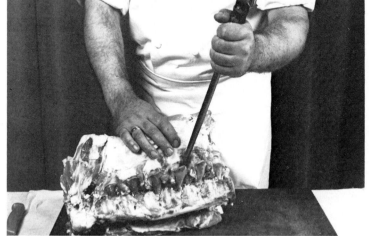

To remove the backbone, proceed as follows: with the aid of a steel (to prevent tearing of the skin) widen the space at the base of the ribs to facilitate separation.

Press the cartilage down on both sides.

Loosen with the steel.

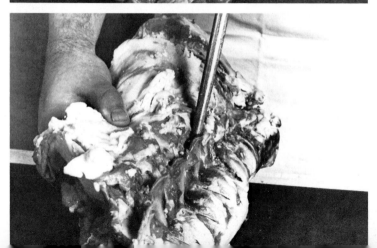

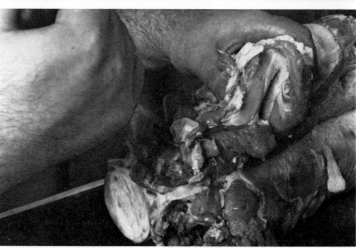

...until the spinous process can be detached.

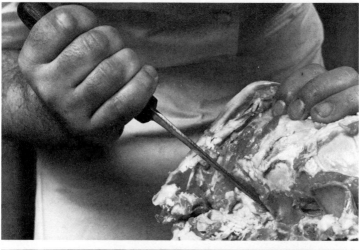

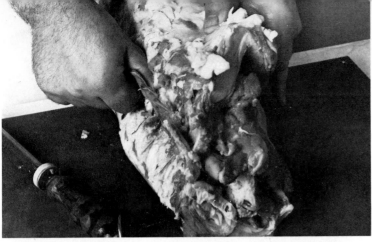

Hold the ribs with the right hand and press down with the left one.

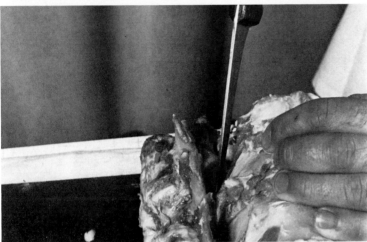

Insert a sharp knife...

...and make an incision towards the spinous process on both sides.

Continue cutting...

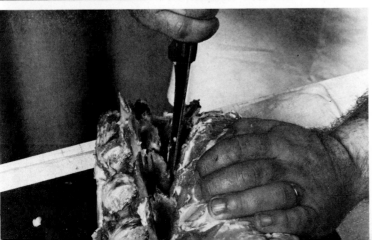

Detaching the spinous process I.

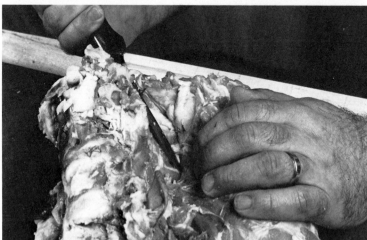

Detaching the spinous process II.

Exposing the spinous process.

Trim the spinous process.

The part of the spinous process which has been exposed ready for severing.

Removing the spinous process cartilage.

Loosen with a steel and pull off the exposed loin.

Use the knife, working towards the top of the backbone, to facilitate removal of the loin.

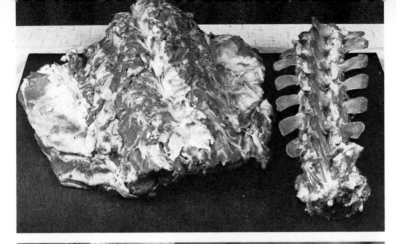

The saddle of veal ready for use, without the loin fillets

Roast leg of lamb

Testing the degree of cooking
Insert the forefinger into the opening on the upper side of the leg bone to determine the temperature of the meat. This will indicate the degree of cooking. If the meat is still cold, the joint is *underdone*. At body temperature the joint is *medium-rare* inside. If the meat is very hot, the joint is *well done*.

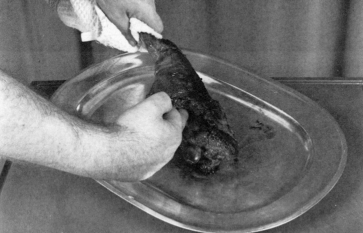

Stuffed shoulder of lamb

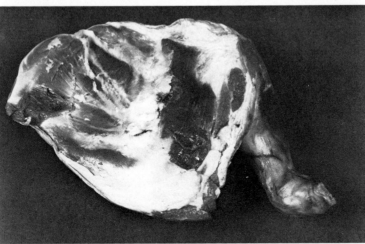

The shoulder of lamb before boning and trimming.

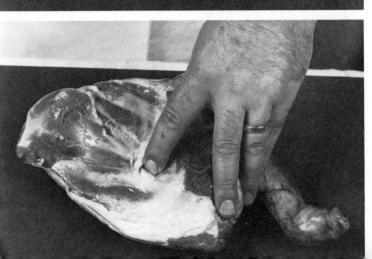

Feel for the blade bone articulation, using the forefinger.

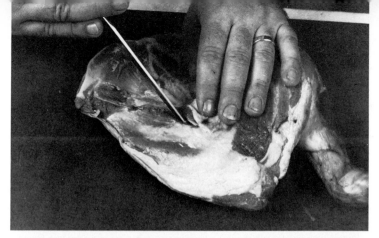

Start cutting with a pointed knife to gain access to the blade bone.

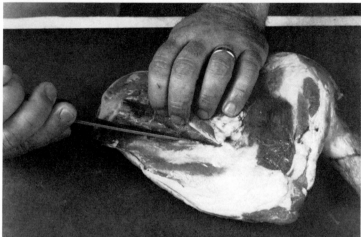

Cutting away the flesh above the blade bone.

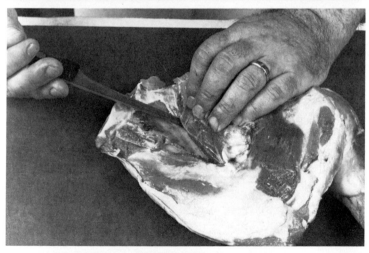

Exposing the blade bone.

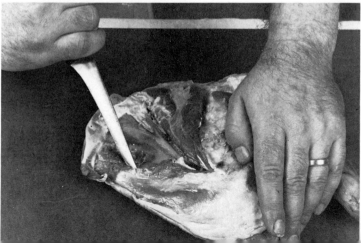

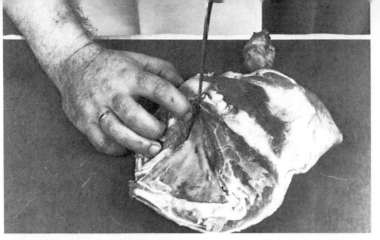

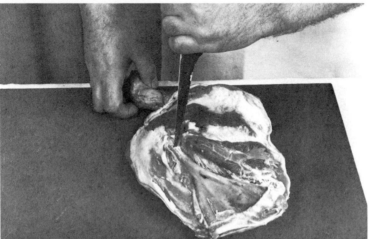

Cutting through the blade bone articulation.

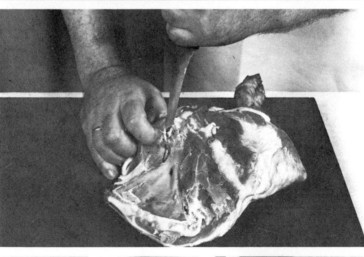

Cutting away the periosteum.

Breaking off the blade bone over the edge of the table.

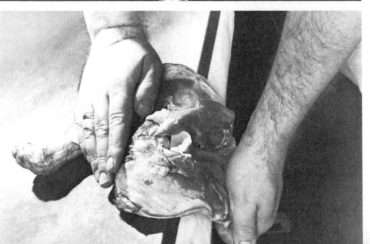

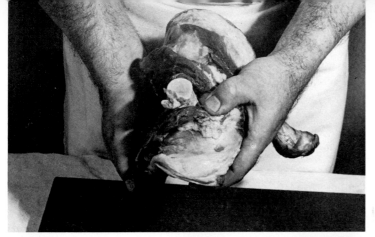

Withdrawing the blade bone.

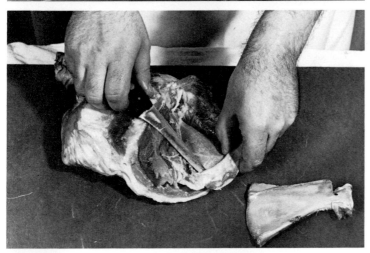

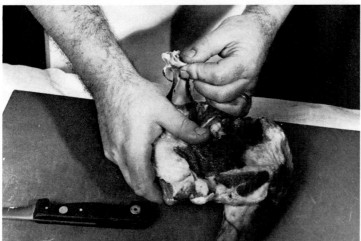

Detaching the cartilaginous process of the blade bone.

The forefinger is used to locate the centre bone.

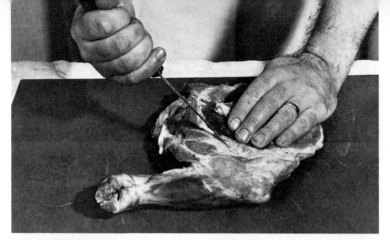

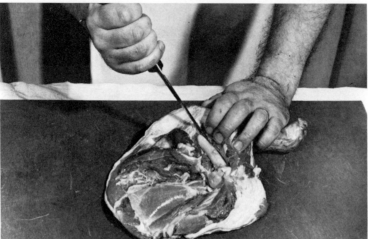

Cutting out the centre bone.

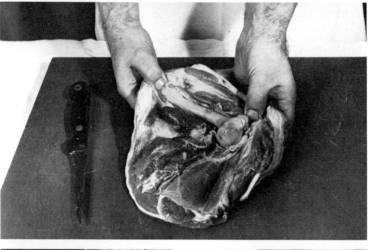

The centre bone has been exposed.

Detaching the centre bone from the flesh.

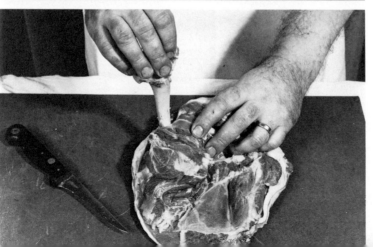

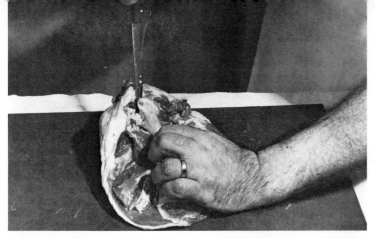

Cutting through the articulation from the centre bone to the shank.

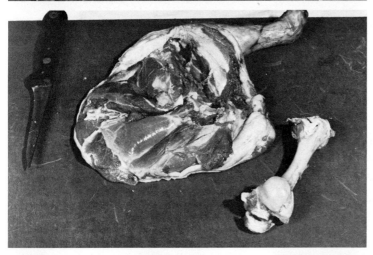

Withdrawing the centre bone.

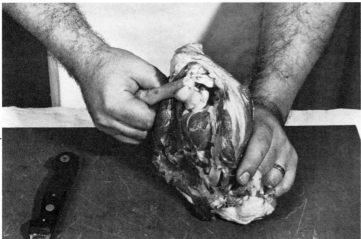

The centre bone has been removed.

Make a circular incision above the articulation.

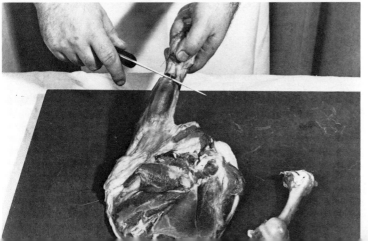

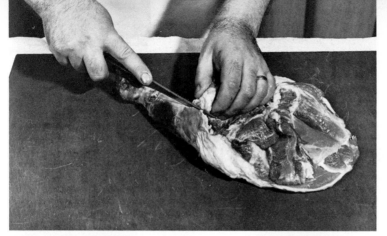

To remove the shank bone,
run the knife up from the
base to the circular incision.

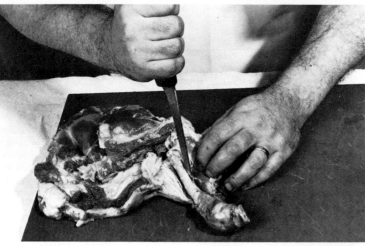

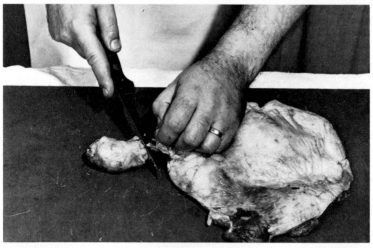

Turn the shoulder over.

Detach the underside of the
shank bone.

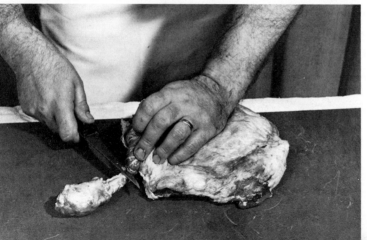

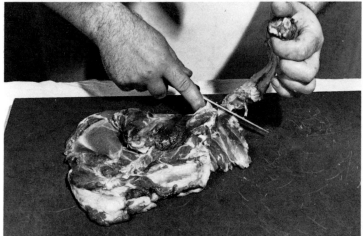

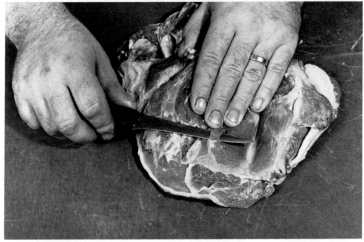

Cut away the periosteum.

Trim the underside of the meat.

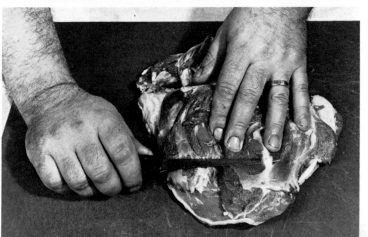

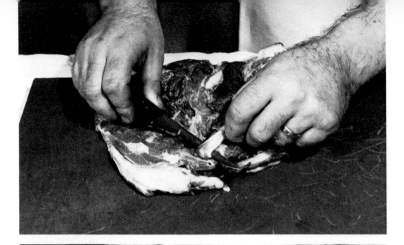

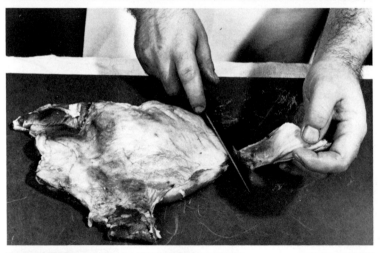

Turn the shoulder over and cut away the unwanted layer of fat.

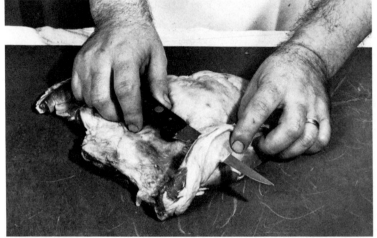

Trim the meat and cut off all unwanted fat.

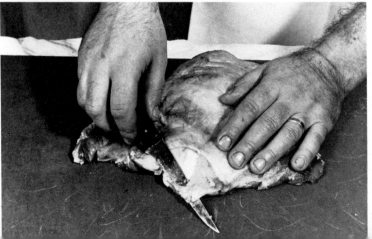

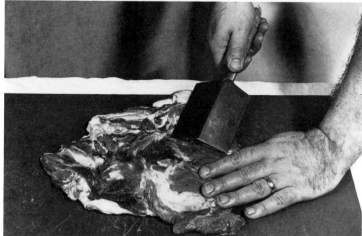

Open out the shoulder with
the underside uppermost
and flatten.

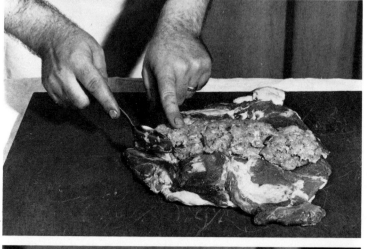

Spread with stuffing.

The stuffed shoulder.

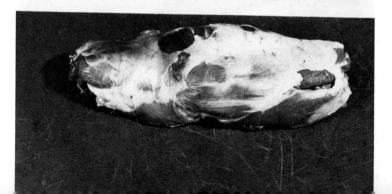

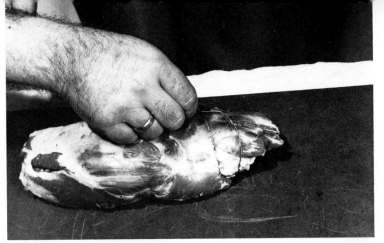

Tie the stuffed shoulder...

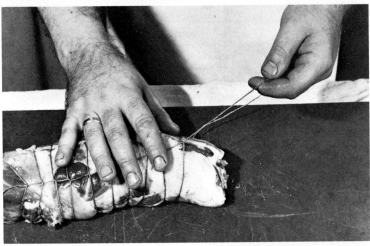

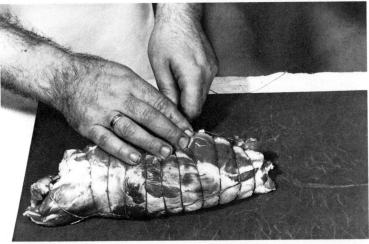

...and fasten off
lengthwise.

The shoulder ready for
roasting.

Trimming a kidney

Remove the surrounding fat with both hands...

...and carefully uncover the kidney first on one side...

...then on the other...

...as far as the point where the fat adheres tightly to the kidney.

Place a sharp knife at this point...

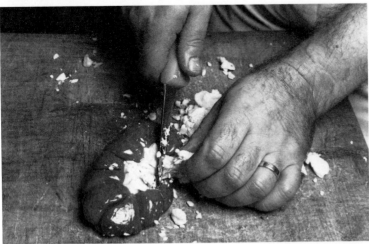

...and carefully cut away the fat.

Bernese potato cake
Rösti nach Berner Art

Cold boiled potatoes are skinned and coarsely grated, lightly fried in hot butter or lard, quickly but carefully turned with a fork, then lightly pressed down with a palette knife. Keep the potatoes away from the side of the pan with the aid of the palette knife so that they do not stick. When the underside is brown, slide the potato cake onto a dish, turn it...

...and brown the other side lightly in hot fat. To serve, slide onto a heated round dish.
Often the potato cake is fried on one side only and served with the brown side uppermost.

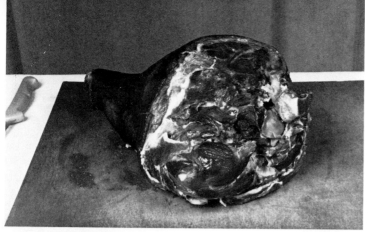

Ham en croûte
(Recipe page 858)

The ham which has been three quarters cooked.

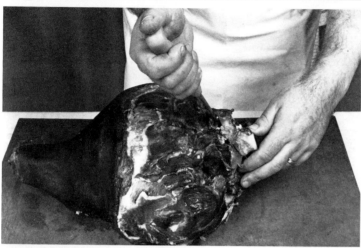

Using a short, sharp knife, expose the bone...

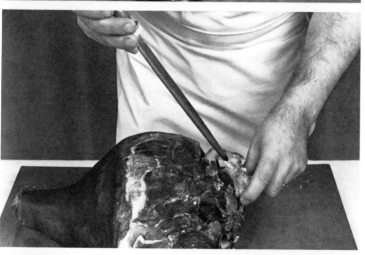

...and remove it with the hand.

Make a circular incision in the skin round the bone.

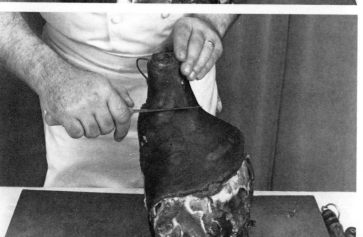

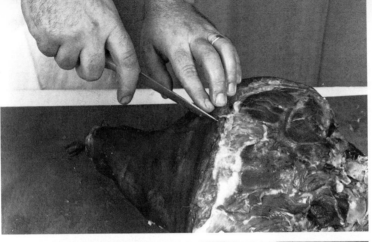

On the inner side of the ham make a diagonal incision in the skin as far as the bone to facilitate removal of the skin.

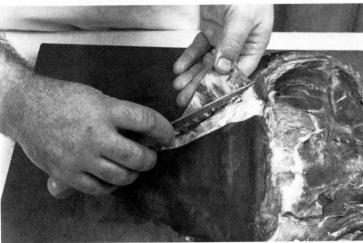

Work the skin loose at first with a knife...

...then pull off with both hands.

The skinned ham.

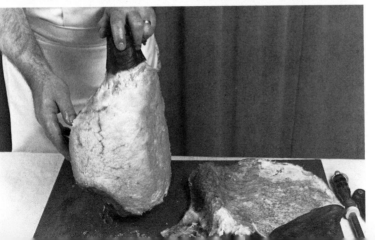

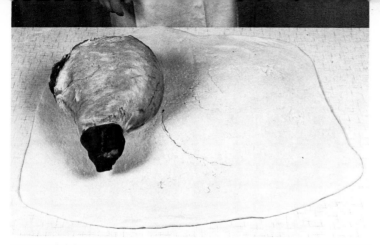

Pin out bread or plait dough about 1 cm (⅜ in) thick and place the ham on top.

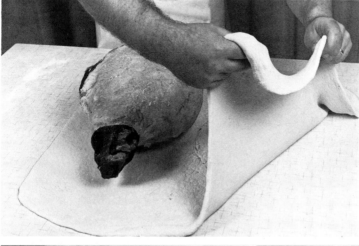

Cover over with enough dough...

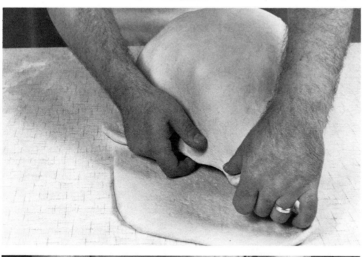

...to leave a free edge.

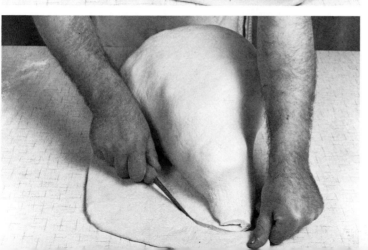

Tuck the free edge under the ham; its weight will press the two pieces of dough together. Cut off the surplus dough.

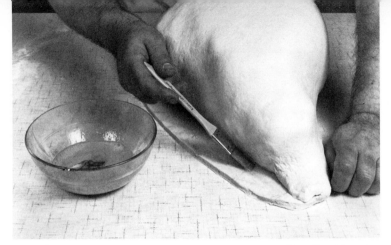

Brush the join with egg.

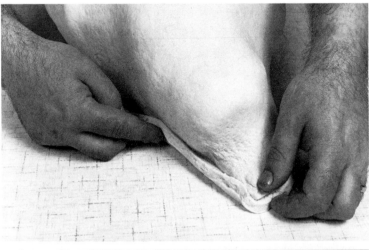

Press upwards the edge of the dough on which the ham is resting and seal well.

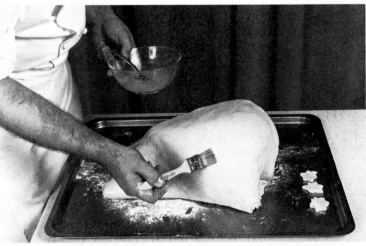

Wash the dough with egg. Pin out the dough trimmings, cut into decorative shapes as desired, place in position and wash with egg.

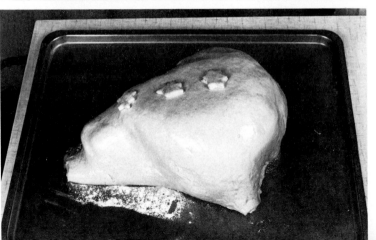

The ham ready for baking.

(Carving ham en croûte, see page 100.)

AT THE TABLE – CARVING, COOKING AND FLAMBÉING

Leg of lamb

Pick up the shank bone in a napkin and transfer the leg of lamb from the dish to the carving board.

Make an incision down to the bone with the carving knife below the articulation.

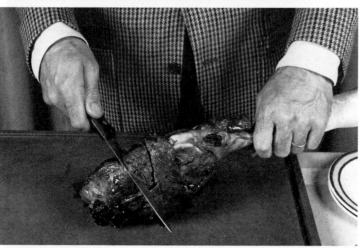

At an oblique angle to this incision cut out the first slice of the upper part of the cushion.

Cut the whole cushion into even slices.

Use the carving knife to transfer the slices of meat to the serving dish.

Turn the leg. Run the knife along the bone...

...to release the cushion on the other side.

Start cutting parallel to the bone.

Working horizontally, carve off the first slice. Continue carving in the same way until the whole cushion has been evenly sliced.

After transferring the slices of meat to the serving dishes with the carving knife, the meat juices from the carving board...

...are poured over the meat.

Saddle of lamb

The fork is inserted into the backbone and remains in the same place throughout. (*Important*)

The saddle fillets are detached from the bone in front and behind, using the point of the knife...

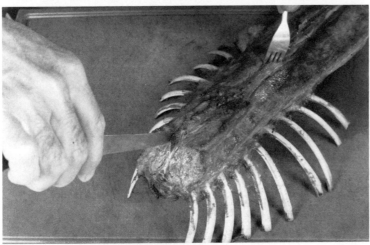

first on one side...

...then on the other.

To cut the fillets away correctly the knife must be flexed a little.

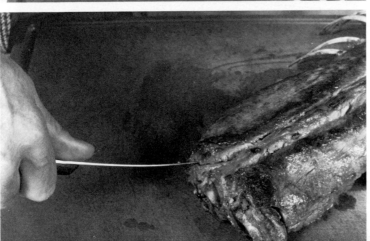

It is important to cut down
onto the ribs along the
backbone. The knife must
be drawn right through.

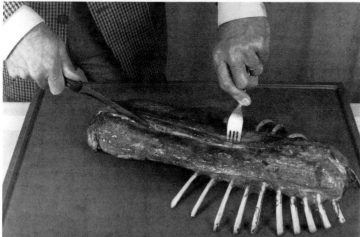

Remove the saddle fillet
from the bone with the
back of a spoon.

98

The fillet after removal.

When both the saddle fillets have been removed, the saddle is turned over and a sickle-shaped cut is made along the bone...

...to remove the two loin fillets.

The saddle fillets are cut into oblique slices which should not be too thin. While cutting, the knife should merely slide along so that the meat retains its juices.

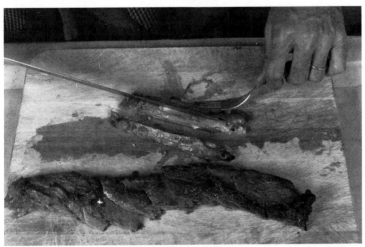

The loin fillets are cut lengthwise into strips (aiguillettes).

Pick up the slices of meat with the carving knife and dress on the saddle bones.

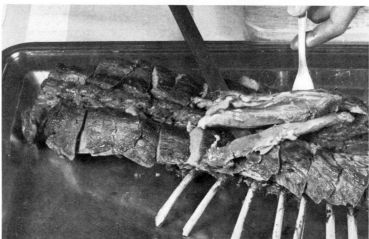

Ham en croûte
(Preparation: illustrations page
(Recipe page 858)

Insert a fork into the top
and cut right round the
crust half way up.

Lift off the top.

Hold the shank of the uncovered ham in a napkin and lift.

Cut straight down to the bone below the knuckle.

Start carving the cushion at an oblique angle to the first incision. Continue at the same oblique angle, cutting the ham into uniform slices.

Cut off a piece of crust and place it with a slice of ham.

After carving the first cushion, turn the ham over and cut up the other cushion in the same way.

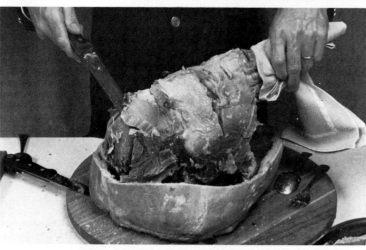

To dress, arrange the pieces of crust with the sliced ham on a serving dish and serve as hot as possible. The ham is more succulent when hot.

Sucking pig

Using a sharp pointed knife, cut away the crackling behind the head all the way round...

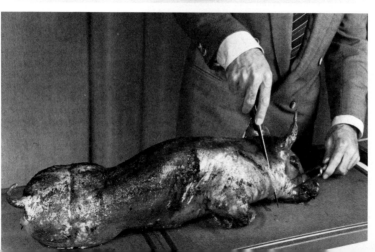

...and firmly and cleanly sever the head from the body.

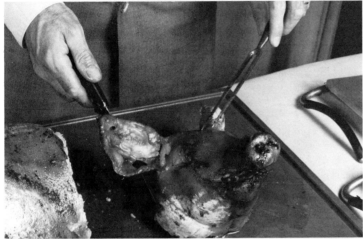

The severed head. When specially requested, the ears, snout and cheeks are removed and served.

Grasp the foot bone at the end of the shoulder in a napkin and lift up, then make a circular cut through the crackling at the shoulder.

Lift the shoulder and run the point of the knife along the bone to detach.

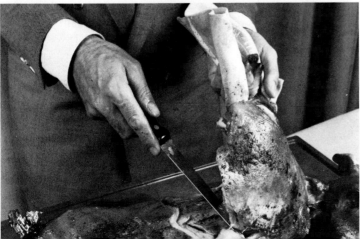

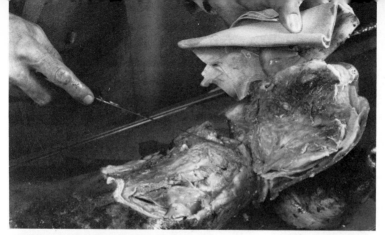

Twist the shoulder joint apart and pull off the shoulder.

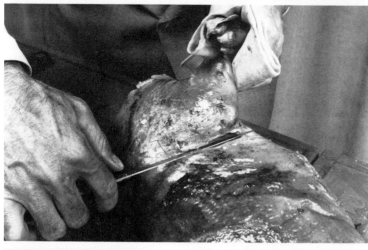

Grasp the end of the leg and cut the crackling with a sharp knife from the back.

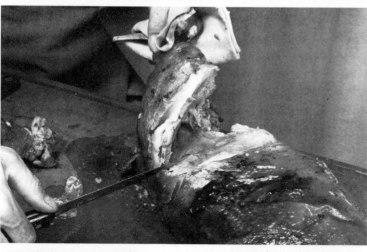

Lift the leg away carefully and run the tip of the knife round to detach.

Twist off the leg and sever from the pelvic bone.

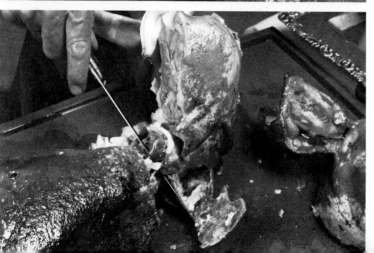

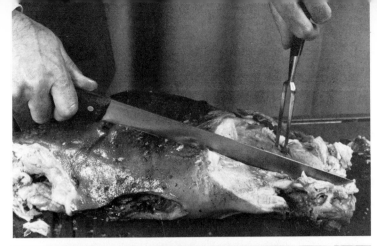

The body without the legs and shoulders is laid in front of the carver.

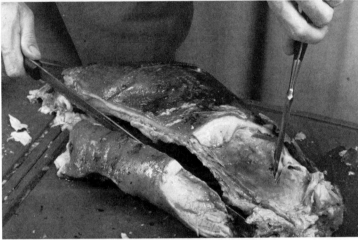

Halfway up the body a slit is made along the belly, separating it from the saddle.

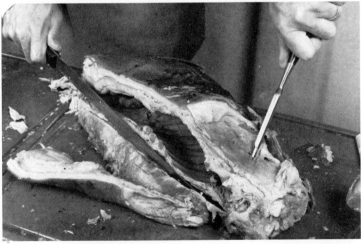

The neck and best end are now cut vertically between the ribs.

If the animal is not too small, the saddle fillet...

...can be detached from the bone.

Cut the belly into even pieces.

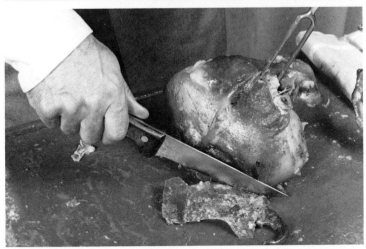

Cut off the crisp, well-browned tail piece.

Cut the leg...

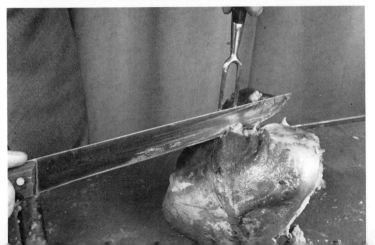

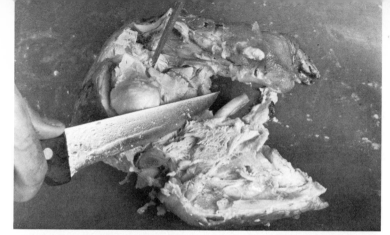

...along the bone...

...into...

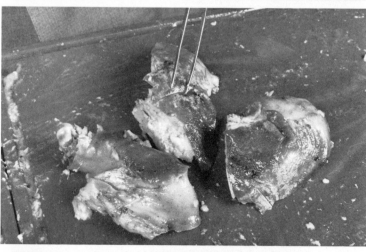

...three pieces.

Depending on the size of
the leg, the three pieces are
cut into smaller ones.

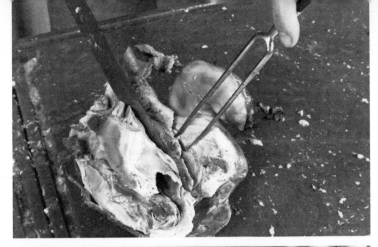

On the inside, cut away the meat on top of the shoulder.

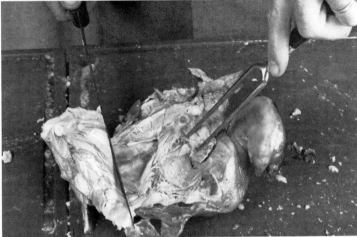

Sever the shoulder from the lower part.

Cut again to obtain at least four servings.

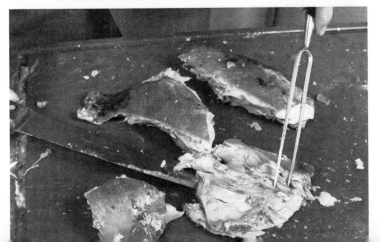

The sucking pig carved ready for serving.

Flambé calf's kidneys
(Recipe page 671)

Assemble the ingredients on a side table next to the flambéing trolley.

Sprinkle a plate with freshly ground pepper. Place the slices of kidney on it and season with more freshly ground pepper.

Place the butter and oil in the pan and heat while tilting the pan from side to side to blend them as well as possible. When brown, add the slices of kidney and fry lightly...

...then turn them.

Pour off the surplus fat.

Add the cognac to the pan
and ignite.

Remove the kidneys from the pan, cover and keep hot.

Place the shallots in the pan, cook gently in the pan juices without colouring...

...then pour in the white wine.

Add the mixed herbs.

Now add the mustard and mix well.

Pour in the thickened veal stock, stir well...

...bind with the cream, reduce.

Season the sauce with salt, pepper and a little paprika.

Finish off with a little cayenne.

Only now are the kidneys lightly seasoned with salt...

...then they are coated with the sauce.

Part 2:

Recipes

Basic Preparations

Basic Stocks

Important: if stock is not intended for immediate use, it *must* be cooled as quickly as possible to prevent souring.

Beef stock

It is impossible to make good consommé or sauce without using a well made basic stock. To prepare beef stock for consommé or for use in various sauces, the bones should be carefully trimmed, blanched and placed in a pan of cold water with flavouring vegetables and herbs. The quantity of vegetables should not exceed ten per cent to avoid too strong a vegetable flavour. Once the water has come to the boil it must be well skimmed and all the fat must be removed.

White veal stock I

Yield: 10 l (17½ pt)

5 kg	veal bones	11 lb
approx. 1 kg	white flavouring vegetables and herbs	2 lb 4 oz
	salt	

Clean and blanch the bones. Place them in a pan of cold water, bring to the boil, skim and add the vegetables and herbs. Season fairly lightly with salt and simmer for 3 to 4 hours. Skim, remove any fat and strain.

White veal stock II

5 kg	veal knuckle bones and veal trimmings	11 lb
250 g	carrots	9 oz
	2 large onions, unpeeled	
	1 leek	
	½ celeriac	
	3 parsley roots	
	½ bay leaf	
	1 tablespoon white peppercorns, crushed	
1 l	dry white wine	1¾ pt
1 dl	tomato purée	3½ fl oz
3½ l	water	6 pt

1 dl	corn oil	3½ fl oz

Chop the bones very small. Cut up the vegetables to make a mirepoix. Fry the bones, meat and mirepoix in the corn oil until golden brown, pour in ½ l (18 fl oz) water and reduce completely. Repeat this procedure six times in the oven. After the last reduction add the tomato purée and continue browning for 1 or 2 minutes. Add the wine and sufficient water to cover and transfer to a stockpot. Continue cooking for an hour while skimming repeatedly, taking care to keep the stock light and clear.

(Gerhard Gartner, Germany)

Brown veal stock I

Yield: 10 l (17½ pt)

5–7 kg	veal bones	11–15½ lb
	dripping	
	bacon trimmings (optional)	
approx. 1 kg	mirepoix	2 lb 4 oz
	2 tablespoons tomato purée	
	a little white wine	
approx. 10 l	water	approx. 17½ pt

Chop up the bones very small and brown in dripping (and bacon trimmings if desired). Add the mirepoix and brown. Pour off the fat, add the tomato purée and brown again, then moisten with a little white wine and reduce while stirring. Moisten again with a little water and stir well. Add the rest of the water, bring to the boil, skim and cook gently for about 4 hours. Skim from time to time and add water if necessary.

Brown veal stock II

Yield: approx. 10 l (17½ pt)

5–7½ kg	veal bones	11–16½ lb
	a few pork rinds (optional)	
80–100 g	fat or oil	3–4 oz
approx. 800 g	mirepoix	1 lb 12 oz
50 g	tomato purée	2 oz
12 l	water	21 pt
½ l	white wine (optional)	18 fl oz
40 g	salt	1½ oz

Chop up the bones small. Brown them in the oven, add the mirepoix and continue browning a little, taking care to avoid burning. Add the tomato purée. Pour off the excess fat, moisten with white wine (optional) or a little water and reduce completely while stirring with a spatula. Pour in sufficient water to cover well, bring to the boil, skim well, season with salt and spices to taste. Cook gently over low heat for 4 hours, removing any fat from time to time. Strain through a cloth and use as required. If not required until the next day, cool at once by standing the pot in running water.

Lamb gravy I

2 kg	lamb bones	4 lb 8 oz
300 g	carrots, diced	10½ oz
200 g	onions, diced	7 oz
	4 cloves of garlic, peeled	
½ l	white wine	18 fl oz
4 l	water	7 pt
	bouquet garni containing:	
	1 sprig rosemary	
	2 sprigs thyme	
	3 bay leaves	
	6 savory stalks	
	10 parsley stalks	
	½ stick celery	
30–50 g	fat	1–2 oz
	salt, pepper	

Chop up the bones, which may be from boned breast or best end, brown them in the oven in the fat, then add the diced vegetables, the garlic and the bouquet garni. Moisten with the white wine, reduce, add the water and boil for 3 to 4 hours, removing the fat repeatedly. Pass through a conical strainer, remove any remaining fat and reduce to ½ litre (18 fl oz). Season with salt and pepper.

This gravy may be used as a basis for various sauces, with the addition of the cooking juices from the meat they are to accompany after these juices have been diluted and freed of fat.

(Pierre Gleize, France)

Lamb gravy II

Chop up lamb bones (shoulder or leg) and colour lightly in butter or oil in the oven. Pour off the fat, add a little mirepoix, two cloves of garlic and a little water, then cook slowly for 45 minutes.

Meat glaze

Reduce strained brown veal stock, turning down the heat considerably, and pour into a smaller pan, then repeat the procedure until the reduced stock is thick enough to coat a spoon. Transfer to small jars or synthetic sausage casings for cold storage.

Meat glaze forms the basis for several sauces. To enhance the flavour of a sauce or increase its spiciness, meat glaze is added to it. Glazes are used for cold dishes to enhance the flavour of joints of meat or give them a glossy coating.

Marinades

To tenderise meat, enable it to be stored for a time or give it an appropriate flavour, it is steeped in a suitable marinade.

Meat for daily requirements
Small individual cuts, such as beef or veal steaks, are marinated in oil to tenderise them.

Meat for pies, galantines and terrines
The trimmed cuts are steeped in Madeira, red or white wine, sherry, Cognac or port, depending on use, and seasoned as desired with the addition of herbs and spices to taste. As a rule the marinade is subsequently mixed with the filling.

Large joints
Large joints are steeped in a raw or cooked marinade for dishes such as braised or stewed marinated beef.

Small cuts
Small cuts should be steeped in a raw marinade or brushed with it. Meat for grilling should always first be brushed with a well-flavoured marinade.

Brining
Wet-salting of pork, bacon, ox tongue, silverside, etc. is a form of marinating, involving the immersion of the meat in brine. It is also called 'pickling'.

Marinade (basic recipe)

Yield: 10 l (17½ pt)

300 g	carrots, diced	10½ oz
300 g	celery, diced	10½ oz
600 g	onions, sliced	1 lb 5 oz
	5 cloves of garlic, crushed	
	5 cloves	
	3 bay leaves	
30 g	peppercorns, crushed	1 oz
	thyme, rosemary to taste	
9 l	wine (usually red)	15¾ pt
approx. 1 l	wine vinegar	approx. 1¾ pt
(depending on strength)		

Place the pieces of meat, which should be of the same size as far as possible, in a suitable container and cover with the marinade. Leave for 8 to 10 days depending on the type of meat and the size of the pieces.

Quick marinade (cooked)

Same ingredients as for basic marinade. Place all the ingredients in a pan, bring to the boil, then cool. Proceed as for basic marinade, but leave to soak for only 2 to 4 days.

Vinegar marinade I (for braised rump of beef)

Yield: 10 l (17½ pt)

300 g	carrots, diced	11 oz
600 g	onions	1 lb 5 oz
	parsley	
300 g	leeks (white), sliced	11 oz
	5 cloves	
	3 bay leaves	
30 g	peppercorns, crushed	1 oz
	3 sprigs thyme	
	5 sprigs marjoram	
8 l	white cooking wine	14 pt
2 l	wine vinegar	3½ pt

Prepare a marinade with all the ingredients. Depending on the strength of the marinade, the meat should be steeped in it for about 8 to 10 days. This marinade may also be used as a quick marinade, but for this purpose the recipe for quick marinade (cooked) is preferable.

Vinegar marinade II

6 l	water	10½ pt
1½ l	wine or tarragon vinegar	⅝ pt
20 g	spiced salt	¾ oz

Boil the water and allow to cool. Add the vinegar and salt. Pour over the meat and marinate for 4 to 6 days.

Milk marinade

2 l	milk	3½ pt
6 g	spiced salt	2 small teaspoons

Scald the milk and allow to cool, then add the salt. Pour over the meat and marinate for 3 to 4 days. In the summer the marinade should be renewed after two days or boiled and allowed to cool before pouring over the meat again.

White wine marinade

3 l	light white wine	5¼ pt
10 g	spiced salt	¼ oz

Pour over the meat and marinate for 4 to 6 days. This recipe is excellent for white meat and mutton.

Pickling brine (for ox tongue, brisket of beef, calf's tongue, knuckle, loin or blade of pork)

Brine:

8 l	water	14 pt
4 kg	salt	8 lb 12 oz
200 g	saltpetre	7 oz
300 g	sugar	11 oz
	20 juniper berries, crushed	
	4 sprigs thyme	
	3 bay leaves	

Salt mixture for rubbing into meat:

500 g	salt	1 lb 2 oz
25 g	saltpetre	1 oz

Place all the ingredients for the brine in a pan and bring to the boil, then leave until cold and pass through a conical strainer or a cloth.
Salinity test: A fresh egg will remain on the surface if the brine contains enough salt. If it does not, more salt should be added.

To pickle a tongue, clean it well, prick the whole surface with a needle and beat well to expel the air. Rub over thoroughly with the salt mixture and leave for 7 to 10 days, depending on size.

(Emil Wälti, Switzerland)

Dry salting

Salt mixture for rubbing in:

500 g	salt	1 lb 2 oz
125 g	sugar	4½ oz
125 g	saltpetre	4½ oz

Salt mixture for dry salting:

1 kg	salt	2 lb 4 oz
35 g	saltpetre	1¼ oz

Clean the tongues well, prick repeatedly with a meat fork, and beat to expel the air. Place on a layer of salt mixture and cover evenly with the mixture. Weight with a board to express the juices and dissolve the salt mixture. Leave in the containers for 10 to 12 days, depending on the size of the tongues, turning them occasionally. The containers should be kept in an even temperature, optimally at about 10°C (50°F).

If light pickling only is desired, the tongues should be removed earlier. Before use, soak them for several hours under running water. To cook them, always place them in a pan of cold water, not hot.

(Emil Wälti, Switzerland)

Roux

Roux are used to thicken sauces. There are three kinds – white, blond and brown. White roux is used for Béchamel sauce, blond for veloutés and brown for brown sauces.

White roux
Roux blanc

Yield: 500 g (1 lb 2 oz)

250 g	butter	9 oz
300 g	flour	10½ oz

Melt the butter and add the flour. Cook over gentle heat while stirring with a whisk until the flour is no longer raw but without colouring.

Blond roux
Roux blond

Yield: 500 g (1 lb 2 oz)

250 g	butter	9 oz
300 g	flour	10½ oz

Proceed in the same way as for white roux, but continue cooking gently until the roux takes on a light fawn colour.

Brown roux
Roux brun

Yield: 500 g (1 lb 2 oz)

250 g	rendered beef suet	9 oz
300 g	flour	10½ oz

After melting the fat stir in the flour. Cook slowly, preferably in the oven, until the roux has taken on an even light brown colour, stirring frequently and taking care to avoid excessive browning or burning of the fat or flour, which would give a bitter flavour to the sauce with which the roux was used.

To ensure absolute smoothness and avoid lumpiness when making a sauce, hot stock is used with cold roux and cold stock with hot roux.

Panadas

A panada is a paste of flour or bread and water, milk or eggs, stirred over heat in the same way as choux paste and seasoned as desired. Panadas are used as binding agents or fillers, or as a foundation for forcemeat. They are always used cold.

Bread panada

1 kg	white bread	2 lb 4 oz
1 l	milk	1¾ pt

Cut off the bread crusts, dice the bread coarsely and soak in the milk which has been brought to the boil. Squeeze out the excess milk and stir over a good heat until dry. Store in a bowl until required.

Flour panada

1 l	water	1¾ pt
20 g	salt	¾ oz
150 g	butter	5¼ oz
600 g	flour	1 lb 5 oz

Place the water, salt and butter in a pan and bring to the boil. Add the flour all at once and stir over the heat until the mixture leaves the sides of the pan. Store in a bowl until required.

Frangipane panada

250 g	flour	9 oz
10 g	salt	¼ oz
	ground pepper	
	nutmeg	
150 g	butter, melted	5¼ oz
	8 egg yolks	
6 dl	milk	1 pt

Place the flour in a pan, add salt, a little ground pepper, nutmeg, the melted butter and the egg yolks. Heat the milk and stir it in a little at a time until the mixture is smooth, then stand on the hotplate and continue stirring until thick enough. Store in a bowl until required.

Rice panada

1 l	beef stock	1¾ pt
350 g	rice	12¼ oz
30–50 g	butter	1–2 oz

Bring the stock to the boil, add the rice and cook until very soft. Add the butter and work to a firm paste over the heat.

Fillings, Forcemeats and Quenelles

In making fillings, forcemeats and quenelles, care should be taken to bind them well, while keeping them light and not too firm. As they have a high fat content, the best binding agent is a panada. They may be enriched with fresh cream if desired.

Simple forcemeat for hot dishes

100 g	pork back fat (larding fat)	3½ oz
400 g	veal or pork, trimmed and without sinew	14 oz
	ice cubes	
500 g	flour or bread panada	1 lb 2 oz
	8–10 egg yolks	
	2–4 eggs	
	dairy cream (optional)	
	salt, pepper	

Chop the meat finely in the processor with the addition of ice cubes. Gradually add the panada, yolks and whole eggs, then the pork fat, and work until finely blended. Season and add cream if desired. Do not allow the mixture to become warm, or it will curdle. If it does become warm, it must be chilled a little.

Half and half forcemeat for hot meat dishes

Proceed as for simple forcemeat for hot dishes, but use half veal and half pork.

(Emil Wälti, Switzerland)

Filling for Basler rissoles

125 g	minced veal	4½ oz
125 g	minced pork	4½ oz
	2 bread rolls, soaked	
	salt	
	nutmeg	
	paprika	
	thyme	
	marjoram	
50 g	onions, softened in butter	2 oz
	juice of half a lemon	

50 g	gherkins, chopped	2 oz

Prepare a forcemeat with the above ingredients.

(Otto Ledermann, Switzerland)

Veal forcemeat

400 g	larding pork fat or bacon	14 oz
1 kg	veal	2 lb 4 oz
	6 egg yolks	
500 g	ice cubes	1 lb 2 oz
	seasonings	

Work the pork fat or bacon in the cutter and remove. Trim the veal, cutting away the sinews, and work in the cutter, adding seasonings, the egg yolks and pork fat or bacon, and then the ice cubes.

Veal forcemeat old style

1 kg	veal	2 lb 4 oz
250 g	flour panada	9 oz
200 g	butter	7 oz
	1 whole egg	
	4 egg yolks	

Trim the veal, remove the sinews, mince finely and mix with the panada, butter, egg, yolks and seasoning. Pass through a sieve and mix well again, adding dairy cream if the forcemeat is too firm.

Bread forcemeat

6 portions

80 g	butter	2¾ oz
200 g	4 bread rolls, weighing	7 oz
3 dl	milk	10 fl oz
	1 whole egg	
	2 egg yolks	
	1 tablespoon finely chopped parsley	
	3 tablespoons canned peas	
100 g	cooked ham, diced	3½ oz

	1 pinch grated nutmeg	
	OR	
	4 white peppercorns, freshly ground	
	salt	
60 g	white flour	2 oz
	OR	
	white breadcrumbs	

Cream the butter. Grate the crust off the rolls, divide each one into four, soak in milk, squeeze dry, pass through a sieve, then add to the butter together with the whole egg and yolks, parsley, peas, ham, salt, nutmeg or pepper, and flour or breadcrumbs. Mix well and stand aside for 30 minutes, then use to stuff breast of veal. This forcemeat is also suitable for belly of pork, chicken, pigeon, etc.

(Vilèm Vrabec, Czechoslovakia)

Forcemeat Falchetti

300 g	chicken livers	10½ oz
100 g	anchovies in oil	3½ oz
100 g	lean pork, diced	3½ oz
100 g	pickled cucumber, chopped	3½ oz
100 g	raw ham, thickly sliced	3½ oz
2 dl	oil	7 fl oz
2 dl	dry white wine	7 fl oz
2 dl	bouillon	7 fl oz
	1 lemon	
	1 sprig rosemary	
	1 bay leaf	
	3 tablespoons capers	
	2 cloves of garlic	
	3 fresh sage leaves	
	salt, freshly ground pepper	

Blanch the chicken livers in lightly salted water. Heat the oil and brown the pork on all sides. Add the ham which has been coarsely diced. Remove from the heat and add the anchovies, herbs and seasonings, then sauter together. Drain the livers, add to the pan, continue sautéing and stir in the wine. Add two fairly thick peeled slices of lemon, pour in the bouillon and stir vigorously over low heat until the livers disintegrate and the mixture is cooked to the consistency of a paste.

(Manfred Wyler, Switzerland)

Gratin forcemeat

500 g	salt belly pork or bacon	1 lb 2 oz
500 g	veal	1 lb 2 oz
500 g	calf's liver	1 lb 2 oz
100 g	shallots, chopped	3½ oz
100 g	fresh mushrooms	3½ oz
	thyme, rosemary	
2–3 dl	Madeira	7–10 fl oz
300 g	butter	10½ oz
	10 egg yolks	
2–3 dl	cold demi-glace sauce	7–10 fl oz
	chopped truffles (optional)	
	salt	

Dice the pork or bacon, brown in 100 g (3½ oz) butter and remove from the pan. Dice the veal after cutting away the sinews and brown in the same pan, then remove. Lightly cook in the same pan the liver which has been diced and soaked in milk. Remove the liver and place the shallots in the pan together with the mushrooms, thyme and rosemary. Cook lightly without colouring, then return the other ingredients to the pan and cook gently for a further 2 to 4 minutes. Turn out on to a metal tray, rinse out the pan with the Madeira to detach the juices and pour over the mixture on the tray.

When cold, mince or chop finely (or pass through a sieve). Work well with a spatula, adding the remaining butter, the egg yolks and salt. Mix in the cold demi-glace and adjust the seasoning. Chopped truffles may be added if desired. Depending on the use to be made of the forcemeat, other kinds of liver may be used instead of calf's liver. The forcemeat is mainly used for hot dishes.

Calf's liver forcemeat old style

1 kg	calf's liver	2 lb 4 oz
500 g	pork back fat	1 lb 2 oz
	4 shallots, chopped	
	bay leaf	
	thyme	
	parsley	
150 g	flour panada	5¼ oz
	2 whole eggs	
	4 egg yolks	

Dice the liver finely and pour boiling water over. Cut the pork fat finely and render down in a pan. Add the shallots, bay leaf, thyme and parsley, then add the liver and brown for 10 minutes. Remove the herbs and allow to cool. Blend to a fine paste, add the panada and work well. Lastly mix in the eggs, yolks and seasoning. If the mixture is not firm enough, add 100 g (3½ oz) veal forcemeat.

Veal sausage meat

Meat mixture:

1 kg – 40%	veal	2 lb 4 oz
700 g – 30%	pork neck fat	1 lb 8 oz
700 g – 30%	milk	1 lb 8 oz
	OR ice and dried milk powder	
2 kg 400 g		5 lb 4 oz

Seasonings:

25 g per kg meat and fat	salt	approx ½ oz per l meat and fat
1½ g per kg meat mixture	white pepper	a pinch per lb meat mixture
5 g per kg meat mixture	mace	a pinch per lb meat mixture
5 g per kg meat mixture	onion	a small teaspoon per lb meat mixture
2 g per kg meat mixture	mixed powdered seasoning	a pinch per lb meat mixture

Blend together the lightly deep-frozen veal, most of the milk and the salt until the mixture begins to hold together. Add the fat which has been chilled and cut up small and work to a fine, homogeneous shiny paste, adding the seasonings towards the end. The final temperature should be about 15–16°C (59–61°F).

To make veal sausages for frying or grilling, the sausage meat is filled into pig casings. The sausages are blanched for 12 to 15 minutes at a maximum temperature of 78°C (172°F), then refreshed under running water.

Pork sausage meat
Same ingredients and quantities as for veal sausage meat, above, using pork instead of veal.
(Sandro Volonté, Switzerland)

Liver quenelles Alsatian
Quenelles de foie à l'alsacienne

4–5 portions

300 g	pig's liver (may be mixed with ox liver)	10½ oz
150 g	lean salt pork or bacon	5¼ oz
100 g	onions, sliced	3½ oz
100 g	white bread	3½ oz
	1 tablespoon chopped parsley or chervil	
	2 cloves of garlic, crushed	
50 g	semolina	1¾ oz
	3 eggs	
	salt, pepper, nutmeg	
	2 tablespoons oil	
	water or milk for soaking bread	

Soften the sliced onions in oil. Using a medium cutter, mince the onions together with the bread which has been soaked and squeezed dry, the pork or bacon and the liver. Add the chopped parsley or chervil, the garlic and the semolina, season with salt, pepper and nutmeg and mix well. Fold in the eggs and shape into quenelles with the help of two tablespoons. Poach (without boiling) for 10 minutes in salted water.

The quenelles are excellent with sauerkraut. Alternatively, they may simply be finished off with onions fried in butter and served with potatoes.

Viennese liver quenelles forcemeat
Farce à quenelles à la viennoise
Leberknödel-Farce nach Wiener Art

1 kg	calf's liver	2 lb 4 oz
500 g	white breadcrumbs	1 lb 2 oz
100 g	white flour	3½ oz
	1 onion, finely chopped	
20 g	parsley, chopped	¾ oz
	5 whole eggs	
	12 egg yolks	
25 g	salt	1 oz
	pepper	
	nutmeg	

Chop the liver or pass through the cutter or a sieve, then mix all the ingredients thoroughly. Either shape into quenelles and poach or alternatively use as forcemeat.

Beef marrow quenelles
Quenelles de moelle

200 g	beef marrow	7 oz
100 g	breadcrumbs	3½ oz
	2 eggs	
30 g	parsley, chopped	1 oz
	salt, pepper	
	nutmeg	

Soak the beef marrow overnight, then crush finely with a fork. Add the breadcrumbs, the beaten eggs, the parsley and seasonings. Mix well with a wooden spatula until thoroughly blended. Shape by hand into small quenelles each weighing about 20 g (¾ oz), rolling them into balls between the palms. Poach in a little bouillon.

(J. P. Bossée-François, France)

Beef marrow paste
Masse de moelle de boeuf

10 portions

300 g	beef marrow (spinal)	10½ oz
80 g	shallots, finely chopped	2¾ oz
60 g	parsley, finely chopped	2 oz
20 g	garlic, finely chopped	¾ oz
100 g	breadcrumbs	3½ oz
1 dl	white wine	3½ fl oz
	salt	
	freshly ground pepper	
	fresh thyme	

Extract the marrow, soak it and cut into ½ cm (¼ in) pieces. Mix with the shallots, garlic, parsley and breadcrumbs, season with salt, pepper and fresh thyme and moisten with the wine.

(Otto Ledermann, Switzerland)

Raw mousseline forcemeat

1 kg	veal	2 lb 4 oz
400 g	ice cubes	14 oz
	10 egg whites	
5–6 dl	dairy cream	about 1 pt

Trim the veal, removing the sinews, and work in the cutter, gradually adding the ice cubes until finely blended. Transfer to a bowl and gradually work in the egg whites and cream with a wooden spatula. Mix well and add the usual seasonings.

Depending on the use to be made of this forcemeat, a variety of ingredients may be mixed with it, such as diced cooked ham, diced ox tongue, truffles, diced goose or chicken liver.

Mousses

Ham mousse I
Mousse de jambon

1 kg	lean ham	2 lb 4 oz
4 dl	aspic jelly	14 fl oz
4 dl	dairy cream	14 fl oz

This recipe is recommended if a mechanical food processor is available. It produces a quickly made, readily digestible mousse.

Remove the outside fat and any gristle from the ham. Dice the ham coarsely, then work in the cutter until finely blended. Pass through a wire sieve if necessary. Place in a bowl and chill. Fold in the aspic jelly, which should be cold and liquid, together with the lightly whipped cream, and use at once.

Ham mousse II
Mousse de jambon
Same ingredients as for ham mousse I, but a little less cream is used. Fold in 2 dl (7 fl oz) cold veal velouté, flavour with Madeira and/or brandy and add the appropriate seasonings.

Pickled ox tongue mousse
Mousse de langue de boeuf salée
Same quantities and procedure as for ham mousse.

Liver mousse I
Mousse de foie de veau

500 g	calf's liver	1 lb 2 oz
2–3 dl	Madeira or port	7–10 fl oz
100 g	butter	3½ oz
2 dl	dairy cream, whipped	7 fl oz
	salt, white pepper	
	spices	

Dice the liver and poach in Madeira until medium done. Leave until cold, then pound well in a mortar and sieve finely. Add spices and Madeira and mix well.

Cream the butter well, then gradually work in the liver purée. Fold in the cream. Add salt and pepper to taste. This mousse is very suitable for spreading on chaud-froids, as a fine forcemeat, or as an hors d'oeuvre when moulded in aspic. It is lighter and finer than mousse made with jelly.

(Pierre Mengelatte, France)

Liver mousse II
Mousse de foie de veau

450 g	calf's liver, coarsely diced	1 lb
2 dl	port or dry white wine	7 fl oz
1½ dl	Béchamel sauce	5 fl oz
4 dl	port jelly	14 fl oz
1½ dl	dairy cream	5 fl oz
1 dl	milk	3½ fl oz
	salt, white pepper	

Reduce the port jelly by half and allow to cool. Cook the liver gently in the port or dry white wine until medium done, leave until cold, then sieve finely. Mix with the Béchamel and the cold but still liquid jelly until well blended, standing the bowl on ice. Carefully mix the milk with the cream and stir in. Season well and refrigerate.

It is always advisable to place a test sample on ice, to find out whether it is firm enough. If not, a little dissolved gelatine may be added. If too firm, dilute with whipped cream.

(Pierre Mengelatte, France)

Aspic and Other Jellies

Aspic (basic recipe)

Calf's head, calf's feet, pig's trotters, pork rinds and bones may be used in preparing aspic. Any of these ingredients used are well blanched, then placed in a pan of cold water with a bouquet garni and brought to the boil. After skimming, the liquid is simmered gently. Repeated skimming is essential to keep it free of fat and as clear as possible. Strain through a fine cloth, then allow to cool and remove any remaining fat. The aspic may be clarified with fresh blood or plasma, or with the help of beef and egg whites.

Clarification of aspic

250 g	lean beef, coarsely chopped	9 oz
	3 egg whites	
	1 leek, finely sliced	
	parsley stalks	
	tarragon (optional)	

Add the beef (preferably shin), egg whites, leek, parsley stalks and a little tarragon if desired to 2 litres (3½ pints) cold basic aspic. Mix well and bring to the boil, then allow to stand below boiling point for about ten minutes and carefully strain through a fine cloth. Season to taste and flavour with Madeira, port, sherry, etc. as desired.

Consommé aspic

If necessary, a light consommé in which 18 to 22 sheets of gelatine have been dissolved produces good results.

Commercial aspic

Good products are available commercially, varying in colour from light to dark. They are labour saving in comparison with the conventional method of preparing aspic. If ready-made aspic is used, it should be flavoured before it sets (tarragon, white wine, sherry, port, etc. may be used for this purpose).

Mint jelly

45 g	gelatine	1½ oz

3 dl	water	10 fl oz
8 dl	white wine vinegar	28 fl oz
325 g	sugar	11 oz
	4 tablespoons finely chopped fresh mint	
	a few drops green colouring	
	a pinch of salt	

Bring the vinegar to the boil, dissolve the sugar in it and boil for a further four minutes. Heat the water, dissolve the gelatine in it and stir into the vinegar syrup together with the chopped mint. Add a pinch of salt, stir, return to the boil and remove from the heat at once. Stir in the green colouring and allow to cool. When the jelly is beginning to set, fill it into jars, cover with greaseproof paper or cellophane and store in the refrigerator. This jelly is served with roast leg of lamb.

(Franco Colombani, Italy)

Pastries and Batter

Beer frying batter

1 kg	flour, sieved	2 lb 4 oz
7 dl	slightly tepid water	1¼ pt
7 dl	beer (or dry cider)	1¼ pt
2 dl	oil	7 fl oz
20 g	salt	¾ oz
	8–10 egg whites	

Place the flour in a bowl, add the salt, oil, beer and water and work to a smooth batter. Shortly before use beat the egg whites to a stiff snow and carefully fold in.

Puff pastry

1 kg	flour, sieved	2 lb 4 oz
4–5 dl	water	14–18 fl oz
800 g	margarine or butter	1 lb 12 oz
20 g	salt	¾ oz

Make a bay in the flour and place in it the salt, the cold water (more or less may be needed depending on the gluten in the flour), and 100 g (3½ oz) margarine or butter. Mix into a dough, shape it into a ball, cut a cross in the top and allow to rest in the refrigerator.

Meanwhile knead the margarine or butter to the same consistency as the dough. Roll out the dough to flatten and widen the cross which was cut in it, place the margarine or butter in the centre and fold the dough over to enclose it. Allow to rest for a time, give two turns, rest for 30 minutes, repeat the procedure once and give two final turns, making six in all. Depending on the purpose for which the pastry is to be used, it may be given two double turns and a single turn. Store in plastic film or a damp cloth.

Choux pastry for hors d'oeuvre

5 dl	water	18 fl oz
5 dl	milk	18 fl oz
15 g	salt	½ oz
500 g	flour	1 lb 2 oz
300 g	butter	10½ oz

16–18 eggs
nutmeg

Place the milk, water, salt, nutmeg and butter in a pan and heat until the butter is melted and the milk and water have come to the boil. Add the flour all at once and stir in with a wooden spatula, cooking the mixture until it leaves the sides of the pan. Allow to cool, then gradually work in the eggs.

Short pastry

1 kg	flour	2 lb 4 oz
4–5 dl	water	14–18 fl oz
20 g	salt	¾ oz
500 g	lard, butter or margarine, depending on use	1 lb 2 oz

Rub the fat into the flour until evenly dispersed. Make a bay, pour in the water, add the salt and quickly work to a smooth paste from the inside outwards. Allow to rest before use.

Pie pastry

1 kg	flour, sieved	2 lb 4 oz
300 g	butter or lard	10½ oz
20 g	salt	¾ oz
4–5 dl	water	14–18 fl oz
	3 eggs	

Place the flour on a marble slab and make a bay. Pour in the water (which should be lukewarm if lard is used) and add the remaining ingredients. Work to a smooth paste from the inside outwards. Allow to rest for some time.

Pizza dough

10 portions (diameter of each pizza 25–30 cm)
Oven temperature: 280–340°C (530–640°F)
Baking time varies, depending on topping

1 kg	flour	2 lb 4 oz

½ l	tepid water	18 fl oz
5 g	yeast	⅕ oz
5 g	sugar	⅕ oz
50 g	salt	1¾ oz
½ dl	olive oil	2 fl oz

Dissolve the sugar in the tepid water and disperse the yeast in it. Add the salt, making sure all the ingredients are completely dispersed. Place the flour in a bowl, slowly pour in the water and work to a soft dough. Add the oil and mix. If the dough sticks to the hands or machine, it is not ready and a little flour should be added. Set aside for at least 2 hours, then divide into 10 portions, mould each one round and allow to recover at room temperature. Store separately in a draught-proof place, preferably a drawer, until required. (This dough is especially suitable for baking in an electric oven.)

(Nico Donato, Italy)

Basic Preparations for Stocks and Sauces

Mirepoix
Carrots, celery and onions are diced as evenly as possible, with the addition of garlic if desired. Mirepoix is used as a flavouring base for roast or braised meat. Depending on the meat with which it is to be used, bay leaf, cloves, thyme, rosemary or other flavourings may be added.

Matignon
The ingredients are the same as for mirepoix, but thinly sliced rather than diced. This preparation is used as a flavouring base for poêlé and braised meat. Its composition may vary; often it contains ham rinds or diced ham.

Bouquet garni
A small bundle of herbs tied within strips of leek. The usual herbs are thyme, basil and parsley, but others such as savory or celery leaves may be added, depending on the purpose for which the bouquet is to be used.

Bouquet garni for white stock
The following ingredients are added to those for an ordinary bouquet garni: – peeled carrots and, in particular, the white part of leek; peeled celeriac instead of celery leaves; a peeled onion stuck with bay leaf and cloves.

Bouquet garni for beef stock
As above; the green part as well as the white part of leek may be used. The onions are left unpeeled, cut in half and lightly browned on the hotplate. A little savoy cabbage and turnip may also be added.

Bouquet garni sachet
A sachet is mainly used for meat dishes where the sauce is not strained and also for marinated meat to prevent ingredients such as crushed peppercorns or juniper berries, mustard seed, etc. from sticking to the meat.

Garnishes for Meat Consommés

Brighton	Veal quenelles, diced calf's head, diced vegetables, flavoured with sherry.
Carnegie	Small ravioli filled with minced veal, truffles, chervil and tarragon.
Charolaise	Glazed pearl onions, rounds of carrot, diced oxtail and tiny stuffed cabbage leaves.
Pot au feu	Finely diced boiled beef, carrots and turnips, finely sliced cabbage, leek and celeriac cooked in bouillon; croûtons are handed separately.
Liver quenelles	Small liver quenelles (recipe page 135).
Lesseps	Royale, poached calf's brains, chervil.
Beef marrow	Poached slices of beef marrow; croûtons are handed separately.
Marrow quenelles	Small beef marrow quenelles (recipe page 136).
Four strips	Thin strips of pickled tongue, chicken breast, truffles and mushrooms.
Mosaic	Small cubes of pickled tongue, carrot, turnip, French beans, poached egg white, truffle, together with peas.
Butcher's style	Strips of cabbage and slices of beef marrow.

Regional Basic Preparations

Kajmak
Boiling hot cow's or ewe's milk is poured into broad, flat containers called 'karlica' and left to cool. During this process the cream separates and forms a thin layer on the surface, which is carefully skimmed off and transferred to a wooden container known as a 'cabrica'. The process is repeated daily, with the addition of salt to each layer.

If kajmak is used before it has matured, that is to say before it has reached the end of the necessary ripening period, it has a pleasant mild flavour. If it is left to stand for a long time, however, it begins to ferment and requires the addition of larger amounts of salt. Fermented, ripe kajmak has a sharper taste and has turned yellow. Kajmak is a popular, typically Serbian product.

Sour milk
Kiselo mleko
This Serbian speciality is made from cow's or ewe's milk, whereas yoghourt is made from cow's milk only. Yoghourt is very similar to sour milk.

To prepare sour milk, cow's or ewe's milk is boiled for 5 to 10 minutes, cooled to a temperature of 42–45°C (108–113°F) and left to stand in a warm place until it is thick. To interrupt fermentation it is then moved to a cold place.

(László Csizmadia, Yugoslavia)

Garnishes for Meat

Alexandra
Artichokes cut in quarters and slices of truffle.

Algérienne
Algerian style. Small cooked tomatoes, thin strips of cooked peppers.

Alsacienne
Alsatian style. Puff pastry tartlets about 8 cm (3½ in) across, baked blind and filled with a garnish of sauerkraut, strips of ham and small smoked sausages.

Ambassadeur
Artichoke bottoms filled with mushrooms in cream sauce. Garnished with Duchesse potatoes.

Américaine
American style. Grilled whole tomatoes and crisply fried bacon rashers.

Andalouse
Andalusian style. Small cooked peppers stuffed with rice. Fried sliced aubergines and tomatoes. Chipolatas.

Argenteuil
Cooked asparagus tips in Hollandaise sauce.

Arlésienne
Arles style. Fried sliced aubergines, thin strips of cooked tomato, fried onion rings.

Armenonville
Morel cream sauce and sliced fried potatoes.

Beaugency
Artichoke bottoms filled with coarsely chopped tomatoes and covered with hot sliced beef marrow.

Bergère
Shepherdess style. Fried breaded ham, strips of onion and morels. Particularly suitable for lamb cutlets.

Berrichonne
Berry style. Egg-size braised cabbage balls, lean bacon rashers braised with the cabbage, glazed pearl onions and chestnuts.

Bonne Femme
Housewife style. Pearl onions and strips of bacon on the meat. Fried diced potatoes. Only suitable for meat in sauce.

Bordelaise
Bordeaux style. (1) Cèpes and Bourguignonne sauce (suitable for any type of meat). (2) Bordelaise sauce (made with red wine and beef marrow – only suitable for beef).

Boulangère
Fried sliced potatoes with strips of cooked onion and gravy. Mainly used with roast lamb.

Bouquetière
Carrots, turnips, sprigs of cauliflower, French beans or leaf spinach, tiny tomatoes, peas and Château potatoes are arranged round the joint, alternating the colours.

Bourgeoise
Family style. Strips of carrot, celeriac and salt belly of pork, together with glazed pearl onions are arranged on meat covered with a sauce.

Bourguignonne
Burgundy style. Same garnish as 'bourgeoise', but with mushrooms cut in quarters instead of the vegetables.

Bruxelloise
Brussels style. Stewed endives and braised Brussels sprouts.

Catalane
Catalonian style. Artichoke bottoms, a small grilled tomato.

Chipolata
Glazed pearl onions, fried chipolata sausages, cooked chestnuts, diced cooked smoked bacon.

Choisy
Braised lettuce, Château potatoes.

Dubarry
Sprigs of cauliflower in Mornay sauce au gratin.

Emmentaloise
Emmental style. With Emmental cheese sauce and thin slices of Emmental au gratin.

Esterhazy
Thin strips of root vegetables in cream sauce.

Favorite
Hot slices of foie gras and asparagus tips.

Flamande
Flemish style. Small balls of braised cabbage, olive-size carrots and turnips, slices of cooked fat pork (or bacon) and sausage.

Florentine
Leaf spinach and slices of semolina mixture cooked with cheese.

Forestière
Morels braised with onions and diced lean bacon. Mushrooms cut in quarters may be used instead of morels.

Givry
Artichoke bottoms cut in quarters and deep-fried onion rings.

Gourmets
Foie gras coated with fresh white breadcrumbs and fried in butter.

Grand-Duc
Grand Duke style. Hot beef marrow is placed on the meat, with a decoration of asparagus tips and slices of truffle.

Helder
Artichoke bottoms with diced tomatoes and Béarnaise sauce.

Henri IV
Artichoke bottoms filled with Noisette potatoes. Béarnaise sauce. Only suitable for steaks such as tournedos or entrecôte.

Holstein
Fried egg topped with anchovy fillets and capers.

Indienne
Indian style. Rice and curry sauce.

Italienne
Italian style. Artichokes cut in quarters and macaroni au gratin.

Jardinière
Gardener style. Surrounded by bouquets of young vegetables.

Judic
Braised lettuce, slices of truffle and gravy.

Languedocienne
Fried aubergines, cèpes and tomatoes cut in slices.

Maraîchère
Salsify, Brussels sprouts and Château potatoes.

Mascotte
Artichoke quarters, slices of truffle, Noisette potatoes.

Masséna
Artichoke bottoms, beef marrow, Béarnaise sauce.

Mexicaine
Mexican style. Diced peppers and mushrooms, sweet corn.

Milanaise
Milan style. Strips of tongue, ham, mushrooms and truffles. Pasta or risotto and tomato sauce.

Mirabeau
Anchovy fillets, stoned olives, tarragon leaves.

Montmorency
Artichoke bottoms filled with finely diced mixed vegetables and decorated with asparagus tips.

Niçoise
Nice style. Diced tomatoes with garlic and tarragon placed on the meat, which is surrounded with French beans and Château potatoes.

Nivernaise
Glazed carrots and pearl onions.

Opéra
Fried chicken liver with Madeira sauce and pearl onions.

Orloff
Onion purée mixed with Hollandaise sauce au gratin.

Parisienne
Parisian style. Braised lettuce, Noisette potatoes. For veal and pork escalopes dipped in egg and fried. Asparagus tips are used for decoration.

Piémontaise
Piedmont style. Risotto with white truffles.

Portugaise
Portuguese style. Stuffed or diced tomatoes. Madeira sauce well flavoured with tomato purée.

Princesse
Asparagus tips with Hollandaise sauce.

Printanière
Spring style. Well surrounded with spring vegetables.

Provençale
Provence style. Tomatoes, mushrooms, olives and anchovy fillets with herbs and garlic.

Rachel
Artichoke bottoms filled with beef marrow, chopped parsley, Bordelaise sauce.

Rossini
Slices of foie gras and truffle. Bourguignonne sauce with truffles.

Saint-Germain
Pea purée, small glazed carrots, fondantes potatoes.

Sarde
Sardinian style. Rice croquettes flavoured with saffron. Stuffed tomatoes and cucumber.

Talleyrand
Pasta mixed with diced truffle and foie gras. Périgueux sauce and grated cheese.

Tyrolienne
Tyrolean style. Fried onion rings and coarsely chopped cooked tomatoes.

Valencienne
Small half peppers filled with rice flavoured with saffron.

Vert-Pré
Cress and straw potatoes.

Zingara
Strips of ham, tongue and mushrooms. Demi-glace sauce flavoured with tomato and tarragon.

Hot Sauces

Basic Sauces and their Derivatives

To make a good sauce, it is essential to use a well made basic stock. Instead of Espagnole sauce, which is still generally used for this purpose in France and certain other regions, we recommend brown veal stock, which is more digestible and contains less flour (recipe page 120 'Brown veal stock II'). Like brown veal stock, any of the following sauces which are prepared in quantities not required on the same day should be rapidly cooled under running water.

Experience shows that good results are often obtained by simplified methods. For instance, brown veal stock may be thickened by simply reducing it by half and adding cornflour. Alternatively, the bones and mirepoix may be dusted with flour after the initial browning of the bones. The flour is allowed to cook to a golden brown colour before proceeding as described above. More prolonged cooking will be required for this alternative method.

Demi-glace I

Yield: 10 litres (17½ pints)
Same ingredients as for 'Brown veal stock II' (recipe page 120)

Reduce the mirepoix by half, dust with 100 g (3½ oz) flour and brown lightly, then moisten with white wine, reduce and add 15–17½ l (26 – 30 pt) brown veal stock. Thicken with cornflour if desired, skim frequently, season, strain and adjust the seasoning.

Demi-glace II (simplified recipe)

Cooking time: about 2 hours

100 g	fat bacon	3½ oz
100 g	ham trimmings	3½ oz
	1 onion, peeled and chopped	
	3 carrots, scraped and chopped	
	4 sticks celery, chopped	
	2 leeks, chopped	
	1 clove of garlic, peeled and chopped	
	2 bay leaves	
	2 sprigs fresh parsley	
	1 teaspoon dried thyme	
60 g	flour	2 oz
⅛ l	dry white wine	5 fl oz
100 g	tomato purée	3½ oz
2 l	brown stock	3½ pt
	salt, pepper	

Preheat the oven to 190°C (374°F). Place the bacon and the ham trimmings in a fireproof dish and render in the oven. Add the onion, carrots, celery, leeks, garlic, bay leaves, parsley and thyme and brown lightly in a moderate oven. Add the flour, mix well and continue cooking in the oven at 190°C (374°F) until the flour is lightly browned.

Remove from the oven and transfer to a large pan. Add the wine, tomato purée and brown stock. Cover and simmer over low heat for 2 hours, skimming from time to time. Strain the sauce through a cloth and allow to cool. Season to taste with salt and pepper. Store in airtight jars in the refrigerator.

(Hermann Rusch, USA)

Some sauces derived from demi-glace

Bordelaise sauce

50 g	shallots, finely chopped	2 oz
250 ml	wine (originally white, but red is now used)	½ pt
	1 sprig thyme	
	1 bay leaf	
750 ml	demi-glace	2½ pt
100 g	beef marrow, finely diced or sliced	3½ oz
	meat glaze (optional)	
	crushed peppercorns	

Sweat the shallots in butter with the peppercorns. Place them and wine (which should be of good quality) in a pan with a little thyme and bay leaf. Bring to the boil, reduce by two thirds and add demi-glace. Strain through a cloth and add the beef marrow which has been poached, also a little meat glaze if desired. Adjust the seasoning.

Brown chaud-froid sauce

1 l	demi-glace	1¾ pt
4–5 dl	aspic	14–18 fl oz
1 dl	truffle essence	3½ fl oz
	OR Madeira	

Add the aspic (a little more may be required) to a good demi-glace sauce. Flavour with the truffle essence or Madeira, check the seasoning and the consistency, then pass through a fine cloth.

Périgueux sauce

	demi-glace	
	truffle essence	
100 g per l	truffles, chopped	2 oz per pt
	Madeira	
	fresh butter (optional)	

Add truffle essence and the chopped truffles to well reduced demi-glace sauce. Flavour with Madeira and finish with fresh butter if desired.

Bourguignonne sauce

50 g	shallots, finely chopped	2 oz
	parsley stalks	
	1 sprig thyme	
	bay leaf	
250 ml	red wine	½ pt
750 ml	demi-glace	2½ fl oz
100 g	fresh butter (optional)	3½ oz
	crushed peppercorns	

Briefly sweat the shallots and peppercorns in butter. Place the shallots in a pan with a little parsley, thyme and bay leaf, pour in the wine, bring to the boil and reduce by half. Fill up with demi-glace, cook well and thicken if necessary. Pass through a cloth and adjust the seasoning. Finish off with the butter if desired.

Italian sauce

Yield: 1½ l (2⅝ pt)

1 l	demi-glace	1¾ pt
150 g	ham, diced	5 oz
150 g	mushrooms, chopped	5 oz
	2 shallots, finely chopped	
2 dl	tomato sauce	7 fl oz
	1 small teaspoon chopped parsley	
	½ small teaspoon tarragon	
	OR chervil	
20 g	butter	¾ oz

Briefly sweat the mushrooms, ham and shallots in butter, then add the demi-glace sauce, together with the tomato sauce. Cook for 6 to 8 minutes and adjust the seasoning. Add the parsley and the chopped tarragon or chervil. Tomato purée may be used instead of tomato sauce, but will require longer cooking.

Chasseur sauce

Yield: 1 l (1¾ pt)

100 g	mushrooms, finely sliced	3½ oz
	2 shallots, finely chopped	
20 g	butter	¾ oz
1 dl	white wine	3½ fl oz
½ l	tomato sauce	18 fl oz
½ l	demi-glace	18 fl oz
	½ small teaspoon chopped tarragon and chervil	
	fresh butter (optional)	

Cook the mushrooms and shallots gently for a few minutes in the butter, add the wine, bring to the boil and reduce by half. Add the tomato sauce and demi-glace, bring to the boil again, cook for a few minutes and adjust the seasoning. If the sauce is too red, add some meat glaze or more demi-glace. Flavour with the tarragon and chervil. Finish off with fresh butter if desired.

Lyonnaise sauce

Yield: 1 l (1¾ pt)

150 g	onions, finely chopped	5 oz
20 g	butter	¾ oz
1 dl	vinegar	3½ fl oz
1 dl	white wine	3½ fl oz
1 l	demi-glace	1¾ pt

Soften the onions slowly in the butter without colouring. Add the wine and vinegar, bring to the boil and reduce by two thirds. Add the demi-glace, cook briefly and adjust the seasoning. This sauce may be served strained or unstrained, depending on the dish with which it is to be used.

Madeira sauce

Add Madeira to good demi-glace sauce. Serve with pickled ox tongue or ham.

Poivrade sauce

Yield: 1 l (1¾ pt)

80 g	onions, finely diced	3 oz
80 g	carrots, finely diced	3 oz
	2 tablespoons oil	
1 dl	vinegar	3½ fl oz
1 l	demi-glace	1¾ pt
	6–8 parsley stalks	
	1 sprig or a pinch of thyme	
	½ bay leaf	
	10 peppercorns, crushed	

Cook the onions and carrots in the oil without colouring. Add the parsley, thyme and bay leaf, together with the vinegar and an equal amount of the marinade used for the meat. Bring to the boil and reduce by two thirds. Add the demi-glace and cook for 30 minutes. Add the peppercorns and continue cooking for a short time, then strain.

If the sauce is too thick, dilute with marinade and cook for a few minutes longer. Finish with fresh butter if desired. This sauce is served with marinated meat or with pork.

Piquant sauce

Yield: 1 l (1¾ pt)

2½ dl	white wine	9 fl oz
2½ dl	vinegar	9 fl oz
	3 shallots, chopped	
7 dl	demi-glace	1¼ pt
100 g	gherkins, chopped	3½ oz
	½ small teaspoon tarragon	
	½ small teaspoon parsley	
	½ small teaspoon chervil	
	Cayenne	

Place the wine, vinegar and shallots in a pan, bring to the boil and reduce. Pour in good demi-glace sauce, bring to the boil and cook for 10 minutes. Add the chopped gherkins, tarragon, parsley and chervil. Adjust the seasoning and add Cayenne to taste.

Portuguese sauce

Yield: 1 l (1¾ pt)

100 g	onions, finely chopped	3½ oz
	1 clove of garlic, grated	
	1 small teaspoon sugar	
20 g	oil	¾ oz
800 g	tomatoes, peeled and coarsely chopped	1 lb 12 oz
	1 tablespoon tomato purée (optional)	
2–2½ dl	demi-glace	7–9 fl oz
	1 tablespoon chopped parsley	

Cook the onions gently in the oil until they begin to colour. Add three quarters of the demi-glace, the tomatoes and a little grated garlic. Season with salt and pepper. Add sugar and tomato purée if desired. Cook until the tomatoes are soft, pour in the rest of the demi-glace and cook well. Adjust the seasoning and add the coarsely chopped parsley.

Robert sauce

Yield: 3 l (5¼ pt)

	1 large onion, finely chopped	
	butter	
½ l	white wine	18 fl oz
3 l	demi-glace	5¼ pt
	mustard	
	a pinch of sugar	

Cook the onion in butter for a few minutes without colouring, then add the wine and reduce by two thirds. Add the demi-glace and cook for 10 minutes. Strain and flavour well with mustard, then add a pinch of sugar and do not cook any more. Adjust the seasoning. This sauce is served with grilled pork.

Charcutière sauce

Same ingredients and method as for Robert sauce, with the addition of short strips of gherkin.

Diable sauce

Yield: 1 l (1¾ pt)

3 dl	dry white wine	10 fl oz
	OR	
1 dl	vinegar	3½ fl oz
100 g	shallots, finely chopped	3½ oz
	12 peppercorns, crushed	
1 l	tomato flavoured demi-glace	1¾ pt
10–20 g	butter	¼–¾ oz

Place the wine or vinegar in a pan with the shallots and peppercorns. Reduce by two thirds, add the demi-glace, cook for a few minutes, season to taste with Cayenne pepper and pass through a tammy cloth. Finish with butter if desired.

Zingara sauce

¼ l	demi-glace	9 fl oz
5 cl	tomato sauce	2 fl oz
5 cl	mushroom cooking liquor	2 fl oz
1 dl	white wine	3½ fl oz
30 g	shallots, chopped	1 oz
50 g	mushrooms	2 oz
50 g	pickled ox tongue	2 oz
30 g	truffles	1 oz

Place the wine, shallots and mushroom liquor in a pan and reduce. Add the demi-glace and the tomato sauce and cook for a short time, then add the mushrooms, truffles and ox tongue cut into julienne strips.

White Sauces

Velouté

Yield: 1 l (1¾ pt)

60 g	butter	2 oz
70–80 g	flour	2½–2¾ oz
1 l	white stock	1¾ pt

Make a roux with the butter and flour (the amount of flour will depend on the consistency required) and allow to cool. Add the stock and cook well for 30 minutes. Strain and adjust the seasoning.

Allemande sauce

1 l	velouté	1¾ pt
1 dl	dairy cream	3½ fl oz
	1 egg yolk	
	lemon juice	

Place the cream and egg yolk in a pan, mix well and heat while gradually stirring in the velouté. Reduce a little, stirring vigorously meanwhile. Flavour with lemon juice and finish with fresh butter.

Tarragon sauce

1 l	Allemande sauce	1¾ pt
	2 tablespoons chopped tarragon	
	a dash of vinegar	

Flavour the Allemande sauce with a little vinegar and add the chopped tarragon. If this sauce is to be served with mutton, it should be made with mutton stock.

Caper sauce

½ l	Allemande sauce	18 fl oz
	2 tablespoons capers	

Restaurant au Crocodile, Strasbourg ▶

164 Parsley ham Burgundy style I, p. 980

Terrine Restaurant au Crocodile, p. 1000

Beef daube in aspic, p. 971 *165*

7

Terrine of sweetbreads with truffle cream, p. 996

Salad Bonne Etape, p. 227

Jellied lamb, p. 977

vinegar

Add the capers to the Allemande sauce and flavour with a little vinegar.

Horseradish sauce

½ l	Allemande sauce	18 fl oz
75 g	horseradish, grated	2¾ oz

Mix together the Allemande sauce and horseradish.

Béchamel sauce

60 g	butter	2 oz
70–80 g	flour	2½–2¾ oz
1 l	milk	1¾ pt

Prepare in the same way as velouté, but use boiling milk instead of white stock. Finish in the same way.

Mornay sauce

½ l	Béchamel sauce	18 fl oz
60 g	Parmesan, grated	2 oz
80 g	OR Gruyère, grated	2¾ oz
	2 egg yolks	
5 cl	dairy cream	2 fl oz

Mix the Béchamel sauce with the cheese. Bind with the egg yolks and cream if desired. Season well.

Poulette sauce

Yield: 1 l (1¾ pt)

1 l	Allemande sauce	1¾ pt

2 dl	mushroom cooking liquor	7 fl oz
	juice of half a lemon	
40–50 g	butter	1½–1¾ oz
	1 tablespoon chopped parsley	

Mix the Allemande sauce with the reduced mushroom cooking liquor and reduce slightly. Flavour with the lemon juice. Pass through a cloth and finish with fresh butter and the parsley. This sauce may also be served with sheep's trotters.

Cream sauce

| ½ l | Béchamel sauce | 18 fl oz |
| 1 dl | dairy cream | 3½ fl oz |

Mix together the Béchamel sauce and cream.

Chaud-froid sauce

Reduce equal amounts of Allemande sauce and light-coloured aspic together. Adjust the consistency with dairy cream and season to taste.

Hot horseradish sauce

| ½ l | cream sauce | 18 fl oz |
| 75 g | horseradish, grated | 2¾ oz |

Add the horseradish to the cream sauce, mix well and remove from the heat.

Mushroom sauce

1 l	Allemande sauce	1¾ pt
3 dl	mushroom cooking liquor	10 fl oz
100 g	mushrooms	3½ oz
30 g	butter	1 oz
30 g	butter to finish (optional)	1 oz

Mix the Allemande sauce with the reduced mushroom liquor, then stir in the mushrooms which have been cooked in butter.

Soubise sauce I

1 kg	onions, finely sliced	2 lb 4 oz
75 g	butter	2¾ oz
1 l	Béchamel sauce	1¾ pt
	butter to finish	

Blanch the onions and stew in butter until soft. Add the Béchamel sauce and cook well. Season carefully, pass through a tammy cloth and finish with butter.

Soubise sauce II

1 kg	onions, finely sliced	2 lb 4 oz
250 g	short-grained rice	9 oz
1½ l	white stock	2⅝ pt
	salt	
	pepper, freshly ground	
	sugar	
	butter	
	1–2 egg yolks	
5 cl–1 dl	dairy cream	2–3 fl oz

Blanch the onions and cook gently with the rice in the stock. Season with salt and pepper. Add a pinch of sugar and a little butter. Sieve to obtain a fine purée and adjust the seasoning. Bind with the egg yolks and cream. This sauce is served with saddle of mutton or veal and with mutton or veal cutlets.

Butter Sauces and their Derivatives

I. Béarnaise sauce (basic sauce)

3 dl	good white wine	10 fl oz
3 dl	tarragon vinegar	10 fl oz
70–80 g	shallots, finely chopped	2½–2¾ oz
	20–24 peppercorns, very finely crushed	
1 kg	best fresh butter	2 lb 4 oz
	12 egg yolks	
	salt	
	Cayenne pepper	
40–50 g	tarragon leaves, chopped	1½–2 oz
20 g	chervil, chopped	¾ oz

Place the wine, vinegar and shallots in a pan and reduce. Add the crushed peppercorns and reduce to less than ½ dl (2 fl oz). Meanwhile clarify the butter. Allow the reduced liquid to cool a little, adding a tablespoon of cold water if necessary. Then add the egg yolks and whisk over gentle heat or in a bain-marie until creamy. Whisk in the clarified butter a little at a time, being careful to avoid excessive heat. Stir in a little cold water if necessary. Season with a little salt and Cayenne and strain through a cloth. Mix in the tarragon, also the chopped chervil if desired. This sauce is especially suitable for red meat, such as roast fillet or sirloin of beef, entrecôte or grilled tournedos.

Sauces derived from Béarnaise

Choron sauce
Add good tomato purée to Béarnaise sauce. Check the flavour.

Foyot or Valois sauce
Mix Béarnaise sauce with slightly warmed, well reduced meat glaze to a light golden brown colour.

Paloise sauce
Prepare in the same way as Béarnaise sauce, adding equal amounts of tarragon and fresh mint.

Rachel sauce
Add tomato purée and meat glaze to Béarnaise sauce without giving the sauce a very pronounced flavour.

II. Hollandaise sauce (basic sauce)

	6 egg yolks	
500 g	butter	1 lb 2 oz
	2 lemons	
	salt	
1–2 dl	water	3½–7 fl oz
1–2 dl	vinegar	3½–7 fl oz
	(depending on strength)	
	2 small teaspoons white pepper, crushed	
	1 tablespoon chopped shallots (optional)	

Place the vinegar in a pan with the shallots and pepper, reduce, add a little water and remove the pan to the side of the stove. Add the egg yolks and whisk continuously while gradually adding the butter which has been melted and clarified. The sauce should have a frothy, creamy consistency. If it is too thick, add a little water. Season with a little salt and Cayenne pepper and flavour with lemon juice. Pass through a cloth and adjust the seasoning if necessary.

Sauces derived from Hollandaise

Maltese sauce

½ l	Hollandaise sauce	18 fl oz
	juice of 1 blood orange	
	and a pinch of grated zest	

Add the orange juice and a little grated zest to the Hollandaise sauce.

Mousseline sauce

½ l	Hollandaise sauce	18 fl oz
	2–3 tablespoons whipped dairy cream	

Fold the whipped cream into the Hollandaise sauce.

Special Sauces

Apple sauce
Flavour apple purée with lemon juice. This sauce, which should be slightly sweet, is served with roast pork.

Avgolémono sauce

	3 eggs	
	juice of 2 lemons	
	1 tablespoon cornflour	
2 dl	meat stock	7 fl oz

Beat the eggs and add the cornflour which has been blended with a little cold water or cold stock. Add the lemon juice drop by drop, stir into the stock and heat to boiling point.

Curry sauce

80 g	onions, chopped	2¾ oz
40 g	butter	1½ oz
	1 tablespoon curry powder	
	(depending on type)	
½ l	white veal stock	18 fl oz
	1 clove of garlic, finely chopped	
	1 apple, finely sliced	
30 g	bouquet garni	1 oz
	salt	
	pepper, freshly ground	
	cornflour	

Fry the onions lightly in the butter until transparent, add the garlic, dust with the curry powder and brown for a few minutes. Add the sliced apple (unpeeled) and cook gently for a moment, then add the stock, bouquet garni, salt and pepper. Simmer for 45 minutes, strain and adjust the seasoning. Thicken with cornflour if necessary.

Dill sauce
6 portions
Prepare in the same way as horseradish sauce (recipe page 179), but instead of horseradish add two tablespoons finely chopped dill to the sauce.

Brie and vermouth sabayon

8 portions

30–60 g	shallots, finely chopped	1–2 oz
	½ teaspoon green peppercorns	
	6 mushroom stalks, finely cut	
	½ teaspoon fresh thyme, chopped	
1 dl	white wine	3½ fl oz
2 dl	veal stock	7 fl oz
	8 egg yolks	
80 g	Brie, cut up small	3 oz
8 cl	dairy cream (35%)	3 fl oz
6 cl	Noilly Prat vermouth	2 fl oz

Place the shallots, peppercorns, mushroom stalks, thyme, wine and stock in a pan and reduce by half, then allow to cool. Beat in the egg yolks, then half the cream and whisk to a thick creamy consistency in a bain-marie as for an ordinary sabayon sauce. Heat the rest of the cream and melt the cheese in it. Mix with the sabayon, beat in the vermouth and adjust the seasoning. Keep the sauce warm but avoid excessive heat.

(Edward Mathis, Canada)

Suprême sauce

Yield: 5 dl (18 fl oz)   Cooking time: about 25 minutes

70 g	butter	2½ oz
	1 onion, peeled and diced	
	1 stalk celery, diced	
	1 carrot, scraped and diced	
	1 clove of garlic, peeled and crushed	
40 g	mushroom stalks, coarsely chopped	1½ oz
	10 peppercorns, crushed	
80 g	flour	3 oz
1 l	chicken stock, lukewarm	1¾ pt
¼ l	dairy cream	9 fl oz
	3 egg yolks	
⅛ l	dry white wine	5 fl oz
	¼ teaspoon salt	
	¼ teaspoon pepper, freshly ground	

Melt the butter in a sauté pan and add the onion, carrot, celery, garlic, mushroom stalks and peppercorns. Cook over medium heat for 5 minutes without colouring. Add the flour, mix well and fry until golden brown. Whisk in the stock and continue whisking until smooth. Bring to the boil, then simmer gently over low heat for 20 minutes and remove.

Place the cream, egg yolks and wine in a bowl, mix well and stir in the hot sauce. Continue stirring until velvety. Strain through a sieve and season to taste with salt and pepper.

Lobster sauce

approx.		approx.
250–300 g	1 lobster	9–10 oz
5 cl	olive oil	2 fl oz
50 g	butter	2 oz
50 g	mirepoix	2 oz
50 g	tomatoes, chopped	2 oz
5 cl	cognac	2 fl oz
	fresh dill	
	fresh tarragon	
1 dl	white wine	3½ fl oz
5 dl	fish stock	18 fl oz
	meat extract	
	salt	
	pepper, freshly ground	

Kill the lobster by plunging it in boiling water and cool at once. Split it in half and cut up. Remove the stomach and set aside the coral. Heat the oil in a sauté pan, add the pieces of lobster and sauter on all sides, turning with a wooden spatula, until the shells have taken on an even red colour. Add the mirepoix and tomatoes and continue cooking. Pour in the cognac, ignite, then add the wine, stock and chopped herbs and boil up well. Remove the pieces of lobster and detach the meat from the shells. Pound these very finely and return to the pan. Cook slowly over gentle heat for about 30 minutes. Add the meat extract and reduce by one third. Mix the coral with the butter and use to bind the sauce. Adjust the seasoning and pass through a fine sieve. The lobster meat may be used elsewhere, e.g. for cold dishes.

(Anton Mosimann, Great Britain)

Moravian liver sauce
Sauce au foie à la moravienne
Játrová omáčka po moravsku

6 portions   Cooking time: 30 minutes (if using bouillon cubes)

200 g	ox *or* calf's liver	7 oz
	a pinch of marjoram	
	3 peppercorns, freshly ground	
	salt	
30 g	smoked bacon, diced	1 oz
20 g	onions, finely cut	¾ oz
6 dl	meat stock	1 pt
	OR bouillon cube stock	
	1 clove of garlic (optional)	
35 g	fat	1¼ oz
30 g	flour	1 oz

Scrape the liver with a knife and pass through a sieve, or mince, and add the pepper and marjoram. Place the bacon in a pan, render down a little, then add the onions and cook until golden. Add the liver together with a little stock and cook for about six minutes. Make a blond roux with fat and flour, blend well with the liver mixture, add the rest of the stock, season with salt and cook for 20 minutes. Add a clove of garlic if desired. This sauce is served with pasta, dumplings or rice.

(Vilèm Vrabec, Czechoslovakia)

Horseradish sauce

6 portions   Cooking time: about 20–25 minutes

40 g	butter	1½ oz
40 g	flour	1½ oz
30 g	horseradish, grated	1 oz
¼ l	milk	9 fl oz
	OR dairy cream	
	1 egg yolk	
½ l	bouillon	18 fl oz
	salt	

Make a roux with the butter and flour and stir in the bouillon a little at a time. Season with salt and cook over low heat for 15 to 20 minutes. Remove from the heat and stir in the egg yolk and milk or cream which have been mixed together. Lastly add the horseradish.

Mole

1 kg	mole powder	2 lb 4 oz

50 g	plain chocolate	2 oz
	3 small teaspoons sugar	
	meat stock or chicken broth	

(Mole powder is a commercial preparation consisting of chillies, sesame seeds, almonds, peanuts, raisins, etc.)

Place all the ingredients in a pan and reduce until fairly thick. This sauce, which is extremely pungent, is also served with poultry.

(Emil Wälti, Mexico)

Pearà sauce

6–10 portions

100 g	beef marrow	3½ oz
300 g	breadcrumbs	10 oz
80 g	Parmesan, grated	3 oz
50 g	butter	2 oz
	black pepper, freshly ground	
	bouillon	

Heat the beef marrow and butter in a pan until liquid, add the breadcrumbs and fry lightly until the fat has been absorbed. Gradually add enough bouillon to obtain the consistency of Béchamel sauce. Cook gently, at the side of the stove if possible, stirring from time to time and adding bouillon as required. Continue cooking until the sauce is very smooth (at least an hour will be needed), then add the Parmesan and sufficient black pepper to give a pungent flavour. This sauce is served with boiled beef.

(Mario Saporito, Italy)

Meat and tomato sauce for pasta

500 g	neck of pork, coarsely chopped	1 lb 2 oz
	OR skinned pork frying sausage	
250 g	tomato purée	9 oz
	1 tablespoon chopped onion	
	1 tablespoon chopped parsley	
5 cl	olive oil	2 fl oz
	water	
	salt and pepper to taste	

Heat the oil in a frying pan, cook the onion in it for a short time without colouring, add the meat and the finely chopped parsley and fry lightly. Stir in the tomato purée with a fork, mix well and pour in enough water to cover. Season with salt and pepper, cover and stew gently over low heat for about 2 hours, stirring repeatedly.

This sauce may be served with any type of pasta. The pasta are well drained and mixed with the sauce before serving. They may be dotted with butter if desired. Grated Parmesan is handed separately.

(Salvatore Schifano, Italy)

Sabayon Villeneuve

10 portions

10 g	shallots, finely chopped	¼ oz
2½ dl	white wine (Villeneuve)	9 fl oz
	2 egg yolks	
	2 whole eggs	
	lemon juice	
	pepper, freshly ground	
	salt	

Place ½ dl (2 fl oz) of the wine in a pan, add the shallots and reduce. Add the eggs and yolks and the rest of the wine and whisk in a bain-marie until frothy. Flavour with lemon juice and season with salt and pepper. This sauce is not prepared until just before serving.

(Otto Ledermann, Switzerland)

Cucumber sauce Vojvodina

6 portions   Cooking time: 15 minutes

30 g	flour	1 oz
30 g	butter	1 oz
½ l	meat stock	18 fl oz
	3–4 pickled cucumbers, finely diced	

Prepare a blond roux with the flour and butter, then stir in the stock to make a smooth sauce. Add the diced cucumbers, also a little sugar if desired, and cook for a few minutes, making sure that the cucumbers are well heated.

(László Csizmadia, Yugoslavia)

Sorrel sauce
Sauce à l'oseille
Sóskamártás

4 portions   Cooking time: about 30 minutes

400 g	sorrel	14 oz
30 g	lard	1 oz
40 g	flour	1½ oz
20 g	onion, finely chopped	¾ oz
1 dl	sour cream	3½ fl oz
	salt	
3 g	sugar	a good pinch
2 dl	water	7 fl oz
	1 small teaspoon monosodium glutamate	

Clean the sorrel, wash well, chop finely and fry gently in the lard together with the chopped onion. Continue cooking until the sorrel has softened to a thick pulp. Sprinkle in the flour, gradually add the water, then the monosodium glutamate, and stir until quite smooth. Add sugar and salt, fold in the sour cream and bring to the boil.

(László Csizmadia, Hungary)

Morello cherry sauce
Sauce aux griottes
Meggymartas

4 portions   Cooking time: 30 minutes

350 g	morello cherries	12 oz
60 g	sugar	2 oz
	salt	
	zest of 1 lemon	
	6–7 cloves	
	1 cinnamon quill	
3 dl	water	10 fl oz
50 g	flour	2 oz
1½ dl	sour cream	5 fl oz
1 dl	red wine	3½ fl oz

Wash the cherries well, stone them and cook in the water together with salt, the sugar, cloves, cinnamon and lemon zest. Place the cherry stones in a separate pan with the wine and cook for about 20 minutes, repeatedly adding more wine as the wine in the pan evaporates.

Mix together the sour cream and flour and use to bind the stewed cherries. Strain the wine and add to the cherries, then boil up again.

(László Csizmadia, Hungary)

Shallot cream
Crème aux échalotes
Schalottencreme

10 portions

200 g	shallots, cut in quarters	7 oz
50 g	maître d'hôtel butter	2 oz
3 dl	double cream	10 fl oz
5 cl	tarragon vinegar	2 fl oz
	juice of 1 lemon	
1 l	tomato sauce	1¾ pt
	a pinch of Cayenne	

Melt the maître d'hôtel butter and gently fry the shallots in it without colouring. When they are transparent, add the vinegar, then the tomato sauce and the cream. Reduce until creamy and of a coating consistency. Flavour with the lemon juice and a pinch of Cayenne, and serve without straining.

(Karl Brunnengräber, Germany)

Mustard cream
Crème de moutarde
Senfcreme

10 portions

125 g	mild mustard	4½ oz
4 dl	sour cream	14 fl oz
	3 egg yolks	
	juice of 2 lemons	
	salt, pepper	
5 cl	brandy	2 fl oz
	1 tablespoon chives, finely chopped	
	a pinch of sugar	

Mix together the egg yolks and mustard, add the brandy and whisk in a simmering bain-marie. Gradually add the sour cream and lemon juice, season with salt and pepper, add a pinch of sugar and the chives, then continue whisking to a smooth cream. This cream should be kept hot in a bain-marie, but under no circumstances should it be allowed to boil.

(Karl Brunnengräber, Germany)

Mushroom Soubise sauce

¼ l	milk	9 fl oz
250 g	onions, sliced	9 oz
125 g	rice	4½ oz
250 g	mushrooms, finely chopped	9 oz
⅛ l	dairy cream	4½ fl oz
	4 egg yolks	
	nutmeg	
	bay leaf	
	cloves	
	salt	
	pepper, freshly ground	

Bring the milk to the boil, add the onions and rice and stir carefully. Add salt, pepper, nutmeg, bay leaf and cloves and mix well. Cover and cook gently in a slow oven. When almost all the milk has been absorbed, pass through a sieve, mix with the mushrooms and cook. Bring to the required consistency with the cream and boil up for a moment or two. Remove from the heat and bind with the egg yolks.

(German Gertsch-Rösner, Luxembourg)

Horseradish Soubise sauce

10 portions

100 g	oil and butter	3½ oz
300 g	larding pork fat or bacon	10½ oz
800 g	rice	1 lb 12 oz
1 kg 500 g	onions, finely sliced	3 lb 5 oz
3 l	bouillon	5¼ pt
50 g	horseradish, fresh, grated	2 oz
	salt	
	spices as desired	

Blanch the onions. Cut up the pork fat or bacon finely. Heat the oil and butter and the pork fat or bacon together, add the onions and cook under cover until soft. Cook the rice in the bouillon under cover in the oven until tender. Pass the onions and rice through a sieve, mix well and season carefully. To serve, mix a heaped tablespoon Soubise sauce with the horseradish.

(Otto Ledermann, Switzerland)

Tokay and walnut sauce
(Recipe page 898)

White wine sauce

4 portions   Cooking time: 45 minutes

150 g	carrots, finely sliced	5 oz
50 g	butter	2 oz
	1 tablespoon flour	
8 cl	sour cream	3 fl oz
¼ l	white wine	9 fl oz
	1 bay leaf	
	salt	
	pepper, freshly ground	

Heat the butter, add the carrots and flour and fry lightly without colouring. Add the bay leaf and season with salt and pepper. Gradually stir in the wine and cook for 45 minutes. Pass through a sieve and return to the pan. Pour in the sour cream and mix well. If the sauce is too thick, add a little more wine. This sauce is handed with fillet of beef or tournedos.

(László Csizmadia, Yugoslavia)

Yorkshire sauce

Yield: ½ l (18 fl oz)

	1 tablespoon orange peel, free of pith, cut into thin strips	
1 dl	port	3½ fl oz
2½ dl	demi-glace	9 fl oz
2½ dl	red-currant jelly	9 fl oz
	a pinch of ground cinnamon	
	a pinch of Cayenne pepper	

Place the orange peel and port in a pan and reduce. Add the demi-glace and red-currant jelly and cook well. Flavour with ground cinnamon and Cayenne. This sauce is served with braised ham.

Tzigane sauce

6 portions

20 g	onion	¾ oz
20 g	shallot	¾ oz
20 g	celery	¾ oz
20 g	carrot	¾ oz
20 g	mushrooms	¾ oz
5 cl	white wine	2 fl oz
5 cl	wine vinegar	2 fl oz
1½ dl	demi-glace	5 fl oz
1 dl	dairy cream	3½ fl oz
	1 tomato	
	1 bouquet garni	
	salt	
	peppercorns, crushed	

Chop the vegetables and mushrooms finely and fry lightly in a little butter without colouring. Stir in the wine and vinegar and reduce by half. Add the peppercorns and the tomato which has been peeled, seeded and coarsely chopped. Lastly add the cream and the bouquet garni. Cook for a few minutes, then strain.

(Emile Jung, France)

Lemon cream sauce

10 portions

70 g	butter	2½ oz
100 g	flour	3½ oz
¾ l	white veal stock	27 fl oz
	OR chicken stock	
	3 lemons	
	1 bouquet garni	
	3 egg yolks	
¼ l	dairy cream	9 fl oz
	salt	
	pepper, freshly ground	
	parsley, chopped	

Make a blond roux with the butter and flour and prepare velouté with the stock. Add thinly pared lemon zest and the bouquet garni and simmer until well cooked. Strain through a cloth, bind with the cream and egg yolks and lastly add salt and pepper, flavour well with lemon juice and stir in the parsley.

Onion sauce Vojvodina style

6 portions   Cooking time: 25 minutes

30 g	vegetable fat or lard	1 oz
50 g	onions, finely chopped	2 oz
½ l	bouillon	18 fl oz
30 g	flour	1 oz
	salt	

Fry the onions lightly in the fat. Add the flour and cook until reddish-brown. Stir in the bouillon, add salt and cook for 20 minutes, stirring repeatedly.

(László Csizmadia, Yugoslavia)

Basel onion sauce
Sauce aux oignons à la bâloise
Zwiebelsauce nach Basler Art

200 g	onions	7 oz
	butter	
¼ l	Béchamel sauce	9 fl oz
	salt	
	pepper, freshly ground	
	dairy cream	

Slice the onions finely and cook in butter until soft. Mix with the Béchamel sauce and season with salt and freshly ground pepper. Strain, boil up and finish the sauce with cream and butter.

(Otto Ledermann, Switzerland)

Cold Sauces

Cumberland sauce (basic sauce)

1 kg	red-currant jelly	2 lb 4 oz
	6 tablespoons French mustard	
	juice and finely pared	
	zest of 2 oranges	
	juice and finely pared	
	zest of 1 lemon	
	red wine	

Melt the jelly and mix with the mustard, orange and lemon juice. Cut the orange and lemon zest into julienne strips and cook in red wine, then add to the jelly. Alternatively, blend a little dry English mustard with red wine until smooth and add to the jelly instead of the French mustard. Season to taste with Cayenne.

Sauce derived from Cumberland sauce

Oxford sauce
Grate the orange and lemon zest instead of cutting into strips, add to the sauce and finish with a little ginger.

Mayonnaise

1 l	oil	1¾ pt
	4–5 egg yolks	
10 g	salt	¼ oz
	1 tablespoon wine vinegar	
	juice of 1 lemon	
	white pepper, freshly ground	

Whisk all the ingredients except the oil until fairly thick, then whisk in the oil a little at a time until smooth and thick. If the mayonnaise becomes too thick, adjust to the desired consistency with a little cold water. Flavour with Worcester sauce and lemon juice if desired.

Sauces derived from mayonnaise

Andalusian sauce

Mix mayonnaise with fine tomato purée and a little white wine. Add Cayenne pepper and Worcester sauce to taste and stir in thin strips of sweet pepper. This sauce is excellent with cold pork.

Bagration sauce

Flavour mayonnaise with anchovy essence; finish off with caviar.

Gloucester sauce

Mix mayonnaise with finely chopped fennel and sour cream. Flavour to taste with lemon juice and Worcester sauce.

Green sauce

Mix mayonnaise with 100 g (3½ oz) very fine spinach purée, adding 1 small teaspoon each of cress, parsley and chervil. The mayonnaise may be mixed with thick juice of blanched spinach which has been squeezed out with the herbs. It should be well seasoned.

Mousquetaire sauce

Mix mayonnaise with melted meat glaze. Stir in finely chopped shallots which have been cooked in white wine, also cut chives. This sauce is served with cold meat.

Rémoulade sauce

Mix mayonnaise with chopped gherkins, capers, tarragon, chervil or parsley and anchovy fillets. Add a little mustard to taste.

Aspic mayonnaise

Mix together two parts mayonnaise and one part cold melted aspic. This mayonnaise is mainly used to bind vegetable salad, also to decorate cold ham, etc.

Tartare sauce

Mix mayonnaise with finely cut chives, chopped tarragon and chervil or parsley, also finely chopped onions. In Switzerland chopped gherkins are added. Alternatively, this sauce may be made by pounding hard-boiled egg yolks to a smooth paste and proceeding as for mayonnaise. In this case onion purée should be used instead of chopped onions.

Egg yolk sauce

6 portions

	3 egg yolks, hard-boiled	
100 g	butter	3½ oz
	2 anchovies	
	OR 1 teaspoon anchovy paste	
	1 teaspoon lemon juice	
	1 teaspoon mustard	
	a pinch of ground pepper	
	salt	
	a few drops Worcester sauce	
	12 black olives	
	parsley	

Cream the butter in a porcelain bowl, add the egg yolks and anchovies which have been sieved, together with the remaining ingredients and mix until smooth. Anchovy paste may be used instead on anchovies if preferred. This sauce is used to decorate stuffed tomatoes and peppers, hard-boiled eggs, canapés, cold meat, etc.

(Vilèm Vrabec, Czechoslovakia)

Gribiche sauce

1 l	oil	1¾ pt
	2 small teaspoons French mustard	
	12 egg yolks, hard-boiled	
100 g	gherkins, chopped	3½ oz
100 g	capers, chopped	3½ oz
	2 tablespoons mixed chopped parsley,	
	tarragon and chervil	
	5 egg whites, hard-boiled	
	salt	
	pepper, freshly ground	
	a little vinegar	

Sieve the egg yolks into a bowl. Mix with the mustard, season and work in the oil a little at a time. Thin down with vinegar if necessary. Add the remaining ingredients and mix well, adjusting the seasoning to taste.

Horseradish cream sauce

1 l	whipped cream	1¾ pt
200 g	horseradish, finely grated	7 oz
	lemon juice	
	Cayenne pepper	
	icing sugar	

Fold the horseradish into the whipped cream with a wooden spatula. Add lemon juice, a little Cayenne and a little icing sugar.

Mint sauce

250 g	fresh mint	9 oz
3–4 dl	boiling water	10–14 fl oz
125 g	caster sugar	4½ oz
6–7 dl	wine vinegar	1–1¼ pt
(depending on strength)		
10 g	salt	¼ oz

Chop the mint or cut it into julienne strips. Blanch in boiling water, add the sugar and allow to cool. Stir in the vinegar and season with salt. If dried mint is used, only a quarter of the quantity given for fresh mint will be required. This sauce is served with mutton or lamb. In the USA mint jelly is preferred. This may be made by adding dissolved gelatine to the sauce, then straining it and allowing it to set.

Picada

Picada is a typical Catalonian savoury sauce which is added to many dishes just before serving. The method of preparation depends on the dish.

The basic ingredients are garlic, roasted nuts such as almonds, pine kernels or hazelnuts, bitter macaroons, fried bread or toast. Saffron is added only to dishes where pale yellow colouring is required and is listed separately in the relevant recipes.

The above ingredients are ground to a fine paste in a mortar, diluted with a little water and added to the dish. For chicken dishes, chicken liver is added to the basic picada ingredients and ground with them. For fish dishes fish liver is used.

(Josep Lladonosa, Spain)

Ravigote sauce

1 l	oil	1¾ pt
4 dl	vinegar	14 fl oz
	4 tablespoon 8 capers, small or chopped	
100 g	parsley, chopped	3½ oz
100 g	mixed chervil, tarragon and chives, chopped	3½ oz
150 g	onions, finely chopped	5¼ oz
	pepper, freshly ground	
	salt	

Make a thick sauce with all the ingredients and adjust the seasoning.

Reform sauce

Yield ½ l (18 fl oz)

½ l	Poivrade sauce	18 fl oz
10 g	truffle, cut in strips (optional)	¼ oz
20 g	pickled ox tongue, cut in strips	¾ oz
20 g	gherkins, cut in strips	¾ oz
20 g	mushrooms, cut in strips	¾ oz
	½ egg white, hard-boiled, cut in strips	

Mix all the ingredients together. This sauce is used for mutton cutlets à la Réforme.

Chive sauce

2 portions

2 dl	mayonnaise	7 fl oz
2 dl	sour cream	7 fl oz
	2 heaped tablespoons chives, finely cut	
	1 tablespoon Dijon mustard	

Add the sour cream to the mayonnaise and mix with the chives and mustard.

(Gerhard Gartner, Germany)

Asparagus sauce

2 portions

> 1 shallot
> 6 white asparagus spears
> dairy cream as required
> butter as required
> sugar

Cook the shallot gently in a little butter until transparent. Cook the asparagus in salted water with the addition of a little sugar, then remove and keep hot. Reduce the cooking liquid well and work the vegetables to a purée in a mixer. Prepare a fine sauce with the purée, the cooking liquid, cream and cold butter. Season.

(Gerhard Gartner, Germany)

Special vinaigrette sauce

> ⅓ nut oil
> ⅔ olive oil
> tarragon vinegar
> salt
> pepper, freshly ground

Prepare vinaigrette sauce with the above ingredients.

(Gerhard Gartner, Germany)

Savoury Butters

Bakonyi butter

4 portions

100 g	butter	3½ oz
10 g	smoked fat pork or bacon	⅓ oz
5 g	onion, very finely sliced	⅙ oz
2 cl	dairy cream	1 fl oz
	1 teaspoon red paprika	
	a good pinch of salt	
	pepper, freshly ground	
40 g	mushrooms, very finely sliced	1½ oz

Dice the pork or bacon very finely and render. Add the onions and mushrooms to the pan and cook gently, then sprinkle with the paprika, add the cream and cook briefly. Allow to cool. Season with salt and pepper and mix with the butter. Wrap in aluminium foil and refrigerate until firm.

Mushroom butter

4 portions

100 g	butter	3½ oz
30 g	mushrooms	1 oz
	½ small teaspoon pepper, freshly ground	
	a good pinch of salt	
	1 tablespoon parsley, finely chopped	

Chop the mushrooms finely in the processor, cook gently with the parsley in 20 g (¾ oz) butter, then allow to cool and harden. Mix well with the rest of the butter and season with salt and pepper. Wrap in aluminium foil and refrigerate until firm.

Herb butter

100 g	butter	3½ oz
	1 tablespoon parsley	
	½ tablespoon dill	

½ tablespoon tarragon
1 tablespoon chives
a good pinch of salt
pepper, freshly ground

Chop all the herbs very finely, season with salt and pepper and mix with the butter. Wrap in aluminium foil and refrigerate until firm.

Morel butter
Proceed as for mushroom butter (page 194), but use 50 g (2 oz) finely chopped drained canned morels instead of mushrooms.

Butter for pörkölt
Beurre pour ragoût hongrois
Pörkölt vaj

100 g	butter	3½ oz
15 g	lard	½ oz
15 g	onion, very finely sliced	½ oz
40 g	green pepper, very finely sliced	1½ oz
	a good pinch of hot paprika	
	1 tablespoon ketchup	
	a good pinch of salt	

Fry the onion and green pepper lightly in the lard without colouring, dust with paprika, add the ketchup and mix thoroughly. Allow to cool and harden. Mix with the butter and season with salt. Wrap in aluminium foil and refrigerate until firm.

(László Csizmadia, Hungary)

Café de Paris butter

Yield: about 5 kg (11 lb)

1 kg 700 g	best butter	3 lb 12 oz
1 kg 700 g	cooking butter	3 lb 12 oz

Flavouring ingredients:

750 g	onions, peeled	1 lb 10 oz
	4 cloves of garlic	
3 dl	oil	10 fl oz

5 g	thyme	⅙ oz
5 g	marjoram	⅙ oz
5 g	rosemary	⅙ oz
15 g	paprika	½ oz
15 g	curry powder	½ oz
15 g	salt	½ oz
12 g	white pepper	½ oz
75 g	Aromat, or other commercial seasoning	2¾ oz
	juice of 1 lemon	
7½ cl	Madeira	2½ fl oz
7½ cl	brandy	2½ fl oz
7½ cl	Worcester sauce	2½ fl oz
25 g	French mustard	1 oz
25 g	chives, cut	1 oz
40 g	parsley, chopped	1½ oz
	12 anchovy fillets, chopped	
	9 eggs	

Cream the butter. Chop the onions and garlic together and soften in oil without colouring. Mix all the flavouring ingredients together in the blender, then add to the butter and cream in the mixer. If margarine is used instead of butter, the resulting preparation is satisfactory but can no longer be called a savoury 'butter'.

Tarragon butter
Blanch 250 g (9 oz) fresh tarragon leaves for a short time, drain and squeeze in a cloth to obtain the juice. Soften the butter (1 kg 700 g), mix the tarragon juice with it and season.

Garlic butter I

500 g	butter	1 lb 2 oz
200 g	garlic	7 oz

Extract the garlic juice, work it into the butter and season.

Garlic butter II

500 g	butter	1 lb 2 oz
150 g	garlic	5 oz

Work the garlic to a fine purée, mix with the butter and season.

Maître d'hôtel butter

500 g	best butter	1 lb 2 oz
100 g	parsley, chopped	3½ oz
	juice of 2–3 lemons	
10 g	salt	⅓ oz

Cream the butter until soft, mix with the remaining ingredients and adjust the seasoning if required.

Flour butter

100 g	butter	3½ oz
75 g	flour	2½ oz

Work the ingredients to a smooth paste. This butter is used as a quick thickening agent for sauces.

Pimiento butter

	2 large red peppers	
250 g	butter	9 oz
	Cayenne pepper	
	salt	

Bake the peppers in a hot oven for a short time, then skin them and remove the seeds. Alternatively, canned peppers may be used. Work to a purée in the processor or pass through a wire sieve. Mix with the butter and seasoning.

Marchand de vins butter

Place finely chopped shallots and red wine in a pan and reduce by half. Add salt, pepper and a little meat glaze, then work into softened butter. Add lemon juice and chopped parsley and check the seasoning.

Anchovy butter

| 250 g | butter | 9 oz |
| 100 g | anchovy fillets | 3½ oz |

Work the anchovy fillets to a purée and pass through a wire sieve. Cream the butter, mix with the anchovy purée and season.

Mustard butter

250 g	butter	9 oz
50 g	medium strong mustard	2 oz
5 g	chopped tarragon (optional)	¼ oz

Cream the butter and mix with the mustard, adding the chopped tarragon if desired. Adjust the seasoning if necessary.

Cold Hors d'Oeuvre

Apple cocktail Eva
Cocktail de pommes Eva
Cocktail di mele Eva

4 portions

	4 Stark Delicious apples	
240 g	beef	8 oz
	half a lemon	
	1 clove of garlic	
	4 tablespoons olive oil	
	salt, pepper	

This variety of apple has an attractive brightly coloured, glossy skin which harmonises with the colour of the meat, and tender aromatic flesh providing a pleasant contrast to the flavour of the meat.

Cut off the stalk end of the apples carefully to make a cover and set aside. Core the apples, then cut out the flesh in the middle with a small ball cutter.

Mince the beef, using the finest cutter, marinate for 2 to 3 hours in the juice of half a lemon and the olive oil, together with the garlic, salt and pepper, then mix with the apple balls. Fill the apples with this mixture, place the covers on top and dress on lettuce leaves. Chill by placing small balls or cubes of ice between the apples and serve very cold.

(Sergio Chiesa, Italy)

Apples stuffed with ham cream
Pommes à la crème de jambon
Jablka plněná šunkovým krémem

6 portions

	3 large sweet crisp apples	
300 g	boiled ham	10 oz
	6 tablespoons whipped cream	
60 g	walnuts	2 oz
	6 choice lettuce leaves	
	1 lemon	
	1 pickled red pepper	

Cut up the ham and mince twice, using the finest cutter. Grind the walnuts and add, together with the cream. Peel, quarter and core the apples. Place them on a board, hollow side uppermost. Pipe on the ham cream, using a star tube. Decorate the top with strips of red pepper. Wash the lettuce leaves, sprinkle with lemon juice, arrange on a flat dish and place the apple quarters on top.

(Vilèm Vrabec, Czechoslovakia)

Aspic southern Norwegian style
Aspic à la norvégienne
Kalvesuss fra Sørlandet

4 portions

500 g	shoulder of veal	1 lb 2 oz
300 g	shoulder of pork	10 oz
	1 onion	
	1 bay leaf	
	pepper, freshly ground	
	bouillon	
	parsley, finely chopped	
	½ teaspoon curry powder	
	thyme	
	powdered aspic	
	white wine vinegar	

Cook the veal and pork in the bouillon with the onion, bay leaf and pepper until tender, then cut into cubes. Mix the parsley with the curry powder. Prepare aspic jelly, sharpen with vinegar and flavour with thyme and the curried parsley. Fill the meat and aspic into a ring mould and leave to set in a cool place.

(Hroar Dege, Günther Rett, Norway)

Avocados stuffed with meat salad
Avocats farcis à la salade de viande
Avocado memule in Salad basar

8 portions

	4 avocados	
300 g	cooked veal	10 oz
	2 salted cucumbers	
	1 small onion	

1 red pepper, seeded
8 black olives, stoned
2 eggs, hard-boiled
salt
pepper, freshly ground
vinegar
oil
lemon juice

Cut the avocados in half lengthways, stone them and remove part of the flesh. Dice the flesh, sprinkle with lemon juice and set aside. Finely dice the meat, cucumbers, red pepper, onion and eggs and carefully mix with the diced avocado flesh. Season with salt and pepper, dress with vinegar and oil and fill into the avocado halves. Decorate each one with a stoned black olive.

(Hermann Wohl, Israel)

French beans with smoked tongue
Haricots verts avec langue fumée
Pasulj sa suvim jezikom

6 portions   Cooking time: 2–3 hours

250 g	French beans	9 oz
	1 large or 2 small smoked tongues (calf, ox or pig)	
2 dl	oil	7 fl oz
200 g	onions, finely chopped	7 oz
3 dl	vinegar	10 fl oz
	1 pickled sweet pepper	
	red paprika	
	salt, pepper	
	1 clove of garlic, finely chopped (optional)	
	water	

Blanch and drain the beans. Wash the tongue carefully in hot water. Place in a pan of hot water with the beans and cook until tender. Remove from the pan and allow to cool. Cook the onions gently in oil without colouring, sprinkle with red paprika, mix with the cold beans and season with salt and pepper. Slice the tongue and place in a bowl with the beans, add the garlic if desired and dress with oil and vinegar. Decorate with pickled sweet peppers and serve cold.

(László Csizmadia, Yugoslavia)

Chopped egg

	10 eggs	
100 g	onions	3½ oz
1 dl	oil	3½ oz
	salt	
	pepper, freshly ground	

Boil the eggs hard and mince finely with the raw onions. Season with salt and pepper and mix with oil to a paste of spreading consistency. Store in the refrigerator.

(Gérard van Dijk, Switzerland)

Prague pork aspic
Aspic de porc de Prague
Rosolový chlebíček

10–12 portions   Cooking time: about 2½ hours

1 pickled pig's trotter
1 fresh pig's trotter
1 onion
salt
10 peppercorns
6 allspice seeds
1 bay leaf
a pinch of thyme

Garnish:

1 lettuce
8 firm tomatoes, cut in quarters

Wash the pig's trotters, place in a fairly large pot and pour in just enough water to cover. Add the onion, salt, herbs and spices and bring to the boil, then cook for about two and a half hours or until tender. Remove the trotters from the pot, bone them and mince the meat and rinds, then transfer to a bowl and pour in sufficient strained cooking liquid to give the consistency of a thin pulp. Pour into a loaf tin and refrigerate until set, then turn out, slice, dress on an oval dish and garnish with lettuce leaves and tomatoes.

This aspic may be served as an hors d'oeuvre, a dish on its own or a snack after supper. It is accompanied by bread and either finely sliced onions and vinegar or vinaigrette sauce.

(Vilèm Vrabec, Czechoslovakia)

Cold vegetable omelettes with tapenade
Omelettes froides de légumes à la tapenade

	12 eggs	
	2 teaspoons chopped truffles	
	1 teaspoon chopped parsley	
	1 teaspoon chopped chervil	
	1 teaspoon chopped chives	
150 g	spinach	5 oz
150 g	Swiss chard	5 oz
	3 tomatoes, skinned and seeded	
	1 shallot, finely chopped	
	a pinch of oregano	
	4 artichoke bottoms	
200 g	chanterelles or flap mushrooms	7 oz
	butter as required	
	olive oil as required	
	¼ clove of garlic	
	salt, pepper	

Tapenade:

100 g	stoned black olives	3½ oz
20 g	capers	¾ oz
40 g	anchovies	1½ oz
	2 teaspoons olive oil	
	pepper, freshly ground	

Blanch the spinach and Swiss chard, chop very finely, add a pinch of garlic and cook lightly in butter without colouring. Dice the tomatoes finely and cook gently in butter with the shallot and oregano. Slice the artichoke bottoms thinly and fry quickly in shallow olive oil. Chop the chanterelles or flap mushrooms and fry quickly in shallow olive oil.

Beat the eggs two at a time and season. Scramble each two eggs with one of the six fillings – truffles, Swiss chard/spinach, tomatoes/shallot, herbs, artichoke bottoms, mushrooms. Place the hot omelettes in separate layers in a buttered earthenware dish to make a pleasing colour combination. Press down carefully and bake in a slow oven for 20 minutes. Allow to cool. Serve from the dish in slices, accompanied by tapenade and finest quality wine vinegar.

To make tapenade, work the ingredients to a purée in the processor and season with a turn of the pepper mill.
(Illustration, page 235)

(Pierre Gleize, France)

Cucumber stuffed with green pepper, morello cherries and Gervais cream
Concombres farcis au poivre vert, griottes et crème de Gervais
Gefüllte Gurke mit grünem Pfeffer, Amarena-Kirschen und Gervaiscreme

	1 cucumber	
150 g	Gervais	5 oz
10 g	stoned morello cherries	½ oz
5 g	chopped parsley	¼ oz
	½ sheet gelatine	
	salt	
	green pepper	

Carefully hollow out the cucumber, leaving a narrow rim, and blanch. Prepare Gervais cream with the Gervais, the cherries which have been chopped and the parsley. Season with salt and green pepper, then fold in the gelatine which has been dissolved. Fill the cucumber with this cream, chill well, then slice.

(Josef Haueis, Austria)

Calf's head with summer garnish and vinaigrette sauce
Tête de veau garnie avec vinaigrette
Sommerlicher Kalbskopf mit Vinaigrette

1 calf's head
2 calves' brains
1 calf's tongue
tomatoes
radishes
finely chopped chives

Cook the calf's head until tender. Cut the meat in thick slices while still warm. When cool dress on lettuce leaves with slices of poached calf's brains and cooked tongue. Decorate with tomatoes and radishes, and sprinkle with vinaigrette sauce (recipe page 193).
(Illustration, page 766)

(Gerhard Gartner, Germany)

Chopped calf's liver Sabta
Foie de veau haché Sabta
Art-Kawet kazuz Sabta

8 portions

800 g	calf's liver, koshered (page 210)	1 lb 12 oz

400 g	onions, finely sliced	14 oz
	8 hard-boiled eggs	
	3 tomatoes	
	10 stoned black olives	
	salt	
	pepper, freshly ground	
	oil	

Dice the liver. Cook the onions lightly in oil without colouring. Add the liver and cook gently. Mince with 7 of the eggs, using the finest cutter. Season with salt and pepper. The mixture should still be lukewarm and soft enough to pipe through the largest tube; if it is too firm, add a little veal gravy.

Cut the tomatoes into 10 large slices. Pipe a large rosette of the liver/egg mixture on to each one. Grate the remaining egg finely and sprinkle on the rosettes. Decorate each rosette with a stoned olive.

(Hermann Wohl, Israel)

Jellied rabbit with basil
Compôte de lapereau au basilic
Compôte van jong konijn met basilicum

6–8 portions

1 kg	young rabbit	2 lb 4 oz
1 dl	dry white wine	3½ fl oz
25 g	smoked streaky bacon	1 oz
25 g	fat bacon	1 oz
	1 bouquet garni	
	1 onion	
	1 carrot	
	15 fresh or dried basil leaves	
	3 tablespoons wine vinegar	
3 dl	veal broth	10 fl oz
	flour as required	
	salt, freshly ground pepper	

Garnish:

	1 curly endive	
	10 fresh basil leaves	
	2 pears, not too ripe	
½ l	red wine	18 fl oz
	1 tablespoon red-currant jelly	
	lemon juice	
	black peppercorns, crushed	

approx. 3–5 cm	cinnamon quill	1–2 in approx.
	salt	
	olive oil	
	lettuce	

Cut up the rabbit. Prepare a marinade with the onion, carrot, bouquet garni, basil, white wine and vinegar, pour over the rabbit and leave for 12 hours. Remove the meat, drain and dry gently with a linen cloth. Strain the marinade and set aside the liquid and the vegetables separately.

Render the bacon over low heat; when all the fat has melted, remove the remaining pieces of bacon. Season the pieces of rabbit with salt and pepper, dust with flour and fry in the hot bacon fat until golden brown. Fry the marinade vegetables lightly in a separate pan without colouring, then transfer to a stew pan with the rabbit. Rinse out the frying pan with a little veal broth, then pour into the stew pan together with the strained marinade and the rest of the veal broth. Cover the pan and cook over very low heat for 1 to 1½ hours. Remove the pieces of rabbit from the cooking liquid, bone them and slice the meat very thinly. Remove all fat from the cooking liquid, strain through a cloth, reduce to 1 dl (3½ fl oz) and adjust the seasoning. Place the meat in a mould or earthenware dish, pour the reduced stock over, allow to cool and refrigerate until set.

Garnish: Peel the pears, place in a pan with the cinnamon quill, lemon juice, red-currant jelly and red wine. Poach for about 15 minutes, depending on the size of the pears, then allow to cool. Cut the pears in quarters and core them. Dress the lettuce leaves with salt, pepper, lemon juice, oil and the basil which has been finely cut.

Dip the mould or dish in hot water for a moment, then turn out on to an oval serving dish. Decorate with an alternating arrangement of pears and lettuce leaves.

(Alexander Koene, Netherlands)

Rabbit in lemon balm aspic
Lapin en gelée à la saveur de mélisse
Coniglio in gelatina al sapore di melissa

8 portions   Cooking time: 2 hours

400 g	rabbit (leg and back fillets)	14 oz
400 g	new carrots	14 oz
100 g	courgettes	4 oz
100 g	extra fine French beans	4 oz
	salt	
	white pepper, freshly ground	
20 g	lemon balm	¾ oz

| 30 g | butter | 1 oz |

Stock:

500 g	rabbit bones	1 lb
80 g	carrots	3 oz
40 g	celery	1½ oz
2 l	water	3½ pt
15 g	coarse salt	½ oz
20 g	lemon balm	¾ oz

To clarify stock:

150 g	tomatoes	5 oz
60 g	carrots	2 oz
40 g	celery	1½ oz
50 g	sheet gelatine	2 oz
	4 egg whites	
10 g	lemon balm	⅓ oz

Wash all the lemon balm, pick off the leaves and set aside the smallest for decoration. Bone and trim the meat, remove the sinews and cut it evenly into 1 cm (½ in) cubes. Fry gently for about 10 minutes without colouring in 40 g (1½ oz) butter containing a few lemon balm leaves. Drain in a conical strainer, allow to cool and refrigerate.

Peel the carrots and courgettes, then wash and drain them, keeping them separate. Turn them to an olive shape 2.5 cm x 0.5 cm (1 in x ¼ in). Cut the beans to the same size. Season these three vegetables with salt and pepper and colour for 2 or 3 minutes in three separate pans each containing 10 g (½ oz) butter. Add 5 cl (2 fl oz) water to each pan, cover with oiled greaseproof paper, leave over low heat for 5 or 6 minutes, drain and mix with the meat.

To make the stock, slice the carrots and celery and place them in a pot with the rabbit bones, lemon balm, water and salt. Bring to the boil, cook over low heat for an hour, skim and remove the fat. Pass through a conical strainer and keep lukewarm.

To clarify the stock and make aspic jelly, first soak the gelatine in ½ l (18 fl oz) cold water, then squeeze out. Peel the carrots and string the celery. Cut the tomatoes in half, remove the stalk and seeds, drain off the liquid and dice the flesh. Place the carrots, celery, tomatoes and lemon balm in a pot and mix well with the egg whites. Using a wooden spoon, slowly stir in the lukewarm stock, then bring to the boil while stirring. Cook for 30 minutes over gentle heat. Strain the stock through a damp cloth, dissolve the gelatine in it and set aside.

When the aspic is beginning to set, line 8 dariole moulds and 8 plates with it, then refrigerate. Decorate the plates with lemon balm leaves. Half fill each mould with the meat and vegetable mixture. Cover with a layer of aspic and refrigerate until set. Fill with the rest of the meat and mask with aspic. Allow to set. To dish, quickly dip the moulds in hot water and turn out on to the plates which have been lined with aspic.
(Illustration, page 411)

(Daniel Drouadaine, Italy)

Rabbit fillet with cabbage and raisin stuffing
Filet de lapin farci aux choux et aux fruits secs
Gefülltes Kaninchenfilet mit Kohl und Trockenfrüchten

4 portions   Cooking time: 1 hour per kg (30 minutes per lb)

200 g	rabbit fillet	7 oz
	2 green cabbage leaves	

Stuffing:

10 g	raisins	½ oz
10 g	candied orange peel, finely chopped	½ oz
50 g	sausage meat	2 oz
	salt; pepper freshly ground	
1 cl	Cognac	½ fl oz

Cut halfway through the flesh down the centre of the rabbit fillet and flatten well. Blanch the cabbage leaves. Prepare stuffing with the sausage meat, salt, pepper and Cognac. Add the raisins and orange peel and mix well. Spread on to the cabbage leaves, cover with the meat and place on a piece of oiled aluminium foil. Roll up and tie. Poach for about 20 minutes at 75°C (167°F) and allow to cool. Remove from the foil and cut in slices.

(Josef Haueis, Austria)

Rabbit leg with saffron stuffing
Cuisse de lapin farcie, parfumée au safran
Gefüllte Kaninchenkeule mit Safranfarce

Cooking time: 1 hour per kg (30 minutes per lb)

	1 rabbit leg	
	salt; pepper freshly ground	
	Cognac	
	rosemary	

Stuffing:

200 g	shoulder of veal, trimmed and minced	7 oz
50 g	bacon, minced	2 oz
20 g	ice	¾ oz
30 g	rabbit liver	1 oz
1 cl	Cognac	½ fl oz
	salt; pepper freshly ground	
5 g	saffron	¼ oz
	fine French beans	

Bone the rabbit leg. Season the meat with salt and pepper, add a little rosemary and sprinkle with a little Cognac. Prepare the stuffing with all the listed ingredients except the beans. Fill the leg with this mixture. Blanch the beans and add to the stuffing. Place the leg on a piece of oiled aluminium foil. Roll up and tie. Poach at 75°C (167°F) and allow to cool. Unwrap and slice.

(Josef Haueis, Austria)

Smyrna meat balls
See 'Hot Hors d'Oeuvre', page 269

Stuffed cabbage leaves
Roulades de choux aux champignons
Gefüllter Kohl mit Champignonfarce

Cooking time: 1 hour per kg (30 minutes per lb)

4 green cabbage leaves, blanched

Stuffing:

200 g	shoulder of veal, trimmed and minced	7 oz
50 g	pork back fat, minced	2 oz
20 g	ice	¾ oz
1 cl	dry white wine	½ fl oz
	salt	
	green pepper	
40 g	small fresh mushrooms, blanched	1½ oz

Place the cabbage leaves on pieces of oiled aluminium foil. Prepare stuffing with the remaining ingredients, divide between the cabbage leaves and roll up in the foil, then tie. Poach for about 20 minutes at 75°C (167°F) and allow to cool. Untie, unwrap and slice.

(Josef Haueis, Austria)

Stuffed leeks with field mushrooms
Poireaux farcis aux morilles et aux girolles
Gefüllter Lauch mit Kalbsbrät, gefüllten Morcheln und Pfifferlingen

Cooking time: 1 hour per kg (30 minutes per lb)

3 large green leek leaves

Stuffing:

200 g	shoulder of veal, trimmed and minced	7 oz
50 g	pork back fat, minced	2 oz
20 g	ice	¾ oz
1 cl	Cognac	½ fl oz
	salt	
	pepper, freshly ground	
10 g	dried morels	½ oz
20 g	small chanterelles	¾ oz

Prepare the stuffing with the veal, pork fat, ice, Cognac, salt and pepper. Soak the morels, then drain and fill with stuffing. Carefully mix the stuffed morels and the chanterelles with the rest of the stuffing. Wash the leek leaves thoroughly, place on a piece of oiled aluminium foil and fill with the stuffing. Roll up in the foil, poach for about 20 minutes and allow to cool. Unwrap and slice.

(Josef Haueis, Austria)

Chopped liver

500 g	liver (chicken, calf or ox), kosher	1 lb 2 oz
	4 eggs, hard-boiled and finely chopped	
100 g	onions	3½ oz
100 g	chicken fat or oil	3½ oz
	salt	
	pepper, freshly ground	
	Aromat	
	oil	

Cut up the liver and slice the onions. Stew lightly in oil and season with salt, pepper and Aromat. Add the eggs and mince finely. Work to a smooth paste with the chicken fat or oil, which should be added in sufficient quantity to bind the paste well. Chill thoroughly. For method of serving, see 'Chopped liver and egg on toast', below.

(Gérard van Dijk, Switzerland)

Chopped liver and egg on toast

10 portions

500 g	chopped liver (recipe above)	1 lb 2 oz
500 g	hard-boiled egg, chopped	1 lb 2 oz
400 g	carrot salad	14 oz
200 g	salted cucumbers	7 oz
	10 slices bread for toasting	

paprika
parsley, chopped

Remove the crusts from the bread, toast and cut each round in half. Using an ice cream scoop, shape the chopped liver and chopped egg each into 10 balls. Place the toast on dessert plates, allowing two half-rounds per portion. Cover one with a ball of chopped liver and the other with a ball of chopped egg. Sprinkle with paprika and chopped parsley and garnish with carrot salad and salted cucumbers.

(Gérard van Dijk, Switzerland)

Chopped liver on toast

10 portions

1 kg	chopped liver (recipe, p. 210)	2 lb 4 oz
	5 slices bread for toasting	
400 g	carrot salad	14 oz
200 g	salted cucumbers	7 oz
	paprika	
	parsley, chopped	

Remove the crusts from the bread, toast and cut each round in half. Place the toast on dessert plates, allowing one half-round per portion. Using an ice cream scoop, shape the chopped liver into 20 balls. Place 2 on each half-round of toast. Sprinkle with paprika and chopped parsley. Garnish with carrot salad and salted cucumbers.

(Gérard van Dijk, Switzerland)

Beef marrow croûtons and lettuce
Croûtons à la moelle sur salade de saison
Markcroûtons auf Salat

beef marrow, sliced
French bread
butter
garlic
pepper, freshly ground
rose pepper, ground
coarse sea salt
lettuce leaves

Vinaigrette dressing:

raspberry vinegar
oil

Cut the bread in lengths and brush the slices with melted butter. Toast to a golden brown colour under the salamander and rub with half a clove of garlic. Cover with slices of beef marrow which have been soaked, blanched and drained. Season with freshly ground pepper, rose pepper and coarse sea salt. Heat for about one minute in a hot oven.

Prepare the vinaigrette dressing, using only a small quantity of oil as the beef marrow is fatty. Dress the lettuce leaves and arrange the slices of bread on top.
(Illustration, page 766)

(Gerhard Gartner, Germany)

Rissoles Vojvodina style
Rissoles à la vojvodine
Pastetice od Sira-Skute

8 portions

250 g	skimmed milk soft cheese (quark)	9 oz
250 g	butter or margarine	9 oz
250 g	flour	9 oz
130 g	smoked neck of pork	4½ oz
	OR ham	
	1 egg	
	a good pinch of salt	

Sieve the cheese or work with a fork until smooth. Add the butter, mix, season with salt and knead to a smooth paste with the flour. Pin out to a thickness of ½ cm (¼ in) and cut with a pastry wheel into 8 x 5 cm (3½ x 2 in) rectangles. Chop the pork or ham finely and mix well with the egg. Place a little of this filling on one half of each pastry rectangle, fold the other half over to enclose the filling and seal the edges well with the fingers. Place on an ungreased baking sheet, egg wash and bake in a preheated oven until light golden. Remove at once; if the rissoles are left to brown, they will taste bitter because of their soft cheese content. These rissoles are served cold with spirits, tea or beer.

(László Csizmadia, Yugoslavia)

Marinated fillet of beef
Filet de boeuf mariné
Gravet Okse

10 portions

1 kg 500	fillet of beef	3 lb 5 oz

Marinade:

4 dl	port	14 fl oz
1½ dl	good Burgundy	5 fl oz
1 dl	olive oil	3½ fl oz
½ dl	sea salt	2 fl oz
½ dl	sugar	2 fl oz
100 g	white pepper, coarsely ground	3½ oz
100 g	cloves	3½ oz
	a little dill and chives	

Sauce:

5 dl	olive oil	18 fl oz
140 g	Colman's dry mustard	5 oz
	3 egg yolks	
	chives, finely cut	
	parsley, finely chopped	
	horseradish, grated	
	a little port	
	a few drops tabasco	

Trim the beef and place on a metal tray. Mix together the ingredients for the marinade and pour over the meat. Place a little dill and chives on top and cover well with aluminium foil to prevent drying out. Refrigerate for about 48 hours, turning the meat regularly so that it is well marinated all over. Remove from the marinade, wrap in aluminium foil and refrigerate for a further 48 hours. The meat is now ready for serving. Unwrap it, cut in paper thin slices and serve with the sauce, allowing 35 g (1¼ oz) per portion.

To make the sauce, mix together the horseradish, chives and parsley and add a little port and a few drops of tabasco. Blend the mustard with the egg yolks and slowly work in the olive oil to a smooth, creamy consistency. Carefully stir in the herb mixture.

(Hroar Dege, Günther Rett, Norway)

Beef fillet with truffled vegetable stuffing
Filet de boeuf farci aux légumes et aux truffes
Gefülltes Rinderfilet mit einer Farce von grünem Paprika, Karotten und Trüffeln

Cooking time: 1 hour per kg (30 minutes per lb)

200 g	fillet of beef	7 oz
	salt	
	pepper, freshly ground	

	Madeira	
200 g	shoulder of veal, minced	7 oz
50 g	pork back fat, minced	2 oz
20 g	ice	¾ oz
10 g	carrots, finely chopped and blanched	⅓ oz
10 g	green pepper, skinned, seeded and finely chopped	⅓ oz
10 g	truffles, finely chopped	⅓ oz

Cut halfway through the flesh down the centre of the fillet of beef and flatten well. Prepare stuffing with the remaining ingredients and spread on the meat. Roll up, wrap in oiled aluminium foil and tie. Poach for about 20 minutes at 75°C (167°F) and allow to cool, then chill. Unwrap and slice.

(Josef Haueis, Austria)

Sliced raw beef Alba
Boeuf cru en tranches d'Alba
Scannello all'albese

1 portion

100 g	raw beef (topside)	4 oz
	⅘ olive oil	
	⅕ lemon juice	
	2 cloves of garlic	

Garnish:

1 tablespoon each:
  pickled courgettes,
  beans,
  carrots
salt and fresh ground pepper as required

Cut the beef in paper-thin slices. Prepare a well flavoured sauce with the garlic which has been pounded in a mortar, olive oil, lemon juice, salt and pepper, and pour over the meat. If desired, the meat may be sprinkled with grated white truffles or Parmesan and fennel.

This Piedmontese speciality is often wrongly called 'Carpaccio', a name chosen by Mr. Cipriani in Venice in honour of the painter Carpaccio, an exhibition of whose paintings was held there.
(Illustration, page 516)

(Franco Colombani, Italy)

Sliced raw beef Bergamo fashion
Boeuf cru en tranches à la bergamasque
Manzo in 'carpaccio' alla bergamasca

4 portions

200 g	beef (sirloin)	7 oz
50 g	Parmesan or other hard cheese	2 oz
100 g	button or flap mushrooms	4 oz
	juice of 1 lemon	
	2 tablespoons olive oil	
	salt, pepper	

Just before serving cut the raw meat in paper-thin slices, using a meat slicer. Also slice the cheese and the mushrooms (raw) very thinly. Place the meat on plates and cover first with sliced cheese, then with mushrooms. Season with salt and freshly ground pepper, sprinkle with olive oil and lemon juice and serve at once.

(Giovanni Maria Tobia, Italy)

Cannelons Basel style
Cannelons à la bâloise
Basler Rollen

10 portions   Baking time: 15–20 minutes

800 g	puff pastry	1 lb 12 oz
	egg	

Filling:

400 g	foie gras trimmings	14 oz
	OR foie gras parfait	
	OR foie gras loaf	
	OR foie gras mousse	
150 g	butter	5 oz
400 g	ham and tongue, finely diced	14 oz
5 cl	Madeira	2 fl oz
30 g	pistachio nuts, chopped	1 oz

Pin out the puff pastry to 2 mm (about ⅛ in) thick and cut into strips 30 cm (12 in) long and 1½ cm (⅝ in) wide. Roll each strip in spiral fashion round small wooden or metal cylinders. Egg wash the top and allow to rest in the refrigerator for 30 minutes, then bake for 15 to 20 minutes at 220°C (428°F). When quite cold pipe in the filling.

To make the filling, prepare fine foie gras purée, cream it with the butter and add the remaining ingredients. Check the seasoning and adjust carefully if necessary.

Pig's or calf's liver sausage may be substituted for foie gras, and margarine for butter.

(Otto Ledermann, Switzerland)

Calf's liver mousse
Mousse de foie de veau
Pâté di fegato

400 g	calf's liver	14 oz
50 g	unsmoked bacon	2 oz
	½ medium onion	
200 g	butter	7 oz
	Marsala	
1 dl	Cognac	3½ fl oz
	a pinch of Cayenne	
	salt	

Slice the liver very finely and soak in water overnight to drain away all the blood. Remove, drain well and dry carefully with a cloth.

Dice the bacon, slice the onion thinly and cook gently together in very little butter without colouring. Add the liver, cook well, season with salt and add sufficient Marsala to detach the cooking juices. Allow to cool, then mince, using the finest cutter, and sieve finely. Transfer to a bowl on ice and work in fresh butter until very smooth and creamy. Add a pinch of Cayenne and the Cognac. Adjust the seasoning if necessary.

Fill the mousse into individual moulds masked with port flavoured aspic (or an oblong fluted mould prepared in the same manner) and refrigerate until set.

(Giulio Gasazza, Switzerland)

Ham shells
Coquilles au jambon
Šunková majonéza na lasturách

6 portions

600 g	lean ham	1 lb 5 oz
	2 apples, peeled and cored	
200 g	mayonnaise	7 oz

	salt	
	1 tablespoon lemon juice	
	1 teaspoon mustard	
	1 teaspoon caster sugar	
	a pinch of white pepper	
	1 teaspoon Worcester sauce	
	2 tablespoons whipped cream	
	OR 1 tablespoon yoghourt	
	6 large choice lettuce leaves	
200 g	canned asparagus	7 oz
	3 firm fresh medium-size tomatoes	
	sprigs of parsley	
	6 clean scallop shells	

Cut the ham and the apples in fairly short, thin strips and mix together in a bowl. Season the mayonnaise with salt and pepper and add the lemon juice, mustard, sugar and Worcester sauce. Fold in the cream or yoghourt and mix with the ham and apples.

Wash and drain the lettuce leaves thoroughly, shred them finely, sprinkle with very little salt and divide between six scallop shells. Cover evenly with the ham/apple/mayonnaise mixture and decorate with asparagus tips, wedges of tomato and sprigs of parsley.

(Vilèm Vrabec, Czechoslovakia)

Ham mousse
Mousse de jambon
Šunková pěna k plnění

Yield: about 800 g (1 lb 12 oz)

500 g	lean ham	1 lb 2 oz
2 dl	double cream	7 fl oz
120 g	butter	4 oz
2 g	sweet paprika	a small pinch
1 g	white pepper	a small pinch
	a pinch of salt	
	3 tablespoons Cognac	

Pass the ham twice through the finest blade of the mincer, or three times if a particularly fine mousse is required. Cream the butter and gradually work in the minced ham, the unwhipped cream, seasoning and Cognac. Beat by hand or in the mixer until light and foamy.

This mousse is used as a filling for eggs, puff pastry cases and horns, and short pastry boats, and as a spread for sandwiches, etc. It may also be used to decorate a wide variety of cold dishes with the aid of a savoy bag and a star pipe.

(Vilèm Vrabec, Czechoslovakia)

Ham cones with horseradish cream
Cornets de jambon à la crème au raifort
Šunkové kornoutky plněné smetanovým křenem

6 portions

| | 6 fairly large slices of ham | |
| | sprigs of parsley | |

Horseradish cream:

40 g	horseradish, grated	1½ oz
	1 tablespoon lemon juice	
	1 teaspoon sugar	
	a pinch of salt	
2½ dl	whipped cream	9 fl oz

Mix together the horseradish, lemon juice, salt and sugar. Fold in the cream. Shape the ham into cones and arrange on a round dish with the tips in the centre. Fill with the horseradish cream just before serving. Decorate the centre with parsley.

(Vilèm Vrabec, Czechoslovakia)

Canapés Hotel Tosco Romagnolo

10 canapés

150 g	veal or tender beef	5 oz
	1 clove of garlic	
1½ dl	olive oil	5 fl oz
	juice of 1 lemon	
	10 slices bread (tin or sandwich loaf)	
100 g	Parmesan cheese, grated	3½ oz
	mayonnaise as required	
	salt, pepper	
	1 courgette	

Leave the garlic overnight in 1 dl (3½ fl oz) olive oil. Next day mince the meat twice, using the finest cutter, season with salt and pepper, add the lemon juice and the garlic-flavoured oil and marinate for 2 hours.

Cut the bread into rounds, sprinkle with the Parmesan and the rest of the oil, place in the oven which has been pre-heated to 200°C (392°F) and leave for a few minutes. Spread with the marinated minced meat just before serving. Cut a marinated courgette (recipe, page 1004) into 5 mm (¼ in) slices and place one in the centre of each canapé. Decorate with mayonnaise.

(Paolo Teverini, Italy)

Stuffed pork fillet
Filet de porc farci aux truffes
Schweinefilet gefüllt mit Schaumfarce, Trüffeln und Speck

Cooking time: 1 hour per kg (30 minutes per lb)

200 g	pork fillet	7 oz
20 g	truffles, sliced	¾ oz
20 g	bacon, sliced	¾ oz
50 g	sausage meat	2 oz
2 cl	dairy cream	1 fl oz
	salt	
	pepper, freshly ground	
	garlic	
	caraway, finely chopped	

Cut halfway through the pork fillet down the centre and flatten. Cover with the bacon which has been thinly sliced and place the slices of truffle on top. Whip the cream, mix with the sausage meat and pipe in a roll along the middle of the fillet. Season with salt and pepper, flavour with garlic and roll up. Sprinkle with caraway. Place on oiled aluminium foil, wrap up and tie. Poach for about 20 minutes at 75°C (167°F) and allow to cool. Chill, unwrap and slice.

(Josef Haueis, Austria)

Pork fillet salad Fodermayer
Salade de filet de porc Fodermayer
Schweinefiletsalat Fodermayer

4 portions

300 g	pork fillet without skin	10 oz
20 g	oil for frying	¾ oz
200 g	carrots	7 oz
80 g	sugar peas, cooked	3 oz
10 g	fresh tarragon	⅓ oz
	1 tablespoon chopped shallots	
	2 tablespoons olive oil	
	salt, pepper	
	lemon juice	
	a little Cognac	
	a pinch of sugar	

Season the pork with salt and pepper, brown lightly all over in hot oil, then roast in a medium oven until medium done. Peel the carrots, cut in thick strips, cook in salted water with the addition of a pinch of sugar, leaving them fairly firm, and allow to cool in the water, then drain well. When the pork is cold, carve into slices 2–3 mm (⅛ in) thick and mix with the carrots, peas, tarragon and shallots. Marinate in a dressing of olive oil, lemon juice, Cognac, salt and pepper. Arrange on a serving dish. This dish may be included in the hors d'oeuvre trolley or served separately as a salad.

(Ewald Plachutta, Austria)

Stuffed pig's tail
Queue de porc farcie
Gefüllter Schweineschwanz mit einer Safran-Pistazienfarce

4 portions   Cooking time: 1 hour per kg (30 minutes per lb)
                 1 pig's tail
                 salt
                 pepper, freshly ground

Stuffing:

200 g	shoulder of veal, minced	7 oz
50 g	pork back fat, minced	2 oz
20 g	ice	¾ oz
1 cl	Cognac	½ fl oz
5 g	saffron	¼ oz
	salt	
	pepper, freshly ground	
5 g	pistachio nuts	¼ oz

Bone the pig's tail and season with salt and pepper. Prepare the stuffing and fill the tail with it. Wrap in oiled aluminium foil and tie. Poach at 75°C (167°F) and allow to cool in the cooking liquid. Chill well, unwrap and slice.

(Josef Haueis, Austria)

Stuffed tomatoes Prague style
Tomates farcies à la pragueoise
Rajčata plnena pràžským salátem

6 portions

	12 firm medium tomatoes	
1 g	pepper	a pinch
400–500 g	Prague meat salad (see p. 222)	14 oz –1 lb

Egg yolk paste to decorate:

	3 hard-boiled egg yolks	
100 g	butter	3½ oz
	2 anchovies	
	OR 1 teaspoon anchovy paste	
	1 teaspoon lemon juice	
	1 teaspoon mustard	
	a pinch of pepper	
	salt	
	a few drops Worcester sauce	
	12 black olives	
	sprigs of parsley	

Scoop out the centres of the tomatoes, sprinkle inside with salt and pepper, invert to drain, then stuff with Prague meat salad. Prepare egg yolk paste and pipe a rosette on each stuffed tomato. Place a black olive in the centre. Finish off with a garnish of fresh parsley.

To make the egg yolk paste, cream the butter in a china bowl and mix to a smooth paste with the sieved yolks, the sieved anchovies (or anchovy paste) and the remaining ingredients. The paste is used to decorate stuffed tomatoes and peppers, hard-boiled eggs, canapés and cold meat dishes.

Stuffed tomatoes Prague style are served as an hors d'oeuvre or snack. They may also be used to garnish cold cuts. Suitable accompaniments include salt sticks, fleurons and similar items.

(Vilèm Vrabec, Czechoslovakia)

Hors d'Oeuvre Salads

Farmer's salad

10 portions

700 g	cooked smoked shoulder of pork	1 lb 8 oz
400 g	onions, finely chopped	14 oz
200 g	cucumber	7 oz
	2 bunches radishes	
300 g	raw sauerkraut	10 oz
	2 bunches parsley	
	chives	
5 cl	oil	2 fl oz
15 g	salt	½ oz
100 g	sugar (optional)	3½ oz
6 cl	vinegar	2 fl oz
60 g	hard-boiled egg yolk	2 oz
	¼ lettuce	
	black pepper	

Cut the pork in thin slices. Blanch the onions and allow to cool. Cut the radishes and cucumber in half, then in thin slices. Wash the sauerkraut thoroughly in cold water, drain well, squeeze dry and cut up if necessary. Finely chop the parsley and chives.

Prepare a dressing with water, vinegar, salt and sugar (optional), place the meat and vegetables in it, season with black pepper, mix lightly, add the oil and mix again. Marinate for a few hours. Drain and refrigerate. Dish on lettuce leaves and sprinkle with grated egg yolk and finely chopped herbs to serve.

(Josef Csanyi, Hungary)

Prague meat salad
Salade de viandes à la pragueoise
Pražský salát

6 portions

200 g	roast pork	7 oz
150 g	roast veal	5 oz
120 g	pickled cucumbers	4 oz
100 g	apples, peeled	3½ oz

80 g	onions	3 oz
	salt	
5 g	white pepper, freshly ground	¼ oz
	1 teaspoon Worcester sauce	
	about 3 tablespoons wine vinegar	
	OR tarragon vinegar	
200–250 g	well seasoned mayonnaise	7–9 oz

Cut the meat, apples and onions in very thin, short strips and place in a bowl. Add the cucumbers which have been cut in strips and squeezed dry. Season with salt and pepper, add the Worcester sauce and vinegar, mix well and stir in the mayonnaise. Transfer to a deep glass bowl and garnish with an arrangement of lettuce leaves and wedges of hard-boiled egg and tomato.

This salad is served as an hors d'oeuvre, a separate course or an evening snack. It may also be used as a topping for canapés or a filling for tomatoes, peppers or hard-boiled eggs. Suitable accompaniments are white bread, rolls or salt bread sticks.

(Vilèm Vrabec, Czechoslovakia)

Grinzing beef salad
Salade de boeuf Grinzing
Grinzinger Heurigensalat

10 portions

1 kg	lean boneless beef, cooked	2 lb 4 oz
400 g	French beans, cooked	14 oz
200 g	salted cucumbers	7 oz
100 g	onions, finely chopped	3½ oz
10 g	parsley, finely chopped	⅓ oz
	10 radishes	
	salt, pepper, mustard	
	vinegar, oil	

Cut the beef, cucumbers and radishes in very thin slices. Mix with the beans, onions and parsley. Prepare a well seasoned dressing with the oil, vinegar, mustard, salt and pepper and pour over the salad. Serve with home-made bread. This is a good way of using up left-over cooked beef.

(Eduard Mayer, Austria)

Israel salad

10 portions

700 g	cucumbers	1 lb 8 oz
700 g	red peppers	1 lb 8 oz
700 g	tomatoes	1 lb 8 oz
	juice of 2 lemons	
2 dl	oil	7 fl oz
1 dl	vinegar	3½ fl oz
	salt	
	pepper, freshly ground	
	Aromat	
	chopped parsley	

Wash the cucumbers, peppers and tomatoes carefully. Peel the cucumbers, peel and seed the tomatoes, seed the peppers. Cut up as for matignon. Mix the lemon juice, oil, vinegar and seasonings well and toss the salad in this dressing. Arrange on salad plates and sprinkle with chopped parsley.

(Gérard van Dijk, Switzerland)

Sweetbread salad
Salade de ris de veau
Kalbsmilchsalat

6 portions

500 g	calves' sweetbreads	1 lb 2 oz
	salt	
	a little leek	
	1 bay leaf	
	1 carrot	
	parsley	
200 g	tomatoes	7 oz
150 g	fresh mushrooms	5 oz
	2–3 canned truffles	
	lemon juice	
	dill, finely cut	
	lettuce leaves	

Dressing:

4 tablespoons olive oil
2 tablespoons red wine vinegar
1 hard-boiled egg yolk, sieved
½ teaspoon Dijon mustard

¼ teaspoon sugar
salt, pepper

Trim the sweetbreads well and soak under cold running water to whiten them. Blanch for about 20 minutes in lightly salted water containing the bay leaf and vegetables. Allow to cool in the water, then remove and break up into small pieces. Skin and hollow out the tomatoes, then cut the flesh in 1 cm (½ in) cubes. Wash the mushrooms well, cut in quarters and blanch in salted water with the addition of lemon juice. Finely slice the truffles. Place the sweetbreads, tomatoes, mushrooms, truffles and dill in a glass bowl and pour the dressing over. Cover and refrigerate for about an hour. To make the dressing, mix all the ingredients together well. To serve, divide the salad between cocktail glasses and decorate with choice lettuce or endive leaves.
(Illustration, page 873)   (Hans Kögl, Austria)

White cabbage salad Serbian style

1 kg	white cabbage	2 lb 4 oz
30 g	paprika	1 oz
2 dl	olive oil	7 fl oz

Remove the outer cabbage leaves and the stump. Cut the cabbage in 1 cm (½ in) cubes. Place in a salad bowl, sprinkle with paprika and pour the oil over. This dish is served either as a salad or as an accompaniment to spirits, especially slivovica.
(László Csizmadia, Yugoslavia)

Pepper salad Serbian style

Bake large, fleshy yellow peppers for 20 to 30 minutes, then set aside for 10 minutes in a sealed container. Skin them carefully while still warm, cut in half, remove the seeds, but leave the stalks in place. Sprinkle with salt on a colander and leave to cool and drain. Transfer to a salad bowl and dress with oil and vinegar, preferably wine vinegar. Add finely chopped garlic to taste; this will give the salad a stronger flavour.
(Lázsló Csizmadia, Yugoslavia)

Brawn salad
Salade au fromage de tête
Tlačenkový salát

6 portions

| 450 g | brawn, thinly sliced | 1 lb |

100 g	green peppers, cut in strips	3½ oz
100 g	firm tomatoes	3½ oz
100 g	pickled cucumbers	3½ oz
100 g	onions	3½ oz
20 g	capers, finely chopped	¾ oz
	1 teaspoon mustard	
	2 teaspoons Worcester sauce	
³⁄₁₆ l	vinegar	7 fl oz
⅛ l	water	4½ fl oz
	salt	
1 g	pepper	a pinch
	2 tablespoons oil	

Peel the tomatoes, cucumbers and onions, slice them and place in a bowl. Mix with the brawn, peppers and capers. Whisk together the mustard, Worcester sauce, vinegar, water, salt, pepper and oil to make a dressing and toss the salad in it. Dish in a glass bowl.

(Vilèm Vrabec, Czechoslovakia)

Fillet of beef salad
Pointe de filet de boeuf en salade

1 portion

150 g	fillet of beef (thin end), cut in thin strips	5 oz
	salt	
	pepper, freshly ground	
	noble-sweet paprika	
	1 tablespoon olive oil	
	1 tomato	
	2 tablespoons sherry vinegar	
	1 tablespoon double cream	
	parsley, chervil, tarragon,	
	finely chopped, to taste	
	lettuce, cress, endive, etc.	

Skin, seed and dice the tomato. Dress the salad as desired and line a deep plate with it. Season the meat with salt, pepper and noble-sweet paprika. Heat the oil until smoking, quickly brown the meat in it, add the tomato and mix for a moment or two. Moisten with the vinegar and pour the cream over. Mix carefully, season with salt and pepper and arrange in the centre of the salad. Sprinkle with the herbs.
(Illustration, page 521)

(Jean Esslinger, France)

Salad Alföld

10 portions

700 g	collared pork	1 lb 8 oz
150 g	onions	5 oz
50 g	onions, finely sliced, for decoration	2 oz
100 g	pickled cucumbers	3½ oz
10 g	tarragon	⅓ oz
	¼ bunch parsley	
200 g	tomatoes, seeded	7 oz
5 cl	oil	2 fl oz
15 g	salt	½ oz
2 g	pepper	a good pinch
8 cl	vinegar	3 fl oz
	¼ lettuce	

First cut the pork in thin slices, then in strips. Finely chop the 150 g (5 oz) onions, the cucumbers, tarragon and parsley. Cut the tomatoes in thin slices. Carefully mix together the chopped ingredients in a suitable bowl and add the oil. Season lightly with salt and pepper, lightly stir in the vinegar, add the pork and tomatoes and mix carefully. Refrigerate for 24 hours. To serve, drain well and sprinkle with the sliced onion and with chopped parsley.

(Josef Csanyi, Hungary)

Salad Bonne Etape

6 portions

180 g	mushroom caps	6 oz
100 g	ham, freshly cooked	4 oz
40 g	2 black truffles, each weighing	1½ oz
	1 chicken breast, poached	
	4 artichoke hearts	
180 g	foie gras terrine, medium done	6 oz
	3 rabbit livers	
	30 crayfish tails, shelled	
	6 chicken hearts	
	salad in season	
	1 teaspoon vinegar	

Vinaigrette sauce:

1 teaspoon mustard
2 teaspoons lemon juice
1 tablespoon wine vinegar

Worcester sauce
salt
pepper, freshly ground
3 tablespoons olive oil
4 tablespoons dairy cream

To make the vinaigrette, whisk together the mustard, lemon juice, vinegar, Worcester sauce to taste, salt and pepper (two turns of the mill) until well blended, then work in the oil a little at a time and lastly add the cream.

Wash and drain the lettuce (or other salad) and place on 6 plates. Cut the ham in strips, the mushroom caps in thin slices, the chicken breast in strips and the artichoke hearts in quarters. Arrange these ingredients tastefully on the plates and dress with the vinaigrette sauce.

Using a knife dipped in hot water, cut 6 thin slices of foie gras out of the terrine. Cut the rabbit livers in half and fry with the chicken hearts until medium done, then season with salt and pepper and moisten with wine vinegar. Fry the crayfish tails lightly in butter for 30 seconds. Arrange these ingredients attractively on the plates and decorate with sliced truffles. (Illustration, page 170)

(Pierre Gleize, France)

Salad Esmeralda

10 portions

150 g	boiled smoked ox tongue	5 oz
500 g	yellow beans	1 lb
	10 hard-boiled eggs	
2 dl	salad oil	7 fl oz
	5 quails' eggs	
13 g	salt	½ oz
50 g	mustard	2 oz
	1 tablespoon Worcester sauce	
	3 lemons	
150 g	carrots, cooked	5 oz
80 g	pickled peppers	3 oz
	1 bunch radishes	
	½ bunch parsley	
	1½ lettuces	

Cut the tongue in slices, then in small strips. Cut the beans in 2 cm (¾ in) lengths. Shred the lettuces finely, setting aside the heart.

Remove the egg yolks while still warm and pass through a sieve (to ensure optimum blending in of the oil). Add the oil, salt and mustard while stirring until smooth and fairly thick, then add the Worcester sauce and the lemon juice and season with black pepper. Set aside.

Cut the egg whites into thin strips. Cut up the carrots into fancy shapes and the quails' eggs into quarters. Cut the peppers in thin strips, finely slice or dice the radishes and finely chop the parsley.

Place all the ingredients except the parsley in a bowl and toss in the dressing. Carefully stir in the parsley, reserving some for decoration. Chill well, then arrange on a serving dish and sprinkle with finely chopped parsley, grated egg yolk and finely cut radish peel. Place the lettuce heart in the centre.

(Josef Csanyi, Hungary)

Salad Greta Garbo

4 portions

200 g	stewed apples	7 oz
100 g	cooked beetroot	3½ oz
100 g	cold roast beef	3½ oz
100 g	matjes herring fillets	3½ oz
30 g	shallots, chopped	1 oz
	2 tablespoons tarragon vinegar	
	1 tablespoon tomato ketchup	
	salt, pepper	

Garnish:

4 hard-boiled egg yolks, chopped
1 green pepper, seeded and chopped

Cut the apples, beetroot, beef and herring fillets in pea-size dice and mix well. Season with salt and pepper, dress with the vinegar and ketchup and refrigerate. Serve in glass bowls or on plates, sprinkled with the chopped egg yolks and green pepper.

(Franz Zodl, Austria)

Greek salad

4 portions

1 lettuce
2 tomatoes
1 onion

	1 cucumber	
	1 sweet pepper, seeded	
	4 anchovy fillets	
	salt, pepper	
¼ dl	vinegar	1 fl oz
1 dl	oil	3½ fl oz

Wash the lettuce well. Cut the tomatoes in quarters, the onion and cucumber in thin slices and the pepper in strips. Mix together well, dress with oil, vinegar, salt and pepper and decorate with the anchovy fillets.

(Emil Wälti, Greece)

Green asparagus salad
Salade d'asperges vertes
Salat von Grünspargel

1 portion

8 green asparagus spears
cress
chicory, thinly sliced
¼ tomato
1 tablespoon small strips of ham or
    boiled pickled ox tongue
3 walnut kernels

Dressing:

1 tablespoon mayonnaise
1 tablespoon dairy cream
1 tablespoon cold asparagus liquor
1 tablespoon cream sherry
1 small teaspoon vinegar
1 small teaspoon chopped dill

If using fresh asparagus cook until half tender and allow to cool. Cut into about 5 cm (2 in) lengths and arrange side by side on a little cress and chicory. Skin, seed and dice the tomato. Chop the nuts. Mix the ingredients for the dressing well.

To serve, sprinkle the tomato, ham or tongue and nuts on the asparagus and pour the dressing over.
(Illustration, page 415)

(Felix Real, Liechtenstein)

Capon salad Bartolomè Stefani
Salade de chapon Bartolomè Stefani
Insalata di cappone Bartolomè Stefani

	4 capon legs	
250 g	cushion of veal	9 oz
	1 tablespoon parsley	
5 cl	muscatel	2 fl oz
100 g	candied citron peel	3½ oz
	olive oil as required	
	wine vinegar as required	
	salt	
	pepper, freshly ground	

Skin the capon legs and poach together with the cushion of veal in stock containing carrots, onions and celery. Allow to cool in the stock.

Cut the capon flesh in long thin strips and mix with the citron peel which has been cut in paper-thin slices. Sprinkle with the muscatel. Prepare a well seasoned dressing with the oil, vinegar, salt and pepper and marinate the capon salad in it before serving. Sprinkle with finely chopped parsley.
(Illustration, page 516)

(Franco Colombani, Italy)

Salad Lady Astor

4 portions

100 g	roast veal	3½ oz
100 g	Westphalian or Parma ham	3½ oz
100 g	smoked salmon and Baltic herring	3½ oz
	4 tablespoons mayonnaise	
	4 tablespoons sour cream	

Garnish:

	8 slices of egg	
80 g	cooked beetroot	3 oz
	lettuce leaves	

Cut the veal, ham, salmon and herring in strips. Mix well and combine with the sour cream.

Dish on a bed of lettuce on individual plates. Mask with mayonnaise and decorate with the sliced egg and the beetroot cut in small thin strips.

(Franz Zodl, Austria)

Lamb's tongue and Roquefort salad
Salade tiède de langues d'agneau au roquefort
Salade met lamstongetjes en roquefort

4 portions

	8 lambs' tongues	
100 g	lettuce	4 oz
10 g	chervil, chopped	½ oz
50 g	Roquefort	2 oz
	butter as required	
	8 croûtons	
	1 clove of garlic	

Stock:

60 g	salt	2 oz
	3 medium carrots	
	2 leeks	
	2 onions	
	4 cloves of garlic, unpeeled	
	40 peppercorns	
	1 celery stalk	
	3 sprigs of parsley	
	2 cloves	
	2 bay leaves	
	1 sprig of thyme	
200 g	ripe tomatoes	7 oz
2 l	water	3½ pt

Vinaigrette sauce:

2 tablespoons walnut oil
2 teaspoons sherry vinegar
1 small shallot, finely chopped
salt and pepper

Boil up the stock well. Cook the tongues in the stock, then skin them. Crush the Roquefort very finely with a fork. Rub the croûtons with garlic on both sides and fry in butter. Dress the lettuce with three quarters of the vinaigrette sauce and arrange on warmed plates. Cut the tongues in half along their length while still warm, dip in the rest of the vinaigrette and place on the lettuce. Sprinkle with Roquefort and chopped chervil and decorate with 2 croûtons per portion, placing one on either side of the tongues.

(Alexander Koene, Netherlands)

Serbian tomato salad
Salade de tomates à la serbe
Srpska Salata od Paradajza

4 portions

500 g	tomatoes	1 lb 2 oz
	4 large fleshy green peppers	
	1 onion	
	oil	
	salt	
	parsley, finely chopped	

Cut the tomatoes in about 2 cm (¾ in) dice, the peppers in thin strips after seeding them, and the onions in thin slices. Place in a salad bowl, season with salt, sprinkle with parsley, dress with oil and mix well.

(László Csizmadia, Yugoslavia)

Vine-growers' salad
Salade des vignerons
Winzersalat

4 portions

200 g	cooked beef	7 oz
	(or left-over roast veal or pork)	
200 g	Cervelat	7 oz
100 g	cooked French beans	3½ oz
150 g	cucumber	5 oz
100 g	mushrooms	3½ oz
80 g	onions rings	3 oz

Dressing:

1¼ dl	diluted vinegar	4½ fl oz
6¼ cl	oil	2¼ fl oz
	2 teaspoons mustard	
	a dash of Worcester sauce	
	2 tablespoons ketchup	
	salt, pepper, a little sugar	

Garnish:

> lettuce leaves
> 2 hard-boiled eggs
> 2 large tomatoes, skinned
> 2 bunches chives

Cut the meat in very thin slices and slice the Cervelat. Leave the beans whole. Peel and slice the cucumber. Slice the raw mushrooms. Mix all the salad ingredients together well. Whisk together the dressing ingredients and toss the salad well in the dressing. Refrigerate before dishing.

To serve, line a glass bowl or individual plates with lettuce leaves. Dress the salad on the lettuce, garnish with slices of tomato and egg and sprinkle well with finely cut chives.

(Ernst Faseth, Austria)

Cold vegetable omelettes with tapenade, p. 203

Truffled sweetbread and cream pie, p. 264

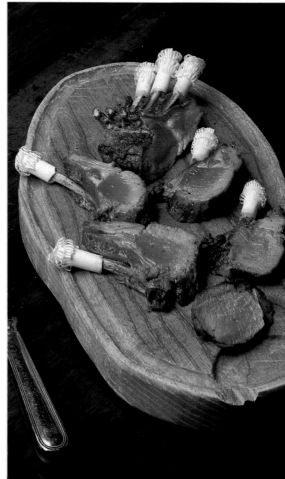

37

◄ Grilled chump chop, p. 782
▼▼ Triple grill of veal Brian, p. 706
▼ Pork chop Frivolité, p. 901

Hot Hors d'Oeuvre

Beef soufflé Scaligera
Soufflé de boeuf Scaligera
Pane di manzo alla Scaligera

6 portions   Cooking time: 45 minutes

500 g	beef (top rump)	1 lb 2 oz
80 g	butter	3 oz
80 g	white flour	3 oz
6 dl	milk	1 pt
	6 eggs (separated)	
	salt	
	pepper, freshly ground	

Trim the meat and mince, using the finest cutter. Make a roux with the butter and flour and prepare a thick Béchamel sauce with the cold milk. Add the meat, then the egg yolks. Beat well, season with salt and pepper and allow to cool. Whip the egg whites to a snow and fold in with a wooden spatula. Fill into a buttered soufflé mould and bake at 180–190°C (355–374°F).

(Mario Saporito, Italy)

Stuffed artichokes
Artichauts farcis soufflés

4 portions

	4 artichokes	
80 g	raw goose or calf's liver	3 oz
20 g	black truffles	¾ oz
2 dl	chicken stock	7 fl oz
1 dl	sour cream	3½ fl oz
	2 eggs (separated)	
	roux	
	salt and pepper	

Cut the base of the artichokes so that they will stand firmly. Cook in unsalted water for about 20 minutes, leaving them fairly firm. While still lukewarm, prepare the artichokes for stuffing, removing the inner leaves and the heart so that the inside is hollow. Dice the liver very finely and cut the truffles in small strips. Place the liver and truffles at the bottom of the hollows. Prepare a roux and blend in the stock and cream to make a thick sauce. Season with salt and pepper, remove from the heat, beat in the egg yolks and, using a wooden spatula, fold

in the egg whites which have been whipped to a snow. Fill the artichokes with this soufflé mixture and bake for 20 minutes at 200°C (392°F). Serve at once.
(Illustration, page 313)   (Roger Souvereyns, Belgium)

Old-fashioned sweetbread pie
Pâté chaud de ris de veau à l'ancienne

10 portions

Sweetbreads:

2 kg	calves' sweetbreads	4 lb 8 oz
400 g	mushrooms	14 oz
20 g	butter	¾ oz
	2 large truffles	
100 g	pistachio nuts	3½ oz

Forcemeat:

250 g	lean pork	9 oz
500 g	fresh pork fat	1 lb 2 oz
	2 eggs, beaten	
4 g	salt	a small teaspoon
1½ dl	Cognac	5 fl oz
2 dl	dairy cream	7 fl oz
	Cayenne pepper	

Pie pastry:

500 g	flour	1 lb 2 oz
300 g	butter	11 oz
	3 eggs	
1½ dl	water	5 fl oz
50 g	sugar	2 oz
10 g	salt	⅓ oz

Sauce:

2 dl	velouté (recipe, page 162)	7 fl oz

Prepare the pastry in the usual manner, using only 1 egg. Mould into a ball, wrap in a cloth and allow to rest in a cold place for at least 2 hours. The remaining eggs are required for brushing the pastry.

Mince the pork and fat finely, place in a large china mortar and pound well with the eggs to make a very fine forcemeat. Stand the mortar on ice, fold in cream and add the seasoning and Cognac.

Wash the sweetbreads thoroughly, trim them, blanch for 3 to 4 minutes and refresh in cold water. Remove all the hard, inedible parts. Place between 2 boards for a few hours under light pressure to compress the fibres and prevent shrinking during cooking. Cut into escalopes 1 cm (⅜ in) thick.

Fry the mushrooms gently in the butter until lightly coloured, allow to cool, then slice coarsely. Slice the truffles. Prepare the pistachios.

Grease a 30 x 10 cm (12 x 4 in) hinged pie mould well. Pin out the pastry 5 mm (¼ in) thick, flour lightly and mark out the base of the mould 4 times. Cut off one of the 4 pieces and set aside to make a lid. Flour the mould and line with the pastry, which should project 1 cm (⅜ in) beyond the top of the mould. Press well against the inside of the mould.

Cover the bottom of the pastry with a 2 cm (¾ in) layer of forcemeat, then place a layer of escalopes of sweetbreads on top, then a layer of sliced mushrooms, then a layer of sliced truffles and cover with forcemeat. Repeat in the same order, finishing with a layer of forcemeat, and smooth the top. Fold the projecting pastry inwards and moisten with beaten egg. Cover with the pastry lid and press down well. Seal and decorate the edge with the help of pastry pincers. If desired, pastry motifs may be added for final decoration, the underside being moistened to fix in position. Cut a 2 cm (¾ in) hole in the centre of the lid and insert a small steam vent made of oiled parchment paper. Egg wash the pastry. Bake in a medium oven for 1¾ hours, and leave to stand for 15 minutes at the side of the oven or stove. Open the hinges, carefully remove the pie and dress on a napkin. Remove the vent and carefully pour the velouté through the hole. Decorate with small bunches of parsley and serve at once.

(André Béghin, Belgium)

Meat balls Turkish style
Boulettes de viande à la turque
Da'ud Pascha

10 portions

2 kg	lean beef or mutton	4 lb 6 oz
	salt	
	herbs and spices to taste	
150 g	pine kernels	5 oz
	oil for frying	

Sauce:

500 g	onions, finely sliced	1 lb 2 oz
150 g	fat	5 oz
800 g	tomatoes, skinned, seeded and diced	1 lb 12 oz
1 dl	white wine	3½ fl oz
	2 cloves of garlic, finely grated	
	salt	
	pepper, freshly ground	

Pound the meat finely in a mortar or chop finely by machine. Add the pine kernels, mix well with seasoning to taste, shape into walnut-size balls and fry quickly in deep oil.

To make the sauce, brown the onions in the fat, add the tomatoes, moisten with the wine, season with salt and pepper and add the garlic. Place the meat balls in the sauce, cover and cook slowly for an hour. Hand pilaf rice separately.

(Otto Ledermann, Turkey)

Lucerne vol-au-vent
Vol-au-vent à la lucernoise
Luzerner Chügelipastete

Yield: 2 vol-au-vent
10 portions as main course or 16–20 portions as hors d'oeuvre
Baking time: 40 minutes

Pastry case:

1 kg–1 kg 200	puff pastry	2 lb 4 oz
		2 lb 10 oz
	2 egg yolks	

Filling:

500 g	shoulder of pork	1 lb 2 oz
500 g	veal	1 lb 2 oz
200 g	veal sausage meat	7 oz
200 g	pork sausage meat	7 oz
	coriander	
	marjoram	
400 g	mushrooms	14 oz
100 g	grapes	4 oz
½ dl	marc brandy	2 fl oz
150 g	apples	5 oz
100 g	onions, chopped	4 oz

Sauce:

150 g	butter	5 oz
90 g	flour	3 oz
1 l	white veal stock	1¾ pt
2 dl	white wine	7 fl oz
1 dl	dairy cream	3½ fl oz
	salt	
	pepper, freshly ground	
	nutmeg	
	juice of 1 lemon	
50 g	almonds, chopped and roasted	2 oz

To make the pastry case, pin out the puff pastry to a thickness of 4 mm (about ⅛ in). Cut out two 24cm (10 in) rounds and two 32 cm (13 in) rounds. Rinse a baking sheet with cold water, place the two smaller rounds of pastry on it and prick with a fork. Shape tissue paper into a tight ball 35–38 cm (14–15 in) across and wrap in aluminium foil. Place in the centre of one of the pastry rounds. Moisten the rim of the pastry with water and carefully lay one of the larger rounds of pastry over the ball of paper. Press the edge on to the moistened rim, pinching up carefully. Lay the pastry trimmings one on another and cut with a pastry wheel into strips 3 mm (⅛ in) thick and 6 mm (¼ in) wide. Brush the pastry case with beaten egg yolk and lay the strips on top, placing one round the edge to cover the ends of the others. Place a ring of pastry in the centre to mark the vol-au-vent cover. Any remaining pastry trimmings may be cut into small shapes (stars, hearts and crescents) to decorate the vol-au-vent. Brush the pastry strips and shapes with egg yolk. Prepare the other vol-au-vent case in the same manner. Refrigerate for 30 minutes, then bake for 40 minutes in an oven preheated to 180°C (355°F), covering the pastry with aluminium foil after 25 minutes.

Remove from the oven and allow to stand for 5 minutes. Cut out the cover with a pointed knife, cut up the paper ball with scissors and carefully remove each piece separately.

To make the filling, dice the meat finely, brown lightly in butter, add the chopped onions and cook gently until soft. Moisten with 1 dl (3½ fl oz) white wine and continue cooking until done. Grate the apples and add. Flavour the sausage meat with coriander and marjoram, mix well and shape into small balls. Poach in the stock. Stew the mushrooms in butter.

Make a roux with 60 g (2 oz) butter and 90 g (3 oz) flour. Blend in veal stock, mushroom cooking liquor and the rest of the wine (1 l – 1¾ pt – in all), stirring well, and simmer over low heat for 20 minutes. Add the diced meat, the sausage meat balls and the mushrooms, together with the marc brandy and the grapes which have been macerated in it. Return to the boil, season, finish with the cream and adjust the seasoning. Heat the vol-au-vent cases in the oven, fill with the sauce, sprinkle with the almonds and replace the cover.

(Otto Ledermann, Switzerland)

Stuffed marrow with dill sauce
Courgettes en sauce à l'aneth
Töltött tök tejfölös-kapros mértással

10 portions   Cooking time: 35–40 minutes

3 kg	3 or 4 marrows	6 lb 10 oz
1 kg	lean pork	2 lb 4 oz
100 g	butter	4 oz
	2 bread rolls	
	2 eggs	
½ l	milk	18 fl oz
30 g	salt	1 oz
1 g	white pepper, freshly ground	a pinch

Sauce:

150 g	lard	5 oz
OR 1½ dl	oil	5 fl oz
150 g	onions, thinly sliced	5 oz
200 g	flour	7 oz
	4 bunches fresh dill	
1 l 2 dl	bouillon	2 pt
6 dl	sour cream	1 pt
2 dl	fresh dairy cream	7 fl oz
40 g	salt	1½ oz
40 g	sugar	1½ oz
4 cl	vinegar *or* lemon juice	1½ fl oz
1 g	white pepper, freshly ground	a pinch
	1 bunch parsley	

Peel the marrows, cut in 4–5 cm (1½–2 in) lengths and hollow these out by removing the seeds and fibres. Blanch for 1 minute in salted water mixed with vinegar and drain. Dry with a clean cloth and arrange side by side in a buttered fireproof dish.

Remove the crusts from the rolls, soak in milk and squeeze dry. Mince the meat and mix well with the rolls, the eggs and the parsley which has been finely chopped. Season with salt and pepper and fill into the marrow rings. Pour a little water or bouillon into the dish, cover with buttered greaseproof paper and cook in the oven until soft.

To serve, mask with the sauce and sprinkle with a little melted butter. To make the sauce, prepare a roux with the lard or oil, the flour, the onions and the dill which has been finely chopped. Blend in the bouillon, add the salt, pepper and sugar, then the vinegar or lemon juice. Lastly add the fresh and sour cream which have been mixed together and cook for 3 or 4 minutes.

(Zsolt Körmendy, Hungary)

Eggs Don Federico
Oeufs Don Federico
Setzeier Don Federico

4 portions

	8 small sausages (chorizos or chipolatas)	
200 g	ham, cut in small pieces	7 oz
150 g	red peppers, stewed and cut in small pieces	5 oz
100 g	stuffed olives	3½ oz
	1 tablespoon olive oil	
50 g	butter	2 oz

| 50 g | onions, cut in strips | 2 oz |
| | 4 eggs | |

At the table heat the butter and oil in a small pan on a spirit stove. Lightly brown the onions and ham, then add the peppers and divide up to form a flat bed between the sausages which have been slowly and lightly browned and arranged in pairs. Break the eggs on to the ham/vegetable mixture, place the olives beside them, cover and allow the eggs to become fairly hard.

(Otto Ledermann, Switzerland)

Pancakes ferryman style
Crêpes du batelier
Crespelle alla moda del passatore
6 portions

Pancakes:

100 g	flour	3½ oz
	2 eggs	
	1 egg yolk	
15 g	butter, melted	½ oz
	a pinch of salt	
¼ l	milk	9 fl oz
	a pinch of grated nutmeg	

Filling:

¼ l	Béchamel sauce	9 fl oz
50 g	raw ham	2 oz
50 g	Mortadella	2 oz
150 g	chicken breast, cooked	5 oz
50 g	Parmesan, grated	2 oz
	a pinch of grated nutmeg	
	1 egg	
	salt and pepper to taste	

Sauce:

	tomato sauce	
	demi-glace	
	butter	
	grated Parmesan	

Make 12 thin pancakes and spread them side by side on aluminium foil. Mince the ham, sausage and chicken several times, using the finest cutter. Add the egg, grated cheese, nutmeg and Béchamel sauce and mix until smooth and of spreading consistency. Spread on the pancakes and fold over wallet fashion.

Cover the bottom of a buttered fireproof dish with tomato sauce, sprinkle with demi-glace, place the pancakes on top, sprinkle with Parmesan, dot with butter and brown under moderate heat for 15 minutes.

(Mario Saporito, Italy)

Meat pita
Pita (stroudel) à la bosnienne
Pita s Mesom (Burek)

10 portions   Baking time: 50–60 minutes

750 g	shoulder of pork *or* veal *or* beef	1 lb 10 oz
	3 onions	
100 g	lard	4 oz
	2 eggs	
	salt; pepper freshly ground	
250 g	strudel dough made with flour	9 oz
	(recipe, page 251)	

Mince the meat. Mince or finely chop the onions. Fry the onions lightly in 1 tablespoon lard without colouring, add the meat and brown until quite dry. Remove from the heat, season with salt and pepper, add the eggs and mix well.

Line a baking sheet with a sheet of strudel dough, sprinkle with melted lard and cover with half the meat mixture. Place a second sheet of dough on top, sprinkle again with melted lard and cover with the rest of the meat mixture. Place a third sheet of strudel dough on top, sprinkle with hot lard and prick with a fork here and there to allow the steam to escape while cooking. Bake in a hot oven for about 50–60 minutes.

(László Csizmadia, Yugoslavia)

Meat strudel
Stroudel à la viande de veau
Husos rétes

4 portions

400 g	shoulder of veal, cooked	14 oz
150 g	butter	5 oz

	2 bread rolls	
2 dl	milk	7 fl oz
	2 eggs (separated)	
	salt	
	Cayenne pepper	
5 cl	fresh dairy cream	2 fl oz

Strudel dough:
6 portions

200 g	flour	7 oz
4 g	salt	a good pinch
	1 egg yolk	
20 g	lard	¾ oz
1 dl	lukewarm water	3½ fl oz
1 dl	sour cream	3½ fl oz

Paprika sauce:
4 portions

30 g	lard	1 oz
40 g	flour	1½ oz
30 g	onion, finely grated	1 oz
20 g	red paprika	¾ oz
	salt	
2 dl	water	7 fl oz
	1 teaspoon consommé granules	
1½ dl	fresh dairy cream	5 fl oz

Bone the shoulder of veal and mince the meat, using the finest cutter. Blend the egg yolk with 100 g (3½ oz) butter and mix well with the rolls which have been soaked in the milk and squeezed dry. Season with salt and Cayenne pepper, mix with the fresh cream and fold in the egg whites whipped to a very stiff snow. Mix with the veal.

Spread the strudel dough on a floured cloth, sprinkle with melted butter, cover evenly with the filling and roll up. Place on a buttered baking sheet, sprinkle with a little melted butter and bake in a preheated medium oven. While still warm, cut evenly in thick slices. Hand paprika sauce or Suprême sauce separately.

To make strudel dough, sieve the flour and make a bay. Place in it the egg yolk, sour cream, lard, salt and water and first mix roughly. If the flour has too high a capacity to absorb, add a little more lukewarm water. The dough should be soft and elastic. Knead well until no bubbles form and the dough does not stick to the hand or board. Mould into a ball, cover with a warm cloth and leave to rest for 10 to 15 minutes. Pin out the dough as large as possible in both directions on a cloth dusted with flour. Slip the hands underneath and stretch to paper thinness without tearing. Cut off the thick edge.

To make paprika sauce, cook the onion gently in the lard, sprinkle with flour and allow to colour. Mix with the paprika, pour in the water, add the granules and mix well. Cook for 15 minutes. Season with salt, stir in the sour cream and return to the boil.

(László Csizmadia, Hungary)

Meat pie Chur style
Gâteau de viande de Coire
Churer Fleischtorte

8 portions   Baking time: about 40 minutes

500 g	short or puff pastry	1 lb
30 g	fat	1 oz
150 g	onions, finely chopped	5 oz
50 g	smoked lean bacon, finely diced	2 oz
250 g	beef, minced	9 oz
250 g	pork, minced	9 oz
40 g	flour	1½ oz
1 dl	Valtellina (red wine)	3½ fl oz
1 dl	thickened gravy	3½ fl oz
	salt	
	pepper, freshly ground	
	paprika	
	marjoram	
	coriander	
	juniper	

Pin out two thirds of the pastry and line a greased cake tin about 24 cm (10 in) across. Prick with a fork. Heat the fat, add the onions and bacon and stew gently. Add the minced meat and continue cooking. Dust with flour, moisten with the wine and gravy, season and cook for a short time. Allow to cool somewhat, then spread evenly on the pastry. Bend the rim back a little and egg wash. Pin out the rest of the pastry to make a cover. Egg wash the edge and place in position. Decorate with fancy shapes cut out of the trimmings. Prick a few times with a fork and egg wash. Refrigerate for 30 minutes, then bake in a preheated oven. If the pie is to be served as a main course, hand a mixed salad separately.

(Otto Ledermann, Switzerland)

Calf's brain pudding
Pouding à la cervelle de veau
Velöpuding

4 portions

1 bread roll

1 dl	milk	3½ fl oz
300 g	calf's brains	11 oz
60 g	butter	2 oz
50 g	Parmesan cheese, grated	2 oz
10 g	salt	⅓ oz
	a good pinch of freshly ground pepper	
	5 eggs (separated)	

Topping:

100 g	mushrooms, sliced	3½ oz
40 g	butter	1½ oz
	1 tablespoon flour	
	Parmesan cheese, grated	

Carefully remove the skin and blood vessels from the brains and soak well. Soak the roll in milk and squeeze dry, then pass through a sieve together with the raw brains. Cream the butter and the egg yolks together, season with salt and pepper and mix well with the sieved brains and the Parmesan. Fold in the egg whites whipped to a very stiff snow. Carefully grease and flour a pudding mould. Fill with the mixture and poach in a bain-marie. Stew the mushrooms in a little butter, dust with the flour and cook until soft. To serve, turn the pudding out on to a warmed dish and sprinkle the top with the mushrooms and with grated Parmesan.

(László Csizmadia, Hungary)

Calf's brains in cocottes my way
Cervelle de veau en cocotte à ma façon
Kalbshirn im Töpfchen auf meine Art

10 portions

1 kg 200	calf's brains, poached	2 lb 10 oz
30 g	butter	1 oz

Duxelles sauce:

100 g	smoked bacon, finely diced	3½ oz
50 g	butter	2 oz
100 g	shallots and onions, chopped	3½ oz
	1 clove of garlic	
400 g	mushrooms, chopped	14 oz
300 g	tomatoes, finely diced	11 oz
3 dl	tomato sauce	10 fl oz
	a pinch of sugar	
	salt	
	pepper, freshly ground	

20 g	parsley, chopped	¾ oz

Carefully remove the skin and blood vessels from the brains, soak and wash them thoroughly, then poach. Cut in slices and arrange in buttered cocottes. Prepare a well-flavoured Duxelles sauce and mask the brains with it. May be served as a main course, with fresh home-made noodles.

(Otto Ledermann, Switzerland)

Calf's brain tartlets
Tartelettes à la cervelle de veau
Kalbshirntörtchen

4 portions

200 g	puff pastry (fresh or frozen)	7 oz

Filling:

200 g	calf's or pig's brains	7 oz
40 g	butter	1½ oz
30 g	onion, finely chopped	1 oz
	1 teaspoon finely chopped parsley	
	2 eggs	
	salt, pepper	

Butter sauce:

	1 egg yolk	
80 g	butter	3 oz
	1 teaspoon lemon juice	
	1 tablespoon clear soup or water	
	salt, pepper	

Garnish (optional):

	4 slices truffle	

Cut the pastry into rounds and line lightly greased patty pans. Bake blind, covering the pastry with paper and dried peas. When partly baked, remove the paper and peas and continue baking until golden brown.

To make the filling, soak and wash the brains in lukewarm water and remove the skin. Chop finely and fry in butter with the onion and parsley. Season with salt and pepper, add the eggs and continue frying until cooked. Fill into the tartlet cases. To make the sauce, beat the egg yolk with a little soup or water in a bain-marie, which should be only moderately warm to prevent curdling. Add clarified butter drop by drop and continue beating until fairly thick. Season with salt and pepper and add the lemon juice. Mask the tartlets with this sauce and decorate with slices of truffle if desired. Serve on individual small plates.

(Ernst Faseth, Austria)

Calf's brain cakes
Galettes à la cervelle de veau
Velöslepények

4 portions   Cooking time: 5–6 minutes

600 g	calf's brains	1 lb 5 oz
	consommé	
	zest of 1 lemon	
	5 eggs	
	4 tablespoons flour	
	1 bunch parsley	
15 g	salt	½ oz
	a good pinch of freshly ground pepper	
160 g	Parmesan cheese, grated	5½ oz
	1 lemon, sliced	
8 cl	oil	3 fl oz
Csiki sauce (Csiki mártás):		
2 dl	Tartare sauce	7 fl oz
	1 apple	
100 g	beetroot	3½ oz
100 g	mushrooms	3½ oz
	1 tablespoon chopped chives	
1 dl	oil	3½ fl oz

Remove the skin and blood vessels from the brains, wash and cook in consommé. Allow to cool and dice finely. Beat the eggs, blend with the flour and Parmesan, season with salt and pepper, add the parsley which has been finely chopped and lastly add the brains. Mix thoroughly. Heat the oil in a small pan, pour in a tablespoonful of the mixture at a time and fry. To serve, dress on a warm dish and decorate with slices of lemon and with parsley. Hand Csiki sauce separately. To make the sauce, cook the beetroot, stew the mushrooms in oil and dice finely, together with the apple. Mix with the Tartare sauce and add the chives. Chill thoroughly.

(László Csizmadia, Hungary)

Calf's brains on fried bread Elisabeth
Croûte à la cervelle de veau Elisabeth
Kalbshirnschnitte Elisabeth

10 portions

	20 slices bread (sandwich loaf)	
30 g	each weighing	1 oz

200 g	butter	7 oz
20 g	20 slices ham, each weighing	¾ oz
1 kg	filling for Basler rissoles (recipe, p. 130)	2lb 4 oz
500 g	calf's brains, poached and sliced	1 lb 2 oz
3 dl	Hollandaise sauce (recipe, p. 175)	10 fl oz

Fry the bread and the ham separately in butter. Place 2 slices of ham, a little rissole filling and slices of brains on each slice of bread, mask with Hollandaise sauce and colour lightly under a salamander.

(Otto Ledermann, Switzerland)

Brain mousselines with green lemon sauce
Mousselines de cervelle – sauce aux citrons verts
Schaumbrötchen von Kalbshirn mit Sauce von grünen Zitronen

10 portions

800 g	calf's brains	1 lb 12 oz
300 g	veal sausage meat	11 oz
4 dl	dairy cream	14 fl oz
5 cl	Cognac	2 fl oz
	4 egg whites, whipped	
50 g	tongue, cut in julienne strips	2 oz
20 g	dried craterelles, soaked	¾ oz
5 g	tarragon	⅕ oz
	salt	
	peppercorns	
	1 clove	
	1 bay leaf	
	1 bouquet garni	
	pepper, freshly ground	
	spices as desired	

Sauce:

	3 green lemons	
5 dl	calf's brain stock	18 fl oz
5 dl	dairy cream	18 fl oz
	2–3 egg yolks	
50 g	butter	2 oz
20 g	shallot, chopped	¾ oz
	Cayenne pepper	

Fleurons:

200 g	puff pastry	7 oz
	1 egg yolk	

Wash and soak the brains for 30–40 minutes, then remove the skin and blood vessels. Poach in about 1½ l (2¾ pt) water containing the bouquet garni, salt, peppercorns, clove and bay leaf. Allow to cool. Reduce the stock to 5 dl (18 fl oz) and reserve for the sauce.

Cut 10 good-size slices of brains and place in buttered timbale moulds. Chop the remaining brains finely in the processor and mix well with the sausage meat, craterelles, tongue, dairy cream, Cognac, tarragon, seasoning and spices as desired. Fold in the egg whites and fill into the moulds. Poach in a bain-marie in a moderate oven.

To make the sauce, thinly pare the lemon zest, cut in thin julienne strips and blanch. Cook gently in butter with the shallot until transparent, moisten with the reduced stock and stir in part of the cream. Add a few drops of lemon juice, salt, Cayenne pepper and tarragon to taste. Shortly before serving mix the egg yolk with the rest of the cream and add to the sauce, but do not boil.

To make the fleurons, pin out the pastry, cut into crescents and wash with egg yolk. Allow to rest. Ten minutes before serving bake in a hot oven.

(Otto Ledermann, Switzerland)

Kohlrabi with brain stuffing
Chou-rave à la cervelle
Keleraba Nadevena Mozgom

4 portions   Cooking time: about 1 hour

	8 fresh kohlrabi globes	
400 g	calves' brains	14 oz
150 g	butter	5 oz
2 dl	sour cream	7 fl oz
	1 small onion	
	1 egg	
	parsley, finely chopped	
	salt	
	pepper, freshly ground	

Peel the kohlrabi. Carefully hollow out, leaving a narrow edge, and boil in salted water. Remove while still fairly firm. Cut up the onion finely and cook gently in butter without colouring.

Remove the blood vessels and skin from the brains, cut in small pieces and fry with the onion. Remove from the heat, season with salt and pepper, add the egg and the parsley and mix carefully. Fill into the kohlrabi globes and place in a fireproof tableware dish. Place a knob of butter on each globe, pour over the sour cream diluted with water and bake in the oven for 30 minutes at the most. Serve very hot.

(László Csizmadia, Yugoslavia)

Calf's liver patties
Petits pâtés au foie de veau
Kalbsleber-Pastetchen

Yield: about 20 patties   Baking time: 20–25 minutes

Pastry:

200 g	flour	7 oz
100 g	butter	3½ oz
	1 egg yolk	
	salt	
	milk	

Filling:

250 g	calf's liver, chopped	9 oz
100 g	smoked pork fat or bacon	3½ oz
50 g	onion, finely cut	2 oz
	1 egg yolk	
	½ roll, soaked	
	salt	
	marjoram	
	thyme	
	nutmeg	
	juice of 1 lemon	

Work the flour, butter, egg yolk, salt and milk to a paste, which should not be too firm, and allow to rest.

To make the filling, dice the pork fat or bacon and brown lightly in a little butter with the onion. Mix with the liver, the egg yolk, the half roll which has been squeezed dry, the seasonings and lemon juice, working the ingredients together thoroughly. Pin out the pastry and line small patty pans which have been well greased. Fill with the filling mixture.

Cut out rounds of pastry to fit the top, wash with egg and place on the filling, pressing the edges of the pastry together firmly to seal. Prick here and there with a fork, egg wash twice and bake off.

(Otto Ledermann, Switzerland)

Calf's liver mousse
Mousse de foie de veau

10 portions

500 g	calf's liver	1 lb 2 oz
500 g	smoked belly of pork (or bacon)	1 lb 2 oz
	5 egg whites	
½ l	dairy cream	18 fl oz
	salt	
	pepper, freshly ground	
	marjoram	
	sugar	
approx. ¾ l	Madeira sauce (recipe, p. 158)	1¼ pt

Remove the skin and pipes from the liver. Cut away the pork rinds and any gristle. Chill all ingredients well before use. Either chop the liver and pork (or bacon) very finely in the processor or pass them through the finest blade of the mincer, then through a sieve. Add the egg whites, seasonings and cream and mix well. Alternatively, whip the whites to a snow and fold in. Fill into lightly buttered individual earthenware moulds and bake for 10 to 12 minutes in an oven preheated to 180–190°C (355–374°F). If preferred, the mousse may be poached in a bain-marie. Hand Madeira sauce separately.

(Germain Gretsch-Rösner, Luxembourg)

Oriental jalousies
Jalousies orientales
Bazek Alim memule misrachit

10 portions   Baking time: 25 minutes

500 g	calf's liver, koshered (see p. 210)	1 lb 2 oz
	1 onion	
	2 cooking apples	
	1 aubergine	
	oil	
50 g	raisins	2 oz
50 g	mushrooms	2 oz
50 g	nuts, chopped	2 oz
	salt	
	pepper, freshly ground	
800 g	puff pastry	1 lb 12 oz
	1 egg	
	cumin	
5 dl	veal gravy	18 fl oz

Finely dice the liver, onion and aubergine, peel the apples and cut in small slices and brown these ingredients lightly in a little oil together with the mushrooms. Add the nuts, season with salt and pepper and flavour with cumin to taste.

Pin out the pastry and cut in four strips 8 cm (3½ in) wide. Make parallel cuts shutter fashion in two of the strips. Cover the other two strips with the filling and place the shutter strips on top. Brush with egg and bake in an oven preheated to 200°C (392°F). Serve at once and hand veal gravy separately.

(Hermann Wohl, Israel)

Meat balls in tomato sauce
Bitoks en sauce à la tomate
Tefteli

10 portions   Cooking time: about 50–60 minutes

750 g	beef	1 lb 10 oz
750 g	pork	1 lb 10 oz
100 g	onions, finely sliced	4 oz
	2 eggs	
	2 bread rolls	
200 g	tomato purée	7 oz
40 g	salt	1½ oz
3 g	black peppercorns	⅛ oz
200 g	flour	7 oz
	1 bay leaf	
400 g	lard	14 oz
OR 4 dl	oil	14 fl oz
	black pepper, freshly ground	

Mince the meat. Add the rolls which have been soaked in milk and squeezed dry and mix well with the eggs. Season with salt and pepper. Moisten the hands and roll into balls 2.5 cm (1 in) across. Roll in flour and fry in lard or oil until well browned but not dry. Remove from the pan.

Fry the onions in the fat remaining in the pan until lightly coloured, add the tomato purée and continue frying for a short time. Add the peppercorns, the bay leaf and salt to taste, moisten with beef stock, cook for about 10 minutes and strain. Place the meat balls in a pan and pour the tomato sauce over. Cover and stew for about 15 minutes, adding a little sugar if desired. To serve, transfer the meat balls and sauce to a bowl and hand cooked rice or boiled potatoes separately.

(Zsolt Körmendy, Hungary–Russia)

American ground beef steak

4 portions

1 kg	beef, coarsely minced	2 lb
	½ teaspoon salt	
	¼ teaspoon pepper	
8 cl	tomato juice	3 fl oz
	1 tablespoon oil	
	4 tablespoons butter	

Season the meat with salt and pepper and mix with the tomato juice. Form into 4 patties in the shape of a steak and brush with oil. Grill about 7½ cm (3 in) from the heat (4 minutes on each side for rare; 6 minutes on each side for medium; 8 minutes on each side for well done). Place the patties on a warm serving dish and top each with 1 tablespoon butter.

(Hermann Rusch, USA)

Hungarian veal and potato pie
Pâté de veau et de pommes de terre à la hongroise
Borjupörkölttel töltött burgonyapástétom

4 portions

1 kg	potatoes, fried in lard	2 lb 4 oz
	4 egg yolks	
30 g	butter	1 oz
600 g	shoulder of veal, finely diced	1 lb 5 oz
40 g	lard	1½ oz
40 g	onion, finely cut	1½ oz
	1 teaspoon red paprika	
15 g	salt	½ oz
1 dl	sour cream	3½ fl oz
5 cl	fresh dairy cream	2 fl oz

Pass the fried potatoes through a hair sieve and mix well with the butter, salt and egg yolks. Cook the onion gently in lard without colouring, add the veal, sprinkle with paprika and mix. Pour in sufficient water to cover the meat and cook until tender.

Butter a pie mould and line with the potatoes. Fill with the meat without the cooking juices and cover with the rest of the potatoes. Poach in a bain-marie in a preheated oven. Mix the sour and fresh cream with the meat cooking juices and bring to the boil. Turn out the pie on to a round dish and hand the sauce separately.

(László Csizmadia, Hungary)

Veal pudding with Suprême sauce
Pouding de veau – sauce suprême
Borjuhusfelfujt

4 portions   Cooking time: 30–50 minutes

600 g	shoulder of veal	1 lb 5 oz
200 g	flavouring vegetables	7 oz
	salt	
25 g	flour	1 oz
2 dl	milk	7 fl oz
	2 egg yolks	
	a good pinch freshly ground white pepper	
	grated nutmeg	
30 g	butter	1 oz
	4 egg whites	
20 g	flour for dusting mould	¾ oz

Cook the veal in salted water containing the flavouring vegetables until tender. Remove the bone and mince the meat twice, using the finest cutter.

Prepare a very thick Béchamel sauce with the flour and milk and allow to cool. Then mix with the egg yolks and add the veal. Season with salt and pepper, add nutmeg to taste and lastly fold in the egg whites which have been whipped to a stiff snow.

Butter and flour a pudding mould. Three quarters fill with the pudding mixture. Poach in a bain-marie for 30 to 50 minutes, depending on the size of the mould. To serve, turn out on to a warm dish and mask with Suprême sauce (recipe, p. 177). Hand the same sauce separately.

(László Csizmadia, Hungary)

Calf's feet Colombani
Pieds de veau Colombani
Piedini di vitello Colombani

4 portions

	2 calf's feet	
50 g	butter	2 oz
1 dl	dairy cream	3½ fl oz
100 g	haricot beans, blanched	3½ oz
	2 tablespoons gravy	
50–60 g	Parmesan, grated	2 oz
	5 sage leaves	

salt
pepper, freshly ground

Clean the calf's feet well and shave off the hairs. Cook in salted water until the skin and sinews easily come away from the bones. Allow to cool.

When cold, finely dice the skin, sinews and meat. Fry lightly in butter together with the sage, season with salt and pepper, add the gravy and stir well. Remove the sage and set aside for decoration. Add the cream, the haricot beans and the Parmesan. Mix carefully, decorate with the sage leaves and serve hot.
(Illustration, page 517)

(Franco Colombani, Italy)

Calves' sweetbreads Princess
Ris de veau princesse
Gespickte Kalbsmilch mit Spargelspitzen

4 portions   Cooking time: about 35 minutes

300 g	calves' sweetbreads	11 oz
40 g	pork back fat or bacon for larding	1½ oz
40 g	butter	1½ oz
50 g	carrots, thinly sliced	2 oz
50 g	celeriac, thinly sliced	2 oz
50 g	leek, thinly sliced	2 oz
50 g	onion, thinly sliced	2 oz
1¼ dl	white wine	4 fl oz
approx. 2½ dl	veal stock	9 fl oz
	salt	
400 g	cooked asparagus, fresh or canned	14 oz

Remove the skin and blood vessels from the sweetbreads. Place in cold water and warm slightly. Change the water frequently until the sweetbreads are white, then blanch by covering with fresh water, bringing to the boil and placing in cold water. When cold, dry well. Remove any remaining blood vessels and skin. Lard with thin strips of pork fat or bacon.

Butter a fireproof casserole and line with the vegetables and onion. Season the sweetbreads with salt, place on the bed of vegetables and sprinkle with the rest of the butter. Pour in the wine and veal stock, cover and cook in the oven for about 35 minutes, basting frequently until the sweetbreads are brown and well glazed. To serve, cut in slices, arrange on a dish on top of the vegetables from the casserole and coat with the cooking liquid. Hand hot asparagus separately.

(Ernst Faseth, Austria)

Small sweetbread soufflés with lemon sauce
Petits soufflés de ris de veau à la sauce au citron
Kalbsmilchauflauf in Zitronensauce mit Pernod abgeschmeckt, Champignonköpfe mit Tomaten und Blattspinat

10 portions   Cooking time: 40 minutes

800 g	calves' sweetbreads	1 lb 12 oz
	8 egg yolks	
	salt, pepper	
⅛ l	dairy cream	4 fl oz
100 g	butter, softened	3½ oz
	5 egg whites	
Sauce:		
100 g	butter	3½ oz
60 g	shallots, finely diced	2 oz
	grated zest and juice of 2 lemons	
	1 clove of garlic, crushed	
	1 teaspoon mustard	
¼ l	thick sour cream	9 fl oz
	2 tablespoons Pernod	
500 g	mushroom caps, stewed	1 lb 2 oz
	4 tomatoes, coarsely chopped	
100 g	leaf spinach, blanched	3½ oz

Soak the sweetbreads in lukewarm running water until no blood escapes. Blanch for 3 minutes in boiling water and plunge into iced water. Cut away the blood vessels and gristle and remove the skin. Cream together the butter, egg yolks and seasonings. Add the sweetbreads which have been worked to a fine purée in a processor, pour in the cream and mix well until smooth. Fold in the stiffly whipped egg whites. Fill into well greased individual fireproof moulds and cook in a bain-marie until firm. To serve, turn out on to warm plates and mask with lemon sauce.

To make the sauce, stew the shallots until transparent with the garlic and lemon zest. Mix well with the mustard, lemon juice and sour cream and cook to a coating consistency. Season with salt and pepper and add the Pernod. Toss the mushroom caps, spinach and tomatoes in butter and season with salt and pepper.
(Illustration, page 696)

(Karl Brunnengräber, Germany)

Truffled sweetbread and cream pie
Feuilleté de ris de veau truffés à la crème

6 portions

1 kg	calves' sweetbreads	2 lb 4 oz

1 l	dairy cream	1¾ pt
100 g	butter	3½ oz
5 cl	Cognac	2 fl oz
80 g	truffles, finely diced	3 oz
150 g	mushrooms, finely diced	5 oz
	juice of 1 lemon	
500 g	puff pastry	1 lb 2 oz
	salt, pepper	
	1 egg to wash pastry	
	flour as required	

Soak the sweetbreads for a long time, then blanch for about 4 minutes and plunge at once into cold water. Remove all gristle and other inedible parts, as well as the fat, season with salt and pepper and coat with flour. Cook over low heat until only lightly coloured, then stir in the Cognac to detach the juices.

Cut the sweetbreads into slices 1 cm (⅜ in) thick, add the truffles and mushrooms, pour in the cream and cook for 15 minutes. The sauce should be rather thick. Season with salt and pepper and add the lemon juice.

Pin out the pastry and cut out two rounds of the same size. Damp the edges. Place one round on a greased baking sheet and cover with the sweetbreads and sauce. Place the other round of pastry on top to make a lid, pressing it down well to seal the edges and pinching these up firmly. Wash with egg yolk and refrigerate for 20 minutes, then bake for 15 to 20 minutes in an oven preheated to 220°C (428°F). This pie should be served immediately after baking. (Illustration, page 235)

(Pierre Gleize, France)

Sweetbread and kidney pie with saffron sauce
Kalbsmilch – und nierenpastete in Safransauce

4 portions

200 g	calves' sweetbreads, blanched	7 oz
250 g	calves' kidneys	9 oz
200 g	calves' brains	7 oz
200 g	flap mushrooms	7 oz
	2 eggs	
	salt, pepper, marjoram	
	2 tablespoons chopped onions	
	2 tablespoons chopped parsley	

40 g	oil	1½ oz
30 g	butter	1 oz
	puff pastry as required	
	egg to wash pastry	

Saffron sauce:

2 dl	dairy cream	7 fl oz
2 dl	veal stock	7 fl oz
	Noilly Prat	
	20 threads of saffron	
100 g	celery	3½ oz
20 g	butter	¾ oz

Garnish:

	4 tomatoes	
240 g	leaf spinach, blanched	8 oz
30 g	Parmesan or breadcrumbs	1 oz
	salt	
	pepper	
	nutmeg	
	a little butter	

Skin the sweetbreads and divide into small segments. Season with salt and pepper. Skin and core the kidneys and cut up somewhat coarsely. Season with salt, pepper and marjoram. Skin the brains, chop coarsely and season with salt and pepper.

Fry the kidneys lightly in 20 g (¾ oz) hot oil. Toss the sweetbreads in hot butter, add the mushrooms which have been cleaned, sliced and seasoned, then cook gently for a short time. Heat the rest of the oil, fry the onions until golden, add the brains, season with salt and pepper and brown well. Add the eggs and continue cooking. Stir in the parsley and mix thoroughly.

Pin out the pastry thinly (no thicker than the back of a knife). Place the offal mixture on the pastry and shape into an oblong with a rounded top. Fold the edges of the pastry over to enclose the filling completely, wash with egg, place on a greased baking sheet and bake for about 20 minutes or until golden brown. The oven temperature should be high at first, then lowered. Hand saffron sauce separately.

To make the sauce, cut up the celery finely and toss lightly in butter. Add the cream and reduce a little. Stir in the veal stock and reduce to a fairly thick consistency. Season with salt, flavour with Noilly Prat and strain. Mix with the saffron and stand over low heat until required.

To make the garnish, skin the tomatoes, scoop out the seeds and season inside and outside with salt and pepper. Season the spinach with salt and pepper, flavour with brown butter and nutmeg and fill into the tomatoes. Sprinkle with grated Parmesan or breadcrumbs and brown quickly in the oven.

(Illustration, page 870)

(Ewald Plachutta, Austria)

Sweetbread pie Villeneuve
Croustade de ris de veau Villeneuve
Kalbsmilch in Teigkruste Villeneuve

10 portions

1 kg	puff pastry	2 lb 4 oz
600 g	leaf spinach, blanched	1 lb 5 oz
100 g	butter	3½ oz
50 g	shallots, finely chopped	2 oz
20 g	dried craterelles, soaked	¾ oz
200 g	chicken livers	7 oz
100 g	foie gras mousse	3½ oz
	salt	
	herbs and spices as desired	
1 kg 200	calves' sweetbreads	2 lb 10 oz

Garnish – vegetable timbale:

1 kg	turnips	2 lb 4 oz
2 dl	dairy cream	7 fl oz
(250 g)	12 egg yolks	(9 oz)
(100 g)	4 egg whites	(3½ oz)
100 g	carrots, cut in julienne strips	3½ oz

– courgettes Provençal style:

1 kg	courgettes	2 lb 4 oz
50 g	butter	2 oz
	shallots, finely chopped	
	herbs, finely chopped	
	spices as desired	
	salt	
	10 small tomatoes	

Villeneuve sauce:

(125 g)	6 egg yolks	(4½ oz)
	spices as desired	
	salt	
½ l	Villeneuve white wine	18 fl oz
1 dl	brown veal stock	3½ fl oz

Pin out the puff pastry and cut in 10 cm x 8 cm (4 in x 3½ in) strips. Season the spinach carefully and arrange evenly on the pastry, leaving 1 cm (⅜ in) free round the edge. Place on top the sweetbreads which have been blanched and skinned, and spread with chicken and foie gras mousse. Drain the craterelles, cut in strips and distribute over the mousse, then cover with another layer of spinach. Wash the edges of the pastry with egg yolk. Cover with a second strip of pastry, press the edges together firmly and decorate with pastry trimmings. Egg wash and refrigerate for about 30 minutes, then bake off. If the pie forms a main course, garnish with vegetable timbale, courgettes Provençal style and a small stewed tomato. Serve with freshly made Villeneuve sauce. To make the sauce proceed as for sabayon.

(Otto Ledermann, Switzerland)

Stuffed kohlrabi Hungarian style
Choux-raves à la hongroise
Töltött kalarábé magyarosan

10 portions	Cooking time: 35-40 minutes	
	20 kohlrabi globes	
	7–8 cm (3½ in) across	
1 kg	shoulder or leg of veal	2 lb 4 oz
40 g	salt	1½ oz
2 g	white pepper, freshly ground	a pinch
	2 bread rolls without crust	
2 dl	milk	7 fl oz
2 dl	sour cream	7 fl oz
100 g	lard	3½ oz
OR 1 dl	oil	3½ fl oz
OR 5 cl	sunflower oil	2 fl oz
and 50 g	lard	2 oz
100 g	butter	3½ oz
100 g	flour	3½ oz
	1 egg	
	1 egg yolk	
30 g	sugar	1 oz
	1 bunch parsley, finely chopped	

Peel the kohlrabi and hollow out each globe, leaving a narrow edge. Boil in lightly salted water until half cooked and leave to dry on a cloth. Cut up very finely the flesh removed from the globes, as well as the fresh leaves and stalks.

To make the filling, mince the meat and mix well with the minced lard (or oil), the rolls which have been soaked in milk, one egg and parsley. Season with salt and pepper and fill into the kohlrabi. Place the globes in a buttered saucepan, sprinkle with the cut up leaves and stalks, add salt and sugar, pour in bouillon or water to half cover the globes, cover and stew until tender. Remove, place in a fireproof dish and set aside.

Prepare a roux with the butter and flour, blend in the cooking liquid from the kohlrabi and bring to the boil. Mix the sour cream with the egg yolk and stir into the sauce to thicken. Add a little lemon juice if desired. To serve, pour the hot sauce over the kohlrabi and sprinkle with chopped parsley, also a little melted butter if desired.

(Zsolt Körmendy, Hungary)

Bosnian meat balls
Boulettes bosniennes
Bosanka Cufte

6 portions   Cooking time: 60-70 minutes

750 g	mutton or beef, minced	1 lb 10 oz
	5 eggs	
½ l	sour milk (see page 147)	18 fl oz
100 g	flour	3½ oz
50 g	lard	2 oz
50 g	butter	2 oz
5 g	caraway, crushed	⅕ oz
	salt	

Mix the meat well with the flour and one egg. Season with salt, work well with the hands and shape into small balls. Place in a buttered and floured fireproof tableware casserole and cook for about 45 minutes in a preheated slow oven, leaving the casserole uncovered. Mix together the rest of the eggs and the sour milk in a bowl, add the caraway and pour over the meat balls. Continue cooking uncovered for about 15 to 20 minutes in a slow oven and serve in the casserole.

(László Csizmadia, Yugoslavia)

Smyrna meat balls
Boulettes à la smyrniote
Smyrna-Kefta

10 portions

800 g	lean beef or mutton	1 lb 12 oz
5 cl	oil	2 fl oz
300 g	onions, chopped	11 oz
300 g	aubergines	11 oz
300 g	courgettes	11 oz
150 g	Parmesan cheese, grated	5 oz
	4 eggs	
	salt	
	pepper, freshly ground	
	herbs	
50 g	flour	2 oz
	oil for frying	

Cook the finely chopped onions in oil. Slice the aubergines and courgettes, add to the onions in the pan and cook until soft without adding any liquid. Leave until quite cold, then chop finely with the meat. Add the cheese and eggs, mix well, season to taste and add herbs as desired. Shape into small balls, roll in flour and fry in deep oil. This dish may be served hot or cold, accompanied by salad.

(Otto Ledermann, Turkey)

Stuffed potato gnocchi Sanzenati
Gnocchi de pommes de terre Sanzenati
Gnocchi Sanzenati ripieni

6 portions

1 kg 500	floury potatoes, peeled and coarsely cut	3 lb 5 oz
450 g	flour	1 lb
200 g	Parmesan, grated	7 oz
	a pinch of nutmeg	
	salt to taste	

Filling:

100 g	neck or shoulder of veal	4 oz
100 g	chicken breast	4 oz
60 g	ham	2 oz
	1 egg	
	1 tablespoon chopped shallot	
80 g	butter	3 oz
1 dl	white wine	3½ fl oz
	salt and pepper to taste	

Boil the potatoes in salted water, drain well and rub through a fine sieve. Mix with the flour, about 50 g (2 oz) grated Parmesan and a pinch of grated nutmeg.

To make the filling, cook the finely chopped shallot in butter without colouring, add the meat which has been coarsely cut, brown over low heat for a few minutes, then stir in the wine and continue cooking until tender. Mince together with the ham, using the finest cutter. Add the beaten egg and the rest of the Parmesan. Adjust the seasoning if necessary.

To make the gnocchi, knead the potato/flour/cheese mixture to a firm dough and shape into long rolls 1½ cm (about ½ in) thick. Cut these into 3 cm (1 in) lengths. Press the thumb into the centre to form a hollow, fill with the meat filling and press the dough round the filling to enclose it completely. Cook in salted water until they rise to the surface. Remove with a skimmer, drain well and place in a warm fireproof dish to keep them hot. Pour melted butter over and sprinkle with Parmesan and brown in a sharp oven.

(Mario Saporito, Italy)

Stuffed kohlrabi
Choux-raves farcis
Töltött kalarábé

5 portions　　　Cooking time: 30 minutes

800 g	shoulder of veal, boned	1 lb 12 oz
	2 rolls	
(800 g)	10 young kohlrabi globes	(1 lb 12 oz)
10 g	salt	1/3 oz
5 g	black pepper, freshly ground	1/6 oz
2 dl	milk	7 fl oz
2½ dl	water	9 fl oz
2½ dl	fresh dairy cream	9 fl oz
100 g	butter	3½ oz
50 g	flour	2 oz
	3 eggs	

Mince the veal, using the finest cutter. Soak the rolls in the milk and squeeze dry. Mix together the veal, the rolls, 2 eggs, salt and pepper and set aside. Remove the tops from the kohlrabi, reserving any small young leaves. Peel the globes and hollow out with a small spoon. Fill with the meat/bread/egg mixture.

Make a roux with the butter and flour, add the kohlrabi leaves which have been finely chopped, then add the cream, diluted with water, stirring constantly. Bring to the boil and season with salt. Place the stuffed kohlrabi in the sauce. Chop the scooped out flesh and sprinkle on top. Cover and cook over low heat for about 30 minutes. When the globes are tender, remove and arrange on a warm dish. Thicken the sauce with 1 egg yolk and pour over. (Illustration, page 622)

(Gyula Gullner, Hungary)

Stuffed cabbage
Paupiettes de choux à la tomate
Gefülltes Kraut

10 portions

1 kg	white cabbage	2 lb 4 oz
900 g	kosher minced beef	2 lb
	(as used for beefburgers)	
200 g	rice	7 oz
2 l	tomato sauce	3½ pt
	10 portions boiled potatoes	

parsley, chopped

Remove the cabbage stump. Blanch the cabbage for 20 minutes in boiling salted water, then drain and allow to cool. Have it divided into separate leaves by the rabbinical representative.

Carefully mix the minced meat with the rice which has been cooked to keep the grains firm. Divide between 20 good-size sound cabbage leaves and roll up. Place on a well oiled roasting tray and sprinkle with the remaining cabbage leaves which have been cut in julienne strips. Pour liquid tomato sauce over until the cabbage rolls are three quarters covered and cook in the oven for 2 hours.

To serve, place 2 cabbage rolls per portion in warmed soup plates and pour the cooking liquid over. Garnish with boiled potatoes and sprinkle with chopped parsley.

(Gérard van Dijk, Switzerland)

Cabbage strudel
Stroudel aux choux
Káposztás rétes

10 portions   Baking time: 15 minutes

Strudel dough:

500 g	strong dry wheat flour	1 lb 2 oz
	2 egg yolks	
40 g	lard	1½ oz
5 g	salt	⅙ oz
	white wine vinegar	
3 dl	water	10 fl oz
50-100 g	butter or lard, melted and lukewarm	2–4 oz

Filling:

2 kg 500	white cabbage	5 lb 8 oz
50 g	salt	2 oz
200 g	lard	7 oz
50 g	sugar	2 oz
5 g	white pepper, freshly ground	⅙ oz

To make the filling, shred the cabbage finely, sprinkle with salt, set aside for 30 minutes, then squeeze dry. Cook the sugar to light caramel in the lard, add the cabbage and fry, stirring frequently. Season with pepper and leave until cold.

To make the strudel dough, sieve the flour and make a bay. Place in it the lard, the egg yolks and the water containing a little salt and a few drops of vinegar. Mix roughly at first. If the flour has too high a capacity to absorb, add a little lukewarm water. The dough should be elastic but not too soft. It must be worked thoroughly until it is smooth and does not stick to the fingers or board. Divide into smaller pieces, knead well again, mould into a ball, lightly brush the surface with fat, place in a warm bowl, cover and leave to rest for about 20 to 25 minutes. Pin out the dough as thinly as possible in both directions on a large floured cloth, then slip the hands underneath with the backs uppermost and stretch out without tearing until paper thin and hanging over the edge of the table. Tear off the thick ends with the hands. Allow to dry for a short time, then splash with melted butter or lard, sprinkle with toasted white breadcrumbs and cover one third of the surface with the cabbage. Starting at this end, roll up the strudel, then place on a baking sheet and brush the top with melted lukewarm butter or with egg. Bake in a hot oven to a good light brown colour.

A great deal of practice and time is required to make strudel. To simplify the procedure, the use of ready-made strudel dough, if available commercially, is to be recommended.

(Zsolt Körmendy, Hungary)

Kreplach

500 g	noodle dough	1 lb 2 oz
250 g	kreplach filling (see below)	9 oz
	1 egg	
	salt	
	water	

Pin out the noodle dough as thinly as possible and cut out 8–10 cm (3½–4 in) rounds. Place a small teaspoonful of filling on each round to cover half of it, wash the edge with egg yolk, fold over to enclose the filling and press the edges together firmly. Simmer in salted water for 20 minutes, refresh under cold running water and drain. Pour oil over the kreplach to prevent drying and refrigerate until required. For method of serving, see *fried kreplach* and *boiled kreplach* (p. 274).

Kreplach filling

50 g	vegetable fat	2 oz
250 g	kosher minced beef	9 oz
50 g	onion, chopped	2 oz
	salt	
	pepper, freshly ground	

Heat the fat in a pan, add the meat and onion and fry for 10 minutes while stirring. Season with salt and pepper and allow to cool.

Fried kreplach

10 portions

	50 kreplach	
3 dl	oil	10 fl oz
8 dl	ketchup	28 fl oz

Heat the oil in a pan and fry the kreplach on both sides until golden brown. To serve, arrange in a ring on individual plates and pour a little ketchup in the centre.

Boiled kreplach

10 portions

	50 kreplach	
8 dl	ketchup	28 fl oz

Heat the kreplach for 5 minutes in boiling salted water. To serve, arrange in a ring on well warmed plates. Pour a little ketchup in the middle and serve hot.

(Gérard van Dijk, Switzerland)

Basler rissoles
Rissoles à la bâloise
Basler Küchenpastetchen

Pastry:

1 kg	flour	2 lb 4 oz
500 g	lard, flaked	1 lb 2 oz
	salt	
	water	

Filling: See recipe, page 130
egg
fat for frying

Sift the flour into a bowl and add the flaked lard. Rub in lightly until evenly distributed. Add the water seasoned with salt and work to a fairly slack paste. Pin out thinly and cut out with a 10–12 cm (4–5 in) cutter. Egg wash the rounds of pastry. Cover one half of each round with a tablespoon of filling and fold the other half over it. Press the edges down well with the back of the cutter to prevent any escape of filling while frying. Fry in hot deep fat and serve at once.

(Otto Ledermann, Switzerland)

Lamb offal with mushrooms
Abats d'agneau aux moucherons

2 portions

	2 lamb's kidneys	
	2 lamb's brains	
	2 lamb's sweetbreads	
	1 lamb's tongue	
100 g	chanterelles or flap mushrooms	4 oz
1 dl	soya sauce	3½ fl oz
1 dl	brown lamb stock	3½ fl oz
1 dl	wine vinegar	3½ fl oz
	1 small teaspoon sugar	
50 g	butter	2 oz
	1 bouquet garni	
	flour	
5 cl	olive oil	2 fl oz

Season the offal well, trim and skin it. Cook the tongue in salted water containing the bouquet garni. Flour the brains and sweetbreads, fry in butter and season. Cut the kidneys in half, remove the fat and fry lightly. Fry the mushrooms in oil. Dissolve the sugar in the lamb stock, add the vinegar and soya sauce, reduce and finish with the butter. To serve, place the mushrooms in the centre of the plate, surround with the offal and mask with the sauce. (Illustration, page 313)

(Roger Souvereyns, Belgium)

Artichoke and tomato moulds
Gâteau à l'artichaut et à la tomate

6 portions

200 g	chicken breast	7 oz
250 g	double dairy cream	9 oz
	2 eggs	
400 g	cold roast lamb, trimmed and finely diced	14 oz

	4 artichoke bottoms	
150 g	tomatoes, skinned and finely diced	5 oz
2 dl	brown veal stock	7 fl oz
	butter as required	

Tarragon sauce:

5 cl	red wine vinegar	2 fl oz
	½ shallot, chopped	
	4 black peppercorns, crushed	
	6 fresh tarragon leaves	
2 dl	lamb gravy (page 121)	7 fl oz
30 g	butter	1 oz

Cook the shallot, peppercorns and tarragon in the vinegar until reduced by two thirds. Add the gravy, then the butter a little at a time, adjust the seasoning and strain.

Prepare a mousse with the chicken, cream and eggs. Butter 6 small dariole moulds well and line with mousse. Place diced tomato at the bottom of the moulds, reserving 1 or 2 tablespoons for decoration. Cover with diced lamb, then with two of the artichoke bottoms which have been finely diced. Add butter to the veal stock to make a thick sauce and pour into the moulds. Cover with mousse. Poach for 20 minutes in a bain-marie.

Turn out on to warm plates and mask with tarragon sauce. Decorate the top with diced tomato and 2 tarragon leaves and surround each mould with wedges of artichoke. (Illustration, page 166)

(Emile Jung, France)

Swedish liver pudding
Pouding de foie de veau à la suédoise

4 portions

150 g	rice	5 oz
8 dl	milk	28 fl oz
50 g	butter	2 oz
	salt	
300 g	calf's or pig's liver	11 oz
100 g	fat bacon or pork fat	3½ oz
	1 medium onion, finely chopped	
100 g	raisins	3½ oz
	2 tablespoons syrup	
	2 teaspoons salt	
	1 teaspoon marjoram	

½ teaspoon pepper and ginger
1 tablespoon potato flour

Accompaniment – cranberry compote:

cranberries
sugar

Place the milk and butter in a pan with a little salt, bring to the boil and add the rice. Cover and cook for about 20 minutes. Mince the liver and bacon or pork fat several times. Add the rice which has been allowed to cool a little, mix with the onion which has been stewed and with the remaining ingredients, then check the seasoning. Fill into a buttered rectangular mould and bake in a bain-marie at 225°C (437°F) for about 40 minutes. Keep hot.

To make the compote, clean and wash the cranberries and bring to the boil. Add one third of the weight of the fruit in sugar and stir well. This procedure produces a jelly-like compote with a natural colour and a fresh flavour.

To serve, cut the pudding into slices about 2 cm (¾ in) thick, sprinkle with a little melted butter and dress on individual plates. Hand the cranberry compote separately.

(Eric Carlström, Sweden)

Stuffed Swiss chard
Feuilles de bettes farcies
Töltött mangold

5 portions   Cooking time: 25 minutes

500 g	Swiss chard	1 lb 2 oz
500 g	cushion of veal	1 lb 2 oz
	OR pork fillet	
	3 bread rolls	
3 dl	milk	10 fl oz
10 g	salt	⅓ oz
5 g	pepper	⅙ oz
5 g	nutmeg, grated	⅙ oz
200 g	mushrooms (cudonia)	7 oz
2 dl	dairy cream	7 fl oz
30 g	flour	1 oz
50 g	butter	2 oz
1 dl	white wine	3½ fl oz
250 g	tomatoes	9 oz

Wash the Swiss chard well, blanch in boiling salted water and set aside. To make the filling, remove the crusts from the rolls, soak in milk and squeeze dry, then mince with the meat and season with salt, pepper and nutmeg.

Remove the thick ribs from the Swiss chard. Divide the filling into 15 portions and wrap each one in a leaf, taking care to prevent the filling from escaping.

Make a roux with the butter and flour, blend in the cream, the wine and 1 dl (3½ fl oz) water, season with salt and bring to the boil. Place the stuffed leaves in the pan, cook for 10 to 15 minutes, add the mushrooms which have been well cleaned and washed and cook for a further 10 minutes.

To serve, arrange the stuffed Swiss chard on a dish, pour the sauce over and decorate each portion with half a fried tomato. Savoy cabbage or swede tops may be used instead of Swiss chard, but the flavour will be different.

(Gyula Gullner, Hungary)

Macaroni with oxtail
Maccaroni à la vachère
Maccheroni alla vaccinara

6 portions

600 g	macaroni	1 lb 5 oz
	butter	
	Parmesan	
	18 tablespoons *oxtail alla vaccinara* (recipe, page 284)	

Cut up the cold cooked oxtail, place in a pan with its stock and heat slowly. Cook the macaroni *al dente* and drain thoroughly. Add to the oxtail in the pan, mix well, heat again for a short time, leave to stand over the heat without boiling and serve hot. Hand the parmesan separately.
(Illustration, page 517)   (Franco Colombani, Italy)

Stuffed squash
Pâtisson farci
Töltött patiszon

4 portions   Cooking time: about 1 hour

	4 medium squash (pâtisson)	
400 g	shoulder of pork	14 oz
50 g	smoked bacon	2 oz
	2 bread rolls	
	1 egg	

	1 small onion, finely cut	
	1 bunch fresh dill	
2 dl	sour cream	7 fl oz
1 dl	fresh dairy cream	3½ fl oz
	1 egg yolk	
10 g	flour	⅓ oz
40 g	butter	1½ oz
	salt	
	pepper, freshly ground	

Peel and hollow out the squash. Place in a pan, add salt and sugar to taste, cover with water and cook until tender. Cut up the bacon finely, render the fat and cook the onion in it until lightly coloured. Add the meat which has been passed through the finest blade of the mincer, season with salt and pepper and stew until tender.

Soak the rolls in milk and squeeze dry. Mix with the meat and 1 egg and blend together well, then fill into the squash and place in a fireproof dish. Mix the sour and fresh cream well with the dill which has been finely chopped, the egg yolk and the flour. Pour over the squash and brown in the oven. All the ingredients must be heated thoroughly.

(László Csizmadia, Hungary)

Moussaka Greek style

6–8 portions

	minced beef or veal	1 lb 2 oz
500 g	minced beef or veal	1 lb 2 oz
100 g	any preferred fat	4 oz
100 g	onions, finely chopped	4 oz
2 dl	tomato sauce	7 fl oz
1 l	Béchamel sauce (recipe, page 171)	1¾ pt
	2 eggs	
	2 tablespoons chopped parsley	
	4 aubergines	
1½ dl	white wine	5 fl oz
	½ cup breadcrumbs	
	2 tablespoons grated Parmesan	
	water	
	nutmeg	
	salt, pepper	

Cook the onions gently in 50 g (2 oz) fat without colouring. Add the meat and brown. Stir in the wine, then the tomato sauce, season and cook over low heat for about an hour.

Slice the aubergines, sprinkle with salt and stand aside under pressure between two plates to drain. Dry and fry in deep fat. Line a buttered shallow fireproof dish with aubergine slices. Mix the meat sauce, which should be rather thick, with a little of the breadcrumbs and grated cheese and place on the aubergines. Cover with the rest of the aubergines and mask with the Béchamel sauce mixed with the remaining Parmesan and the eggs after removing from the heat. Sprinkle with the rest of the breadcrumbs, then with the rest of the fat which has been melted, and brown for 15 minutes in a hot oven (200–225°C/392–437°F). Remove from the oven, allow to rest for a short time, then slice and serve.

(Emil Wälti, Greece)

Three frontiers toast
Croûte aux morilles trois frontières
Morchelschnitte Dreiländereck

10 portions

	20 slices bread (tin or	
30 g	sandwich loaf), each weighing	1 oz
1 kg 200	calves' sweetbreads	2 lb 10 oz
50 g	butter	2 oz
5 cl	oil	2 fl oz
	salt	
	spices as desired	
50 g	flour	2 oz
	2 eggs	
50 g	morels, fresh or dried	2 oz
400 g	asparagus	14 oz
¾ l	cream sauce (recipe, page 172)	27 fl oz
3 dl	Hollandaise sauce (recipe, page 175)	10 fl oz

Toast the bread, allowing 2 slices per portion. Blanch and skin the sweetbreads, then flour them and coat with beaten egg. Fry on both sides until golden yellow and place on the toast. Wash the morels very carefully and stew until soft. Cut the asparagus into 2 cm (¾ in) lengths – trimmings are generally used if available – and cook without allowing the asparagus to become completely soft. Discard the cooking liquid.

Carefully stir the morels and asparagus into the cream sauce and spoon evenly over the sweetbreads. Mask with Hollandaise sauce and brown for a short time under a salamander. Serve at once to prevent the toast becoming soft.

(Otto Ledermann, Switzerland)

Moussaka Serbian style
Moussaka à la serbe
Musaka od Plavih Patlidžana

6 portions   Cooking time: 1–1½ hours

	4 large aubergines	
250 g	pork, finely minced	9 oz
250 g	beef, finely minced	9 oz
	8 eggs	
250 g	lard	9 oz
OR 2½ dl	oil	9 fl oz
½ l	milk	18 fl oz
	1 onion, finely cut	
	3 tomatoes, finely diced	
	flour	
	salt	
	pepper, freshly ground	
	parsley, finely chopped	

Peel the aubergines, slice thinly along the length, sprinkle with salt and set aside in a bowl. Lightly cook the onion and tomatoes in 1 tablespoon lard or oil without colouring. Add the meat, season with salt and brown lightly. Remove from the heat, season with pepper, add the parsley and mix well. Squeeze each slice of aubergine dry separately. Beat 3 of the eggs well. Dip the aubergine slices in the beaten egg, coat with flour and fry in hot shallow lard.

Arrange alternate layers of aubergines and meat in a fireproof dish, finishing with a layer of aubergines. Beat the remaining eggs with the milk and pour over. Bake in a preheated oven for 1 to 1½ hours. The top should be crisp and golden yellow. Serve in the same dish.

(László Csizmadia, Yugoslavia)

Pasta shells maison
Coquillettes maison
Conchiglie della casa

2 tablespoons finely cut boiled beef
3 tablespoons cooked peppers
pasta shells
butter as required
salt
Parmesan, grated

Heat the peppers in a sauteuse, add the beef, stir over low heat for a short time and leave to stand. Cook the pasta *al dente,* drain thoroughly, add to the meat and peppers, mix well, cook for a few moments over low heat and serve. The pasta should remain firm after cooking. (Illustration, page 517)

(Franco Colombani, Italy)

Peasants' gratin Bergamo
Gratin des paysans bergamasques
Fojade del contadino

1 kg	aubergines	2 lb 4 oz
	2 eggs	
	white flour as required	
	oil as required	
	4–6 slices Mortadella	

Meat sauce:

300 g	pork	11 oz
400 g	beef	14 oz
	1 clove of garlic	
	½ medium onion	
	1 tablespoon parsley, finely chopped	
200 g	streaky bacon	7 oz
1 dl	red wine	3½ fl oz
	2 tablespoons tomato purée	
approx. 1 dl	bouillon	3½ fl oz
1 dl	oil	3½ fl oz
100 g	butter	3½ oz
	1 bay leaf	
	1 sprig thyme	
	1 sprig rosemary	

Noodle dough:

1 kg	white flour	2 lb 4 oz
	8 eggs	
	salt	
	water	

Meat balls:

400 g	beef	14 oz
100 g	breadcrumbs	3½ oz
100 g	Parmesan, grated	3½ oz
	1 clove of garlic, very finely chopped	
	2 tablespoons parsley, chopped	
	4 eggs	

Peel the aubergines a day ahead, slice thinly along the length and sprinkle with salt. Arrange the slices in layers in a china bowl and cover with a weighted plate or lid without crushing the aubergines. Leave to drain until the next day, then pour off the water; egg and flour the slices, fry in deep oil and keep hot.

Make the noodle dough, pin out thinly and cut in strips 1½ to 2 cm (about ¾ in) wide. Cook *al dente* in salted water and spread on a cloth to dry.

To make the sauce, mince the meat, using the finest cutter, and add the parsley. Brown lightly in butter and oil together with the bacon which has been finely diced and the onion which has been finely chopped. Stir in the wine and reduce completely, then stir in the tomato purée, moisten well with bouillon and cook over low heat for at least 2 hours without allowing the liquid to boil away completely.

Mix together the ingredients for the meat balls, shape into walnut-size balls and cook in the sauce for an hour. Sprinkle the base of a buttered fireproof dish with very little chopped garlic or rub the dish with garlic. Fill with alternate layers of noodles, aubergines, Mortadella, Parmesan and meat balls in sauce, repeating until all the ingredients have been used up. Dot with butter, sprinkle with grated Parmesan and bake for 45 minutes in an oven preheated to 200°C (392°F).

(Maurizio Tassi, Italy)

Ox cheek pudding or Mudlarks' prize
Mudlarks were barefoot urchins in Victorian times who combed the muddy banks of the Thames for usable items and collected the refuse from merchant ships and barges at low tide. They sold their finds in the local public houses, sometimes for a few coppers, but often in exchange for a huge meat pudding.

6 portions   Cooking time: 5 hours

Suetcrust:

450 g	self-raising flour	1 lb
225 g	suet, shredded	8 oz
60 g	fresh breadcrumbs	2 oz
	1 level teaspoon salt	
	1 level teaspoon white pepper	
2½ dl	cold water	10 fl oz

Filling:

1 kg 500	ox cheek	3 lb
450 g	ox kidneys	1 lb
250 g	onions, chopped	9 oz
150 g	carrots, sliced	5 oz

	1 pig's trotter	
	8 anchovy fillets	
	8 prunes, stoned	
200 g	mushrooms, sliced	7 oz
	1 tablespoon parsley, chopped	
	2 tablespoons salt	
	1 teaspoon white pepper	
60 g	flour	2 oz
	2 tablespoons vinegar	

Cook the pig's trotter in 1 l (2 pt) water for 2 hours. Remove, reduce the water to ½ l (1 pt) and allow to cool. Remove the meat and skin from the bone and cut into small strips.

Sieve the flour into a mixing bowl; add the suet, breadcrumbs, salt and pepper. Mix carefully with a spatula, slowly pouring in the water until completely absorbed by the flour. Handle the pastry as little as possible. Mould into a ball and place on a floured board. Pin out into a round 8 mm (¼ in) thick. Stand a pudding basin on the pastry upside down and cut round it, leaving a 2 cm (¾ in) edge. Cut out a wedge-shaped quarter segment of the pastry and set aside. Fold the remaining pastry in three parts and carefully place it in the pudding basin which has been well greased, then spread it out to line the basin, pressing it firmly against the sides. Damp the cut edges and press together firmly.

Trim the ox cheek and kidneys, cut into 3 cm (1 in) cubes and coat with flour. Replace each prune stone with a rolled anchovy fillet. Fill the lined pudding basin with all the ingredients in alternating layers. Sprinkle the top with salt, pepper and vinegar. Add any remaining flour and fill to within 2 cm (¾ in) of the top edge with the reduced liquid in which the pig's trotter was cooked.

Roll out the remaining pastry into a round to fit the top of the pudding basin. Damp the edges and press firmly on to the pastry lining the basin. Cover with buttered greaseproof paper. Place a pudding cloth on top, make a 6 cm (2 in) inverted pleat in the centre and tie round. Open the pleat to leave room for the pudding to rise. Steam for 5 hours or cook in a bain-marie for 4 hours, keeping the pan covered and making sure there is always sufficient water to come halfway up the basin. When the pudding is cooked, remove the cloth and paper and turn out on to a warm dish to serve.

(Victor Sassie, Great Britain)

Oxtail alla vaccinara
Queue de boeuf à la vachère
Coda di manzo alla vaccinara

8 portions

2 kg	oxtail and ox cheek	4 lb 8 oz
100 g	bacon or fat pork	3½ oz

30 g	lard	1 oz
30 g	parsley	1 oz
	1 carrot	
	1 onion	
	2 celery stalks	
1½ dl	white wine	5 fl oz
	2 tablespoons tomato purée	
	water	
	salt and pepper, freshly ground	
	1 clove garlic	

Peel the onion, carrot and garlic and chop very finely together with the parsley. Dice the bacon or pork finely, then chop. Cut up the meat in small pieces, rinse under running water and place in boiling water. When the water returns to the boil, remove the meat.

Brown the bacon (or pork) and the vegetables in the lard, add the meat to the pan and brown lightly. Season with salt and pepper and moisten with a little of the wine, reduce completely and repeat until all the wine has boiled away. Now add the tomato purée which has been blended with ½ l (18 fl oz) water. Cover and braise over low heat for 4 hours, adding water or stock if the pan becomes dry. String and wash the celery, cut in small pieces, add to the pan after 4 hours' cooking time and cook for a further 30 minutes. Transfer to a deep serving bowl and serve at once.

(Franco Colombani, Italy)

Easter meat loaf Prague style
Gratin de pâques de Prague
Pražská velikonoční nádivka

6 portions   Baking time: 45 minutes

600 g	cooked Kasseler (lightly pickled and smoked fore loin of pork)	1 lb 5 oz
OR 400 g	cooked belly of pork	14 oz
and 200 g	cooked shoulder of pork	7 oz
OR 300 g	cooked smoked beef	11 oz
150 g	cooked pork	5 oz
and 150 g	cooked veal	5 oz
100 g	raw calf's liver	4 oz
	6 eggs	
	salt	
	6 peppercorns, freshly ground	
	2 tablespoons chopped parsley *or* chives	

150 g	white bread *or* rolls	5 oz
60 g	butter	2 oz

Chop the meat and liver finely, place in a bowl and mix well with the beaten eggs, salt, pepper, parsley or chives and the bread or rolls previously diced and moistened with bouillon. Transfer to a well buttered fireproof dish and bake at 200–220°C (392–428°F) for about 45 minutes.

White bread flour may be used instead of bread or rolls, with the addition of ⅛ l (4½ fl oz) milk to the beaten eggs. If desired, the egg yolks only may be mixed with the meat at first and the whites whipped to a stiff snow which is folded in last. Serve with spinach or vegetable salad.

(Vilèm Vrabec, Czechoslovakia)

Stuffed pancakes Hortobágyi
Crêpes farcies Hortobágyi
Hortobágyi husos Palacsinta

10 portions   Cooking time: 35–40 minutes

Filling:

600 g	boned shoulder of veal	1 lb 5 oz
100 g	lard	3½ oz
OR 1 dl	oil	3½ fl oz
150 g	onions, finely chopped	5 oz
10 g	paprika	⅓ oz
20 g	salt	¾ oz
100 g	yellow peppers, seeded	3½ oz
50 g	tomatoes, cut in quarters	2 oz
30 g	flour	1 oz
5 dl	sour cream	18 fl oz

Pancakes:

350 g	flour	12 oz
150 g	lard	5 oz
OR 1½ dl	oil	5 fl oz
3 dl	milk	10 fl oz
3 dl	mineral water (soda or other aerated water)	10 fl oz
	3 eggs	
10 g	salt	⅓ oz

(Instead of milk, fresh dairy cream may be used, which will give a finer flavour to the pancakes.)

To make the filling, fry the onions in lard or oil until lightly coloured, sprinkle with paprika, moisten with a little water and stew for a few seconds. Add the veal which has been finely diced, cover and cook in very little liquid. Shortly before the meat is tender, add the tomatoes and the peppers which have been cut in strips and continue cooking. Remove the meat from the cooking liquid and chop finely. It is better not to mince the meat as the filling should not have the consistency of a purée. Keep the meat stock hot.

To make the pancakes, prepare a thick, smooth batter with the sieved flour, the milk, mineral water, eggs and salt. Heat very lightly oiled omelette pans and pour in a very thin layer of batter. As soon as the underside is light brown, turn the pancake either by tossing or with the aid of a fork. Cook the other side to the same colour. With a properly oiled pan and batter of the correct thickness there is no danger of sticking. Place one tenth of the filling on each pancake and roll up. Transfer the filled pancakes to a fireproof dish and place in a preheated oven.

Mix the sour cream with the flour and blend into the hot meat stock to thicken. Pour over the hot pancakes while boiling hot. Decorate with rings of seeded peppers and tomatoes. The veal may be replaced by boned paprika chicken, in which case the appropriate sauce is used instead of one based on the veal stock.

(Zsolt Körmendy, Hungary)

Hungarian ham pancakes
Crêpes au jambon gratinées à la hongroise
Sonkás rakott palascinta

6 portions

	6 eggs (separated)	
120 g	flour	4¼ oz
3 dl	dairy cream	10 fl oz
50 g	butter, melted	2 oz
300 g	ham	11 oz
1½ dl	sour cream	5 fl oz
80 g	lard	3 oz
	salt	

Prepare a pancake batter with the egg yolks, the flour, fresh cream and melted butter. Season with a little salt. Whip the egg whites to a very stiff snow and fold in very lightly. Cook the pancakes on one side only. They should not be too large; 6 or 7 are required for 6 portions.

Butter a fireproof dish and place a pancake on the bottom with the cooked side underneath. Sprinkle with small strips of ham and pour a little sour cream over, then place another pancake on top and repeat the procedure until all the pancakes have been used up. Brown in a hot oven for 8 to 10 minutes. Cut into slices in the same way as a cake and serve very hot.

(László Csizmadia, Hungary)

Stuffed peppers

4 portions

	8 plump green peppers	
	5 large tomatoes	
500 g	beef and pork, minced	1 lb 2 oz
	1 onion, finely cut	
	3 tablespoons oil	
	1 tablespoon flour	
	1 tablespoon paprika	
	1 egg	
	salt	
	pepper, freshly ground	
50 g	rice, washed	2 oz
	parsley, finely chopped	
	sour milk (see page 147)	

Seed the peppers and wash well. Fry the onion lightly in 1 tablespoon oil until it takes on a little colour, add the uncooked rice and the minced meat and brown well. Remove from the heat, mix well with the egg and parsley and season with salt and pepper. Fill into the peppers and cover the top with a slice of tomato. Place the peppers in a pan, add a little water and the remaining tomatoes and braise. If necessary, add a little more water while cooking. When the peppers are soft, blend in a roux made with 1 tablespoon each of oil and flour and seasoned with paprika. Cook for a further 30 minutes. Serve with sour milk.

(László Csizmadia, Yugoslavia)

Turnovers belle strasbourgeoise
Chaussons belle strasbourgeoise

8 portions

600 g	puff pastry	1 lb 5 oz

Filling:

150 g	shoulder of veal, trimmed and free from sinew	5 oz
1½ dl	dairy cream	5 fl oz
	2 eggs	
	½ shallot, finely cut	
150 g	cooked ham	5 oz
100 g	cooked foie gras	3½ oz

250 g	calves' sweetbreads, skinned	9 oz
150 g	mushrooms	5 oz
50 g	cooked cocks' combs	2 oz
2 cl	Cognac	1 fl oz

Sauce:

2 dl	demi-glace sauce (recipe, page 155)	7 fl oz
1 dl	Madeira	3½ fl oz
50 g	foie gras purée	2 oz
40 g	butter	1½ oz

To make the filling, cook the shallot gently in a little butter without colouring. Pass the veal through the finest blade of the mincer. Add the cream, the beaten eggs and the shallot and mix well. Dice the ham and foie gras. Divide the sweetbreads into small segments. Dice and poach the mushrooms. Slice the cocks' combs. Mix all the ingredients for the filling together, adding salt, pepper and the Cognac.

Divide the puff pastry into 8 oval pieces, pin each one out to an oval shape, cover half of each oval with filling, fold over and press the edges well to seal. Wash with egg yolk. Decorate with puff pastry trimmings as desired and egg wash. Bake for 20 minutes in an oven preheated to 220°C (428°F). Serve hot and hand the sauce separately.

To make the sauce, reduce the Madeira by half and add the demi-glace. Remove from the heat and work in the foie gras purée, then the butter a little at a time.
(Illustration, page 166)

(Emile Jung, France)

Pelmeni

10 portions

Noodle dough:

800 g	flour	1 lb 12 oz
	8 eggs	
1½–2½ dl	water	5–9 fl oz
	(the amount of water depends on the quality of the flour)	

Filling:

500 g	beef	1 lb 2 oz
500 g	pork	1 lb 2 oz
200 g	lard	7 oz
150 g	onions, finely cut	5 oz
30 g	salt	1 oz
3 g	pepper, freshly ground	a pinch
½ g	ginger	a small pinch
½ g	marjoram	a small pinch

	1 bunch parsley	
	5 eggs	
200 g	butter	7 oz
200 g	Parmesan, grated	7 oz
5 dl	sour cream	18 fl oz

Work the flour, eggs and water with a pinch of salt to a fairly firm dough (as for noodles), cover and allow to rest. Mince the beef and pork. Cook the onions in lard until lightly coloured, add the meat and fry. Season with salt, pepper, marjoram and ginger. Add the parsley which has been finely chopped, then the eggs and mix well.

Pin out the dough thinly and cut with a round cutter. Place a teaspoonful of filling in the centre of each round, wash the edges with egg, fold over to a half-moon shape and press the edges together firmly. Poach for 8 to 10 minutes in a large pan of salted water and drain well. Transfer to a fireproof dish, sprinkle with melted butter and grated cheese and place in the oven until the cheese has melted, but do not allow to brown. Serve in the same dish and hand the sour cream separately. In some regions hot gravy sharpened with lemon juice and sprinkled with chopped parsley is served as well as sour cream.

(Zsolt Körmendy, Russia)

Filled pancakes Chiesa

4 portions

Batter:

	3 eggs	
80 g	white flour	3 oz
5 cl	milk	2 fl oz
	salt	

Filling:

	½ medium onion, finely cut	
50 g	cushion of veal	2 oz
50 g	pork	2 oz
50 g	chicken	2 oz
5 cl	white wine	2 fl oz
	juice of 1 lemon	
	2 eggs	
100 g	Parmesan	3½ oz
5 cl	dairy cream	2 fl oz
20 g	butter	¾ oz
5 dl	Béchamel sauce (recipe, page 171)	18 fl oz
	4 slices Vezzena or	
	Emmental cheese	

Beat the eggs and carefully blend with the flour. Stir in the milk carefully to make a very smooth batter. Season with salt. Heat a 10 cm (4 in) pancake pan, brush with oil, pour in very little batter with the aid of a ladle and fry without browning. Make 7 more thin pancakes in the same manner. Allow to cool side by side on a sheet of aluminium foil.

To make the filling, fry the onion in a little butter until coloured and add a little lemon juice. Cut up the veal, pork and chicken coarsely and add to the pan. Brown lightly, stir in the wine and cook until tender, adding a little water or bouillon from time to time to prevent burning. Reduce the cooking liquid, remove from the heat, allow to cool a little and mince, using the finest cutter. Mix with the beaten eggs, the cream and 50 g (2 oz) grated Parmesan. Season with salt and pepper, mix thoroughly and spread on the pancakes. Fold twice. Lightly butter a fireproof dish and sprinkle with lemon juice. Place the pancakes inside and coat with ¼ l (9 fl oz) Béchamel sauce.

Place a slice of cheese on alternate pancakes. Coat with the rest of the Béchamel sauce, sprinkle with the remaining Parmesan and dot with butter. Brown for 10 minutes in an oven preheated to 200°C (392°F).

(Sergio Chiesa, Italy)

Macedonian meat and chilli custard
Gratin macédonien
Crvene Paprike sa Suvim Mesom i Jajima

4 portions   Cooking time: about 1½ hours

	10 small dried red chillies	
300 g	smoked ribs of beef	11 oz
	6 eggs	
1 dl	oil	3½ fl oz
	salt	
	pepper, freshly ground	

Wash the meat in warm water and cut into 4 cm (about 1½ in) cubes. Place in a pan with the chillies, cover with water and cook for an hour or until the meat and chillies are tender. Drain well and mince finely. Mix thoroughly with the oil and the beaten eggs and place in a fireproof dish. Bake in a preheated slow oven until the eggs have set. Serve hot.

(László Csizmadia, Yugoslavia)

Transylvanian stuffed peppers
Poivrons doux farcis à la transylvanienne
Erdélyi töltött paprika

5 portions   Cooking time: 30 minutes

500 g	shoulder of pork, minced	1 lb 2 oz

10 g	noble sweet paprika	⅓ oz
	2 medium onions	
	1 bunch dill	
3 dl	sour cream	10 fl oz
	10 medium yellow peppers	
	oil	
	salt, pepper	
	2 eggs	
100 g	rice, blanched	3½ oz
	1 level tablespoon flour	

Chop one onion finely and colour lightly in oil. Beat the eggs and mix well with the meat, rice and onion, season with salt and pepper, sprinkle with half the paprika and mix again. To remove the stalks from the peppers, press them down with the thumb, then twist and pull. This will leave the top of the peppers uneven and prevent escape of the filling while cooking.

Seed the peppers and wash thoroughly. Fill with the meat/rice mixture. Finely chop the other onion, fry lightly in oil until coloured, sprinkle with the rest of the paprika, pour in about 1 l (1¾ pt) water, season with salt and bring to the boil. Blend the flour with the sour cream and add, together with the dill which has been finely chopped.

Place the stuffed peppers in the pan, cover and cook over low heat for about 30 minutes, stirring from time to time. Add a little water if the sauce becomes too thick. When the peppers are cooked, remove from the pan and arrange on a dish. Strain the sauce and pour over. Sprinkle with a little sour cream and decorate with finely chopped dill.

(Gyula Gullner, Hungary)

Stuffed peppers in tomato sauce
Poivrons farcis en sauce aux tomates
Töltött paprika

10 portions

1 kg	shoulder of pork, minced	2 lb 4 oz
	20 yellow peppers	
50 g	lard	2 oz
100 g	onions, finely chopped	3½ oz
5 g	clove of garlic	⅙ oz
30 g	salt	1 oz
2 g	black pepper	a small pinch
1 g	marjoram	a small pinch
	3 eggs	
200 g	rice	7 oz
	1 bunch of parsley, finely chopped	

Tomato sauce:

2 l (3½ pt)

600 g	tomato purée	1 lb 5 oz
200 g	lard	7 oz
OR 2 dl	oil	7 fl oz
200 g	flour	7 oz
14 dl	bouillon	2½ pt
100 g	onions, finely chopped	3½ oz
40 g	salt	1½ oz
	2 bunches celery leaves	
200 g	sugar	7 oz

Wash the peppers. To remove the stalk end, proceed as follows. Hold the pepper in the hand with the stalk end downwards so that thumb pressure all the way round the stalk will make the upper part of the pepper come away and the seeds and fibres may be pulled out with the stalk. Remove any remaining seeds and fibres without damaging the outer shell. Wash well inside and outside, invert and allow to drain.

Cook the rice, leaving the grains firm, and allow to cool. Place the meat in a bowl and add the other ingredients in the following order: rice, 30 g (1 oz) onion lightly fried in lard, parsley, eggs, salt, pepper, marjoram, crushed garlic and the rest of the onion lightly fried in lard. Mix thoroughly and fill into the well drained peppers. Transfer to a saucepan, add the tomato sauce and braise under cover. If the peppers have too strong a flavour, they should be blanched and refreshed before use.

To make the sauce, prepare a blond roux with the flour and lard or oil, add the tomato purée, mix well and stir in the bouillon. Add the finely chopped onions and celery leaves, mix well and cook, then strain. Serve boiled potatoes with the stuffed peppers and sauce.

(Zsolt Körmendy, Hungary)

Pirochki
Piroguis à la russe

10 portions

Fermented dough:

1 kg	flour	2 lb 4 oz
20 g	sugar	¾ oz
10 g	salt	⅓ oz
	6 egg yolks	
100 g	butter	3½ oz
5 dl	milk	18 fl oz
20 g	yeast	¾ oz

Filling:

400 g	beef	14 oz
400 g	pork	14 oz
100 g	onions, finely chopped	3½ oz
	2 hard-boiled eggs, finely chopped	
30 g	salt	1 oz
3 g	black pepper, freshly ground	a pinch
200 g	lard	7 oz

Accompaniment:

5 dl	sour cream	18 fl oz

Prepare a light fermented dough with the ingredients indicated. Pin out finger thick, cut out with a floured round cutter, place on a floured board, cover with a warm cloth and leave to rise. To make the filling, fry the onions in lard until lightly coloured, add the beef and pork which have been finely minced, season with salt and pepper and cook gently. When cooked, add the hard-boiled eggs and set aside until lukewarm. Using a savoy bag and plain tube, pipe the filling into the risen rounds of dough from the side. Prove, then fry in deep hot oil. The pirochki should be pale golden in colour. Serve on a paper lined silver dish and hand the sour cream separately. The pirochki may be filled after frying, but the filling should then be used hot. They should be roughly egg-sized when cut out.

(Zsolt Körmendy, Russia)

Porrada

6 portions

600 g	almonds	1 lb 5 oz
1½ l	chicken broth	2¾ pt
	4 medium leeks	
	2 medium onions	
1–2 dl	wine vinegar	3½–7 fl oz
50 g	lard	2 oz
100 g	streaky bacon, diced	3½ oz
100 g	old or dry cheese, finely diced	3½ oz

Almond milk: skin the almonds, pound very finely in a mortar and slowly stir in the broth. Stand aside for 5 or 6 hours and strain through a cloth.

Meanwhile slice the leeks and onions, blanch for 3 minutes in boiling water, then drain well. Brown lightly in a little lard. Fry the bacon lightly in lard until transparent, moisten with the vinegar, add the browned vegetables and cook over low heat for about 25 minutes. Add the almond milk and the cheese. Continue cooking slowly over low heat to the consistency of a thick purée.

Make short pastry in the usual manner, mould into a ball, wrap in a cloth and leave to rest in the refrigerator for about 3 hours. Divide into 6 portions, pin out and line cake tins about 16 –20 cm (6–8 in) across. Spread the porrada purée on top (as when making pizza) and bake for 15 minutes in an oven preheated to 215°C (419°F). Serve hot.

(Josep Lladonosa, Spain)

Ravioli Bergamo
Ravioli à la bergamasquaise
Ravioli alla bergamasca

12 portions

Dough:

1 kg (2 lb 4 oz)		
800 g	flour	1 lb 12 oz
	4 eggs	
	a pinch of salt	
	water as required	

Filling:

1 kg	left-over roast meat	2 lb 4 oz
400 g	Parmesan, grated	14 oz
200 g	breadcrumbs	7 oz
200 g	Mortadella	7 oz
	6 eggs	
	6 amaretti	
	1 clove of garlic	
	salt, pepper	
	24 sage leaves	

Chop the garlic finely. Mince the meat and Mortadella, using the finest cutter. Add the beaten eggs, the breadcrumbs and the finely ground amaretti and mix thoroughly. If the mixture does not hold together, add a small quantity of breadcrumbs which have been soaked in milk. Season with salt and pepper.

Pin out the dough thinly to a rectangular shape. Mark half of it into squares. Using a savoy bag and plain tube, pipe a little filling on to each square. Lightly moisten the dough round the filling. Fold the other half of the dough over to cover the filling and press down, first with the hand, then with the back of a cutter. Cut out the squares with a pastry wheel. Alternatively, ravioli moulds are available commercially which make the process less time-consuming.

Cook the ravioli in salted water for about 12 to 15 minutes, drain and sprinkle with Parmesan. Brown some diced smoked bacon in melted butter together with the sage leaves and pour over the ravioli to serve.

(Guido Belotti, Enzo Ronzoni, Carlo Calvetti, Italy)

Ravioli Slovenian style
Ravioli à la slovène
Idrijski Žlikrofi

8 portions   Cooking time: about 25 minutes

Dough:

700 g	flour	1 lb 8 oz
	4 eggs	
	water	

Filling:

500 g	potatoes	1 lb 2 oz
360 g	smoked neck or fore loin of pork	12 oz
	3 eggs	
	1 small onion, chopped	
100 g	lard	3½ oz
	chopped parsley	
	pepper, freshly ground	
	salt	

Prepare a fairly firm noodle dough with the flour, eggs and water. Peel the potatoes, cut in quarters, boil in salted water, drain off the water, dry over low heat and pass through a sieve. Cook the meat and chop finely. Mix well with the potatoes, 1 egg, the onion and the parsley. Season with salt and pepper. Pin out the dough no thicker than the back of a knife and brush with beaten egg. Mark half into squares and pipe hazelnut-size balls of filling on each. Fold the other half of the dough over to cover the filling and press down, first with the hand, then with the back of a round cutter. Cut out the squares with a pastry wheel. Make a small dent in the centre of each ravioli. Cook in salted water for 20 to 25 minutes. This dish may be served either as a hot hors d'oeuvre or as an accompaniment to mutton.

(László Csizmadia, Yugoslavia)

Individual rice rings

Yield: 15 to 20 small borders

350 g	Vialone rice	12 oz
100 g	butter	3½ oz
	1 small onion, chopped	
1 l	bouillon	1¾ pt
½ g	saffron	a small pinch
1 dl	white wine	3½ fl oz
50 g	Parmesan, grated	2 oz
	1 egg, beaten	

breadcrumbs

Filling:

200 g	pork, finely chopped	7 oz
	OR pork frying sausage	
200 g	veal, finely chopped	7 oz
1 dl	white wine	3½ fl oz
1 dl	tomato sauce	3½ fl oz
	5 basil leaves, finely chopped	
	1 tablespoon parsley, finely chopped	
	15–20 small sprigs parsley	
	1 clove of garlic, crushed	

Fry the onion in 50 g (2 oz) butter without colouring. Add the rice and stir until transparent, then moisten with the wine. Gradually stir in the bouillon, cook for about 10 minutes, add the saffron and continue cooking, keeping the grains of rice firm. Allow to cool a little and stir in the Parmesan and egg. Butter small ring moulds, sprinkle with breadcrumbs and fill with the risotto. Sprinkle the top with breadcrumbs and bake at 175°C (347°F) until the top is crusted over.

To make the filling, brown the meat in butter with the garlic, stir in the wine, add the chopped herbs and the tomato sauce and cook until fairly thick. Turn out the ring moulds on to warm plates, place the filling in the centre, decorate each one with a sprig of parsley and serve hot.

(Franco Colombani, Italy)

The Szechuan hot, chewy, shredded beef

4 portions

500 g	beef steak (rump or leg)	1 lb 2 oz
2 g	salt	a pinch
	pepper	
	1 large carrot	
	2 sticks celery	
	oil for deep frying	
1 cl	soya sauce	½ fl oz
8 ml	hoisin sauce	1 dessertspoon
3 ml	chilli sauce	1 teaspoon
5 g	cornflour	⅕ oz
	2 stalks spring onion	
15 g	lard	½ oz
8 ml	dry sherry	1 dessertspoon
3 g	sugar	½ teaspoon

Cut the beef into 5–6 cm (about 2 in) double matchstick strips. Rub with salt, pepper to taste, and cornflour. Scrape and cut the carrot and celery into similar size shreds. Mix the sauces, sugar and sherry together until well blended. Cut the spring onions into 4–5 cm (1½–2 in) sections.

Heat the oil in the deep fryer. When a breadcrumb will sizzle on being dropped into it, add the beef, shaking off any excess cornflour. Fry over medium heat until the beef is crisp (this will take about 5 minutes). Remove and drain.

Heat the lard in a frying pan. Add the carrot, spring onion and celery. Stir-fry them together over high heat for 1½ minutes. Add the sauce mixture and the beef. Stir and turn them all together until every strip of beef is well covered by the sauce. Reduce the heat to medium. Continue to stir and turn until the sauce in the pan is almost dried and coagulated (this will take about 3 to 3½ minutes). Serve in a well heated serving dish. This is an excellent first course for a meal comprising several courses.

(Kenneth Lo, China)

Rissoles Château de Gruyères
Rissolen oder Halbmondpastetchen Schloss Greyerz

10 portions

35 g	butter	1¼ oz
60 g	flour	2 oz
2 dl	milk	7 fl oz
1 dl	dry white wine	3½ fl oz
	salt	
	nutmeg	
	pepper, freshly ground	
	3 egg yolks (1 to brush pastry)	
100 g	Gruyère cheese, grated	3½ oz
50 g	ham, diced	2 oz
400 g	puff pastry	14 oz

Make a roux with the butter and flour. Blend in the milk and wine and cook well. Add the cheese and the finely diced ham and season very carefully. Remove from the heat, add 2 egg yolks and spread at once on an oiled metal tray to a thickness of about 1½ cm (⅝ in). Leave until quite cold.

Pin out the pastry and cut into rounds. Cut the cold cheese filling into 30 g (1 oz) cubes and place one on one side of each round of pastry. Brush the edge with egg yolk and fold over to a half-moon shape. Press the edges together very firmly. Refrigerate for an hour, wash with egg yolk and bake. Serve very hot. Hand tomato sauce separately.

(Otto Ledermann, Switzerland)

Artichoke risotto
Risotto aux artichauts
Risotto con i carciofi

4 portions

500 g	rice	1 lb 2 oz
	6 tender whole artichokes (Italian)	
200 g	butter	7 oz
1½ l	bouillon	2¾ pt
2 cl	oil	1 fl oz
5 cl–1 dl	dairy cream	2–3½ fl oz
30 g	Parmesan, grated	1 oz
	salt and pepper	

Trim the artichokes (depending on quality) to within 2 cm (¾ in) of their base. Cut away the hard outer leaves and remove the heart. Cut up the artichokes finely and fry lightly in oil and butter without colouring in a wide pan. Stir in the rice and continue stirring until transparent. As soon as the rice has absorbed the fat, slowly stir in the bouillon. When the rice is almost cooked, stir in the cream, then the Parmesan and lastly a knob of butter. Stir well again and leave to stand for about 5 minutes. If desired, more grated Parmesan may be added when serving.

(Mario De Filippis, Italy)

Sausage risotto
Risotto à la saucisse à rôtir
Risotto alla pilota

6 portions   Cooking time: 18–20 minutes

600 g	Vialone rice	1 lb 5 oz
150 g	butter	5 oz
2 l	bouillon	3½ pt
100 g	Parmesan, grated	3½ oz
	1 tablespoon chopped onion	
300 g	pork frying sausage	11 oz

Heat half the butter in a fairly deep saucepan. Fry the onion lightly in it without colouring, add the rice and stir until transparent. Moisten with bouillon, then add the rest of the bouillon a little at a time, stirring constantly until the rice is cooked.

Skin the sausage, fry in a frying pan and mash well with the aid of two forks until cooked. Drain off the fat and work the sausage into the risotto. Fold in the cheese and finish off with the rest of the butter which has been well softened.

(Mario Saporito, Italy)

Scrambled eggs Schoenenbourg

4 portions   Cooking time: 5 minutes

	12 eggs	
150 g	fillet of beef, chopped	5 oz
150 g	spinach, blanched and chopped	5 oz
	1 tablespoon chopped shallots	
16 cl	dairy cream, whipped	6 fl oz
	butter as required	
	salt	
	pepper, freshly ground	
	8 fleurons	

Lightly beat the eggs in a large bowl and season with salt and pepper. Fry the shallots in butter over low heat, add the meat and spinach with a knob of butter, stand the pan in a bain-marie and whisk in the eggs. When fairly thick remove the pan and lightly stir in the cream until all the ingredients are well blended. Dress on warm plates and garnish with fleurons.

(François Kiener, France)

Filled loaf Croatian style
Pain farci à la croate
Vekna a Umakom od Paradajza

6 portions   Cooking time: 50–60 minutes

500 g	veal	1 lb 2 oz
	1 sandwich or rye loaf	
400 g	fresh tomatoes	14 oz
1 dl	oil	3½ fl oz
	3 tablespoons bouillon	
	OR warm water	
	1 egg	
	1 small onion, finely cut	
	salt	
	pepper, freshly ground	
	parsley, finely chopped	
50 g	butter	2 oz

Mince the meat. Lightly fry the onion in oil without colouring, add the meat and fry. Remove from the heat, add the egg and parsley and season with salt and pepper. Cut off the ends of the loaf, carefully remove the crumb from the centre and fill with the meat. Replace the ends of the loaf to cover the filling. Place in a buttered roasting pan, sprinkle with bouillon or warm water, then with melted butter, and bake for 25 minutes in a preheated moderate oven. Serve tomato sauce separately.

(László Csizmadia, Yugoslavia)

Sauerkraut balls

Yield: 60 to 80 balls

225 g	lean boneless ham	8 oz
225 g	lean boneless pork	8 oz
225 g	salt beef, cooked	8 oz
	1 medium onion, peeled and quartered	
	1 teaspoon fresh parsley, chopped	
	3 tablespoons fat	
240 g	flour	8½ oz
	1 teaspoon dry mustard	
	1 teaspoon salt	
½ l	milk	18 fl oz
1 kg	sauerkraut, cooked, drained and finely chopped	2 lb
	2 eggs, slightly beaten	

Mince the meats and onion. Add the parsley and blend well. Heat the fat in a large frying pan. Add the meat mixture and sauter until browned. Add the flour, mustard, salt, milk, eggs and sauerkraut. Blend well. Cook over medium heat, stirring constantly, until thick. Cool and form into balls about the size of a walnut. Pour oil to a depth of 5 cm (2 in) into a deep fryer or heavy saucepan and heat to about 190°C (375°F). Fry the sauerkraut balls a few at a time for about 2 minutes, until browned. Drain on paper towels. Serve hot on a warmed dish. This dish is an excellent appetiser and a good way to use left-over meat.

(Hermann Rusch, USA)

Cauliflower and ham au gratin
Choux-fleurs au jambon gratinés
Květák so šunkou zapečený

6 portions   Cooking time: 1 hour

1 kg 500	cauliflower	3 lb 5 oz
	salt	
400 g	cooked ham	14 oz
	OR cooked Kasseler	
	3 egg yolks	

⅛ l	dairy cream	4 fl oz
20 g	breadcrumbs	¾ oz
40 g	Parmesan cheese, grated	1½ oz
30 g	butter	1 oz
50 g	breadcrumbs	2 oz
50 g	butter for soufflé mould	2 oz

Clean the cauliflower, cook in salted water, keeping it firm, and divide into sprigs. Chop the ham finely. Butter a soufflé mould and sprinkle with breadcrumbs. Fill with alternate layers of cauliflower and ham, finishing with cauliflower. Beat the egg yolks and cream together, season with salt and pour over the cauliflower. Sprinkle with grated cheese and breadcrumbs, dot with butter and bake at 225–250°C (437–482°F) for 40 to 50 minutes to brown the top well.

(Vilèm Vrabec, Czechoslovakia)

Baked pasta with ham I
Gratin de nouilles au jambon
Schinkenfleckerl

4 portions

300 g	pasta squares	11 oz
	OR ribbon noodles	
80 g	butter	3 oz
160 g	cooked ham, finely diced	6 oz
	4 eggs (separated)	
1¼ dl	sour cream	4 fl oz
	salt, pepper	
	marjoram	
20 g	butter to grease dish	¾ oz
20 g	butter for topping	¾ oz
20 g	breadcrumbs	¾ oz
30 g	Parmesan, grated	1 oz

Cook the pasta in boiling salted water for about 8 minutes. Drain and rinse well in cold water. Cream the butter and work in the egg yolks and sour cream a little at a time. Add salt, pepper and marjoram to taste. Mix with the ham and pasta. Whip the egg whites to a stiff snow with a pinch of salt and fold in. Butter a shallow fireproof dish and sprinkle with breadcrumbs. Fill with the pasta and ham mixture, sprinkle with grated Parmesan and melted butter and bake at 200°C (392°F) for about 20 minutes to a golden brown colour. Serve in the same dish, cut into portions. Fresh green salad is recommended as an accompaniment.

(Ernst Faseth, Austria)

Baked pasta with ham II
Gratin de nouilles au jambon
Sonkaskocka

4 portions   Cooking time: about 25–30 minutes

Pasta dough:

	2 eggs	
500 g	flour	1 lb 2 oz
	water	
	salt	
100 g	lard	3½ oz
2 dl	sour cream	7 fl oz
200 g	smoked ham, finely cut	7 oz
	3 egg yolks	
	3 egg whites, stiffly whipped	
	2 good pinches freshly ground pepper	
	salt	
	2 tablespoons flour for dusting dish	

Prepare a firm noodle dough, pin out thinly and cut into small squares or finger thick noodles. Cook in salted water. Cream 80 g (3 oz) lard and beat in the eggs until smooth. Carefully stir in the ham and the sour cream, season with salt and pepper, add the cooked pasta and lastly fold in the very stiffly whipped egg whites. Grease an ovenproof dish with the rest of the lard and dust with flour. Fill with the pasta and ham mixture and bake in a moderate oven for about 25 to 30 minutes to a golden brown colour.

(László Csizmadia, Hungary)

Deep-fried ham pancakes
Crêpes au jambon frites
Rantott sonkás palacsinta

4 portions   Cooking time: 10–12 minutes

	8 pancakes	
320 g	cooked ham	11 oz
	2 egg yolks	
1½ dl	sour cream	5 fl oz
	a good pinch freshly ground pepper	
	2 eggs	
200 g	white breadcrumbs	7 oz
3 dl	oil	10 fl oz
4 dl	tomato sauce	14 fl oz

Pancakes:
Yield: 10

150 g	flour	5 oz
	2 eggs	
2 dl	milk	7 fl oz
	a good pinch of salt	
1 dl	mineral water	3½ fl oz
1 dl	oil	3½ fl oz

Cut up the ham finely. Mix with the sour cream and egg yolks and season with salt and pepper. Fill the cooked pancakes with this mixture, fold the ends over to enclose the filling well and roll up. Coat with beaten egg and white breadcrumbs and deep fry in hot oil until golden on both sides. Serve on a well-heated dish and hand well-seasoned tomato sauce separately.

To make the pancakes, prepare a smooth batter with the flour, eggs, milk, mineral water and salt. Heat a tablespoonful of oil in a pancake pan and pour in a little batter at a time to make 10 small pancakes.

(László Csizmadia, Hungary)

Ham roll
Roulade de jambon
Sonká terkecs

4 portions   Cooking time: about 10 minutes

	6 egg yolks	
	6 egg whites	
250 g	flour	9 oz
10 g	salt	⅓ oz
300 g	cooked ham	11 oz
20 g	flour	¾ oz
20 g	butter	¾ oz
2 dl	milk	7 fl oz
	grated nutmeg	
	a good pinch freshly ground pepper	
	2 egg yolks	

Eger sauce (Egri martas):

4 dl	brown sauce	14 fl oz
	Eger bull's blood (red wine)	
2 cl	Cognac	1 fl oz

Whisk 6 egg yolks with a little salt until foamy. Mix with the flour and fold in the stiffly whipped egg whites. Spread evenly to the thickness of one finger on a baking sheet lined with parchment paper. Bake in even heat for about 10 minutes. Prepare a thick Béchamel sauce with 20 g (¾ oz) each flour and butter and 2 dl (7 fl oz) milk, season with nutmeg and mix with the ham which has been finely minced. Add 2 egg yolks, season with pepper and spread on the sponge while still warm. Roll up and slice. Serve with Eger sauce.

To make the sauce, mix the brown sauce with Eger bull's blood and bring to the boil. Add the Cognac and boil again. The total cooking time for the sauce is 10 to 12 minutes.

(László Csizmadia, Hungary)

Bombay butterflies

8 portions

500 g	veal, medium minced	1 lb
500 g	onions, chopped	1 lb
	1 tablespoon garlic, finely chopped	
	2 tablespoons fresh ginger, chopped	
	1 tablespoon curry powder	
	1 tablespoon garam masala	
	1 tablespoon tomato purée	
	1 tablespoon meat glaze	
	½ tablespoon Indian chilli powder	
	½ tablespoon ground cardamom	
	1 teaspoon ground cinnamon	
5 g	saffron	⅙ oz
200 g	clear butter	7 oz
5 cl	olive oil	2 fl oz

Pastry:

1 kg	fine flour	2 lb 4 oz
200 g	melted butter	7 oz
	salt to taste	
	water	

Heat the butter and oil in a well-tinned thick-bottomed copper pan and fry the onions until lightly coloured. Add the meat, stirring constantly, then the spices, tomato purée, meat glaze and salt to taste. Cook for a few minutes and set aside.

Make a soft dough with the flour, butter, salt and water. Divide into pieces the size of dinner rolls. Pin out and cut into rectangles 15 x 5 cm (6 x 2 in). Place a tablespoon of the filling in the centre of each and fold over into a triangle to enclose the filling. Seal with a little pastry. Fry the butterflies in oil at 160°C (320°F) to a crisp golden brown. Serve with mint chutney or plain yoghourt whipped and blended with chopped onion.
(Illustration, page 695)

(Percy Sullivan, India)

Tuscan toast
Croûtes à la toscane
Crostini casalinghi alla toscana

200 g	chicken livers	7 oz
100 g	butter	3½ oz
30 g	capers	1 oz
50 g	pickled gherkins and onions	2 oz
200 g	calf's milt	7 oz
30 g	anchovy paste	1 oz
	1 onion, sliced	
	1 stick celery, cut in pieces	
	2 tablespoons parsley, chopped	
1 dl	dry white wine	3½ fl oz
	bread	
	bouillon	

Brown the onion and celery in the butter with the addition of the parsley. Add the chicken livers and the milt which has been skinned and cut in pieces. Fry gently for about 30 minutes, add the capers, pickled gherkins and onions, anchovy paste and wine, stir well and cook for a further 10 minutes. Remove from the heat and pass through the finest blade of the mincer or work to a smooth purée in the processor. Cut household bread in slices ½ cm (about ¼ in) thick, toast or fry them, dip quickly in bouillon and spread with the purée. Serve lukewarm if possible, accompanied by a dry white wine. This is a classic Tuscan hors d'oeuvre which is often served with raw ham or Tuscan sausage (recipe, page 979).

(Mario De Filippis, Italy)

Spinach and mushroom slices
Florentiner Schnitten mit Champignons

800 g	puff pastry	1 lb 12 oz
600 g	leaf spinach, blanched	1 lb 5 oz
	oil and butter	
20 g	shallots, finely chopped	¾ oz
300 g	mushrooms, finely sliced	11 oz
1 dl	dairy cream	3½ fl oz
200 g	Parmesan cheese, grated	7 oz
	seasonings to taste	

Pin out the pastry to a rectangle 3 mm (⅛ in) thick and cut in 10 x 6 cm (4 x 2½ in) oblongs. Cover with the spinach which has been squeezed dry. Cook the shallots gently in oil and butter without colouring, add the mushrooms and seasoning, stew for a short time, then pour

Stuffed leg of lamb en croûte, p. 727▶

Ribs of beef with pine kernels and green pepper au gratin, p. 511

Tongue and brains with spring vegetables, p. 955

Tournedos with lavender honey and thyme, p. 446

Fillet of beef with leek and onion sauce, p. 409

◄ Sauté fillet of beef with artichokes, p. 509
▼ Knuckle of veal with oranges and Rosé de Provence, p. 615

310

Calf's sweetbreads with three sauces; calf's kidneys and sweetbreads on endives with white truffles; mignons of veal with onions on raw spinach; sweetbreads Vincent, pp. 661, 668, 659, 667 ►

◄ Pickled leg of pork with cider vinegar sauce, p. 860
▼ Shoulder of lamb with passion fruit; lamb fillet with candied garlic, pp. 749, 756

312

Lamb's tongue Indian style; stuffed artichokes and lamb fillet with rosemary; lamb fillet Van Dijck; lamb offal with mushrooms, pp. 786, 1007, 756, 757, 275 ►

in the cream and reduce a little. Spread on the spinach, sprinkle with Parmesan and bake in a medium oven.

(Otto Ledermann, Switzerland)

Chopped pork in pie pastry
Jambon haché en croûte
Ham gehakt in deeg gebakken

4 portions

600 g	lean pork, chopped	1 lb 5 oz
	2 eggs	
50 g	shallots, finely chopped	2 oz
4 cl	dairy cream	1½ fl oz
50 g	breadcrumbs	2 oz
	salt	
	pepper, freshly ground	
	nutmeg, grated	
	pie pastry (recipe, page 143)	
	tomato sauce	

Carefully mix the pork with the egg, shallots, breadcrumbs and cream. Add salt, pepper and nutmeg to taste. Shape into a ham and chill well. Insert a well cleaned chicken bone into the centre, enclose completely in pie pastry and bake quickly in a hot oven. Hand tomato sauce separately.

(Bernard van Beurten, Netherlands)

Pork tamales
Quenelles de porc à la mexicaine
Tamales con carne de cerdo

6–10 portions

1 kg	tamales flour (available commercially)	2 lb 4 oz
500 g	cornflour	1 lb 2 oz
250 g	rice flour	9 oz
	¼ teaspoon baking powder	
150 g	lard or butter	5 oz
	bouillon	
	corn husks or parchment paper	
500 g	roast pork	1 lb 2 oz
	mole (Mexican sauce) (recipe, page 179)	

Cut the pork into very thin strips. Mix the lard, flour, baking powder and bouillon to a firm paste in the mixer, but do not mix for more than 5 minutes to avoid toughening the paste. Using a tablespoon, divide the paste into pieces the size of an egg. Wrap these round the strips of meat, shape into cones and enclose in preserved corn husks or parchment paper cut to size. Cook for about 10 to 15 minutes in a pressure cooker. Serve masked with mole.

(Emil Wälti, Mexico)

Meat balls Norwegian style
Fricadelles de porc à la norvégienne
Medisterkaker

8–10 portions   Cooking time: about 15 minutes

1 kg	shoulder or leg of pork	2 lb 4 oz
250 g	shoulder of beef	9 oz
	2 teaspoons salt	
	1 teaspoon freshly ground pepper	
	½ teaspoon ginger	
	3 tablespoons potato flour	
½ l	cold milk	18 fl oz
½ l	stock or water	18 fl oz

Trim the meat and mince finely several times. Add the salt, pepper and ginger and mix very carefully with the potato flour. Gradually add the milk. If desired, 2 or 3 eggs may be mixed with the milk before adding, to make the mixture firmer. With the help of a tablespoon, shape the mixture into balls each weighing about 80 g (3 oz) and fry in butter on all sides to brown well. Remove and place in a roasting tin, add about ½ l (18 fl oz) stock or water and cook uncovered in an oven preheated to 200°C (392°F). To serve, dress on a warmed dish. Thicken the cooking liquid with a little potato flour and hand separately. This is a popular Norwegian Christmas dish.

(Otto Ramsbacher, Norway)

Spaghetti Hungarian fashion
Spaghetti à la hongroise
Spaghetti magaarosan

10 portions   Cooking time: 30 minutes

1 kg	spaghetti	2 lb 4 oz
100 g	smoked bacon	3½ oz
100 g	lard	3½ oz

OR 1 dl	oil	3½ fl oz
800 g	shoulder of veal, boned	1 lb 12 oz
200 g	onions, finely chopped	7 oz
40 g	salt	1½ oz
20 g	paprika	¾ oz
150 g	yellow peppers	5 oz
150 g	tomatoes, sliced	5 oz
200 g	Parmesan cheese, grated	7 oz

Dice the bacon finely and fry in lard or oil until transparent. Add the onions and fry until lightly coloured. Sprinkle with the paprika and cook for a few seconds. Add the veal which has been cut in pea-size pieces, season with salt, cover and stew until half cooked. Add the tomatoes, together with the peppers which have been washed, seeded and cut in rings. Mix well, cover again and stew until all the ingredients are cooked.

Cook the spaghetti *al dente* in salted water. Rinse in cold water and drain well. In Hungary spaghetti are dipped in hot water and well drained before serving. Transfer to a fireproof dish and cover with the meat sauce. Sprinkle with Parmesan and stand in a hot oven for a few minutes. Decorate if desired with sliced tomatoes and seeded peppers cut in rings. Serve very hot. The grated cheese may be handed separately if desired.

(Zsolt Körmendy, Hungary)

Pasta spirals gourmet style
Spirales du gourmet
Spirali de buongustaio

4 portions

250 g	canned peeled tomatoes (including juice)	9 oz
approx. 50 g	smoked fat pork or bacon, approx. cut in 3 slices	2 oz
approx. 50 g	ham, cut in 3 slices approx.	2 oz
	4 tablespoons fresh or canned peas	
10 g	butter	⅓ oz
	2 cloves of garlic	
	1 medium onion	
	1 bouquet garni made up of rosemary sage bay leaf	
350 g	pasta spirals	12 oz
5 cl	white wine	2 fl oz

Cut the onion into very fine julienne strips and brown in butter together with the garlic and bouquet garni. Add the ham and pork or bacon which have been cut in thin strips, brown lightly, moisten with the wine, add the tomatoes and peas and mix carefully. Cook over low heat for 30 minutes. Add little, if any, salt as the meat is salty.

Cook the pasta *al dente* in lightly salted water, drain well and mix with the sauce in a warm dish. Sprinkle with Parmesan and serve at once. Instead of spirals, noodles or any other pasta except spaghetti may be mixed with the sauce.

(Sergio Chiesa, Italy)

Toast Aix-les-Bains

10 portions

	10 slices bread for toasting	
1½ l	mushroom sauce	2¾ pt
400 g	cooked ham	14 oz
500 g	Fontina (or Emmental) cheese	1 lb
	parsley	

Toast the bread. Cut the ham and cheese in slices of the same size. Place the toast on warm plates and coat with mushroom sauce. Cover first with a slice of ham, then with a slice of cheese and brown under a salamander. Decorate with parsley.

(Manfred Wyler, Switzerland)

Toast Caroline

10 portions

	10 slices bread for toasting	
400 g	ham, cut into 20 slices	14 oz
1 kg	leaf spinach	2 lb 4 oz
100 g	butter	3½ oz
1½ l	Mornay sauce (recipe, page 171)	2¾ pt
	parsley	

Cut the slices of bread in half and toast. Cover the slices of ham with the spinach which has been blanched and stewed in butter. Roll up and keep hot. To serve, place a ham and spinach roll on each half round of toast, mask with Mornay sauce, brown under a salamander and decorate with parsley.

(Manfred Wyler, Switzerland)

Toast Colombo

10 portions

500 g	bread for toasting	1 lb 2 oz
1 kg	neck of pork	2 lb 4 oz
	OR cushion of veal	
	Aromat	
	flour	
	4 eggs	
	10 bananas	
1 dl	oil	3½ fl oz
	10 cherries, stoned	
1½ l	curry sauce (recipe, page 176)	2¾ pt
	10 lettuce leaves	
	10 slices tomato	
	parsley	
	salt and pepper	

Cut the bread into 10 slices and cut each one across into 2 triangles. Toast the bread. Cut the meat into 20 escalopes, flour, season with salt, pepper and Aromat and coat with egg. Fry in oil. Place 2 triangles of toast on each plate (well warmed) and cover each triangle with an escalope. Mask with curry sauce and decorate with 2 half bananas browned in butter and a stewed cherry. Garnish with a lettuce leaf, slice of tomato and parsley.

(Manfred Wyler, Switzerland)

Toast Bordelaise

1 portion

	1 small teaspoon onion, finely chopped	
	2 teaspoons parsley, chopped	
	1 slice bread for toasting	
10 g	butter	⅓ oz
	beef marrow, sliced	
	Bordelaise sauce (recipe, page 156)	
	pepper	
	chives, chopped	

Mix together the onion and parsley, cook gently in butter and spread on toast. Cover with slices of beef marrow, mask with Bordelaise sauce, sprinkle with freshly ground pepper and decorate the centre with chives.
(Illustration, page 415)

(Felix Real, Liechtenstein)

Toast Simmental

10 portions

	10 slices bread for toasting	
800 g	cooked pig's tongue	1 lb 12 oz
OR 890 g	raw pig's tongue	2 lb
	water	
	spices, bouquet garni	
12 dl	Madeira sauce (recipe, page 158)	2 pt
	parsley, chopped	

Blanch the tongue in stock and cook, then leave in the stock to cool. Peel, slice very thinly in lengths and stand in a warm place. Toast the bread, arrange the slices of tongue evenly on top and mask with Madeira sauce. Sprinkle with parsley.

(Manfred Wyler, Switzerland)

Stuffed tomatoes and peppers Macedonian style
Tomates et poivrons doux farcis á la macédonienne
Punjeni Paradajz i Paprike

6 portions   Cooking time: about 40–50 minutes

250 g	beef (shoulder cut)	9 oz
250 g	shoulder of pork	9 oz
2 dl	oil	7 fl oz
	4 red peppers	
1 kg	tomatoes	2 lb 4 oz
	parsley, finely chopped	
	pepper, freshly ground	
	salt	
	1 onion, chopped	
50 g	rice	2 oz
	3 eggs	
2½ dl	sour milk (see page 147)	9 fl oz
	OR sour cream	
	1 tablespoon flour	
	butter	

Cut the peppers open at the stalk end, then carefully remove the seeds and fibres. Blanch in boiling water and invert on a colander to drain and cool. Cut off the tops of the tomatoes, hollow out a little with a teaspoon and reserve the flesh. Cook the rice in salted water. Fry the onion lightly in oil without colouring.

Mince the meat. Mix well with the onion, cooked rice, egg and parsley and season with salt and pepper. Fill into the peppers and tomatoes and place in a greased fireproof casserole. Make a fairly thin roux with oil and the flour, mix with the flesh removed from the tomatoes and pour over the stuffed peppers and tomatoes. Place a small knob of butter on each one and bake in a moderate oven for about 40 minutes. Before serving, mix together the sour milk and eggs, pour over the stuffed vegetables and brown lightly in the oven.

(László Csizmadia, Yugoslavia)

Stuffed tomatoes Veronese style
Tomates farcies à la véronèse
Pomodori ripieni al forno

6 portions   Cooking time: 20–30 minutes

	6 medium tomatoes	
60 g	dried flap mushrooms	2 oz
	½ onion	
	1 clove of garlic	
300–350 g	pork frying sausage, skinned	11–12 oz
	12 slices Mozzarella cheese	
	parsley, chopped	
	a little flour	
	8 tablespoons olive oil	

Soak the flap mushrooms in lukewarm water, squeeze dry and chop finely. Cut the onion, garlic and sausage finely and brown lightly in the oil, add the mushrooms, season with salt and pepper and cook over low heat for 15 minutes. Add the parsley and a little flour to thicken. Wash the tomatoes, cut in half horizontally, hollow out, season lightly and fill with the sausage mixture. Cut the cheese into semicircles of the same diameter as the tomatoes and place one on each stuffed half tomato to cover half the surface. Oil a fireproof dish, arrange the tomatoes in it and cook in a hot oven (200–210°C/392–410°F).

(Mario Saporito, Italy)

Masked tomatoes Czech fashion
Tomates enrobées à la tchèque
Rajčata zapečená v sekané

6 portions   Cooking time: about 30 minutes

	6 medium-size firm tomatoes	
350 g	beef (preferably a hind-quarters cut)	12 oz
250 g	fat pork	9 oz
	1 egg	

	2 bread rolls	
OR 100 g	white bread	3½ oz
¼ l	milk	9 fl oz
	salt	
1 g	pepper	a pinch
	a good pinch of marjoram	
	1 tablespoon fresh parsley, finely chopped	
20 g	onion, diced	¾ oz
110 g	lard	4 oz
	2 tablespoons water	
30 g	breadcrumbs	1 oz
	bouillon	

Garnish:

pickled cucumbers
radishes
lettuce

Wash and dry the tomatoes, prick the skin several times with a needle and season with salt and pepper. Trim and wash the meat, mince twice, transfer to a bowl, season with salt and pepper, add the water and mix well. Brown the onion lightly in 30 g (1 oz) lard and add to the meat together with the egg, the rolls which have been soaked in milk, squeezed dry and sieved or minced, and the parsley. Mix thoroughly, adding breadcrumbs if not firm enough. Divide into six portions, enclose a tomato in each, press firmly in place and coat with breadcrumbs. Place in a roasting tin, pour over the rest of the lard which has been heated and cook in the oven at 220°C (428°F) for about 30 minutes, basting from time to time and adding a little bouillon if necessary. Transfer to a serving dish and garnish with pickled cucumbers, radishes and lettuce. Pour away the fat remaining in the roasting tin, add a little bouillon to detach the meat juices, blend in 20 g (¾ oz) butter, boil for a moment, season with salt to taste and strain. Pour a little of the hot gravy over the disguised tomatoes and hand the rest in a sauce boat. The tomatoes may be served hot or cold.

(Vilèm Vrabec, Czechoslovakia)

Hot hors d'oeuvre Ristorante Bianchi

3 portions

3 slices bread (tin or sandwich loaf)
1 slice cooked ham
1 slice Gruyère or Fontina cheese
2 tablespoons mushrooms in cream sauce

2 slices Mozzarella cheese
2 tablespoons very thick Mornay sauce
  (made with Emmental, Gruyère or
   Tilsit cheese)
flour
2 eggs
oil

Cut one slice of bread into six rectangles. Cut the Mozzarella cheese to the same size and impale on silver or wooden skewers alternately with the bread. Cut the second slice of bread in half, toast and cover with the mushrooms (mushroom canapés). Cut two identical rounds out of the third slice of bread. Cut two disks of Gruyère or Fontina cheese and a disk of ham of the same size. Cover one round of bread with a disk of cheese, then the ham, then another disk of cheese and lastly the remaining round of bread. Dip into beaten egg and fry quickly on both sides (croque-monsieur).

Thicken the Mornay sauce sufficiently to make it set when cold. When it has set, cut out small rounds, dip into milk and beaten egg and deep fry in oil, to make cheese balls. Place the skewers, mushroom canapés and croque-monsieur in a fireproof dish and brown lightly under a salamander. Serve very hot together with the cheese balls.

(Giulio Casazza, Switzerland)

Greek stuffed vine leaves
Feuilles de vigne farcies ou dolmas à la grecque
Dolmades

4–6 portions

500 g	minced meat (mixed)	1 lb
100 g	onions, chopped	3½ oz
	3 tablespoons butter	
100 g	rice, washed	3½ oz
	3 tablespoons parsley, chopped	
	48 vine leaves, fresh or canned	
	aniseed, salt, pepper	
	Avgolémono sauce	
	(recipe, page 176)	

Fry the onions lightly in 2 tablespoons butter without colouring, add the meat, rice and parsley and brown lightly. Add 2 dl (7 fl oz) water, season with salt and pepper, flavour to taste with aniseed, cover and cook gently for 10 minutes. Allow to cool and adjust the seasoning if necessary.

Blanch the vine leaves, allow to cool, dry with a cloth and spread on the table. Cut away the thick ribs. Place a teaspoonful of meat and rice filling on each leaf and roll up to enclose the filling, tucking in the ends. (If the leaves are small, use two for each roll). Arrange in a greased braising pan, add 1 tablespoon butter and 2 cups water, cover and stew gently for 40 minutes. Dress the stuffed vine leaves on a dish, mask with Avgolémono sauce and serve very hot.

(Emil Wälti, Greece)

Stuffed vine leaves Macedonian style
Feuilles de vigne farcies à la macédonienne
Sarma od Lisčá Vinove Loze

6 portions   Cooking time: about 30 minutes

500 g	shoulder of lamb or veal, minced	1 lb
2 dl	oil	7 fl oz
80 g	rice	3 oz
	1 small onion, chopped	
	30 large young vine leaves	
	1 egg	
	1 tablespoon flour	
	1 bunch dill, finely chopped	
½ l	water	18 fl oz
2 dl	white wine	7 fl oz
	red paprika	
	salt	
	pepper, freshly ground	
2 dl	sour milk (see page 147)	7 fl oz

Fry the onion lightly in 5 cl (2 fl oz) oil without colouring and remove from the heat. Boil the rice until half cooked, then mix with the onion, meat, egg and dill. Season with salt and pepper.

Wash the vine leaves carefully. Pour boiling salted water over them and leave until soft. Drain on a colander. Place a teaspoonful of the meat/rice filling in the centre of each vine leaf and shape into small rolls 3 cm (1¼ in) long and 2 cm (¾ in) wide. Pack upright in a saucepan, pour in the water and simmer over very low heat for about 30 minutes. Make a roux with 1 tablespoon flour and the rest of the oil, season with a good pinch of paprika, blend in a little water and pour over the stuffed vine leaves evenly.

On no account should the stuffed vine leaves be stirred while cooking. Instead, the pan should be carefully shaken now and then. Pour the wine over just before serving. Hand sour milk separately.

(László Csizmadia, Yugoslavia)

Stuffed onions Bosnian fashion
Oignons farcis à la bosnienne
Solgan-Dolma

6 portions   Cooking time: 1 hour

	6 large onions	
500 g	shoulder of mutton	1 lb
30 g	rice, blanched	1 oz
1 dl	oil	3½ fl oz
1 dl	water	3½ fl oz
150 g	kajmak (see page 147)	5 oz
	1 tablespoon flour	
	1 tablespoon tomato purée	
	1 tablespoon vinegar	
	finely ground hot red paprika	

Skin the onions and blanch in boiling water. Cut off the tops and hollow out carefully. Reserve the tops. Mince the meat, mix with the rice and season with salt and pepper. Fill into the onions, replace the tops and arrange in a fireproof tableware dish.

Make a roux with the oil and flour, add the tomato purée, the kajmak and a little hot water and pour over the stuffed onions. Cook slowly for 40 to 50 minutes, adding vinegar towards the end of the cooking time to keep the onions whole.

(László Csizmadia, Yugoslavia)

Stuffed onions Makó
Oignons farcis Makó
Makói töltött hagyma

10 portions   Cooking time: 45 minutes

	boneless shoulder or leg of pork	2 lb 4 oz
1 kg	boneless shoulder or leg of pork	2 lb 4 oz
	20 medium onions 5–6 cm (2 in) across	
	2 bread rolls	
	2 eggs	
100 g	lard	3½ oz
OR 1 dl	oil	3½ fl oz
100 g	butter	3½ oz
	1 bunch parsley, finely chopped	

Mornay sauce:

(1 l 1¾ pt)

60 g	butter	2 oz
50 g	flour	2 oz
¾ l	milk	27 fl oz
20 g	salt	¾ oz
5 g	Cayenne pepper	⅙ oz
5 g	nutmeg, grated	⅙ oz
	4 egg yolks	
1 dl	dairy cream	3½ fl oz
80 g	Parmesan cheese, grated	3 oz

Skin the onions and cut off the tops. Hollow out with a round vegetable scoop, leaving a narrow rim. Chop the meat finely. Remove the crusts from the rolls and soak in milk. Finely chop the flesh removed from the onions and fry in lard or oil until lightly coloured. Mix well with the meat, the rolls which have been squeezed dry and the parsley. Season with salt and pepper and fill into the onions. Arrange in a buttered casserole, pour in a little water or bouillon, bring to the boil, cover and cook in the oven until soft. Transfer to a fireproof serving dish, pour the Mornay sauce over, sprinkle with a little melted butter and return to the oven until a golden crust has formed.

To prepare the sauce, make a blond roux with the butter and flour. Whisk in the milk which has been heated. Season with salt, Cayenne and nutmeg and cook slowly over low heat. Season with salt, Cayenne and nutmeg and cook slowly over low heat. Pass through a tammy cloth and bind with the cream which has been mixed with the egg yolks, but do not return to the heat. Fold in the cheese with a wooden spoon.

(Zsolt Körmendy, Hungary)

Stuffed onions Halasch
Oignons farcis Halasch
Halasi töltött hagyma

10 portions   Cooking time: 45 minutes

1 kg	boneless shoulder of veal	2 lb 4 oz
	20 medium onions 5–6 cm (2 in) across	
200 g	lard	7 oz
OR 2 dl	oil	7 fl oz
50 g	salt	2 oz
3 g	black pepper, freshly ground	a good pinch
10 g	garlic, crushed	⅓ oz
400 g	smoked fat pork or bacon	14 oz
1 l	sour cream	1¾ pt
	1 bunch parsley, finely chopped	
	paprika	

Skin the onions and cut off the tops. Hollow out with a round vegetable scoop, leaving a narrow rim. Blanch in salted water, but keep the onions very firm, then remove, invert on a cloth, allow to drain, dry and fill with the meat filling (see below). Place in a buttered fireproof dish. Cover each onion with a thin slice of fat pork or streaky bacon, coat with sour cream, sprinkle with a little paprika and brown the top in the oven.

To prepare the filling, chop the flesh removed from the onions and fry in lard or oil until lightly coloured. Add the garlic, the veal cut into small cubes, salt and pepper and fry lightly for a few minutes. Add the parsley and stew without adding liquid until the meat is cooked. Chop the meat finely and mix with the cooking juices.

(Zsolt Körmendy, Hungary)

Avocado Mokolo

4 portions

	2 avocados	
1 dl	bouillon	3½ fl oz
50 g	lean smoked bacon	2 oz
	1 clove of garlic	

Chop the garlic very finely. Cut the bacon in very thin strips and blanch in the bouillon. Cut the avocados in half along the length, remove the stones and fill the hollows with bouillon containing the bacon.

(Silvio Ballinari, Cameroon)

Savouries to Accompany Wine and Beer

Filled rolls

Yield: 10 rolls

100 g	10 rolls each weighing	4 oz
80 g	butter	3 oz
15 g	mustard (for butter)	½ oz
2 cl	water	1 fl oz
	salt	
	pepper, freshly ground	
100 g	salted cucumbers	4 oz
150 g	lettuce	5 oz
	4 eggs, hard-boiled	
1½ dl	mayonnaise (for eggs)	5 fl oz
	Aromat	
300 g	left-over meat (roast or boiled)	11 oz
300 g	left-over ham or pickled tongue	11 oz
½ dl	mayonnaise (for meat)	2 fl oz
20 g	mustard (for dressing)	¾ oz
150 g	tomatoes, skinned	5 oz

Split the rolls. Cream the butter, mustard and water, season with salt and pepper and spread on the rolls. Cut the salted cucumbers and the lettuce in thin strips. Dice the eggs. Dress with mayonnaise and season with Aromat and pepper. Cover the lower half of each roll with this salad, reserving half of it for later use.

Cut the meat into thin strips about 2 cm (¾ in) long. Mix the mayonnaise and mustard together, then mix with the meat and place on the salad-covered rolls. Slice the tomatoes thinly and arrange on the meat. Season with Aromat and cover lightly with the remaining salad. Place the other half of the rolls on top and press down lightly. Wrap the filled rolls in plastic film and place on the table to provide a substantial snack.

(Haco, Switzerland)

Alsatian surprise loaf
Pain, vin et fantaisie

20 portions

Filling I:

1 knuckle of veal, boned
1 knuckle of pork, boned
5 shallots, peeled and thinly sliced

	5 cloves of garlic	
200 g	parsley	7 oz
500 g	smoked fat pork or bacon, cut in strips	1 lb 2 oz
	1 sprig thyme	
	about 10 rosemary leaves	
7 dl–1 l	Alsatian Tokay	1¼–1¾ pt
4 kg	bread dough (1 kg for 5 portions)	9 lb

Filling II:

500 g	smoked fat pork or bacon, cut in thin strips	1 lb 2 oz
120 g	fillet of veal, finely diced	4 oz
240 g	fillet of pork, finely diced	8 oz
320 g	fillet of lamb, finely diced	11 oz
	1 carrot, finely diced	
	1 leek, finely diced	
	1 red pepper, finely diced	
	1 green pepper, finely diced	

Liaison:

	6 eggs	
1 dl	dairy cream	3½ fl oz
	nutmeg, salt, pepper	

Cut the meat for *Filling I* in small pieces, place in a pan with the strips of fat pork or bacon and brown lightly, then add the shallots, garlic, parsley, thyme, rosemary leaves, salt and pepper. Stir in the wine and cook over very low heat for 2 to 2½ hours. Mash well with a fork and add the ingredients for *Filling II* which have been browned together just before they are required. Blend together the ingredients for the liaison and stir into the filling. Mix well and adjust the seasoning. Enclose in bread dough, shape into a loaf and bake off. In Alsace the meat filling is taken to the baker, who provides the bread dough and bakes the loaf. (Illustration, page 520).

(Jean Esslinger, France)

Viennese snack meal

8 portions

400 g	roast ribs of pork	14 oz
400 g	salmon-ham	14 oz
400 g	collared pork	14 oz
400 g	pressed ham	14 oz
400 g	Tilsit cheese	14 oz

Garnish:

800 g	mixed pickles	1 lb 12 oz
	8 radishes	
	2 heads of chicory	
	4 tomatoes	
	1 lettuce	
	3 green peppers	
	4 eggs, hard-boiled	

Cut the meat and cheese in thin slices and arrange on a flat plate. Place the pickles on a lettuce leaf next to the meat. Seed the peppers and slice finely, divide each tomato in eight and each egg in half. Arrange the garnish on the plate as desired.

(Eduard Mayer, Austria)

Cold Hungarian liver sausage
Boudin hongrois froid
Hideg májashurka

10 portions

1 kg	pig's liver	2 lb 4 oz
1 kg	smoked neck of pork	2 lb 4 oz
	2 rolls	
300 g	goose liver	11 oz
200 g	onions, finely cut	7 oz
50 g	lard	2 oz
	2 eggs	
40 g	salt	1½ oz
10 g	pepper, freshly ground	⅓ oz
	1 tablespoon forcemeat flavouring herbs and spices	
	bouillon	

Place half the pig's liver and the smoked pork in a saucepan and pour in sufficient bouillon to cover. Simmer until the liver is cooked. Finely mince the cooked liver and pork twice, together with the rolls which have been soaked and squeezed dry. Fry the onions in lard and mince finely with the raw half of the pig's liver. Dice the goose liver finely and mix with the cooked and raw pig's liver and the eggs. Season with salt, pepper and the herbs and spices. Shape into a sausage and wrap in double cellophane. Tie round carefully, interlacing the twine. Tie off both ends well. Poach for about 30 minutes in well-seasoned bouillon. Chill well. Serve with various salads and cold sauces.

(László Csizmadia, Hungary)

Beef sausage Amsterdam style
Saucisson de boeuf à la façon d'Amsterdam
Osseworst (Amsterdam)

2 kg	lean beef	4 lb 8 oz
500 g	smoked fat pork or bacon	1 lb 2 oz
	peppercorns	
	salt	
	cloves	

Mince all the ingredients finely. Fill into well cleaned sausage casings and smoke in the chimney for 14 days.

(Bernard van Beurten, Netherlands)

Ham focaccia
Galette au jambon de Parme
Focaccia con prosciutto di Parma

1 portion

	1 portion pizza dough (recipe, page 143)	
50 g	Parma ham	2 oz
	1 tablespoon olive oil	

Roll out the dough into a disk 25–30 cm (10–12 in) in diameter. Sprinkle with olive oil and bake. Remove from the oven, cover with the Parma ham which has been cut paper thin, and divide into eight with a sharp knife. Serve at once. Instead of Parma ham, paper thin slices of cooked ham may be used.

(Nico Donato, Italy)

Plated pork in aspic
Aspic de porc en assiette
Tellersülze

8 portions

	4 pig's trotters	
400 g	shoulder of pork	14 oz
2 l	water	3½ pt
⅛ l	vinegar	4 fl oz

40 g	onion	1½ oz
300 g	flavouring vegetables	10 oz
	10 peppercorns	
	4 allspice berries	
	1 small bay leaf	
	thyme	
	salt	

Cook the pig's trotters and shoulder of pork until tender in the water containing all the remaining ingredients. Remove the meat, leave until quite cold, cut in small pieces and divide between 8 plates. Strain the cooking liquid, remove the fat, then pour over the meat and refrigerate until set. Garnish as desired with cucumber, hard-boiled egg, beetroot and horseradish.

(Illustration, page 942)

(Eduard Mayer, Austria)

Canapés Falchetti

10 portions

500 g	forcemeat Falchetti	1 lb
	(recipe, page 132)	
	10 rolled anchovy fillets	
	OR 5 stuffed olives	
	10 slices white bread	
	OR 20 polenta canapé bases	

Cut the slices of bread in half diagonally and toast. Warm the forcemeat in a bain-marie and spread on the toast. Decorate with half an olive or an anchovy fillet and serve lukewarm.

Polenta may be used instead of bread. It is cut cold into 10 x 5 cm (4 x 2 in) oblongs 5 mm (¼ in) thick, fried in butter or browned under a salamander, then spread with the warm forcemeat and served. The lukewarm forcemeat may be spread on crackers to make party savouries.

(Manfred Wyler, Switzerland)

Prague canapés

6 portions   Cooking time: 20 minutes

800 g	boneless pork (shoulder if possible)	1 lb 12 oz
	2 rolls	

OR 100 g	white bread	3½ oz
	1 cup water *or* milk	
	salt	
2 g	sweet paprika, ground	a pinch
1 g	pepper, ground	a small pinch
100 g	lard	3½ oz
OR 1 dl	oil	3½ fl oz
	3 onions, finely chopped	
	3 tablespoons mustard	

Remove the crusts from the rolls, cut them in quarters, soak in water or milk and squeeze dry. Cut the pork in pieces and mince finely with the rolls. Season with salt, pepper and paprika, mix well and shape into 18 flat cakes. Fry quickly in hot fat on both sides until golden brown. Spread the top with mustard and sprinkle with onion. Serve on thinly sliced bread or toast, or arranged on a dish with a garnish of parsley.

(Vilèm Vrabec, Czechoslovakia)

Pizza Donato

1 portion

	1 portion pizza dough	
	(recipe, page 143)	
100 g	veal or pork fillet, cut into 6 thin slices	3½ oz
	2 tablespoons fresh tomatoes,	
	skinned, seeded and finely diced,	
	or canned tomatoes ('pelati')	
50 g	Mozzarella cheese, finely diced	2 oz
	1 clove of garlic, finely chopped	
	2 tablespoons olive oil	
	salt, pepper	
	6 basil leaves	

Lightly fry the garlic in a little olive oil without colouring. Roll out the pizza dough into a disk 25–30 cm (10–12 in) in diameter. Cover with the tomatoes and sprinkle the cheese on top, leaving a border of about 1 cm (⅜ in) round the edge. Season to taste with salt and pepper. Place in a preheated oven. Meanwhile season the slices of meat with salt and pepper and briefly pass through the oil.

When the pizza is half baked, remove from the oven carefully but quickly and cover with the slices of meat, arranging them concentrically. Decorate the meat with the basil leaves. Sprinkle the pizza with the garlic and with oil, then quickly bake off and serve at once.

(Nico Donato, Italy)

Pizza Bismarck

1 portion

	1 portion pizza dough (recipe, page 143)	
100 g	pork frying sausage or minced pork	3½ oz
100 g	Mozzarella cheese, finely diced	3½ oz
10 g	Parmesan cheese, grated	½ oz
	6 basil leaves	
	1 teaspoon olive oil	
	2 tablespoons fresh tomatoes, skinned, seeded and finely diced, or canned tomatoes ('pelati')	
	1 egg	
	salt, pepper	

If using minced pork, first season it with salt and pepper and flavour with chopped thyme. Mix the sausage meat or pork well to a spreading consistency with the Parmesan, tomatoes and olive oil. Add salt and pepper if required.

Roll out the pizza dough into a disk 25–30 cm (10–12 in) in diameter. Sprinkle with the diced Mozzarella and top with a ring of meat mixture, leaving about 1 cm (⅜ in) round the edge and about 6 cm (2½ in) in the centre uncovered. Build up the meat mixture inwards crater fashion so that the uncovered central part of the pizza becomes an empty container. Place the pizza in a preheated oven. When half baked, carefully remove from the oven and break the egg into the centre. Decorate the ring of meat with the basil leaves and return to the oven. Continue baking until the egg is just set. Season it with salt and pepper, and serve at once.

(Nico Donato, Italy)

Meat balls Turkish style
Boulettes de mouton à la turque
Kadin Köfte

5 portions

500 g	mutton		1 lb
50 g	onion, finely chopped		2 oz
50 g	cooked rice		2 oz
	salt, pepper		
	2 eggs		
approx. 5 dl	oil for frying	approx.	1 pt

Mince the meat finely, add the rice, onion, salt and pepper and mix well. Shape into small balls no bigger than 3 cm (1¼ in) across, drop them into boiling salted water and simmer very gently for 25 to 30 minutes once the water has returned to the boil. Transfer the meat balls to a cloth to dry, then dip in beaten egg and deep fry in hot oil until golden. Impale on toothpicks and serve very hot.

(Emil Wälti, Turkey)

Meat pie Vigneron
Pâté vigneron

4–5 portions

250 g	shoulder of pork, free from sinew	9 oz
250 g	shoulder of veal, free from sinew	9 oz
½ dl	white wine	2 fl oz
25 g	shallot, chopped	1 oz
	1 tablespoon parsley, chopped	
	1 tablespoon chervil, chopped	
	pepper	
	nutmeg	
	salt	
	forcemeat flavouring herbs and spices	
500 g	puff pastry	1 lb 2 oz
2½ dl	dairy cream	9 fl oz
	3 egg yolks	

Mince the meat coarsely. Add the wine, shallot, parsley, chervil and other seasonings with the exception of salt. Marinate for 8 hours.

Pin out about two thirds of the pastry into a round base, 24 cm (10 in) across. Season the meat filling with salt to taste and place in the centre of the pastry, flattening it a little. Pin out the rest of the pastry into a round of the same size as the base, lay it over the filling and seal the edges well. Cut a hole in the top. Egg wash and bake for 30 to 35 minutes at 200–225°C (392–437°F). Mix the egg yolks well with the cream and pour into the pie through the hole in the top, then bake for a further 20 to 25 minutes. Serve very hot.

(Emil Wälti, France)

Sausage rolls Basel style
Feuilletés bâlois
Wurstweggen

puff pastry
egg

Filling:

500 g	fat and lean pork	1 lb 2 oz
100 g	white bread, soaked in milk	3½ oz
	salt	
	pepper, freshly ground	
	nutmeg	
	1 onion, finely cut	

Chop or mince the pork finely. Squeeze the bread dry and mix with the meat. Season with salt, pepper and nutmeg and add the onion which has been lightly cooked without colouring. Pin out the pastry to a thickness of about 4 mm (⅛ in) and cut into oblongs 14 x 11 cm (5½ x 4½ in). Wash half of these with egg and pipe on the filling, leaving a 2 cm (¾ in) edge. Cover with the remaining oblongs, pressing the edges together well. Wash the top with egg and bake in a hot oven until golden.

(Otto Ledermann, Switzerland)

Onion tart
Tarte aux oignons
Zwiebelkuchen

500 g	onions, thinly sliced	1 lb 2 oz
100 g	bacon, finely diced	3½ oz
	1 tablespoon flour	
	salt	
	5–6 eggs	
½ l	full cream milk	18 fl oz
	short pastry	

Cook the onions gently with the bacon. Blend the eggs and flour together carefully, adding a little salt. Mix well with the onions and bacon, then stir in the milk. Grease a tart mould and line with short pastry. Fill with the onion and bacon custard and bake until golden yellow in a hot oven. The baking time is 30 to 40 minutes, depending on the thickness of the filling.

(Otto Ledermann, Switzerland)

Onion tartlets Merian
Tartelettes à la Merian
Zwiebeltörtchen Merianische Art

Yield: 16 tartlets

500 g	onions	1 lb 2 oz
200 g	lean bacon	7 oz

10 g	chives	⅓ oz
¼ l	dairy cream	9 fl oz
	4 eggs	
20 g	butter	¾ oz
350 g	puff pastry	12 oz

Dice the bacon finely and chop the onions. Cook together in butter until lightly coloured, then allow to cool. When cold, stir in first the eggs, then the finely chopped chives and then the cream a spoon at a time. Line tartlet pans with puff pastry and divide the filling between them. Bake in a medium oven.

(Otto Ledermann, Switzerland)

Soups

Mock turtle soup
Braune Kalbskopfsuppe (falsche Schildkrötensuppe)

5–6 portions

250 g	calf's head	9 oz
150 g	veal bones	5 oz
	1 onion stuck with a clove	
	1 carrot	
100 g	celery or celeriac	3½ oz
	thyme, parsley	
	salt	
	water	
1 l	thickened brown veal stock	1¾ pt
	1 tablespoon tomato purée	
	infusion: a pinch each of	
	rosemary, basil, marjoram and	
	mushroom trimmings	
	1 teaspoon chervil, finely chopped	
3 cl	sherry	1 fl oz

Blanch the calf's head and veal bones, place in a pan of cold water and bring to the boil. Add the onion, carrot, celery or celeriac, thyme, parsley and salt. Simmer until the calf's head is cooked, then remove it from the pan, cool and cut into small cubes. Pass the cooking liquid through a conical strainer and reduce a little if necessary. Add the veal stock mixed with the tomato purée and bring to the boil.

Meanwhile place the ingredients for the infusion in a little water, boil up with the mushroom trimmings, leave to stand in a warm place for a short time, then strain into the soup. Add the pieces of calf's head and the chopped chervil and check the seasoning. Add the chervil and sherry and serve very hot.

(Emil Wälti, Switzerland)

Consommé with meat balls
Consommé aux quenelles de viande
Kraftbrühe mit Fleischknödeln

10 portions

2 l	consommé	3½ pt
500 g	kosher minced beef	1 lb 2 oz
	(beefburger mince)	
	parsley, chopped	

Shape the minced meat into 20 small balls and poach in salted water. Serve in hot bouillon sprinkled with parsley, allowing 2 meat balls per portion.

(Gérard van Dijk, Switzerland)

Consommé with kreplach
Consommé aux kreplacs
Marak Kreplach (Kisanim)

8 portions   Cooking time: 10 minutes

| 1½ l | consommé | 2¾ pt |

Dough:

400 g	flour	14 oz
	3 egg yolks	
	½ glass water	
	salt	

Filling:

	1 onion	
200 g	cooked veal	7 oz
	oil	
	1 tablespoon breadcrumbs	
	1 egg	
	salt	
	pepper, freshly ground	

Prepare a noodle dough with the flour, egg yolks, water and salt. Leave to rest for 30 minutes. Slice the onion, fry in oil until lightly coloured and remove from the pan. Mince finely with the meat, mix with the egg and breadcrumbs and season with salt and pepper.

Pin out the dough thinly and cut into 7 cm (3 in) squares. Using a savoy bag and plain tube, pipe a little of the filling on to one side of each square. Moisten the edge, fold into a triangle and seal well. Moisten the two acute-angled corners and press together. Cook for 10 minutes in salted water. To serve, pour hot consommé into each plate and add three kreplach.

(Hermann Wohl, Israel)

Consommé with matzo dumplings I
Consommé aux quenelles azymes
Kraftbrühe mit Matzeknödel

10 portions

2 l	consommé	3½ pt
	20 matzo dumplings (page 1024)	
	parsley, chopped	

Heat the soup, add the dumplings and poach gently for 5 minutes. Serve sprinkled with parsley, allowing two dumplings per portion. Individual portions of consommé and matzo dumplings may be heated in a microwave oven.

(Gérard van Dijk, Switzerland)

Consommé with matzo dumplings II
Consommé aux quenelles azymes
Marak im Kaduri Mazza

8 portions   Cooking time: 5 minutes

1½ l	consommé	2¾ pt
	2 matzos	
150 g	matzo meal	5 oz
	2 eggs	
	1 onion	
	oil	
	salt; pepper freshly ground	
	nutmeg	
	parsley, chopped	

Soak the matzos in water and squeeze dry. Dice the onion finely and fry in oil until lightly coloured. Mix well with the matzos, matzo meal, eggs, seasonings and parsley. Mould into balls 2 cm (¾ in) across and poach gently in salted water for 5 minutes. Serve in very hot consommé.

(Hermann Wohl, Israel)

Consommé Serenella

6 portions   Cooking time: 5 hours

4 l	water	7 pt

| 1 kg 100 | oxtail | 2 lb 8 oz |
| 10 g | coarse salt | 1/3 oz |

Garnish:

30 g	radishes	1 oz
30 g	Patna rice	1 oz
10 g	butter	1/3 oz
2 dl	oxtail stock	7 fl oz
2 g	saffron	a good pinch

Cut the oxtail into 10 cm (4 in) pieces, place in a pan with the water and salt, bring to the boil, then cook slowly for 4 hours over low heat, skimming repeatedly. Remove the oxtail when it is cooked, leave until cold, cut off 180 g (6 oz) meat and cut this evenly into 4 mm (1/8 in) cubes. Set aside in 2 l (3½ pt) oxtail stock.

Wash the radishes, slice them very finely and wash and blanch the leaves. Prepare a risotto in the usual manner with the butter, rice, saffron and 2 dl (7 fl oz) or more oxtail stock. Allow to cool and set aside.

To serve, heat the reserved oxtail stock, add the risotto which has been heated separately, then the radishes, and decorate with the blanched radish leaves.
(Illustration, page 411)

(Gualtiero Marchesi, Italy)

Clear oxtail soup
Consommé de queue de boeuf
Klare Ochsenschwanzsuppe

5–6 portions

500 g	oxtail	1 lb 2 oz
	1 calf's foot, cut in half	
100 g	matignon vegetables	3½ oz
1 l	veal stock	1¾ pt
1 l	water *or* bone stock if available	1¾ pt
1 dl	white wine	3½ fl oz
	1 tomato	
	1 egg white	
200 g	shin of beef or lean cow meat, chopped	7 oz
20 g	fat	¾ oz
	brunoise, made up of	
30 g	carrot	1 oz
30 g	celery	1 oz

30 g	turnip	1 oz
	salt, pepper, herbs and spices	
	1 teaspoon chives, finely cut	

Brown the oxtail in the oven, add the calf's foot and brown well, then add the matignon and stir in the wine. Transfer to a large pot. Pour a little water into the pan to detach the juices and add to the pot, together with the veal stock. Season and cook until the oxtail is tender. Remove it from the soup, place on a metal tray, cut off the meat, allow to cool and press flat.

Pass the soup through a cloth. If it is too thin, reduce a little, then leave to cool. Mix the chopped meat with the egg white and water. Add the cold soup. Cook the brunoise separately in water or bouillon and add to the soup. Dice the oxtail meat and add. With careful preparation, there is no need to clarify the soup, but constant skimming is essential (the flavour is better if the soup is unclarified). If desired, flavour with a dash of brandy. Sprinkle with chives and serve very hot.

(Emil Wälti, Switzerland)

Beef bouillon with bone marrow quenelles
Bouillon de boeuf aux quenelles de moelle

Bouillon:

3 l	water	5 pt
1 kg	shin of beef	2 lb 4 oz
250 g	marrow bones	9 oz
	1 onion stuck with a clove	
500 g	beef bones, blanched	1 lb 2 oz
300 g	bouquet garni	10 oz
	salt, pepper	

Bone marrow dumplings:

75 g	white breadcrumbs	2½ oz
125 g	beef marrow	4½ oz
25 g	semolina	1 oz
	2 eggs	
	1 teaspoon parsley, chopped	
	salt, pepper, nutmeg	

Prepare a strong bouillon, cooking the meat until tender. Remove the meat, which may be used elsewhere. To make the dumplings, remove the marrow from the bones and mash with a fork or pass through a fairly coarse sieve. Add the remaining ingredients, seasoning well, and mix thoroughly. Shape into small dumplings with a teaspoon and poach for 8 to 10 minutes in a little bouillon, but do not boil. Drain the dumplings on a cloth. Cool if not required immediately, otherwise pour the boiling bouillon over and serve, sprinkled with finely cut chives if desired.

(Emil Wälti, France)

Brain soup Basel style
Potage de cervelle à la bâloise
Basler Hirnsuppe

10 portions   Cooking time: about 15 minutes

800 g	2 calves' brains weighing	1 lb 12 oz
1 l	water	1¾ pt
1 dl	wine vinegar	3½ fl oz
	1 onion stuck with a clove	
	salt	
100 g	butter	3½ oz
150 g	onions, finely chopped	5 oz
1½ dl	strong light veal stock	5 fl oz
1 l	milk	1¾ pt
60 g	rice flour	2 oz
	salt	
	nutmeg	
	pepper, freshly ground	
20 g	chives, freshly cut	¾ oz
	2 egg yolks	
2 dl	dairy cream	7 fl oz

Soak the brains well, then remove the skin and any splinters of bone. Prepare stock with the water, vinegar, whole onion and salt. Poach the brains in this stock for about 10 minutes. Cook the chopped onions gently in butter without colouring, moisten with the veal stock and add the flour which has been blended with the milk. Cook over low heat for about 15 minutes. Drain the brains well, cut into 1½ cm (⅝ in) dice and add to the soup. Bring to the boil, thicken with the egg yolks and cream, then pour at once into a tureen. Sprinkle with the chives and serve. Croûtons may be handed separately if desired.

(Otto Ledermann, Switzerland)

Wedding soup Prague fashion
Potage de mariage à la pragueoise
Pražská svatebníz polévka

6 portions   Cooking time: 25 minutes (apart from bouillon)

2 l	clear meat broth *or* bouillon made with cubes	3½ pt
60 g	butter	2 oz
50 g	flour	2 oz
30 g	onion, finely cut	1 oz
150 g	ham, diced	5 oz
120 g	canned peas	4 oz
100 g	mushrooms, cleaned and finely diced	3½ oz
20 g	butter (to cook mushrooms)	¾ oz
	salt to taste	
	a pinch of grated nutmeg	
	1 egg yolk	
⅛ l	milk *or* dairy cream	4 fl oz

Melt 60 g (2 oz) butter in a saucepan, soften the onion in it for a few moments and add the flour. Cook over gentle heat for about a minute without colouring, while stirring constantly with a whisk. Gradually stir the cold broth into the roux, bring to the boil, cook for 20 minutes and strain. Add the nutmeg, ham, peas and the mushrooms which have been stewed in butter. Season to taste and cook for a short time, then remove from the heat, thicken with the egg yolk and milk or cream which have been beaten together and serve at once.

(Vilèm Vrabec, Czechoslovakia)

Oxtail soup
Potage de queue de boeuf
Gebundene Ochsenschwanzsuppe

5–6 portions

500 g	oxtail	1 lb 2 oz
	1 calf's foot	
100 g	matignon vegetables	3½ oz
20 g	tomato purée	¾ oz
50 g	flour, browned	2 oz
1 l	veal stock	1¾ pt
1 l	water *or* bone stock if available	1¾ pt
1 dl	white wine	3½ fl oz
20 g	fat	¾ oz
	brunoise, made up of	
30 g	carrot	1 oz
30 g	celery	1 oz
30 g	turnip	1 oz
	salt, pepper, paprika, spices	
	1 teaspoon chives, finely cut	

Brown the oxtail in the oven, add the calf's foot and continue browning, then add the matignon, brown a little and stir in the tomato purée and wine. Transfer to a large pot. Pour a little water into the pan to detach the juices and add to the pot, together with the veal stock and seasoning. Cook until the oxtail is tender. After half the cooking time, blend the flour with the water or bone stock and add to the soup. When the oxtail is cooked, remove it from the soup, cut off the meat, place on a metal tray, allow to cool and press flat.

Pass the soup through a conical strainer. Check the consistency and reduce a little if too thin. Cook the brunoise separately in water or bouillon and add to the soup, together with the oxtail meat which has been cut into cubes. If desired, flavour with a dash of brandy. Sprinkle with chives to serve.

(Emil Wälti, Switzerland)

Velouté of fillet of veal and cucumber Val di Chiara
Velouté de filet-mignon de veau aux concombres Val di Chiara
Vellutato di filetto-mignon di vitello di cetrioli Val di Chiara

4 portions   Cooking time: 1½ hours

300 g	veal bones, chopped	11 oz
120 g	fillet of veal	4 oz
450 g	cucumber	1 lb
1½ l	light veal stock	2¾ pt
50 g	flour	2 oz
1 dl	double dairy cream	3½ fl oz
4 dl	milk	14 fl oz
10 g	butter	⅓ oz
	2 egg yolks	
15 g	coarse salt	½ oz
	table salt	
	pepper, freshly ground	
10 g	chives cut into 3 cm	⅓ oz
	(1 in) lengths	

Trim the fillet of veal and set aside. Place the veal bones in a pan of cold water, bring quickly to the boil, refresh and drain. Wash and peel the cucumbers. Using a special cutter, cut out 6 cm (2½ in) balls, then cut each cucumber in half lengthwise, remove the seeds and set aside.

Heat the milk and allow to cool. Heat the veal stock and keep hot. Heat 50 g (2 oz) butter, add the cucumber halves and peel to the pan and fry lightly for 5 minutes without colouring, stirring constantly with a wooden spoon. Add the flour, mix well and cook over gentle heat for 10 minutes, again without colouring. Pour in the veal stock and bring to the boil while whisking. Add the veal bones, the fillet of veal in one piece and the salt. Cover and cook over gentle heat for 1¼ hours, stirring frequently. Skim off the excess butter that rises to the surface.

Meanwhile melt 10 g (⅓ oz) butter in a small pan, add the cucumber balls which have been seasoned with salt and pepper, and fry gently for 10 to 12 minutes. Drain and keep hot. Place the egg yolks, cream and cold milk in a bowl, mix well and season lightly with salt and pepper.

When the velouté is cooked, remove the bones and veal. Cut the veal into 1 cm (⅜ in) cubes and keep hot. Allow the soup to cool until lukewarm, then pass through a conical strainer, add the egg yolk/cream/milk mixture, stir well, return to the saucepan and finish cooking over low heat without boiling, while stirring constantly. Adjust the seasoning and add the diced meat and the cucumber balls. Sprinkle with chives just before serving. This soup may be served hot or cold.
(Illustration, page 411)

(Daniel Drouadaine, Italy)

Haricot bean and pasta pot
Potée aux haricots blancs et aux pâtes
Maltagliati alla brentatora

6 portions

Soup:

600 g	haricot beans, soaked overnight	1 lb 5 oz
1 dl	tomato sauce	3½ fl oz
2 l	bouillon	3½ pt
250 g	pork rinds	9 oz
100 g	streaky bacon, finely cut	3½ oz
	½ medium onion	
	salt, pepper	

Pasta dough:

	4 eggs	
400 g	flour	14 oz
	a pinch of salt	

For the dough, make a bay with the flour and pour in the eggs which have been beaten with the salt. Mix until smooth, pin out to the same thickness as noodle dough, and allow to dry on a linen cloth. Roll up and cut through the dough criss-cross fashion to make diamond-shaped *maltagliati* ('badly cut' pasta).

To make the soup, brown the bacon and onions in a saucepan, add the beans, bouillon, tomato sauce, and salt and pepper to taste. Cook slowly until the beans are soft, then remove from the heat. Keep half the beans hot and sieve the rest. Return all the beans to the stock in the saucepan, add the pasta, together with as much extra bouillon as required, and bring to the boil. Blanch the pork rinds in lightly salted water, cut into very fine julienne strips and add to the soup.

(Mario Saporito, Italy)

Aubergine soup
Potage aux aubergines
Marak Chazilim

6 portions

1½ l	bouillon	2¾ pt
	1 medium aubergine	
	1 onion	
	1 tablespoon mushroom soup mix, dried	
50 g	flour	2 oz
	2 eggs yolks	
	salt	
	pepper, freshly ground	
	nutmeg	

Dice the aubergine and cut up the onion finely. Stew lightly in oil, add the flour and mushroom soup mix and continue stewing for a short time. Slowly pour in the bouillon, stirring carefully to avoid crushing the aubergine cubes. Stand over the heat without boiling for 10 minutes. Carefully season with salt, pepper and nutmeg. Thicken the soup with the egg yolks just before serving.

(Hermann Wohl, Israel)

Avgolemono soup

5 portions

Lamb stock:

1½ l (2¾ pt)			
1 kg	lamb bones and trimmings		2 lb 4 oz
approx. 2 l	water	approx.	3½ pt
80 g	carrots		3 oz
	⅛ celeriac		
	1 onion		
	4 parsley stalks		
	1 sprig thyme		
	½ bay leaf		
	salt, pepper		
100 g	rice		3½ oz
	2 egg yolks		
1 dl	milk		3½ fl oz
30 g	butter		1 oz

1 tablespoon cornflour
juice of half a lemon
1 teaspoon parsley, chopped
salt
pepper, freshly ground

To make the stock, cook the lamb bones and trimmings in water with the carrots, celeriac, onion, parsley, thyme and bay leaf. Season with salt and pepper.

Beat the egg yolks well in a bowl, stir in the cornflour blended with the milk, and pour into the stock after cooking the rice in it. Stir in the lemon juice drop by drop and add the butter. Sprinkle with parsley.

The soup may be made more nourishing by adding shredded meat and also potatoes. In this case it is served as a main course.

(Emil Wälti, Greece)

Pot goulash
Goulasch en chaudron
Bográcsgulyás

5 portions

800 g	beef (chuck or shin)	1 lb 12 oz
60 g	lard	2 oz
300 g	onions, finely cut	11 oz
800 g	potatoes, peeled and evenly diced	1 lb 12 oz
	1 clove of garlic, crushed	
100 g	green peppers, cut into even strips	3½ oz
100 g	fresh tomatoes, cut into quarters	3½ oz
	salt	
	noble-sweet paprika	
	marjoram	
	caraway	

Nockerln:

100 g	flour	3½ oz
	1 egg	
	salt	
	water	

Fry the onions gently in lard, sprinkle with noble-sweet paprika and add a little water. Cut the meat into small cubes and add to the pan, together with the garlic, caraway, marjoram and salt. Cover and stew, stirring frequently, until the liquid has boiled away and the meat is beginning to brown. If the pan becomes dry too quickly, add a little water to prevent burning. When the meat is half cooked, add the potatoes, peppers and tomatoes, together with sufficient water to cover well. Simmer over low heat until the meat and potatoes are cooked. Add small *nockerln* and decorate with rings of sweet pepper to serve.

To make the *nockerln*, prepare a firm dough with the flour, egg, salt and a little water. Roll out, pinch off small even-size pieces, and cook in boiling soup or salted water. The cooking time for the goulash depends on the quality of the meat; the older the animal, the longer the time required.

(Gyula Gullner, Hungary)

Bortsch

10 portions
Cooking time: about 2 hours (depending on the quality of the meat)

500 g	beef (topside or top rump)	1 lb 2 oz
100 g	butter	3½ oz
OR 1 dl	oil	3½ fl oz
500 g	potatoes	1 lb 2 oz
400 g	raw beetroots	14 oz
400 g	white cabbage	14 oz
100 g	fresh tomatoes	3½ oz
100 g	onions	3½ oz
300 g	mixed root vegetables	11 oz
60 g	flour	2 oz
½ dl	vinegar	2 fl oz
3 dl	sour cream	10 fl oz
	1 bay leaf	
2 g	black pepper, freshly ground	a good pinch
30 g	salt	1 oz
30 g	tomato purée	1 oz
	lemon juice	

Wash the meat well. Place it in a pan containing about 4 l (7 pt) salted water with the bay leaf, bring to the boil and cook, skimming well. Cut the onions, beetroots and root vegetables into julienne strips, brown lightly in butter, add a little bone broth and stew gently. Stir in the tomato purée and vinegar, then add to the soup. Continue cooking for a time, then add the cabbage, finely shredded, and the potatoes cut into dice. Remove the meat when tender but still fairly firm and cut into cubes.

Make a roux and stir into the bouillon. Add the meat together with the tomatoes cut in quarters and continue cooking for a few minutes. Season with pepper and add lemon juice to taste. To serve, pour into a warmed tureen and sprinkle with sour cream.

Bortsch may also be made with pickled beetroot juice or brine from sauerkraut or pickled cucumbers. In this case the lemon juice is omitted. There are different ways of preparing bortsch in various countries – Russia, Poland or China, for example – and it may be served hot or cold. It is sometimes made without roux. There is one common feature, however; beetroots are invariably used. If the soup is not red enough, the juice of grated raw beetroots is added.

(Zsolt Körmendy, Russia)

Bortsch Kiev style

10 portions
Cooking time: 80 to 110 minutes, depending on the quality of the meat

300 g	leg of beef	11 oz
300 g	leg of mutton	11 oz
600 g	beetroots	1 lb 5 oz
800 g	white cabbage	1 lb 12 oz
750 g	potatoes	1 lb 10 oz
100 g	dried beans	3½ oz
100 g	carrots	3½ oz
70 g	celeriac	2½ oz
80 g	tomato purée	3 oz
150 g	onions	5 oz
80 g	parsley roots	3 oz
50 g	butter	2 oz
OR 5 cl	oil	2 fl oz
50 g	smoked bacon	2 oz
30 g	sugar	1 oz
30 g	salt	1 oz
3 g	black pepper, freshly ground	a good pinch
	1 bunch parsley	
2 dl	sour cream	7 fl oz
	1 bay leaf	
	lemon juice	

Wash the beef carefully and place in a pan with about 5 l (9 pt) water or bone broth. Bring to the boil, cook for a short time, then add the mutton which has been washed. Cook slowly over low heat, skimming repeatedly and adding salt to taste. Pick over the beans carefully, wash them and cook in water until soft.

Cut the bacon into julienne strips and brown in butter or oil. Cut the onions in julienne strips and add to the bacon. Fry until the onions are lightly coloured. Cut the beetroots, carrots, parsley roots and celeriac into julienne strips and add to the onions, together with the parsley, finely chopped, and the tomato purée. Stew for a short time, then add to the meat, season with salt and pepper, add the bay leaf and continue cooking until the meat is tender.

Remove the meat from the pan, allow to cool, then cut into cubes. Add the cabbage, cut into julienne strips, to the soup together with the potatoes which have been finely diced. Continue cooking, then add the beans with their cooking liquid and the cubes of meat. Cook until the soup is ready to be served, then add a little sugar and lemon juice. Serve very hot in a warmed earthenware dish or a tureen, sprinkled with sour cream and chopped parsley.

(Zsolt Körmendy, Russia)

Bridegroom's soup
Soupe du fiancé
Legényfogóleves

4 portions   Cooking time: about 1 hour

150 g	shoulder of pork	5 oz
150 g	breast of veal	5 oz
150 g	calf's liver	5 oz
150 g	mushrooms	5 oz
200 g	mirepoix	7 oz
100 g	peas	3½ oz
1½ l	bouillon	2¾ pt
30 g	butter	1 oz
50 g	flour	2 oz
1 dl	dairy cream	3½ fl oz
	1 egg yolk	
	juice of half a lemon	
	salt	
	pepper, freshly ground	
	½ bunch parsley, chopped	

Butter dumplings:

50 g	fine semolina	2 oz
30 g	butter	1 oz
	1 egg	

Finely dice the pork, veal, liver and mushrooms. Place in a pan with the mirepoix and peas and mix well. Pour in the bouillon and cook until all the ingredients are tender. Prepare the butter dumpling dough, shape into dumplings with a tablespoon and cook in the soup.

Make a blond roux with 30 g (1 oz) butter and 50 g (2 oz) flour. Mix with chopped parsley, blend in a little cold water and stir into the soup. Return the soup to the boil. Just before serving, flavour with a little lemon juice and add the cream and egg yolk which have been beaten together.

(László Csizmadia, Hungary)

Mutton goulash with red wine
Goulasch de mouton au vin rouge
Uerügulyas Vörösborban

10 portions   Cooking time: 1 hour

2 kg 500	shoulder of mutton	5 lb 8 oz
200 g	lard	7 oz
400 g	onions, finely chopped	14 oz
20 g	garlic, crushed	¾ oz
30 g	paprika	1 oz
3 l	water	5 pt
2 g	caraway, ground	a pinch
50 g	salt	2 oz
200 g	yellow peppers	7 oz
100 g	tomatoes	3½ oz
2 dl	red wine	7 fl oz
1 kg 500	potatoes	3 lb 5 oz
	pasta squares	

Bone the shoulder of mutton and cut the meat into pieces weighing about 30 g (1 oz). Blanch in hot water, refresh in cold water and wash well.

Fry the onions in hot lard until lightly coloured, sprinkle with paprika and add the water, meat, caraway and garlic. Season with salt, pour in the wine, cover the pan and cook until the meat is almost tender. Peel, wash and dice the potatoes. Seed the peppers and cut in quarters lengthwise. Cut the tomatoes in wedges and add to the pan with the potatoes, peppers and sufficient water to provide 3 dl (10 fl oz) soup per portion. Cook until ready to serve. Cook the pasta squares separately and add just before serving.

(Zsolt Körmendy, Hungary)

Mutton soup with French beans
Soupe de mouton aux haricots verts
Palócleves

4 portions   Cooking time: 1 hour

600 g	shoulder of mutton	1 lb 5 oz
200 g	onions, finely chopped	7 oz
40 g	lard	1½ oz
	1 teaspoon red paprika	
300 g	French beans	11 oz
200 g	potatoes	7 oz

2 dl	sour cream	7 fl oz
	1 bay leaf	
	1 small clove of garlic, crushed	
	salt	
	pepper, freshly ground	
	caraway	
	1 teaspoon flour	
	dill	

Fry the onions in the lard until lightly coloured and sprinkle with the paprika. Add the meat, cut into small cubes, pepper, a little salt and caraway, the bay leaf and garlic. Pour in a little water and stew until the meat is cooked.

Cut the potatoes in small pieces and the beans in 3 cm (1¼ in) lengths. Cook in salted water, add to the meat together with the water in which they were cooked, and mix well. The total liquid yield should be 8 dl–1 l (28–36 fl oz), allowing 2–2½ dl (7–9 fl oz) per portion. Carefully mix the sour cream and flour together and blend into the soup to thicken it. Sprinkle with a little finely chopped dill before serving.

(László Csizmadia, Hungary)

Shepherds' soup
Soupe des bergers
Csordásleves

4 portions   Cooking time: about 1½–2 hours

300 g	beef (short ribs)	11 oz
150 g	shoulder of mutton	5 oz
150 g	boned chicken	5 oz
150 g	carrots	5 oz
100 g	parsley roots	3½ oz
150 g	savoy cabbage	5 oz
	2 celery leaves	
	parsley	
	2 green peppers	
50 g	onions	2 oz
	salt	
	pepper, freshly ground	
60 g	pasta squares, dried	2 oz
1½ l	water (hot)	2¾ pt

Dice the beef and mutton and place in a pan with the water. Add all the vegetables and seasoning, mix well and cook. Dice the chicken and add to the soup shortly before the meat is tender. Continue cooking until all the meat is tender, add the pasta squares and cook until ready to serve.

(László Csizmadia, Hungary)

Potato dumpling soup Nyirség style
Potage aux quenelles de pommes de terre Nyirség
Nyirségi gombócleves

10 portions   Cooking time: 1 hour

600 g	shoulder or knuckle of veal	1 lb 5 oz
200 g	carrots and parsley roots	7 oz
100 g	celeriac	3½ oz
400 g	cauliflower	14 oz
100 g	mushrooms	3½ oz
100 g	cooked peas	3½ oz
50 g	onions, finely chopped	2 oz
	1 yellow pepper, seeded and diced	
	1 medium tomato, diced	
40 g	salt	1½ oz
3 g	black pepper, freshly ground	a good pinch
	1 lemon	
120 g	lard	4 oz
OR 12 cl	oil	4 fl oz
80 g	flour	3 oz
2 dl	dairy cream	7 fl oz
	2 egg yolks	
	1 bunch parsley	
3 l	bouillon	5 pt

Potato dumplings:

400 g	potatoes, boiled in their jackets	14 oz
60 g	lard or butter	2 oz
100 g	flour	3½ oz
	1 egg	
5 g	salt	⅙ oz
2 g	black pepper, freshly ground	a good pinch
	½ bunch parsley, finely chopped	

Fry the onions in a little lard or oil until lightly coloured. Dice the carrots, parsley roots, celeriac and veal, and chop the parsley finely. Add the rest of the lard or oil to the onions, together with the diced vegetables, meat and chopped parsley. Season with the juice of 1 lemon, salt and pepper, mix well and stew under cover without adding liquid until almost cooked.

Carefully clean the mushrooms, dice them and add to the meat. Cook for a short time, dust with the flour, mix well and pour in the bouillon. Divide the cauliflower into florets and add to the soup together with the pepper and tomato. Cook until ready to serve, then thicken with the egg yolks mixed with the cream and add the peas and potato dumplings.

To make the dumplings, peel the freshly cooked potatoes and pass through a sieve. Mix with the lard or butter, flour, egg, parsley, salt and pepper. Shape into small dumplings and cook in salted water.

(Zsolt Körmendy, Hungary)

Pot goulash
Goulasch en chaudron
Bográcsgulyás

10 portions   Cooking time: 1½ hours

1 kg 600	lean stewing beef (short ribs)	3 lb 8 oz
150 g	lard	5 oz
500 g	onions, finely chopped	1 lb 2 oz
20 g	garlic, finely chopped	¾ oz
40 g	paprika	1½ oz
2 g	caraway seeds, crushed	a good pinch
50 g	salt	2 oz
100 g	yellow peppers, seeded and cut in strips	3½ oz
100 g	tomatoes, cut in quarters	3½ oz
1 kg 600	potatoes, diced	3 lb 8 oz
	marjoram (optional)	

Pasta squares:

100 g	flour	3½ oz
	1 egg	

Fry the onions in the lard until lightly coloured. Sprinkle with paprika and crushed caraway seeds and mix well. Wash and dice the meat and add to the pan, together with the garlic, salt and a little marjoram if desired. Pour in a little water, mix well and braise under cover, adding water from time to time to prevent burning. When the meat is almost cooked, add the peppers, potatoes and tomatoes cut in quarters. Pour in sufficient water to cover the meat and vegetables and finish cooking.

To make the pasta squares, prepare a firm paste with the flour and egg. Do not add salt, which would make the paste too soft. Roll out no thicker than the back of a knife on a floured board. Pinch off ½ cm (¼ in) squares with the fingers, or cut into squares with a knife. Cook separately in salted water. Add to the goulash when ready to serve. Serve in the cooking pot, decorated with peppers cut into strips or rings.

(Zsolt Körmendy, Hungary)

Kharcho
Potée de mouton

10 portions
Cooking time: about 30 minutes for lamb, or about 60–80 minutes for mutton

1 kg	breast of lamb or mutton, boned	2 lb 4 oz
200 g	onions, thinly sliced	7 oz
200 g	rice, washed and well drained	7 oz
100 g	pickled plums	3½ oz
	1 bunch dill, finely chopped	
	1 head celery	
120 g	butter	4 oz
60 g	tomato purée	2 oz
10 g	garlic, crushed	⅓ oz
	1 bay leaf	
2 g	black peppercorns	1 teaspoon
20 g	salt	¾ oz
	bouquet garni	

Wash, dice and blanch the meat, place it in a pan with 3 l (5 pt) cold water, bring slowly to the boil and skim. Add the salt, the onions and a muslin bag containing the bouquet garni, the washed celery leaves, the bay leaf, garlic and peppercorns. Continue cooking slowly. Cook the tomato purée in butter for a moment and add to the soup. When the meat is almost tender, add the rice and the pickled plums and finish cooking. If desired, a few diced potatoes may be cooked in the soup. Remove the muslin bag, pour the soup into an earthenware dish or a tureen and sprinkle with dill to serve.

(Zsolt Körmendy, Russia)

Tripe soup Bohemian style
Soupe aux tripes à la bohémienne
Drštková polévka

6 portions   Cooking time: 4–5 hours

3 l	water	5 pt
600 g	tripe	1 lb 5 oz
120 g	flavouring vegetables	4 oz
60 g	onions, finely cut	2 oz
	a pinch of marjoram	
	a pinch of pepper	
	salt	
2 g	paprika	a good pinch

a pinch of ginger
2 cloves of garlic, crushed
parsley, finely chopped

Roux:

50 g	butter	2 oz
50 g	flour	2 oz

Wash the tripe well, rub with salt, blanch and wash again in cold water. Place in a pan of cold water, bring to the boil and cook for about 40 minutes. Discard the water, fill the pan with fresh water, season with salt and cook for about 3 hours, or until the tripe is tender. Add the vegetables which have been cleaned and washed and cook for a further 20 minutes. Remove the tripe, drain, allow to cool and cut in narrow strips. Prepare a blond roux with the butter, flour, onions and paprika. Add the garlic and blend in 1¾ l (3 pt) strained tripe stock. Season to taste, cook for 20 minutes and strain. Add the tripe, return to the boil and sprinkle with parsley to serve.

The soup has a particularly good flavour if 100 g (4 oz) smoked loin of pork (Kasseler) is cooked with the tripe. As soon as it is tender, it is removed from the stock and finely diced, then served in the soup. The flavouring vegetables may be finely cut and used as a garnish. Tripe soup is a typical Bohemian dish.

(Vilèm Vrabec, Czechoslovakia)

Turkish tripe soup
Potage de tripes à la turque
Iskembe Korbasi

5 portions

500 g	lamb's stomach *or* crow of veal	1 lb 2 oz
200 g	onions, finely chopped	7 oz
50 g	flour	2 oz
1 l	bouillon	1¾ pt
180 g	natural yoghourt	6 oz
	1 egg yolk	
80 g	butter	3 oz
100 g	white bread	3½ oz
	1 teaspoon parsley, finely chopped	
	1 teaspoon dill, finely chopped	
	2 tablespoons vinegar	
	2 cloves of garlic, finely chopped	
	salt, pepper, paprika	

Clean the lamb's stomach or crow of veal thoroughly and cut in small cubes or strips. Cook half the onions gently in 40 g (1½ oz) butter until transparent, add the stomach or crow, continue cooking gently, dust with the flour, pour in the bouillon, season and continue cooking until the stomach or crow is tender. Remove from the heat, add the egg yolk well mixed with the yoghourt and check the seasoning. Dice the bread and fry in butter. Prepare a relish with the rest of the onions, the garlic, parsley, dill, vinegar, salt and pepper. Hand croûtons and the relish separately.

(Emil Wälti, Turkey)

Country style soup
Potage du comtat
Zuppa del contado

6 portions   Cooking time: 2–3 hours

700 g	neck of beef	1 lb 8 oz
	3 carrots	
	3 potatoes	
	2 onions	
	1 medium celeriac	
200 g	fresh peas, shelled	7 oz
	1 tablespoon tomato purée	
	2 tablespoons olive oil	
1 dl	red wine	3½ fl oz
3 l	water	5 pt
	salt, pepper	

Finely dice the meat, carrots, potatoes, onions and celeriac. Brown the meat in the oil, add the diced vegetables and the peas and allow to colour. Stir in the wine, add salt, the tomato purée and the water. Bring to the boil, reduce the heat and simmer until cooked. Adjust the seasoning. Serve with croûtons of stale bread fried in butter.

(Mario Saporito, Italy)

Sheep's head soup
Soupe à la tête de mouton
Bárányfejleves

4 portions   Cooking time: about 1½ hours

	2 sheep's heads	
150 g	carrots	5 oz
100 g	parsley roots	3½ oz
50 g	onion	2 oz
	3–4 peppercorns	

	salt	
	1 green pepper	
	2 eggs	
	2 egg yolks	
150 g	flour	5 oz
	½ bunch parsley	
20 g	lard	¾ oz
	1 teaspoon tarragon	
1 dl	sour cream	3½ fl oz

Wash the heads well, then blanch them. Slice the carrots and parsley roots thinly and place in a pan with the heads. Add about 1 l (1¾ pt) water and cook until the heads are tender. Remove them from the pan, then remove the brains and cut off the meat. Slice the brains and meat very thinly. Finely chop the onion and parsley. Mix the brains, meat, onion and parsley with one egg and salt to taste to make forcemeat.

Prepare a dough with the flour and one egg. Pin it out thinly and divide in half. Mark one half into small squares. Pipe a little forcemeat on to each square and lightly moisten the edges. Place the other half of the dough on top and press down. Cut out the squares with a pastry wheel.

Chop the tarragon very finely and place it in a saucepan. Strain the sheep's head stock into the saucepan and cook the ravioli in it. To serve, mix the 2 egg yolks with the sour cream and pour into the tureen. Strain in the soup and add the ravioli.

(László Csizmadia, Hungary)

Minestrone Genoese style
Minestrone à la génoise
Minestrone alla Genovese

4 portions   Cooking time: at least 2 hours

vegetables in season – carrots,
    savoy cabbage, leeks, beans, peas,
    Swiss chard, courgettes, potatoes,
    onions as required
olive oil as required
streaky bacon
salt

Pesto (basil sauce):

36 fresh young basil leaves
1 tablespoon Sardo Pecorino cheese, grated
1 tablespoon Parmesan cheese, grated
3 tablespoons pine kernels

1–2 cloves of garlic
spaghetti (30 g/1 oz per 1 l/1¾ pt water)

Cut up the vegetables finely and brown lightly in olive oil together with the bacon. Add at least 2–3 l (3½–5 pt) water and cook for minimum 2 hours, adding water if necessary. The soup should be fairly thin.

Cook broken spaghetti separately. Add to the soup when cooked and return to the boil for a moment. Remove from the heat and stir in 2 teaspoons pesto per portion.

To make pesto, pound the basil, pine kernels and garlic very finely in a mortar, then add both the grated cheeses, work to a fine purée with a little olive oil and mix thoroughly. Add olive oil as required to make a thick sauce.
(Illustration, page 517)

(Franco Colombani, Italy)

Orosz soup
Potage Oros
Orosz leves

10 portions   Cooking time: about 60–80 minutes

1 kg	beef (top side or top rump)	2 lb 4 oz
	2 eggs	
40 g	salt	1½ oz
5 g	black pepper, freshly ground	⅙ oz
	1 bunch parsley, chopped	
	1 bunch chives, chopped	
10 g	garlic, crushed	⅓ oz
400 g	carrots and parsley roots	14 oz
150 g	onions	5 oz
1 kg	white cabbage	2 lb 4 oz
500 g	fresh tomatoes, cut in quarters	1 lb 2 oz
400 g	potatoes, diced	14 oz
3 dl	sour cream	10 fl oz
	chives	

Carefully wash the carrots and parsley roots, scrape them and slice finely. Dice the cabbage and finely chop the onions. Place these ingredients in a pan with about 4 l (7 pt) water or bouillon, salt, pepper and the garlic, and bring to the boil, then reduce the heat and simmer. Mince the meat finely, season with salt and pepper and shape into small balls with wet hands. Drop into the soup and cook for about 30 to 40 minutes. Add the potatoes, tomatoes and parsley and finish cooking.

To serve, pour the hot soup into a warmed tureen and sprinkle with chives and sour cream.

The flavour of the soup may be greatly improved by the addition of sliced flap mushrooms.

(Zsolt Körmendy, Russia)

Easter soup
Potage pascal
Mayeritsasoupa

5 portions

	1 lamb's head	
200 g	lamb's liver	7 oz
200 g	other lamb's offal	7 oz
	(heart, stomach, etc.)	
200 g	celery	7 oz
100 g	green shallots	3½ oz
	1 tablespoon parsley, chopped	
	1 teaspoon dill, chopped	
	juice of half a lemon	
	1 cup milk *or* sour milk	
100 g	rice	3½ oz
30 g	butter	1 oz
	1 tablespoon cornflour	
	2 egg yolks	
	salt, pepper	
	water	

Cut the head in half. Wash thoroughly together with the offal and soak for about 2 hours. (Other items of lamb's offal may be used if desired). Blanch, then cook the head and heart in water. Chop the celery, shallots and liver and cook in water until soft. Remove the meat and brains from the bones and slice thinly. Cook the rice in the lamb stock, then add the meat, liver and vegetables. Beat the egg yolks in a bowl and blend in the milk and cornflour, mixing well. Add to the soup, then stir in the lemon juice drop by drop. Season to taste with salt and pepper, add the butter and sprinkle with the chopped herbs. Serve very hot. The addition of lemon juice gives the soup a slightly acid taste.

(Emil Wälti, Greece)

Transylvanian soup with horseradish
Potage transylvanien au raifort
Erdélyi tormáslé

4 portions   Cooking time: about 1 hour

500 g	shoulder of pork	1 lb 2 oz
100 g	carrots	3½ oz
50 g	lard	2 oz
50 g	flour	2 oz
50 g	onion, finely chopped	2 oz
50 g	parsley roots	2 oz
5 g	red paprika	⅙ oz
1 l	sauerkraut brine	1¾ pt
1 dl	sour cream	3½ fl oz
200 g	horseradish	7 oz
	salt	

Dice the pork and place in a pan with 1 l (1¾ pt) water. Cut the carrots and parsley roots into fine julienne strips and stew in a little lard, then add to the meat. Bring to the boil and cook until the meat is tender. Make a roux with the flour, 1 tablespoon lard and the onion. Sprinkle with paprika and stir in the sauerkraut brine. Boil up well, strain in the meat stock, return to the boil and season with salt. Stir in the sour cream to serve. Hand grated horseradish separately.

(László Csizmadia, Hungary)

Pohljebka

10 portions
Cooking time: about 80 minutes, depending on the quality of the meat

750 g	pork (leg)	1 lb 10 oz
750 g	1 boiling fowl weighing	1 lb 10 oz
500 g	pickled cucumbers	1 lb 2 oz
300 g	potatoes	11 oz
500 g	white cabbage	1 lb 2 oz
200 g	mixed root vegetables	7 oz
100 g	onions	3½ oz
	1 bunch dill	
30 g	salt	1 oz
2 g	black pepper, freshly ground	a good pinch
60 g	butter	2 oz
80 g	flour	3 oz
2 dl	sour cream	7 fl oz

Draw and wash the fowl. Place it in a pan with about 2½ l (4½ pt) cold water. Bring slowly to the boil, skim, season with salt, reduce the heat and simmer. Dice the pork, add to the pan and continue cooking, adding water from time to time. Dice the root vegetables, cabbage and potatoes. Slice the onions thinly and chop the dill finely. Add the vegetables to the pan and continue cooking over low heat. When all the ingredients are cooked, add the cucumbers cut in slices. Lift out the bird, bone it and dice the meat. Make a roux with the butter and flour.

Pour the broth into a separate pan, thicken with the roux, flavour well with the pickled cucumber liquid and with freshly ground pepper, then pour the broth back into the cooking pot. Add the diced chicken. Serve very hot in a warmed tureen, sprinkled with sour cream.

(Zsolt Körmendy, Russia)

Sharp beef soup
Soupe aigre de boeuf
Vetreceleves

4 portions   Cooking time: about 1½ hours

250 g	beef (rump)	9 oz
60 g	onion	2 oz
	2 bay leaves	
	salt	
	pepper, freshly ground	
40 g	flour	1½ oz
5 g	red paprika	⅙ oz
60 g	lard	2 oz
1 dl	sour cream	3½ fl oz
	1 tablespoon vinegar	
1 l	bone stock	1¾ pt

Dice the onion finely and cook gently in a little lard without colouring. Add the beef, cut in thin strips, and the bay leaves. Season with salt and pepper. Gradually add 3 dl (10 fl oz) bone stock and cook until the meat is tender, then pour in the rest of the stock. Make a roux with the flour and a little lard, sprinkle with the paprika and stir into the soup to thicken. Before serving, mix the soup with the vinegar and sour cream.

(László Csizmadia, Hungary)

Ham dumpling soup
Consommé aux quenelles de jambon
Sonkagaluska leves

4 portions   Cooking time: about 30 minutes

Ham dumplings:

50 g	butter	2 oz
	3 egg yolks	
	3 eggs	

250 g	lean cooked ham	9 oz
60–70 g	white breadcrumbs	2–2½ oz
	salt	
	pepper, freshly ground	
1½ l	bouillon	2¾ pt

Cream the butter. Mince the ham finely, then mix well with the butter, the eggs and yolks, the breadcrumbs and salt and pepper to taste. If the mixture is too soft, add a small amount of breadcrumbs. Flour the hands and shape the mixture into small dumplings the size of a walnut. Cook in the bouillon and serve.

(László Csizmadia, Hungary)

Reaper's soup
Potage du moissonneur
Kaszásleves

4 portions   Cooking time: 2–2½ hours

	4 pig's trotters	
	1 large clove of garlic, crushed	
2 dl	sour cream	7 fl oz
	1 tablespoon flour	
	pepper, freshly ground	
	vinegar	
	smoked bacon rind	
	horseradish, grated	

Cook the trotters in salted water with the garlic and bacon rind until tender. Remove from the stock, cut off the meat, dice finely and place in a tureen. Reduce the stock and thicken with the sour cream mixed with the flour. Return to the boil, add pepper and vinegar to taste and pour over the meat. Serve very hot with grated horseradish.

(László Csizmadia, Hungary)

Solianka

10 portions
Cooking time: 80–110 minutes, depending on the quality of the meat

800 g	fillet of beef	1 lb 12 oz
400 g	smoked raw ham	14 oz
300 g	boiling sausages	11 oz
400 g	calf's kidneys	14 oz

400 g	pickled cucumbers, peeled and sliced	14 oz
150 g	onions	5 oz
150 g	butter	5 oz
100 g	tomato purée	3½ oz
100 g	capers, finely chopped	3½ oz
100 g	olives, stoned and thinly sliced	3½ oz
20 g	salt	¾ oz
15 g	black pepper, freshly ground	½ oz
	1 bay leaf	
	juice of 2 lemons	
	1 bunch parsley, finely chopped	
	½ bunch chives, chopped	
3 dl	sour cream	10 fl oz

Wash the beef, place it in a pan with 3½ l (6 pt) cold water, bring to the boil slowly over gentle heat, skim, season with salt and add the bay leaf. Wash the ham well and cook in a large pan of water until tender, then cut into cubes.

Peel and chop the onions, fry in butter or oil until lightly coloured, add the tomato purée and continue frying for a few seconds. Add the kidneys, cut into triangles, and cook gently for a few minutes. Add to the beef shortly before it has finished cooking, together with the sausage, cut in slices, the cucumbers, ham, capers, olives and parsley. Carefully pour in a little of the ham stock, making sure that the soup does not become too salty. Continue cooking over low heat for 5 to 10 minutes. Add lemon juice and season well with freshly ground pepper.

Carve the beef into 10 slices. Transfer the soup to a tureen. When serving, place a slice of beef on each plate, pour the hot soup over and sprinkle with sour cream and chives.

(Zsolt Körmendy, Russia)

Pig's brain soup
Soup à la cervelle de porc
Sertésagy leves

4 portions   Cooking time: about 30 minutes

250 g	pig's brains	9 oz
50 g	onions, finely chopped	2 oz
1½ l	sauerkraut brine	2¾ pt
30 g	tomato purée	1 oz
2 dl	sour cream	7 fl oz
60 g	flour	2 oz
30 g	lard	1 oz
10 g	red paprika	⅓ oz

5 g	pepper, freshly ground	⅙ oz
	salt	

Make a roux with the flour, lard and onions, dust with paprika and pour in the brine. Season with salt and pepper. Cut the brains into cubes and cook in the brine until tender. Add the sour cream to serve.

(László Csizmadia, Hungary)

Galician vegetable soup
Potage aux légumes à la galicienne
Caldo gallego

8 portions   Cooking time: about 2 hours

300 g	smoked ham, finely diced	11 oz
	2 chorizo sausages	
180 g	pork garlic sausage	6 oz
100 g	salt fat pork or bacon	3½ oz
250 g	haricot beans, soaked	9 oz
250 g	turnip tops	9 oz
250 g	potatoes	9 oz
	1 onion, finely chopped	
	salt, pepper	

Place the beans and water in a pan, bring to the boil and pour off the water. Cover them with cold water, add the ham, pork or bacon, and onion and cook for about 1½ hours. Cut the potatoes into about 5 mm (¼ in) cubes and the turnip tops into strips about 1½ cm (½ in) long. Add these ingredients to the pan, together with the chorizo, salt and pepper, and simmer over low heat until cooked.

Remove the chorizo and the pork or bacon. Slice the chorizo finely, cut away the pork rind and cut the pork into small pieces. Return the chorizo and pork to the pan and check the seasoning. Serve very hot in earthenware bowls.

(Emil Wälti, Spain)

Pigeon pea soup Puerto Rican style
Soupe aux pois à la portoricaine
Sopa de gandules

8 portions

150 g	smoked pickled loin of pork	5 oz

150 g	ham	5 oz
150 g	onions, finely chopped	5 oz
	2 clovers of garlic, finely chopped	
150 g	green peppers	5 oz
150 g	tomatoes	5 oz
600 g	pigeon peas (canned)	1 lb 5 oz
600 g	pumpkin, courgettes or cucumbers	1 lb 5 oz
1 l	chicken broth	1¾ pt
	salt, black pepper	

Cut the pork (raw) into small cubes and brown in a braising pan. Add the onions and garlic and cook gently until transparent. Dice the ham finely; seed and chop the green pepper; skin, seed and chop the tomatoes. Add all these to the pan and stew for a short time. Add the pumpkin and continue stewing, then the pigeon peas and the broth, cover as tightly as possible and continue cooking for about 20 minutes, or until all the ingredients are tender. Season to taste with salt and pepper and serve very hot in earthenware bowls. The soup should be fairly thick but not smooth.

(Emil Wälti, Puerto Rico)

Tschulent I

30 portions   Cooking time: 7–8 hours

5 dl	oil	18 fl oz
100 g	garlic	3½ oz
1 kg 500	onions	3 lb 5 oz
3 kg	kosher stewing beef	6 lb 10 oz
1 kg 200	chicken gizzards	2 lb 10 oz
	16–24 potatoes	
2 kg 500	white beans, soaked	5 lb 8 oz
400 g	hulled barley	14 oz
8 l	water or bouillon	14 pt
	salt	
	pepper, freshly ground	
	Aromat	
	paprika	

Brown the onions and garlic in oil in a heavy pan with a well-fitting lid. Dice the meat and brown in oil in a frying pan, then add to the onions together with the gizzards and cook gently for about 10 minutes. Pour in the water or bouillon. Add the potatoes, barley and drained beans. Cover tightly and cook for 3 to 4 hours, adding water or bouillon from time to time. Season with salt, pepper, Aromat and paprika. Continue cooking for 4 hours, or until required, over the lowest possible heat or in a steamer, stirring occasionally.

(Gérard van Dijk, Switzerland)

Chamim (Tschulent II)
Déjeuner du sabbat

8 portions

200 g	white beans	7 oz
50 g	pearl barley	2 oz
500 g	veal knuckle bones	1 lb 2 oz
	OR beef shank bones	
600 g	beef, diced	1 lb 5 oz
	1 onion	
	3 cloves of garlic	
1½ l	bouillon	2¾ pt
	pepper, freshly ground	
	salt	
	paprika	
500 g	raw potatoes, cut in half	1 lb 2 oz

Place all the ingredients in a casserole, cover tightly, bring to the boil and adjust the seasoning if necessary. Cover tightly again and place in a slow oven. Cook for 20 hours, checking frequently and adding water to replace the liquid which has evaporated. This is a very substantial dish which is served as a main course on the sabbath.

(Hermann Wohl, Israel)

Vipava soup
Soupe Vipava
Vipavska Corba

8–10 portions   Cooking time: about 3 hours

600 g	sauerkraut, finely cut	1 lb 5 oz
500 g	potatoes	1 lb 2 oz
400 g	dried white beans	14 oz
100 g	lard	3½ oz
20 g	flour	¾ oz
500 g	smoked pork	1 lb 2 oz
	5 tablespoons sour cream	
	1 onion	
	3 cloves of garlic	
	peppercorns	
	2 bay leaves	
	salt	

Soak the beans for 12 hours before use. Cook the sauerkraut, the beans and the potatoes (unpeeled) separately. Cook the meat in about 3 l (5 pt) water, remove, bone and dice. Mash the beans. Peel and dice the potatoes. Make a roux with the lard, flour, garlic and onion. Place the meat and vegetables in a pan, add the roux, bay leaves, peppercorns, salt and pork stock, then cook for a further 8 to 10 minutes. Add the sour cream just before serving. The soup should be very thick.

(László Csizmadia, Yugoslavia)

Sausage soup
Soupe à la saucisse
Kolbászleves

4 portions   Cooking time: 1–1½ hours

200 g	smoked sausage	7 oz
100 g	carrots	3½ oz
50 g	parsley roots	2 oz
50 g	kohlrabi	2 oz
50 g	Brussels sprouts	2 oz
30 g	onion	1 oz
	1 green pepper	
	salt	
	3–5 peppercorns	
	4 eggs	
	1 roll	

Wash the sausage carefully and cook in 1½ l (2¾ pt) water with the Brussels sprouts, the rest of the vegetables cut in small pieces, and the peppercorns. Season with salt.

To serve, strain the hot soup into a fireproof dish and carefully break one egg per portion into it. The whites should become hard enough to enclose the soft yolks. Slice the sausage thinly and add to the soup. Cut the roll into small cubes, fry in butter and hand separately.

(László Csizmadia, Hungary)

Hot and Cold Buffet Dishes

Meat Dishes for Hot and Cold Buffets

This modern method of entertaining is on the increase, both in the home and at large functions in hotels or restaurants and in industry. The recipes in this book provide many opportunities of adding interest and novelty to the menu and offering guests particularly inviting dishes, both familiar and out of the ordinary, whatever the type of occasion.

It is hard to imagine a buffet without a meat dish, unless the intention is to serve a vegetarian or fish buffet. There is a wide variety of dishes to choose from. The book includes recipes for hot and cold savouries, hors d'oeuvre salads, simple rustic style dishes or elaborate ones for special celebrations. By consulting the various chapters on hors d'oeuvre and main meat dishes, a selection may be made of the items most suitable for any particular type of buffet. Preference should be given to dishes which can be served in individual portions.

As a general rule buffet menus include a clear soup – hot or cold, depending on the time of year – which is handed on a tray. At a dance, especially one for young people, individual plate service should be used for the supper buffet. There is an endless number of possible combinations.

The best meat dishes to select for a hot buffet are those which remain succulent for some time, even though the meat has to be carved in advance. Ragoûts of all kinds and certain sautés are also suitable.

Cold Buffets

Galantine Colombani

5 kg	cushion of veal	11 lb
3 kg	chicken legs and breasts	6 lb 10 oz
2 kg	fresh pig's cheek	4 lb 8 oz
2 kg	sausage meat (pork if possible) (recipe, page 134)	4 lb 8 oz
400 g	white truffles	14 oz
150 g	pistachio nuts, shelled	5 oz
300 g	salt	10 oz
	2 teaspoons mace, pepper,	

	freshly ground, to taste	
	1–2 teaspoons monosodium glutamate	
	or Aromat	
2½ dl	Marsala	9 fl oz
½ dl	rum	2 fl oz
	2 teaspoons Worcester sauce	
	1 teaspoon saltpetre	
200 g	gelatine	7 oz
	parchment or oiled paper	
	2 carrots	
	2 sticks celery	
	1 onion	
	4 cloves	
	1 cinnamon quill	

Slit the chickens down the centre of the back and cut the flesh off the carcase without damaging the skin. Detach the breasts and bone the legs. Spread out the skin on a rectangular piece of oiled or parchment paper. Cut the pig's cheek, the veal and the flesh from the chicken breasts and legs into small strips the thickness of one finger. Marinate in the Marsala mixed with the rum. Dice the truffles and chop the nuts coarsely.

To make the forcemeat, thoroughly mix together the truffles, pistachio nuts, mace, salt, monosodium glutamate, Worcester sauce, saltpetre, sausage meat and the gelatine which has been soaked. Add freshly ground pepper to taste and mix again. Drain the meat well and mix the marinade with the forcemeat.

Cover the chicken skin with a layer of forcemeat, then with the strips of chicken and meat and finally with another layer of forcemeat. Roll up the galantine carefully and tie firmly round the ends and middle to prevent the roll opening while cooking. Leave to pickle at room temperature for about 8 hours, preferably overnight. Then place in a pan of water with 2 carrots, 2 sticks celery, 1 onion stuck with 4 cloves, a piece of cinnamon quill about 2 cm (¾ in) long, the chicken carcases and 2 veal bones. Cook over fairly low heat, allowing 2 hours for a galantine weighing 3 kg (6 lb 10 oz). Leave to cool slowly in the stock. Remove while the stock is still lukewarm, untie and carefully place the roll on a dry rectangular piece of oiled paper. Roll up firmly, tie and leave until completely cold, then refrigerate for at least 12 hours or until firm. Serve cut into 1 cm (⅜ in) slices with pickled cucumbers or marinated flap mushrooms.
(Illustration, page 576)

(Franco Colombani, Italy)

Galantine Achenbach

20 portions	Cooking time: 75 minutes	
125 g	pork back fat, sliced paper thin	4½ oz

Forcemeat:

300 g	shoulder of pork, boned	11 oz
300 g	shoulder of veal, boned	11 oz
250 g	smoked pork neck fat (or bacon)	9 oz
200 g	leg of pork, cut into 1 cm (⅜ in) cubes	7 oz
200 g	ox tongue, cut into 5 mm (¼ in) cubes	7 oz
50 g	truffles, finely chopped	2 oz
50 g	split pistachio nuts	2 oz
2½ g	Achenbach forcemeat flavouring	a good pinch
1 g	nutmeg	a pinch
	1 tablespoon white wine	
½ g	marjoram	a small pinch
½ g	rosemary	a small pinch
⅛ l	dairy cream	4 fl oz
10 g	onion, grated	⅓ oz
	foie gras parfait	

Garnish:

artichoke bottoms, canned
Achenbach foie gras parfait
truffles, finely chopped

Line a galantine mould with paper thin slices of pork back fat and set aside in a cold place. Mince the shoulder of pork and veal two or three times with the neck fat or bacon using the finest cutter. Carefully fold in the cream. Add the diced leg of pork and ox tongue, the pistachio nuts, truffles, herbs and spices, wine and onion. Place a layer of forcemeat at the base of the galantine mould. Lay a roll of foie gras parfait the thickness of a thumb in the centre. Carefully fill the space round it with forcemeat and cover with forcemeat to fill the mould up to the top edge. Place slices of pork fat on top and cover with the lid of the mould. Tie round firmly to prevent expansion of the contents while cooking. Poach in a bain-marie at about 70–72°C (158–162°F) for 1¼ hours. Plunge into cold water, then refrigerate overnight under light pressure. To serve, unmould and cut in 1 cm (⅜ in) slices.

Artichoke bottoms with truffle surprise: Mix foie gras parfait with finely chopped truffles, shape into small balls and arrange on artichoke bottoms. Dish with the sliced galantine. Serve with curried rice salad, Waldorf salad, chanterelle salad and slices of peach.

(Erwin Frohmann, Bernd Moos, Werner Schall,
Rudolf Achenbach Delicatessen, Germany)

Stuffed breast of veal Genoese style
Poitrine de veau farcie à la mode de Gênes
Cima ripiena alla genovese

1 kg 200	breast of veal, boned	2 lb 10 oz

	1 calf's sweetbread	
100 g	cushion of veal	3½ oz
80 g	cow's udder	3 oz
	1 calf's brain	
	3 pickled ox tongues, cut	
	in thick slices	
100 g	butter	3½ oz
	8 eggs	
50 g	pistachio nuts	2 oz
200 g	Parmesan cheese, grated	7 oz
	2 cloves of garlic, crushed	
250 g	canned peas	9 oz
	fresh marjoram to taste	
30 g	dried flap mushrooms, soaked	1 oz
	4 carrots, blanched and diced	
2 l	clear meat or vegetable broth	3½ pt
	2 tablespoons parsley, chopped	

Cut a pocket for the forcemeat in the breast of veal in the usual manner. To make the forcemeat, brown the sweetbread, cushion of veal, udder and brains in butter, remove from the pan and drain. Chop the cushion of veal, sweetbread and udder very finely, cut up the brains, place in an earthenware bowl and mix well. Add the peas, garlic and parsley, the tongues which have been finely diced, the marjoram, finely chopped, the flap mushrooms which have been squeezed dry and chopped, and the carrots. Beat the eggs and stir into the forcemeat while standing the bowl on ice if possible. Season with salt and pepper, add the Parmesan, mix carefully and add a little more marjoram if required (to give the forcemeat its typical flavour).

When all the ingredients are well blended, stuff the breast of veal with three quarters of the forcemeat. (The veal shrinks and the forcemeat swells while cooking.) Sew up the pocket opening, wrap the veal in a linen cloth and tie. Heat the broth, place the veal in it, cook for 1 hour uncovered, then cover the pan and continue cooking for a further 2 hours. Leave in the stock until cold. Cut into 1 cm (⅜ in) slices and serve with courgettes (recipe, page 1004) or salad as desired.
(Illustration, page 515)

(Franco Colombani, Italy)

Stuffed breast of veal Hoge Veluwe
Poitrine de veau Hoge Veluwe
Gevulde kalfsborst met champignons Hoge veluwe

	breast of veal (quantity as required)	
900 g	lean veal, chopped	2 lb
200 g	calves' sweetbreads, cooked and chopped	7 oz
	4 eggs	
¼ l	dairy cream	9 fl oz

1 kg	large mushrooms	2 lb 4 oz
500 g	carrots, diced	1 lb 2 oz
	Cognac (optional)	
	salt	
	pepper, freshly ground	

Remove the flat bones from the breast of veal and slit with a sharp knife to make a pocket. To make the forcemeat, mix the chopped veal and sweetbreads well and stir in the eggs and cream. Season with salt and pepper and flavour with Cognac if desired. Continue working until very smooth and pliable. Carefully fold in the carrots and the mushrooms which have been coarsely sliced. Stuff the breast of veal with the forcemeat and sew up the opening well. Roast in a moderate oven. This dish is particularly suitable for buffets and may be served either hot or cold.
(Illustration, page 945)

(Bernard van Beurten, Netherlands)

Veal cutlets in aspic
Côtelettes de veau en gelée
Kalbskoteletts in Aspik

6 portions

150 g	6 veal cutlets, each weighing	5 oz
50 g	butter	2 oz
1 dl	white wine (optional)	3½ fl oz
1 l	aspic jelly (flavoured as desired)	1¾ pt
	garnish as desired	

Trim the cutlets very carefully. Fry them slowly in the butter, keeping them very juicy, then add the wine to the pan if desired. Leave the cutlets under light pressure until cold.

Mask suitable moulds with aspic jelly and let it set. Decorate the bottom as desired with slices of egg, gherkins, sliced truffles, tarragon leaves, etc. and fix in position with aspic. Carefully brush the garnish with aspic or pour in a thin layer of aspic. Let it set, then place the cutlets in the moulds and fill up with aspic. Refrigerate until set. Turn out just before serving.

(Sandro Volonté, Switzerland)

Lamb ballottine Geigy
Ballottine d'agneau Geigy
Lammballotine Geigy

10 portions   Cooking time: 90 minutes

1 kg 500	shoulder of lamb	3 lb 5 oz

Forcemeat:

100 g	lamb trimmings	3½ oz
300 g	shoulder of pork	11 oz
	shoulder of veal	
100 g	larding bacon	3½ oz
30 g	dried morels	1 oz
	dried craterelles	
10 g	pistachio nuts	⅓ oz
150 g	ham, diced	5 oz
	larding bacon, diced	
	salt	
	flavourings as desired	

Garnish:

10 olivette tomatoes
sweet corn salad as required
10 pears
3 tablespoons mustard pickles, chopped
10 chicory leaves
celery salad as required

Bone out the shoulder of lamb, taking care to keep its shape. Leave the shoulder joint in place for decoration. Remove the inside sinews.

Prepare the forcemeat as for a galantine. Stuff the shoulder to the shape of a sitting hen. Sew up carefully and tie, but not too tightly, to avoid cutting the flesh while cooking. Heat the oven to 240°C (464°F). Poêler the meat at this temperature for a time, then reduce the heat to 200°C (392°F) and continue cooking. The total cooking time is 1½ hours. If desired, the meat may be cooked in a forced convection oven.

For a cold buffet, two gallottines are prepared, one of them as a showpiece. Both are well chilled and the second one is cut into slices which are glazed with aspic and arranged on an aspic-coated buffet dish. The garnish consists of olivette tomatoes stuffed with sweet corn salad, small pears with mustard pickles and chicory leaves stuffed with celery salad.

(Otto Ledermann, Switzerland)

Stuffed saddle of lamb modern style
Selle d'agneau farcie moderne
Gefüllter Lammrücken Moderne Art

8 portions   Cooking time: 1½ hours

2 kg 500	saddle of lamb	5 lb 8 oz
	4 lamb fillets	
50 g	dried morels, soaked	2 oz

	8 green cabbage leaves, blanched	
100 g	pickled ox tongue	3½ oz
50 g	truffles	2 oz
300 g	veal	11 oz
300 g	pork	11 oz
250 g	fresh pork fat	9 oz
300 g	ice cubes	11 oz
	salt	
	pepper, freshly ground	
	rosemary	
	mint	
6 cl	Cognac	2 fl oz
6 cl	egg white	2 fl oz
4 l	aspic jelly	7 pt
	lamb stock as required	
	meat glaze	

Garnish I:

2 cucumbers, 5 cm (2 in) in diameter
8 cherry-size tomatoes
2 palm hearts

Garnish II:

200 g	Gervais	7 oz
100 g	carrots, cooked	3½ oz
	8 artichoke bottoms	
	10 green peppers	
	juice of 1 lemon	
	2 cabbage leaves, blanched	

Carefully bone the saddle of lamb from underneath. Remove and skin the fillets. Drain and chop the morels. Cover four pieces of foil with a layer of morels, place a lamb fillet in the centre of each, wrap up and freeze.

To make the forcemeat, pass the veal, pork and pork fat through the medium blade of the mincer, then work with the ice cubes in the processor. Add the egg white and Cognac, season with salt and pepper, flavour to taste with rosemary and mint, then refrigerate for an hour. Add the finely diced truffles and tongue and mix well.

Invert the saddle of lamb and line the inside with the blanched cabbage leaves. Stuff with the forcemeat, unwrap the frozen fillets and place in the centre, cover with forcemeat and fold the thin flanks inwards. Tie round with stretch tape. Poach in lamb stock at 120°C (248°F) for 1½ hours. Leave until cold, then brush with meat glaze. Cut into 1½ cm (⅝ in) slices, lay these on a wire tray and glaze with several layers of aspic. Coat a silver serving dish with aspic. Place a piece of saddle about 8 cm (3½ in) long in the centre of the upper edge of the dish. Arrange the 16 slices of meat in closely spaced pairs down the dish with rows of garnish to the left and right.

To make *Garnish I*, peel the cucumbers and cut into 1 cm (⅜ in) slices. Blanch in boiling salted water and refresh in cold water. Transfer to a wire tray and place a skinned tomato the size of a cherry on top. Cut the palm hearts into ½ cm (¼ in) slices and place on the tomatoes. Glaze with several layers of aspic. To make *Garnish II*, seed the green peppers and cut up very finely. Dice the carrots finely. Mix the Gervais with the lemon juice and add the peppers and carrots. Season the cabbage leaves with salt and pepper. Stuff with the Gervais and shape into a roll 5 cm (2 in) thick. Chill well, then cut into 1 cm (⅜ in) slices with a sharp knife. Place the artichoke bottoms on a wire tray and cover each one with a slice of Gervais roll. Glaze several times with aspic.

(Illustration, page 868)

(Gottfried Albert, Austria)

Stuffed pickled saddle of lamb
Selle d'agneau salée farcie
Gepökelter gefüllter Lammrücken

8 portions

1 kg 600	saddle or best end of lamb, boned	3 lb 8 oz

Pickling salt:

1 kg	salt	2 lb 4 oz
10 g	saltpetre	⅓ oz
2 g	sugar	a pinch

Forcemeat:
Yield: 800 g (1 lb 12 oz)

400 g	fresh pork fat		14 oz
300 g	lean pork		11 oz
100 g	foie gras trimmings		3½ oz
approx. 25 g	spiced salt	approx.	1 oz
100 g	truffles, diced		3½ oz
	OR half a can truffle substitute		
100 g	pistachio nuts		3½ oz
100 g	dried morels, blanched and finely sliced		3½ oz
200 g	pork caul		7 oz
500 g	fresh pork fat, thinly sliced		1 lb 2 oz
200 g	leaf spinach, blanched		7 oz
	2 lamb fillets		

Asparagus ring:

asparagus tips
aspic mayonnaise
vegetable mayonnaise
vegetables as desired

Bean purée:

300 g	French beans	11 oz
	salt, pepper	

Rub the pickling salt into the meat well, cover with the salt and leave to stand under pressure for a week, turning the meat daily. To make the forcemeat, mince the pork fat, pork and foie gras, pass through a hair sieve and season. Mix half the forcemeat (400 g – 14 oz) with diced truffles and pistachio nuts. Fill into sausage casing, cook, allow to cool, then remove the casing. Mix the rest of the forcemeat with the morels.

Trim the pickled lamb. Spread out the pork caul on a piece of foil and cover with a thin layer of morel forcemeat. Place the lamb on top, cover with thin slices of truffle, then with morel forcemeat, place slices of pork fat on top and cover these with spinach. Lay the cooked forcemeat on top, together with the two lamb fillets wrapped in slices of pork fat, and roll up. Tie securely and simmer for about 50 minutes in water flavoured with a bouquet garni. Re-tie and leave until cold. Mask with several layers of aspic mayonnaise, cut half the roll in slices and either brush with aspic or dip in aspic.

To make the asparagus ring, mask a ring mould with aspic. Line with asparagus tips cut in half and pour aspic into the spaces between them. Mask with aspic mayonnaise and fill up with vegetable mayonnaise mixed with aspic. When set, dip quickly in hot water and unmould. Fill the hollow centre with vegetables as desired.

To make the bean purée, blanch the beans, work them to a purée and season with salt and pepper. Dress on artichoke bottoms. A further accompaniment to this dish is fennel cut in half and cooked with saffron.
(Illustration, page 939)

(Adolf Meindl, Austria)

Fillet of beef for a country buffet
Filet de boeuf pour buffet campagnard

30 portions

3 kg	fillet of beef	6 lb 10 oz
	60 medium tomatoes	
	3 medium onions, very finely chopped	
100 g	ground paprika	3½ oz
200 g	parsley, very finely chopped	7 oz
200 g	capers	7 oz
	15 egg yolks	
50 g	pepper	2 oz
	2 teaspoons Cayenne pepper	
	5 tablespoons mustard	
2 dl	vinegar	7 fl oz

4 dl	oil	14 fl oz
70 g	salt	2½ oz
1 dl	Worcester sauce	3½ fl oz
1½ l	liquid aspic jelly	2¾ pt
	watercress	

Trim the beef, removing any sinew and skin, then mince finely or scrape with a knife. Cut a cross in the top of the tomatoes, place them in hot water, skin and allow to cool. Hollow out from the underside and drain on a rack.

Prepare mayonnaise with the egg yolks, mustard, oil and vinegar, add the seasonings, onions and parsley and mix thoroughly. Stir in the raw meat a little at a time, then add most of the aspic and mix well again. Fill the mixture into the tomatoes, stand them on a wire tray, glaze with the rest of the aspic when it is beginning to set, and decorate each one with a watercress leaf. Refrigerate. Line a basket with watercress and arrange the tomatoes on it. (Illustration, page 521)

(Jean Esslinger, France)

Stuffed fillet of beef Consignorio
Filet de boeuf farci Consignorio
Filetto di manzo alla Consignorio

10 portions

1 kg 500	fillet of beef	3 lb 5 oz
	calf's liver mousse (page 138)	
	a thick stick of juniper wood	
	same length as the meat	

Trim the meat. Pierce the centre from end to end with a tranchelard, then push the stick into the hole. Roast the meat in a preheated oven for 20 minutes and allow to cool. Remove the stick. Using a savoy bag and plain tube, pipe calf's liver mousse, which has not set, into the cavity. Refrigerate again. The meat may be brushed with aspic or masked with calf's liver mousse.

(Giulio Casazza, Switzerland)

Smoked ox tongue modern style
Langue de boeuf fumée moderne
Fustolt Marhanyel Módern Módra
10 portions

1 kg 800	pickled ox tongue (smoked)	4 lb

200 g	carrots	7 oz
	1 bouquet garni	
	1 stick celery	
500 g	calf's brains	1 lb 2 oz
2 g	salt	a pinch
1 g	peppercorns	half a teaspoon
	2 bay leaves	
20 g	onion	¾ oz
	juice of 2 lemons	
1 kg 200	vegetable salad	2 lb 10 oz
150 g	royale	5 oz
3 dl	Rémoulade sauce (recipe, page 189)	10 fl oz
	6 globes kohlrabi	
180 g	pâté de foie gras	6 oz
300 g	tomatoes	10 oz
150 g	button onions	5 oz
200 g	mushrooms	7 oz
1 g	salt	a small pinch
10 ml	citric acid	2 teaspoons
	¼ bunch radishes	
	¼ lettuce	
	parsley	
20 g	truffles	¾ oz
2½ l	white chaud-froid sauce	4½ pt
2 l	aspic jelly	3½ pt
	18 black olives, stoned	

Soak the tongue in water for at least 12 hours. Place in a large pan of cold water with the bouquet garni, bring to the boil and cook, adding the carrots and celery later.

Remove the blood vessels from the brains, soak in tepid water and remove the skin. Poach in water containing the lemon juice (or citric acid), onion, bay leaves, and peppercorns, then cool.

Prepare well-seasoned vegetable salad, also the required amount of Rémoulade sauce. Poach the royale in a small sausage casing and allow to cool. Turn the mushrooms and blanch them. Slice the kohlrabi fairly thickly, hollow out the centre of the slices and blanch in salted water. Have ready for use lightly seasoned pâté de foie gras flavoured with Cognac. Prepare crystal-clear aspic jelly with the tongue stock, cool, then leave to set at −4°C (25°F). Prepare the garnishes and other ingredients required for dressing – tomatoes, olives, button onions, parsley, lettuce. Lastly, prepare white chaud-froid sauce.

Carefully coat the inside of a dish of suitable size with the chaud-froid sauce and place in the refrigerator to set quickly. Make 4 bases of identical shape with the vegetable salad which has been mixed with aspic. Arrange on top thin slices of tongue alternating with slices of royale, decorate symmetrically with button onions and carefully glaze with aspic, then refrigerate until set.

Meanwhile mask a round mould with aspic and decorate with sliced radishes and truffle motifs round the upper edge. Place the brains inside, cover with aspic and leave to set, then fill up with Rémoulade sauce stiffened with aspic. Stand the mould in ice-cold water and chill thoroughly. Fill the centres of the kohlrabi slices which have been cut zigzag fashion with pâté de foie gras and invert on to slices of tomato. Decorate the top with small slices of tomato and with black olives. Glaze carefully with aspic and garnish with sprigs of parsley. Unmould the brains and refrigerate for a short time. Brush the mushrooms with aspic. Arrange the garnishes on the dish as shown in the illustration.
(Illustration, page 943)

(Josef Csanyi, Hungary)

Stuffed pig's trotter
Pied de porc farci
Gefüllter Schweinsfuss

14–18 portions   Cooking time: 2½ hours

(1)	1 kg 500– 2 kg 500	1 pig's trotter weighing	3 lb 5 oz– 5 lb 8 oz

(2) *Pork forcemeat:* total weight 1 kg 500 (3 lb 5 oz)

1 kg	leg of pork trimmings onions, caraway seeds, thyme, pepper, nutmeg, white wine	2 lb 4 oz
500 g	sausage meat	1 lb 2 oz

(3) *Sausage meat for forcemeat:*

approx. 250 g	veal, minced	approx. 9 oz

approx. 250 g	pork fat, minced coriander,
	    caraway seeds, nutmeg, pepper
	    (freshly ground)
		approx. 9 oz

(4)	1 kg 100	leg of pork, cut into 1½ cm (⅝ in) dice	2 lb 8 oz
	300 g	ox tongue, diced	11 oz
	100 g	split pistachio nuts	3½ oz
	50 g	truffles	2 oz
	6 g	forcemeat flavouring	¼ oz
	60 g	salt	2 oz
	1½ g	thyme, finely ground	a good pinch
	3 g	coriander	a good pinch
	3 g	caraway seeds	a good pinch

		very little garlic, grated	
(5)		foie gras parfait	
(6)	1 dl	brandy	3½ fl oz
	1 g	saffron	a pinch

Wash pig's trotter carefully in warm water, shave off the bristles, then bone out, cutting through skin and removing bone as far as hoof.

Mix the pork forcemeat with the remaining ingredients except the foie gras parfait and brandy. Stuff trotter with half the forcemeat. Insert a roll of foie gras parfait 2–3 cm (about 1 in) thick and cover with the rest of the forcemeat. Fold the skin over to enclose the stuffing, wrap in a cloth and tie securely. Cook in a bain-marie at 75°C (165°F) for 2½ hours. Refresh in cold water for about 5 minutes, then refrigerate overnight at about 1–3°C (34–37°F). Unwrap and wash in warm water. Wipe off the fat left on the surface after poaching.

Mix together the brandy and saffron and brush on to the trotter to give the skin a bright yellow sheen. Decorate with a flower consisting of petals out of a red pepper with a small disk of pepper in the centre. Finish off with leaves made out of leek leaves.

(Erwin Frohmann, Bernd Moos, Werner Schall,
Rudolf Achenbach Delicatessen, Germany)

Stuffed ham Igeho
Jambon de jeune porc Igeho
Jungschweinkeule Igeho

12 portions   Cooking time: about 2 hours

		ham	5 lb
	2 kg 300	mustard pickles	

Ham mousse:

		dairy cream	10 fl oz
	3 dl	gelatine	⅓ oz
	10 g	tomato-flavoured chaud-froid sauce	

Aspic jelly:
1 l (1¾ pt)

		consommé double, well	1¾ pt
	1 l	clarified and seasoned	
	70 g	powdered aspic	2½ oz

Garnishes:
I. Vegetables in aspic:

cucumber balls
carrot balls
celeriac balls
peas
12 cherry-size tomatoes
12 quails' eggs

II.   500 g   apple slices, fluted   1 lb 2 oz
                and stewed
                12 plums
                1 stalk angelica

III.   6 small tomatoes
        12 stuffed olives
        12 artichoke bottoms
        ham mousse
        vinegar
        bay leaf
        parsley
        lemon
        salt
        pepper, freshly ground

Poach the ham in water at 80°C (176°F) for 2 hours. Leave in a cool place until cold, then cut out the cushion. Fill the cavity with ham mousse and smooth off to the original shape of the ham. Carve the cushion and arrange the slices on the ham. Decorate the top with mustard pickles. Decorate the ham rolls with truffle motifs and brush with aspic.

Make the mousse with the ham trimmings, the cream, gelatine and chaud-froid sauce. For the ham rolls, fill the centre of small, thin, rolled-up slices of ham with ham mousse.

To make the aspic jelly, stir the powdered aspic into the consommé and warm to 90°C (194°F) over gentle heat. The total quantity of aspic required is 3 l (5 pt), including the amount needed to coat the serving dish.

For the vegetables in aspic, mask a 20 cm (8 in) cake mould with aspic jelly. Line the bottom alternately with the vegetable balls, which have been briefly marinated and well drained, the peas and the quails' eggs in a symmetrical pattern. Lightly coat with aspic, allow to set, then arrange a second layer of vegetable balls on top. Fill up with aspic which is just beginning to set and refrigerate for a few hours.

For garnish II, stone the plums and surround each one with stewed apple slices. Decorate with two thin strips of angelica. To make garnish III, cut the tomatoes in half, scoop out the seeds and sprinkle inside with salt. Fill with ham mousse and invert on the artichoke bottoms. Glaze with aspic and decorate with a stuffed olive.

To serve, line a rectangular dish with aspic. Dress the ham in the top lefthand corner and the vegetables in aspic in the bottom righthand corner. Finish off with a harmonious arrangement of ham rolls, tomatoes on artichoke bottoms, and apple slices.

(Franz Sailer, Austria)

Parsley ham Burgundy style I and II
Recipes, page 980

Shoulder of pork Belle Epoque
Epaule de porcelet belle époque
Schweineschulter Belle Epoque

25 portions

	1 small shoulder of pork with foot (from a 4 to 5 month old pig)	
4 kg	weighing about	8 lb 12 oz
300 g	sausage meat (recipe, page 134)	11 oz
150 g	pickled pork, poached in blood and finely diced	5 oz
300 g	ham and pig's tongue, finely diced	11 oz
50 g	pistachio nuts	2 oz

Accompaniments:

500 g	small tomatoes	1 lb 2 oz
200 g	sweet corn	7 oz
200 g	mayonnaise	7 oz
	10 small corn cobs	
600 g	cucumbers	1 lb 5 oz
200 g	chanterelles for salad	7 oz
	10 tartlet cases	
150 g	celery salad	5 oz
	10 cherries with stalks	
	salt, spices	
	onions, chopped	
10 g	truffles, sliced	1/3 oz
4 l	aspic jelly	7 pt

Bone the shoulder of pork, leaving a cavity for stuffing, and remove the sinews. Pickle and smoke very lightly. Carefully mix the sausage meat with the diced pork, ham and tongue and the nuts. Stuff the shoulder with this forcemeat. Tie in a cloth and poach over low heat in good stock. Cool in the stock.

Cut out the thick part of the shoulder carefully and remove the skin. Carve off some slices, place these on a wire tray and glaze lightly with aspic. The rest of the joint is used as a showpiece and harmoniously arranged with the accompaniments to provide an attractive display. This dish may also be served hot as part of a hot buffet, with hot potato salad or Dauphinoise potatoes and mixed salad.

(Otto Ledermann, Switzerland)

Stuffed shoulder of pork autumn style
Epaule de porc farcie automnale
Gefüllte Schweineschulter herbstliche Art mit Essigkräutersauce

12 portions   Cooking time: 2 hours

3 kg	2 small shoulders of pork each weighing	6 lb 10 oz
300 g	fresh pork fat	11 oz
250 g	truffles, finely cut	9 oz
300 g	pickled tongue, finely diced	11 oz
300 g	pistachio nuts	11 oz
500 g	goose liver free from sinew	1 lb 2 oz
⅛ l	sherry	4 fl oz
⅛ l	Madeira	4 fl oz
	salt	
	white pepper, freshly ground	
	allspice	
	forcemeat flavouring	
6 l	aspic jelly	10½ pt
⅛ l	egg white	4 fl oz
½ l	meat glaze	18 fl oz
500 g	ice cubes	1 lb 2 oz
	potato flour	

Garnish:

	4 courgettes 4 cm (1½ in) in diameter	
	2 celeriac	
200 g	carrots	7 oz
	½ avocado	
25 g	cauliflower	1 oz
	1 large white radish	
	20 green peppers	
	20 red peppers	
	20 yellow peppers	
	15 small corn cobs	
	20 black olives	
	24 piri-piri	

100 g	Gervais	3½ oz
	lemon juice	
	liquid aspic	
	2 tablespoons dairy cream	

Vinaigrette sauce:

	2 tablespoons parsley, finely chopped	
	1 tablespoon chives, finely chopped	
	1 tablespoon chervil, finely chopped	
	1 tablespoon tarragon, finely chopped	
	1 tablespoon onion, finely chopped	
	1 tablespoon capers, finely chopped	
	½ tablespoon lemon balm, finely chopped	
¼ l	olive oil	9 fl oz
¹⁄₁₆ l	wine vinegar	2 fl oz
¹⁄₁₆ l	water	2 fl oz
	salt	
	pepper, freshly ground	
	a pinch of salt	

Carefully bone out the shoulders of pork as far as the foot bone, as for zampone. Cut the meat and fat off the skin. Leave the skin and feet in cold water for about 2 hours.

To make forcemeat, mince 2 kg (4 lb 8 oz) pork cut from the shoulders, using the medium blade of the mincer. Pass the fresh pork fat separately through the same blade. Season the minced pork with salt, place in the processor with the ice cubes and work until finely blended. Add the minced fat a little later and work together. Mix with the egg white and add salt, pepper, allspice and forcemeat flavouring. Refrigerate for about an hour.

Marinate the truffles in sherry. Dip the tongue, pistachio nuts and truffles in potato flour and mix with the forcemeat. Marinate the fresh goose liver in Madeira, drain well and pass through a fine wire sieve. Transfer to a savoy bag and pipe on to aluminium foil to make two rolls 1½ cm (⅝ in) across. Roll up in the foil and place in deep freeze until firm. Drain the pork skins well and dry carefully with absorbent kitchen paper.

Fill the forcemeat into the skins, shape each into a sausage, divide along the middle with the side of the hand and place a roll of goose liver in the groove. Fold the skin over the forcemeat and carefully sew up the ends. Shape neatly as required and enclose in foil. The diameter should be 8 cm (3½ in). Wrap in damp cloths and tie separately on to boards 12 cm (5 in) wide. Fill the rest of the forcemeat into an 8 cm (3½ in) bombe mould which has been brushed with butter. Steam at 70°C (158°F) for 2 hours together with the stuffed shoulders, allow to cool, then chill well for 6 hours.

Cut each stuffed shoulder in two. Place the back piece on a wire tray, brush with meat glaze and allow to cool. Cut the front half in 1 cm (⅜ in) slices, place these on a wire tray and glaze with several layers of clear light aspic. When the back half is quite cold, glaze it in the same way.

Coat a 90 x 52 cm (36 x 20 in) rectangular silver dish with amber coloured aspic to a thickness of about 4 cm (1½ in). Place the autumn vegetable arrangement in the centre near the upper edge, with the two stuffed shoulders on a slant on either side towards the ends of the dish. Arrange the slices of meat one overlapping another at 2 cm (¾ in) intervals. Surround the vegetable arrangement with the celeriac garnish necklace fashion. Place the courgette garnish in the empty triangles next to the slices of meat. Hand the vinaigrette sauce separately. For the centrepiece, make an autumnal bouquet arrangement with the cold meat bombe, the corn cobs, cauliflower florets, peppers and olives.

To make the courgette garnish, cut the courgettes obliquely into slices 1 cm (⅜ in) thick and 8½ cm (3½ in) long. Blanch in boiling salted water and refresh in cold water. Place on a wire tray and pipe 3 dots of creamed Gervais on to each slice. Top each dot with a 1 cm (⅜ in) disk of white radish. Arrange 2 piri-piri in the shape of a V on the front of each slice of courgette, with a half-slice of olive at the point of the V. Glaze with clear light aspic.

To make the celeriac garnish, peel the celeriac and rub at once with lemon juice. Cut 12 disks ½ cm (¼ in) thick out of the centre. Prepare an oval stencil 8 cm (3½ in) long. Place it on the slices of celeriac and cut out with a pointed knife. Blanch in boiling water containing a little lemon juice, refresh in iced water and place on a wire tray. Peel the carrots and cook in lightly salted water. Cut into slices, then into 2½ cm (1 in) disks. Place these in the centre of the celeriac slices.

Peel the avocado half and sieve finely. Add a little lemon juice and liquid aspic, together with 2 tablespoons dairy cream, and mix well. Spread to a thickness of ½ cm (¼ in) on a small metal tray and refrigerate until firm, then cut into 12 mm (½ in) disks and place in the centre of the carrot slices. Glaze with clear aspic.

To make the vinaigrette sauce, mix the oil, salt and pepper together well. Add the vinegar and water, then the herbs, and mix well again.
(Illustration, page 868)

(Siegfried Seelos, Austria)

Galantine of sucking pig Noblesse
Galantine de cochon de lait noblesse
Spanferkelgalantine Noblesse

8 portions

1 kg 800	saddle of sucking pig	4 lb
400 g	pork fillet	14 oz
200 g	mushrooms, very finely chopped	7 oz
100 g	onions, very finely chopped	3½ oz
150 g	panada	5 oz
300 g	pork free from sinews	11 oz

	1 red pepper	
	1 green pepper	
	1 cucumber	
200 g	pickled tongue (point end only)	7 oz
	1 pork caul	
	salt, pepper, forcemeat flavouring	
	Cognac	
1½ dl	dairy cream	5 fl oz
5 dl	pork stock	18 fl oz
	aspic for glazing	
	a little meat glaze	
	a little oil	

Bone the saddle without damaging the skin. Rub with salt, pepper and forcemeat flavouring. Lightly brown the onions and mushrooms, season with salt and pepper and allow to cool. Trim the pork fillet, season with salt, brown lightly in hot oil, allow to cool and cut in half. Cover with the browned onions and mushrooms and wrap in a pork caul.

Clean the peppers and cut into cubes. Dice the tongue. Mince the 300 g (11 oz) pork, using the finest cutter, and mix well with the panada. Stir in the cream, peppers and tongue, season with salt and pepper and flavour to taste with forcemeat flavouring and Cognac.

Spread out the saddle with the inside uppermost, cover with half the forcemeat, place the pork fillet on top, then cover with the remaining forcemeat. Fold the ends together and roll in a damp cloth. Tie securely and poach for about 90 minutes in well flavoured pork stock. Leave until cold, then unwrap the galantine, roll tightly in a clean cloth, tie and press. Coat with meat glaze, slice, then glaze the slices with aspic and cut in half.

Garnish with peeled, hollowed out cucumber filled with Gervais cream and very finely diced radishes, also with skinned, seeded tomatoes filled with herb cream.

To decorate, cut out small balls of cucumber with a round vegetable scoop and place them on the galantine to resemble a bunch of grapes. Finish off with a short pastry vine loaf. (Illustration, page 869)

(Ewald Plachutta, Austria)

Hot Buffets

Stuffed breast of veal Hoge Veluwe
Recipe, page 376

Shoulder of beef after my own fashion

10 portions

3 kg	shoulder of beef	6 lb 10 oz
1 kg	salt belly of pork or streaky bacon, thinly sliced, for barding	2 lb 4 oz
450 g	pork fat	1 lb
300 g	fat pork or streaky bacon for forcemeat	11 oz
200 g	veal	7 oz
250 g	breadcrumbs	9 oz
500 g	onions	1 lb 2 oz
	5 shallots	
200 g	carrots	7 oz
	bouquet garni of	
	3 sprigs rosemary	
	4 bay leaves	
	parsley root	
	3 cloves of garlic	
3 g	saffron	a good pinch
2 g	powdered sage	a good pinch
250 g	butter	9 oz
2 dl	light stock	7 fl oz
1 dl	Espagnole sauce	3½ fl oz
2 dl	dairy cream	7 fl oz
	6 eggs	
400 g	green peppers	14 oz
300 g	red peppers	11 oz
70 g	black truffles	2½ oz
	2 calves' feet	
3 kg	veal bones	6 lb 10 oz
1 l	dry white wine	1¾ pt
	1 pork caul	
12 cl	Cognac	4 fl oz
1 g	powdered mace	a pinch
500 g	rice	1 lb 2 oz
300 g	small peas	11 oz

Seed half the red and green peppers and cut them in strips. Cut the pork fat in strips. Prepare a marinade with the wine, the herbs and the garlic which has been finely chopped. Trim the beef, lard it with the strips of fat and thread it alternately with strips of red and green pepper between the lardons. Marinate for 5 hours, then remove, drain, dry well with a cloth and season. Set aside the marinade. Heat 100 g (3½ oz) butter in a braising pan, brown the meat well in it, add the veal bones, the calves' feet and a mirepoix of carrots, onions and 2 shallots, fry lightly, cover and braise lightly in a very hot oven in the classic manner. Remove the bones, calves' feet and mirepoix. Pour off the fat.

Wrap the beef in the pork caul and return to the braising pan with the vegetables and calves' feet. Stir in the marinade to detach the cooking juices, cover and reduce, then add the light stock and the Espagnole sauce and braise for 4 hours, checking occasionally. When the calves' feet are cooked, remove them, rinse and bone, then cool the meat under pressure. When the beef is tender, remove from the pan, allow to cool, then chill. Lay the slices of pork belly (or streaky bacon) side by side on a napkin and sprinkle with powdered sage and Cognac.

Prepare a salpicon with the remaining peppers, 1 onion and 2 shallots. Cook gently in a little butter, then add the truffles, finely diced, and the meat from the calves' feet which has been cut into small cubes. Season with salt and pepper.

Coarsely dice the fat pork (or bacon) for the forcemeat, also the veal. Fry lightly together with a sliced onion and a chopped shallot until golden brown, remove from the heat and pour off the fat. Add the breadcrumbs which have been soaked in the cream, and mince twice, using the finest cutter. Transfer to a bowl and stir in the eggs, well beaten, 5 cl (2 fl oz) Cognac, salt and pepper. Add half the salpicon and mix thoroughly. Spread part of this forcemeat on to the slices of pork belly (or bacon). Remove the caul from the beef and carve the meat evenly. Spread the slices with the rest of the forcemeat, replace in their original position, place on the slices of pork belly and wrap these round the meat to enclose it completely. Tie round closely and sprinkle with salt and pepper. Roast for 1¼ hours in a very hot oven or on a spit, basting very frequently.

Meanwhile cream 150 g (5 oz) butter, blend in the saffron and mace, season with salt and mix with the rest of the salpicon. Work the ingredients together well and refrigerate. Mould into 10 egg-shaped quenelles with a dessertspoon and refrigerate until firm, then egg and bread-crumb them and refrigerate again. Prepare a thick Italian risotto (without cheese) with the rice and as much bouillon as required. Cook the peas in boiling salted water. Fill the risotto into 10 buttered savarin moulds. Strain the braising stock and adjust the seasoning. Pass through a hair sieve and keep hot over very low heat until required.

When the meat is roasted, remove the twine. Using a sharp carving knife, make a horizontal incision through the joint to cut off the top quarter in the form of a lid. Cover the lower part with a thin layer of peas, pour a little stock over, replace the lid and brush with hot stock.

Brush a serving dish with melted butter and place the meat on it. Turn out the rice moulds to form a ring round the meat. Fill the centre of each with peas. Cover the whole dish with buttered paper and place in a hot oven. Meanwhile deep-fry the quenelles, then arrange them on the dish between the rice moulds. Present the dish, handing the sauce separately. For each portion, pour a little sauce on to a well-warmed plate, then serve two slices of meat, a ring mould with peas and a fried quenelle.

(Jean Esslinger, France)

Roast sucking pig
Porcelet (cochon de lait) rôti au four
Péceno Prase

12–14 portions   Cooking time: 3½–4 hours

	1 sucking pig, prepared for cooking,	6½–
3–4 kg	weighing	8¾ lb
150 g	lard	5 oz
5 cl	oil	2 fl oz
	salt	

Carefully sprinkle the sucking pig inside with salt and lay on its back for an hour. To prevent it from losing its shape while roasting, insert into the belly a beer bottle which has been thoroughly washed inside and outside, then sew up the opening. Place a rack in the roasting pan, or arrange 4 metal rods or wooden stakes to make a grid. Rub the pig with lard and place on top. Roast at 220°C (428°F) for 3½ to 4 hours, basting with oil frequently. Allow to cool a little before serving, then carve and dress on a hot dish (illustrations, page 102). Cold sucking pig is a very popular supper dish, as well as providing a satisfying light meal at other times of the day.

(László Csizmadia, Yugoslavia)

Stuffed sucking pig

8–10 portions   Roasting time: about 5 hours

4 kg 500–	1 sucking pig weighing	10–15 lb
6 kg 500		
	2 tablespoons dried thyme leaves	
100 g	mushrooms	4 oz
	2 tablespoons onions, minced	
50 g	apples, peeled and diced	2 oz
	2 tablespoons butter	
40 g	dry breadcrumbs	1½ oz
	2 eggs, slightly beaten	
	½ teaspoon nutmeg	
	½ teaspoon salt	

	½ teaspoon pepper	
50 g	melted bacon fat	2 oz
50 g	onions, peeled and chopped	2 oz
25 g	celery, chopped	1 oz
50 g	ham, diced	2 oz
	2 small carrots, scraped and chopped	
	1 sprig fresh thyme	
	1 bay leaf	
40 g	dry mustard mixed with	1½ oz
	3 tablespoons water	
	1 red apple	
⅛ l	apple cider	4 fl oz
⅛ l	brown stock	4 fl oz
	1 tablespoon cornflour mixed with	
	1 teaspoon water	

Wash the sucking pig thoroughly inside and out. Dry with paper towels and sprinkle thyme in the cavity. Place in the refrigerator for 12 hours. Preheat the oven to 175°C (350°F). Sauter the mushrooms, minced onion and diced apples in the butter, mix with the breadcrumbs and eggs to make a stuffing and season with nutmeg. Sprinkle the cavity of the pig with the salt and pepper. Fill with the stuffing mixture and sew up carefully. Cover the snout, ears and tail with foil to protect them from burning. Pull the hindlegs backward and the forelegs forward and tie securely. Place the bacon fat in a large roasting pan and add the chopped onions and celery, the ham, carrots, thyme and bay leaf. (These may be added in the form of a mirepoix tied together in cheesecloth). Set the pig on a bed of vegetables as desired. Roast at 175°C (350°F) for 5 hours, basting every 10 minutes or so with the drippings in the pan.

For a crisp skin and a spicy flavour, brush the pig with mustard every 15 minutes. When cooked, remove the pig and transfer to a large dish. Place the apple (whole) in the mouth. Drain the fat from the pan and pour the drippings into a saucepan. Add the cider, brown stock and cornflour blended with the water. Simmer for 10 minutes. Strain the gravy into another saucepan. Bring to the boil and add any remaining mustard paste. Season to taste with salt and pepper. Hand the sauce separately. This is an excellent main course for a special dinner party or buffet.

(Hermann Rusch, USA)

Hot Main Dishes

Beef

Stuffed beefsteak Styrian style
Steak de boeuf farci à la styrienne
Gefülltes Beefsteak Steirischer Herbst

4 portions

160 g	4 beefsteaks each weighing	5½ oz
4 cl	oil	1½ fl oz
	salt, pepper	

Filling:

20 g	butter	¾ oz
	2 tablespoons onions, finely chopped	
20 g	ham or smoked meat	¾ oz
50 g	mushrooms *or* chanterelles	2 oz
	if in season	
20 g	gherkins	¾ oz
	1 egg	
	2 tablespoons breadcrumbs	
	2 tablespoons parsley, chopped	
	salt, Aromat	

Sauce:

4 cl	fruit brandy	1½ fl oz
20 g	butter	¾ oz
1¼ dl	dairy cream	4 fl oz
	1 tablespoon ketchup	
1¼ dl	gravy or bouillon	4 fl oz

Garnish:

	2 fried chicken livers	
	black grapes	

Accompaniment – green polenta slices:

3 dl	milk	10 fl oz
120 g	coarse maize meal	4 oz
	1 egg	
	4 anchovy fillets, chopped	
250 g	fresh leaf spinach	9 oz
40 g	butter	1½ oz
	2 cloves of garlic	
	salt, pepper, nutmeg	

Beat the steaks lightly, season and cut a pocket in each one with a pointed knife. To make the filling, chop the ham, mushrooms and gherkin finely and fry in the butter together with the onions and parsley. Season, bind with the egg and breadcrumbs and stand over moderate heat for a short time. Stuff the steaks with this filling, secure with toothpicks and fry until medium done.

To make the sauce, pour off the oil in which the steaks were fried, flamber the steaks with fruit brandy and transfer them to a warmed serving dish. Add the butter, cream, ketchup, remaining fruit brandy and gravy or bouillon to the pan to make a thin sauce.

To make the polenta slices, season the milk, bring to the boil and stir in the maize meal. Return to the boil, cover and cook gently for 10 minutes. Blanch the spinach and squeeze dry. Add to the cooked polenta together with the egg and anchovy fillets, and mix well. Adjust the seasoning. Spread on a greased baking sheet to the thickness of one finger and dry for a short time in a moderate oven, then allow to cool. Cut into diamond shapes and fry in butter on both sides.

To serve, pour the sauce over the steaks, fix the liver and grapes in position with cocktail sticks and surround with polenta slices. This dish is also suitable for individual plate service. (Illustration, page 626)

(Ernst Faseth, Austria)

Braised beef
Geschmortes Beinfleisch

4 portions

1 kg 200	braising beef (rib)	2 lb 10 oz
	1 calf's or pig's foot, blanched	
6 cl	oil	2 fl oz
approx. 30 g	flour approx.	1 oz
150 g	mirepoix, consisting of carrots, celeriac, onions	5 oz
	1 bacon rind	
	1 bouquet garni, consisting of leek, parsley, garlic, bay leaf, thyme	
	1 tablespoon tomato purée	
3¾ dl	red wine	13 fl oz
1 l	brown stock	1¾ pt
	salt, pepper	

Semolina dumplings:

2½ dl	milk	9 fl oz
120 g	semolina	4 oz

	2 eggs	
30 g	butter	1 oz
	2 rolls without crusts	
	salt, nutmeg	

Cabbage balls:

800 g	cabbage	1 lb 12 oz
50 g	carrots	2 oz
50 g	onions	2 oz
	8 rashers bacon	
	salt, pepper	
	brown stock	

Cut the meat into portions, season with salt and pepper and fry in hot oil to brown. Add the mirepoix, the bacon rind and tomato purée and fry well. Moisten with 2½ dl (9 fl oz) red wine, then pour in the brown stock. Add the calf's or pig's foot and the bouquet garni. Braise slowly in the oven for about 1½ to 2 hours. After three quarters of the cooking time, reduce the liquid, dust with flour, add the rest of the wine and finish cooking. Strain the sauce and adjust the seasoning.

To make the dumplings, bring the milk to the boil with a little butter, add the semolina, season with salt, cook and allow to cool. Bind with the eggs and mix with the rolls which have been diced and fried in butter. Shape into dumplings and poach gently in salted water for about 10 to 15 minutes.

To make the cabbage balls, cut the cabbage in quarters, blanch in salted water, refresh, separate the leaves and season. With the aid of a cloth, shape the cabbage leaves into balls. Wrap these in rashers of bacon and stew under cover in brown stock on a bed of carrots and onions.

(Frank Zodl, Austria)

Bitok Russian style
Bitoks à la russe

10 portions

1 kg 500	fillet of beef	3 lb 5 oz
500 g	butter	1 lb 2 oz
5 g	black pepper, freshly ground	⅙ oz
1 g	nutmeg, grated	a pinch
20 g	capers, finely chopped	¾ oz
150 g	flour	5 oz
2 kg	potatoes	4 lb 8 oz
	1 bunch parsley, finely chopped	
1 dl	milk	3½ fl oz

4 dl	sour cream	14 fl oz
4 dl	fresh dairy cream	14 fl oz
300 g	onions Lyons style	11 oz
20 g	mustard	¾ oz
	salt	
	lard	

Mince the beef finely and place in a bowl. Season with salt, pepper and nutmeg, add about 300 g (11 oz) softened butter, mix well with the hands and knead. Mould into small, flat, oval shapes, flour them and shallow-fry in hot clarified butter. Transfer to a fireproof dish and keep hot. Pour away the butter remaining in the pan, then stir in the sour and fresh cream and the milk which have been blended with a little flour. Bring to the boil and add the mustard and capers.

Peel and slice the potatoes which have been boiled in their skins, sauter them in a little hot lard, season with salt and mix with the parsley. Dress the bitok in the centre of a warmed dish, surround with the potatoes and pour the sauce over. Top with fried onion rings Lyons style.

To make the onion rings, thinly slice the onions and separate the rings. Season lightly with fine salt, flour them and fry in very hot deep or shallow oil until crisp and golden.

(Zsolt Körmendy, Russia)

Brisket of beef with horseradish
Poitrine de boeuf au raifort
Tornás hus

5 portions   Cooking time: 2½ hours

1 kg 250	brisket of beef	2 lb 12 oz
200 g	carrots	7 oz
100 g	celeriac	3½ oz
100 g	leeks	3½ oz
10 g	peppercorns	⅓ oz
5 g	saffron	⅙ oz
10 g	ginger	⅓ oz
	1 clove of garlic	
250 g	horseradish, grated	9 oz
	1 bunch chives, finely chopped	
2 dl	sour cream	7 fl oz
300 g	salt	10 oz

Garnish:

fried potatoes with onions
(recipe, page 1021)

Cut the meat in pieces along the bone, carefully rub in the salt and stand in a cool place for 2 days, then remove from the brine. Cook in water containing the vegetables, peppercorns, saffron, ginger and garlic to make a strong, well-flavoured broth.

Mix the freshly grated horseradish and the chives with the sour cream and season with salt and pepper. To serve, carve the meat and dress in a deep dish. Surround with the cooked carrots, celeriac and leeks, and pour the bouillon over. Hand the potatoes and horseradish sauce separately.
(Illustration, page 622)

(Gyula Gullner, Hungary)

Salt brisket of beef Norwegian fashion
Poitrine de boeuf salée à la norvégienne
Lettsprengt oksebryst

8 portions

2 kg	salt brisket of beef	4 lb 8 oz
	2 tablespoons sugar	
100 g	French mustard	3½ oz
	2 tablespoons white wine	
50 g	coriander	2 oz
	bouquet garni	

Swedes with Béchamel sauce:

1 kg	swedes	2 lb 4 oz
30 g	flour	1 oz
30 g	butter or margarine	1 oz
6 dl	milk	1 pt
	salt, pepper	
20 g	clarified butter	¾ oz

Cook the brisket until tender in water containing the bouquet garni. Cool for a short time, then bone and trim the meat. Spread on all sides with a mixture of mustard, sugar and white wine, and sprinkle with coriander. Brown in the oven at about 200°C (392°F). To serve, cut in slices. The accompaniments are swedes in Béchamel sauce and mashed potatoes with clarified butter.

To make the Béchamel sauce, prepare a roux with the butter (or margarine) and the flour, stir in the cold milk, bring to the boil and season with salt and pepper. Pour over the boiled swedes.
(Illustration, page 625)

(Rolf Fröshaug, Norway)

Salt brisket of beef with beetroot and horseradish
Poitrine de boeuf aux betteraves rouges et au raifort

8 portions   Cooking time: 3–3½ hours

1 kg 800	salt brisket of beef	4 lb
	2 beetroots	
100 g	horseradish	3½ oz
	vinegar	
	salt	
	sugar	
	pepper, freshly ground	

Cook the brisket slowly over gentle heat for 3 to 3½ hours. Cut into slices, dress on a hot dish and pour a few spoonfuls of the hot stock over.

Cook the beetroots, keeping them somewhat firm, peel them and grate together with the horseradish. Add vinegar, salt, sugar and pepper to give a sweet and sour flavour, and serve with the brisket.

(Hermann Wohl, Israel)

Brussels sweetbreads
Choesels à la bruxelloise

10 portions

1 kg	oxtail	2 lb 4 oz
250 g	beef dripping	9 oz
500 g	onions, chopped	1 lb 2 oz
½ l	water	18 fl oz
1 l	veal stock	1¾ pt
1 kg	ox kidney	2 lb 4 oz
1 kg	breast of veal	2 lb 4 oz
	2 sheep's trotters	
	salt, pepper	
	5 sprigs thyme	
	3 bay leaves	
	1 knob of garlic cloves	
	3 cloves	
2 l	Gueze (Belgian beer)	3½ pt
1 kg 500	calf's sweetbreads, trimmed and blanched	3 lb 5 oz
2 dl	Madeira	7 fl oz

Garnish:

2 kg	boiled potatoes	4 lb 8 oz

Cut the oxtail into 3 cm (about 1 in) lengths and brown lightly on all sides in the dripping, then add the onions and brown lightly. Pour the dripping into a second pan. Stir the water into the pan containing the oxtail, add the veal stock and cook for 30 minutes.

In the second pan brown the kidney which has been well washed and trimmed and cut into 3 cm (about 1 in) pieces; also brown the veal cut into 3 cm (about 1 in) pieces, and the sheep's trotters, cut in quarters. Pour off the fat, add salt and pepper, the thyme, bay leaves and cloves, and the cloves of garlic. Pour in the beer and cook for 35 minutes. Add the sweetbreads, cut into 4 cm (1½ in) pieces, cook for a further 20 minutes, then add the oxtail with the onions and cooking liquid. Adjust the seasoning. Carefully remove the fat, add the Madeira and serve very hot. Hand the potatoes separately.

(André Béghin, Belgium)

Fillet of beef Old Vienna style
Filet de boeuf vieille Vienne
Altwiener Lungenbraten

8 portions

1 kg 200	fillet of beef	2 lb 10 oz
	salt, pepper	

Forcemeat:

150 g	veal	5 oz
150 g	pork	5 oz
	2 rolls	
	1 small onion, finely chopped	
50 g	butter	2 oz
	1 clove of garlic	
	1 teaspoon parsley, chopped	
50 g	dried flap mushrooms, chopped	2 oz
	1 egg	
	salt, pepper, paprika	
100 g	chicken livers	3½ oz
5 cl	oil	2 fl oz
2 l	cream sauce	3½ pt

Trim the fillet of beef and cut round it lengthwise so that it can be opened out into a large escalope the thickness of one finger. Beat lightly, season with salt and pepper, spread evenly with the forcemeat, place the chicken livers, cut into strips, in the centre and roll up. Tie securely and brown lightly in the oil. Add the cream sauce and stew until tender, then untie and carve. Serve with home made noodles.

To make the forcemeat, mince the veal and pork, mix well with the rolls which have been soaked and squeezed dry and the onion which has been lightly fried in butter. Season with salt, pepper and paprika, add the clove of garlic, crushed, the parsley, mushrooms and egg, and mix well.

(Eduard Mayer, Austria)

Fillet of beef with artichoke hearts
Rinderfilet mit Artischockenvierteln (bürgerliche Art)

4 portions

800 g	fillet of beef, trimmed	1 lb 12 oz
40 g	butter	1½ oz
2½ dl	thickened veal stock	9 fl oz
	salt, pepper	

Garnish:

	16 artichoke hearts, fresh or canned	
100 g	smoked bacon, cut in julienne strips	3½ oz
150 g	potatoes (raw), finely diced	5 oz
150 g	shallots	5 oz
	2 cloves of garlic	
50 g	butter	2 oz
1¼ dl	bouillon	4 fl oz
1¼ dl	white wine	4 fl oz
	1 teaspoon parsley, chopped	
	1 teaspoon lemon juice	

Rub salt and pepper into the beef and roast slowly at 220°C (428°F) until brown on all sides. The roasting time should be about 35 minutes, leaving the meat medium rare. Keep hot, rinse the roasting pan with the veal stock to detach the juices, reduce a little, thicken with cornflour and strain.

To make the garnish, cut the artichoke hearts in quarters and blanch in salted water. If using fresh artichokes, trim and cut in to quarters, remove the chokes and blanch for about 10 to 12 minutes in water containing a little lemon juice. Brown the shallots, garlic and bacon lightly in butter. Add the artichokes and potatoes. Stir in the wine, then the bouillon, season with salt and pepper and stew for 15 minutes.

Add the parsley to browned butter while it is foaming, then add the lemon juice and pour over the vegetables. Hand the beef gravy separately.

(Franz Zodl, Austria)

Fillet of beef Cecil
Filet de boeuf Cecil

4 portions

approx. 600 g	fillet of beef (middle cut)	approx.	1 lb 5 oz
100 g	butter mixed with oil		3½ oz
	salt, pepper		
	4 large potatoes		

Garlic butter:

100 g	fresh butter	3½ oz
	1 clove of garlic	
	a little lemon juice	

Stand the fillet of beef on end, compress with the flat of the hand and reduce its height to 5 or 6 cm (about 2 in) with the aid of a cutlet bat. Fry in half the butter and oil until medium rare, then remove from the pan. Pour in a little water to detach the cooking juices and make gravy.

To make the garlic butter, mix the butter with the juice of the garlic clove and a few drops of lemon juice. Shape into a roll on aluminium foil and refrigerate.

Peel and wash the potatoes, cut them very thinly and dry well on a cloth. Heat the rest of the butter/oil mixture and sauter the potatoes in it. Season with salt and pepper and place in a fireproof serving dish to form a base for the meat.

Carve the meat on the slant and dress on the potatoes. Place thin slices of garlic butter between the slices of meat and sprinkle with the gravy. Melt the butter slightly under a salamander. Serve with fresh salad dressed with olive oil and lemon juice.

(Eric Carlström, Sweden)

Fillet of beef Vurro
Filet de boeuf Vurro
Filette di manzo alla Vurro

1 portion

180 g	fillet of beef	6 oz
	butter as required	
	oil as required	
1 dl	dairy cream	3½ fl oz
	1 tablespoon mustard	
	1 tablespoon ketchup	
	2 teaspoons gravy or	
	a few drops Worcester sauce	

Cognac
salt, pepper
1 sprig rosemary
3 sage leaves

Season the fillet of beef. Heat the butter and oil with the rosemary and sage, add the meat and fry as desired. Remove the herbs and pour off the fat. Add Cognac to the pan, ignite, remove the meat and keep hot. Whisk together the cream, mustard and ketchup, then cook to a fairly thick sauce in the same pan. Add the gravy or Worcester sauce, boil up again briefly and adjust the seasoning. Dress the meat on a warmed plate and coat with the fairly thick sauce. Serve with pilaf rice, vegetable purée or mashed potatoes.

(Franco Vurro, Italy)

Fillet of beef Charlois
Filet de boeuf farci Charlois
Rinderfilet Charlois

4 portions

600 g	fillet of beef	1 lb 5 oz
200 g	foie gras	7 oz
	2 small truffles	
2½ dl	Madeira sauce	9 fl oz
	a little Madeira	
	salt, pepper	
	oil	

Cut the fillet of beef to open out flat. Cut the foie gras in sufficient pieces to cover the fillet. Fry the pieces lightly and allow to cool, then make a lengthwise incision in each and insert the truffles, cut in quarters. Sprinkle with a little Madeira. Beat the beef lightly, cover with the foie gras, roll up and tie securely. Season with salt and pepper, freshly ground. Brown the meat well for 15 minutes at 200°C (392°F), then leave to stand in the oven at 80°C (176°F) for 15 minutes. The meat should remain pink. Pour a little Madeira sauce over if desired. Serve with fresh vegetables and parsley potatoes. Hand Madeira sauce separately.
(Illustration, page 939)

(Adolf Meindl, Austria)

Fillet of beef Francis
Filet de boeuf François
Mastochsenfilet Franz

About 12 portions   Cooking time: 20–30 minutes

2 kg	fillet of beef	4 lb 8 oz

300 g	foie gras purée	11 oz
300 g	parsley, celery and dill	11 oz
100 g	unsmoked bacon or fat pork, thinly sliced	3½ oz
500 g	broccoli	1 lb 2 oz
300 g	tomatoes	11 oz
300 g	kohlrabi	11 oz
1 kg	Château potatoes	2 lb 4 oz
	chanterelles	
	butter	
	2 truffles, finely sliced	
	gravy	
	salt	
	pepper, freshly ground	
	mustard	
	butter	
	oil	
	beaten eggs for omelette	

Carefully trim the fillet of beef. Using a tranchelard, bore a hole 5 cm (2 in) in diameter through the centre from end to end by inserting the knife, twisting it and pulling it out together with the core of meat which has been cut away.

Spread the very thinly sliced bacon on aluminium foil to the shape of a rectangle 6 cm (2½ in) wide and of the same length as the fillet of beef. Arrange the truffle slices on top side by side. Using a savoy bag fitted with a plain tube about 3–4 cm in diameter (1½ in), pipe a roll of foie gras purée lengthwise right down the centre. Fold the bacon over to enclose the purée and insert the roll into the hollow centre of the fillet. Brown on all sides.

Chop the parsley, celery and dill very finely, or work to a purée. Cook lightly in butter and season to taste. Cook the omelette on one side only, making it large enough to enclose the meat. Place it in the centre of a piece of foil with the cooked side underneath. Cover with the parsley, celery and dill mixture. Place the meat on top, roll up and place on a roasting tray with the outside edge of the omelette underneath. Roast for 20 to 30 minutes in a preheated oven.

To serve, carve the meat and dress on a warmed dish. Garnish with broccoli, kohlrabi, stuffed tomatoes, chanterelles stewed in butter, and Château potatoes. Serve with truffle sauce made with truffle trimmings.

(Franz Sailer, Austria)

Fillet of beef Gundel
Filet de boeuf Gundel
Bélszintokany Gundel modra

10 portions

1 kg 600	fillet of beef	3 lb 8 oz
400 g	goose liver, diced	14 oz
350 g	butter	12 oz
40 g	salt	1½ oz
5 g	pepper, freshly ground	⅙ oz
	parsley, finely chopped	
100 g	onions, finely chopped	3½ oz
100 g	mushrooms, diced	3½ oz
300 g	cooked peas	11 oz
300 g	cooked peas	11 oz
½ l	Espagnole sauce (5 portions)	18 fl oz
2 dl	red wine	7 fl oz
300 g	cooked French beans	11 oz

Garnish:

300 g	cooked asparagus	11 oz
	5 portions scrambled egg	
	10 portions gaufrette potatoes	

Colour the onions lightly in butter. Add the meat, cut into strips, and brown lightly. Add the mushrooms, goose liver, peas and parsley, season with salt and freshly ground pepper, and mix well. Stir in the Espagnole sauce and the wine and cook for a few minutes. Remove from the heat and finish with butter (optional). Dress on a round dish and top with a nest of scrambled egg. Surround with the gaufrette potatoes and the asparagus which have been tossed in butter. Pour a little butter over the asparagus.

Alternatively, this dish may be prepared at the table. Prepare a thick sauce with butter, the onions, goose liver, mushrooms and parsley, salt and pepper, the Espagnole sauce which has been heated, and the wine. Keep hot. Sauter the strips of meat separately in hot butter over fierce heat for 2 to 3 minutes, pour Cognac over and ignite. Mix the meat with the sauce. Flavour to taste with Worcester sauce and finish with knobs of butter. Serve with the potatoes, scrambled egg and asparagus which have been prepared in the kitchen.

(Zsolt Körmendy, Hungary)

Fillet of beef with leek and onion sauce
Filet de boeuf aux poireaux et aux oignons

4 portions

800 g	fillet of beef	1 lb 12 oz
	2 strips fat pork	
	4 leeks	
	3 onions, sliced	

	2 medium potatoes, finely diced	
1 l	bouillon	1¾ pt
	2 tablespoons sour cream	
100 g	butter	3½ oz
	1 bay leaf	
	1 clove of garlic	
	sea salt	
	black pepper, chopped	

Sprinkle the fat pork with sea salt and pepper, wrap round the beef, tie in position, and fry in 50 g (2 oz) butter for 15 minutes. Add the onions, bay leaf and garlic, the white part of 3 leeks, thinly sliced, and the potatoes. Pour in the bouillon, bring to the boil, cook for 5 minutes and remove the meat. Continue cooking the vegetables in this stock, then either pass through a fine sieve or blend to a purée in the processor. Season to taste and stir in the sour cream and the rest of the butter. Cut the remaining leek into strips lengthwise and arrange on the meat. Surround with the sauce.
(Illustration, page 309)

(Roger Souvereyns, Belgium)

Fillet of beef Csongrade style
Filet de boeuf à la Csongrade

5 portions   Cooking time: 20–25 minutes

800 g	fillet of beef, trimmed	1 lb 12 oz
400 g	shoulder of pork, finely minced	14 oz
200 g	pork caul	7 oz
30 g	salt	1 oz
50 g	garlic, crushed	2 oz
20 g	pepper, freshly ground	¾ oz
30 g	noble sweet red paprika	1 oz

Garnish I:

	3 yellow peppers	
300 g	broccoli	11 oz
10 g	salt	⅓ oz
10 g	nutmeg	⅓ oz
5 g	pepper, freshly ground	⅙ oz
50 g	butter	2 oz

Garnish II:

300 g	cauliflower florets, cooked	11 oz
	6 tablespoons Béchamel sauce	
60 g	Parmesan, grated	2 oz
30 g	ham, finely cut	1 oz

11

413

◀ Rabbit leg with juniper berries and fresh noodles, p. 928

▼ Best end of lamb Harlequin, p. 761

414

Green asparagus salad, p. 230 ▶▲
Toast Bordelaise, p. 319 ▶▲▲
Mignons of veal First Lady, p. 660 ▶▼
Fricassée of fillet of beef Felice, p. 507 ▶▼▼

17

Sweetbreads with truffles and leeks, p. 587

Stuffed knuckle of veal, p. 560

	chives, finely chopped	
60 g	butter	2 oz

Season the beef with salt and pepper. Brown in a little oil over fierce heat for 2 or 3 minutes. Season the minced pork with salt, paprika and pepper. Add the well crushed garlic (or garlic juice). Mix well, adding 1 tablespoon water if too firm. Cover the fillet of beef all round with the pork mixture to a thickness of about one finger and wrap in the prepared pork caul. Refrigerate for 30 minutes, then roast for 20 to 25 minutes in an oven preheated to 180°C (355°F). Serve very hot, cut into slices and garnished with peppers and cauliflower.

To make *Garnish I,* seed the peppers and remove the fibres. Place in a hot oven and leave until the skin can be pulled off. Stuff with broccoli purée.

For *Garnish II,* mask the cauliflower florets with Béchamel sauce and sprinkle with the Parmesan, ham and chives, then gratinate in the oven.
(Illustration, page 623)

(Gyula Gullner, Hungary)

Fillet of beef Pieter Breughel
Filet de boeuf Pieter Breughel

6 portions

1 kg 500	fillet of beef	3 lb 5 oz
	6 tomatoes	
150 g	carrots, diced	5 oz
150 g	celeriac, diced	5 oz
400 g	French beans, blanched	14 oz
600 g	asparagus, blanched	1 lb 5 oz
	1 medium cucumber	
	watercress	
200 g	aspic jelly	7 oz
1 dl	aspic mayonnaise	3½ fl oz

Trim and season the fillet of beef, then roast until medium rare or medium done. Allow to cool. Blanch the vegetables, except the tomatoes, separately; drain and allow to cool.

Cut the tomatoes in half, scoop out the seeds, season and invert on a wire tray to drain. Mix half the carrots and all the celeriac separately with the mayonnaise and fill into the tomatoes. To serve, carve the beef and dress on a dish. Garnish with chopped aspic jelly, the asparagus and the French beans separately arranged in small bundles and alternating with the stuffed tomatoes.

Peel the cucumber and cut evenly into 6 cylinders. Hollow out with a vegetable scoop (as for noisette potatoes) and blanch briefly. Allow to cool and fill the centre with the rest of the carrots which have been trimmed into balls and blanched. Place three cylinders at each end of the dish and garnish with small bunches of watercress.

(André Béghin, Belgium)

Fillet of beef with rosemary
Filet de bouef au romarin
Filetto di manzo al rosmarino

4–6 portions

1 kg	fillet of beef	2 lb 4 oz
	3 sprigs rosemary	
	12 juniper berries	
	salt, pepper	
1 dl	olive oil	3½ fl oz

Brown the fillet of beef on all sides in oil and season with salt and pepper. Place the rosemary and the juniper berries in a roasting pan with the meat and roast in the oven for 15 minutes. Carve into slices 1 cm (⅜ in) thick, season with salt and pepper and pour the gravy over. (Illustration, page 518)

(Franco Colombani, Italy)

Fillet of beef Rydberg
Filet de boeuf Rydberg

4 portions

600 g	fillet of beef	1 lb 5 oz
50 g	oil and butter	2 oz
	salt	
	pepper, freshly ground	
	2 medium onions	
	4 potatoes	
30 g	butter for frying potatoes	1 oz

Dice the beef finely. Heat the oil and butter mixture, add the meat and brown lightly, then season with salt and a fair amount of freshly ground pepper. Remove the meat from the pan and keep hot. Chop the onions coarsely and cook gently in the same pan until soft.

Peel, finely dice and blanch the potatoes. Fry to a golden colour in a little butter and season with salt. To serve, arrange the meat in the centre of a suitable dish and surround with the onions and potatoes.

(Eric Carlström, Sweden)

Fillet of beef Stroganoff I
Filet de boeuf sauté Stroganov
Rinderfilet Stroganow

2 portions

300 g	fillet of beef	11 oz
50 g	shallots, chopped	2 oz
50 g	salted cucumbers, cut in julienne strips	2 oz
50 g	sweet peppers, cut in julienne strips	2 oz
50 g	mushrooms, cut in julienne strips	2 oz
1 dl	dairy cream	3½ fl oz
50 g	butter	2 oz
	2 tablespoons olive oil	
	sherry, vodka, cognac (to taste)	
	rose paprika	
	pepper, salt	
	1 tablespoon parsley, chopped	

Cut the meat into strips 4–5 cm (about 2 in) long and ½ cm (¼ in) wide. Heat the butter and oil in a flambéing pan, moving the butter backward and forward with a fork to melt it more quickly. When hot, add the meat, brown quickly on one side, turn and brown the other side, then sprinkle well with paprika and add freshly ground pepper, then a little salt. Splash with Cognac and vodka and ignite. Transfer the meat, which should be medium rare, to a warmed serving dish, cover and keep hot.

Stew the shallots in the cooking juices, stir in the cucumber, peppers and mushrooms, moisten with sherry and reduce. Flavour with vodka and add the cream to thicken. Reduce the sauce, add salt and freshly ground pepper as required and turn down the flame. Add the juice which has escaped from the meat, reduce and heat without boiling. Pour over the meat and serve at once.

(Otto Franz Müller, Switzerland)

Fillet of beef Stroganoff II
Boeuf Stroganov
Bélszin Stroganov

10 portions

1 kg 600	fillet of beef	3 lb 8 oz

250 g	butter	9 oz
OR 2½ dl	oil	9 fl oz
100 g	onions, sliced	3½ oz
300 g	mushrooms, sliced	11 oz
300 g	pickled cucumbers, peeled and thinly sliced	11 oz
	1 bunch parsley, chopped	
120 g	flour	4 oz
40 g	salt	1½ oz
4 g	white pepper, freshly ground	2 good pinches
20 g	capers, finely chopped	¾ oz
20 g	mustard	¾ oz
	juice of 2 lemons	
3 dl	sour cream	10 fl oz
2 dl	fresh dairy cream	7 fl oz
2 dl	white wine	7 fl oz

Sauté semolina:

600 g	semolina	1 lb 5 oz
200 g	butter	7 oz
OR 2 dl	oil	7 fl oz
30 g	salt	1 oz
9 dl–1 l	water	1½–1¾ pt

Cut well-hung fillet of beef in strips and season with salt and pepper. Heat the butter or oil in a large frying pan and cook the onions until lightly coloured. Add the meat and mushrooms, sprinkle with finely chopped parsley and sauter quickly over very fierce heat. Add the pickled cucumbers and the capers, sauter very briefly, dust with flour, pour in the sour cream which has been mixed with the fresh cream, add the wine and bring to the boil very quickly. Blend in small knobs of butter to finish off, then flavour well with lemon juice and mustard. If the sauce is too thick, dilute with a little bouillon, but it should not be too thin.

It is essential for this dish to be cooked over fierce heat for a short time only, to ensure that the meat is medium rare. Serve in a fireproof dish, sprinkled with chopped parsley. Hand boiled rice, sauté semolina or potato fritters separately.

To prepare the semolina, sieve it, then sauter in butter or oil until light brown. Add hot salted water, mix quickly, cover and cook gently for a few minutes. Fluff up with a fork before serving.

To make potato fritters, rub boiled potatoes through a sieve while still hot. Add the butter, dry well over heat, season and stir in the egg yolks. Roll out, cut into small rounds, egg and breadcrumb and deep fry in lard or margarine. Alternatively, commercial ready-made potato croquettes may be served.

(Zsolt Körmendy, Russia)

Beef pot-au-feu with Tzigane sauce
Pièce de boeuf en pot-au-feu à la sauce tzigane

6 portions

1 kg	fillet of beef	2 lb 4 oz
	12 carrots, turned	
	12 turnips, turned	
	12 celeriac, turned	
	12 small potatoes, turned	
	6 whites of leek	
	12 slices beef bone marrow	
	Tzigane sauce	
	(recipe, page 185)	

Cook the meat in a pan of water with the vegetables for about 10 to 15 minutes, skimming frequently. The meat should be medium rare. Poach the slices of bone marrow separately. To serve, cut the beef into 6 slices, place on a dish, cover with the bone marrow, pour the sauce beside the meat and surround with the vegetables.
(Illustration, page 168)

(Emile Jung, France)

Fillet of beef in puff pastry Jean-Pierre Clause
Filet de boeuf en croûte Jean-Pierre Clause

6 portions

	3 fillets of beef (middle cut)	
320 g	each weighing	11 oz
120 g	foie gras	4½ oz
5 cl	port	2 fl oz
5 cl	Madeira	2 fl oz
1½ dl	brown stock	5 fl oz
	1 shallot, finely cut	
	1 pinch black pepper	
20 g	sieved foie gras	¾ oz
40 g	butter	1½ oz
10 g	truffle, finely chopped	½ oz

4 cl	truffle liquor	1½ fl oz
	salt, pepper, freshly ground	
420 g	puff pastry	15 oz
	egg yolk	

Garnish:

24 asparagus tips
6 artichoke bottoms
potatoes Maxim's
6 small bundles French beans
tomatoes

Hollow out the centre of the three fillets with a tranchelard and fill each one with 40 g (1½ oz) foie gras. Season with salt and pepper, brown on all sides in a frying pan for 2 or 3 minutes and allow to cool. Pin out the puff pastry and enclose the fillets in it, decorate with pastry trimmings, wash with egg yolk and bake at 220°C (428°F) for 20 to 30 minutes.

Fry the shallot lightly in a knob of butter without colouring, moisten with the port, reduce by half, add the pepper, moisten with the Madeira, reduce by half, add the brown stock and bring to the boil. Thicken the sauce with the sieved foie gras, work in the butter a little at a time, add the truffle liquor and the truffle, and adjust the seasoning if required. Garnish with asparagus tips, stuffed tomatoes, French beans, artichoke bottoms au gratin and potatoes Maxim's.

(Emile Jung, France)

Stuffed fillet of beef in puff pastry Maître Thoeni
Filet de boeuf farci en croûte Maître Thoeni
Gefülltes Rinderfilet in der Teigkruste nach Meister Thoeni

12 portions

	1 fillet of beef	
½ dl	oil	2 fl oz
	salt, pepper	
500 g	raw foie gras, sliced	1 lb 2 oz

Forcemeat:

500 g	veal	1 lb 2 oz
200 g	foie gras	7 oz
500 g	chicken livers	1 lb 2 oz
250 g	butter	9 oz
50 g	fresh mushrooms	2 oz

50 g	dried morels	2 oz
50 g	truffle trimmings	2 oz
	12 egg yolks	
5 g	thyme	⅙ oz
8 g	pepper	¼ oz
35 g	salt	1¼ oz
30 g	shallots	1 oz
5 g	forcemeat flavouring	⅙ oz
1 dl	Madeira	3½ fl oz
1 dl	brandy	3½ fl oz
1½ dl	demi-glace sauce	5 fl oz
170 g	white breadcrumbs	6 oz
	1 bay leaf	
500 g	lean bacon	1 lb 2 oz
	half puff pastry	

Trim the fillet of beef well, season and brown on all sides in hot oil. Slit lengthwise, insert the raw foie gras and refrigerate.

To make the forcemeat, mince the veal, foie gras, chicken livers, mushrooms, morels and truffle trimmings. Work to a fine forcemeat with the remaining ingredients. Cover the fillet on all sides with the forcemeat and wrap in the bacon which has been thinly sliced. Roll out the pastry and wrap round the fillet, then allow to rest for a time.

Bake in a moderately hot oven until golden. Use a meat thermometer to check whether the meat is sufficiently cooked. The fillet may be served hot with Périgueux sauce, or cold with horseradish cream sauce. (Sauces, pages 157, 171)

(Emil Wälti, Switzerland)

Fillet of beef Empal-Pedis
Pointes de filet de boeuf Empal-Pedis
Rinderfiletspitzen Empal-Pedis

4 portions

720 g	fillet of beef (point)	1 lb 8 oz
	salt	
	pepper	
40 g	butter	1½ oz
6 cl	brandy	2 fl oz

| 1¼ dl | dairy cream | 4 fl oz |
| 3¾ dl | demi-glace sauce | 13 fl oz |

Sauce:

50 g	onions, finely chopped	2 oz
80 g	mushrooms	3 oz
40 g	preserved hot peppers	1½ oz
	3 tablespoons soya sauce	
	1 tablespoon Worcester sauce	
	1 teaspoon curry powder	

Accompaniment – rice with almonds and raisins:

200 g	rice	7 oz
400 g	water	14 fl oz
50 g	butter	2 oz
	salt	
80 g	almonds, blanched and flaked	3 oz
80 g	raisins	3 oz

Cut the fillet of beef in thin slices and season with salt and pepper. Heat the butter, brown the meat in it quickly and flamber with the brandy. Add the cream and the demi-glace sauce to thicken, heat without boiling and serve.

To make the sauce, wash the mushrooms and slice them very thinly. Chop the peppers coarsely and the onions finely. Place the curry powder in a bowl, blend with the soya and Worcester sauce, add the onions, peppers and mushrooms, and mix well. Set aside for 3 to 4 hours. Serve separately.

Brown the rice in butter, season with salt and stir in the water. Bring to the boil, then cook in the oven. Roast the almonds. Pick over the raisins, wash in hot water and drain. Add to the cooked rice.

(Frank Zodl, Austria)

Fillet of beef with Calvados
Filet de boeuf au Calvados
Rinderfiletwürfel mit Calvados

6 portions

900 g	fillet of beef, cut into 2 cm (¾ in) cubes	2 lb
400 g	apples	14 oz
300 g	fresh mushrooms, cut in quarters	11 oz
200 g	lean bacon	7 oz
3 dl	demi-glace sauce	10 fl oz

1 dl	Calvados	3½ fl oz
150 g	butter	5 oz
	pepper, salt	
	oil	

Peel and slice the apples. Stew them in 50 g (2 oz) butter, keeping them fairly firm, add half the Calvados and keep hot. Cut the bacon into thick strips, sauter in 50 g (2 oz) butter, add the mushrooms and continue cooking. Add the rest of the Calvados to the demi-glace sauce, then work in the rest of the butter a little at a time. Brown the meat in oil for 2 or 3 minutes only, keeping it very rare. Season with salt and pepper.

Dress the meat in the centre of a round dish, topped with the bacon and mushrooms, and coated with the sauce. Decorate with the apple slices. Serve with boiled potatoes or rice pilaf.

(Willi Bartenbach, Switzerland)

Meat brochettes Bosnian style
Brochettes de viande à la bosnienne
Sis-Cevap

6 portions   Cooking time: 12–14 minutes

500 g	fillet of beef	1 lb 2 oz
	OR leg of mutton	
	4 green or red peppers	
	4 tomatoes	
200 g	onions	7 oz
300 g	potatoes	11 oz

Cut the meat into fairly thick pieces 3 cm (about 1 in) square, and season with salt. Cut up the peppers fairly coarsely and cut the onions, tomatoes and potatoes into fairly thick slices. Thread the pieces of meat on to skewers alternately with the slices of pepper, onion and potato, repeating until each skewer has been filled. Shallow-fry in hot oil on all sides until the meat is cooked, sprinkling with water frequently and taking care to prevent the vegetables from disintegrating.

(László Csizmadia, Yugoslavia)

Meat balls grandmother's fashion
Fricadelles à la grand'mère
Polpette della nonna

4 portions

300 g	beef, boiled or roasted	11 oz

3 eggs
4 salami
2 potatoes, boiled in their skins
1 tablespoon Parmesan, grated
1 tablespoon pine kernels
1 tablespoon raisins
egg white
white breadcrumbs

Chop the beef, salami, pine kernels and raisins finely. Mash the potatoes. Mix together all the ingredients except the egg white and breadcrumbs. Shape into small balls, dip in lightly beaten egg white, then in breadcrumbs and fry in butter.

(Guido Belotti, Enzo Ronzoni, Carlo Calvetti, Italy)

Meat and curd cheese fricadelles mountain style
Fricadelles des montagnards au sérac
Morbidelle di ricotta del montanaro

6 portions   Cooking time: 18–20 minutes

600 g	beef	1 lb 5 oz
250 g	curd cheese	9 oz
70 g	Parmesan cheese, grated	2½ oz
80 g	ham, diced	3 oz
1 dl	oil for frying	3½ fl oz
	2 egg yolks	
	1 egg	
	2 tablespoons milk	
50 g	breadcrumbs	2 oz
	3 tablespoons flour	
	salt and pepper as required	

Mince the meat finely and mix with the ham, curd cheese and Parmesan. Add the egg yolks beaten with the milk, season with salt and freshly ground pepper, mix until well blended and shape into round flat cakes, allowing 3 per portion. Flour, egg and breadcrumb, and fry on both sides in oil.

(Mario Saporito, Italy)

American ground beef steak

4 portions

1 kg	beef, coarsely minced	2 lb

	½ teaspoon salt	
	¼ teaspoon pepper	
8 cl	tomato juice	3 fl oz
	1 tablespoon oil	
	4 tablespoons butter	

Season the meat with salt and pepper and mix with the tomato juice. Form into 4 patties in the shape of a steak and brush with oil. Grill about 7½ cm (3 in) from the heat (4 minutes on each side for rare; 6 minutes on each side for medium; 8 minutes on each side for well done). Place the patties on a warm serving dish and top each with 1 tablespoon butter.

(Hermann Rusch, USA)

Turkish beef fricadelles
Fricadelles de boeuf à la turque
Terbiyéli Köfte

500 g	beef, minced	1 lb 2 oz
100 g	white bread, soaked in water	4 oz
	1 egg	
	1 onion, grated	
	a handful fresh parsley, finely chopped	
	pepper, freshly ground	
	salt	
	butter	
	rounds of toast	
	2 cups bouillon	

Sauce:

	1 tablespoon rice flour	
¼ l	boiling water	9 fl oz
	2 egg yolks	
	dairy cream	
	juices of 1 lemon	
	ginger	
	salt	

Mix the beef well with the bread which has been squeezed dry, the egg, onion and parsley. Season with a little salt and a fair amount of pepper. Shape into round flat cakes and brown quickly on both sides in hot butter. Line the bottom of a well-greased fireproof dish with rounds of toast and place the fricadelles on top. Pour the bouillon over, cover and cook in the oven.

To make the sauce, blend the rice flour to a paste with a little cold water and stir into the boiling water. Return to the boil for a moment and remove from the heat. Stir in the egg yolks, mixed with cream, and the lemon juice, then add ginger and salt to taste. Pour over the fricadelles to serve.

(Otto Ledermann, Turkey)

Chili con carne

10 portions

2 kg	stewing beef		4 lb 8 oz
2 dl	olive oil		7 fl oz
	1 tablespoon paprika		
200 g	onions, chopped		7 oz
	2 cloves of garlic, chopped		
1 kg	speckled beans, soaked		2 lb 4 oz
250 g	peppers		9 oz
1 kg	tomatoes, skinned and diced		2 lb 4 oz
approx. 5 dl	veal stock	approx.	18 fl oz
	salt, pepper		
	Cayenne pepper		
	chili powder		
	coriander		

Cut the beef into about 1½ to 2 cm (¾ in) cubes, place in a bowl with the olive oil and paprika, and marinate overnight. Brown lightly in a braising pan, add the veal stock and the seasonings, and stew under cover.

Heat the peppers in the oven, remove the skins, cut in half and seed, then dice and add to the meat while cooking. Fry the onions and garlic lightly in a separate pan without colouring, add the tomatoes and stew. Cook the beans separately, after soaking them overnight. Lastly mix all the ingredients together, thicken with a little cornflour if necessary, and adjust the seasoning, if required, to give the dish a strong, pungent flavour. Serve very hot in earthenware bowls.

(Emil Wälti, Mexico)

Beef stew with green beans and courgettes
Estouffade de boeuf aux haricots verts et aux courgettes
Mole de Olla

10 portions

2 kg	stewing beef	4 lb 8 oz
5 dl	bouillon	18 fl oz

200 g	onions, finely cut	7 oz
	2 cloves of garlic, finely chopped	
600 g	green beans (French or runner)	1 lb 5 oz
800 g	courgettes	1 lb 12 oz
	1 can sweet corn	
	salt, paprika	
	cloves	
	a little chili powder	
	mint leaves, chopped	

Dice the meat and stew in the bouillon together with the onions. Add the garlic and season with salt and paprika. Flavour to taste with cloves and a little chili powder. When three quarters cooked, add the beans, cut into 2 to 3 cm (about 1 in) pieces and continue simmering, then add the courgettes, cut into 8 mm (⅓ in) slices. When almost cooked, add the sweet corn and the mint. Check the seasoning and serve very hot in individual earthenware bowls or a large earthenware pot.

(Emil Wälti, Mexico)

Shin of beef with young vegetables
Jarret de boeuf aux petits légumes

4 portions

600 g	shin of beef	1 lb 5 oz
250 g	carrots	9 oz
250 g	turnips	9 oz
80 g	button onions	3 oz
100 g	runner beans	4 oz
100 g	dwarf tomatoes	4 oz
	2 leeks	
100 g	onion, finely cut	4 oz
100 g	celeriac, finely cut	4 oz
100 g	parsley root, finely cut	4 oz
600 g	potatoes	1 lb 5 oz
	salt	
	pepper, freshly ground	
	thyme	
	bay leaf	
	cloves	
	bouillon	

Place the beef in a saucepan and add the onion, celeriac, parsley root, salt, pepper, thyme, bay leaf and cloves. Cover with bouillon and cook until the beef is tender.

Turn the carrots and turnips. Peel the button onions. Cut the beans into long strips. Divide each leek in half, keeping the white part only. Cook each vegetable separately in bouillon, keeping it firm to the bite. Wash the tomatoes carefully (use ordinary small ones if dwarf, cherry-size ones are not available) and cook briefly in the oven at 180°C (355°F). Peel and turn the potatoes. Boil them in salted water. To serve, dress the beef in a shallow dish, garnish with the vegetables and potatoes, and pour a little hot bouillon over.

(Germain Gertsch-Rösner, Luxembourg)

Austrian beef offal stew
Ragoût d'abats de boeuf à l'autrichienne
Bruckfleisch

8 portions

1 kg 500	beef offal (ox milt, sweetbreads, liver, lights, etc.)	3 lb 5 oz
100 g	lard	3½ oz
200 g	onions	7 oz
80 g	parsley root	3 oz
80 g	carrots	3 oz
40 g	swedes	1½ oz
40 g	celeriac	1½ oz
40 g	flour	1½ oz
¼ l	red wine	9 fl oz
¼ l	bouillon or water	9 fl oz
	salt, pepper	

Chop the onions finely and brown lightly in the lard. Add the root vegetables, grated, and brown well. Add the offal, cut into cubes, season with salt and pepper, and cook until tender. Sprinkle with the flour, brown well, add the wine and bouillon (or water), bring to the boil and stew until ready to serve. This dish is served with dumplings.

(Eduard Mayer, Austria)

Boiled beef and tongue Hofrat style
Assiette du conseiller
Hofratteller

4 portions

350–400 g	pickled tongue	12–14 oz

| 350–400 g | beef (top rump) | | 12–14 oz |
| approx. 3 dl | bouillon | approx. | 10 fl oz |

Horseradish sauce:

15 g	butter	½ oz
15 g	flour	½ oz
2½ dl	dairy cream	9 fl oz
	horseradish, grated	
	salt, sugar	
	nutmeg	
	Cayenne pepper	

Boil the tongue and beef. Carve thinly and serve very hot with boiling-hot bouillon poured over the slices.

To make the sauce, prepare a roux with the butter and flour and blend in the cream. Bring to the boil, then add salt, sugar, nutmeg, Cayenne and grated horseradish to taste. The accompaniments for this dish are boiled potatoes and hot tomatoes stuffed with horseradish sauce.

(Helmut Stadlbauer, Austria)

Steak Yucatan
Bifteck à la Yucatan
Bistec a la Yucateca

6 portions

1 kg	rump steak, cut into 6 portions	2 lb 4 oz
	2 cloves of garlic	
	juice of 1 lemon	
1 dl	oil	3½ fl oz
	salt	

Sauce:

200 g	green peppers	7 oz
200 g	red peppers (or half a can)	7 oz
200 g	onions, finely chopped	
200–300 g	tomatoes (ripe)	7–9 oz
	salt, pepper, paprika	
1 kg	potatoes	2 lb 4 oz

Rub the steaks with garlic, marinate in lemon juice, then fry in hot oil and season with salt.

To make the sauce, cut the peppers into strips after cooking them in salted water. Skin, seed and coarsely cut up the tomatoes. Cook the onions in a little oil without colouring, add the tomatoes and peppers, season with salt, pepper and paprika, and reduce to a fairly thick sauce.

Boil the potatoes separately in salted water. Serve the steaks very hot on individual plates, coated with the sauce. Hand the potatoes separately.

(Emil Wälti, Mexico)

Carbonades of beef Gambrinus
Carbonades de boeuf Gambrinus

4 portions

180 g	4 rump steaks, each weighing	6 oz
400 g	onions	14 oz
100 g	butter	3½ oz
½ l	beer	18 fl oz
4 dl	brown stock	14 fl oz
250 g	white cabbage	9 oz
250 g	red cabbage	9 oz
	2 courgettes	
600 g	potatoes	1 lb 5 oz
100 g	lean bacon, diced	3½ oz
	flour	
½ l	beef bouillon	18 fl oz
	salt	
	pepper, freshly ground	
	thyme	
	cloves	
	bay leaf	

Peel and slice the onions. Fry them in butter until lightly coloured. Beat the steaks, season with salt and pepper, then flour them and brown on both sides in 50 g (2 oz) butter. Add the onions, beer, brown stock, thyme, cloves and bay leaf. Place in the oven which has been preheated to 190 to 200°C (374 to 392°F) and cook for about 35 minutes.

Blanch the white and red cabbage separately. Divide into leaves, cover with the bacon, shape into balls and place on a linen cloth. Gather up the cloth to enclose the cabbage balls and tie firmly to make a bag. Place in a shallow braising pan and cook in a little beef bouillon, then season with salt and pepper. Cut the courgettes into thick slices and fry lightly in butter. Turn the potatoes and boil in salted water. Remove the thyme, cloves and bay leaf from the stock, but do not strain. Work in the rest of the butter to make a sauce.

Serve the steaks on warmed plates with the sauce poured over and garnished with a white and a red cabbage ball, sliced courgettes and boiled potatoes.

(Germain Gertsch-Rösner, Luxembourg)

Ribs of beef in a salt crust with bone marrow
Côte de boeuf sous sel à la moelle

4 portions

2 kg	ribs of beef	4 lb 8 oz
	4 beef or veal bones	
100 g	beef marrow, sliced	3½ oz
200 g	turnips	7 oz
200 g	carrots	7 oz
500 g	spinach	1 lb 2 oz
7 dl	red Pinot (wine)	1¼ pt
	oil as required	
	butter	

Sauce:

1 onion, finely diced
1 tomato, skinned, seeded
   and coarsely chopped
1 carrot, finely diced
1 bunch parsley
1 sprig thyme
4 cloves of garlic
crushed peppercorns
1 calf's tail
2 tablespoons flour

Salt crust:

600 g	coarse salt	1 lb 5 oz
	2 egg whites	
	1 tablespoon flour	

Cut the calf's tail into pieces and fry lightly in oil. Add the carrot and onion and brown lightly, dust with the flour and stir over low heat until the flour is light brown. Add the tomato, garlic and parsley, and season with peppercorns (crushed) and a little salt. Mix well and stir in the wine, then cook for 10 minutes while stirring. Add 5 dl (18 fl oz) water and simmer over low heat until the pieces of calf's tail are cooked. Remove them from the pan, strain the sauce and keep hot. Meanwhile turn the turnips and carrots for the garnish and glaze them separately. Blanch the spinach, squeeze it dry and stew in butter.

Mix the coarse salt well with the flour and egg whites. Brown the ribs of beef (in one piece) on all sides and roast for 10 minutes in an oven preheated to 300°C (572°F). Remove and coat the top with a thick layer of salt crust. Return to the oven and roast for a further 30 minutes. The layer of salt will keep the inside of the meat rare.

The joint is presented on the carving board, then the salt crust is carefully removed and the meat is evenly carved into four rib portions. It is garnished with the turnips, carrots and spinach. The sauce is brought to the boil, the slices of bone marrow are placed in it and left to stand for a few moments, then the marrow and sauce are served with the meat.

The calf's tail may be served later or on another day. The pieces are brushed with hot mustard, sprinkled with chopped peppercorns, placed in a fireproof dish, coated with the rest of the sauce or with light stock and heated briefly in a hot oven before serving. (Illustration, page 619)

(Jean Esslinger, France)

Red-cooked leg of beef in pieces with cowheel

4–5 portions for 2 meals to be served with 2 or 3 other dishes

1 kg 250	leg of beef	2 lb 12 oz
300–400 g	cowheel*	11–14 oz
2½ cl	soya sauce	1 fl oz
1 dl	water	3½ fl oz
3 cl	rice wine or dry sherry	1 fl oz
4 g	sugar	⅙ oz
	4 slices root-ginger	
	1 bouquet garni	
1½ cl	vegetable oil	½ fl oz

(*If cowheel is unobtainable, it may be replaced by 1 or 2 pig's trotters cut in half.)

Cut the beef and cowheel into 2 or 3 cm (about 1 in) cubes. Plunge them into a large pan of boiling water and boil for 10 minutes. Drain and transfer to a casserole in which the oil has been heated over high heat. Turn the beef to fry in the hot oil for 3 to 4 minutes. Add all the other ingredients, and mix well. Bring the contents of the casserole to the boil on the cooker. Transfer them to an oven preheated to 180°C (355°F) and cook for 1 hour, turning the contents over once every 30 minutes. Reduce the heat to 160°C (320°F) and cook for a further 2½ hours. If the contents become too dry, add 1 dl (4 fl oz) water. To serve, bring the casserole to the table. Rice and vegetable dishes go well with this dish. Beef cooked in this manner is suitable for reheating.

(Kenneth Lo, China)

Braised beef tripe with coriander

3–4 portions

750 g	beef tripe	1 lb 10 oz

	4 slices root-ginger	
25 g	salt	1 oz
	1 medium green pepper	
	1 medium red pepper	
	2 stalks spring onion	
100 g	transparent pea flour noodles	4 oz
30 g	lard	1 oz
15 g	salted black beans	½ oz
2 dl	good stock	7 fl oz
	1 chicken stock cube	
2 cl	rice wine (or sherry)	1 fl oz
2 cl	soya sauce	1 fl oz
2 cl	hoisin sauce	1 fl oz
2 cl	sesame oil	1 fl oz
3 cl	vinegar	1 fl oz
5 g	sugar	⅕ oz
30 g	coriander leaves	1 oz

Boil the tripe in 2 l (3½ pt) water with the ginger and salt for 1½ hours. Drain and cut into chopstick-thick long slivers. Cut the green and red pepper into similar size slivers after discarding the seeds. Cut the spring onion into 4–5 cm (1½–2 in) lengths. Soak the black beans in water for 10 minutes and drain. Soak the noodles for 10 minutes and drain. Crumble the stock cube.

Heat the lard in a heavy saucepan. Add the black beans and the peppers, and stir in the hot fat for 3 minutes. Add the tripe and turn and stir-fry with the other ingredients over high heat for 3 minutes. Add the noodles, spring onion, soya and hoisin sauce, stock, stock cube, sugar and vinegar. Reduce the heat to very low and allow the contents to simmer very gently for 30 minutes, turning the contents over every 10 minutes. Sprinkle with half the wine and coriander and mix well a few times. Sprinkle with the remainder of the wine and coriander leaves to serve. This is a good domestic dish to consume with rice, suitable for reheating. (Illustration, page 694)

(Kenneth Lo, China)

Tripe Florentine style
Tripes à la florentine
Trippa alla fiorentina

6–8 portions

2 kg	raw undressed tripe	4 lb 8 oz
	2 large onions	
10 g	butter	⅓ oz
	2 medium carrots	

	2 stalks celery	
	1 bunch parsley, finely chopped	
	1 red pepper	
1 dl	olive oil	3½ oz
	1 lemon	
250 g	tomato purée	9 oz
	water as required	
	1 bay leaf	
	grated Parmesan	

Wash the tripe well, place in a pan of lightly salted water with 1 onion, the bay leaf and a wedge of lemon, and cook for 2½ hours, skimming from time to time. Add water if required while cooking. Leave until cold, then cut the tripe into thin strips. Slice the carrots, celery and remaining onion thinly and colour lightly in the olive oil. Add the tripe and cook for 20 minutes, then stir in the parsley, the pepper, which has been finely cut, and the lemon zest, cut into very thin strips. Add the tomato purée together with hot water as required, and cook over low heat for an hour, stirring now and again and adding water if necessary. The consistency should be fairly thick. Finish with the butter, stir, transfer to a serving dish and sprinkle well with grated Parmesan. Serve with boiled potatoes.

(Mario De Filippis, Italy)

Tripe Thurgau style
Tripes à la thurgovienne
Kutteln nach Thurgauer Art

4 portions

750 g	tripe, cooked and cut into strips	1 lb 10 oz
100 g	onions, finely chopped	3½ oz
	2 cloves of garlic, finely chopped	
750 g	fresh tomatoes	1 lb 10 oz
3 dl	cider	10 fl oz
1 dl	bouillon	3½ fl oz
40 g	butterfat	1½ oz
	salt	
	pepper	
	1 teaspoon caraway	

Cook the onions and garlic gently in the butterfat, add the tripe and continue cooking for a few minutes.

Meanwhile skin the tomatoes, cut them in half, seed and squeeze out the liquid, then dice the flesh coarsely and add to the tripe in the pan. Cook gently for a short time and add the cider. Season with salt and pepper, add the caraway, continue cooking for a time, then pour in a little bouillon. Cook for a total of 30 to 40 minutes, or until the tripe is very tender. Check the seasoning and serve with boiled potatoes.

(Emil Wälti, Switzerland)

Tripe Macedonian fashion
Tripes à la macédonienne
Skembici

6 portions   Cooking time: about 5 hours

1 kg	tripe	2 lb 4 oz
20 g	lard	¾ oz
200 g	onions	7 oz
	1 tablespoon flour	
2½ l	water	4½ pt
	parsley, coarsely chopped	
	dill, coarsely chopped	
	2–3 cloves of garlic	
	red paprika (optional)	
	salt	
	pepper, freshly ground	

Clean and wash the tripe thoroughly. Place in a pan of cold water, bring to the boil and simmer gently for 20 minutes. Pour off the water and refill with fresh hot water. Add the onions and garlic, and cook for 3 to 4 hours, adding water if required. When the tripe is half cooked, add the parsley and dill and season with salt and pepper. The tripe is cooked when a fork may be inserted easily and the stock has become cloudy and thick.

Cut the cooked tripe into 4 x 1 cm (1½ x ⅜ in) rectangles. Make a roux with flour and lard, sprinkle with paprika, mix with the tripe and cook gently for a short time. Pour in sufficient tripe stock to cover, and cook for 30 minutes. This dish is served with grated Kackavalj cheese, but Parmesan cheese, which is similar, may be substituted for it.

(László Csizmadia, Yugoslavia)

Tripe Val Mesocco
Tripes Val Mesocco
Trippa Val Mesocco

10 portions   Braising time: about 40 minutes

1 kg 500	tripe in one piece, cooked	3 lb 5 oz
50 g	butter	2 oz

200 g	onions, chopped	7 oz
250 g	apples, thinly sliced	9 oz
15 g	parsley, chopped	½ oz
150 g	ham, finely diced	5 oz
300 g	veal sausage meat	11 oz
2 dl	oil	7 fl oz
5 dl	cider	18 fl oz
5 dl	brown veal stock	18 fl oz
	salt; pepper, freshly ground	

Garnish:

1 kg	10 tomatoes, weighing a total of approx.	2 lb 4 oz
500 g	frozen leaf spinach	1 lb 2 oz
50 g	butter	2 oz
25 g	shallots	1 oz
	salt; pepper, freshly ground	
	nutmeg	

Trim the tripe to an oblong shape and cut the trimmings into julienne strips. To make the filling, cook the onions lightly in butter. Add the strips of tripe, the ham, parsley and apples. Season with salt and freshly ground pepper. Cook gently for a further 10 minutes, then remove from the heat and leave until quite cold. Carefully mix with the sausage meat and check the seasoning.

Spread the filling evenly on the inside of the oblong of tripe, roll up firmly and tie. Heat the oil in a fireproof casserole and brown the tripe well on all sides. Pour off the oil, add the cider and reduce a little. Pour in the veal stock, cover and braise in the oven for about 40 minutes. Remove the tripe, untie and leave to stand for about 15 minutes. Cut into 20 slices, allowing 2 per portion.

Cut off the top of each tomato to make a lid. Carefully hollow out with a vegetable scoop and season. Quickly toss the spinach and shallots in brown butter and season to taste. Fill into the tomatoes, replace the lid and cook in a preheated oven shortly before serving.

Dress the slices of stuffed tripe on a large plate or dish, coat with the sauce and garnish with the stuffed tomatoes. Serve with polenta, rice pilaf or mashed potatoes.

(Otto Ledermann, Switzerland)

Norwegian sailor's beef stew
Poêlée des marins à la norvégienne
Sjφmanns Lapskaus

8 portions

1 kg	leg or shoulder of beef	2 lb 4 oz

1 kg	potatoes, peeled	2 lb 4 oz
	3 onions, chopped	
	2–3 teaspoons salt	
	½ teaspoon pepper, freshly ground	
60 g	butter or margarine	2 oz
4–5 dl	brown stock or water	14–18 fl oz

Cut the meat and potatoes into 1½ cm (⅝ in) cubes. Fry the onions gently in the butter or margarine until lightly coloured. Add the meat and brown. Transfer the meat and onions to a large stew pan. Brown the potatoes in the butter or margarine and add to the meat. Season with salt and pepper. Pour in sufficient stock or water to cover. Simmer under cover over low heat until the meat is tender and the potatoes are cooked to a purée. If using meat which requires more prolonged cooking, do not add the potatoes until the meat is half cooked. Serve in a well warmed dish and hand crispbread separately. Root vegetables may be cooked with the meat if desired.

(Otto Ramsbacher, Norway)

Fillet of beef Bohemian style
Filet de boeuf à la bohémienne
Svíčková pečeně na smetaně

6 portions   Cooking time: 1½ hours

900 g	fillet of beef	2 lb
	salt	
	8 peppercorns, freshly ground	
80 g	smoked bacon or fat pork	3 oz
80 g	lard	3 oz
150 g	root vegetables (carrot, parsley root, celeriac)	5 oz
	2 onions, sliced	
	6 allspice seeds	
	8 peppercorns	
	1 bay leaf	
	a pinch of thyme	
	nutmeg, grated	
	3 lemons	
40 g	flour	1½ oz
¼ l	sour cream	9 fl oz
1 l	bouillon	1¾ pt
	1 teaspoon mustard	
	Worcester sauce	

Garnish:

| | 1 lemon | |
| | stewed cranberries | |

Trim the beef of sinew and membranes, rinse, dry, and lard along the grain with thin strips of bacon or fat pork. Rub with salt and pepper, and brown quickly on all sides in hot lard. Add the onions and the root vegetables which have been cleaned, washed and sliced. Fry until the vegetables are lightly coloured, but not brown. Add the herbs, spices and lemon zest, together with a little bouillon. Cover and place in the oven which has been preheated to 230°C (445°F). Cook for about 1 hour, uncovering after a time. Turn the meat several times, baste occasionally and add a little bouillon as required.

When the meat is cooked, remove it and keep hot. Pour off the fat, sprinkle the flour into the pan, stir well and brown for a short time. Add bouillon and lemon juice and cook for about 15 minutes, stirring frequently. Strain, remove the herbs and spices, return to the pan, add the vegetables which have been sieved, season with salt, mustard and Worcester sauce, bring to the boil and enrich with the sour cream.

Carve the beef into ½ cm (¼ in) slices and pour a little sauce over. Decorate the edge of the dish with slices of lemon topped with a little cranberry compote. Hand the rest of the sauce separately. Serve with Bohemian bread dumplings (recipe, page 1025). This is the most popular beef dish in Czechoslovakia.

(Vilèm Vrabec, Czechoslovakia)

Beef brochettes
Filet de boeuf en brochettes
Bélszin spiz szalonnás zöldbabbal

5 portions

700 g	well-hung fillet of beef	1 lb 8 oz
300 g	smoked streaky bacon	11 oz
20 g	salt	¾ oz
5 g	pepper, freshly ground	⅙ oz
5 g	ground caraways	⅙ oz
10 g	garlic	⅓ oz
	1 tablespoon mustard	
100 g	butter	3½ oz
	1 carrot	
100 g	leeks	3½ oz
	celeriac	

Garnish:
I.

	5 medium tomatoes	
250 g	spinach	9 oz
1 dl	dairy cream	3½ fl oz

	garlic	
	salt, pepper	
	nutmeg, grated	

II.

300 g	French beans	11 oz
20 g	smoked streaky bacon, thinly sliced	¾ oz

Divide the beef evenly into 5 portions and beat into flat steaks about 20 x 10 cm (8 x 4 in). Spread with mustard and crushed garlic, and season with salt, pepper and ground caraways. Cut the bacon into 5 slices of the same size and place one on each steak. Roll up and cut each roll evenly into 5 slices. Thread the slices on to skewers, 5 on each.

Thinly slice the carrot, a little celeriac and the leek. Sprinkle on to the skewers and leave to stand for half a day. Remove the vegetables and fry the meat quickly in a little butter, then remove and set aside. Toss the vegetables in the butter remaining in the pan. Dress the vegetables in the centre of a warmed dish to make a base for the brochettes. Surround with the garnish and serve hot immediately.

To make *Garnish I,* blanch and skin the tomatoes, cut them in half and scoop out the seeds with a small spoon. Pick over the spinach and wash it well, cook, squeeze dry and cut finely, then stew in butter. Add the cream, return to the boil, season with salt and pepper, add a little crushed garlic and flavour with nutmeg to taste. Fill into the tomatoes. To make *Garnish II,* clean the beans well and blanch in salted water. Divide into 5 portions and roll each in a thin strip of bacon.

(Gyula Gullner, Hungary)

Tournedos as I like them

8 portions

200 g	8 tournedos each weighing	7 oz
	4 tablespoons butter, clarified	
	4 tablespoons port	
	1 small truffle, chopped	
	OR 2 teaspoons preserved truffles, chopped	
1 dl	veal stock, reduced and flavoured with port	3½ fl oz
	1 tablespoon dairy cream	
	32 small white onions	
	foie gras mousse as required	
	salt	

pepper, freshly ground

Season the tournedos with pepper and salt. Heat the butter in a sauté pan and fry the tournedos medium rare, medium or as desired. Dress on a warmed metal serving dish and keep hot. Hollow out the onions, blanch them, drain well, stuff with foie gras mousse and arrange round the tournedos.

Detach the cooking juices with the port, add the chopped truffle, stir in the veal stock, heat gently, then add the cream and mix well. Add salt, and especially pepper, to taste. Pour over the tournedos.

(Patrick Klipfel, Armand Roth, France)

Tournedos Budapest style I
Tournedos Budapest
Bélszin Budapest modón

5 portions   Cooking time: about 40 minutes

120 g	6 tournedos each weighing	4 oz
5 dl	water	18 fl oz
12 cl	oil	4 fl oz
80 g	smoked bacon, finely diced	3 oz
150 g	goose liver, very finely diced	5 oz
150 g	mushrooms	5 oz
100 g	onions, finely chopped	3½ oz
30 g	tomato purée	1 oz
150 g	green peppers	5 oz
150 g	morello cherries, poached	5 oz
300 g	pork or veal bones, chopped	11 oz
	salt	
	red paprika	

Cook the onions gently in oil until lightly coloured, add the tomato purée, dust with paprika, pour in the water and season with salt. Add the bones and stew under cover for 30 minutes. Remove the bones and strain the stock. Fry the bacon until transparent, then add the mushrooms which have been well washed and very finely diced, together with the liver and the peppers, seeded and very finely diced. Season with salt, mix, fry for a short time, pour in the stock and bring to the boil.

Season the tournedos with salt, fry in a little oil until medium rare, dress on a warmed dish and coat with the hot sauce. Garnish with the morello cherries and serve with pear shaped Duchesse potatoes.

(Gyula Gullner, Hungary)

Tournedos Budapest style II
Tournedos Budapest
Bélszínjava Budapest modra

10 portions   Cooking time: meat 10 minutes, sauce 25–30 minutes

1 kg 800	fillet of beef	4 lb
500 g	pork or veal bones, chopped	1 lb 2 oz
350 g	lard	12 oz
40 g	salt	1½ oz
150 g	smoked bacon	5 oz
250 g	goose liver*	9 oz
250 g	mushrooms	9 oz
200 g	onions, chopped	7 oz
20 g	noble sweet paprika	¾ oz
50 g	tomato purée	2 oz
250 g	yellow peppers, seeded	9 oz
150 g	peas, cooked	5 oz

Garnish:

boiled rice
OR gaufrette potatoes

(*Chicken or duck liver may be used instead of goose liver.)

Cook the onions gently in lard until lightly coloured, season with salt and paprika, add a little water and mix well. Add the bones and cook for 25 to 30 minutes, then remove the bones and pass the stock through a strainer.

Finely dice the bacon, mushrooms, liver and peppers. Fry the bacon lightly in lard, add the mushrooms, liver and peppers, season with salt and fry briskly. Add the stock, mix and bring to the boil. Cut the beef into steaks 3 cm (1¼ in) thick, season and grill.

To serve, place the steaks on croûtons made with rolls, cover with the sauce and sprinkle with a few peas. Decorate with raw peppers, seeded and cut into rings, and with slices of raw tomato. Hand boiled rice or gaufrette potatoes separately.

(Zsolt Körmendy, Hungary)

Tournedos Cordon rouge
Lendenschnitten Cordon Rouge

6 portions

140 g	6 tournedos each weighing	5 oz

20 g	6 slices goose liver each weighing	¾ oz
	6 slices of raw ham	
3 dl	Madeira sauce	10 fl oz
5 cl	Cognac	2 fl oz
7 cl	oil	2½ fl oz
130 g	butter	4½ oz
	salt	
	pepper	

Season the tournedos, fry in oil for about 7 minutes, keeping them medium rare, and set aside for about 5 minutes. Make an incision in the side with a small paring knife and fill with goose liver. Wrap each tournedos in a slice of raw ham and fry in 80 g (3 oz) hot butter in a braising pan for a further 5 minutes or so. Remove and keep hot.

Flamber the cooking juices with Cognac, add the Madeira sauce and finish with the rest of the butter. Serve the sauce separately. The accompaniments are Berny potatoes and fresh vegetables.

(Willi Bartenbach, Switzerland)

Tournedos with lavender honey and thyme
Tournedos au miel de lavande et fleur de thym

4 portions

200 g	4 tournedos, barded, each weighing	7 oz
2 dl	veal stock	7 fl oz
	1 teaspoon honey	
	2 sprigs thyme	
	8 lavender flowers	
	1 tablespoon Cognac	
	1 tablespoon honey vinegar	
80 g	butter	3 oz
	salt	
	pepper	

Season 50 g (2 oz) butter with salt and pepper. Sauter the tournedos in it, remove them from the pan and keep hot. Pour off the butter and stir the Cognac, vinegar and veal stock into the pan to detach the cooking juices. Add the lavender flowers together with the thyme sprigs, stripped of their leaves, reduce, adjust the seasoning and pass through a conical strainer. Add the thyme leaves and finish the sauce with the rest of the butter. Dress the tournedos on a dish and coat with the sauce. Serve with a potato and leek gratin.
(Illustration, page 309)

(Roger Souvereyns, Belgium)

Tournedos Hussar style
Tournedos à la mode des hussaires
Husarenfilet

4 portions

90 g	8 tournedos each weighing	3 oz
130 g	larding bacon	4½ oz
30 g	butter	1 oz
1¼ dl	red wine	4 fl oz
5 dl	brown stock	18 fl oz
	1 bouquet garni	
30 g	tomato purée	1 oz
30 g	flour	1 oz
	salt, pepper	

Garnish:

50 g	ham, cut in julienne strips	2 oz
50 g	red or green pepper, seeded	2 oz
50 g	onions, sliced	2 oz
50 g	pickled cucumber, cut in julienne strips	2 oz
30 g	butter	1 oz
	1 teaspoon parsley, chopped	

Beat the tournedos lightly and lard with strips of bacon. Season with salt and pepper, brown quickly in butter on both sides, and transfer to a braising pan. Dust the cooking juices in the frying pan with flour, add the tomato purée and brown for a short time, then stir in the wine and add the brown stock. Pour over the tournedos, add the bouquet garni and braise slowly in the oven for about 45 minutes. Dress the meat on a serving dish. Strain the sauce, check the seasoning, pour a little over the tournedos and hand the rest separately.

To make the garnish, fry the onion slices in hot butter, together with the pepper, cut into strips. Add the ham and cucumber, and heat. Spoon over the tournedos and sprinkle with parsley. Rice, parsley potatoes or mashed potatoes may be served with this dish.

(Franz Zodl, Austria)

Tournedos with green pepper
Tournedos au poivre vert
Filetto di manzo al pepe verde

6 portions   Cooking time: about 15 minutes

220 g	6 tournedos each weighing	8 oz
1 dl	demi-glace sauce	3½ fl oz

1 dl	dairy cream	3½ fl oz
120 g	green Madagascar pepper	4 oz
200 g	butter	7 oz
	1 tablespoon Cognac	
	6 slices bread (sandwich loaf)	
	a few drops Worcester sauce	
	salt	

Cut the bread to the same size as the tournedos and fry in butter. Season the meat with salt, fry in the butter as long as desired, remove and keep hot.

Remove the pepper from its preserving liquid, drain well, add to the cooking juices in the pan while still hot, stand over the heat for a short time, then add the Cognac. Stir in the demi-glace sauce and the cream, season with salt, pepper and Worcester sauce, and reduce a little.

Place the hot slices of fried bread on a warmed dish, cover with the tournedos and pour the sauce over.

(Mario Saporito, Italy)

Tournedos with bone marrow
Pavé de boeuf à la moelle

6 portions

180 g	6 tournedos each weighing	6 oz
180 g	butter	6 oz
20 g	shallots, chopped	¾ oz
2 dl	veal stock, reduced	7 fl oz
½ l	red wine (Brouilly)	18 fl oz
200 g	beef bone marrow	7 oz
	salt	
	pepper, freshly ground	

Soak the bone marrow for 12 hours before use. Season the tournedos with salt and pepper and fry for 6 minutes on both sides in 40 g (1½ oz) nut-brown butter. Place on an inverted plate to drain off the juices, which should be collected for use in the sauce. Meanwhile cut the bone marrow into 1 cm (⅜ in) thick slices, place in a pan with sufficient salted water to cover, bring to the boil and remove from the heat.

Pour off the butter in which the tournedos were fried, place the shallots in the pan and cook gently in the remaining cooking juices. Pour in the wine and reduce to three quarters. Add the veal stock and reduce to half. The sauce should have a slightly syrupy consistency. Remove from the heat and slowly whisk in the rest of the butter to bind the sauce. Adjust the seasoning and pass through a conical strainer. Stir in the juices collected from the meat.

Place the tournedos on warmed plates and mask with the sauce. Drain the slices of bone marrow well and place on top.
(Illustration, page 764)

(Jean-Paul Bossée-Francois, France)

Tournedos Mexican style
Tournedos à la mexicaine
Carne asada Mexicana

4 portions

160 g	4 tournedos each weighing about	5½ oz
	8 tortillas	
	4 tablespoons guacamole	
4 dl	brown bean purée	14 fl oz
	4 medium tomatoes	
	pepper, salt	

Tortillas:
EUROPEAN STYLE:

500 g	fine maize meal	1 lb 2 oz
	1 tablespoon oil	
	salt	

MEXICAN STYLE:

500 g	minza flour (available commercially)	1 lb 2 oz
75 g	plain flour	2½ oz
	salt	

GUACAMOLE (avocado sauce):

	5 avocados	
	5 large tomatoes	
	5 medium onions	
	salt, pepper, coriander	
	chilli powder	
5 cl	oil	2 fl oz

BEAN PUREE:

	brown or speckled beans
	1 onion stuck with a clove
	a little lard
	salt, chilli powder
	bouillon

GARNISH:

> 4 lettuce leaves
> 12 raw onion rings
> 12 strips of raw sweet pepper

The tournedos should be cut from the thin part of the fillet. Cut each one horizontally and flatten to make a long strip about 6–7 cm (2½ in) wide and about 7–8 mm (⅓ in) thick. Grill lightly, season and transfer to a warmed plate.

To make tortillas in the European manner, mix the maize meal with the oil and work to a pliable dough with tepid salted water. To make them in the Mexican way, mix together the minza flour and the plain flour, season with salt and add sufficient water to make a firm dough. Divide into pieces the size of an egg and either flatten with the hand or pin out into smooth rounds. This may conveniently be done between two sheets of plastic foil. Cook the tortillas one at a time in an ungreased frying pan for about 2 minutes on each side and fold over.

To make guacamole, peel the avocados, remove the stones and mash finely with a fork. Skin, seed and very finely dice the tomatoes. Chop the onions finely. Mix all these ingredients together well, season with coriander, salt, pepper and chilli powder, and lastly blend with the oil. The sauce should be very pungent.

To make bean purée, soak the beans overnight, then place in a pan of cold water containing an onion stuck with a clove, bring to the boil and simmer gently. When the beans are almost cooked, add a little lard, season with salt, and finish cooking. Work the beans in a blender or pass through a sieve, then mix to a thick purée with bouillon and season with a little chilli powder.

Dish the tournedos on individual plates and garnish with the bean purée, a grilled tomato, guacamole on a lettuce leaf and a tortilla. For a colourful finish, top the guacamole with the onion rings and the bean purée with the strips of sweet pepper.

(Emil Wälti, Mexico)

Tournedos with fresh morels
Tournedos aux morilles fraîches

4 portions

125 g	4 tournedos each weighing	4½ oz
150 g	butter	5 oz
250 g	fresh morels	9 oz
	2 carrots	
	2 turnips	
	2 whites of leak	

2 dl	dairy cream	7 fl oz
	60 noisette potatoes	
	salt, pepper	
	parsley, chopped	

Sauter the tournedos as long as desired, transfer to a warmed dish and keep hot. Add the vegetables, cut into fine julienne strips, to the pan and stir-fry until lightly coloured. Season with salt and pepper and keep hot. Wash the morels carefully and sauter in butter. Detach the cooking juices in the cream and reduce.

Dress the tournedos in the centre of a warmed oval dish. Place the vegetable julienne on one side and the morels on the other. Coat the tournedos with the sauce and decorate each one with a morel. Sprinkle with chopped parsley if desired. Serve noisette potatoes separately. (Illustration, page 621)

(Jean Esslinger, France)

Tournedos with prickly pear
Tournedos Sabre

6 portions

	6 tournedos	
	oil	
	6 slices orange	
	6 prickly pears (cactus fruit)	
	salt	
	pepper, freshly ground	
	sugar	

Season the tournedos with salt and pepper. Fry in oil on both sides, remove and dress on a hot dish. Cook the orange slices and the prickly pears gently in the same pan with very little sugar. Cover each tournedos with a slice of orange and place a prickly pear on top.

(Hermann Wohl, Israel)

Tournedos with saffron and tarragon sauce
Tournedos – sauce au safran et à l'estragon
Runderhaas biefstuk met saffransaus en dragon

4 portions

160 g	4 tournedos each weighing	5½ oz

Béarnaise sauce:

	3 peppercorns, crushed	
	2 shallots, finely chopped	
	½ tablespoon tarragon, finely chopped	
5 cl	wine vinegar	2 fl oz
	3 egg yolks	
250 g	butter	9 oz
	a pinch of chervil, finely chopped	
	saffron	

Fry the tournedos as long as desired. Cook the tarragon, shallots, peppercorns and saffron in the vinegar until the liquid has boiled away to a tablespoonful. Pass through a fine strainer and transfer to a second pan. Whisk with the egg yolks until very thick, then whisk in the butter a little at a time. Lastly stir in the chervil.

(Bernard van Beurten, Netherlands)

Grilled tournedos with fried eggs and stuffed cucumber
Tournedos grillés aux oeufs et aux concombres farcis
Řezy ze svckové se sázenými vejci a plněnými okurkami

6 portions   Cooking time: 20 minutes

150 g	6 tournedos each weighing about and 2 cm (¾ in) thick	5 oz
	salt	
1 g	pepper	a pinch
	2 tablespoons oil	
	6 fried eggs	

Stuffed cucumber:

	1 large cucumber	
300 g	mixed minced meat	11 oz
	1 egg	
	1 egg yolk	
	1 roll	
OR 50 g	white bread	2 oz
⅛ l	milk	4 fl oz
	1 onion, finely cut	
	parsley, chopped	
	salt	
1 g	pepper	a pinch
	2 firm tomatoes	
	oil	
	bouillon	

Trim the tournedos, beat them lightly, season with salt and pepper and sprinkle with oil. Grill for 3½ minutes on each side. They should be brown outside, but red or pink in the centre. Dress on a warmed dish and place a trimmed fried egg on each. Garnish the dish with stuffed cucumber and serve Béarnaise sauce separately.

To make stuffed cucumber, peel the cucumber, cut into 4 cm (1½ in) lengths and hollow out. Mix together the flesh removed from the cucumber, the minced meat, the egg and yolk, the roll which has been soaked in milk and squeezed dry, the onion and parsley. Season with salt and pepper and fill into the cucumber. Cover each piece with a slice of tomato. Heat a little oil in a braising pan, cook the cucumber gently for a few moments, add a little bouillon, cover the pan and cook slowly for 10 to 15 minutes, taking care to keep the pieces of cucumber firm.

(Vilèm Vrabec, Czechoslovakia)

Oven busters and champ, or Dockyard workers' dinner

This dish made its appearance at the turn of the century on the north-west coast of England with the arrival of Irish immigrant farm labourers. They had come in the hope of finding well paid work in the industrial centres. In particular, the nearby ports such as Liverpool and Barrow were able to provide them with employment as unskilled labourers.

The staple food of these indigent immigrants was the potato, and 'champ' became a highly popular dish as a change. It consisted of mashed potatoes mixed with spring onions and buttermilk. A popular addition to these ingredients was the swede, which grew only sparsely in the saline soil of the coastal farms, but was well liked for its flavour and texture. Swedes were particularly appreciated when mixed with dripping and liberally seasoned with black pepper. This simple meal became a classic dish when served with short ribs, the cheapest cut of beef.

6 portions

Six operations are involved in preparing this dish: –
(1) Roasting the short ribs.
(2) Preparing the vegetables for braising.
(3) Braising the short ribs.
(4) Preparing the ingredients for 'champ'.
(5) Making 'champ'.
(6) Dressing and serving.

Cooking time: 2½ hours

3 kg	short ribs	6 lb 10 oz
	2 onions	
	2 carrots	
	2 leeks	
250 g	overripe tomatoes	8 oz
	1 teaspoon white pepper for sauce	
	½ teaspoon white pepper for meat	

	2 level teaspoons salt for roasting meat	
	1 dessertspoon flour	
½ l	bouillon	1 pt
50 g	dripping	2 oz
	1 teaspoon salt for sauce	

Champ:

	potatoes	
1 kg	potatoes	2 lb 4 oz
1 kg	swedes	2 lb 4 oz
100 g	beef dripping	4 oz
	12 spring onions	
	1 heaped teaspoon salt	
	1 heaped teaspoon pepper	
	1 heaped tablespoon parsley, chopped	

(1) ROASTING THE SHORT RIBS: Season the meat with 1 teaspoon salt and half a teaspoon white pepper, rub with the dripping, place in a roasting tray and roast for 30 minutes in an oven preheated to 240°C (465°F).

(2) PREPARING THE VEGETABLES FOR BRAISING: While the ribs are roasting, carefully wash the vegetables. Scrape the carrots, peel the onions and cut the leeks in half lengthwise. Cut the tomatoes in half without skinning or seeding. Cut the onions into thick half rings, the potatoes into thick slices and the leeks into small pieces.

(3) BRAISING THE SHORT RIBS: After 30 minutes' roasting time, reduce the oven temperature to 180°C (355°F), remove the meat and pour off the fat. Line the bottom of the roasting dish with the prepared vegetables, sprinkle with salt and pepper, add the bouillon, place the ribs on the bed of vegetables, cover and braise in the oven for 2 hours.

(4) PREPARING THE INGREDIENTS FOR 'CHAMP': Clean and peel the vegetables. Cut the potatoes in half and the swedes in 3 cm (1 in) cubes. Chop the spring onions coarsely.

(5) MAKING 'CHAMP': Begin making the 'champ' when the ribs have been cooking for 1½ hours. Place the potatoes and swedes in a pan of cold water, bring to the boil and cook over high heat for 20 minutes. When cooked, pour off the water and dry off over low heat. Sieve into a bowl, season with salt and pepper, then add the dripping, parsley and spring onions, and mix well. To serve, divide into portions on a warm dish and keep hot.

(6) DRESSING AND SERVING: Remove the meat from the roasting dish and pour off most of the fat. Boil up the remaining stock, season with the salt and pepper, add the flour and stir over the heat until thick. Bone the meat and cut into thick slices. Dish in the centre of the portions of 'champ'. Make a hollow in the centre of these and fill up with sauce.

(Victor Sassie, Great Britain)

Ribs of beef stewed in brown ale
Côtes de boeuf étuvées dans la bière brune
Ossekoteletten in bruin bier gestoofd

4 portions

| 1 kg 200 | ribs of beef, cut in four | 2 lb 10 oz |

100 g	butter	3½ oz
	2 small bottles brown ale	
100 g	onions	3½ oz
100 g	carrots	3½ oz
100 g	leeks	3½ oz
100 g	celery	3½ oz
	1 nut-size piece of ginger	
	1 bay leaf	
	12 white peppercorns	

Brown the meat in butter, stir in the brown ale, add the bay leaf, the ginger which has been finely cut and the peppercorns. Cover and stew until tender. Fry the vegetables and add to the cooked meat. If necessary, thicken the sauce with a little potato flour.

(Bernard van Beurten, Netherlands)

Oxtail

Oxtail makes a more succulent stew than almost any other meat. Nowadays less and less butchers will take the trouble to scald the tails before skinning them; as a result, an increasing number of oxtails are sold unscalded, impairing their cooking qualities. This is probably the reason for the virtual disappearance of oxtail from menus.

The best oxtails for use in the kitchen are fairly large – but not too large – and have been scalded. They are cut into sections, any section which is too large for requirements being further sawn across. The thicker end pieces are best divided up lengthwise and the excess fat is removed at the same time. The sections are blanched for a short time and well drained before use.

If oxtail is to provide a palatable meal, it should be cooked until tender enough for the meat to come away from the bone very easily.

(Karl Brunnengräber, Germany)

Stewed oxtail Old Vienna
Queue de boeuf étuvée vieille Vienne
Gedünsteter Ochsenschwanz Alt Wien

4 portions

1 kg 200	oxtail	2 lb 10 oz
4 cl	oil	2 fl oz
	salt, pepper	
70 g	carrots	2½ oz
70 g	celeriac	2½ oz
70 g	parsley root	2½ oz

150 g	onions	5 oz
40 g	flour	1½ oz
40 g	tomato purée	1½ oz
	1 bouquet garni (thyme, bay leaf, garlic)	
	1 tablespoon mustard	
70 g	stewed cranberries	2½ oz
	1 teaspoon vinegar	
1¼ dl	red wine	4 fl oz
2 l	stock or bouillon	3½ pt

Garnish:

100 g	mushrooms	4 oz
100 g	onions	4 oz
100 g	carrots	4 oz

Wash and dry the oxtail and cut through the joints. Season with salt and pepper. Place in a braising pan in hot oil and brown in the oven on all sides. Add the root vegetables, coarsely diced, and continue browning. Add the onions, colour lightly, dust with flour and brown well. Now add the tomato purée, moisten with the wine and pour in the stock. Add the bouquet garni and cook slowly in the oven under cover for about 2½ to 3 hours, turning several times. When the meat is tender enough to come away from the bone without cutting, transfer to a dish and keep hot. Remove the fat from the sauce, strain and season with salt and mustard, then add the vinegar and cranberries. Thicken with a little cornflour if required.

Cook the vegetables for the garnish separately, then mix together and dress on the oxtail. Suitable accompaniments are bread or ham dumplings, or Austrian dumplings cooked in a napkin.
(Illustration, page 770)

(Frank Zodl, Austria)

Stuffed oxtail Salzburg style
Queue de boeuf farcie à la salzbourgeoise
Gefüllter Ochsenschwanz auf Salzburger Art

6 portions

2 kg	oxtail	4 lb 8 oz
1½ dl	oil	5 fl oz
	salt, pepper	
	mirepoix	
	bacon trimmings	
40 g	flour	1½ oz
	1 tablespoon tomato purée	
3 l	brown stock	5 pt
3 dl	dry red wine	10 fl oz

	2 bay leaves	
	8 juniper berries	
	8 allspice seeds	
	8 peppercorns	
50 g	butter	2 oz

Stuffing:

150 g	neck of pork	5 oz
50 g	pig's liver	2 oz
100 g	pressed ham	3½ oz
50 g	pistachio nuts	2 oz
80 g	carrots	3 oz
80 g	mushrooms	3 oz
	salt, pepper	
	French mixed herbs, consisting of	
	thyme, basil, savory, fennel,	
	lavender flowers, tarragon,	
	aniseed, rosemary, marjoram	
6 cl	dairy cream	2 fl oz
	1 teaspoon parsley, chopped	

Slit the oxtail lengthwise on the inside and remove the bones one by one without piercing the outside. Beat to open out flat. To make the stuffing, mince the pork and liver finely. Cut the ham, mushrooms and carrots into 1 cm (⅜ in) cubes. Blanch the carrots and mushrooms separately, then add to the meat and liver, together with the ham and pistachio nuts. Season with salt and pepper, add the mixed herbs, cream and parsley, and mix thoroughly.

Stuff the oxtail so that the cut edges will meet, sew up with twine and tie round firmly to make sure that it keeps its shape. Season, brown on all sides in oil, and remove. In the same pan brown the tail bones, finely chopped, together with mirepoix vegetables and bacon trimmings. Add the flour, continue browning, then add the tomato purée and fry for a few moments longer. Stir in the brown stock and the wine, and add the bay leaves, peppercorns, juniper berries and allspice. Stew the oxtail in this sauce for about 2 hours, then remove. Pass the sauce through a fine hair sieve and finish with the butter. Serve with spinach dumplings, salsify and whole, small young turnips.

(Illustration, page 872)

(Helmut Stadlbauer, Austria)

Stewed oxtail Lorraine
Ragoût de queue de boeuf à la Lorraine
Ochsenschwanzragoût auf Lothringer Art mit gedünsteten Kohlköpfchen und Magerspeckstreifen

10 portions
Cooking time: about 3 hours, depending on size and age of tails

3 kg	oxtail, scalded if possible	6 lb 10 oz
400 g	mirepoix of onions, celery, carrots	14 oz
	1 bouquet garni (marjoram, basil, rosemary)	
1 l	dry red wine	1¾ pt
1 l	Espagnole sauce	1¾ pt
1½ l	brown stock	2¾ pt
150 g	red currant jelly	5 oz
	a little lemon zest	
	a little lemon juice	
5 cl	brandy	2 fl oz
	a pinch of Cayenne pepper	
1 dl	oil	3½ fl oz
100 g	lard	3½ oz

Stuffed cabbage leaves:

	20 white cabbage leaves	
200 g	minced meat	7 oz
	2 rolls	
250 g	lean bacon	9 oz

Cut up the oxtail, blanch it and season with salt and pepper. Heat the oil and lard together and brown the oxtail on all sides. Add the mirepoix and bouquet garni, then stir in the wine and bring to the boil. Cover tightly and cook in a moderate oven until the pan is almost dry. Add the brown stock and the Espagnole sauce, together with a little lemon zest and the red currant jelly. Finish cooking in the oven under cover. Remove the meat and keep hot.

Remove all fat from the sauce, adjust the seasoning, check the consistency and pass through a strainer. Add the brandy, a little lemon juice and a pinch of Cayenne. Pour over the oxtail, surround with the stuffed cabbage leaves and decorate with strips of fried bacon.

To prepare the stuffed cabbage leaves, cut away the cabbage stumps, blanch the leaves, refresh in iced water and drain. Mix the minced meat with the rolls which have been soaked and squeezed dry to make a smooth forcemeat. Season well and divide between the cabbage leaves which have been spread flat. Roll up and stew until cooked.

(Karl Brunnengräber, Germany)

Grilled oxtail with sauerkraut
Queue de boeuf grillée avec choucroute
Grilovaná hovězí oháňka s dušeným kysaným zelím

6 portions   Cooking time: about 3 hours

1 kg 500	oxtail	3 lb 5 oz

3 l	water	5 pt
	salt	
40 g	lard	1½ oz
60 g	carrots	2 oz
40 g	celeriac	1½ oz
60 g	parsley root	2 oz
40 g	savoy cabbage	1½ oz
	1 clove of garlic	
	1 onion	
	8 peppercorns	
80 g	butter	3 oz
200 g	white breadcrumbs	7 oz
600 g	sauerkraut, cooked	1 lb 5 oz

Rinse and joint the oxtail. Place the sections in boiling salted water and cook under cover for 2 to 2½ hours, skimming from time to time. Half an hour before the end of the cooking time, add the root vegetables and cabbage which have been cleaned, washed, thinly sliced and browned in lard, together with the onion, garlic and peppercorns. Cook until the meat is very tender and comes away from the bone easily. Leave until cold, then dip the pieces of meat in melted butter, coat with white breadcrumbs and grill over very moderate heat until golden brown. Serve on a bed of cooked sauerkraut with parsley potatoes as an accompaniment.

The stock in which the oxtail was cooked makes an excellent soup, which may be served with various types of dumpling or with royale as a garnish.

(Vilèm Vrabec, Czechoslovakia)

Oxtail stew
Ragoût de queue de boeuf
Oksehaleragoût

1 portion   Cooking time: about 2 hours

350 g	oxtail	12 oz
	3 fresh tomatoes, skinned	
	OR 4–5 canned tomatoes	
	OR 1 teaspoon tomato purée	
¾ l	water	1¼ pt
	1 bay leaf	
	black pepper, freshly ground	
	1 small sprig thyme	
30 g	lard	1 oz
	mirepoix, consisting of	
	1 carrot	
	¼ celeriac	

> 1 leek
> 2 medium onions, all cut into
> 1 cm (⅜ in) cubes

Joint the oxtail and remove surplus fat. Melt the lard and brown the pieces of oxtail quickly over high heat. Season with salt and pepper, add the mirepoix and tomatoes, cook for 3 or 4 minutes and pour in the water. Bring to the boil, skim and add the thyme. Cover, place in a preheated oven and braise for 2 hours. The meat should be cooked until very tender. Remove and keep hot.

Reduce the stock, bind with flour butter, adjust the seasoning and pass through a cloth. Pour this sauce over the oxtail, adding a little Cognac or sherry, if desired, to give a finer flavour. Garnish with turned carrots and glazed or lightly caramelised button onions. Serve with mashed potatoes.

Alternative – ragoût of oxtail Indian style
Instead of tomatoes or tomato purée, add 2–3 teaspoons best quality curry powder with the mirepoix. Before serving, blend in 2–3 dl (7–10 fl oz) dairy cream. Serve with boiled firm-grained rice, allowing 80 g (3 oz) raw rice per portion.

(Karl-Otto Schmidt, Denmark)

Debrecen oxtail stew
Ragoût de queue de boeuf à la debrecenne
Ochsenschwanzragoût auf Debreziner Art mit Pfefferschotenstreifen

10 portions
Cooking time: about 3 hours, depending on size and age of tails

3 kg	oxtail, scalded	6 lb 10 oz
	1 bouquet garni (leek, celery, carrots, thyme, rosemary)	
200 g	onions, finely diced	7 oz
300 g	lean bacon, cut into strips	11 oz
250 g	tomato purée	9 oz
	2 tablespoons noble-sweet paprika	
2 dl	dairy cream	7 fl oz
3 dl	sour cream	10 fl oz
400 g	red, green and yellow peppers, cut into strips and stewed	14 oz
	a pinch of sugar	
	2 tablespoons cornflour	

Joint, blanch and drain the oxtail. Cook until very tender together with the bouquet garni in a small amount of stock. Remove and drain on a colander.

Meanwhile fry the onions and bacon until lightly coloured, add the tomato purée and cornflour, brown well and dust with the paprika. Add two thirds of the strained stock, the fresh cream and the sour cream. Mix well, add salt and sugar and reduce to a thick coating consistency. Place the pieces of oxtail in the sauce and bring to the boil. To serve, place the strips of red, yellow and green pepper on top and pour a small spoonful of sour cream over.

(Karl Brunnengräber, Germany)

Ragoût of oxtail Palatinate fashion
Ragoût de queue de boeuf à la palatine
Ochsenschwanzragoût auf Pfälzer Art, mit Maronen und Champignons

10 portions
Cooking time: about 3 hours, depending on size and age of tails

3 kg	oxtail, scalded	6 lb 10 oz
400 g	mirepoix (onions, celeriac, carrots)	14 oz
	1 bouquet garni (basil and lemon balm)	
1 l	white wine	1¾ pt
1 l	Espagnole sauce	1¾ pt
1½ l	brown stock	2¾ pt
600 g	small mushrooms	1 lb 5 oz
300 g	small onions	11 oz
300 g	marrons glacés	11 oz
	lemon juice	
	Cayenne pepper	
40 g	parsley, chopped	1½ oz
1 dl	oil	3½ fl oz
100 g	lard	3½ oz

Potato dumplings:

160 g	butter	5½ oz
	5 eggs	
	4 egg yolks	
60 g	flour	2 oz
750 g	potatoes, cooked on the previous day	1 lb 10 oz
	salt	
	mace	
	parsley, chopped	
100 g	breadcrumbs fried in butter	3½ oz

Cut up and blanch the oxtail. Season with salt and freshly ground pepper and brown well in the lard. Add the mirepoix, which has been browned, the bouquet garni, wine, Espagnole sauce and brown stock, and braise until tender. Transfer the meat to a second pan. Pass the braising stock and vegetables through a sieve into the pan containing the meat. Add the onions which have been lightly fried, the mushrooms and the marrons glacés, and mix carefully.

Remove some of the fat from the ragoût if necessary. Flavour to taste with lemon juice, Cayenne and chopped parsley. Serve with potato dumplings.

To make the dumplings, cream the butter and gradually stir in the egg yolks and whole eggs, the flour and the potatoes which have been grated. Season with salt and mace, and add chopped parsley to taste. Shape into dumplings with a dessertspoon and poach in boiling salted water. Coat with buttered breadcrumbs to serve.

(Karl Brunnengräber, Germany)

Stewed beef Puszta
Ragoût de boeuf Puszta

10 portions   Cooking time: 1–1½ hours

2 kg	beef (brisket or shoulder or similar coarse cut)	4 lb 8 oz
500 g	onions, finely cut	1 lb 2 oz
2 kg	potatoes, cut into strips	4 lb 8 oz
400 g	yellow peppers, seeded and cut into strips	14 oz
200 g	tomatoes, cut into quarters	7 oz
20 g	garlic, crushed	¾ oz
4 dl	white wine	14 fl oz
50 g	salt	2 oz
40 g	noble-sweet paprika	1½ oz
2 g	ground caraways	a pinch
1 g	marjoram	a small pinch
200 g	lard	7 oz

Fry the onions in lard until lightly coloured. Add the meat, coarsely diced, together with the garlic and caraways. Season with salt and add the marjoram. Fry quickly until the meat is golden brown. Sprinkle with paprika, add a little water, cover and braise. When the meat is half cooked, add the peppers, tomatoes, potatoes and wine, then continue braising until the meat is tender. It should be noted that the meat must be braised in very little liquid, not boiled.

To serve, mix with cooked pasta squares and decorate with raw peppers which have been seeded and cut into rings or strips, and with sliced raw tomatoes.

The main difference between this dish and pot goulash is that the latter is cooked with a large quantity of water and served as a soup, whereas Puszta pörkölt is braised with very little liquid.

(Zsolt Körmendy, Hungary)

Ragoût of beef Erdberg style
Ragoût de boeuf à la Erdberg
Erdberger Rahmfleisch mit Brimsennockerln

4 portions

1 kg 200	stewing beef	2 lb 10 oz
60 g	carrots	2 oz
40 g	larding bacon	1½ oz
60 g	gherkins	2 oz

Marinade:

1¼ dl	white wine	4 fl oz
6¼ cl	vinegar	2½ fl oz
1 l	water	1¾ pt
150 g	root vegetables (carrot, swede, celeriac), very thinly sliced	5 oz
50 g	onions	2 oz
	salt, thyme	
	2 bay leaves	
	8 cloves	
	8 peppercorns	
30 g	sugar	1 oz
5 cl	oil	2 fl oz
50 g	flour	2 oz
	1 dessertspoon tomato purée	

Sauce:

3¾ dl	sour cream	13 fl oz
	1 tablespoon flour	
	mustard, Worcester sauce	

Garnish:

500 g	fresh cucumbers	1 lb 2 oz
30 g	butter	1 oz
	1 tablespoon sugar	
	a dash of vinegar	
	a little bouillon	
	salt, pepper	
	a little dairy cream	
	2 teaspoons dill, chopped	
	2 red peppers	
	a little oil	

Accompaniment: cottage cheese dumplings

300 g	cottage cheese	11 oz

160 g	flour	5½ oz
80 g	ham or cooked smoked meat, finely chopped	3 oz
	2 egg yolks	
	nutmeg	
	parsley, chopped	
	salt, pepper	
40 g	brown butter	1½ oz

Lard the meat and thread with strips of carrot and gherkin. Bring to the boil the ingredients for the marinade, cool and pour over the meat. Refrigerate and marinate for 1 or 2 days. Remove the meat, dry and season. Brown in oil on both sides and arrange in a casserole. Drain the marinade vegetables and brown in the pan which was used to brown the meat. Dust with flour, add the tomato purée and fry for a short time. Pour in a little of the marinade. Transfer to the casserole containing the meat, cover and cook in the oven for about 1½–2 hours, adding the rest of the marinade if necessary. Remove the meat when it is tender.

To make the sauce, blend the sour cream and flour into the cooking liquid to thicken, and flavour with mustard and Worcester sauce. Bring to the boil for a moment, strain and adjust the seasoning.

To make the garnish, peel the cucumbers, cut them in half, remove the seeds and slice coarsely. Brown lightly in the butter, adding the sugar, half the dill, and a little salt and pepper. When browned, add a dash of vinegar and a little bouillon, and bring to the boil for a moment. Mix the rest of the dill with a little cream and spoon over the cucumber. Cover with the red peppers which have been seeded, cut into rings and browned in a little oil.

To make the dumplings, mix together all the ingredients except the brown butter. Shape with a dessertspoon and poach for 8 minutes in boiling salted water, then drain and pour brown butter over. To serve, carve the meat, arrange on a dish, pour a little sauce over and surround with the garnish. Hand the rest of the sauce and the dumplings separately.

(Ernst Faseth, Austria)

Beef stew Swedish fashion
Ragoût de boeuf à la suédoise

4 portions

approx. 1 kg	beef (best shoulder cut)	approx.	2 lb 4 oz
	salt, pepper		
	a little flour		
1 dl	oil		3½ fl oz
	3 medium onions		
	1 carrot		

1 celeriac
1 bouquet garni, consisting of
  6 bay leaves,
1 teaspoon pimento,
  dried marjoram
2 tablespoons tomato purée

Cut up the beef, allowing 4 pieces per portion. Season with salt and pepper, coat lightly with flour and brown well in hot oil. Pour off the oil, coarsely slice the onions, carrot and celeriac, and add to the meat. Add the tomato purée and the bouquet garni and brown well. Pour in sufficient water to cover the meat, then cover the pan tightly and cook for about 2 hours, or until the meat is tender. Remove the meat and discard the bouquet garni. Pass the stock and vegetables through a sieve, place in a pan with the meat and return to the boil.

Transfer to a deep serving dish and hand boiled potatoes and pickled beetroot separately. If home-made pickled beetroot is preferred to the commercial product, prepare the beetroots by boiling and peeling them. Pickle them either whole or sliced in vinegar containing allspice and bay leaves.

(Eric Carlström, Sweden)

Stewed beef Hussar fashion
Roastbeef à la hussarde
Gedünstetes Roastbeef (Beiried) nach Husaren Art

4 portions

800 g	beef (contrefilet)	1 lb 12 oz
8 cl	oil	3 fl oz
150 g	mirepoix	5 oz
100 g	onions, finely chopped	3½ oz
	1 tablespoon tomato purée	
1½ l	brown stock	2¾ pt
½ l	white wine	18 fl oz
150 g	mushrooms, sliced	5 oz
	1 tablespoon parsley, chopped	
	2 tablespoons sour cream	
40 g	flour	1½ oz
	3 tablespoons tomatoes, finely diced	
	2 bay leaves	
	salt, peppercorns	
	English mustard powder	
	Béarnaise sauce	

Pasta squares with cabbage:

	3 tablespoons onion, diced	
500 g	white cabbage trimmed of stump	1 lb 2 oz
	1 tablespoon granulated sugar	
3 cl	oil	1 fl oz
	a little bouillon	
200 g	pasta squares	7 oz
	salt, black pepper	

Rub the meat thoroughly with salt, pepper and mustard. Brown in hot oil in a braising pan. Remove, add the mirepoix to the pan and brown, then add the tomato purée and stir in the brown stock. Return the meat to the pan, add the seasonings and stew until tender. Blend the flour with the sour cream and stir into the stock to thicken.

Brown the onions in 3 cl (1 fl oz) oil, add the mushrooms and a little tomato purée, and fry for a few moments. Stir in the wine, then the thickened stock, and cook for 10 minutes. Slice the meat and dress on a serving dish. Pour the mushroom sauce over, cover with the diced tomatoes and mask with Béarnaise sauce.

To prepare the cabbage, heat the oil in a pan, add the sugar and allow it to caramelise, then add the onions together with the cabbage which has been diced, and brown well. Stir in a little bouillon, season with salt and pepper and stew gently until soft, keeping the contents of the pan as dry as possible.

Cook the pasta squares in a large pan of salted water, drain and rinse in cold water, then mix with the cabbage and season to taste with salt and pepper.

(Ewald Plachutta, Austria)

Ragoût of beef with flap mushrooms
Ragoût de boeuf aux cèpes
Geretto di manzo con funghi

6 portions

1 kg	stewing beef (shin)	2 lb 4 oz
	1 medium onion	
	2 cloves of garlic	
40 g	dried flap mushrooms	1½ oz
5 cl	olive oil	2 fl oz
½ l	dry white wine	18 fl oz
40 g	flour	1½ oz
60 g	parsley, chopped	2 oz
	salt, pepper	

Soak the mushrooms in lukewarm water, squeeze dry and chop finely. Strain half the water and set aside. Chop the onion and garlic finely, fry in the oil until lightly coloured and add the mushrooms. Dice the meat, flour lightly and add to the pan. Brown well on all sides, season with salt and pepper, stir in the strained water, then add the wine. Bring slowly to the boil, then cook over moderate heat. Adjust the seasoning. Dress in a warm, deep serving dish and sprinkle with the chopped parsley.

(Mario Saporito, Italy)

Ragoût of beef Quatro Barres with pickled flap mushrooms
Ragoût de boeuf aux cèpes en saumure Quatre Barres
Guisado de buey Quatro Barres con setas saladas

6 portions

1 kg 200	shin of beef, boned	2 lb 10 oz
1 kg	fresh flap mushrooms	2 lb 4 oz
	OR chanterelles	
5 l	dry red wine	9 pt
	2 leeks, cleaned and finely sliced	
	3 medium onions, peeled and finely sliced	
	2 carrots, peeled and chopped	
	1 bay leaf	
	1 sprig thyme	
	4 cloves	
15–20 g	black peppercorns	½–¾ oz
	2 tablespoons sugar	
50 g	flour	2 oz
250 g	lard	9 oz
1 dl	vinegar	3½ fl oz
	4 cloves of garlic	
30 g	pine kernels	1 oz
	salt as required	

Clean the mushrooms, wash well several times, drain, cut into pieces, place in an earthenware container and cover with boiling water. Leave until cold, pour off the water, drain the mushrooms well and arrange in layers in an earthenware pot, covering each layer with salt. They will keep for a long time, remaining firm and sound. Before using them, soak them in cold water for 4 hours, changing the water meanwhile, then place in fresh water and cook for 10 minutes. Pour off the water, drain the mushrooms, add the vinegar and set aside until required. Trim the beef of all sinew, cut into 25 g (1 oz) cubes and marinate in the red wine with the onions, carrots, leeks, herbs, spices and salt for 24 hours.

Remove the meat, drain on a sieve, then brown on all sides in about 175 g (6 oz) lard. Place the meat in an aluminium pan. Remove the vegetables and herbs from the marinade, drain well, brown in the lard, place in the pan with the meat, add the wine in which the meat was marinated, cover and cook over low heat for 3–4 hours. Remove the meat and pass the stock and vegetables through a conical strainer.

In a separate pan, make a roux with the flour and the rest of the lard. Gradually stir in the liquid part (i.e. the wine) of the stock, then cook slowly while skimming well. Lastly stir in the solid part of the stock, i.e. the vegetable purée. Place the meat in this sauce. Add the garlic, mushrooms and pine kernels which have been well pounded in a mortar, cook for a further 10 to 15 minutes and season with salt. If the stock has a sour taste, stir in the sugar to neutralise it. Serve hot.

(Josep Lladonosa, Spain)

Beef roll Capuchin style with Amarone
Roulade du capuchin à l'Amarone
Rotolo del cappuccino all'amarone

6 portions

1 kg	beef (shoulder cut)	2 lb 4 oz
350–400 g	1 cotechino (boiling sausage) weighing	12–14 oz
60 g	dried flap mushrooms	2 oz
	6 rashers bacon	
1 l	Amarone (Italian red wine)	1¾ pt
	1 onion	
	1 carrot	
	1 stick celery	
	1 bouquet garni (sage, thyme, rosemary, bay leaf, parsley)	
	2 cloves of garlic, finely chopped	
1 dl	oil	3½ fl oz
100 g	butter	3½ oz
	salt	
	pepper, freshly ground	

Open out and flatten the meat. Season with salt and freshly ground pepper. Cover with the bacon, then with the flap mushrooms which have been soaked, squeezed dry and coarsely chopped. Sprinkle with the garlic and a little salt. Place the sausage, which has been blanched and skinned, in the centre, roll up and tie.

Finely dice the onion, carrot and celery, then brown in butter and oil. Add the meat roll and brown all round for 5 minutes. Stir in the wine, add the bouquet garni, bring to the boil for a moment, then continue cooking over low heat. To serve, slice and dress on polenta croûtons of the same size. Strain the stock and pour over the slices of meat.

(Mario Saporito, Italy)

Braised beef ribs with salted black beans

3–4 portions   Cooking time: 2 hours

1 kg 500	meaty beef ribs	3 lb 5 oz
30 g	black beans	1 oz
2 cl	soya sauce	1 fl oz
	2 large onions	
10 g	lard	⅓ oz
1 dl	water	3½ fl oz
½ cl	chilli sauce	1 teaspoon
	pepper to taste	
	3 slices root ginger	
5 cl	red wine	2 fl oz
1½ cl	oil	1 fl oz

Use a sharp Chinese chopper to cut the ribs into sections 5–6 cm (about 2 in) in length. Cut the onions into thin slices, the ginger into shreds. Soak the black beans in water for 10 minutes and drain. Heat the oil in a large casserole. Add the onions and ginger and stir-fry over high heat for 3 minutes. Add the black beans and the ribs. Turn them together for 3 minutes. Add the black beans and the ribs. Turn them together for 3 minutes. Add all the other ingredients and continue to turn and stir them together for 5 minutes. Cover the casserole and transfer to an oven preheated to 160°C (320°F). Cook for 2 hours, turning the contents over every 30 minutes and adding water or wine if the contents become too dry. Serve by bringing the casserole to the table. This dish is eaten with rice, bread or steamed buns, using the fingers.

(Kenneth Lo, China)

Beef olives Znojmo style
Roulades de boeuf à la Znaim
Znojemské závitky z hovězího masa

6 portions   Cooking time: 50 minutes

900 g	beef (boned ribs *or* rump)	2 lb
	salt	
1–2 g	pepper	a pinch
20 g	butter	¾ oz
100 g	smoked shoulder of pork, cooked	3½ oz
60 g	smoked bacon	2 oz
	2 anchovies, sieved	
20 g	capers	¾ oz

	1 pickled cucumber	
	parsley	
200 g	onions	7 oz
	1 clove of garlic, crushed	
60 g	lard	2 oz
20 g	flour	¾ oz
⅛ l	dairy cream	4 fl oz
	1 teaspoon mustard	
	1 teaspoon Worcester sauce	
¾ l	bouillon	1¼ pt

Rinse and dry the meat. Cut it into 6 slices across the grain, snip the edges and beat flat, then sprinkle with salt and pepper. Chop (or work in the processor) the shoulder of pork, bacon, cucumber, capers, parsley and 80 g (3 oz) onion. Mix with the garlic, the butter which has been creamed, and the anchovies. Spread this filling on to the slices of meat, roll up, starting from the narrow side and secure with thread. Brown quickly in hot lard on all sides, add the rest of the onions, finely cut, cook for a few moments, dust with flour, brown lightly, add the bouillon, bring to the boil and braise for 30 to 45 minutes.

Thicken with the cream, flavour with mustard and Worcester sauce, and bring to the boil for a moment. Remove the meat, untie and dress on a dish. Strain the sauce, pour part of it over the meat, and hand the rest separately. If a coarser cut such as topside is used, it will require more prolonged braising. Suitable accompaniments are rice and stewed cranberries or rowan berries.

(Vilèm Vrabec, Czechoslovakia)

Braised beef Italian fashion
Boeuf braisé à l'italienne
Stracotto classico all'italiana

2 kg	beef (topside)	4 lb 8 oz
1 l	young, full-bodied red wine (Barbera)	1¾ pt
	butter and oil as required	
	1 ox foot, skinned	
	2 medium onions	
	2 sticks celery	
	4 carrots	
	4 cloves	
	2 cm (¾ in) cinnamon quill	
	salt, pepper	
	nutmeg, grated	
	2 cloves of garlic	
	2 tablespoons concentrated tomato purée	

Trim the meat and thread with the garlic cut into small strips. Prepare well-flavoured bouillon with the meat trimmings, the ox foot, 2 carrots, the celery, water, nutmeg, salt and pepper. Keep hot. Brown the meat on all sides in butter and oil, moisten with a little wine, then pour in wine to a depth of 4 cm (1½ in). Cook for a short time over high heat, then reduce the heat and add the bouillon with its vegetables, the onions, cut in quarters and stuck with the cloves, the remaining 2 carrots (raw), the crushed cinnamon and the tomato purée. Cover and braise for 2 hours, turning the meat occasionally.

Remove the meat and keep hot. Add the boned ox foot cut into small cubes and cook for a further 30 minutes, then pass the stock and its contents through a vegetable mill. Carve the beef and mask with the sauce. Serve with courgette purée and polenta croûtons. (Illustration, page 519)

(Franco Colombani, Italy)

Braised beef Renaissance
Estouffade de boeuf Renaissance
Stufato di manzo Rinascimento

6 portions   Cooking time: 2–3 hours

800 g	beef (shoulder cut)	1 lb 12 oz
80 g	beef bone marrow	3 oz
100 g	Mortadella, diced	3½ oz
60 g	butter	2 oz
	1 medium onion	
	1 carrot	
	1 stick celery	
	1 clove of garlic	
	3 tablespoons tomato sauce	
3 dl	red wine	10 fl oz
50 g	ground cloves	2 oz
½ l	bouillon	18 fl oz
	salt, pepper	

Rub the meat well with the ground cloves, season with salt and pepper, and set aside for 2 hours. Heat the butter and bone marrow in a braising pan and add the vegetables and garlic, very finely sliced. Fry until lightly coloured, then add the meat and brown on all sides. Cook gently over low heat, add a little red wine, reduce completely, add wine again and repeat until all the wine has been used. Add the Mortadella and the tomato sauce, pour in the bouillon and finish cooking. Carve the meat. Pass the stock and vegetables through a vegetable mill, or work to a purée in the processor, and spoon over the meat.

(Mario Saporito, Italy)

Shoulder of beef bourgeois style
Paleton de boeuf à la bourgeoise

10 portions

2 kg 500	beef (shoulder cut), boneless	5 lb 8 oz
	1 calf's foot	
150 g	onions, finely diced	5 oz
150 g	carrots, finely diced	5 oz
1 kg	potatoes	2 lb 4 oz
	1 clove of garlic	
	1 bouquet garni	
	2 tomatoes, skinned and seeded	
100 g	concentrated tomato purée	3½ oz
1 l	Côtes du Rhône (red wine)	1¾ pt
	oil as required	
	salt, pepper	
	butter	

Panada:

150 g	white breadcrumbs	5 oz
5 cl	milk	2 fl oz
	1 shallot, finely chopped	

To make the panada, place the milk in a pan with the shallot, bring to the boil, and stir in the breadcrumbs with a spatula. Season the meat with salt and pepper. Fry in oil in a braising pan until golden brown. Add the onions and carrots, the calf's foot, the garlic and herbs, the tomatoes and the tomato purée. Stir in the wine and add water if necessary. Cover, place in the oven which has been preheated to 200°C (392°F) and cook gently for 2½ to 3 hours.

Remove the meat, allow to cool, then carve. Mask the slices of meat with the panada. Peel the potatoes, slice them thinly, dip in melted butter and place on the meat. Arrange the slices of meat in a lightly buttered fireproof dish and brown lightly in the oven. Strain the stock and pour round the meat just before serving.
(Illustration, page 166)

(Emile Jung, France)

Boiled beef Grand'mère Madeleine
Le pot-au-feu de grand'mère Madeleine

6 portions   Cooking time: 2 to 3 hours

1 kg 500	shin of beef	3 lb 5 oz
1 kg	flat ribs of beef	2 lb 4 oz

500 g	chuck steak	1 lb 2 oz
	horseradish, grated	
300 g	leeks	11 oz
200 g	carrots, scraped	7 oz
200 g	swedes, peeled	7 oz
	1 celeriac, peeled	
300 g	onions	11 oz
	5 cloves	
	1 knob garlic	
	coarse salt	
	(10 g per l, ¼ oz per pt)	
	black peppercorns	

Place the flat ribs at the bottom of a large pot, cover with the shin of beef, then the chuck steak and pour in sufficient water to cover well. Bring to the boil with the pot uncovered. Skim after 10 minutes. Reduce the heat a little, season with salt, and add a few peppercorns, together with 2 onions stuck with the cloves. Cut the rest of the onions in half, place on a roasting tray, brown them lightly on top of the stove, and add to the broth to give it colour.

Tie the leeks together and add to the pot with the carrots, swedes, celeriac and garlic. Skim continually while cooking. When the various vegetables are tender, lift them out with a skimmer and place in a casserole at the side of the stove. Add 2 ladles broth and cover. When cooked, slice the meat and place on a serving dish or warmed plates. Pour a little broth over and garnish with the vegetables. Pour the rest of the broth into a tureen and add beef marrow quenelles (recipe, page 136). Serve very hot. Serve warm horseradish as accompaniment. (Illustration, page 765)

(Jean-Paul Bossée-François, France)

Alsatian beef casserole
Paleron de boeuf dans sa potée

6–8 portions   Cooking time: 3 hours

| 1 kg 500 | beef (shoulder cut) | 3 lb 5 oz |
| | 1 pork caul | |

Stuffing:

1 kg 500	onions	3 lb 5 oz
100 g	butter	3½ oz
100 g	parsley, chopped	3½ oz
25 g	salt	1 oz
2 g	pepper	a good pinch
	nutmeg, grated	

Casserole vegetables:

	3 shallots	
	3 leeks (white part only)	
	3 carrots	
1 kg	swedes	2 lb 4 oz
1 kg 500	potatoes	3 lb 5 oz
1½ l	water	2¾ pt
	4 tablespoons parsley, chopped	

Trim the meat and cut a pocket for stuffing. Cut up the onions very finely and cook gently in the butter. Add the parsley and seasonings. Mix well and fill into the pocket. Enclose the meat in the pork caul. Peel and dice the vegetables.

Fry the meat in butter in a cast iron casserole until golden brown on both sides. Remove and set aside. Fry the vegetables in the same casserole and season with salt and pepper. Place the meat on the vegetables and spoon these over until the meat is covered. Pour in the water, cover tightly and cook for 2 hours in an oven preheated to 250°C (482°F).

Remove the meat and carve into 2 cm (¾ in) thick slices. Add seasoning to the vegetables if required, transfer to a deep china or earthenware dish, arrange the meat on top and sprinkle with chopped parsley. This is a classic dish of the Alsatian cuisine.
(Illustration, page 520)

(Jean Esslinger, France)

Beef olives Appenzell style
Paupiettes de boeuf à l'appenzelloise
Appenzeller Rindfleischröllchen

4 portions

120 g	4 rump steaks, thinly cut, each weighing	4 oz
160 g	8 slices smoked beef, thinly cut	5½ oz
	veal sausage meat *or* Appenzell	
	boiling sausage	
100 g	onions, finely chopped	3½ oz
50 g	dried flap mushrooms	2 oz
2 dl	cider	7 fl oz
2 dl	demi-glace sauce	7 fl oz
	1 tablespoon oil	
	1 bay leaf	
	1 clove	
	½ teaspoon caraway seeds	
	salt, pepper	

Flatten the steaks and cover with the smoked beef, then the sausage meat. Sprinkle with caraway and roll up. Secure with twine or toothpicks. Season with salt and pepper and brown all round in hot oil in a braising pan. Add the onions and cook gently for a short time, then add the mushrooms which have been soaked and squeezed dry, and continue cooking. Stir in the cider, reduce a little, then add the demi-glace sauce, the bay leaf and clove, and braise slowly for about 45 minutes, adding a little water if necessary. Remove the twine or toothpicks and dress the beef olives on a serving dish. Remove the bay leaf and clove from the sauce, adjust the seasoning, and pour over the meat. Serve with rice, pasta or potatoes as desired.

(Emil Wälti, Switzerland)

Beef olives Hagolan
Roulades de boeuf Hagolan

8 portions

125–150 g	8 slices beef (shoulder cut) each weighing	4–5 oz
	2 avocados (not too ripe)	
	8 slices smoked breast of goose	
	mustard	
	pepper, freshly ground	
	salt	
	paprika	
	mirepoix	
	bouillon	
	red wine	
	cornflour	
	oil	

Peel the avocados, cut in quarters and wrap each in a slice of smoked breast of goose. Flatten the slices of beef, spread with mustard and roll up round the rolled slices of goose. Brown in oil, season with pepper, salt and paprika, add the mirepoix, fry until lightly coloured and moisten with the bouillon. Cook until the beef olives are tender, then remove and dress on a warmed dish. Strain the stock. Blend the cornflour with a little water and stir into the stock to thicken. Finish with a good red wine. Pour over the beef olives.

(Hermann Wohl, Israel)

Beef olives Zeeland style
Paupiettes de boeuf à la zélandaise
Opgerolde lende biefstuk Zeelandia

4–6 portions

800 g	beef (contrefilet), trimmed	1 lb 12 oz
200 g	onions, very finely chopped	7 oz
30 g	pink peppercorns	1 oz
40 g	mustard	1½ oz
	1 tablespoon tomato purée	
	salt	

	pepper, freshly ground	
	1 tablespoon flour	
	½ egg	
8 cl	veal gravy	3 fl oz
8 cl	dairy cream	3 fl oz
	milk	
100 g	butter	3½ oz

Garnish:

1 large onion
oil

Make a horizontal cut through the beef so that it can be opened out and flattened. Cook the onions gently in butter without colouring, dust with a little flour, add half the mustard, half an egg, beaten, the pink pepper and a little milk. Mix well and work to a forcemeat of spreading consistency. Spread on the beef, roll up and secure. Chill thoroughly until very firm. Cut into 20 small rolls and impale on skewers. Fry in butter over medium heat.

To make the sauce, pour off the butter in the pan, add the rest of the mustard and the tomato purée, and cook gently for a moment. Stir in the veal gravy, then the cream, and bring to the boil for a few moments. Season with salt and freshly ground pepper. To serve, mask the skewered meat with the sauce and garnish with onion rings deep-fried in oil.

(Bernard van Beurten, Netherlands)

Shoulder of beef with mashed potatoes
Paleron de boeuf avec purée de pommes de terre
Bankekød med kartoffelmos

6 portions   Cooking time: 1½ hours

1 kg 500	shoulder of beef, evenly cut	3 lb 5 oz
1 kg 500	onions, sliced	3 lb 5 oz
	3 bay leaves	
	5 peppercorns	
1½ l	water	2¾ pt
60 g	fat	2 oz
100 g	flour	3½ oz
	salt	
	pepper, freshly ground	

Mashed potatoes:

2 kg	potatoes	4 lb 8 oz
1½ l	milk	2¾ pt
300 g	butter	11 oz

Cut the beef into 18 slices 2 cm (¾ in) thick and flatten well. Season with salt and pepper, sprinkle well with flour and brown in very hot fat in a sauté pan. Remove the meat and keep hot. Fry the onions in the same pan until well browned. Place them in a large stew pan together with the meat, bay leaves and peppercorns. Add the water and cook for 1½ hours.

Remove the meat and dress in a warm serving dish. Bring the stock to the boil, remove the fat and strain over the meat. Serve with mashed potatoes.

To prepare the potatoes, peel them, boil in unsalted water, drain and dry off well, then pass through a sieve. Add the butter, boil the milk and stir in gradually. Season to taste.

(Eric Cederholm, Denmark)

Rib steak Esterházy
Petite côte de boeuf en daube Esterházy
Esterházy Rostélyos

5 portions

200 g	5 rib steaks each weighing	7 oz
1 dl	oil	3½ fl oz
50 g	butter	2 oz
150 g	carrots	5 oz
150 g	parsley roots	5 oz
100 g	onions	3½ oz
	zest and juice of half a lemon	
4 dl	sour cream	14 fl oz
30 g	flour	1 oz
	salt	
	pepper, freshly ground	
	1 bay leaf	
	capers	
	1 teaspoon mustard	
	parsley, chopped	

Beat the steaks lightly and season with salt and pepper. Brown in hot oil on both sides in a sauté pan and transfer to a stew pan. Scrape the carrots and parsley roots well. Slice 50 g (2 oz) of each and fry in the oil remaining in the sauté pan. Dust with flour and mix well, then add water and bring to the boil. Pour over the steaks, season to taste, add the lemon zest and braise under cover.

Cut the rest of the carrots and parsley roots and the onions into fine julienne strips, brown lightly in butter, pour in a little water and cook under cover.

When the meat is tender, transfer it to a clean saucepan and strain the sauce over. Add the cooked vegetable julienne, the sour cream, a few capers, the mustard and the lemon juice. Adjust the seasoning and bring to the boil. Sprinkle with chopped parsley to serve. Hand pear-shaped potato fritters separately.

(Gyula Gullner, Hungary)

Entrecôte steak gourmet style
Entrecôte du gourmet
Gourmetrostbraten

4 portions

200 g	4 entrecôte steaks each weighing	7 oz
	salt, pepper	
	flour	
50 g	butter (for frying meat)	2 oz
6 cl	white wine	2 fl oz
6 cl	gravy	2 fl oz
130 g	mushrooms, coarsely chopped	4½ oz
30 g	onions, chopped	1 oz
20 g	butter (for topping)	¾ oz
80 g	ham, coarsely chopped	3 oz
	1 teaspoon tomato purée	
	2 cloves of garlic	
	1 tablespoon each dill,	
	parsley, basil, tarragon	
	12 slices beef bone marrow	
80 g	Parmesan cheese, grated	3 oz

Beat the steaks and snip the edges. Season with salt and pepper and dip one side in flour. Fry quickly in hot butter, transfer to a serving dish and keep hot. Stir in the wine to detach the cooking juices, then add the gravy.

To make the topping, brown the onions lightly in butter, then add the mushrooms and ham, and continue frying for a short time. Add the tomato purée, garlic and herbs. Pour in the steak gravy, reduce well and season with salt and pepper. Spread on the steaks, cover with cooked, sliced beef bone marrow, sprinkle with Parmesan and brown in an oven with good top heat (about 220°C–428°F).

(Franz Zodl, Austria)

Entrecôte steak with letcho
Entrecôtes au letcho
Letschorostbraten

4 portions

200 g	4 entrecôte steaks each weighing	7 oz
	salt, pepper	
	flour	

| 50 g | butter | 2 oz |
| 6 cl | gravy or bouillon | 2 fl oz |

Letcho:

150 g	peppers, diced	5 oz
150 g	tomatoes, skinned and seeded	5 oz
30 g	onion	1 oz
30 g	smoked bacon, cut into strips	1 oz
20 g	butter	¾ oz
	1 teaspoon rose paprika	
	1 teaspoon tomato purée	
	2 cloves of garlic	
	salt, pepper, sugar	
	parsley, chopped	

Beat the steaks, snip the edges and season with salt and pepper. Dip one side in flour and fry quickly in hot butter. Transfer to a serving dish and keep hot. Rinse the pan with gravy or bouillon to detach the cooking juices.

To make letcho, brown the bacon, onion and garlic in butter. Add the peppers and continue frying briefly, then add the paprika, tomato purée and tomatoes. Stir in steak gravy and cook gently for about 5 minutes. Add salt, pepper and sugar to taste. To serve, cover the steaks with the letcho and sprinkle with chopped parsley.

N.B. Letcho is a Hungarian vegetable dish.

(Frank Zodl, Austria)

Rib steak with chanterelles
Petite côte de boeuf aux chanterelles
Marhaborda friss erdei gombával

5 portions   Cooking time: 20–25 minutes

1 kg	beef (wing rib) on the bone	2 lb 4 oz
10 g	pepper, freshly ground	⅓ oz
20 g	salt	¾ oz
50 g	mustard	2 oz
2 dl	oil	7 fl oz
250 g	chanterelles	9 oz
250 g	button onions, peeled	9 oz
250 g	spinach	9 oz
150 g	tomatoes, skinned	5 oz
50 g	lean bacon	2 oz
100 g	butter	3½ oz
1 dl	dry white wine	3½ fl oz

salt and pepper for sauce

Rub the pepper and mustard into the meat thoroughly, pour 1 dl (3½ fl oz) oil over, and marinate in the refrigerator for 3 to 4 days. Season with salt and brown well in a little oil on all sides. Place in an oven preheated to 180°C (355°F) and roast for 20 to 25 minutes, turning once.

Clean the chanterelles, wash them carefully and leave to drain. Clean and wash the spinach thoroughly, blanch in boiling water for 1 or 2 minutes and drain.

Cut the bacon into fine julienne strips and brown in a little butter. Cut up the onions, chanterelles and tomatoes and add to the pan. Fry quickly over high heat and season with salt and pepper. When the contents of the pan are cooked, pour in the wine. Place the beef in the centre of a warmed dish, cover with the spinach and spoon the chanterelle sauce over. Carve the meat at the table.

(Gyula Gullner, Hungary)

Stuffed steak in paprika sauce
Paupiettes de boeuf en sauce au paprika
Gefüllter Rostbraten in Paprikasauce

4 portions

160 g	4 entrecôte steaks each weighing	5½ oz
	salt, pepper	

Stuffing:

120 g	marcaroni	4 oz
20 g	butter	¾ oz
100 g	ham	3½ oz
1¼ dl	sour cream	4 fl oz
	1 egg	
	parsley, chopped	
	paprika, salt	

Sauce:

40 g	oil *or* butter	1½ oz
70 g	onions	2½ oz
40 g	paprika	1½ oz
60 g	tomato purée	2 oz
40 g	flour	1½ oz
1¼ dl	sour cream	4 fl oz
1¼ dl	fresh dairy cream	4 fl oz
7½ dl	beef bouillon	1¼ pt
	1 slice lemon	

2 cloves of garlic
salt

Beat the steaks, snip the edges and season with salt and pepper. To make the stuffing, break the macaroni into about 10 cm (4 in) lengths and cook 'al dente' in salted water, then drain well. Dice the ham finely and brown in butter, season with paprika and add the sour cream. Reduce a little, then add the parsley and the egg. Mix with the macaroni and spread on the steaks. Roll up and tie with twine. Flour the meat and fry in hot fat in a braising pan until golden brown on all sides. Remove and keep hot.

To make the sauce, dice the onions and glaze them in the cooking juices. Season with paprika, add the tomato purée and the garlic which has been finely chopped, dust with flour and add the beef bouillon together with the sour and fresh cream. Season with salt, flavour with lemon zest and juice and boil up well. Place the meat in the pan, cover and cook in the oven at 220°C (428°F) for about 1½ hours. When the meat is tender, remove it from the pan and strain the sauce. To serve, cut each steak obliquely into three or four slices and surround with the sauce.

(Johann Kögl, Austria)

Braised entrecôte Hungarian style
Entrecôtes braisées à la hongroise
Serpenyös Rostélyos

10 portions   Cooking time: 40–50 minutes

180 g	10 entrecôte steaks each weighing	6 oz
50 g	salt	2 oz
100 g	flour	3½ oz
300 g	lard	11 oz
400 g	onions, finely chopped	14 oz
20 g	garlic, chopped	¾ oz
30 g	noble-sweet paprika	1 oz
2 g	ground caraways	a pinch
200 g	tomatoes, cut in quarters	7 oz
300 g	yellow peppers, seeded and cut into strips	11 oz
2 kg 500	potatoes, cut into strips	5 lb 8 oz

Beat the steaks lightly, season with salt, flour them and brown quickly in very little lard, then transfer to a braising pan of suitable size. Fry the onions in the rest of the lard until lightly coloured, add the garlic and caraway, dust with the paprika, stir in a little water, cook for a few minutes, then pour over the meat. Add sufficient water to cover the meat and braise slowly, turning the steaks repeatedly and adding water if required.

When the steaks have begun to cook, add the peppers and tomatoes. Cook for a few minutes, add the potatoes, pour in sufficient water to cover all the contents of the pan and finish cooking. Serve very hot, decorated with raw yellow peppers, seeded and cut into rings, and with sliced raw tomatoes.

(Zsolt Körmendy, Hungary)

Garlic steak Viennese style
Entrecôte à l'ail à la viennoise
Vanillerostbraten

10 portions

180 g	10 entrecôte steaks each weighing	6 oz
3 dl	oil	10 fl oz
	salt, pepper	
½ l	brown stock	18 fl oz
	10 cloves of garlic, finely crushed	
	10 salted cucumbers, peeled	

Flatten the steaks, which should be very well hung and tender. Season with salt and pepper and fry quickly in very hot oil until brown, but still pink and succulent inside. Remove from the pan and place on a warm dish. Add the garlic to the pan and fry for a few moments. Pour in the brown stock, stir well and pour over the steaks. Serve with fried potatoes and salted cucumbers.

(Eduard Mayer, Austria)

Rump steak Auersperg

4 portions

180 g	4 rump steaks each weighing	6 oz
	12 slices beef bone marrow	
	4 teaspoons Parmesan, grated	
30 g	butter	1 oz
	salt, pepper	

Sauce:

50 g	mushrooms, chopped	2 oz
50 g	onions, chopped	2 oz
50 g	ham, chopped	2 oz
30 g	parsley, chopped	1 oz
20 g	garlic, chopped	¾ oz
	1 teaspoon tomato purée	

	1 tablespoon oil	
6 cl	white wine	2 fl oz
12 cl	demi-glace sauce	4 fl oz
	salt, pepper	

Season the steaks with salt and pepper and fry on both sides for about 2 or 3 minutes. Transfer to a serving dish and keep hot. To make the sauce, heat the oil in a frying pan, fry the onions until golden, add the mushrooms and continue frying. Add the ham, parsley, garlic and tomato purée, stir in the wine and stew until cooked. Thicken with the demi-glace sauce and season with salt and pepper to taste. Pour over the steaks, cover with the slices of bone marrow which have been blanched, sprinkle with Parmesan and butter, and gratinate in the oven with high top heat or under a salamander.

(Franz Zodl, Austria)

Rump steak Hacarmel

8 portions

200 g	8 rump steaks each weighing		7 oz
	oil		
	2 onions, finely cut		
100 g	pine kernels		3½ oz
100 g	raisins		3½ oz
200 g	chicken livers, finely cut		7 oz
	salt		
	pepper, freshly ground		
	paprika		
approx. 2 dl	red wine	approx.	7 fl oz

Season the steaks with salt, pepper and paprika. Fry in oil until cooked as desired and transfer to a well warmed dish. Add the onions and livers to the pan, together with the raisins which have been soaked in red wine and drained. Fry lightly and spoon over the steaks. Sprinkle with roasted pine kernels.

(Hermann Wohl, Israel)

Rump steak Rasumofsky

4 portions

200 g	4 rump steaks each weighing	7 oz
40 g	larding bacon	1½ oz
	salt, pepper	
6 cl	oil	2 fl oz

120 g	mirepoix, consisting of carrot, celeriac, swede, onion	4 oz
1¼ dl	game stock, gravy or bouillon	4 fl oz
1¼ dl	red wine	4 fl oz
20 g	flour	¾ oz
	2 teaspoons tomato purée	
6¼ cl	Madeira	2 fl oz
	1 teaspoon mustard	
	1 teaspoon cornflour	
⅕ cl	Cognac	a dash
20 g	butter	¾ oz

Garnish:

100 g	2 apples, each weighing	3½ oz
20 g	butter	¾ oz
	1 teaspoon sugar	
	8 button onions	
40 g	bacon, cut into small strips	1½ oz
60 g	mushrooms cut into six pieces	2 oz

Accompaniment: Austrian corn dumpling

400 g	white bread without crust	14 oz
5 dl	milk	18 fl oz
100 g	butter	3½ oz
	4 eggs	
150 g	sweet corn, cooked	5 oz
	1 bunch chives	
	salt, nutmeg	
10 g	butter, melted	⅓ oz

Lard the meat and marinate for 2 hours in 2 cl (1 fl oz) oil. Season, brown on both sides in the rest of the oil, and arrange in a stew pan. Brown the mirepoix in the oil, dust with flour, add the tomato purée and continue frying for a short time. Stir in the wine and add the stock, gravy or bouillon. Bring to the boil and pour over the meat. Cover and stew for about 1 hour, or until the meat is tender. Remove from the pan and keep hot. Blend together the Madeira, mustard and cornflour, add to the stock and bring to the boil. Strain this sauce and finish with the Cognac and 20 g (¾ oz) butter.

To make the garnish, peel, core and slice the apples into rings (or cut into rings with a fluted cutter). Fry lightly in butter on both sides. Brown the sugar in butter, add the onions, bacon and mushrooms, stir gently over low heat for a few moments, then fill into the hollow centres of the apple slices.

To make the dumpling, dice the bread and moisten with the milk. Cream the butter, then mix with the eggs, or add the egg yolks only and fold in the stiffly whipped whites at the end. Season, add the bread, mix well and stir in the sweet corn. Shape into a roll on a damp napkin, roll in the napkin and tie up the ends. Place in an oblong pan of boiling water and simmer for about 25 minutes. Unwrap the dumpling and slice.

To serve, arrange the steaks on a dish and mask with sauce. Place the filled apple slices on top and the slices of dumpling all round. Brush the dumpling with melted butter and sprinkle with chopped chives.

(Ernst Faseth, Austria)

Braised beef bonne bourgeoise
Aiguillette de boeuf à la bonne bourgeoise

5 portions

2 kg	topside of beef	4 lb 8 oz
1 dl	oil	3½ fl oz
250 g	larding bacon, diced	9 oz
	5 cloves of garlic, well mashed	
	1 calf's foot	
	2 onions	
	2 carrots	
	10 small shallots	
	1 bunch parsley	
1 dl	vinegar	3½ fl oz
	salt, pepper	
	2 bay leaves	
	1 pork rind	

Garnish:

350 g	turnips	12 oz
350 g	carrots, glazed	12 oz
200 g	smoked bacon, diced	7 oz
	potatoes, boiled	
	parsley, chopped	
	butter	

Marinate the larding bacon overnight in the oil together with the garlic, then lard the meat. Brown it lightly on both sides, add the calf's foot, cut into 1 cm (⅜ in) slices, the onions, carrots, shallots, pork rind, parsley and bay leaves, and continue frying. Pour off the fat, add the vinegar, cover and braise in the oven at 200°C (392°F) for 15 minutes. Pour in 1½ l (2¾ pt) water, season with salt and pepper, and return to the oven. Braise slowly for 1¾ hours, or until the meat is tender.

Remove the meat and sliced calf's foot and keep hot. Reduce the stock, adjust the seasoning and strain. Slice the meat and dress on a warmed, buttered dish on top of the slices of calf's foot. Pour the sauce over, keeping some back to hand separately. Serve with boiled potatoes

and the turnips and carrots, boiled and tossed in butter. Sprinkle the meat and accompaniments with chopped parsley before serving.
(Illustration, page 619)

(Jean Esslinger, France)

Braised beef Danish style
Estouffade de boeuf à la danoise
Dansk Surstek

8 portions   Cooking time: 2½ hours

2 kg 500	haunch of beef	5 lb 8 oz
	2 teaspoons salt	
	a pinch of pepper, freshly ground	
	a pinch of ground cloves	
75 g	butter or margarine	2½ oz

Marinade:

2 dl	vinegar (5% proof)	7 fl oz
½ l	beer	18 fl oz
	8 peppercorns	
	2 bay leaves	
	2 large onions, chopped	

Sauce:

50 g	butter or margarine	2 oz
50 g	flour	2 oz
¾ l	brown stock	1¼ pt
	1 teaspoon sugar	
	1 teaspoon vinegar	
2 dl	sour cream	7 fl oz
	salt	
	redcurrant juice to taste	

Prepare a raw marinade. Trim the beef carefully, rub with salt and pepper and leave in the marinade in a cool place for 2 or 3 days, turning frequently. Remove the beef and dry well. Brown on all sides in butter or margarine, place in a stew pan with the marinade and add water to cover if necessary. Cook slowly under cover for about 2½ hours, depending on the quality of the meat.

When the meat is tender, reduce the stock to about 1 l (1¾ pt). Prepare a brown roux with the butter (or margarine) and flour, stir in the stock, then add the sugar and vinegar, together with redcurrant juice to taste, and cook until thick. Add the sour cream and strain.

To serve, slice the meat and dress on a warm dish. Hand the sauce separately, also vegetables as desired. Haunch of elk is prepared in the same way in Norway.

(Otto Ramsbacher, Norway)

Braised beef Rhenish style I
Rheinischer Sauerbraten mit Kartoffelklössen und Apfelmus

10 portions

2 kg 500	lean beef (shoulder cut)	5 lb 8 oz
200 g	lard	7 oz

Marinade:

¼ l	red wine vinegar	9 fl oz
¼ l	red wine	9 fl oz
¼ l	water	9 fl oz
	2 bay leaves	
20 g	black peppercorns	¾ oz
	2 cloves of garlic	
	1 teaspoon salt	
	1 teaspoon sugar	
	1 medium onion, sliced	
	2 cloves	

Sauce:

100 g	carrots	3½ oz
100 g	leeks	3½ oz
100 g	celery	3½ oz
50 g	smoked bacon	2 oz
200 g	tomato purée	7 oz
100 g	flour	3½ oz
50 g	raisins	2 oz
2 dl	red wine	7 fl oz
2 l	bouillon	3½ pt

Potato dumplings:

2 kg 500	floury potatoes (raw), peeled	5 lb 8 oz
100 g	semolina	3½ oz
50 g	potato flour	2 oz
	1 teaspoon salt	
	6 eggs	
	½ onion, finely diced and fried	
	a pinch of nutmeg	
	a pinch of pepper, freshly ground	

Stewed apples:

2 kg	cooking apples	4 lb 8 oz
	½ cinnamon quill	
100 g	sugar	3½ oz
	juice of half a lemon	
1 dl	white wine	3½ fl oz
	10 prunes	

Mix the ingredients for the marinade together well and marinate the beef for a week. Remove and drain. Strain the marinade and set aside the solid contents. Macerate the raisins in red wine. Heat the lard in a stew pan and brown the meat well on all sides, then remove and place on a wire rack. Cut the carrots, leeks and celery into 1 cm (⅜ in) cubes and add to the stew pan. Fry the bacon lightly, add the contents of the marinade and brown well.

Add the tomato purée and brown over medium heat for about 15 minutes, repeatedly stirring in a little marinade. Dust with flour, pour in the bouillon, add the meat and braise over medium heat for 1½ hours. Remove the meat, slice and dress on a well warmed dish. Strain the sauce, adjust the seasoning and add the macerated raisins.

To make the dumplings, boil the potatoes and pass through a ricer. Mix with the remaining ingredients and knead thoroughly. Shape with the hands into dumplings each weighing about 80 g (3 oz). Drop into boiling salted water, reduce the heat to just below simmering point and poach for about 10 minutes. Remove with a skimmer and dress on a warm dish.

To prepare the stewed apples, peel and core the apples, place them in a pan with the cinnamon, sugar, lemon juice and wine, and cook gently for about 15 minutes. Rub through a coarse sieve and leave until quite cold. Dish on dessert plates and decorate with the prunes.

(Erwin Frohmann, Bernd Moos, Werner Schall,
Rudolf Achenbach Delicatessen, Germany)

Braised beef Rhenish style II
Estouffade de boeuf à la rhénane
Rheinischer Sauerbraten mit Rosinen

4 portions

1 kg 800	shoulder of beef (middle cut)	4 lb

Marinade:

⅛ l	strong red wine vinegar	4 fl oz
½ l	water	18 fl oz
½ l	wine	18 fl oz
	salt	
	½ cup sugar	
	mirepoix, consisting of	

	1 leek, diced	
	2 medium carrots, diced	
	1 unpeeled onion, diced	
	½ celeriac, diced	
	lard	
	1 tablespoon peppercorns, crushed	
	1 teaspoon juniper berries	
	1 tablespoon tomato purée	
	1 tablespoon mustard	
	½ bay leaf	
	2 cloves	
	2 allspice seeds	
5 dl	red wine	18 fl oz
5 dl	beef broth	18 fl oz
60 g	raisins	2 oz
	potato flour	

Trim the meat of skin and sinew. Mix the marinade ingredients together well. Place the meat and mirepoix in the marinade, cover tightly and marinate in the refrigerator for a week. Remove the meat, drain and dry. Brown the meat in lard in a large casserole and place in the oven. Add the mirepoix from the marinade, the peppercorns, juniper berries, tomato purée, mustard, bay leaf, cloves and allspice. Pour the marinade over a little at a time, reduce and repeat until all the marinade has boiled away, then add the wine and broth, cover and braise until the meat is tender. Press the mirepoix and stock through a conical strainer. Stir the raisins, which have been soaked, into the sauce. If necessary, thicken with a little potato flour mixed with water. Alternatively, before straining the sauce a spiced Lebkuchen may be crumbled into it and boiled up in it. To serve, slice the meat, dress on a well warmed dish and hand the sauce and potato cakes (recipe, page 1020) separately.

(Gerhard Gartner, Germany)

Braised beef Vestland fashion
Estouffade de boeuf à la westlandaise
Vestlands surstek

4 portions

1 kg 500	beef (haunch or ribs)	3 lb 5 oz
	vegetable oil	
	pepper, freshly ground	

Marinade:

1½ l	pale ale	2¾ pt
	3 tablespoons vinegar	
	1 onion	

cloves
white peppercorns
1 bay leaf
juniper berries
dairy cream

Mix the marinade ingredients together well. The marinade should taste slightly of juniper. Marinate the meat for 48 hours, then remove, dry well with a cloth and rub with pepper. Brown in oil in a braising pan over low heat. Moisten with a little marinade and braise for 2 hours, frequently adding a little marinade meanwhile. Remove the meat from the pan and add a little cream to the stock. Carve the meat into thin slices and dress on a warmed dish with the sauce poured over. Serve with boiled potatoes, peas and carrots in Béchamel sauce, and sweet and sour pumpkin.

(Hroar Dege, Günther Rett, Norway)

Braised beef with mustard sauce
Boeuf en daube à la moutarde
Sanyú–Vetrece

10 portions   Cooking time: 1–1½ hours

2 kg	beef (shoulder or fore rib)	4 lb 8 oz
200 g	smoked bacon or pork fat	7 oz
150 g	lard	5 oz
400 g	onions, finely chopped	14 oz
4 dl	white wine	14 fl oz
6 dl	sour cream	1 pt
40 g	flour	1½ oz
40 g	salt	1½ oz
2 g	pepper, freshly ground	a good pinch
	3 bay leaves	
10 g	garlic, crushed	⅓ oz
50 g	lemon	2 oz
20 g	mustard	¾ oz
10 g	noble-sweet paprika	⅓ oz
	sugar	

Cut up the bacon or pork fat finely, brown in lard, add the onions and garlic and fry until lightly coloured. Add the bay leaves together with the meat which has been cut into strips the thickness of a pencil. Brown well, stirring constantly. Season with salt, pepper and paprika, and stir in a little water. Cover and braise, stirring and adding a little water from time to time if required.

When the meat is half cooked, add the wine a little at a time. When the meat is tender, stir in the sour cream which has been whisked with the flour. Flavour with mustard and lemon juice, and add a little sugar to taste. (The sugar will give the sauce a milder flavour.) Continue cooking for a few minutes. Sprinkle with a few drops of sour cream to serve, and hand boiled rice as an accompaniment. This dish should have a strong, acid taste.

(Zsolt Körmendy, Hungary)

Pot-roast of beef Norwegian castle style
Rôti di boeuf du château à la norvégienne
Gammeldags Slott Stek

4 portions   Cooking time: 2 hours

1 kg	topside of beef, boned	2 lb 4 oz
	salt	
	pepper, freshly ground	
	1 bay leaf	
	allspice	
	3 tablespoons vegetable fat	
	1 tablespoon vinegar	
	anchovy fillets, finely chopped	
	2 tablespoons dark syrup	
	cloves	
5 dl	bouillon	18 fl oz
2 dl	dairy cream	7 oz
50 g	flour butter	2 oz

Season the meat with salt and pepper and tie round. Heat the fat in a braising pan and brown the meat on all sides. Stir in 2 dl (7 fl oz) bouillon and add the bay leaf, allspice, anchovy fillets, syrup, vinegar and cloves. Braise for about 2 hours, then remove the meat and set aside in a warm place for 15 minutes.

Add the rest of the bouillon to the cooking liquid, thicken with flour butter and cream, reduce a little and strain. Slice the meat, dress on a well warmed dish and pour the sauce over. Serve with boiled carrots, cauliflower, peas and potatoes and with red currant jelly. This dish is traditionally served on Sunday in Norway.

(Hroar Dege, Günther Rett, Norway)

Braised beef bourgeois
Boeuf braisé à la bourgeoise

6 portions

approx. 2 kg	boneless beef	approx.	4 lb 8 oz
	larding bacon		

	salt, pepper	
	oil	
	mirepoix consisting of	
	1 large onion, coarsely diced	
	1 medium carrot, coarsely diced	
	1 celeriac, coarsely diced	
	2 tablespoons tomato purée	
	1 small can anchovies	
	1 teaspoon peppercorns, crushed	
	1 teaspoon allspice	
1½ dl	syrup	5 fl oz
½ dl	wine vinegar	2 fl oz
1½ dl	brown stock	5 fl oz
1 dl	dairy cream	3½ fl oz
	1 tablespoon arrowroot	
3 dl	sherry	10 fl oz
	Mesost (whey cheese), grated	
	lemon juice	

Pickled tomatoes:

1 kg	small green tomatoes	2 lb 4 oz
	salt	
	marinade consisting of	
5 dl	vinegar	18 fl oz
500 g	sugar	1 lb 2 oz
	1 teaspoon cloves	
	1 small cinnamon quill	
	1 piece ginger	

Lard the beef, tie round with twine, and season with salt and pepper. Heat oil in a braising pan and lightly brown the meat on all sides. Add the mirepoix, peppercorns and allspice, cover and cook gently until moist. Add the anchovies and tomato purée and fry for a short time. Stir in the vinegar and syrup and add sufficient brown stock to cover the meat. Bring to the boil, reduce the heat and braise slowly under cover for about 2½ hours. Remove the meat, wrap in greaseproof paper and keep hot. (The meat will remain very succulent with this procedure.)

Remove the grease from the stock, pass through a conical strainer and reduce a little if necessary. Blend the arrowroot with the cream and add to the sauce to give a smooth, thick consistency. Flavour with sherry, a few drops of lemon juice and grated Mesost cheese. Keep hot.

Serve with boiled potatoes or potato croquettes, redcurrant jelly or cranberries, and pickled green tomatoes. To pickle tomatoes, rinse them in cold water and prick with a needle. Simmer in salted water, keeping them firm, then rinse in cold water. Cook the marinade until thick, add the tomatoes and cook until soft, then place in a suitable container, cover tightly, allow to cool and refrigerate.

(Eric Carlström, Sweden)

Stewed seamen's steak
Steak de boeuf des marins

6 portions

	12 slices beef (thick flank or topside)	
100 g	each weighing	4 oz
	salt, pepper	
1 dl	oil	3½ fl oz
	3 large onions, finely sliced	
	10 medium potatoes, blanched	
	bouquet garni consisting of	
	4 bay leaves	
	1 teaspoon pimento	
5 dl	brown stock	18 fl oz
3 dl	beer	10 fl oz
	Worcester sauce	
	2 tablespoons parsley, finely chopped	

Flatten the meat well, season and brown well in hot oil. Pour off the oil and lightly brown the onions in the remaining cooking juices. Add the bouquet garni and brown stock, cover with greaseproof paper, then with a tightly-fitting lid, and simmer for about 35 minutes, when the meat should be half cooked. Remove the bouquet garni, add the potatoes and pour in the beer which should barely cover the meat. Cover tightly and cook until the meat is tender. To serve, flavour with a little Worcester sauce and sprinkle with the parsley.

(Eric Carlström, Sweden)

Braised steak Hagalil
Steak de boeuf braisé Hagalil

8 portions

180 g	8 beefsteaks (shoulder) each weighing	6 oz
	flour	
	oil	
5 dl	gravy	18 fl oz
	8 prunes	
	8 dried apricots	
	8 dried apple rings	
	lemon zest, grated	
50 g	almonds, chopped	2 oz
	pepper, freshly ground	
	salt	
	paprika	

approx. 5 dl	red wine	approx. 18 fl oz

Macerate the dried fruit in the wine. Season the steaks with salt, pepper and paprika, flour them and brown on both sides in oil. Place in a fireproof dish. Add the gravy to the pan, stir to detach the cooking juices, bring to the boil and pour over the steaks. Cover with greaseproof paper, place in a preheated oven and braise until the meat is half cooked. Remove the dried fruit from the wine, add to the meat and braise until tender. Finish with the remaining wine and sprinkle with the lemon zest and almonds.

(Hermann Wohl, Israel)

Braised silverside of beef Catalan style
Cuisse de toreau étouffée à la catalane
Estofado de toro de lidia a la catalana

6 portions   Cooking time: about 3 hours

1 kg 500	silverside	3 lb 5 oz
300 g	streaky pork fat or bacon in one piece	11 oz
300 g	Butifarra (Catalan sausage)	11 oz
800 g	potatoes, peeled and cut in pieces	1 lb 12 oz
	6 onions, cut in fairly small pieces	
	3 carrots, cut in fairly small pieces	
	6 ripe tomatoes, cut in pieces	
350 g	button onions	12 oz
	1 sprig thyme	
	1 bay leaf	
	1 cinnamon quill	
	1 leek	
300 g	lard	11 oz
60 g	flour	2 oz
1 dl	aniseed liqueur	3½ fl oz
1 dl	Muscat wine	3½ fl oz
	pepper, salt	

Cut the meat into pieces weighing about 50 g (2 oz). Melt the lard, brown the pork fat or bacon in it and remove from the pan. Season the meat with salt and pepper and brown in the hot lard. Add the carrots and onions, brown lightly, then add the tomatoes, herbs, cinnamon, leek, sausage and pork fat or bacon. Dust with flour and stir with a wooden spoon. Pour in sufficient water to cover and cook under cover until the meat is almost cooked. Transfer the meat to a second pan. Strain the stock over the meat and bring to the boil. Add the button onions and the potatoes and finish cooking. (It may be necessary to add the potatoes earlier, as all the ingredients should be tender and ready for serving at the same time.) Finish off with the liqueur and the wine, adding a little salt if required. Cut up the pork fat and sausage evenly and arrange in a round dish with the meat. Peas are sometimes served with this dish. In Barcelona many restaurants serve this popular dish on Tuesdays. It is made with meat from the bulls killed in the ring at the traditional bullfight on the previous Sunday.

(Josep Lladonosa, Spain)

Braised beef Viennese style
Estouffade de boeuf à la viennoise
Stoffade

4 portions

1 kg	beef (top rib)	2 lb 4 oz
60 g	ham	2 oz
60 g	cooked smoked tongue	2 oz
60 g	larding bacon	2 oz
100 g	mirepoix	3½ oz
100 g	onions, coarsely chopped	3½ oz
	6 slices smoked pork fat (or bacon)	
20 g	each weighing	¾ oz
	12 walnuts, coarsely chopped	¾ oz
	3 dried figs, finely sliced	
approx. 100 g	1 slice brown bread	approx. 4 oz
	10 juniper berries	
	10 green peppercorns, crushed	
5 dl	red wine	18 fl oz
2½ dl	bouillon	9 fl oz
	salt, pepper	

Trim the meat, season with salt and pepper, and thread alternately with strips of larding bacon, ham and tongue. Line a braising pan with slices of smoked pork fat or bacon, and cover with the mirepoix, onions, walnuts and figs and with the bread which has been cut into cubes. Sprinkle with the crushed peppercorns and the juniper berries. Place the meat on top and cook gently under cover for about 10 minutes. Add the bouillon and wine, cover and braise for about 1½ hours. Remove the meat, pass the sauce through a conical strainer and season with salt to taste. Carve the meat and pour the sauce over to serve.

(Franz Zodl, Austria)

Boiled beef with horseradish sauce Prague fashion
Pointe de culotte de boeuf avec sauce au raifort à la pragueoise
Hovězí květová špička s křenavou omáčkou

6 portions   Cooking time: 2 hours

800 g–1 kg	rump of beef	1¾–2¼ lb
150 g	flavouring vegetables	5 oz
	salt	
	1 bay leaf	
	1 onion, thickly sliced	
	parsley *or* chives, chopped	

Potato cake:

750 g	potatoes	1 lb 10 oz
⅛ l	oil	4 fl oz
	salt	

Horseradish sauce:

40 g	butter	1½ oz
40 g	flour	1½ oz
¼ l	milk	9 fl oz
¼ l	bouillon	9 fl oz
	2 tablespoons horseradish, grated	
	salt	
10 g	sugar	⅓ oz
	1 tablespoon lemon juice	
	4 tablespoons dairy cream	

Place the beef in a pan containing about 3 l (5 pt) lightly salted boiling water and add the flavouring vegetables, the bay leaf and the onion which has been lightly browned without fat. Cook the meat slowly for about 1½ to 2 hours, skimming occasionally. Slice, pour a little broth over and sprinkle with parsley or chives just before serving.

Boil the potatoes, peel and allow to cool, then grate coarsely. Heat the oil, add the potatoes, season with salt and fry over low heat until the underside is crisp and well browned. Turn carefully, add a little oil and brown on the other side.

To make the sauce, prepare a white roux with the butter and flour, blend in the milk (cold) and bouillon, bring to the boil and cook for 10 minutes. Add the horseradish, salt to taste, sugar and lemon juice and finish with the cream.

(Vilèm Vrabec, Czechoslovakia)

Norwegian beef olives
Oiseaux sans tête
Benløse fugler

4 portions

80 g	8 slices beef (topside or similar) each weighing	3 oz

2 tablepoons vegetable fat
bouillon
salt
pepper, freshly ground
dairy cream

Stuffing:

	1 onion, chopped	
	4 anchovy fillets, cut into strips	
100 g	bacon, cut into strips	3½ oz

Flatten the meat, season on one side with salt and pepper and cover with the bacon, anchovy fillets and onion. Roll up and secure with a small wooden skewer or toothpick. Carefully brown in vegetable fat, add bouillon and braise until tender. Remove from the pan and thicken the stock with a little cream. Dress the beef olives on a well warmed dish, pour the sauce over and hand purée of peas, gherkins and cranberry preserve separately.

(Hroar Dege, Günther Rett, Norway)

Double entrecôte steak patron
Entrecôte double du patron
Zwischenrippenstück Patron

4 portions

650 g	boned sirloin	1 lb 7 oz
150 g	white bread without crust	5 oz
150 g	beef bone marrow, blanched	5 oz
80 g	shallots, chopped	3 oz
	mixed herbs, consisting of	
	chopped parsley, chervil, basil	
	salt, pepper, English mustard powder	
20 g	breadcrumbs	¾ oz
30 g	butter	1 oz
5 cl	oil	2 fl oz
2½ dl	Chambertin for sauce	9 fl oz

Potato gnocchi:

400 g	floury potatoes	14 oz
	1 egg	
30 g	butter	1 oz
	flour as required	
	salt	
	oil	

Stewed fennel:

2 fennel

80 g	streaky pork fat or bacon	3 oz
150 g	carrot and celery brunoise	5 oz
	white stock	
	salt, pepper	
	parsley, chopped	

Cut the meat into 4 steaks, flatten gently, and season with salt, pepper and mustard powder. Fry quickly in oil and cool. Soak the bread in bouillon and mash well. Dice the bone marrow. Sauter the shallots in butter, mix with the bone marrow, bread and herbs, and season with salt and pepper. Spread in a thick layer on to the steaks, sprinkle with breadcrumbs and brown in the oven; the meat should be medium done. Serve with Chambertin sauce, potato gnocchi and stewed fennel.

To make the gnocchi, peel the potatoes, boil them, sieve and allow to cool. Mix with the egg, flour as required, butter and salt. Shape into small dumplings, roll over the inside of a grater, and deep fry in hot oil.

To prepare the fennel, clean it, cut in half and remove the stumps. Parboil in salted water, pour off the water, cover with the brunoise and the bacon, add white stock and stew under cover. Sprinkle with chopped parsley.

To make the sauce, stir the Chambertin into the pan in which the meat was fried, mix well with the cooking juices and reduce to the desired consistency. Keep hot.

(Ewald Plachutta, Austria)

Entrecôte steak with Teroldego
Entrecôte au Teroldego
Costata di manzo al Teroldego

4 portions

150 g	4 entrecôte steaks each weighing		5 oz
10–20 g	flour butter	approx.	½ oz
	sunflower or corn oil as required		
1 dl	Teroldego (red wine)		3½ fl oz
	1 tablespoon gravy		
	2 cloves of garlic		
	1 sprig rosemary		
	6 sage leaves		
	salt, pepper		

Flour the steaks very lightly and brown on both sides in hot oil, then season with salt and freshly ground pepper. Add the herbs and garlic, then the wine and gravy. Fry the steaks as desired, remove from the pan and dress on a warmed dish. Reduce the cooking juices, thicken with the flour butter and pour over the meat.

(Sergio Chiesa, Italy)

Boiled ribs of beef with peppers
Côte de boeuf bouillie avec poivrons
Costata bollita con peperonata

Trim the meat well and tie so that it keeps its shape. Bring to the boil a strong bouillon
flavoured with carrots, celery and onions. Place the meat in it and boil over high heat to prevent escape of the juices. Allow 15 minutes per kg (7 minutes per lb). Serve with peppers
Italian style (recipe, page 1012).
(Illustration, page 518)

(Franco Colombani, Italy)

Entrecôte steak Villette
Entrecôte Villette
Zwischenrippenstück Villette

10 portions   Cooking time: 8 minutes

1 kg 600	entrecôte steak	3 lb 8 oz
	seasonings as desired	
30 g	butter	1 oz
300 g	ox spine marrow	11 oz
80 g	shallots, finely chopped	3 oz
60 g	parsley, finely chopped	2 oz
20 g	garlic, finely chopped	¾ oz
100 g	breadcrumbs	3½ oz
1 dl	white wine	3½ fl oz
	salt	
	pepper, freshly ground	
	fresh thyme	

Beaujolais sauce:

	3 shallots, finely chopped	
50 g	butter	2 oz
2 dl	Beaujolais	7 fl oz
	a pinch of fresh thyme	
	1 bay leaf	
2 dl	brown veal stock	7 fl oz

	seasonings as desired	
300 g	watercress	11 oz

Trim the meat of sinew and fat, cut it into four and beat each piece lightly. Season and brown quickly in butter. Remove from the pan and cover with a 1 cm (⅜ in) layer of ox marrow paste. Brown for about 8 minutes in an oven with 200°C (392°F) top heat.

To make the ox marrow paste, prepare and soak the marrow, then cut into 5 mm (¼ in) pieces. Mix with the shallots, garlic, parsley and breadcrumbs, add salt, pepper and fresh thyme, and moisten with the wine.

To make the sauce, stew the shallots carefully in 30 g (1 oz) butter without colouring. Add the Beaujolais, thyme and bay leaf, and reduce by two thirds. Add the stock and reduce by half. Season with salt and pepper, add the rest of the butter a little at a time, and strain. To serve, pour the sauce on to warmed plates, dress the meat in the centre, cut into slices the thickness of one finger, and garnish with watercress.

(Otto Ledermann, Switzerland)

Ox tongue Mazuba
Langue de boeuf Mazuba

8 portions
Cooking time: 2½ hours, or 50 minutes in a pressure cooker

1 kg 500–	pickled ox tongue	3 lb 5 oz–
2 kg		4 lb 8 oz
200 g	mushrooms	7 oz
	2 tomato peppers	
	(gamba)	
	2 tomatoes	
	1 onion	
1 dl	red wine	3½ fl oz
1 dl	veal gravy	3½ fl oz

Soak the tongue for 24 hours before use. Boil in water for 2½ hours, refresh in cold water and skin. Slice and keep hot.

Cut the onion into julienne strips. Slice the mushrooms finely. Skin and seed the tomatoes and cut into julienne strips, together with the peppers. Cook the onion gently in oil until lightly coloured. Add the mushrooms, peppers and tomatoes, cook for a few minutes, then add the gravy and wine and boil up for a moment. Pour over the tongue.

(Hermann Wohl, Israel)

Pickled ox tongue with asparagus
Langue de boeuf aux asperges
Vařený hovězí jazyk s chřestem

6 portions   Cooking time: about 2½–3½ hours

1 kg	asparagus	2 lb 4 oz
	salt	
30 g	sugar	1 oz
	1 pickled ox tongue	
	2 cloves	
	4 peppercorns	
	allspice	
	1 bay leaf	
	1 onion	
150 g	flavouring vegetables	5 oz
40 g	butter	1½ oz
	1 tablespoon parsley, chopped	

Clean and scrape the asparagus. Place in a pan of lightly salted boiling water with the sugar and cook for about 15 minutes or until tender. (The cooking time depends on the thickness of the asparagus.) Place 3 l (5 pt) water in a pan with the spices, bay leaf and onion. Bring to the boil, add the tongue, which has been well washed, reduce the heat and cook for 2½ to 3 hours, or until the tip of the tongue is tender. Add the flavouring vegetables 45 minutes before the end of the cooking time.

Rinse the cooked tongue in cold water, skin at once and remove the gristle. Slice and dress on a heated dish with the asparagus. Serve with new potatoes which have been boiled in their skins, then peeled and tossed in hot butter with chopped parsley. Hand Hollandaise sauce separately (recipe, page 175).

(Vilèm Vrabec, Czechoslovakia)

Wine-cooked beef with turnips

4–5 portions for 2 meals, to be served with 2–3 other dishes
Cooking time: 3 hours

1 kg 250	stewing beef	2 lb 12 oz
500 g	turnips	1 lb 2 oz
2 cl	soya sauce	1 fl oz
6 cl	white wine	2 fl oz
6 cl	water	2 fl oz
	4 slices root ginger	
3 g	salt	a good pinch

	pepper to taste	
6 cl	rice wine or dry sherry	2 fl oz
	1 beef or chicken stock cube	

Cut the beef into 3–4 cm (about 1½ in) cubes and the turnips into similar size wedge shaped pieces. Plunge the beef into a large pan of boiling water and boil vigorously for 5 or 6 minutes, then drain. Transfer to a large heatproof basin, add the turnips and all the other ingredients and mix them together. Close the top of the basin with tinfoil. Simmer in a bain-marie for 3 hours, adding boiling water to the pan when necessary. To serve, either bring the basin used for cooking to the table, or transfer to a suitable serving dish. This dish is suitable for reheating.

(Kenneth Lo, China)

Quick-fried shredded ribbons of beef (or lamb) with bean sprouts

4 portions

500 g	beef (fillet or rump steak)	1 lb 2 oz
	2 stalks spring onion	
330 g	bean sprouts	12 oz
2 cl	oil	1 fl oz
3 g	salt	a good pinch
3 g	sugar	a pinch
	pepper to taste	
5 cl	soya sauce	½ fl oz
5 g	lard	¼ oz
1 cl	good stock	½ fl oz

Cut the beef with a sharp knife into matchstick shreds. Cut the spring onions into 4–5 cm (about 2 in) sections. Rub the beef with a little of the oil and salt. Heat the rest of the oil in a large frying pan or saucepan. Add the beef and stir-fry over high heat for 1 minute, then push it to one side of the pan. Add the lard to the other side of the pan. When it has melted, add the spring onions, the remaining salt and the bean sprouts. Turn them over quickly for 1½ minutes. Sprinkle the contents of the pan with soya sauce, pepper and stock. Mix, then turn all the contents together quickly for 1½ minutes. Dress on a well heated serving dish and serve immediately.

(Kenneth Lo, China)

Quick-fried shredded ribbons of beef (or lamb) with onion and young leeks

4 portions

500 g	beef (fillet or rump steak)	1 lb 2 oz

	1 large onion	
	3–4 young leeks	
	3 cloves of garlic	
2 cl	oil	1 fl oz
5 g	lard	¼ oz
3 g	salt	a good pinch
	pepper to taste	
⅘ cl	soya sauce	½ fl oz
1 cl	good stock	½ fl oz
½ cl	rice wine or sherry	¼ fl oz

Cut the beef with a sharp knife into matchstick shreds. Cut the onion into 4 or 5 slices. Crush the garlic and chop coarsely. Clean the leeks and cut on the slant into 4–5 cm (about 2 in) sections. Rub the beef with a little of the salt and oil, and with pepper to taste. Heat the rest of the oil in a large frying pan or saucepan. Add the onion and garlic and stir-fry over high heat for half a minute. Add the beef and stir-fry again for 1 minute, then push aside. Add the leeks, lard, soya sauce, stock and wine (or sherry). Continue to stir-fry and mix all the contents together for 2½ minutes. Dress on a well heated dish and serve immediately. (Illustration, page 694)

(Kenneth Lo, China)

Quick-fried sliced beef with mushrooms

4 portions

500 g	beef (fillet or rump steak)	1 lb 2 oz
250 g	firm button mushrooms	9 oz
3 g	salt	a good pinch
	pepper to taste	
1½ cl	oil	½ fl oz
1 cl	soya sauce	½ fl oz
2 cl	good stock	1 fl oz
5 g	lard	¼ oz
½ cl	hoisin sauce	¼ fl oz
1 cl	rice wine or sherry	½ fl oz
2 g	sugar	a pinch
3 g	cornflour	1 level teaspoon

Cut the beef into thin slices 4 cm x 5–6 cm (1½ x 2–2½ in). Rub with salt, pepper and a little of the oil. Wash the mushrooms thoroughly, remove the stalks, and cut each stalk and cap in half. Mix the cornflour with the stock until well blended.

Heat the rest of the oil in a frying pan. Add the mushroom stalks, stir-fry for 1 minute, then add the lard, beef and mushroom caps. Stir and turn them together over high heat for 1½ minutes. Add the soya sauce, hoisin sauce and wine (or sherry). Turn and stir for 1½ minutes. Pour the stock and cornflour mixture evenly over the contents of the pan. Continue to stir-fry quickly for half a minute. Dress on a well heated dish and serve immediately. (Illustration, page 694)

(Kenneth Lo, China)

Pumpkin Argentinian style
Potiron à l'argentine
Criolla carbonada

10 portions   Cooking time: 1¼ hours

6 kg	1 pumpkin weighing approx.	13 lb 4 oz
250 g	butter	9 oz
300 g	sugar	11 oz
1 dl	oil	3½ fl oz
1 kg 500	lean boneless beef	3 lb 5 oz
	2 large onions, finely diced	
150 g	peppers, finely diced	5 oz
10 g	garlic, crushed	⅓ oz
1½ l	bouillon	2¾ pt
500 g	tomatoes, skinned, seeded and coarsely diced	1 lb 2 oz
800 g	potatoes, diced	1 lb 12 oz
700 g	kohlrabi, diced	1 lb 8 oz
500 g	courgettes, diced	1 lb 2 oz
300 g	sweet corn	11 oz
	salt	
	pepper	
	oregano	

Wash the pumpkin well, cut off the top to make a lid and carefully remove the seeds and fibres. Butter the inside evenly and sprinkle with the sugar. Bake in a moderate oven for 35 minutes.

Cook the peppers, onions and garlic gently for a few moments in a little butter, add the bouillon and bring to the boil. Add the beef, which has been cut into 30 g (1 oz) cubes and browned in hot oil, together with the beef cooking juices, the tomatoes, a small pinch of oregano, salt and pepper. Stew for 15 minutes, then add the potatoes and the kohlrabi. Cook for a further 10 minutes, then add the courgettes and sweet corn. Finish cooking and season well. Fill into the baked pumpkin, replace the lid at once, and serve.

(Karl Brunnengräber, Argentine)

Grilled ribs of beef with flap mushrooms
Côte de boeuf grillée riche de cèpes
Costata di manzo alla griglia ricca di funghi

2 portions   Cooking time: mushrooms 1 hour; beef 16 minutes

800 g	ribs of beef	1 lb 12 oz
70 g	4 flap mushrooms each weighing	2½ oz
20 g	4 black Narcia truffles each weighing	¾ oz
40 g	clarified butter	1½ oz
	12 basil leaves	
3 cl	olive oil	1 fl oz
	salt	
	white pepper, freshly ground	

Wash the basil and set aside. Wash the flap mushrooms quickly and carefully under running water, drain and dry with a cloth. Arrange them side by side in a sauté pan containing the clarified butter. Season with salt and pepper, cover and cook slowly over low heat for 1 hour, turning them carefully from time to time. Add 6 basil leaves and the truffles (whole) after 30 minutes. When cooked, keep hot.

Preheat a grill for 30 minutes. Oil the meat lightly and grill on both sides as desired, turning it four times in all in order to produce the grid marks characteristic of grills. While cooking the first side, season the other side with salt and pepper, then turn and season the grilled side. If necessary, brush the grill thinly with oil from time to time.

Dress on an oval dish with an alternating arrangement of flap mushrooms and truffles, and decorate with the remaining basil leaves.

(Daniel Drouadaine, Italy)

Tripe with chanterelles or flap mushrooms
Tripes aux girolles ou aux cèpes
Überbackene Kutteln auf di Art des Pilz–Peter

10 portions   Cooking time: 40 minutes

1 kg 500	tripe, cooked	3 lb 5 oz
700 g	carrots	1 lb 8 oz
250 g	celery	9 oz
250 g	leeks	9 oz
250 g	onions	9 oz
150 g	butter	5 oz
	2 cloves of garlic, crushed	

750 g	chanterelles *or* flap mushrooms	1 lb 10 oz
160 g	Parmesan cheese, grated	5½ oz
2½ l	concentrated gravy	4½ pt
¼ l	white wine	9 fl oz
	salt	
	pepper, freshly ground	
	monosodium glutamate	
	oil	
	flour	
	melted butter	

Cut the tripe into strips or pieces as desired, dust with a little flour and fry lightly in hot oil. Meanwhile heat part of the butter in a second pan, add the carrots, leeks, celery and onions which have been coarsely sliced, together with the garlic, and cook gently without colouring. Stir in the wine, add the gravy and the tripe and cook for about 30 minutes.

Clean the mushrooms carefully, wash thoroughly, dry with a cloth and slice fairly coarsely. Heat the rest of the butter in a frying pan, sauter the mushrooms in it, season and stew for a few minutes.

Transfer the tripe with a little of the stock (which should not be too liquid) to a fireproof serving dish. Cover with the mushrooms, sprinkle with the cheese and melted butter, and brown quickly in an oven with good top heat. Hand egg 'spätzle' and mixed salad separately.

(Karl Brunnengräber, Germany)

Hot Beef Dishes for Individual Plate Service

Animelles with spring onions and diced tomato salad
Animelles aux oignons printaniers et à la compôte de tomates
Animelles vom Stier mit Frühlingszwiebelchen und Tomatenkompott

1 portion

> 1 bull's animelles
> pepper, freshly ground
> salt
> olive oil
> ½ shallot, finely chopped
> 3 spring onions

Diced tomato salad:

> 1 large tomato (raw)
> 1 tablespoon tomato ketchup
> a few drops Worcester sauce
> 1 teaspoon olive oil
> lemon juice
> a pinch of sugar

Skin the animelles with a sharp knife and soak under running water for 2 to 3 hours. Place on a cloth and dry well. Slice, season with salt and pepper and coat with the olive oil mixed with the shallot. Grill over high heat for half a minute on each side.

Blanch the spring onions in salted vegetable broth with a pinch of sugar, keeping them firm. Skin, seed and dice the tomato. Mix carefully with the ketchup, Worcester sauce, lemon juice and oil. Add salt to taste and a pinch of sugar. Decorate the top with basil leaves cut into strips. Serve with basil butter.
(Illustration, page 768)

(Gerhard Gartner, Germany)

Fricassée of fillet of beef Felice
Fricassée de filet de boeuf Felice
Frikassee von Rinderfilet Felice

4 portions

400 g	fillet of beef (thin end)	14 oz

100 g	butter	3½ oz
	1 tablespoon onion, finely chopped	
	salt	
50 g	flap mushrooms	2 oz
	12 pieces soft ox marrow	
2 dl	veal gravy	7 fl oz
1 dl	port	3½ fl oz
	1 tablespoon brunoise of black truffles	
	1 tablespoon meat glaze	

Cut the fillet of beef into 5 cm (2 in) strips the thickness of one finger. Brown quickly in 50 g (2 oz) butter. Season lightly with salt. Add the onion and continue frying briefly. The meat should be medium rare. Keep hot on a plate.

Cut the flap mushrooms and bone marrow into slices 3 mm (⅛ in) thick. Stir the gravy and port into the pan in which the meat was fried, add the flap mushrooms and reduce by half. Add the truffles, bone marrow, meat glaze and meat. Bring to the boil and gradually add the rest of the butter, which has been softened. Serve with leaf spinach.
(Illustration, page 415)

(Felix Real, Liechtenstein)

Charolais rissoles with sherry sauce
Rissoles de Charolais au xérès

1 portion   Cooking time: 15 minutes

100 g	puff pastry	3½ oz
200 g	fillet of beef	7 oz
5 cl	sherry	2 fl oz
	1 shallot	
	1 teaspoon meat glaze	
	butter as required	
	a few cubes fresh black truffle	
	fat for deep frying	

Sherry sauce:

1 dl	veal stock	3½ fl oz
5 cl	sherry	2 fl oz
	a little arrowroot	
15 g	butter	½ oz
	salt, pepper	

Pin out the puff pastry into a 10 cm (4 in) square 3 mm (⅛ in) thick. Moisten the edges well with water. Trim the meat, cut into 1 cm (⅜ in) cubes and macerate in the sherry. Chop the shallot finely and cook gently in a little butter until transparent. Add the meat glaze and about 1 teaspoon butter, season well, then add the meat and truffle. Place this filling in the centre of one half of the pastry square, fold the other half over to make a rissole and seal the edges well. Wrap in greaseproof paper, tie at both ends and deep fry. Remove after 15 minutes, unwrap and dish on a napkin. Serve with sherry sauce.

(André Béghin, Belgium)

Sauté beef fillet with scallops
Sauté de filet de boeuf et coquilles St. Jacques
Ragoût von ossehaas met jakobschelpen

4 portions

200 g	fillet of beef, cut into thin strips	7 oz
	8 scallops, well cleaned	
¼ l	American sauce	9 fl oz
1 kg	spinach	2 lb 4 oz

Brown the meat lightly, add the scallops and continue frying for a few minutes. Pour in the sauce and mix well. Serve on a bed of blanched spinach.

(Bernard van Beurten, Netherlands)

Sauté fillet of beef with artichokes
Sauté de filet de boeuf au ragoût d'artichauts

2 portions

300 g	fillet of beef (thin end)	11 oz
	2 artichoke bottoms	
2 dl	sour cream	7 fl oz
5 cl	gin	2 fl oz
5 cl	veal stock	2 fl oz
	1 tablespoon mustard seed	
	1 teaspoon chives, chopped	
	1 tablespoon flour	
	½ lemon	
30 g	butter	1 oz
	salt, pepper	

Blanch the artichoke bottoms, keeping them firm, in salted water with the addition of the lemon juice and flour. Cut them into 4 cm x 1 cm (1½ x ⅜ in) strips. Cut the meat into strips of the same size and sauter in butter over high heat for 2 minutes together with the artichokes. Season with salt and pepper. Remove from the pan and keep hot. Stir in the gin to detach the cooking juices, add the veal stock, sour cream and mustard seed, and reduce a little. Add the chives and adjust the seasoning. Carefully toss the meat and artichokes in the sauce and dress on individual plates.
(Illustration, page 310)

(Roger Souvereyns, Belgium)

Sauté fillet of beef with juniper berries
Sauté minute de filet de boeuf aux baies de genièvre

6 portions

1 kg	fillet of beef (thin end)	2 lb 4 oz
100 g	butter	3½ oz
1 l	red wine	1¾ pt
3 dl	demi-glace sauce	10 fl oz
	a pinch of finely chopped shallot	
	salt, pepper	
	6 juniper berries	
	oil as required	

Place the wine in a pan with the shallot, reduce by a third, strain and add the butter a little at a time to make a sauce. Season with salt and pepper and keep hot. Cut the meat into 5 cm x 1½ cm (2 in x ⅝ in) strips. Season with salt, pepper and the juniper berries which have been finely crushed. Sauter in butter over fierce heat, keeping the meat rare, and transfer to a strainer. Dish on warmed plates and mask with the sauce. Hand purée of celery separately. This dish should be cooked at the last minute.

(Emile Jung, France)

Ribs of beef with vegetable purée
Côte de boeuf aux purées de légumes

4 portions

1 kg 400	ribs of beef	3 lb
1 dl	olive oil	3½ fl oz
	1 small sprig thyme	
	1 small sprig rosemary	

	4 sage leaves	
	8 basil leaves	
	1 clove of garlic	
	salt	
	black pepper, freshly ground	
	garden cress	
3 dl	Béarnaise sauce (recipe, page 174)	10 fl oz

Trim the beef carefully. Prepare a marinade with the oil, thyme, rosemary, sage, basil and garlic. Place the meat in it and leave for 12 hours, turning the meat several times. Remove, drain and season with salt and pepper. Grill, then leave to stand in a warm place for 10 minutes to prevent escape of the juices when carving. Serve on warm plates, garnished with vegetable purées. Hand Béarnaise sauce separately. Garden cress may be used as a garnish instead of vegetables.
(Illustration, page 238)

(Anton Mosimann, Great Britain)

Ribs of beef with pine kernels and green pepper au gratin
Côte de boeuf aux noix de pinède et au poivre vert gratinée

4 portions

800 g	2 ribs of beef each weighing	1 lb 12 oz
100 g	breadcrumbs	3½oz
50 g	pine kernels, chopped	2 oz
1 dl	nut oil	3½fl oz
	2 tablespoons olive oil	
	2 tablespoons fine herbs (chervil, tarragon, marjoram), chopped	
20 g	green pepper in preserving liquid	¾oz
3½ dl	white wine (Chiroubles)	12 fl oz
½ l	veal stock	18 fl oz
400 g	parsley	14 oz
100 g	butter	3½oz
	salt, pepper	

Fry the meat in butter, season with salt and pepper and keep hot. Rinse out the pan with the wine, add the stock, reduce over low heat, pass through a conical strainer and finish with butter. Pound the breadcrumbs, oil, herbs, green pepper and preserving liquid, and the pine kernels to a paste of spreading consistency in a china mortar. Spread on top of the meat and briefly brown under a salamander. Dress the meat on individual plates and surround with the sauce. Garnish with parsley deep fried in fat at 130°C (265°F).
(Illustration, page 308)

(Roger Souvereyns, Belgium)

Viennese fiacre goulash
Goulash fiacre viennois
Fiakergulyas

8 portions

1 kg 500	beef (cut from the haunch)	3 lb 5 oz
150 g	lard	5 oz
1 kg	onions, chopped	2 lb 4 oz
60 g	noble-sweet paprika	2 oz
	1 teaspoon vinegar	
	1 tablespoon caraway seeds, finely chopped	
	1 tablespoon marjoram	
	4 cloves of garlic	
	2 peppers, cut into strips	
	8 fried eggs	
	8 frankfurters	
	8 gherkin fans	
	boiled potatoes	
	salt	

Cook the onions gently in hot lard until golden, add the paprika and vinegar, then pour in a little water. Add the meat, cut into cubes, and season with salt, marjoram, caraways and garlic juice. Stew slowly, adding the peppers shortly before the end of the cooking time. Dish on individual plates, allowing about 4 pieces of meat per portion. Pour a little of the cooking liquid over and garnish each portion with a fried egg, a frankfurter, boiled potatoes and a gherkin fan.

(Eduard Mayer, Austria)

Tournedos with oysters and vegetable julienne
Tournedos aux huîtres et à la julienne de légumes
Lendenschnitte mit Austern und Gemüsestreifen

2 portions

140 g	2 tournedos each weighing	5 oz
	6 oysters (Maremmes or Bélon)	
40 g	butter	1½ oz
	1 shallot, chopped	
	1 thin leek, cut into strips	
	1 small carrot, cut into strips	
	1 slice celeriac, cut into strips	
1 dl	white wine	3½ fl oz

| 5 cl | dairy cream | 2 fl oz |

Saffron potatoes:

1 clove of garlic, peeled
4 potatoes
a small pinch of saffron

Open the oysters and set aside the liquor. Fry the tournedos in 20 g (¾ oz) butter until medium done. Pour off the butter and stand the pan containing the meat in a warm place. Heat 10 g (¼ oz) butter in a second pan, cook the shallot gently until transparent, add the vegetable julienne and sauter, keeping the vegetables firm. Add the oyster liquor and the wine, and stir well. Remove the vegetables and keep hot.

Add the cream to the stock, reduce to the desired consistency, add the oysters at the last minute and carefully blend in the rest of the butter. Return the vegetables to the pan. Dress on warmed plates and place the fried tournedos on top. Serve with saffron potatoes. Turn the potatoes to the desired size, and blanch in salted water containing the garlic and saffron. (Illustration, page 768)

(Gerhard Gartner, Germany)

Tournedos Bercy with mint mousseline potatoes
Tournedos Bercy, pommes de terre mousseline à la menthe
Lendenschnitte Bercy mit Minz-Schaumkartoffeln

10 portions   Cooking time: 20 minutes

| 150 g | 10 tournedos each weighing | 5 oz |
| 1 dl | oil | 3½ fl oz |

Bercy butter:

200 g	butter, softened	7 oz
	salt	
	pepper, freshly ground	
	Cayenne pepper	
	juice of 1 lemon	
100 g	ox bone marrow	3½ oz
60 g	shallots, finely chopped	2 oz
	1 teaspoon parsley, chopped	
1 dl	white wine	3½ fl oz

Mint mousseline potatoes:

800 g	floury potatoes	1 lb 12 oz
⅓ l	milk	12 fl oz
	½ cup single dairy cream	

	1 egg yolk	
75 g	butter	2½ oz
	2 tablespoons mint, finely chopped	

Stew the shallots briefly in the wine, allow to cool, then mix well with the butter. Add the lemon juice, a pinch of Cayenne, freshly ground pepper to taste, the bone marrow which has been finely diced and the parsley. Mix well, spread on wet parchment paper, shape into a roll and leave in a cool place until cold.

Fry the tournedos in oil, medium done, and dress on individual plates with a slice of Bercy butter on each. Hand the potatoes separately. To prepare the potatoes, peel them and boil in salted water until soft. Press through a ricer and cream with the milk and cream which have been heated together. Beat in the egg yolk and add the butter a little at a time. Season with salt and pepper and fold in the mint.

(Karl Brunnengräber, Germany)

Grilled tournedos with red butter
Tournedos grillés au beurre rouge

6 portions

200 g	6 tournedos each weighing	7 oz
200 g	best butter	7 oz
3½ dl	Burgundy *or* Côtes du Rhône	12 fl oz
	salt, pepper	
	juice of half a lemon	

Bring the wine to the boil and reduce to 1 tablespoon. Cream the butter, carefully whisk in the wine, season with salt and pepper and add a few drops of lemon juice. Trim the tournedos, season on both sides with salt and pepper and grill as desired on a very hot grill which has been thoroughly cleaned. Dish on individual plates.

(Pierre Gleize, France)

Tournedos Anton Mosimann

4 portions

160 g	4 tournedos each weighing	5½ oz
2 cl	groundnut oil	1 fl oz
15 g	4 slices goose liver each weighing	½ oz
120 g	chicken mousse	4 oz
	salt	

Ristorante Albergo del Sole, Maleo: stuffed breast of veal Genoese style, p. 375 ▶

516 Veal with tuna sauce; sliced raw beef Alba, pp. 973, 214 ▲
Capon salad Bartolomè Stefani; best end of pork Florentine style; galantine Colombani;
marinated flap mushrooms, pp. 231, 983, 373 ▼

Macaroni with oxtail; minestrone Genoese style; pasta shells maison, pp. 278, 359, 281

Calf's feet Colombani, p. 262

518

520 Alsatian surprise loaf, p. 328

Alsatian beef casserole, p. 473

Fillet of beef salad, p. 226

Fillet of beef for a country buffet, p. 381

Stuffed breast of veal Alsatian style, p. 537

Knuckle of veal Alsatian style, p. 556

	pepper, freshly ground	
2 dl	Madeira sauce (recipe, page 158)	7 fl oz

Chicken mousse:

250 g		9 oz
80 g	chicken breast, skinned	3 oz
2 dl	dairy cream	7 fl oz
	salt	
	pepper, freshly ground	

Trim the tournedos carefully and brown quickly and briefly on one side in groundnut oil. Cover the browned side of each with a slice of goose liver and spread with chicken mousse. Arrange in a sauté pan and place in a preheated medium oven. Roast for 4 to 5 minutes for medium rare meat, or for 7 to 8 minutes if well done meat is required. Pour the sauce on to heated plates and place the meat on top. Hand young carrots and spinach sauté in butter separately.

To make the mousse, trim the chicken carefully and remove any sinew. Mince finely and pass through a sieve. Place in a bowl and stand on ice. Beat the cream in vigorously a little at a time to make a light frothy forcemeat. Season with salt and pepper.

(Illustration, page 239)

(Anton Mosimann, Great Britain)

Tournedos with snails
Tournedos aux escargots
Lendenschnitte mit Schnecken

1 portion

120 g	tournedos	4 oz
20 g	butter	¾ oz
	5 snails cut in half, in their liquor	
5 cl	veal stock	2 fl oz
	1 tablespoon brunoise of carrot, leek and celery	
	Cognac	
	salt	
	pepper, freshly ground	

Heat 10 g (⅓ oz) butter in a copper pan and fry the tournedos until medium done. Remove and keep hot. Pour off the butter. Melt the rest of the butter in the same pan, add the vegetable brunoise, brown, then add the snails and liquor, together with the veal stock, and reduce. Season the sauce with salt and pepper, flavour with Cognac and add fresh garlic juice to taste (optional). Pour the sauce over the tournedos to serve.

(Gerhard Gartner, Germany)

Tournedos Giannino Medagliani
Filetto di manzo Giannino Medagliani

4 portions

180–200 g	4 tournedos each weighing	6–7 oz
80 g	butter	3 oz
10 g	tarragon leaves	⅓ oz
2 dl	brown stock	7 fl oz
1 dl	dry white wine	3½ fl oz

Garnish:

160 g	4 courgettes each weighing	5½ oz
5 cl	water	2 fl oz
30 g	butter	1 oz
	salt	
	white pepper, freshly ground	
60 g	Patna rice	2 oz
1 g	saffron	a pinch
30 g	Canadian wild rice	1 oz
15 g	onion, finely chopped	½ oz
	hot water or light stock as required	
	coarse salt	
	oiled parchment paper or greased aluminium foil	

Wash the tarragon and chop finely. Wash the courgettes and cut into 3 cm (1¼ in) lengths, hollow these out carefully and season with salt and pepper. Melt 30 g (1 oz) butter in a vegetable stew pan, place the pieces of courgette in it side by side, add the water, cover with the parchment paper or foil and poach over low heat for 15 minutes, turning the courgettes after half the cooking time so that they are evenly cooked on both sides. Remove from the pan and keep hot.

Divide the onion between three separate pans and cook gently without colouring. Add the wild rice to one pan and divide the Patna rice between the other two. Stir with a wooden spoon for 2 minutes. Stir the saffron into one of the pans of Patna rice. Add about 4 cl (1½ fl oz) hot water or light stock to each of the pans of Patna rice and 6 cl (2 fl oz) to the pan containing the wild rice. Bring to the boil, cover the three pans with oiled parchment paper and cook in the oven at 200°C (392°F), allowing 15 to 18 minutes for the Patna rice and 30 to 40 minutes for the wild rice. Separate the grains with a fork while cooking. Keep the three pans hot.

Season the tournedos with salt and pepper, fry in nut-brown butter on both sides, then remove from the pan. Pour off the butter, add the tarragon, stir in the wine at once, reduce for 1 minute, add the brown stock, reduce for 4–5 minutes and finish with 20 g (¾ oz) butter,

adjusting the seasoning if required. Pour the sauce on to warm plates and place the tournedos in it. Stuff the courgettes with the rice and arrange on the plates.
(Illustration, page 412)

(Gualtiero Marchesi, Italy)

Tournedos with garlic and orange
Tournedos à l'ail et aux oranges
Lendenschnitten mit Knoblauch

10 portions   Cooking time: 25 minutes

125 g	10 tournedos each weighing	4½ oz
	4 cloves of garlic, peeled	
	3 tablespoons lemon juice	
8 cl	oil	3 fl oz
	1 teaspoon rosemary	
	pepper, freshly ground	
	salt	
	3 oranges, divided into segments	
100 g	butter	3½ oz
50 g	shallots, finely diced	2 oz
½ l	thickened veal gravy	18 fl oz
	2 egg yolks	
3 dl	yoghourt	10 fl oz
	3 tablespoons parsley, coarsely chopped	
	1 tablespoon pink peppercorns	

French beans with chanterelles:

500 g	fresh French beans	1 lb 2 oz
400 g	small chanterelles, fresh or canned	14 oz
60 g	lean bacon, diced	2 oz
70 g	shallots, diced	2½ oz
	1 bunch chives	
	1 bunch parsley	
50 g	butter	2 oz
	a pinch of sugar	
	black pepper, freshly ground	
	½ cup veal gravy	

Flatten the tournedos slightly. Pound the garlic with salt and place in a bowl. Add the lemon juice, oil and rosemary, season with pepper and mix carefully to a smooth emulsion. Spread on the meat and marinate under cover for 2 hours. Remove the meat, heat the remaining emulsion in a sauté pan, add a little butter and fry the meat on both sides until medium done. Cover and keep hot.

Cut the pulp of the orange segments away from the surrouding skin, fry the segments lightly in butter in the same pan, and arrange on the tournedos. Add the shallots to the pan, stir in the thickened veal gravy and boil up to detach the sediment. Pass through a strainer and thicken with the egg yolks which have been mixed with the yoghourt. Stir in the parsley and the pink peppercorns, and pour over the meat. Serve with French beans and chanterelles.

To prepare the beans, clean them carefully and cook in lightly salted water, keeping them firm to the bite. Drain on a colander. Carefully clean and wash the chanterelles. Cook them with the bacon and shallots, if possible without adding any water. Toss the beans and chanterelles in butter with chopped parsley, finely cut chives and veal gravy. Add a pinch of sugar and season with black pepper.

(Karl Brunnengräber, Germany)

Mexican peppered steak
Entrecôte poivrée des Mexicains
Mexikanisches Feuersteak

10 portions   Cooking time: meat, 15 minutes; sauce, 1 hour

1 kg 700	boned sirloin, well hung	3 lb 12 oz
125 g	green and red chillies, fresh or preserved	4½ oz
15 g	20 rashers lean bacon each weighing	½ oz

Pepper sauce:

100 g	butter	3½ oz
600 g	root vegetables	1 lb 5 oz
250 g	onions	9 oz
1 dl	red wine vinegar	3½ fl oz
¼ l	red wine	9 fl oz
200 g	redcurrant jelly	7 oz
2 l	brown stock	3½ pt
1½ l	demi-glace sauce	2¾ pt
	white peppercorns, coarsely crushed	

Cut the meat evenly into 10 steaks, flatten a little and thread across the grain with strips of red or green chilli. Fry or grill until medium done. Serve on individual plates, coated with pepper sauce and decorated with crisply fried bacon. Hand the rest of the sauce separately, with Dauphine potatoes and broccoli which has been stewed with finely cut onions and coarsely chopped tomatoes.

To make the sauce, finely dice the root vegetables and onions, cook them gently in butter until lightly coloured, then detach the sediment twice with redcurrant jelly, a little vinegar and red wine. Add the brown stock and the demi-glace sauce, and cook for 1 hour, skimming frequently. When the sauce has reached the desired consistency, add a few coarsely crushed white peppercorns to give it a moderately pungent flavour, cook for a few moments and strain. (Illustration, page 697)

(Karl Brunnengräber, Germany)

Pepper steak Maman Yvette
Steak au poivre Maman Yvette

4 portions   Cooking time: 20 minutes

250–300 g	4 entrecôte steaks each weighing	9–10 oz
	salt	
	white peppercorns, crushed	
	oil as required	
15 g	butter (for tomatoes)	½ oz
	4 tomatoes, skinned, seeded and finely diced	
	8 tablespoons dairy cream	
50 g	butter (to finish sauce)	2 oz
15 g	tarragon, finely chopped	½ oz

Trim the steaks well, season with salt, then coat with the crushed peppercorns, pressing them down lightly. Fry in oil until cooked as desired, dish on warmed plates and keep hot. Pour off the oil, melt 15 g (½ oz) butter in the same pan and cook the diced tomatoes gently in it. Season with salt and stir in the cream to detach the cooking juices. Mix thoroughly, remove from the heat, finish with 50 g (2 oz) butter and add the tarragon. Pour over the steaks and serve with fried potatoes sprinkled with chopped parsley.
(Illustration, page 621)

(Jean Esslinger, France)

Mignons of beef Frigara Romanesca
Mignons de boeuf Frigara Romanesca

4 portions

50 g	12 filets mignons each weighing	2 oz
2 cl	oil	1 fl oz
80 g	button onions	3 oz
	sage, finely chopped	
1½ dl	brown veal stock	5 fl oz
20 g	butter for sauce	¾ oz

salt
pepper, freshly ground

Trim the meat carefully, season with salt and pepper and rub in a little oil. Grill on both sides over high heat, keeping the meat medium rare. Dish on heated plates and surround with the onions which have been glazed and rolled in the sage. Heat the brown veal stock, season carefully and work in the butter a little at a time. Pour this sauce round the meat. Serve with fine French beans which have been tossed in butter and with Cocotte potatoes.

For Cocotte potatoes, peel medium potatoes and carefully turn them with a small knife. Blanch in boiling water, drain and leave on a cloth until cold. Fry in oil and butter until golden. Sprinkle lightly with salt just before serving.
(Illustration, page 239)

(Anton Mosimann, Great Britain)

Quick-fried sliced beef with mussels (or oysters) in oyster sauce with celery

4 portions

500 g	beef steak (rump or fillet)	1 lb 2 oz
	12 large mussels (or oysters)	
	3 slices root ginger	
	3 stalks spring onion	
1½ cl	oil	½ fl oz
2 g	salt	half a small teaspoon
1 cl	rice wine or sherry	½ fl oz
3 g	cornflour	half a teaspoon
	3 cloves of garlic	
	3 sticks celery	
10 g	lard	⅓ oz
1 cl	soya sauce	½ fl oz
1 cl	oyster sauce	½ fl oz
1½ cl	mussel water	½ fl oz

Cut the beef into thin slices 4 x 5 or 6 cm (1½ x 2 in). Rub with salt and 3 ml (half a teaspoon) oil. Shred and chop the ginger into small grains. Crush the garlic and chop into small grains. Cut the spring onion and celery into 4 cm (1½ in) sections. Poach the mussels (or oysters) for 1½ minutes in ¼ l (9 fl oz) water. Remove the mussel flesh from the shells and collect 1½ cl (½ fl oz) of the water in which the mussels were cooked. Mix this with the cornflour until well blended.

Heat the rest of the oil in a frying pan. Add the ginger, garlic and beef. Stir-fry over high heat for 1 minute. Add the soya sauce, oyster sauce, celery, spring onions and mussels. Turn and stir together for 2 minutes. Pour in the wine or sherry and continue to stir and turn for 2 minutes. Finally add the thickened mussel water and continue to stir and turn for half a minute. Serve on a well heated dish to be consumed immediately.

This is a very savoury dish which makes an excellent accompaniment for drinks or for serving with rice.

(Kenneth Lo, China)

Oxtail with dumplings or pasta
Queue de boeuf avec quenelles de pommes de terre
Ochsenschlepp mit Knödeln oder Teigwaren

10 portions   Cooking time: 3–4 hours

3 kg 500	oxtail, scalded but not skinned	7 lb 12 oz
150 g	lard	5 oz
1 kg	mirepoix of carrots, celery, parsley roots, leeks, coarsely cut	2 lb 4 oz
	2 cloves of garlic, crushed	
1 l	red wine	1¾ pt
150 g	French mustard	5 oz
	1 lemon, sliced	
250 g	redcurrant jelly	9 oz
	OR cranberries	
200 g	flour	7 oz
2½ l	brown stock	4½ pt
	thyme	
	2 bay leaves	
1 kg	onions, coarsely diced	2 lb 4 oz
	vinegar	
	salt, pepper	

Joint the oxtails, season with salt and pepper, place in a roasting tray and brown in the lard in a hot oven. Add the mirepoix and onions, and roast with the oxtails until coloured. Dust with a little flour, add the bay leaves, garlic, thyme, wine and stock, and cook slowly for 3 to 4 hours. After half the cooking time, add a little stock, together with the mustard, the slices of lemon and a dash of vinegar. Stir in the redcurrant jelly, or cranberries if preferred.

Remove the meat when it is tender and keep hot. Pass the sauce, including the vegetables, through a sieve and pour over the meat. Serve either with bread or potato dumplings or with 'spätzle' or broad ribbon noodles.

(Karl Brunnengräber, Germany)

Ox tongue with orange
Pointes de langue de boeuf à l'orange
Ochsenzungenspitzen mit Orangen

1 portion

approx. 150 g	ox tongue (tip end), pickled and boiled	approx.	5 oz
	2 oranges		
	1 tablespoon caster sugar		
5 cl	red wine		2 fl oz
5 cl	orange juice		2 fl oz
5 cl	veal gravy		2 fl oz
	1 level teaspoon potato flour		
10 g	butter		⅓ oz
	Grand Marnier (optional)		
	lemon juice (optional)		

Skin the tongue, cut into 5 slices lengthwise and marinate in the wine. Finely pare half an unsprayed orange with a sharp knife and cut the zest into thin julienne strips. Blanch in fresh water, pour off the water and set aside the zest.

Boil the sugar in a copper pan until it turns to light caramel. Stir in the juice of 1 orange and the veal gravy, boil up and add the orange zest julienne. Reduce to the amount of sauce required, thicken with the potato flour and finish with a knob of butter. Flavour with Grand Marnier and lemon juice according to personal taste.

Peel the second orange, cut into segments and remove the skin. Arrange the slices of tongue on a warmed plate fanwise, coat with the sauce, place the orange segments on top and garnish with a piece of Parmesan pancake (recipe, page 1024).
(Illustration, page 769)

(Gerhard Gartner, Germany)

Stewed beef with red wine
Boeuf en daube au vin rouge
Gestovtes Rindfleisch in Rotwein

10 portions   Cooking time: 3½ hours

1 kg 200	chuck steak	2 lb 10 oz
1 kg 200	topside or thick flank of beef	2 lb 10 oz
	5 large onions, finely diced	
	5 carrots, finely diced	
	2 large cloves of garlic, finely chopped	

	1 bouquet garni (parsley, thyme, bay leaf)	
½ l	dry red wine	18 fl oz
	2 tablespoons red wine vinegar	
5 cl	brandy	2 fl oz
250 g	pork rinds	9 oz
120 g	black olives, stoned	4 oz
	5 tomatoes, skinned and seeded	
150 g	mushrooms	5 oz
100 g	fresh pork fat	3½ oz
	flour	
	salt	
	pepper, freshly ground	
	a pinch of ground cloves	
	oil	

Cut the meat into pieces weighing about 65 g (2 oz) and mix carefully with the onions, carrots, garlic, salt, pepper, ground cloves, wine and vinegar. Marinate overnight in a cool place. Dice the pork fat and render down in a little oil. Add the meat which has been well drained, together with the vegetables, and cook gently for 20 minutes. Reduce the marinade by half and strain, then add to the meat, together with a little water, the bouquet garni and the pork rinds. Cover tightly and seal with a band of flour and water paste. Cook for about 3 hours in a moderate oven.

Strain off the stock and transfer the meat to a second pan or fireproof casserole. Dice the pork rinds and add to the meat, together with the mushrooms which have been stewed, the tomatoes which have been chopped and lightly stewed, and the olives. Remove all fat from the stock, add to the meat, mix very carefully and simmer over very low heat for 15 minutes. This dish is served with various fresh salads and with pasta or French bread.

(Karl Brunnengräber, Germany)

Entrecôte Girardi
Girardi-Rostbraten

4 portions

180 g	4 entrecôte steaks each weighing	6 oz
	salt, pepper	
	1 onion, finely chopped	
4 cl	oil	1½ fl oz
	1 glass white wine	
½ l	bouillon, brown stock or water	18 fl oz
20 g	butter	¾ oz
50 g	smoked bacon, finely chopped	2 oz
80 g	mushrooms, finely chopped	3 oz

	1 teaspoon lemon zest, finely chopped	
	1 teaspoon capers, finely chopped	
	1 small onion, finely chopped (for sauce)	
	1 small teaspoon parsley, finely chopped	
20 g	flour	¾ oz
¼ l	sour cream	9 fl oz
	a little mustard	

Flatten the steaks and snip the edges. Season with salt and pepper and fry quickly on both sides in hot oil. Remove and keep hot. Add the onion to the pan and fry until golden, stir in the wine and boil up to detach the sediment, pour in the bouillon, stock or water, return the steaks to the pan and cook under cover until tender.

Lightly cook the bacon, mushrooms, small onion, lemon zest, capers and parsley in hot butter, dust with flour and stir in half the sour cream. Add this sauce to the meat shortly before the end of the cooking time. Season with a little mustard before serving. Dish on warm plates and top with the rest of the sour cream. Serve with Austrian dumpling (recipe, page 1026) or ribbon noodles.

(Eduard Mayer, Austria)

Entrecôte steak with shallot butter
Entrecôte au beurre d'échalotes
Entrecôte met sjalotenboter

2 portions

400 g	entrecôte steak	14 oz
100 g	shallots, finely chopped	3½ oz
1 dl	Beaujolais	3½ fl oz
200 g	butter	7 oz
	1 tablespoon meat glaze	
	salt	
	pepper, freshly ground	

Place the shallots and wine in a pan and reduced completely until the shallots turn red. Stir in the meat glaze and work in 150 g butter. Season with salt and freshly ground pepper.

Fry the meat quickly on both sides in 50 g (2 oz) butter, allowing 5 minutes each side. Remove from the pan, allow to rest for 10 minutes, then cut into oblique slices. Dish on 2 heated plates, coat with shallot butter and surround with fresh vegetables such as sugar peas.

(Paul Fagel, Netherlands)

Entrecôte Strindberg
Zwischenrippenstück Strindberg

1 portion

160 g	1 entrecôte steak weighing	5½ oz
	1 teaspoon English mustard powder	
	1 heaped teaspoon shallot, finely chopped	
100 g	butter	3½ oz
	parsley	
	meat glaze	
	salt	
	pepper, freshly ground	

Blend the mustard powder with a few drops of water. Cook the shallot gently in a little butter. Flatten the steak, season with salt and pepper, and spread one side with the mustard. Cover evenly with the shallot. Heat the butter in a cast iron pan and place the steak in it with the coated side undermost. Fry for 1 or 2 minutes, then turn and fry for 1 minute.

Dish on a heated plate, sprinkle with chopped parsley, then with a few drops of meat glaze, and pour the butter remaining in the pan over the meat. Serve with potatoes and vegetables or salad.

(Otto Brust, Germany)

Entrecôte steak with four varieties of pepper
Entrecôte aux quatre poivres

4 portions

180 g	4 entrecôte steaks each weighing	6 oz
5 cl	oil	2 fl oz
	white peppercorns, crushed	
	black peppercorns, crushed	
20 g	butter	¾ oz
4 cl	Cognac	1½ fl oz
2 dl	brown veal stock	7 fl oz
2 dl	dairy cream	7 fl oz
3 g	green peppercorns	1 teaspoon
3 g	pink peppercorns	1 teaspoon
	salt	
	pepper, freshly ground	

Trim the steaks carefully and season with salt and a few crushed white and black peppercorns.

Brown well on both sides in 5 cl oil, then add 10 g butter. Remove the meat and keep hot. Pour off the fat remaining in the pan. Stir in the Cognac and ignite. Add the stock and reduce by half. Pour in the cream and reduce to the required consistency.

Add the green and pink peppercorns to the sauce just before serving. (If they are added earlier, the sauce will be too hot.) Finish with the rest of the butter and check the seasoning. Dress the steaks on warmed plates and coat with the sauce. Serve with soufflé potatoes and broad beans. (Illustration, page 239)

(Anton Mosimann, Great Britain)

Entrecôte with rosemary
Entrecôte au romarin

4–5 portions

400 g	2 entrecôte steaks each weighing	14 oz
100 g	butter	3½ oz
2 dl	white wine vinegar	7 fl oz
2 dl	Riesling	7 fl oz
	1 onion, chopped	
	2 teaspoons white pepper, chopped	
	4 sprigs rosemary	
2 dl	dairy cream	7 fl oz
	1 tablespoon Dijon mustard	

Fry the steaks on both sides in butter and keep hot. Pour off the butter, detach the sediment with the vinegar and the Riesling, add the onion, 2 sprigs rosemary and the pepper, reduce, then add the cream. Reduce again, adjust the seasoning, stir in the mustard and strain the sauce. Strip the leaves off the 2 remaining sprigs of rosemary, chop finely and mix with the sauce. Cut the meat into oblique slices and coat with the sauce. Hand Macaire potatoes separately.

(André Béghin, Belgium)

Entrecôte with Stilton cheese and cider

8 portions

150–175 g	8 entrecôte steaks each weighing	5–6 oz
375 g	Stilton cheese, grated	13 oz
5½ dl	cider	1 pt
	2 egg yolks	
7 cl	double cream	3 fl oz

2 cloves of garlic, crushed
salt
pepper, freshly ground

Reduce the cider by half. Blend with the cheese, egg yolks, cream and garlic. Season to taste with salt and pepper. Grill the steaks as required, then cover the top with the Stilton paste and baste under a very hot salamander until the cheese is glazed.

(Samuel J. Chalmers, Great Britain)

Veal

Roast veal with tchina and pine kernels
Rôti de veau au tchina et aux pignons

8 portions   Cooking time: 1½ hours

1 kg 600	shoulder of veal	3 lb 8 oz
	mirepoix	
	pepper, freshly ground	
	salt	
	paprika	
100 g	tchina	3½ oz
	lemon juice	
	3 cloves of garlic, finely pounded	
	parsley, chopped	
50 g	pine kernels, roasted	2 oz

Season the veal with salt, pepper and paprika and place it in a roasting pan. Add the mirepoix and roast for 1½ hours in an oven preheated to 200°C (392°F). Remove the meat and carve. Arrange the slices on a fireproof dish. Reduce and strain the gravy.

Tchina is made with ground sesame seeds or peanuts. The former type is preferable as it has a finer flavour. Mix the tchina to a thick paste with a little water and lemon juice, the garlic, salt and pepper to taste, and chopped parsley. Add a little of the strained gravy and spread on the slices of meat. Sprinkle with the pine kernels.

(Hermann Wohl, Israel)

Stuffed breast of veal with prunes
Poitrine de veau farcie aux pruneaux

8 portions

2 kg	breast of veal	4 lb 8 oz
	3 rolls, soaked and squeezed dry	
	1 onion, finely chopped	
	oil	
	parsley, chopped	
	2 eggs	
	20 prunes, soaked and stoned	

	pepper, freshly ground	
	salt	
	nutmeg	
	mirepoix	
1 dl	red wine	3½ fl oz
	2 oranges	
	cornflour	
3–5 dl	veal gravy	10–18 fl oz

Bone the veal and cut a pocket for the stuffing in the centre with a sharp knife. To make the stuffing, mix the rolls well with the onion which has been lightly fried without colouring, the eggs and the parsley. Season with salt, pepper and nutmeg, add the prunes which have been blanched briefly, and mix well again. Fill into the pocket in the veal and sew up the opening.

Brown the meat on both sides in oil together with the mirepoix. Detach the sediment with the wine and the veal gravy, place in a preheated oven and roast, basting very frequently. Remove the meat and strain the sauce. Blend the cornflour with a little water and carefully stir into the sauce to thicken. Peel the oranges, cut the segments smoothly out of the skins and add to the sauce. To serve, carve the meat, arrange on a heated dish and pour the orange sauce over.

(Hermann Wohl, Israel)

Stuffed breast of veal Alsatian style
Poitrine de veau farcie à l'alsacienne

20 portions

5–6 kg	breast of veal	11–13¼ lb
	1 pork caul	
	2 calves' feet, chopped	
	5 onions, diced	
	3 carrots, diced	
½–1 l	white wine	18 fl oz–1¾ pt
	water as required	

Stuffing:

800 g	white bread	1 lb 12 oz
½ l	dairy cream	18 fl oz
	15 egg yolks	
100 g	chives, finely chopped	3½ oz
100 g	parsley, finely chopped	3½ oz
500 g	veal trimmings, browned	1 lb 2 oz
40 g	salt	1½ oz
10 g	pepper	⅓ oz
	ground nutmeg to taste	
	thyme flowers to taste	
	8 large onions	

100 g	butter	3½ oz

Gnocchi Roman style:

1 l	water	1¾ pt
2 l	milk	3½ pt
200 g	butter	7 oz
	2 cloves of garlic, pounded	
	salt, pepper, nutmeg	
750 g	semolina	1 lb 10 oz
300 g	Gruyère cheese, grated	11 oz
	6 egg yolks	
¼ l	dairy cream	9 fl oz

Bone and trim the veal. Slit it lengthwise to make a pocket. To make the stuffing, soak the bread in the cream and mash well with a fork. Peel and finely chop the onions, brown them lightly in the butter and set aside. Mince the bread and the veal trimmings finely, add the herbs and egg yolks, mix well and add the seasonings. Lastly stir in the onions. Stuff the veal and roll in the pork caul.

Preheat the oven to 300°C (572°F). Place the veal in a braising pan, brown in the oven, add the diced onions and carrots together with the calves' feet and roast for 2½ hours, reducing the oven temperature to 200°C (392°F) after 1 hour and basting frequently with the cooking juices. Remove the meat from the pan and keep hot. Pour off the fat in the pan, stir in the wine and as much water as required, bring to the boil and reduce to a syrupy consistency. Bone the calves' feet, finely dice the meat from the feet and add to the sauce after straining it.

Carve the breast of veal into 2 cm (¾ in) thick slices. Serve with gnocchi Roman style. To prepare the gnocchi, place the water and milk in a pan with the butter, salt, pepper and ground nutmeg. Bring to the boil. Pour in 600 g (1 lb 5 oz) semolina in a thin stream, stir well and continue stirring for 5 minutes. Add the rest of the semolina, then the egg yolks which have been beaten with the cream. Then mix in 200 g grated cheese. Pour this mixture in a buttered and floured baking sheet about 1″ thick, and flatten lighly. Allow to cool. Cut into half moons or medallions with a cutter. Transfer them to shallow fireproof dishes, sprinkle with the remaining grated cheese, and brown in the oven.
(Illustration, page 522)

(Jean Esslinger, France)

Glazed breast of veal Mère Merian
Poitrine de veau glacée Mère Merian
Glacierte Kalbsbrust Mama Merian

10 portions

2 kg 500	breast of veal, boned and trimmed of gristle, 18 cm (7 in) wide	5 lb 8 oz

	oil	
	salt	
	herbs and spices as desired	
5 dl	thickened veal stock	18 fl oz
3 dl	dry white wine	10 fl oz
60 g	tomato purée	2 oz
800 g	mixed vegetable brunoise, coarsely cut	1 lb 12 oz
300 g	mirepoix	11 oz

Soubise sauce with fresh horseradish:

100 g	oil and butter	3½ oz
300 g	pork back fat or bacon, finely diced	11 oz
800 g	rice	1 lb 12 oz
1 kg 500	onions, finely cut and blanched	3 lb 5 oz
3 l	bouillon	5 pt
50 g	horseradish	2 oz
	salt	
	herbs and spices as desired	

Florentine mushroom slices:

800 g	puff pastry	1 lb 12 oz
600 g	leaf spinach, blanched	1 lb 5 oz
	oil and butter	
	shallots, finely chopped	
300 g	mushrooms	11 oz
1 dl	dairy cream	3½ fl oz
200 g	Parmesan cheese, grated	7 oz
	salt	
	spices as desired	

Season the veal carefully and brown in hot oil on all sides. Add the mirepoix, brown lightly and add a little tomato purée. Stir in the wine and stock, bring to the boil and glaze in the oven, basting frequently. Leave to stand in moderate heat for about 30 minutes before serving.

To serve, mix a heaped tablespoon Soubise sauce with the fresh grated horseradish and spread on a dish. Carve the veal and arrange on top. Coat with the stock which has been reduced and mixed with the vegetable brunoise. Serve with puff pastry slices covered with mushrooms and spinach, sprinkled with Parmesan and gratinated.

To make the Soubise sauce, stew the onions under cover in the oil and butter together with the pork fat or bacon. Cook the rice under cover in the oven in a pan of bouillon. Pass the onions and rice through a sieve, mix well and season carefully.

(Otto Ledermann, Switzerland)

Stuffed breast of veal Prague style
Poitrine de veau farcie à la pragueoise
Pražské telecí hrudí nadívané

6 portions   Cooking time: about 1½ hours

1 kg 200	breast of veal	2 lb 10 oz
100 g	butter	3½ oz
	bouillon	
	salt	
	2 lettuces	
	6 firm tomatoes OR	
600 g	peas, cooked	1 lb 5 oz

Stuffing:

80 g	butter	3 oz
200 g	rolls (4)	7 oz
3 dl	milk	10 fl oz
	1 egg	
	2 egg yolks	
	1 tablespoon parsley, finely chopped	
	3 tablespoons canned peas	
100 g	ham, diced	3½ oz
	a pinch of nutmeg OR	
	4 white peppercorns, freshly ground	
	salt	
60 g	white flour *or* breadcrumbs	2 oz

Rinse and dry the meat. Make an incision along the rib joints and bend the breast over the edge of the table to break the ribs free. Using a small, sharp knife, slit the skin round the ribs lengthwise, twist the ribs and pull them out. Turn the meat over, make a slit in the thin connective tissue between the upper and the lower part, and enlarge the opening evenly with the help of a small ladle to make a deep pocket. This pocket must be kept dry to prevent the stuffing from falling out when carving. Season the pocket with salt, insert the stuffing and sew up. Often there is only a thin skin connecting the rib meat with the rest of the breast. In this case the breast should also be sewn up at this point.

Melt 80 g (3 oz) butter in a roasting pan. Place the rib bones, which have been chopped up, in the centre, together with any veal trimmings, and place the breast of veal on top with the underside uppermost. Roast at about 230°C (445°F) for 1½ hours, basting frequently and adding a little bouillon if necessary. Turn the meat after 45 minutes.

When cooked, remove from the pan and prick with a fork several times to allow the steam to escape so that the stuffing will remain in place while carving. Stand the meat aside to cool for a short time, then remove the thread, carve and dress on a heated dish. Garnish with lettuce and either tomatoes cut into quarters or cooked peas. Remove the fat from the cooking juices and add a little bouillon, salt and the rest of the butter.

If desired, double the quantity of stuffing required may be prepared. The surplus is shaped into small cylinders on a floured board and added to the meat 50 minutes before the end of the roasting time, or cooked separately in butter for about 10 minutes if the roasting pan is not large enough. Serve with roast, fried or mashed potatoes and boiled vegetables or vegetable salad.

To make the stuffing, cream the butter, remove the crust from the rolls, cut each one in quarters, soak in milk, squeeze dry, pass through a sieve, then add to the butter with the whole egg and yolks, the parsley, peas, ham, seasonings and flour or breadcrumbs. Mix well and set aside for 30 minutes before use. This stuffing is also suitable for belly of pork, chicken, pigeon, etc.

(Vilèm Vrabec, Czechoslovakia)

Breast of veal with spinach stuffing
Poitrine de veau farcie aux épinards
Teléce Grudi Punjene Spanácem

6 portions   Cooking time: about 60–70 minutes

1 kg 500	breast of veal, boned and trimmed of skin	3 lb 5 oz
2 dl	oil	7 fl oz
OR 200 g	butter	7 oz
750 g	spinach	1 lb 10 oz
1 kg	potatoes	2 lb 4 oz
50 g	butter (for potatoes)	2 oz
	2 rolls	
	1 tablespoon flour	
20 g	butter (for stuffing)	¾ oz
¼ l	milk	9 fl oz
1 dl	sour cream	3½ fl oz
	1 egg	
	salt	
	pepper, freshly ground	

Slit the veal with a sharp knife to make a pocket for the stuffing and season it with salt. Prepare a thick Béchamel sauce with the flour, 20 g (¾ oz) butter and 1½ dl (5 oz) milk. Soak the rolls in a little milk. Clean the spinach, cook it and drain well. Mix thoroughly with the rolls which have been squeezed dry, the Béchamel sauce, the rest of the milk, the sour cream and the egg. Season with salt and pepper. Fill into the pocket in the veal and sew up the opening. Place in a roasting pan of suitable size, baste with hot oil or melted butter and roast for 60 to 70 minutes.

Serve with potatoes which have been boiled in their skins, peeled and sprinkled with 50 g (2 oz) melted butter, and with green salad.

(László Csizmadia, Yugoslavia)

Stuffed breast of veal Viennese style
Poitrine de veau farcie à la viennoise
Gefüllte Kalbsbrust auf Wiener Art

8 portions

2 kg	breast of veal	4 lb 8 oz
100 g	butter	3½ oz
	1 tablespoon flour	
	salt	

Stuffing:

60 g	butter		2 oz
	3 eggs		
	4 rolls		
OR 200 g	white bread		7 oz
	1 small onion, finely chopped		
60 g	mushrooms, thinly sliced		2 oz
20 g	parsley, chopped		¾ oz
approx. ⅛ l	milk	approx.	4 fl oz
	nutmeg, grated		
	salt		

Bone the meat, but do not remove the gristle. Slit to make a pocket for the stuffing. To make the stuffing, remove the crust from the rolls and dice these finely. Cook the onion gently in hot butter without colouring, add the mushrooms and parsley and fry together. Spoon over the rolls. Mix the milk and eggs together, adding salt and a little grated nutmeg, pour over the rolls and leave to soak, then mix thoroughly

Season the veal with salt, stuff and sew up the opening. Chop up the bones removed from the meat, place in a roasting pan and lay the meat on top. Pour melted butter over and brown in a hot oven, then reduce the heat, add a little water and roast for about 90 minutes, basting frequently. Stand the meat in a warm place for 20 minutes before carving.

Reduce the cooking juices a little, dust with flour, bring to the boil, add ½ l (18 fl oz) water and reduce well. Strain and hand separately.

(Eduard Mayer, Austria)

Breast of veal with mushroom and parsley stuffing
Poitrine de veau farcie aux champignons et au persil
Zsöld séges töltött borjuszegy

5 portions   Cooking time: about 2 hours

1 kg	breast of veal	2 lb 4 oz
150 g	butter	5 oz
20 g	onion, finely chopped	¾ oz
	3 rolls	
	3 eggs	
2 dl	milk	7 fl oz
	1 bunch parsley, chopped	
	salt, pepper	
500 g	carrots	1 lb 2 oz
500 g	green beans	1 lb 2 oz
500 g	sugar peas	1 lb 2 oz
150 g	mushrooms	5 oz

Carefully wash and dry the veal. Bone it without damaging the flesh and slit in the centre of one side to make a pocket for the stuffing, using a sharp knife.

To make the stuffing, remove the crust from the rolls and soak these in milk. Wash the mushrooms thoroughly, trim them, then dice finely and stew in a little butter together with the onion. Cream 100 g (3½ oz) butter, mix well with the eggs, then stir in the mushrooms and onion and season with salt and pepper. Mix with the rolls which have been squeezed dry, and add the parsley. Fill into the pocket in the veal and either secure in place with small skewers or sew up. Place the meat on a roasting tray, together with half a peeled onion, and season with salt. Pour in 1 dl (3½ fl oz) water and roast for about 1½ hours in an oven preheated to 150°C (302°F).

Meanwhile cook the vegetables separately in boiling salted water, drain, toss in butter and add a little sugar if desired. Wrap the meat in a wet cloth and leave for about 30 minutes to facilitate carving. To serve, reheat in the oven, carve, dress on a hot dish and surround with the vegetables.

(Gyula Gullner, Hungary)

Sliced breast of veal Holsteiner Hof
Tranches de poitrine de veau Holsteiner Hof
Kalbsbrustschnitte Holsteiner Hof

6 portions

900 g	sliced breast of veal	2 lb

	groundnut oil		
100 g	mirepoix		3½ oz
approx. 5 cl	white wine	approx.	2 fl oz
approx. ½ l	demi-glace sauce, thickened	approx.	18 fl oz

Garnish:

60 g	dessert apples, diced		2 oz
60 g	peppers, diced		2 oz
60 g	sultanas, soaked		2 oz
60 g	dates, diced		2 oz
15–20 g	butter	approx.	½ oz

Accompaniments:

approx. 300 g	lettuce	approx.	11 oz
	2 hardboiled eggs, chopped		
20 g	parsley, chopped		¾ oz
360 g	green noodles		13 oz
approx. 50 g	butter	approx.	2 oz
	salt		
	Aromat to taste		

Season and flour the slices of veal. Brown in hot groundnut oil on all sides and remove from the pan. Lightly brown the mirepoix in the oil remaining in the pan, stir in the wine to detach the sediment, then add the slightly thickened demi-glace sauce and bring to the boil. Add the veal and cook over gentle heat.

To prepare the garnish, melt the butter, add the apples and peppers which have been blanched, together with the sultanas and dates, and heat through. Spoon over the meat.

To prepare the accompaniments, cook the noodles in boiling salted water, keeping them firm to the bite, drain and toss in about 50 g (2 oz) warmed butter. Season with salt and a little Aromat. Dress the lettuce in the usual manner and mix with the eggs and parsley. If possible, dress the meat in an oval copper pan and the noodles in a round copper pan. Pour about 1½ dl (5 fl oz) sauce over the meat and hand the rest in a sauce-boat. Serve the lettuce on salad plates.

(Otto Ledermann, Switzerland)

Emincé of veal Zurich style I
Emincé de veau à la zurichoise
Geschnetzeltes Kalbfleisch auf Zürcher Art

6 portions

720 g	cushion of veal, thinly sliced	1 lb 9 oz
300 g	fresh mushrooms, thinly sliced	11 oz
3 dl	dairy cream	10 fl oz
2 dl	Stäfner white wine	7 fl oz
50 g	shallots, finely chopped	2 oz

150 g	butter	5 oz
	parsley, finely chopped	
	salt, pepper	
	lemon juice	
	a little paprika	

Sauter the mushrooms in 50 g (2 oz) butter. Season and add a few drops of lemon juice. Brown the meat quickly (for about 2 to 3 minutes) in a second frying pan and add the shallots which have been sweated in butter. Season with salt, pepper and a little paprika and transfer to a colander to drain. Detach the meat cooking juices with the wine and reduce. Add the mushrooms and cream and season well. Add the meat and reheat without boiling. Dish at once, sprinkled with the parsley. Serve with Swiss potato cake *(rösti)* or noodles. This is a very old dish originating in blanquette of veal.
(Techniques, page 52)

(Willi Bartenbach, Switzerland)

Emincé of veal Zurich style II
Emincé de veau à la zurichoise
Geschnetzeltes Kalbfleisch auf Zürcher Art

4 portions

200 g	cushion of veal, thinly sliced	7 oz
200 g	calf's kidneys without fat, thinly sliced	7 oz
200 g	mushrooms, sliced	7 oz
	2 tablespoons oil	
50 g	onions, chopped	2 oz
1 dl	white wine	3½ fl oz
20 g	butter	¾ oz
1 dl	brown stock, thickened	3½ fl oz
1 dl	dairy cream	3½ fl oz
	lemon juice	
	pepper, freshly ground	
	paprika	
	salt	
	chopped herbs	

Quickly brown the veal, then the kidneys, in hot oil with the onions. Transfer to a bowl and season. Detach the cooking juices with the wine, reduce a little and pour over the meat. Cook the mushrooms gently in butter. Mix the stock with the cream and reduce to the desired consistency. Add the meat and reheat without boiling. Dress the meat on a dish, cover with the mushrooms and sprinkle with chopped herbs. Serve with Swiss potato cake *(rösti)*, noodles or rice.

(Otto Ledermann, Switzerland)

Sauté of veal with vegetable pudding
Sauté de veau et pouding de légumes
Sformato di verdure con carne in umido

4 portions

1 kg	veal fricandeau	2 lb 4 oz
300 g	white onions	11 oz
1 dl	olive oil	3½ fl oz
½ l	white wine	18 fl oz
500 g	peeled tomatoes, canned	1 lb 2 oz
	flour as required	
	salt, pepper	

Cut the meat into cubes and flour lightly. Slice the onions and fry in the oil until lightly coloured, add the meat, stir-fry until browned, then cook gently for 20 minutes, turning from time to time. Slowly pour in the wine and reduce slowly. Season with salt and pepper. After 1 hour add the tomatoes in their juice, cover and continue cooking over low heat. Turn out the vegetable pudding (recipe, page 1010) on to a heated dish and surround with the meat.

(Mario De Filippis, Italy)

Fillet of veal Albert Szent-Györgyi
Filet de veau à la Albert Szent-Györgyi
Borjuszelet Albert Szent-Györgyi módra

10 portions   Cooking time: 15-20 minutes

1 kg 800	fillet of veal	4 lb
250 g	lard	9 oz
200 g	butter	7 oz
500 g	red peppers, seeded and finely diced	1 lb 2 oz
500 g	yellow and green peppers, seeded and finely diced	1 lb 2 oz
800 g	mushrooms, finely sliced	1 lb 12 oz
100 g	onions, finely chopped	3½ oz
20 g	paprika	¾ oz
50 g	salt	2 oz
	pepper	
50 g	flour	2 oz
8 dl	gravy	1¼ pt
	parsley, finely chopped	
	10 portions cooked rice	

Trim and beat the veal fillets, season with salt and flour them, then brown in hot lard and braise under cover without adding liquid. Fry the onions in half the butter until lightly coloured, add the mushrooms and peppers, season with salt and pepper, sprinkle with paprika and fry quickly.

To serve, shape the rice into a base for the meat, arrange the slices of meat on top and cover with the fried vegetables. Work the rest of the butter into the gravy to make a sauce and pour over. Sprinkle with finely chopped parsley.

(Zsolt Körmendy, Hungary)

Veal medallions Bartenbach
Médaillons de filet de veau Bartenbach
Gefüllltes Kalbsfilet Bartenbach

6 portions

	12 veal medallions cut from the fillet,	
60 g	each weighing about	2 oz
100 g	butter	3½ oz
3 cl	whisky	1 fl oz
2½ dl	dairy cream	9 fl oz
	salt, pepper, Cayenne	
	a little flour	

Forcemeat:

50 g	dried morels	2 oz
180 g	veal sausage meat	6 oz
	2 shallots, chopped	
50 g	butter	2 oz
5 cl	dairy cream	2 fl oz
2 cl	whisky	1 fl oz
	salt, pepper	

Beat the medallions well to flatten, and season with salt and pepper. To make the forcemeat, chop the morels which have been soaked and well washed. Cook gently in butter together with the shallots. Add the whisky, reduce and allow to cool. Mix with the sausage meat and cream, and season with salt and pepper.

Spread half the medallions with the forcemeat and cover with the other half. Coat lightly with flour and fry carefully in butter for about 10 minutes. Remove from the pan and keep hot. Stir the whisky into the pan to detach the sediment, add a little veal stock and the cream, and reduce a little. Season and pour a little of this sauce over the meat, handing the rest separately. Serve with fresh noodles.

(Willi Bartenbach, Switzerland)

Veal medallions with goose liver, grapes and wine sauce
Médaillons de veau avec foie d'oie et raisin-sauce au vin blanc
Kalfs Haas met witte wijnsaus, ganzelever en druiven

4 portions

75 g	8 veal medallions each weighing	2½ oz
30 g	8 slices goose liver each weighing	1 oz
200 g	grapes, peeled and seeded	7 oz
50 g	shallots, finely chopped	2 oz
4 dl	veal gravy	14 fl oz
4 dl	white wine	14 fl oz
100 g	butter	3½ oz

Fry the veal in butter. Fry the goose liver for a few minutes. Cook the shallots gently in the same pan without colouring, stir in the wine and reduce. Add the gravy and reduce to the required consistency.

Warm the grapes. Dress the medallions on a dish, cover with the goose liver, coat with the sauce and decorate with the grapes.

(Bernard van Beurten, Netherlands)

Crépines of veal and lobster
Crépines de mignons de veau homardine

4 portions   Cooking time: 30 minutes

800 g	fillet of veal	1 lb 12 oz
600 g	lobster American style (classic recipe)	1 lb 5 oz
	3 eggs	
2 dl	dairy cream	7 fl oz
	1 pig's caul	
	2 tablespoons dairy cream to thicken sauce	
	thyme, bay leaf, tarragon	
	salt	
	pepper, freshly ground	
	1 small teaspoon cayenne pepper	
60 g	butter	2 oz
	1 tablespoon oil	
	flour for coating	
	2 eggs for coating	
	breadcrumbs for coating	

Prepare lobster American style. Remove the meat. Cut four medallions from the tail and set aside for decoration. Dice the rest of the lobster meat. Set aside the coral and the sauce in which the lobster was cooked. There should be at least ½ l (18 fl oz) sauce. Dice the veal finely. Mince one third of it coarsely and place in a bowl. Mix with the diced veal and lobster meat, the coral, 2 dl (7 fl oz) dairy cream and the eggs. Add powdered thyme, bay leaf and tarragon, season with salt, pepper and cayenne, and mix this forcemeat again until well blended.

Cut the caul into slices about 18 cm (7 in) in diameter. Using a savoy bag fitted with a plain tube, pipe a medallion 2 cm (¾ in) thick and about 7½ cm (3 in) across on to each slice of caul. Fold in the edges of the caul to enclose the forcemeat completely. Plunge the crépines into the lobster sauce and cook over low heat for 30 minutes. Carefully remove, drain and allow to cool. When cold, remove the pieces of caul carefully. Flour, egg and crumb the crépines. Heat them in the butter and oil in a fireproof casserole on top of the cooker, then transfer to an oven preheated to 165–175°C (330–350°F) and bake until golden brown, basting from time to time, but not turning them.

Thicken the lobster sauce with dairy cream and heat without boiling. Dress the crépines on a heated dish, cover with the lobster medallions and coat with the sauce, keeping some back to hand separately.
(Illustration, page 763)   (Patrick Klipfel, Armand Roth, France)

Fillet of veal Jutland style
Kalvefilet på jysk maner

4 portions

180 g	4 fillets of veal each weighing	6 oz
200 g	lean ham	7 oz
200 g	butter	7 oz
	salt	
	pepper, freshly ground	
100 g	medium rye flour	3½ oz

Garnish:

	4 puff pastry tartlet cases	
400 g	mushrooms	14 oz
¼ l	dairy cream	9 fl oz
	1 small bunch dill	

Coat the veal fillets with rye flour under pressure and season with salt and pepper. Heat 150 g (5 oz) clarified butter in a sauté pan, fry the meat until medium-done (about 7 or 8 minutes) and transfer to a heated dish.

Cut the ham into strips 1 cm (⅜ in) wide and sauter in the same pan. Spoon over the veal fillets, decorate each one with a few sprigs of dill and surround with the mushroom cream tartlets. To make the tartlets, cut the mushrooms into thick slices. Heat the rest of the butter in a stew pan and cook the mushrooms gently without colouring, turning them constantly. Reduce the cream by about a third and thicken with a little flour butter if necessary. Strain and add to the mushrooms. Season with salt and pepper. Finish with a little port if desired. Fill into the tartlet cases which have been heated.

(Karl-Otto Schmidt, Denmark)

Roast fillet of veal with tomato sauce and mint
Filet de veau rôti avec coulis de tomates à la menthe
Gebraden kalfshaas, tomaatsaus met verse mint blaadjes

4 portions

600–700 g	fillet of veal	1¼–1½ lb
	salt, pepper	
80 g	butter	3 oz
5 cl	dry white wine	2 fl oz
	8 mint leaves	
	4 small tomatoes	

Sauce:

200 g	tomatoes, finely diced	7 oz
	1 clove of garlic (unpeeled), roughly crushed	
	¼ medium onion	
	1 tablespoon olive oil	
⅛ l	light veal stock	4 fl oz
	1 bouquet garni	
	salt, pepper	
	12–16 mint leaves	

Garnish:

1 kg	tomatoes	2 lb 4 oz
50 g	butter	2 oz
	salt	

To make the sauce, cook the onion and garlic gently in olive oil without colouring, add the tomatoes, bouquet garni and veal stock, and cook over low heat for 10 minutes. Remove the herbs and garlic, strain and adjust the seasoning. Chop the mint and add to the sauce just before serving.

To prepare the garnish, skin, seed and finely dice the tomatoes. Melt the butter and cook the tomatoes gently in it, then season with salt.

Roast the veal until medium done, carve into thin slices and arrange these in a ring on a round dish. Pour the sauce round them. Place the mint leaves on the meat and fill the centre of the dish with the cooked diced tomatoes.

(Alexander Koene, Netherlands)

Mignons of fillet of veal Suzanne
Mignons de filet de veau Suzanne
Kalbsfiletschnitten Suzanne

6 portions

30 g	24 small slices fillet of veal each weighing	1 oz
150 g	fresh mushrooms, very thinly sliced	5 oz
150 g	calf's sweetbreads	5 oz
400 g	Patna rice	14 oz
600 g	leaf spinach	1 lb 5 oz
300 g	tomatoes	11 oz
3 dl	concentrated veal stock	10 fl oz
1 dl	port	3½ fl oz
	6 small puff pastry cases	
	12 asparagus tips	
1 dl	dairy cream	3½ fl oz
150 g	butter	5 oz
	1 small teaspoon shallot, finely chopped	
	1 small teaspoon garlic, finely chopped	
1 dl	white wine	3½ fl oz
	salt, pepper	
	oil	
	a little sugar	

Cook the mushrooms gently in 50 g (2 oz) butter, season and add half the cream. Beat the veal well to flatten, cover half the slices with the mushrooms and place the other half on top. Season and fry carefully in butter. Stir in the port to detach the sediment and add the veal stock. Finish the sauce with butter. Blanch the sweetbreads in water and white wine, cut up very finely and prepare in the same way as the mushrooms, finishing with the rest of the cream. Skin the tomatoes, cut them in half, seed them and cut into small cubes (about 1 cm–⅜ in). Cook gently in oil or butter and add the shallot and garlic, salt and pepper to taste, and very little sugar.

Dress 12 small bases of rice pilaf on a serving dish and cover with the meat. Place the tomatoes on top, together with the asparagus tips which have been thinly sliced. Serve with sweetbread bouchées and leaf spinach. Hand the sauce separately.

(Willi Bartenbach, Switzerland)

Fillet of veal Valenciennes
Filet de veau Valenciennes
Kalbsfilet Valenciennes

5 portions   Cooking time: about 25 minutes

750 g	fillet of veal	1 lb 10 oz
⅛ l	olive oil	4 fl oz
100 g	butter	3½ oz
	1 onion, chopped	
	4 shallots, finely chopped	
	5 tomatoes, skinned, seeded and coarsely diced	
150 g	red and green peppers, seeded, cut into strips and blanched	
300 g	fresh mushrooms, thinly sliced	11 oz
300 g	fresh young peas	11 oz
250 g	long grain rice	9 oz
	salt	
	pepper, freshly ground	
	saffron	
	bouillon	

Cut the veal into strips the thickness of the little finger. Brown for 3 minutes in hot oil, then season with salt and pepper. Add the onion, shallots, mushrooms, peppers, peas, tomatoes and rice. Mix carefully and cook gently for 1 minute without colouring the onion. Add a pinch of saffron and mix well. Stir in 5 dl (18 fl oz) boiling hot bouillon, cover and cook in a preheated oven for 18 minutes. Remove, dot with butter, cover again and leave to stand at the side of the stove for 5 minutes. Fluff up the rice with a fork and dress in a heated ovenware casserole. Serve with a light curry or Madeira sauce.

(Otto Brust, Germany)

Veal fricandeau in vegetables
Fricandeau de veau en croûte de légumes
Kalbsfricandeau in der Germüsehülle

8 portions   Cooking time: 1½ hours

1 kg 800	veal fricandeau	4 lb
5 cl	oil	2 fl oz
100 g	larding bacon	3½ oz

100 g	mushrooms	3½ oz
100 g	celeriac	3½ oz
100 g	carrots	3½ oz
100 g	leeks	3½ oz
	1 teaspoon each chervil, parsley, dill, chopped	
80 g	butter	3 oz
2 dl	veal stock	7 fl oz
	salt, pepper	
	1 pig's or calf's caul	

Remove any skin from the veal, lard it, season with salt and pepper and brown in the oven for about 15 minutes. Refrigerate. Wash the carrots, celeriac, leeks and mushrooms and cut into coarse julienne strips. Cook gently in hot butter for about 8 minutes, season with salt and pepper and stir in the herbs. Spread evenly over the veal and enclose in the caul. Roast slowly in the oven for about 30 minutes. Add the veal stock and glaze. Serve with Parisienne or parsley potatoes.

(Franz Zodl, Austria)

Fricandeau of veal with cream sauce
Fricandeau de veau à la crème
Kalvestek med Fløtesaus

4 portions

900 g	veal fricandeau	2 lb
	pepper, freshly ground	
	salt	
	coarse mustard seed	
	3 tablespoons vegetable fat	
1½ dl	bouillon	5 fl oz
1 dl	demi-glace sauce	3½ fl oz
2 dl	dairy cream	7 fl oz

Cucumber salad:

500 g	cucumber	1 lb 2 oz
7½ cl	vinegar	2½ fl oz
2½ dl	water	9 fl oz
	sugar	
	parsley, finely chopped	

Rub the veal with a mixture of salt, freshly ground pepper and mustard seed. Brown in the fat in an oven preheated to 175°C (350°F), stir in the bouillon and continue roasting. When the meat is cooked, remove from the pan, reduce the stock and thicken with demi-glace sauce and cream.

To serve, cut the meat into slices and dress on a heated dish. Hand the sauce and cucumber salad separately. To make the salad, slice the cucumber finely. Dress with the vinegar and water which have been well mixed with a little sugar. Add the parsley and toss carefully in the dressing, then leave to stand for 1 hour.

(Hroar Dege, Günther Rett, Norway)

Grenadins of veal with capers and courgettes
Grenadins de veau aux câpres et courgettes

4 portions

400 g	veal fricandeau	14 oz
approx. 400 g	courgettes	approx. 14 oz
	4 teaspoons capers	
	4 teaspoons parsley, chopped	
	1 tablespoon veal stock	
	juice of 1 lemon	
60 g	butter, softened	2 oz
	1 tablespoon white wine	
	flour as required	
	salt, pepper	

Cut the meat into 4, then into 16 small slices. Beat between 2 sheets of plastic film until very thin. Cut each courgette evenly into 12 slices, season with salt and pepper, coat with flour and shake off the excess. Fry lightly in clarified butter, wiping away any excess fat to keep the courgettes crisp.

Fry the veal in the same way as the courgettes. Pour off the butter and detach the sediment with the lemon juice and wine. Add the parsley, capers and stock. Thicken the sauce with the softened butter. Arrange the veal grenadins and the courgettes alternately in a ring on a heated dish and coat with the sauce.

(François Kiener, France)

Veal grenadins with Champagne Georges Prade
Grenadins de veau au champagne Georges Prade
Kalbsgrenadins mit Champagner Georges Prade

4 portions

160 g	4 veal grenadins each weighing	5½ oz
	½ bottle Champagne brut	
250 g	mushrooms or chanterelles, thinly sliced	9 oz

	1 calf's liver	
¼ l	dairy cream	9 fl oz
70 g	butter	2½ oz
5 cl	white wine	2 fl oz
	salt	
	pepper, freshly ground	
	parsley, finely chopped	
	3 tablespoons veal stock	
	flour as required	

Wash and soak the kidney well, trim and cut into 8 slices. Season the veal with salt and pepper, dust with flour and brown quickly in 30 g (1 oz) hot butter on both sides. Pour off the butter, stir in ¼ bottle Champagne, bring to the boil, cover and cook over moderate heat for 20 minutes. Remove the meat and keep hot.

Add the mushrooms and cook for 5 minutes. Thicken with a little potato flour and add 20 g (¾ oz) butter, the cream and the rest of the Champagne. Brown the slices of kidney on both sides in the remaining butter, stir in the white wine and 2 tablespoons veal stock, boil up and season to taste. Remove the kidney and keep hot. Mix the two sauces together, boil up for a moment and adjust the seasoning.

To serve, dress the veal grenadins on a warmed dish, coat with sauce and place the slices of kidney on top. Spoon a few drops of veal stock over each slice.

(Roger Parrot, François Perret, Switzerland)

Danish veal goulash
Goulasch à la danoise

4 portions   Cooking time: about 1 hour

750 g	shoulder of veal	1 lb 10 oz
200 g	butter	7 oz
350 g	onions	12 oz
½ l	dairy cream	18 fl oz
1 l	water or veal stock	1¾ pt
	pepper, freshly ground	
	salt	
35 g	tomato purée	1¼ oz
80 g	flour butter	3 oz

Cut the veal and the onions evenly into 2 cm (¾ in) cubes. Place the butter in a stew pan, melt and colour lightly, then add the onions and cook gently until transparent without colouring. Add the veal and season with salt and freshly ground pepper. Add the tomato purée and mix well. Stir in the water or stock, bring to the boil and simmer over low heat for about 1 hour. Remove the meat and reduce the stock. Bind with flour butter and add the cream. Season to taste with salt and pepper and pass through a cloth.

Dress the meat in a heated serving dish and pour the sauce over. Hand mashed potatoes or boiled rice separately. Beetroot salad or cucumber salad sprinkled with dill also makes a suitable accompaniment.

(Karl-Otto Schmidt, Denmark)

Knuckle of veal Alsatian style
Jarret de veau à l'alsacienne

6 portions

	6 knuckles of veal	
150 g	mushrooms, turned and stewed	5 oz
150 g	button onions, blanched	5 oz
	2 egg yolks	
2 dl	dairy cream	7 fl oz
	1 small black truffle, cut into julienne strips	
1 dl	oil	3½ fl oz
100 g	butter	3½ oz
	pepper, freshly ground	
	salt	
	nutmeg, grated	
1 l	fairly dry white wine (Riesling)	1¾ pt
5 dl	water	18 fl oz
	6 onions, finely cut	
100 g	flour	3½ oz
	6 cloves of garlic, finely chopped	

Spätzle:

500 g	flour	1 lb 2 oz
	9 eggs	
	salt, pepper	
	nutmeg, grated	
150–200 g	butter	5–7 oz

Season the knuckles with salt and pepper, flour them and brown in butter and oil. Remove from the pan. Add the onions to the pan and colour lightly. Place the knuckles on top. Add the wine, salt and pepper as required, and the garlic, cover and cook slowly over low heat for 1½ hours, adding the water after half the cooking time. Remove the knuckles and keep hot. Pass the stock through a conical strainer, then add the mushrooms and button onions.

Remove from the heat, bind with the egg yolks and cream, flavour with nutmeg and adjust the seasoning. Dress the knuckles on a warmed dish and pour the sauce over. Serve the *spätzle* separately.

To make the *spätzle,* beat the eggs and season with salt, pepper and nutmeg. Prepare a dough with the eggs and flour. Force a soup plateful at a time through a large-holed sieve or colander into a pan of boiling salted water. As soon as they rise to the surface remove with a skimmer, transfer to a colander and allow to cool. Toss in melted butter, place in a fireproof dish and heat in the oven at 200°C (392°F) for 10 minutes. The dough may be shredded into the boiling water with a knife instead of being forced through a sieve.
(Illustration, page 522)

(Jean Esslinger, France)

Knuckle of veal with Canadian russets
Jarret de veau aux reinettes du Canada
Muscoletto con la renetta del Canada

4 portions

800 g	knuckle of veal in one piece	1 lb 12 oz
	2 apples (russets), sliced	
100 g	pork fat or fat bacon, sliced	3½ oz
50 g	butter	2 oz
	oil	
	powdered rosemary and sage as required	
	salt, pepper	
	2 onions, finely chopped	
	bouquet garni (rosemary, sage leaves, sprig of thyme, parsley, bay leaf)	
¼ l	white wine	9 fl oz
	1 tablespoon wine vinegar	
½ l	bouillon	18 fl oz
Accompaniments:		
400 g	sweet and sour onions	14 oz
500 g	carrots, buttered	1 lb 2 oz

Remove the knuckle bone, skin the meat and marinate well. Season well with salt, pepper and the powdered herbs, bard with the slices of pork fat or bacon and tie securely. Dust with flour and fry in butter for 5 minutes until brown on all sides. Add the onions, a clove of garlic and the bouquet garni. Cover the meat with the sliced apples and season with salt and pepper. Add the wine, sprinkle the apples with the vinegar and pour in sufficient bouillon to cover the meat. Braise under cover for 2 hours in an oven preheated to 200°C (392°F). Remove the meat and keep hot.

Pass the stock and the apples through a conical strainer and return to the pan. Place the meat in the pan, dot with butter and return to the oven which has been heated to 250°C (482°F). Reduce for about 1½ hours. Carve the meat, coat with the sauce and hand the accompaniments separately.

(Sergio Chiesa, Italy)

Braised knuckle of veal with orange zest and ginger
Jarret de veau braisé aux zestes d'oranges et de gingembre

6 portions

250–280 g	6 pieces knuckle of veal each weighing	9–10 oz
50 g	onions, finely cut	2 oz
50 g	carrots, finely cut	2 oz
50 g	celery, finely cut	2 oz
	1 bouquet garni	
1 dl	light stock	3½ fl oz
1 dl	brown stock	3½ fl oz
	2 tomatoes, skinned, seeded and diced	
40 g	concentrated tomato purée	1½ fl oz
20 g	orange zest	¾ oz
10 g	ginger, finely cut	⅓ oz
5 cl	white wine	2 fl oz
	salt, pepper	
	oil and butter as required	

Flour the veal lightly and colour in butter and oil. Add the onions, carrots and celery and continue frying. Stir in the wine to detach the sediment, add the light stock, then the brown stock, and continue cooking. Add the tomatoes, purée and bouquet garni and cook for about 40 minutes.

Meanwhile blanch the orange zest for about 5 minutes and cut into julienne strips, together with the ginger. Dress the veal on a warmed dish. Strain the stock, add the orange zest and ginger and pour over the veal. Hand home-made noodles separately.

(Emile Jung, France)

Stuffed knuckle of veal Peterskeller
Jarret de veau farcie Peterskeller
Gefüllte Kalbshachse Peterskeller

4 portions

approx. 1 kg	1 large knuckle of veal weighing approx.	2 lb 4 oz

6 cl	oil	2 fl oz
	salt	
	pepper	

Stuffing:

100 g	veal sausage meat	3½ oz
60 g	leaf spinach, blanched	2 oz
60 g	pressed ham	2 oz

Cauliflower balls:

	1 cauliflower		
	salt		
approx. 10 g	butter	approx.	½ oz

Tomatoes with mushroom stuffing:

	4 tomatoes		
approx. 200 g	mushrooms	approx.	7 oz
	(exact quantity depends on size of tomatoes)		
30 g	butter		1 oz
1 dl	dairy cream		3½ fl oz
	salt		
	1 tablespoon parsley, chopped		

Bone the knuckle of veal and make two incisions lengthwise to enlarge the surface a little. To make the stuffing, mix the sausage meat well with the spinach and the ham which has been cut into 1 cm (⅜ in) cubes. Place on the meat, fold the meat over to enclose, and sew up. Season, place in a braising pan with the oil and roast at 200°C (392°F) for about 2 hours, reducing the oven temperature after a time. Moisten the meat frequently with a little water to make gravy.

Cook the cauliflower in salted water. Enclose 50 g (2 oz) at a time in a cloth and twist gently to shape into a ball. Carefully place the balls on a buttered fireproof tray, mask with Hollandaise sauce and brown in a hot oven.

Blanch the tomatoes for 6 to 10 seconds in boiling water, refresh in cold water and skin. Cut off the top of each and hollow out. Slice the mushrooms thinly and cook in butter. Add the cream and reduce until thick. Add salt and chopped parsley to taste and fill into the tomatoes.

Slice the meat and dress with the garnish. Remove the fat from the stock and pour over the meat. Mix saffron rice with diced red and green peppers, diced ham and peas to make an additional garnish.
(Illustration, page 872)

(Helmut Stadlbauer, Austria)

Knuckle of veal Munich style
Jarret de veau à la munichoise
Kalbshachse aus dem Wurzelsud auf Münchner Art

3–4 portions

approx. 2 kg	knuckle of veal	4 lb 8 oz
4 l	veal bone stock, clarified	7 pt
	1 tablespoon white vinegar	
	½ celeriac	
	1 leek	
	1 carrot	
	½ onion	
100 g	butter	3½ oz

Garnish:

6 potatoes
1 tablespoon parsley, chopped
butter
1 small teaspoon caraway

Boil the knuckle of veal whole in the stock and vinegar, skimming constantly to keep the meat white. Cut the vegetables into julienne strips and cook in part of the stock, keeping them firm to the bite. Slice the knuckle lengthwise and sprinkle with hot butter.

Turn the potatoes, cook in salted water, toss in butter and sprinkle with parsley and caraway. Dress the vegetable julienne on top of the meat and garnish with the potatoes. If desired, serve with horseradish which has been grated by hand.

(Gerhard Gartner, Germany)

Stuffed knuckle of veal
Jarret de veau farci
Giretto o Muscolo di vitello farcito

4 portions

1 kg 500	knuckle of veal	3 lb 5 oz
200 g	butter	7 oz
150 g	mirepoix	5 oz
	1 sprig rosemary	
2 dl	white wine	7 fl oz
3 dl	brown stock	10 fl oz
	oil	

Stuffing:

50 g	veal	2 oz
50 g	pork or ham	2 oz
30 g	bacon or pork fat	1 oz
	2 eggs	
	2 rolls, soaked in milk	

Garnish:

	4 artichoke bottoms	
	bone marrow	
300 g	Brussels sprouts	11 oz
300 g	carrots, turned	11 oz
300 g	Pont-Neuf potatoes	11 oz

Prepare the stuffing. Carefully bone the veal and set aside the bone. Replace the bone with the stuffing, cover with pork fat or bacon, roll up and tie. Place in an oven preheated to 220°C (428°F), together with the knuckle bone, baste with a little oil and roast for 1 hour. Remove the fat from the pan, add the butter which has been melted, the mirepoix and rosemary, and continue roasting. Moisten with the wine, reduce, add the brown stock and baste the meat frequently with the cooking juices.

Meanwhile cook the vegetables and keep hot, leaving the potatoes until last. Stuff the artichoke bottoms with bone marrow, taken from the knuckle bone. Serve the meat with the vegetables. Carve at the table to prevent the stuffing from breaking up.
(Illustration, page 418)

(Ivo Balestra, Switzerland)

Veal cutlets Bakony style
Côtelettes de veau Bakony
Bakonyi Borjuborda

10 portions   Cooking time: 15-20 minutes

180 g	10 veal cutlets each weighing		6 oz
300 g	lard		11 oz
50 g	salt		2 oz
200 g	onions, finely chopped		7 oz
600 g	mushrooms, sliced		1 lb 5 oz
30 g	paprika		1 oz
250 g	yellow peppers		9 oz
8 dl	sour cream	approx.	1¼ pt
200 g	flour		7 oz
2 g	caraway (optional)		a pinch
10 g	garlic (optional)		⅓ oz
	tomatoes and peppers to decorate		

Nockerln:

800 g	flour	1 lb 12 oz
50 g	salt	2 oz
100 g	lard or butter	3½ oz
	3 eggs	

Beat the cutlets, season with salt and flour; fry on both sides in lard, then set aside. Fry the onions gently in lard until lightly coloured, sprinkle with paprika, add the mushrooms, season with salt, add caraway and garlic to taste and continue cooking for a short time. Add the yellow peppers which have been seeded and diced, then the sour cream which has been blended with the flour. Mix well and cook for 4 or 5 minutes. Pour over the cutlets and stew under cover for a short time.

To serve, remove the cutlets and dress on a dish. Pour the sauce over together with the vegetables and decorate with seeded peppers cut into rings and with tomato quarters. Sprinkle with a little sour cream. Hand the *nockerln* separately. To make the *nockerln,* prepare a soft dough with the flour, salt, eggs and as much lukewarm water as required. Beat until smooth and forming air bubbles. Either force through a *nockerln* maker or large-holed sieve into a pan of boiling, salted water, or place on a small board and scrape off into the water with a knife. The *nockerln* are cooked when they rise to the surface. Remove them, rinse in cold water and toss in hot lard or butter.

(Zsolt Körmendy, Hungary)

Veal cutlets Arnold Böcklin
Côtelettes de veau Arnold Böcklin
Kalbskoteletts Arnold Böcklin

10 portions

120 g	10 veal cutlets each weighing	4 oz
	salt	
	spices as desired	
30 g	flour	1 oz
1 dl	oil	3½ fl oz
25 g	10 small slices ham each weighing	1 oz
	10 fresh eggs	
	10 slices truffle	
400 g	leaf spinach, frozen	14 oz
50 g	butter	2 oz
25 g	shallot, chopped	1 oz
4 dl	veal stock, thickened	14 fl oz

Trim the cutlets neatly, season with salt and spices as desired and coat with flour. Heat the oil and fry the cutlets on both sides until golden. Pour off the oil and glaze the cutlets lightly.

Dress on a heated serving dish. Cover with the ham which has been rolled up round the cooked spinach. Place a small poached egg on top of each and decorate with a slice of truffle. Pour a little of the veal stock round the cutlets and hand the rest separately, together with olivette potatoes, boiled Chinese artichokes and tomatoes stuffed with peppers Italian style (recipe, page 1012).

(Otto Ledermann, Switzerland)

Veal cutlets Bregentved
Côtelettes de veau Bregentved
Kalvekotelet Bregentved

6 portions
Cooking time: 1½ hours (including sauce and Duchesse rings)

180 g	6 veal cutlets each weighing	6 oz
500 g	chanterelles	1 lb 2 oz
150 g	bacon rashers	5 oz
500 g	spinach, blanched	1 lb 2 oz
125 g	butter	4½ oz
	salt	
	pepper, freshly ground	

Madeira sauce:

1 kg	veal bones	2 lb 4 oz
	3 onions, coarsely sliced	
	1 carrot, coarsely sliced	
	1 celeriac, coarsely sliced	
100 g	tomato purée	3½ oz
	2 bay leaves	
1 l	water	1¾ pt
3 dl	Madeira	10 fl oz
75 g	fat for frying	2½ oz
60 g	flour	2 oz
	salt	

Duchesse rings:

1 kg	potatoes	2 lb 4 oz
	3 egg yolks	
50 g	butter	2 oz

To make the sauce, fry the vegetables and bones in the fat until lightly coloured. Add the flour and cook gently, then add the tomato purée and brown a little. Stir in the water and add the bay leaves. Bring to the boil and reduce well. Remove the fat, strain, season to taste and finish with the Madeira.

To make the Duchesse rings, peel the potatoes and boil in salted water. Pour off the water, dry very well over low heat and quickly pass through a wire sieve. Return to the heat, mix well with the butter, season, remove from the heat and add the egg yolks. Using a savoy bag fitted with a star tube, pipe on to a carefully greased baking sheet in rings the size of the veal cutlets. Bake until golden yellow.

Flatten the cutlets a little, season and fry on both sides in butter. Sauter the chanterelles with the bacon and keep hot. Stew the spinach in butter.

Dress the spinach on a warmed dish and place the cutlets on top. Using a spatula, arrange a Duchesse ring on each cutlet. Fill the centre with the chanterelle/bacon mixture. Hand the Madeira sauce separately.

(Eric Cederholm, Denmark)

Veal cutlets Brno musicians' style
Côtelettes de veau des musiciens à la brunnoise
Muzikantzké kotlety po brněnsku

6 portions   Cooking time: about 8 minutes

150 g	6 veal cutlets each weighing	5 oz
	salt	
approx. 2 g	pepper	a pinch
8 cl	oil	3 fl oz
	6 fried eggs	
	12 anchovy fillets	
	parsley to garnish	

Snip the cutlets round the edges, beat lightly, season with salt and pepper and fry in hot oil for 3 or 4 minutes on each side. Dress on a heated dish, place a fried egg on each cutlet and decorate with an anchovy fillet in the shape of a clef. Pour off the fat in which the meat was fried, rinse out the pan with a little bouillon to detach the sediment, work in 20 g (¾ oz) butter, season with salt and serve separately.

(Vilèm Vrabec, Czechoslovakia)

Veal cutlets Cornabuse
Côtelettes de veau Cornabuse
Costelette di vitello alla Cornabuse

4 portions

200 g	4 veal cutlets each weighing	7 oz

2 cloves of garlic, crushed
oregano
Worcester sauce
olive oil
salt

Prepare a marinade with the oil, garlic, oregano, salt and Worcester sauce. Marinate the cutlets for at least 2 hours, turning several times. Grill the cutlets, garnish with wedges of lemon and serve with mixed salad.

(Franco Boffetti, Italy)

Veal cutlets Denise
Côtelettes de veau Denise
Kalbskoteletts Denise

4 portions

220 g	4 veal cutlets each weighing	7½ oz
4 cl	oil	1½ fl oz
	a little flour	
	salt, pepper	
	brown stock	
2 cl	Noilly Prat	1 fl oz
50 g	butter	2 oz
	3 tomatoes	
80 g	ham	3 oz
80 g	mushrooms or flap mushrooms	3 oz
	2 eggs	
100 g	Gruyère cheese, grated	3½ oz

Stuffed kohlrabi:

	2 kohlrabi	
	2 tablespoons onions, cooked	
20 g	butter	¾ oz
	salt, pepper	
	a little bouillon	
	parsley, chopped	

Potato pancakes:

400 g	floury potatoes	14 oz
	salt, nutmeg	
	1 egg yolk	
	1 egg	
	a little dairy cream	
30 g	butter	1 oz

Trim the cutlets, flatten them lightly, season with salt, dust with flour and fry on both sides in hot oil until medium done. Pour off the excess oil, add 20 g (¾ oz) butter, allow to melt, stir to detach the cooking juices and add a little brown stock. Cook gently without boiling, turning the meat frequently. Flavour the stock with the Noilly Prat.

Skin, seed and dice the tomatoes. Season with salt and pepper and toss for a moment in 10 g (⅓ oz) butter. Set aside 2 tablespoons of the tomatoes for the kohlrabi. Cut the ham into strips and the mushrooms into slices, brown lightly in the rest of the butter and season with salt. Mix the cheese, mushrooms, ham and tomatoes with the 2 eggs which have been beaten, and adjust the seasoning. Set aside to use as a topping for the cutlets.

Peel the kohlrabi, cut them in half, hollow out with a vegetable scoop and boil in salted water, keeping them firm. Toss the onions in butter, add the flesh scooped out of the kohlrabi globes, season with salt and pepper and stir in a little bouillon. Cook gently under cover, then mix with the diced tomatoes which have been set aside. Sprinkle with chopped parsley and fill into the kohlrabi globes, then reheat.

To make the pancakes, peel the potatoes, cut them in quarters, boil in salted water, keeping them firm, drain and sieve. Mix with the egg yolk, whole egg and cream, and season with salt and nutmeg. Fry in hot butter until golden brown to make small pancakes. Dress the cutlets on a dish, spread with the topping and brown in the oven or under a salamander. Serve with the stuffed kohlrabi and potato pancakes. Hand the sauce separately.
(Illustration, page 870)

(Ewald Plachutta, Austria)

Veal cutlets General Leclerc
Côtes de veau Général Leclerc

4 portions

175–200 g	4 veal cutlets each weighing	6–7 oz
500 g net	morello cherries, stoned and poached	1 lb 2 oz net
80 g	butter	3 oz
4 dl	double cream	14 fl oz
1 dl	kirsch	3½ fl oz

Drain the cherries and set aside the juice, but add a little of it to the cherries and keep hot. Fry the cutlets on both sides in 70 g (2½ oz) butter, allowing about 5 to 7 minutes a side, then keep hot. Pour off the butter, stir in the cherry juice to detach the sediment, bring to the boil and reduce. Sweeten with very little sugar if too acid. Add the cream, reduce, season to taste with salt and pepper, stir in the kirsch, reduce again and finish with about 10 g (½ oz) butter. Dress the cutlets on a round dish with the cherries in the centre. Hand green noodles tossed in butter separately as an accompaniment.

(André Béghin, Belgium)

Veal cutlets Gundel style
Côtelettes de veau Gundel
Borjuborda Gundel módra

10 portions   Cooking time: 10-15 minutes

160 g	10 veal cutlets each weighing	5½ oz
150 g	butter	5 oz
150 g	lard	5 oz
300 g	mushrooms	11 oz
	parsley	
500 g	spinach	1 lb 2 oz
200 g	ham	7 oz
1 l	milk	1¾ pt
60 g	flour	2 oz
	10 eggs	
400 g	white breadcrumbs	14 oz
200 g	Parmesan cheese, grated	7 oz
50 g	salt	2 oz
3 g	black pepper, freshly ground	a good pinch
2 g	nutmeg, grated	a pinch

Beat the cutlets, flour them, season with salt, then egg and breadcrumb, using 2 eggs and, if desired, egg whites not required for the sauce. Sauter the cutlets in hot lard or butter.

Wash the spinach well, boil it in salted water over high heat, remove, refresh well in cold water, squeeze in a cloth and season with salt and pepper. Butter a fireproof dish and line the bottom with the spinach. Arrange the cutlets on top, cover with the mushrooms which have been sliced and sautéd and with the finely chopped parsley, and season to taste with salt and pepper.

Make a roux with 70 g (2½ oz) butter and the flour. Stir in the milk (cold) and bring to the boil. Remove from the heat, add 8 egg yolks, the cheese and the ham which has been finely cut, mix well and season with salt and nutmeg. Pour over the cutlets, sprinkle with grated cheese and breadcrumbs, dot with butter, surround with Duchesse potatoes and brown quickly under a salamander.

(Zsolt Körmendy, Hungary)

Veal cutlets with button onions and glazed carrots
Côtes de veau aux petits oignons confits et carottes glacées

6 portions

250 g	6 veal cutlets each weighing	9 oz
	50 button onions	

1 kg	veal bones	2 lb 4 oz
100 g	butter (for stock)	3½ oz
1 l	light stock	1¾ pt
	1 onion, chopped	
	salt	
	pepper, freshly ground	
2½ dl	olive oil	9 fl oz
110 g	butter	4 oz
1 kg	carrots	2 lb 4 oz
	sugar	
	6 medium potatoes	
5 cl	Madeira	2 fl oz

Pancake batter:

1½ dl	milk	5 fl oz
1½ dl	beer	5 fl oz
100 g	flour	3½ oz
	2–3 eggs	
40 g	butter	1½ oz
	2 pinches chopped parsley	
	2 pinches salt	
	1 pinch sugar	

Cook the button onions gently in a mixture of oil and butter, then season with salt and pepper. Brown the bones in 100 g (3½ oz) hot butter, add the chopped onion and brown for 5 minutes. Stir in the light stock, bring to the boil, reduce by two thirds and pass through a conical strainer. Fry the cutlets in 20 g (¾ oz) butter and 2 cl (1 fl oz) oil. Season with salt and pepper and keep hot.

Pour off the fat, stir in the strained veal stock to detach the sediment, add the Madeira, reduce and finish with 20 g (¾ oz) butter. Dress the cutlets on a warm dish, coat with the sauce and garnish with the button onions and the blanched carrots. Hand potatoes in pancake batter separately. Peel the potatoes, boil them, keeping them very firm, cut each one into 4 or 5 slices, dip in the pancake batter and fry in butter.

(Emile Jung, France)

Veal cutlets Saxonne
Côtelettes de veau Saxonne
Kalbskoteletts Saxonne

4 portions

220 g (with bones)	4 veal cutlets each weighing	7½ oz

2½ dl	veal stock, thickened	9 fl oz
50 g	butter	2 oz
	salt	

Garnishes:

	16 asparagus tips or scorzonera	
	4 tablespoons Hollandaise sauce	
20 g	greenhouse cress	¾ oz
	broccoli or leaf spinach	

Endive with scrambled egg:

	2 endives or lettuces (large)	
40 g	butter	1½ oz
6 cl	bouillon	2 fl oz
	salt, pepper	
	scrambled egg	

Trim the cutlets, scrape the bones clean and snip the edges. Season with salt and fry in butter on both sides for about 5 minutes. Dress on a serving dish and keep hot. Stir the veal stock into the pan to detach the sediment, bring to the boil and reduce a little. Strain over the meat. Place 4 asparagus tips or scorzonera on each cutlet, coat with Hollandaise sauce and sprinkle with cress.

Make a conical cut at the end of the endive roots to remove the bitter section. Blanch in salted water for about 3 minutes and cut in half lengthwise. Place in a pan with the butter, bouillon, salt and pepper and cook gently for about 5 minutes. Arrange beside the cutlets with the inside uppermost, press down a little and fill with the scrambled egg.
(Illustration, page 770)

(Franz Zodl, Austria)

Veal cutlets Westland style
Côtelettes de veau à la Westland
Kalfskoteletten westlandstijl

4 portions

200 g	4 veal cutlets each weighing	7 oz
150 g	butter	5 oz
	salt	
	pepper, freshly ground	
50 g	carrots	2 oz

50 g	leek	2 oz
50 g	celeriac	2 oz
80 g	mushrooms	3 oz
50 g	red and green peppers	2 oz

Sauce:

10 g	green peppers, finely cut	½ oz
	veal gravy	
	Cognac	

Cut up the mushrooms finely and cut the carrots, leek, celeriac and peppers into thin julienne strips. Sauter the vegetables in butter and allow to cool. Fry the cutlets in the rest of the butter and cut a pocket in the centre with a sharp knife. Fill with the vegetables.

To make the sauce, brown the green pepper lightly in the pan used to fry the cutlets. Stir in veal gravy to detach the sediment and cook for a few minutes, then add the Cognac, bring to the boil and strain. Hand the sauce separately, together with boiled potatoes as an accompaniment.

(Bernard van Beurten, Netherlands)

Calf's liver medallions on croûtons with apples and honey sauce
Médaillons de foie de veau aux croûtons – sauce aux pommes et au miel
Schijfjes kalfslever op gebakken brood met appel en honingsaus

4 portions

90 g	4 calf's liver medallions each weighing	3 oz
	salt	
	pepper, freshly ground	
	flour	
	3 apples	
	4 round slices white bread	
60 g	honey	2 oz
1 dl	veal gravy	3½ fl oz
40 g	carrot *or* leek, cut into fine julienne strips	1½ oz
1 cl	Calvados	½ fl oz
80 g	butter	3 oz

Flour the liver and fry in butter. Fry the bread in butter. Peel and core the apples and cut them into thick slices. Fry lightly in butter and stir in the Calvados. Mix together the veal gravy and honey and reduce to the required consistency. Pour the honey sauce on to a serving dish, place the croûtons on it, arrange the liver medallions on top and cover with the apple slices. Place a teaspoonful of apple purée in the centre of each slice and sprinkle with leek or carrot julienne. (Illustration, page 945)

(Bernard van Beurten, Netherlands)

Stuffed calf's liver Croatian style
Foie de veau farci à la croate
Nadevena Teleća Džigerica

4 portions   Cooking time: 1 hour

500 g	calf's liver	1 lb 2 oz
100 g	bacon, finely cut	3½ oz
100 g	lard *or* margarine	3½ oz
OR 1 dl	oil	3½ fl oz
	1 onion	
50 g	white breadcrumbs	2 oz
	1 egg	
6 cl	sour cream	2 fl oz
	parsley, chopped	
	pepper, freshly ground	
	salt	

Cut a pocket in the centre of the liver with a sharp knife. Heat half the fat or oil. Add the bacon, the chopped onions, the parsley and breadcrumbs and mix well. Fry and allow to cool, then mix with the egg and sour cream and season with salt and pepper. Carefully enlarge the pocket in the liver with the hand, fill with the stuffing and sew up. Place the liver in a roasting pan, sprinkle with the rest of the fat or oil and roast in a moderate oven for 1 hour. Season with salt, slice thinly with a sharp knife, dress on a serving dish and pour the gravy over. Serve with vegetable dumplings (recipe, page 1010).

(László Csizmadia, Yugoslavia)

Flambé larded calf's liver
Froie de veau lardé et flambé
Telecí játra pečená flambovaná

2 portions   Cooking time: about 6 minutes

400 g	calf's liver	14 oz
100 g	larding bacon or pork fat	3½ oz
	salt	

	4 peppercorns, freshly ground	
100 g	butter	3½ oz
6 cl	Cognac	2 fl oz
	4 pineapple slices	

Wash, dry and trim the liver, removing any skin present, then cut into slices 1 cm (⅜ in) thick, flatten lightly and lard with strips of bacon or pork fat which have been dipped in Cognac. Season with pepper and fry in 80 g (3 oz) hot butter for about 2½ minutes on each side. Season shortly before the liver is cooked. Warm the rest of the Cognac in a small ladle over a spirit stove, ignite and pour over the contents of the pan, which should be very hot.

(Vilèm Vrabec, Czechoslovakia)

Calf's liver with glazed carrots
Foie de veau aux carottes glacées
Gedünstete Kalbsleber mit glacierten Karotten

4 portions

800 g	calf's liver in one piece	1 lb 12 oz
150 g	larding bacon or salt pork fat	5 oz
200 g	swedes, thinly sliced	7 oz
50 g	onions, finely chopped	2 oz
1¼ dl	bouillon	4 fl oz
1¼ dl	white wine	4 fl oz
	1 bay leaf	
	2 cloves of garlic, finely chopped	
	salt, pepper	

Glazed carrots:

600 g	carrots, peeled	1 lb 5 oz
50 g	butter	2 oz
3¾ dl	water	13 fl oz
	salt, sugar	
	1 teaspoon parsley, chopped	

Skin the liver and lard with strips of bacon or salt pork fat the thickness of a pencil and the length of a finger. Sprinkle a braising pan with the onions, swedes and garlic. Add the bay leaf. Season the liver with salt and pepper and place in the pan with the larded side uppermost. Pour the bouillon and wine over and bring to the boil, then cook in the oven under cover for about 45 minutes. Slice as desired to dish, remove the fat from the sauce and serve separately.

To prepare the carrots, cut them into wedge-shaped pieces of the desired size. Cook them in salted water and butter with a little sugar. When the water has boiled away, the carrots should be tender. Sprinkle with chopped parsley to serve.

(Franz Zodl, Austria)

Calf's liver Mamma Rosa
Foie de veau Maman Rose
Fegato di vitello Mamma Rosa

10 portions

2 kg	calf's liver	4 lb 8 oz
300 g	bacon	11 oz
500 g	onions	1 lb 2 oz
500 g	carrots	1 lb 2 oz
500 g	celeriac	1 lb 2 oz
2 l	red wine	3½ pt
	bouquet garni	

Mashed potatoes:

2 kg	potatoes	4 lb 8 oz
	salt, pepper	
¼ l	dairy cream	9 fl oz
100 g	butter	3½ oz
100 g	Parmesan, grated	3½ oz

Coarsely dice the vegetables. Remove any skin and tubes from the liver. Place it in an earthenware dish with the vegetables and the bouquet garni, pour in the wine and marinate for 48 hours.

Finely dice the bacon and brown in very little oil. Add the liver and brown on all sides. Drain the marinade vegetables, add to the pan and brown a little. Pour in the marinade to cover the liver, adding extra red wine if necessary. Cover and braise slowly over gentle heat for 2 hours.

Remove the liver. Sieve the stock and vegetables to make a dark, smooth sauce. Keep the liver and sauce hot. Prepare the mashed potatoes, add the Parmesan, dress in a lighlty buttered fireproof dish and cover with the liver, cut into 20 slices. Coat with the sauce and serve hot.

(Fiorenzo Boroni, Italy)

Calf's liver Venetian style
Emincé de foie de veau à la vénitienne

4 portions

600 g	calf's liver	1 lb 5 oz
40 g	butter	1½ oz
100 g	onions, finely cut	3½ oz

2 dl	Madeira	7 fl oz
2 dl	brown veal stock	7 fl oz
	1 sage leaf, chopped	
60 g	butter (to finish sauce)	2 oz
	salt	
	pepper, freshly ground	

Trim the liver of skin and tubes and cut into thin slices about 3 cm (1¼ in) long. Season with salt and pepper. Cook the onions gently in half butter until lightly coloured, while stirring constantly. Detach the sediment with 1½ dl (5 fl oz) Madeira, add the sage and reduce by half. Stir in the veal stock and reduce to the required consistency.

Heat the rest of the butter in a sauté pan, add the liver and sauter quickly, turning the pieces two or three times. Add to the sauce. Soften the 60 g (2 oz) butter and add to the sauce a spoonful at a time over low heat. Finish with the rest of the Madeira and adjust the seasoning. Serve the liver in a little sauce only, together with Swiss potato cake (recipe, page 1017). (Illustration, page 240)

(Anton Mosimann, Great Britain)

Calf's liver Hungarian style
Foie de veau à la hongroise
Piritott Borjumaj Magyarosan

10 portions   Cooking time: 2-3 minutes

1 kg 800	calf's liver	4 lb
50 g	salt	2 oz
400 g	lard	14 oz'
500 g	onions, cut into rings	1 lb 2 oz
5 g	black pepper, freshly ground	⅙ oz
4 g	marjoram	⅙ oz
20 g	paprika	¾ oz
300 g	yellow peppers, seeded and cut into strips	11 oz
200 g	tomatoes, cut in quarters	7 oz

Fry the onions lightly in lard until pale golden. Add the peppers, the tomatoes and the liver which has been cut into short, thin strips. Season with salt, pepper and marjoram, sprinkle with paprika and sauter over high heat while stirring. The liver should remain pink.

Dress on a serving dish and decorate with raw peppers which have been seeded and cut into rings, and with sliced raw tomatoes. Hand boiled potatoes separately.

(Zsolt Körmendy, Hungary)

Stuffed calf's liver Schloss Klessheim
Foie de veau farci Château Klessheim
Gefüllte Kalbsleber Schloss Klessheim

8 portions

1 kg 200	calf's liver	2 lb 10 oz
120 g	ham, diced	4 oz
120 g	mushrooms	4 oz
350 g	veal sausage meat	12 oz
1¼ dl	Madeira	4 fl oz
100 g	butter	3½ oz
80 g	morels	3 oz
1 kg	veal bones	2 lb 4 oz
	salt, pepper	
	parsley	

Accompaniments:

	8 small Golden Delicious apples	
5 cl	white wine	2 fl oz
	juice of 3 lemons	

Potato croquettes:

1 kg 200	potatoes	2 lb 10 oz
	4 egg yolks	
	parsley, finely chopped	
	nutmeg, salt, pepper	

Selection of vegetables:

800 g	courgettes	1 lb 12 oz
	4 beef tomatoes	
80 g	mushrooms	3 oz
80 g	morels	3 oz
	1 leek	
50 g	butter	2 oz
1¼ dl	Madeira	4 fl oz
	salt, pepper	

Cut a pocket in the liver and pour in 6 cl (2 fl oz) Madeira. Season with salt and pepper, and flavour with parsley. Leave to marinate for 2 hours.

Mix the sausage meat well with the ham, mushrooms, morels and the Madeira used to marinate the liver. Season with salt and pepper, fill into the liver and sew up the pocket. Place the bones in a braising pan with the liver on top. Cook in the oven at about 160–170°C (320–340°F) for 2 hours 10 minutes. Rinse out the pan with the remaining Madeira to detach the cooking juices and finish with the butter.

Peel the apples, leaving them whole, and cook gently in the wine and lemon juice. Peel, boil and sieve the potatoes. Mix them with the egg yolks and add parsley, nutmeg, salt and pepper. Shape into small cakes or balls and deep-fry in vegetable fat.

Blanch the vegetables separately and toss in fresh butter. Marinate the mushrooms and morels in the Madeira, then cook in a little stock. Mix carefully with the vegetables. Pour a little gravy on to the dish. Slice the liver and arrange in the centre, with the apples on one side and the vegetables and potato croquettes on the other.
(Illustration, page 940)

(Werner Dabernig, Austria)

Calf's liver Riehen style
Foie de veau à la Riehen
Kalbsleberschnitten auf Riehener Art

10 portions

1 kg 500	calf's liver	3 lb 5 oz
	salt	
	spices as desired	
30 g	flour	1 oz
1 dl	oil	3½ fl oz
700 g	apples	1 lb 8 oz
	juice of 1 lemon	
150 g	butter	5 oz
4 dl	thickened veal stock	14 fl oz

Garnish:

700 g	noodles	1 lb 8 oz
100 g	butter	3½ oz
	salt	
	spices as desired	

Remove any skin from the liver and cut evenly into 20 slices (2 per portion). Season and flour them, then sauter quickly on both sides in hot oil in an omelette pan until medium done. Dress on a bed of fresh buttered noodles.

Peel and core the apples, then cut them into 30 g (1 oz) rings, rub with lemon juice and fry in butter until golden. Place them on the slices of liver and coat with the rest of the butter which has been browned. Hand the thickened veal stock separately. Alternatively, grill the liver and serve with fried onions or onion rings in addition to the apple rings.

The following additional accompaniments are suitable: tomatoes stuffed with peas or mushrooms; leaf spinach with roasted pine kernels; asparagus tips mimosa; broccoli.

(Otto Ledermann, Switzerland)

Braised calf's lights
Mou de veau braisé
Polmone in umido

4 portions	Cooking time: 1 hour	
400 g	calf's lights	14 oz
60 g	butter	2 oz
20 g	bacon, chopped	¾ oz
	3 small onions	
	2 carrots	
	2 tomatoes	
	celery leaves	
	4 sage leaves	
approx. 1½ l	bouillon	approx. 2¾ pt
	salt, pepper	

Boil the lights for 20 minutes and remove the white parts, then cut into small cubes. Cut the onions and carrots into Julienne strips and chop the celery leaves coarsely. Brown lightly in butter together with the chopped bacon and sage leaves. Add the lights and seasoning. Skin, seed and finely dice the tomatoes, then add to the pan. Pour in the bouillon and cook for 1 hour over low heat, or until the liquid has boiled away. Remove from the heat and sprinkle with grated Parmesan to serve.

(Guido Belotti, Enzo Ronzoni, Carlo Calvetti, Italy)

Calf's lights Prague fashion
Mou de veau à la pragueoise
Telecí plíčky po pražsku

6 portions	Cooking time: about 1 hour	
900 g	calf's lights, trimmed	2 lb
	salt	
150 g	root vegetables (carrot, celery, parsley root)	5 oz
	1 onion	
	3 allspice berries	
	5 peppercorns	

	1 bay leaf	
60 g	butter	2 oz
50 g	flour	2 oz
10 g	mustard	⅓ oz
10 g	capers	⅓ oz
2 dl	sour cream	7 fl oz
	1 tablespoon vinegar (approx.)	
100 g	ham	3½ oz
	parsley, finely chopped	
	2 lemons	

Wash the lights thoroughly in cold water and cook in salted water with the root vegetables, onion, bay leaf and spices. When tender, remove the lights, allow to cool and slice very thinly. Make a blond roux with the butter and flour. Stir in the sour cream and sufficient cold bouillon to make a thick, smooth sauce. Add the capers and mustard and cook for 15 minutes, stirring frequently. Add the lights and 80 g (3 oz) ham cut into strips. Mix well, season with salt and add vinegar to taste.

Dress in a deep dish, sprinkle with the parsley and with the rest of the ham which has been finely cut, and garnish with lemon slices. Serve with Bohemian bread dumplings (recipe, page 1025).

(Vilèm Vrabec, Czechoslovakia)

Veal medallions Falchetti
Médaillons de veau Falchetti
Medaglioni di vitello Falchetti

10 portions

	fillet of veal	3 lb 5 oz
1 kg 500	fillet of veal	3 lb 5 oz
1 dl	oil	3½ fl oz
50 g	butter	2 oz
5 cl	white wine	2 fl oz
	30 triangular croûtons, toasted	
	30 slices Fontina cheese	
	forcemeat Falchetti (recipe, page 132)	

Prepare the forcemeat and mince finely. Warm slightly just before use. Cut the veal into 30 medallions, season with salt and pepper, brown in the oil and butter, and add the wine. Keep hot. Remove the medallions and spread with forcemeat. Reduce the stock until thick. Dress the medallions on the croûtons, cover each with a thin slice of Fontina cheese and gratinate under a salamander. Pour the sauce into a warmed serving dish, place the medallions in it and serve at once.

(Manfred Wyler, Switzerland)

Veal medallions Hungarian style
Médaillons de veau à la hongroise
Piritott Borjuérmék magyarosan

10 portions   Cooking time: 10-15 minutes

1 kg 800	fillet of veal	4 lb
50 g	salt	2 oz
100 g	flour	3½ oz
300 g	lard	11 oz
200 g	onions, finely cut	7 oz
20 g	paprika	¾ oz
300 g	yellow peppers	11 oz
200 g	tomatoes	7 oz
2 kg	potatoes	4 lb 8 oz

Cook the onions in lard until lightly coloured, sprinkle with paprika, mix well, add a little water and season with salt. Stew under cover, sieve and keep hot.

Cut 5 veal medallions per portion, beat, season with salt, flour and sauter in lard. Remove and place in the onion purée. Set aside the lard remaining in the pan. Add the peppers, seeded and cut into strips, and the tomatoes, cut into quarters, to the meat, mix thoroughly, cover and stew for a short time.

Boil the potatoes in their skins, peel them, slice and sauter quickly over high heat in the lard which has been set aside. Add a little of the onion purée.

Dress the potatoes in the centre of a dish and surround with the medallions. Sprinkle these with onion purée. Decorate with raw peppers which have been seeded and cut into rings, and with sliced raw tomatoes, and serve very hot.

(Zsolt Körmendy, Hungary)

Veal medallions Magyaróvár fashion
Médaillons de veau Magyaróvár
Borjuszelet Magyaróvári módra

10 portions   Cooking time: 15-20 minutes

600 g	3 fillets of veal each weighing	1 lb 5 oz
40 g	salt	1½ oz
100 g	flour	3½ oz
250 g	lard	9 oz
400 g	ham	14 oz

| 400 g | cheese | 14 oz |
| 3 dl | gravy thickened with butter | 10 fl oz |

Duxelles:

400 g	fresh mushrooms, finely chopped	14 oz
100 g	butter	3½ oz
50 g	onions, finely cut	2 oz
	parsley, finely chopped	
10 g	salt	⅓ oz
10 g	white pepper, freshly ground	⅓ oz
10 g	nutmeg, grated	⅓ oz
	2 egg yolks	
50 g	flour	2 oz
2 dl	milk	7 fl oz
1 dl	dairy cream	3½ fl oz

Garnish:

5 portions risi-bisi
5 portions straw potatoes (optional)

Fry the onions lightly in butter until pale golden, add the mushrooms and parsley, season with salt, pepper and nutmeg, dust with flour and immediately pour in the milk, which has been heated, and the cream. Cook to a paste of spreading consistency, remove from the heat, add the egg yolks and mix well.

Trim the fillets of veal and cut each one into 10 medallions. Flatten, season with salt, flour and sauter in hot lard. Spread with duxelles, cover with a slice of ham cut to size, cover this with a slice of cheese of the same size and brown under a salamander. Dress on a base of risi-bisi and pour the gravy over. Surround with straw potatoes if desired.

(Zsolt Körmendy, Hungary)

Veal medallions Palatinus style
Médaillons de veau Palatinus
Piritott Borjuérmék Palatinus módra

10 portions

1 kg 500	fillet of veal	3 lb 5 oz
600 g	goose liver	1 lb 5 oz
50 g	salt	2 oz
100 g	flour	3½ oz
350 g	lard	12 oz
200 g	onions	7 oz
20 g	paprika	¾ oz
250 g	peas, cooked	9 oz

300 g	yellow peppers	11 oz
200 g	tomatoes	7 oz
2 kg	potatoes	4 lb 8 oz

Prepare in the same way as **Veal medallions Hungarian style.** Slice the goose liver, season with salt, flour and sauter in lard. To serve, dress the potatoes in the centre of the dish and arrange the veal medallions and slices of goose liver alternately round them. Top with the onion purée mixed with the peppers and tomatoes. Sprinkle with peas.

(Zsolt Körmendy, Hungary)

Veal medallions surprise
Médaillons de veau surprise
Kalfsbiefstuk Surprise

4 portions

150 g	4 veal medallions each weighing	5 oz
	4 slices of calf's sweetbreads	
30 g	each weighing	1 oz
160 g	mushroom duxelles	5½ oz
240 g	pie pastry	8 oz
100 g	butter	3½ oz
	2 eggs	
	salt; pepper, freshly ground	
5 cl	veal gravy	2 fl oz
	Madeira	

Fry the veal medallions in butter until medium done and allow to cool. Fry the slices of sweetbreads (which have been previously blanched) very lightly and allow to cool.

Spread the medallions with the duxelles, cover each with a slice of sweetbreads and spread this with duxelles. Pin out the pastry and divide evenly into four pieces. Enclose each medallion in pastry as smoothly and evenly as possible, making sure the ends are no thicker than the centre. Decorate the top with pastry shapes as desired, brush with egg yolk and bake in a hot oven. Serve with Madeira sauce.

(Bernard van Beurten, Netherlands)

Mignons of veal with tarragon
Mignons de veau à l'estragon
Kalbsmignons mit Estragon

5 portions

| 70 g | 10 veal medallions each weighing | 2½ oz |

100 g	butter	3½ oz
10 g	tarragon leaves	⅓ oz
3 dl	dairy cream	10 fl oz
1 dl	veal stock	3½ fl oz
1 dl	white wine	3½ fl oz
	spices as desired	

Flap mushroom risotto:

300 g	Patna rice	11 oz
120 g	butter	4 oz
100 g	dried flap mushrooms	3½ oz
40 g	onion	1½ oz
6 dl	bouillon	1 pt
	cloves	
	bay leaf	
	salt	
	a little garlic	

Season the veal medallions with salt and pepper. Fry them slowly in butter over low heat. Remove and dress on a heated serving dish. Place a blanched tarragon leaf on each one.

Detach the cooking juices with the wine, then add the veal stock, the cream and the rest of the tarragon. Season and reduce by half. Pour over the medallions. Serve with flap mushroom risotto.

To make the risotto, chop the onion finely and cook gently in 60 g (2 oz) butter until lightly coloured. Add the rice and fry for a short time without colouring. Stir in the bouillon, add the seasonings, cover and cook for about 12 minutes, stirring from time to time. The rice should be kept firm to the bite.

After half the cooking time, add the flap mushrooms which have been soaked and squeezed dry. When the rice is cooked, fold in the rest of the butter. Add a little bouillon if necessary. Serve in a deep earthenware dish.

(Otto Ledermann, Switzerland)

Sauté sweetbreads maison
Ris de veau sauté maison

4 portions

400 g	calf's sweetbreads	14 oz
	salt, pepper	
	lemon juice	
	1 egg	

	breadcrumbs as required	
100 g	butter	3½ oz

Morel tartlets:

200 g	fresh morels	7 oz
	1 tablespoon onion, finely chopped	
30 g	butter	1 oz
2 dl	dairy cream	7 fl oz
	1 teaspoon flour butter	
	4 dariole tartlets, baked blind	

Parisienne potatoes

500 g	potatoes	1 lb 2 oz
50 g	butter	2 oz
	salt	

Accompaniments:

300 g	young peas	11 oz
	4 rashers bacon	

Trim the sweetbreads, dry them in a cloth and slice thinly. Season with salt and pepper and sprinkle with a few drops of lemon juice. Egg and crumb them and fry until golden in lightly browned butter. Blanch the morels which have been well soaked. Squeeze them dry and chop coarsely. Cook the onion gently in butter and add the morels. Stir in the cream, thicken with the flour butter and season to taste. Fill into the tartlets.

Cut the potatoes into balls with a small vegetable scoop, blanch them, roast in butter in the oven until golden, and season with salt. Toss the peas in butter and season. Fry the bacon until crisp. Dress the sweetbreads on a serving dish and garnish with the bacon. Arrange the tartlets and the potatoes alternately round the sweetbreads. Serve the peas separately.

(Eric Carlström, Sweden)

Sweetbreads in Champagne sauce Polignac
Ris de veau au Champagne Polignac

6 portions

1 kg	calf's sweetbreads	2 lb
	1 teaspoon salt	
40 g	flour	1½ oz
	¼ teaspoon salt	
	¼ teaspoon pepper	
40 g	butter (to cook sweetbreads)	1½ oz

¼ l	Champagne	9 fl oz
⅛ l	dairy cream	4 fl oz
¼ l	Suprême sauce (recipe, page 177)	9 fl oz
	juice of 1 lemon	
	2 tablespoons truffles or morels, chopped	
80 g	mushrooms, sliced	3 oz
	1 tablespoon butter (to cook mushrooms)	

Blanch the sweetbreads for 5 minutes in boiling water containing 1 teaspoon salt. Drain and plunge into cold, running water. Slip off the thin outside membrane with the fingers. Cut away any dark veins and thick, connective tissue. Combine the flour, salt and pepper in a shallow dish. Melt the butter in a saucepan.

When it foams, roll the sweetbreads in the seasoned flour, then sauter in the butter until uniformly golden brown. Pour off the excess butter, add the Champagne and reduce by half. Pour in the cream and bring to the boil. Add the Suprême sauce and simmer for 40 minutes.

Remove the sweetbreads from the sauce and place in a shallow dish. Strain the sauce, add the lemon juice, truffles or morels, and the mushrooms which have been sautéd in 1 tablespoon butter. Simmer for a further 5 minutes and pour over the sweetbreads.

(Hermann Rusch, USA)

Sweetbread croustade Florentine with sabayon Villeneuve
Croustade de ris de veau florentine – sabayon Villeneuve
Krustade von Kalbsmilch auf florentiner Art mit Sabayon Villeneuve

10 portions

1 kg 200	calf's sweetbreads	2 lb 10 oz
2 kg	spinach	4 lb 8 oz
400 g	puff pastry	14 oz
100 g	butter	3½ oz
10 g	truffles, sliced	⅓ oz
	seasonings to taste	
50 g	onions	2 oz
20 g	shallots	¾ oz

Sabayon Villeneuve:

10 g	shallot, finely chopped	⅓ oz
2½ dl	white wine (Villeneuve)	9 fl oz
	2 egg yolks	
	2 eggs	
	lemon juice	

pepper, freshly ground
salt

Pin out the pastry and cut into rounds. Egg wash and rest for 30 minutes, then bake in an oven preheated to 200°C (392°F). Wash and soak the sweetbreads in cold water, then blanch for 3 to 4 minutes. Allow to cool, trim carefully, then stand aside for a few hours between two boards with a small weight on top. Cut into slices, season and fry on both sides in butter without colouring. Clean the spinach thoroughly and stew in butter with the onions and shallots. Season to taste.

To make the sabayon, place 5 cl (2 fl oz) white wine in a pan with the shallot and reduce well. Add to the egg yolks and whole eggs together with the rest of the wine and whisk in a bain-marie. Add lemon juice, pepper and salt to taste. This sauce is made at the last minute, just before serving.

To serve, dress the pastry bases on a well warmed silver dish, place the spinach on top, cover with the slices of sweetbread and garnish with the truffles. Hand the sauce separately.

(Otto Ledermann, Switzerland)

Spring sweetbreads
Ris de veau à la printanière
Borjumirigy tavaszi köritéssel

5 portions   Cooking time: 20 minutes

160 g	calf's sweetbreads each weighing	5½ oz
200 g	butter	7 oz
	1 bay leaf	
	5 choice chanterelles	
100 g	carrots, sliced	3½ oz
100 g	celeriac, sliced	3½ oz
100 g	leeks, sliced	3½ oz
2 dl	white wine	7 fl oz
	1 bunch parsley, chopped	
	salt, pepper	

Soak the sweetbreads in cold water, blanch in boiling salted water, refresh and dry with a cloth. Line a stew pan with the carrots, celeriac and leeks. Place the sweetbreads on top, sprinkle with melted butter, add the wine and bay leaf, cover and cook for 20 minutes in an oven preheated to 200°C (392°F).

Meanwhile clean and wash the chanterelles carefully, sauter them in a little butter and season with salt and pepper. To serve, place the vegetables on a dish and dress the sweetbreads on top.

Decorate each portion with a chanterelle. Sprinkle with the cooking juices and the parsley.

(Gyula Gullner, Hungary)

Sweetbreads Schloss Fuschl
Ris de veau Château Fuschl
Kalbsmilch Schloss Fuschl

6 portions

500 g	calf's sweetbreads, blanched	1 lb 2 oz
2½ dl	white wine	9 fl oz
	1 lemon	
	2 fresh bay leaves	
	5 sprigs fresh rosemary	
	4 juniper berries	
5 dl	veal stock	18 fl oz

Veal forcemeat:

250 g	veal	9 oz
	1 egg	
150 g	leaf spinach, blanched	5 oz
	2 ice cubes	
	Aromat, salt	

Sauce:

800 g	carrots	1 lb 12 oz
2½ dl	white wine	9 fl oz
	juice of 2 lemons	
	juice of half an orange	
2½ dl	carrot juice	9 fl oz
60 g	mushrooms	2 oz
	1 teaspoon cornflour	
	a few Swiss chard leaves cut in strips	
	salt, pepper	

Accompaniments:

480 g	fresh asparagus	1 lb
	6 Swiss chard leaves	
50 g	butter	2 oz
	potatoes	
10 g	parsley, chopped	⅓ oz

Clean and trim the sweetbreads. Place in a pan with the veal stock, wine, lemon, bay leaves, rosemary and juniper berries, cook gently for 20 minutes and leave in a cool place. To make the forcemeat, work the veal to a fine purée in the mixer with the egg, Aromat, salt and ice.

Drain the spinach and squeeze dry. Mix the sweetbreads with the spinach and about 120 g (4 oz) forcemeat and shape into a roll.

Cut the carrots into thin julienne strips and marinate in the lemon and orange juice together with 1¼ dl (4 fl oz) white wine for 6 to 8 hours. Squeeze them dry and mix with the rest of the forcemeat. Place on a piece of aluminium foil and wrap round the sweetbreads. Bake at 160°C (320°F) for 35 to 40 minutes.

Prepare the sauce with the marinade, the rest of the wine, a little veal stock and the carrot juice. Cook the strips of Swiss chard in it, together with the mushrooms which have been cut in half. Thicken the sauce with the cornflour and season with salt, pepper and Aromat. Cook the asparagus and wrap in the Swiss chard leaves which have been blanched. Sprinkle with butter. Boil the potatoes in salted water, and sprinkle with butter and with parsley.

To serve, slice the sweetbreads, dress on a dish and pour a little sauce round the slices. Garnish with the asparagus and the parsley potatoes. Hand the rest of the sauce separately. (Illustration, page 941)

(Werner Dabernig, Austria)

Sweetbreads with truffles and leeks
Ris de veau aux truffes et aux poireaux
Animelle di vitello al tartufo e porri

4 portions

1 kg	calf's sweetbreads	2 lb 4 oz
100–150 g	black truffles	4–5 oz
3 dl	white wine	10 fl oz
150 g	butter	5 oz
600 g	leeks	1 lb 5 oz
2 dl	brown stock	7 fl oz
	juice of 1 lemon	
150 g	mirepoix	5 oz
1 dl	white vinegar	3½ fl oz
20 g	shallots	¾ oz

Blanch the sweetbreads for 4 to 5 minutes in salted water containing the lemon juice, vinegar and mirepoix. Refresh in cold water. Remove any inedible gristly tissue and fat, then carefully slip off the outer membrane.

Brown the shallots in the butter, add the sweetbreads and colour lightly on both sides, turning carefully. Detach the sediment with the white wine and reduce. Brush and wash the truffles and add to the pan. Transfer to an oven preheated to 220°C (428°F) and cook for 35 to 50 minutes, depending on the size of the sweetbreads. After the first 20 minutes or so, add 50 g

(2 oz) melted butter, together with the brown stock. Baste and turn the sweetbreads and truffles frequently while cooking.

Cut up the leeks and blanch in salted water. Prepare a sauce with the stock in which the sweetbreads were cooked and the rest of the butter. Dress the sweetbreads on a serving dish and arrange the truffles and leeks alternately round the edge. Coat the sweetbreads with the sauce. (Illustration, page 418)

(Ivo Balestra, Switzerland)

Calf's kidneys with sausage and flap mushrooms
Rognons de veau avec saucisse à rôtir et cèpes
Rognone di vitello con salsiccia e funghi

4 portions

	2 calf's kidneys	
	1 clove of garlic	
1–2 dl	bouillon	4–7 fl oz
	4 tomatoes, peeled (canned)	
20 g	dried flap mushrooms	¾ oz
300 g	continental frying sausage	11 oz
1–2 dl	white wine	4–7 fl oz
	oil and butter as required	

Soak the flap mushrooms in lukewarm water. Trim the kidneys, wash thoroughly and slice. Brown the garlic in oil and butter, add the kidneys and sauter, season with a little freshly ground pepper, pour in the bouillon, add the tomatoes which have been crushed, then add the flap mushrooms which have been soaked, and cook slowly over low heat.

Cut up the sausage and poach in white wine in a separate pan. When the wine has boiled away, allow the sausage to cook in its own fat. Pour off the fat and add the sausage to the pan containing the kidneys. Mix carefully, dish and serve hot, with polenta as an accompaniment. (Illustration, page 519)

(Franco Colombani, Italy)

Calf's kidneys with chipolatas
Rognons de veau et chipolatas
Kalbsnieren mit Chipolata

6 portions

approx. 750 g	calf's kidneys, sliced (12 slices)	approx.	1 lb 10 oz

	with a layer of external fat	
	½ cm (¼ in) thick	
	6 chipolatas	
	6 slices dried meat	
200 g	Brussels sprouts, trimmed	7 oz
200 g	Parisian carrots	7 oz
200 g	chestnuts	7 oz
	potato croquettes	
	salt	
	pepper, freshly ground	
	celery salt	
	sage	
120 g	foie gras loaf	4 oz
	oil	
	butter	
¼ l	demi-glace sauce	9 fl oz
	Madeira	
50 g	truffles, chopped	2 oz

Fry the slices of kidney in a sauté pan in hot oil, then season with salt, pepper and sage. Drain on a wire rack. Pour off the oil and stir in the demi-glace sauce, together with a little Madeira, to detach the sediment. Add the foie gras loaf and pass through a fine sieve. Add the truffles which have been finely chopped. Fry the chipolatas and the dried meat lightly in butter. Prepare the Brussels sprouts, carrots and chestnuts separately and glaze them. Season the chestnuts with celery salt.

To serve, dress the slices of kidney on one side of a heated dish. Cover the other side with an alternating arrangement of sliced dried meat, Brussels sprouts, carrots, chipolatas and chestnuts. Sprinkle the contents of the dish with brown butter. Serve with the sauce and with potato croquettes which have been deep-fried in oil.

(Otto Brust, Germany)

Calf's kidneys Greenbrier
Rognons de veau Greenbrier

4 portions

	4 calf's kidneys	
	½ teaspoon salt	
	½ teaspoon pepper	
	¼ teaspoon dried thyme leaves	
	4 tablespoons butter	
	2 tablespoons shallots, peeled and chopped	
40 g	dried morels, soaked in lukewarm water	1½ oz

¼ l	dry white wine	9 fl oz
¼ l	dairy cream	9 fl oz
	1 teaspoon meat glaze (recipe, page 122)	
	juice of 1 lemon	
	2 tablespoons brandy	
	8 toasted croûtons, cut into heart shapes	
	2 tablespoons melted butter	

Trim the fat from the kidneys. Scald them in boiling water for 2 minutes, then rinse in cold water. Remove the skin and cut the kidneys into quarters. Cut away and discard the white veins and hard portions. Slice the kidneys in thin slivers. Season with salt, pepper and thyme. Melt the 4 tablespoons butter in a frying pan and sauter the kidneys for 2 minutes. Transfer to a heated dish. Add the shallots to the pan and brown them over medium heat. Add the drained morels and heat them well. Pour in the wine and reduce by half, then add the cream and meat glaze and bring to the boil. Reduce the heat and simmer for 5 minutes. Add the kidneys and lemon juice and return to the boil. Transfer to a serving dish and sprinkle with brandy. Brush the croûtons with the melted butter and place on top.

(Hermann Rusch, USA)

Calf's kidney Liége style
Rognon de veau à la liégeoise

2 portions   Cooking time: 15 minutes

500–600 g	1 calf's kidney weighing	1–1¼ lb
50 g	butter	2 oz
	1 teaspoon juniper berries, chopped	
5 cl	gin	2 fl oz

Wash and soak the kidney thoroughly, trim and remove the fat, then cut the kidney in half. Fry it on both sides in butter in a copper pan. Add the juniper berries, cook for a further 2 minutes, then stir in the gin to detach the sediment. Serve in the pan surrounded with potatoes trimmed to the size and shape of olives.

(André Béghin, Belgium)

Stuffed calf's kidney on Swiss chard
Rognon de veau farci sur blettes
Gefüllte Kalbsniere auf Mangold

2 portions

| | 1 calf's kidney | |

5 cl	milk	2 fl oz

Veal forcemeat:

300 g	veal trimmed of sinew	11 oz
	2 ice cubes	
	1 egg	
	salt, pepper	
40 g	white bread without crust	1½ oz
20 g	dried morels, soaked and sliced	¾ oz
	1 tablespoon brandy	
8 g	green pepper	¼ oz
	1 pork caul	
	1 tablespoon parsley, chopped	
	3 fresh mushrooms	
	2 tomatoes, coarsely diced	

Swiss chard:

300 g	Swiss chard	11 oz
	salt, pepper	

Soak the kidney, remove the fat, slit open and cut away the white vessels and hard tissue. Steep in the milk for 1 day. To make the forcemeat, work the veal to a purée in the mixer with the ice, egg, bread, salt and pepper. Mix half the forcemeat with the morels and fill into the kidney. Mix the remainder with the brandy and the green pepper, then spread on the caul and roll up to enclose the kidney. Braise in the oven for 30 to 35 minutes.

Remove the kidney, add the parsley, mushrooms and tomatoes to the pan and cook gently for a time. Blanch the Swiss chard and season well. To serve, slice the kidney and dress on the Swiss chard. Pour the sauce over. Serve with fried potatoes.
(Ilustration, page 942)

(Werner Dabernig, Austria)

Veal and kidney roast
Rognonnade de veau
Gerollter Kalbsnierenbraten

20 portions

approx. 5 kg	boned loin of veal	approx.	11 lb
1¼ dl	oil		4 fl oz
OR 120 g	vegetable fat		4 oz
	salt, pepper		
	a little water		
	mirepoix of		
100 g	carrots		3½ oz

100 g	onions	3½ oz
80 g	celery	3 oz
	1 tablespoon tomato purée	
3 l	veal stock	5 pt
	3-4 calf's kidneys	

Stuffing:

500 g	veal sausage meat	1 lb 2 oz
100 g	white bread without crust	3½ oz
approx. 1 dl	cold milk	approx. 4 fl oz
300 g	veal, trimmed of sinew	11 oz
	1 egg	
6 cl	dairy cream	2 fl oz
	a pinch of nutmeg	
	salt	
	forcemeat flavouring	

To make the stuffing, soak the bread in the cold milk and squeeze dry. Mince finely with the veal. Mix with the egg and cream, then with the sausage meat. Add seasonings to taste and mix well. Trim the loin of veal neatly and spread with the stuffing. Remove most of the fat from the kidneys and season them. If they are large, cut in half lengthwise. Arrange along the saddle fillet of the loin and roll up the meat tightly, starting at the fillet. Tie round securely with twine, starting at the ends to keep the kidneys in place. Season with salt and pepper and place in a braising pan on a bed of veal bones which have been chopped into small pieces. Add the oil or vegetable fat and roast at 200°C (392°F) for about 2 hours, basting frequently and adding only sufficient water to prevent excessive browning.

When cooked, remove the meat and finish the sauce. Add the mirepoix to the bones in the pan and brown, together with the tomato purée. Stir in the veal stock and reduce to 2 l (3½ pt). Pass the sauce through a hair sieve and hand separately.

The meat may be roasted without the veal bones, but in this case the bones should be used to prepare stock and the sauce should be made separately. Serve with glazed carrots, asparagus tips, artichoke bottoms filled with peas, and parsley potatoes.
(Illustration, page 871)

(Helmuth Stadlbauer, Austria)

Escalopes of veal kidney Père André
Escalopes de rognons de veau Père André

2 portions

| 500 g | calf's kidney | 1 lb 2 oz |
| | salt, white pepper | |

100 g	fresh breadcrumbs	3½ oz
60 g	Gruyère cheese, grated	2 oz
80 g	butter	3 oz
100 g	noodles	3½ oz
30 g	ham	1 oz
	2 mushrooms	
	1 tomato, skinned and seeded	
	garlic	

Sauce:

5 cl	veal stock	2 fl oz
3 cl	Cognac	1 fl oz
15 g	butter	½ oz
	salt, pepper	

Wash and soak the kidney well, trim and remove the fat and core, then cut in half. Slice each half obliquely into escalopes about 1 cm (⅜ in) thick. Season with salt and finely chopped white pepper. Coat with flour, then with the breadcrumbs which have been mixed with the cheese. Fry over gentle heat in 50 g (2 oz) butter. Arrange the escalopes in a ring on a round dish and keep hot.

Cut the ham and mushrooms into fine julienne strips and sauter in butter together with the tomato which has been diced and flavoured with very little garlic. Blanch and drain the noodles, toss them in 15 g (½ oz) butter, add the ham and mushroom julienne, mix well and dress in the centre of the dish. Discard the butter in the sauté pan, stir in the Cognac to detach the sediment, add the veal stock, reduce, finish the sauce with butter and adjust the seasoning.

(André Béghin, Belgium)

Cushion of veal Aurélie
Noix de veau Aurélie

8 portions

approx. 2 kg	cushion of veal	approx.	4 lb 8 oz
	3 eggs		
	1 broad slice pork fat		
	2 carrots		
	2 onions		
	5 sprigs thyme		
	2 bay leaves		
4 dl	light stock		14 fl oz
2 dl	whisky		7 fl oz
500 g	mushrooms		1 lb 2 oz
2 kg	potatoes		4 lb 8 oz
	1 clove of garlic		
1 dl	dairy cream		3½ fl oz

	1 slice ham	
	8 medium tomatoes	
200 g	breadcrumbs	7 oz
500 g	butter	1 lb 2 oz
2 kg	leaf spinach	4 lb 8 oz

Forcemeat:

200 g	chicken livers	7 oz
200 g	lean pork	7 oz
100 g	cushion of veal trimmings	3½ oz
	2 eggs	
12 g	salt	½ oz
3 g	allspice	a good pinch
2 g	pepper	a pinch
1 dl	whisky	3½ fl oz
	1 tablespoon chives, chopped	
	1 tablespoon parsley, chopped	

To make the forcemeat, mince the meat and chicken livers twice, using the finest cutter, then add the beaten eggs, the whisky, chives, parsley and seasoning. Mix very well. Remove any skin from the veal, trim it and slit to make a pocket. Brush inside with egg white and stuff with the forcemeat. Sew up the opening, tie round, wrap in the slice of pork fat and braise with the vegetables. Remove the pork fat after 45 minutes, detach the sediment with white wine and 1 dl (3½ fl oz) whisky, and cook for a further 20 minutes over very low heat.

Meanwhile prepare the garnish. Make a Duchesse mixture with potatoes, butter and eggs. Using a savoy bag fitted with a tube, pipe 8 bouchées on to a greased baking sheet, brush with egg yolk and bake. Prepare a duxelles with the mushrooms which have been finely chopped, except for 8 of them which have been turned and grooved to be used for decoration, the ham which has been finely diced, and the butter.

Fill the potato bouchées with the duxelles. Decorate each one with a grooved mushroom. Hollow out the tomatoes, stuff them with the rest of the forcemeat, and cook carefully in the oven. Blanch the spinach, squeeze it dry, cook gently in butter and fill into 8 small round moulds. Carve the veal, strain the stock and pour over the meat, and arrange the items of garnish alternately on the same dish.

(André Béghin, Belgium)

Cushion of veal with peas
Noix de veau aux petits pois
Ternera Asada con Guisantes

6 portions   Cooking time: about 1 hour

1 kg 200	cushion of veal	2 lb 10 oz

400 g	peas	14 oz
150 g	lard	5 oz
	1 onion, sliced	
	1 clove of garlic	
	1 bay leaf	
	1 sprig thyme	
	1 cinnamon quill	
	1 sprig oregano	
	8 peppercorns	
	3 cloves	
1 dl	white wine	3½ fl oz
5 cl	marc brandy (grappa)	2 fl oz

Melt the lard in a casserole and brown the veal which has been seasoned with salt. Transfer to a preheated oven and roast under cover. Add the onion, herbs and spices. When the onion is lightly browned, stir in the wine and grappa, reduce completely, add a little water and braise until the meat is tender. Remove, cut into slices and place in another casserole. Strain the sauce over the meat, sprinkle with the peas which have been cooked and continue cooking in a cool oven for a few minutes before serving.

(Josep Lladonosa, Spain)

Veal paprika
Ragoût de veau au paprika
Borjupaprikás

10 portions

2 kg	shoulder or knuckle of veal	4 lb 8 oz
250 g	lard	9 oz
300 g	onions, finely chopped	11 oz
30 g	paprika	1 oz
50 g	salt	2 oz
300 g	yellow peppers, seeded and cut into strips	11 oz
150 g	tomatoes, cut into quarters	5 oz
5 dl	sour cream	18 fl oz
2 dl	dairy cream	7 fl oz
	flour	

Bone the meat and cut into 3 cm (1¼ in) cubes. Wash these well. Fry the onions gently in the lard until lightly coloured, sprinkle with the paprika, add a little water and boil for 1 or 2 minutes while stirring. Add the meat, season with salt and stir-fry until lightly browned. Add a little water if necessary, cover and braise, stirring frequently and adding a little warm water if required. When the meat is half cooked, add the tomatoes and peppers and finish cooking.

Mix the sour cream and fresh cream with a little flour, add to the meat and cook for a further 3 or 4 minutes. If the sauce is too thick, dilute it with a little water. Serve with *nockerln* (recipe, page 962) or boiled rice.

(Zsolt Körmendy, Hungary)

Veal pörkölt
Ragoût de veau à la hongroise
Borjupörkölt

10 portions   Cooking time: 30–40 minutes

2 kg	shoulder or knuckle of veal	4 lb 8 oz
300 g	lard	11 oz
400 g	onions, finely chopped	14 oz
20 g	garlic, crushed	¾ oz
40 g	paprika	1½ oz
50 g	salt	2 oz
50 g	tomato purée	2 oz
300 g	yellow peppers, seeded and cut into strips	11 oz
150 g	tomatoes, cut in four or six, depending on size	5 oz

Bone the meat, cut into 3 cm (1¼ in) cubes, and wash. Fry the onions gently in the lard until lightly coloured, sprinkle with the paprika and mix with the garlic. Stir in the tomato purée, add a little water and boil for a few minutes while stirring. Add the meat, season with salt, cover and braise over high heat, stirring occasionally and adding warm water if required. When the meat is half cooked, add the tomatoes and peppers and finish cooking. Dust with flour and cook for a few minutes longer without allowing the sauce to become too thick.

Serve in a deep dish with *nockerln* (recipe, page 962) or boiled potatoes as an accompaniment. If the pörkölt is preferred with a little fatty gravy instead of sauce, the flour should be omitted and the amount of water reduced.

(Zsolt Körmendy, Hungary)

Veal sauté with tomatoes
Sauté de veau aux tomates

4 portions

700–800 g	shoulder of veal	1½–1¾ lb
1 kg	beef tomatoes	2 lb 4 oz
200 g	mirepoix of leeks, carrots, celery, onion, parsley	7 oz

100 g	smoked bacon rind	3½ oz
50 g	butter	2 oz
60 g	flour	2 oz
1 l	brown veal stock	1¾ pt
½ l	dry Moselle wine	18 fl oz
300 g	macaroni	11 oz
	1 tablespoon tomato purée	
	salt	
	pepper, freshly ground	
	marjoram	
	thyme	
	cloves	

Dice the meat and fry in butter until lightly coloured. Add the mirepoix, tomato purée and bacon rind. Dust with the flour, cover and cook in the oven without adding liquid. Skin and seed the tomatoes, and cut them in quarters. Add the skins and seeds to the meat and then the wine together with the herbs and spices; stir in the veal stock. Cover and braise over low heat or in an oven preheated to 180 to 190°C (355 to 375°F) for about 40 minutes.

When the meat is tender, pass the sauce through a strainer and add the tomato quarters. To serve, place the meat in a warmed deep dish and pour the sauce with the tomato quarters over. Hand macaroni separately.

(Germain Gertsch-Rösner, Luxembourg)

Ragoût of veal Hasharon

6 portions

1 kg 200	shoulder of veal, diced	2 lb 10 oz
	cloves	
	bay leaves	
	bouillon	
	cornflour	
	white pepper, freshly ground	
	salt	
	white wine	
	2 avocados	
200 g	sweet corn	7 oz
	1 tomato pepper (gamba), cut into	
	julienne strips	

Place the veal, salt, pepper, cloves and bay leaves in a stew pan and pour in sufficient white wine and bouillon to cover. Cook until tender. Blend the cornflour with a little water and stir into the ragoût to thicken. Cut out small balls of avocado and add to the ragoût, together with the cooked sweet corn and the gamba which has been lightly cooked in oil. Return to the boil. Dress in a heated serving dish and hand curried rice separately.

(Hermann Wohl, Israel)

Skewered beef olives Hôtel des Bergues
Brochettes de paupiettes de veau Hôtel des Bergues
Gefüllte Kalbsröllchen Hôtel des Bergues

10 portions

1 kg	loin of veal, boned	2 lb 4 oz
1 l	thickened brown veal stock	1¾ pt
200 g	raw ham	7 oz
600 g	duxelles	1 lb 5 oz
100 g	foie gras mousse	3½ oz
	oil	

Rice pilaf:

800 g	rice	1 lb 12 oz
50 g	butter	2 oz
100 g	onions	3½ oz
1 l	light veal stock	1¾ pt

Ratatouille:

1 kg	courgettes	2 lb 4 oz
50 g	onions	2 oz
500 g	tomatoes	1 lb 2 oz
500 g	red, green and yellow peppers	1 lb 2 oz
500 g	aubergines	1 lb 2 oz
2 dl	oil	7 fl oz
	parsley	
	oregano	

Cut the veal and the raw ham into 40 slices. Beat the veal to flatten the slices evenly. Cover with the duxelles and the foie gras mousse, roll up and wrap in the slices of ham. Impale on small wooden skewers, four veal birds on each one. Fry in oil over gentle heat until golden. Dress the skewered veal birds on rice pilaf, garnish with the ratatouille and pour the thickened brown veal stock round the edge.

(Otto Ledermann, Switzerland)

Veal olives Marienbad style
Paupiettes de veau Marienbad
Mariánskolázeňské závitky

6 portions   Cooking time: 50-60 minutes

150 g	6 veal escalopes each weighing	5 oz
50 g	white bread *or* rolls	2 oz
⅛ l	milk	4 fl oz
	2 egg yolks	
	1 teaspoon parsley, chopped	
100 g	ham, chopped	3½ oz
100 g	mushrooms, cleaned and diced	3½ oz
20 g	butter	¾ oz
10 g	onion, finely chopped	⅓ oz
	salt, a large pinch of pepper	
80–100 g	lard	3–3½ oz
1 dl	white wine	3½ fl oz
1½ dl	sour cream	5 fl oz
	1 tablespoon cornflour	
	flour	

Snip the edges of the escalopes a few times, flatten and season lightly with salt. Soak the bread in milk, squeeze dry or sieve, and mix with the egg yolks, parsley and ham, the mushrooms which have been stewed in the butter with the onion, and salt and pepper to taste. Spread on the escalopes, roll up and secure with small wooden skewers or special clamps. Dust the top lightly with flour and brown on all sides in hot lard. Stir in the wine to detach the sediment, cover and cook until tender. Blend the cornflour with the sour cream, stir into the sauce to thicken and add salt to taste.

(Vilèm Vrabec, Czechoslovakia)

Veal roll Casareccia style
Roulade de veau à la bourgeoise
Rotolo di carne alla casareccia

8 portions   Cooking time: 1½ hours

1 kg 500	breast of veal	3 lb 5 oz
300 g	curd cheese	11 oz
150 g	ham	5 oz
50 g	butter	2 oz
150 g	walnut kernels	5 oz
150 g	pistachio nuts	5 oz
150 g	olives, stoned	5 oz
	1 onion, diced	
	2 carrots, diced	
5 cl	Cognac	2 fl oz
½ l	bouillon	18 fl oz
2 dl	white wine	7 fl oz

rosemary, sage
celery leaves
salt
pepper
oil

Beat the veal well to flatten and sprinkle with salt and pepper. Chop the ham, nuts and olives very finely, mix with the cheese to a paste of spreading consistency, season and spread on the meat. Roll up and tie securely. Heat the butter in a braising pan with a little oil until melted, brown the meat on all sides, add the vegetables and brown, stir in the wine to detach the sediment, bring to the boil, then braise in the oven for 1½ hours, basting very frequently with Cognac and bouillon.

(Guido Belotti, Enzo Ronzoni, Carlo Calvetti, Italy)

Saddle of veal with green asparagus
Selle de veau aux asperges vertes
Borjugerinc zöld spàrgável

5 portions

1 kg 500	saddle of veal with kidney	3 lb 5 oz
250 g	goose liver, finely diced	9 oz
200 g	butter	7 oz
100 g	onions, finely cut	3½ oz
1 dl	sweet red wine	3½ fl oz
50 g	flour	2 oz
1 kg	green asparagus	2 lb 4 oz
	salt	
	pepper	

Trim the veal, cutting away all sinew. Season well with salt to ensure that the salt penetrates the thick parts of the saddle while roasting. Place the meat in a roasting tray with the kidney. Add 100 g (3½ oz) butter and a little water, and roast in an oven preheated to 150°C (302°F), basting frequently.

Melt a little butter in a sauté pan and fry the onions gently until lightly coloured. Add the goose liver and sauter over high heat until no blood escapes from the pieces of liver. Season with salt and pepper while cooking. Dust with the flour, moisten with the wine and bring to the boil. Remove from the heat and mash the liver well with a wooden spoon.

When the veal is cooked, carefully cut the meat and kidney off the bone. Spread the saddle bone with the goose liver purée, slice the meat and kidney and arrange on top.

To serve, dress on a heated dish, cover with the asparagus and sprinkle with the cooking juices. Decorate with fried tomatoes if desired.

(Gyula Gullner, Hungary)

Veal roll Karlsbad style
Roulade de veau à la Karlsbad
Karlovarská ruláda

6 portions   Cooking time: about 1½ hours

900 g	boneless veal (shoulder or breast)	2 lb
	salt	
150 g	lean smoked bacon, thinly sliced	5 oz
130 g	butter	4½ oz
	4 eggs	
15 g	capers, finely chopped	½ oz
	bouillon	
	12 firm medium tomatoes, skinned and stewed	
	6 gherkins	

Rinse the meat, remove any skin, slit to open out into a large oblong, flatten well and season with salt. Cover with the slices of bacon. Scramble the eggs with 10 g (⅓ oz) butter, spread on the bacon and sprinkle with the capers. Roll up and tie round with thread spiral fashion. Brown well on all sides in hot butter, add the chopped up veal bones and roast for 1¼ to 1½ hours at 230–240°C (445–465°F). Baste frequently with the cooking juices, adding a little bouillon if necessary.

Remove from the pan, untie and keep hot. Add a little bouillon and butter to the pan, season with salt to taste, boil up for a moment and strain. Slice the meat, dress on a heated dish and garnish with stewed tomatoes and gherkin fans. Hand the gravy separately. Alternatively the meat may be spread with mustard and covered with slices of ham and Emmental cheese instead of bacon before roasting. Serve with fried potatoes and vegetable salad.

(Vilèm Vrabec, Czechoslovakia)

Veal olives with blackberry sauce
Paupiettes de veau truffées avec sauce aux mûres
Farseret Kalverulle i Brombar

4 portions

500 g	cushion of veal	1 lb 2 oz

100 g	butter	3½ oz
	2 carrots, sliced	
	2 onions, sliced	
	1 bouquet garni	
10 g	flour	⅓ oz
50 g	fresh spinach, blanched	2 oz

Forcemeat:

200 g	boneless veal (shoulder)	7 oz
200 g	pork fat or bacon	7 oz
10 g	parsley, chopped	⅓ oz
	1 egg	
	salt, pepper	
20 g	truffle, chopped	¾ oz
100 g	chicken liver	3½ oz

Sauce:

200 g	blackberries	7 oz
80 g	sugar	3 oz
¼ dl	lemon juice	1 fl oz
½ dl	orange juice	2 fl oz
½ dl	wine vinegar	2 fl oz
½ dl	plum brandy	2 fl oz
4 dl	water	14 fl oz
50 g	butter	2 oz
	salt, pepper	

To make the forcemeat, pass the pork fat or bacon and the veal through the finest blade of the mincer, season and add the parsley, the truffle, the beaten egg and the chicken liver which has been diced; sauté and allow to cool. The forcemeat should be smooth and light.

Brown the veal in butter, pour off the butter and add 1½ l (2¾ pt) water. Cook under cover and allow to cool. Cut the meat evenly into 5 slices, trim to an oval shape, season with salt and pepper and cover with the spinach. Divide the forcemeat between the 5 slices of meat and roll up to make veal birds 10 cm (4 in) long and 4 cm (1½ in) thick. Sew up the ends with thread.

Sauter the onions and carrots in 25 g (1 oz) butter, add the bouquet garni and the veal birds, dust with flour and roast for 15 minutes at 220°C (428°F), turning the meat from time to time. Add the veal gravy, cover and braise in the oven for 1 hour, then remove the thread and keep the veal birds hot. Strain the stock, remove the fat and reduce to about 3 dl (10 fl oz). Use for the sauce.

Make a syrup from 50 g (2 oz) sugar and 2 dl (7 fl oz) water. Bring to the boil and add 100 g (3½ oz) blackberries, using the choicest ones for this purpose. Set beside for decoration. Boil together the rest of the sugar and 2 dl (7 fl oz) water and allow to caramelise lightly. Stir in the vinegar, add the rest of the blackberries immediately, then the orange and lemon juice, the plum brandy and the reduced stock, and reduce for 10 minutes, stirring and skimming constantly. Check the seasoning, strain and finish with the butter. Place the veal birds in this sauce and warm slightly over gentle heat.

To serve, place a veal bird on each plate and coat with sauce. Cut the fifth veal bird into eight slices and place two on each plate next to the whole veal bird. Surround with the stewed blackberries which were set aside. Hand Duchesse potatoes separately.

(Jens Peter Kolbeck, Denmark)

Best end of veal Donizetti
Carré de veau Donizetti
Carré di vitello alla Donizetti

10 portions

3 kg	best end of veal	6 lb 10 oz
1 kg	fresh flap mushrooms	2 lb 4 oz
1 kg	white beans	2 lb 4 oz
500 g	streaky bacon, diced	1 lb 2 oz
	6 egg yolks	
	1 large onion, coarsely diced	
	3 sticks celery, coarsely diced	
	3 carrots, coarsely diced	
	3 bay leaves	
	1 sprig rosemary	
	3 cloves of garlic	
½ l	white wine	18 fl oz
100 g	parsley, finely chopped	3½ oz
500 g	maize meal	1 lb 2 oz
2½ l	water (for polenta)	4½ pt
2–2½ dl	sunflower oil	7–9 fl oz
	bouillon as required	
	water as required	
	salt, pepper	

Soak the beans on the previous day. Place in a bain-marie before use. Brown the bacon in a little butter or oil, add the beans, cover with bouillon and water and cook, stirring repeatedly. Add a little bouillon if necessary. The cooked beans should be dry. Pass through a sieve or vegetable mill, mix well with the egg yolks and keep hot.

Make fairly thick polenta from the maize meal and water, stirring vigorously while cooking. Pour on to a buttered rectangular tray 2 cm (¾ in) deep and of the same size as the best end of veal, and leave until cold, to make a base for the meat.

Trim the best end neatly, cut away the fat and brown on both sides in oil in a frying pan over high heat. Add the vegetables, herbs and garlic. Wrap the bones in aluminium foil to prevent burning. Place the pan with its contents in an oven preheated to 200–220°C (392–428°F) and roast for about 2 hours, turning the meat frequently so that it cooks evenly and moistening frequently with white wine.

Meanwhile wash and clean the flap mushrooms thoroughly and marinate the caps and stalks in very little oil, salt and pepper. Slice thinly, sauter in very little oil containing a clove of garlic and keep hot.

Turn out the polenta and hollow out a little. Fill with a thin layer of bean purée and one of flap mushrooms and smooth over. Remove the veal from the oven and carve to provide one slice with bone and one without per portion. Spread each slice with bean purée. Place a thin layer of mushrooms between the slices and restore the best end to its original shape. Spread carefully with the rest of the bean purée and dress on the polenta base. Brown in the oven at 220°C (428°F). Before serving place a cutlet frill on the end of each bone.

(Francesco Borari, Italy)

Veal quenelles with rice pilaf
Quenelles de veau en bordure de riz
Kalbfleischklösschen im Reisrand

6 portions

400 g	lean veal without sinew	14 oz
1/8 l	dairy cream	4 fl oz
	salt	
	bouillon as required	
1/8 l	water	4 fl oz
35 g	white vegetable fat	1¼ oz
65 g	flour	2¼ oz
	2-3 eggs	

Rice pilaf:

300 g	long grain rice	11 oz
	1 onion, finely chopped	
	bouillon	
250 g	butter	9 oz

Suprême sauce:

50 g	flour	2 oz
50 g	butter	2 oz
¼ l	light stock *or* chicken velouté	9 fl oz
1/8 l	dry white wine	4 fl oz
1/8 l	dairy cream	4 fl oz
	2 egg yolks	

Place the water, salt and vegetable fat in a pan and bring to the boil. Remove from the heat, add the flour all at once, stir well, return to the heat and work well with a spatula until the panada leaves the side of the pan without sticking. Remove from the heat and beat in the eggs, then allow to cool. Mince the veal several times, using the finest cutter. Add the panada and pass through a hair sieve. Add the cream, season with salt and mix very lightly. Using a dessertspoon, shape the mixture into quenelles the size of a pigeon's egg. Place in a buttered pan, add boiling hot bouillon and poach gently for 5 minutes.

To make rice pilaf, melt the butter in a saucepan, fry the onion until lightly coloured, add the rice and stir in double the amount of boiling bouillon. Place in a preheated oven and cook for 18 minutes. Fluff up with a fork, dot with butter, cover and leave to stand away from the heat.

To make the sauce, prepare a roux with the flour and butter, blend in boiling hot stock or chicken velouté, add the wine, remove from the heat and bind with the cream and egg yolks.

Fill the rice pilaf into a buttered ring mould and press down a little. To serve, unmould on to a heated round dish. Drain the quenelles well and dress in the centre of the ring. Coat with Suprême sauce and sprinkle with truffle julienne. Hand lettuce salad separately.

(Otto Brust, Germany)

Veal steak Old Vienna
Steak de veau Vieille Vienne
Kalbssteaks Alt Wien

4 portions

600 g	fillet of veal	1 lb 5 oz
80 g	chicken liver	3 oz
80 g	calf's sweetbreads, blanched, skinned and coarsely diced	3 oz
60 g	mushrooms or flap mushrooms	2 oz
	2 tomatoes, skinned, cut in half and seeded	
	2 egg yolks	
	2 tablespoons bouillon	
230 g	butter	8 oz
8 cl	oil	3 fl oz
20 g	flour	¾ oz
50 g	shallots, finely chopped	2 oz
	1 dessertspoon parsley, chopped	
	8 fleurons	
	a little brown stock	
	salt, pepper	
	lemon juice	

Noilly Prat, Madeira, Cognac
commercial seasoning
maize cakes (recipe, page 1028)

Cook the shallots gently in 2 cl (about 1 fl oz) oil without colouring. Add the chicken liver which has been coarsely diced and sauter carefully. Season with salt and pepper and flamber with Cognac. Dice the mushrooms, sauter in 20 g (¾ oz) butter and season. Add the sweet-breads, mix well, then add the contents of the pan to the chicken liver. Flavour with Noilly Prat and Madeira and stir in the parsley.

Whisk the egg yolks in a bain-marie with the bouillon, a little commercial seasoning, lemon juice, white pepper and salt. Beat in 180 g (6¼ oz) hand-hot clarified butter and keep hot. Season the tomatoes with salt and pepper and fry lightly in 1 cl (about ½ fl oz) oil.

Cut the fillet of veal into 4 slices. Flatten well, season with salt and dust with flour. Heat the rest of the oil in a braising pan and brown the meat on both sides. Pour off excess oil, add 30 g (1 oz) butter and a little brown stock to the pan, stir to detach the sediment and simmer very gently, but do not boil.

Dress on a serving dish, spoon the chicken liver/sweetbread mixture on top and press down a little. Coat with the Hollandaise sauce and brown in the oven. Pour gravy round and garnish with hot fleurons, the tomatoes and maize cakes.

(Ewald Plachutta, Austria)

Veal steak Fiora
Steak de veau Fiora
Kalbssteak Fiora

4 portions

	4 veal steaks (cut from the fillet)	
130 g	each weighing	4½ oz
350 g	Swiss chard	12 oz
180 g	calf's brains	6 oz
200 g	butter	7 oz
4 cl	oil	1½ fl oz
	1 egg	
	1 egg yolk	
	1 tablespoon Parmesan cheese, grated	
	1 tablespoon parsley, chopped	
	1 tablespoon onion, finely chopped	
	4 tablespoons bouillon or brown stock	
	a little flour	
	nutmeg	
	salt, white pepper	

lemon juice
commercial seasoning

Remove the stalks from the Swiss chard, wash the leaves, blanch them in salted water and allow to cool (chopping them if they are too large). Toss in 20 g (¾ oz) brown butter and season to taste. Skin and coarsely chop the brains. Melt 30 g (1 oz) butter and cook the onion lightly without colouring, then add the brains, season with salt and pepper and fry. Add the egg and continue frying. Finish with chopped parsley.

Flatten the meat well, season with salt and dust lightly with flour. Heat the oil in a frying pan and fry the meat on both sides until brown. Pour off excess oil, add 20 g (¾ oz) butter and bouillon or stock, stir and simmer gently, but do not boil. Cover the veal with the Swiss chard and dress the brains on top. Whisk the egg yolk in a bain-marie with 2 tablespoons bouillon, lemon juice, commercial seasoning, salt and pepper. Whisk in 130 g (4½ oz) hand-hot clarified butter. Coat the veal with this sauce, sprinkle with the Parmesan and brown in the oven. Serve with saffron risotto.

(Ewald Plachutta, Austria)

Veal steak Florida
Steak de veau Florida
Kalbssteak Florida

6 portions

150 g	6 veal steaks each weighing about	5 oz
300 g	apples	11 oz
	6 slices pineapple	
	6 peach halves	
	a few sultanas	
30 g	strip almonds, roasted	1 oz
150 g	butter	5 oz
5 dl	curry sauce	18 fl oz
400 g	Patna rice	14 oz
7 cl	white wine	2½ fl oz
30 g	sugar	1 oz
	salt, pepper	
	a few dessert cherries	

Peel, core and slice the apples. Stew them with the sugar and a few sultanas in the white wine and 30 g (1 oz) butter. Fry the pineapple in 40 g (1½ oz) butter. Warm the peach halves and cherries. Season the veal and fry slowly in the rest of the butter for about 10 minutes.

To serve, dress the veal on a round silver dish. Place the stewed apples in the centre and decorate with the pineapple, peaches and cherries. Sprinkle with the almonds. Hand rice pilaf and curry sauce separately.

(Willi Bartenbach, Switzerland)

Veal steak Karlsbad style
Steak de veau Karlsbad
Telecí stejky po karlovarsku

6 portions   Cooking time: about 6 minutes

	12 veal steaks about 2 cm (¾ in) thick	
80 g	(cut from the fillet) each weighing	3 oz
	salt	
	2-3 eggs	
80 g	flaked almonds	3 oz
100 g	butter	3½ oz
	bouillon	
750 g	rice, boiled	1 lb 10 oz
	curry powder	

Garnish:

	lettuce
	lemon
	4 tomatoes

Beat the steaks a little to flatten, season with salt, dip in beaten egg, coat with the flaked almonds and fry over high heat for 2½ minutes on each side in 80 g (3 oz) hot butter. Blend the curry powder with the rest of the butter which has been melted, or with 2 cl (about 1 fl oz) oil, and mix with the cooked rice.

Dress in a warm dish and place the veal on top. Stir a little bouillon into the pan in which the meat was fried, season with salt, bring to the boil and strain. Coat the veal with a little of this gravy and hand the rest separately. Garnish the meat with lemon wedges and tomatoes cut in quarters. Serve vegetable salad separately.

(Vilèm Vrabec, Czechoslovakia)

Veal steak Klöntal fashion
Steak de veau Klöntal
Kalbssteak Klöntalerart

6 portions

150 g	6 veal steaks each weighing about	5 oz
200 g	small chanterelles	7 oz
3 dl	dairy cream	10 fl oz
2 dl	white wine	7 fl oz
150 g	butter	5 oz

20 g	shallots, finely chopped	¾ oz
10 g	parsley, chopped	⅓ oz
	salt, pepper	
	1 teaspoon chives	
	1 teaspoon chervil	
	1 teaspoon basil	
	1 teaspoon tarragon	
	1 small teaspoon thyme	
	1 small teaspoon garlic	

Spinach spätzle:

800 g	flour	1 lb 12 oz
	8 eggs	
100 g	spinach, finely chopped	3½ oz
6 dl	water	1 pt
	salt, nutmeg	

Season the meat and fry slowly in 80 g (3 oz) butter for about 10 minutes. Remove and keep hot. Add the rest of the butter to the pan together with the shallots and fresh chanterelles. Cook gently for a short time, then stir in the wine to detach the sediment. Add the garlic, salt and pepper, and all the herbs except the parsley. Reduce by half, add the cream and reduce slowly to the required consistency. Pour over the veal and sprinkle with the parsley.

Place all the ingredients for the *spätzle* in a bowl and work with the hand to a smooth dough. Force in small amounts through a *spätzle* maker or large-holed sieve into a pan of boiling salted water. Transfer to a fireproof dish in layers, pouring a little melted butter over each layer, then mix very carefully with a fork. Sprinkle with grated Parmesan and brown briefly in the oven or under a salamander.

(Willi Bartenbach, Switzerland)

Minced veal steak Wallenberg
Steak de veau haché Wallenberg

4 portions

250 g	veal	9 oz
2 dl	dairy cream	7 fl oz
	3 egg yolks	
	salt, pepper	
	breadcrumbs	
approx. 100 g	butter	approx. 4 oz

Trim the veal, chill well and mince twice. Chill again, season with salt and pepper and mix with the egg yolks. Work in the cream a little at a time. Divide into four portions and form into flat round or oval cakes. Coat with breadcrumbs, flatten lightly with a palette knife and fry in clarified butter until golden. Transfer to a heated dish and coat with brown butter. Serve with freshly boiled potatoes which have been passed through a ricer. Hand cranberries or pickled cucumbers separately.

(Eric Carlström, Sweden)

Escalope of veal Antwerp style
Escalopes de veau à l'anversoise

6 portions

150 g	6 escalopes of veal each weighing	5 oz
2 dl	veal stock	7 fl oz
65 g	butter	2¼ oz
500 g	hop shoots	1 lb 2 oz
2 dl	dairy cream	7 fl oz
	6 puff pastry tartlet cases	
	6 cm (2½ in) in diameter	
1 dl	mousseline sauce	3½ fl oz
500 g	asparagus, poached	1 lb 2 oz
½ dl	dry white wine	2 fl oz
	6 tomatoes	
	1 tablespoon parsley, finely chopped	

Sauter the escalopes in 50 g (2 oz) butter and keep hot. Add the wine to the pan to detach the cooking juices, pour in the stock, reduce a little, season and finish with butter. Mix together the hop shoots and the cream, fill into the tartlet cases and mask with mousseline sauce. Cook the tomatoes under cover in the oven, then cover with the asparagus tips which have been tossed in butter. Arrange the escalopes on an oval dish, pour the sauce over and garnish alternately with the accompaniments.

(André Béghin, Belgium)

Escalope of veal Caravaggio

4 portions   Cooking time: 15 minutes

400 g	cushion of veal	14 oz
	8 large slices Gruyère *or* Fontina cheese	
	4 slices Parma ham	
	flour as required	
100 g	butter	3½ oz
½–1 dl	sherry	2–3 fl oz
4 dl	dairy cream	14 fl oz
	2 teaspoons Cognac	

Cut the veal evenly into 8 thin escalopes. Flatten them well and season with salt and pepper. Cut the cheese to the same size. Cover four of the escalopes with a slice of cheese, then with a slice of ham, folded over, then with another slice of cheese and lastly with another escalope. Coat with flour and fry in butter over very low heat. When cooked, dress in a fireproof dish. Pour off the butter, detach the sediment with sherry, add the cream, stir well, flavour with the Cognac and pour over the escalopes.

(André Béghin, Belgium)

Escalope of veal Mechlin style
Escalopes de veau à la malinoise

6 portions

150–160 g	6 escalopes of veal each weighing	5–5½ oz
50 g	butter (for frying)	2 oz
1 kg	Duchesse potato mixture	2 lb 4 oz
	2 eggs	
	1 carrot	
	1 stick celery	
	2 artichoke bottoms	
	2 mushrooms	
3 dl	Béchamel sauce	10 fl oz
1 dl	dairy cream	3½ fl oz
40 g	Parmesan cheese, grated	1½ oz
	6 small tomatoes	
	24–36 asparagus tips (depending on size)	
300 g	French beans, blanched	11 oz
2 dl	veal stock	7 fl oz
15 g	butter (for sauce)	½ oz

Garnish:

noisette potatoes

Season the escalopes with salt and pepper and fry in butter for 15 minutes. Transfer to an oval dish and keep hot. Pour off the butter. Dice the carrot, celery stick, artichoke bottoms and mushrooms. Blanch, drain and mix with the Béchamel sauce, then finish with the cream and keep hot.

Using a savoy bag fitted with a star tube, pipe out 6 borders of Duchesse potato mixture on a greased baking sheet. Egg wash and bake. Fill with the vegetable mixture, sprinkle with Parmesan and brown under a salamander. Cut the tomatoes in half, poach or grill them, season and cover with the asparagus tips. Toss the beans in butter and arrange in bundles.

Stir the veal stock into the pan in which the escalopes were fried, finish with the butter, adjust the seasoning and pour this sauce over the meat. Arrange the garnish on the same dish.

(André Béghin, Belgium)

Stuffed escalope of veal
Escalopes de veau farcies
Jägertaske

4 portions   Cooking time: 25 minutes

200 g	4 escalopes of veal each weighing	7 oz
200 g	butter	7 oz
175 g	ham, finely chopped	6¼ oz
100 g	onions, finely chopped	3½ oz
200 g	mushrooms, well cleaned and finely chopped	7 oz
	4 egg yolks	
	salt	
	pepper, freshly ground	

Accompaniments:

400 g	sugar peas	14 oz
50 g	butter	2 oz
	4 large potatoes	
1 l	oil	1¾ pt

Flatten the escalopes well and season. Cover half of each one with the ham, onions and mushrooms. Make a well in the centre and place an egg yolk in it. Fold the other half of the escalope over to enclose the filling and carefully knock the edges together with the back of a knife. Melt the butter in a sauté pan and fry the escalopes slowly over low heat.

To serve, dress on a warmed dish and pour the cooking juices over. Hand the sugar peas which have been cooked in the butter as an accompaniment, together with straw potatoes. To make these, peel the potatoes, cut them into very thin strips, wash, dry carefully and deep-fry in hot oil.

(Eric Cederholm, Denmark)

Hungarian veal paupiettes
Paupiettes de veau à la hongroise
Polpetti magyarosan

10 portions   Cooking time: 10-15 minutes

70 g	20 escalopes of veal each weighing	2½ oz
400 g	smoked pork fat or bacon	14 oz

400 g	Parmesan cheese, grated	14 oz
50 g	salt	2 oz
	4 eggs	
200 g	flour	7 oz
400 g	breadcrumbs	14 oz
	lard	
50 g	capers	2 oz

Paprika sauce:
1 l (1¾ pt)

500 g	pork or veal bones	1 lb 2 oz
200 g	lard	7 oz
40 g	salt	1½ oz
20 g	paprika	¾ oz
200 g	onions, finely cut	7 oz
100 g	yellow peppers, seeded and finely cut	3½ oz
100 g	tomatoes	3½ oz
100 g	flour	3½ oz
½ l	sour cream	18 fl oz
1 dl	fresh dairy cream	3½ fl oz

Garnish:

boiled rice

Slice the pork fat or bacon thinly. Beat out the escalopes well, cover each one with a slice of pork fat or bacon and sprinkle with Parmesan. Fold the two ends towards the centre, beat to keep in position, flour, egg and breadcrumb, and fry in hot lard. Dress the rice on a dish and arrange the escalopes on top. Hand paprika sauce mixed with finely cut capers separately.

To make the sauce, cook the onions in lard until lightly coloured, sprinkle with paprika, stir in hot water to detach the sediment, season with salt, then add the tomatoes, peppers and bones. Pour in sufficient hot water to cover, bring to the boil and cook, then strain the sauce and return to the boil. Blend the flour with the sour cream and a little water, mix with the sauce and boil for 2 or 3 minutes. Add the fresh cream and return to the boil. Adjust the seasoning and serve hot.

(Zsolt Körmendy, Hungary)

Sautée escalope of veal Westhoek
Escalopes de veau sautées Westhoek

6 portions   Cooking time (escalopes): 12 minutes over gentle heat

150–160 g	6 escalopes of veal each weighing	5–5½ oz
100 g	butter	3½ oz
	3 shallots, finely cut	
500 g	mushrooms, coarsely sliced	1 lb 2 oz

	2 tomatoes, skinned and seeded	
1 dl	dry white wine	3½ fl oz
4 dl	dairy cream	14 fl oz
	1 tablespoon tarragon leaves, chopped	
	salt, pepper	

Garnish:

	6 artichoke bottoms, blanched	
	18-24 asparagus tips (depending on size), stewed in butter	
	noisette potatoes as required	

Season the escalopes with salt and pepper, sauter in butter, remove from the pan and keep hot. Add the shallots to the pan, cook gently without colouring, then add the mushrooms and allow to colour well. Dice the tomatoes and add to the pan. Mix and cook over low heat to extract the juice from the tomatoes, then stir in the wine, bring to the boil and reduce. Add the cream, reduce to the required consistency and season to taste. Coat the escalopes with this sauce and sprinkle with finely chopped tarragon. Fill the artichoke bottoms with the asparagus tips and arrange on the same dish. Serve noisette potatoes separately.

(André Béghin, Belgium)

Escalopes of veal with lemon
Escalopes de veau au citron
Scaloppine di vitello al limone

6 portions

500 g	cushion of veal	1 lb 2 oz
	breadcrumbs as required	
	2 eggs	
	juice of 2 lemons	
	½ medium onion	
50 g	ewe cheese	2 oz
60 g	butter	2 oz
3–4 dl	bouillon	10–14 fl oz
	salt and pepper as required	

Cut the veal evenly into small escalopes as for piccata. Dip in the eggs which have been beaten with the cheese and seasoned with salt and pepper and then breadcrumb. Fry lightly on both sides in 30 g (1 oz) butter without allowing the butter to brown. Remove the meat and drain on absorbent paper, then arrange in a fireproof dish, dot with the rest of the butter, cover with the onion which has been coarsely cut and pour the lemon juice over. Add the bouillon and braise in a moderate oven for 45 minutes, adding bouillon if required.

(Salvatore Schifano, Italy)

Knuckle of veal with braised lettuce
Jarret de veau aux laitues braisées
Borjucsülök párolt fejessalátával

6 portions   Cooking time: 2-2½ hours

900 g	3 knuckles of veal each weighing	2 lb
	3 choice lettuces	
200 g	carrots	7 oz
100 g	lean bacon	3½ oz
10 g	garlic	⅓ oz
80 g	butter	3 oz
	salt, pepper	

Garnish:

	6 large potatoes	
120 g	butter	4 oz
	1 bunch chives	
	salt, pepper	

Remove the skin from the knuckles of veal, season with salt, place in a roasting tray, sprinkle with a little melted butter, add the garlic and carrots, and roast in an oven preheated to 150°C (300°F) for 2 to 2½ hours until tender. Wash the potatoes carefully, wrap separately in aluminium foil and bake round the meat. Wash the lettuces well, blanch in boiling salted water for 1 or 2 minutes and drain. Cut the bacon into fine julienne strips and fry in a little butter. Cut the lettuces into wedges, mix with the bacon and warm in the veal cooking juices. Carefully cut the meat off the bone and carve each boned knuckle into 4 to 6 slices, then replace these on the bone to serve. Unwrap the cooked potatoes, cut a cross in the top of each and squeeze the inside up through the incision from underneath. Cut the chives finely, mix with butter, salt and pepper and place a teaspoonful of the mixture on top of each potato. (Illustration, page 624)

(Gyula Gullner, Hungary)

Knuckle of veal with oranges and Rosé de Provence
Jarret de veau aux oranges et au rosé de Provence

8 portions

3 kg	2 knuckles of veal weighing about	6 lb 10 oz
	8 oranges	
3½ dl	rosé wine (Provence)	12 fl oz
½ l	veal gravy	18 fl oz
100 g	butter	3½ oz
	3 tablespoons olive oil	

1 tablespoon Curaçao
mirepoix of
  4 shallots
  2 carrots
  2 leeks (white part only)
  2 bay leaves
  1 sprig thyme
  6 coriander seeds

Blanch the knuckles of veal briefly in boiling water, then refresh under cold running water and dry well. Place the olive oil in a roasting tray, season with salt and pepper, add the meat and roast at 250°C (482°F), basting frequently. Add the mirepoix after 30 minutes.

Remove the zest of 2 oranges and cut into very fine julienne strips. Squeeze all 8 oranges and reserve the juice. When the meat is cooked, stir the orange juice into the roasting tray to detach the cooking juices, then add the veal gravy. Reduce over low heat. Remove the knuckles of veal and cover with the rest of the orange segments. Pass the sauce through a conical strainer, add the butter a little at a time, then add the orange zest julienne. (Illustration, page 310)

(Roger Souvereyns, Belgium)

Calf's liver brochettes Basle style
Brochettes de foie de veau à la bâloise
Basler Leberspiesschen

10 portions

1 kg 200	calf's liver	2 lb 10 oz
300 g	pork caul	11 oz
300 g	lean bacon	11 oz
400 g	mushroom caps, cooked	14 oz
	salt	
	pepper, freshly ground	
	sage	
1 dl	oil	3½ fl oz
3 dl	thickened veal stock	10 fl oz
50 g	butter	2 oz
10 g	parsley, chopped	⅓ oz

Remove all skin from the liver and cut into pieces 3 cm (1¼ in) long and 1½ cm (⅝ in) thick. Cover each piece with sage and wrap in the caul. Cut the bacon into rashers 2 mm (¹⁄₁₂ in) thick and cut these into 3 cm (1¼ in) squares. Impale the liver, bacon and mushroom caps alternately on skewers, allowing a total of 180 g (6 oz) ingredients per skewer. Season with salt and freshly ground pepper.

Heat the oil in an omelette pan (without allowing it to become too hot) and carefully fry the brochettes on all sides until medium done. To serve, dress the brochettes on sautés fine French beans. Pour brown butter over and sprinkle with freshly chopped parsley. Hand boiled potatoes and thickened veal stock separately.

(Otto Ledermann, Switzerland)

Veal ragoût Viennese style
Ragoût de veau à la viennoise
Pilzlingfleisch mit Griesskrapfen

4 portions

800 g	shoulder of veal, boned	1 lb 12 oz
6 cl	oil	2 fl oz
200 g	onions	7 oz
	1 tablespoon flour	
	2 teaspoons tomato purée	
3¾ dl	bouillon	13 fl oz
250 g	flap mushrooms, chanterelles or mushrooms	9 oz
2½ dl	sour cream	9 fl oz
	2 teaspoons parsley, chopped	
	salt, pepper	

Accompaniment: Gnocchi Roman style

5 cl	milk	2 fl oz
120 g	semolina	4 oz
	1 egg	
20 g	butter	¾ oz
	salt, nutmeg	
	Parmesan, grated	
	butter, melted	

Dice the meat, season with salt and dust with flour. Chop the onions finely, brown lightly in the oil, add the meat and stir-fry, then add the tomato purée and stir in the bouillon. Cook gently for 40 minutes. Slice the mushrooms coarsely and add together with a little pepper, then cook gently for a further 20 minutes. Thicken with flour and sour cream and finish with the parsley.

To make the gnocchi, bring the milk to the boil with the butter and salt and nutmeg to taste. Stir in the semolina, whisk well until thick, then stir well with a spoon. Draw to the side of the stove, cover and leave to stand for 10 minutes. Remove and quickly stir in the egg. While still warm, spread on a greased baking sheet with a 3 cm (1¼ in) rim, then sprinkle with butter and Parmesan. Chill for a short time and cut out into rounds or crescents. Place in a greased fireproof dish or on a greased baking sheet and bake in a hot oven (220°C–430°F) for

15 minutes or until golden brown. To serve, dress the ragoût in a deep dish and hand the gnocchi separately.

(Ernst Faseth, Austria)

Blanquette of veal with sorrel
Blanquette de veau à l'oseille

6 portions

1 kg 200	shoulder of veal	2 lb 10 oz
	1 onion	
	3 carrots	
	1 leek	
	¼ celeriac	
	1 clove	
	1 bay leaf	
	1 sprig thyme	
2 dl	white wine	7 fl oz
1 dl	Noilly Prat	3½ fl oz
	salt	
	peppercorns	
	2 egg yolks	
1½ dl	dairy cream	5 fl oz
40 g	flour	1½ oz
60 g	butter	2 oz
	2 tablespoons sorrel, chopped and blanched	

Garnish:

	30 small spring onions	
200 g	mushrooms	7 oz
	6 croûtons	
	rice pilaf (see page 1030)	

Dice the meat and blanch in boiling water for 3 or 4 minutes. Pour off the water, transfer the meat to a colander and rinse in cold water. Place the meat in a clean stew pan together with the onion, carrots, leek, celeriac, clove, bay leaf, thyme, wine and Noilly Prat. Cover with water and cook for about 50 minutes.

To make the sauce, prepare a roux with the butter and flour, stir in 1 l (1¾ pt) stock from the veal, after straining, and reduce for 10 minutes. Remove from the heat, thicken with the egg yolks, add the cream which has been whipped and stir in the sorrel. Dress in a warmed deep serving dish and coat with sauce. Garnish with blanched spring onions, mushrooms sautés in butter and bread croûtons fried in butter until golden brown. Hand rice pilaf apart.

(Emile Jung, France)

Ribs of beef in a salt crust with bone marrow, p. 435

Braised beef bonne bourgeoise, p. 485

Pepper steak Maman Yvette, p. 527

Tournedos with fresh morels, p. 450

622

Best end of pork Csaba, p. 833

Knuckle of veal with braised lettuce, p. 615

(Previous page) Salt brisket of beef Norwegian style, p. 402

◄ Stuffed beefsteak Styrian style, p. 398
▼ Viennese potpourri, p. 627

626

Viennese potpourri

4 portions

80 g	4 veal medallions each weighing	3 oz
	1 egg	
	2 tablespoons flour	
	4 tablespoons breadcrumbs	
1 dl	oil for frying veal	3½ fl oz
80 g	4 fillets mignons of beef each weighing	3 oz
5 cl	oil for frying beef	2 fl oz
500 g	chicken, cooked (half a chicken)	1 lb 2 oz
	salt, pepper	

Risotto:

160 g	rice	5½ oz
20 g	butter (for rice)	¾ oz
	2 teaspoons onion, chopped	
3 dl	bouillon	10 fl oz
40 g	mushrooms, thinly sliced	1½ oz
40 g	chicken liver, diced	1½ oz
10 g	butter (for liver)	⅓ oz
	2 tablespoons peas, cooked	
	salt, parsley	
	1 tablespoon Parmesan, grated	
	1 egg	
10 g	butter (for mould)	⅓ oz

Cold garnish:

150 g	cucumber pickled with mustard, cut into strips	5 oz
	salad in season	

Hot garnish:

200 g	asparagus	7 oz
200 g	cauliflower	7 oz
200 g	French beans	7 oz
60 g	butter	2 oz
	salt, pepper	

Beat the veal medallions to flatten, season with salt, then flour, egg and breadcrumb, and fry in oil. Season the filets mignons and fry until medium done in oil. Skin and bone the chicken. Slice the breast obliquely and set aside. Cut up the rest of the chicken finely.

To make the risotto, brown the finely chopped onion in butter, add the rice and fry for a short time. Stir in the bouillon, season with salt, cover and cook in the oven for 20 minutes. Brown the mushrooms and chicken liver in butter. Mix the peas, the parsley and the finely cut chicken with the cooked rice. Add the egg and the Parmesan and leave to stand on the stove for a short time. Butter a bombe mould, line with the slices of chicken breast, fill with the risotto and smooth the top.

Boil the vegetables for the hot garnish, drain and toss in butter. Dress as shown in the illustration. Turn the risotto out on to a round dish and insert a small skewer in the top. Surround alternately with the veal, beef and garnishes.
(Illustration, page 626)

(Ernst Faseth, Austria)

Hot Veal Dishes for Individual Plate Service

Emincé of veal Ibn Saud
Emincé de veau Ibn Saud
Sminuzzato di vitello Ibn Saud

1 portion

100 g	cushion of veal, finely sliced	3½ oz
5 cl	white wine	2 fl oz
5 cl	dairy cream	2 fl oz
	a pinch of sambal oleg	
	a small pinch of curry powder	
	¼ apple, peeled and finely diced	
	¼ banana, finely diced	
	½ slice canned pineapple, finely diced	
	flour	
	butter	
	salt	
	pepper, freshly ground	

Season the veal and flour lightly. Sauter in butter and detach the cooking juices with the white wine. Reduce completely, add the cream, then the sambal oleg and curry powder, and stir well. Add the diced fruit, stir and dish. Serve with rice pilaf or mashed potatoes.

(Giulio Casazza, Switzerland)

Emincé of veal exotic style
Emincé de veau à l'exotique
Geschnetzeltes Kalbfleisch in Curry-Sauce mit exotischen Früchten

2 portions

300 g	cushion of veal, cut into strips	11 oz
	1 tablespoon onion, finely chopped	
30 g	butter	1 oz
	1 tablespoon desiccated coconut	
	1 tablespoon curry powder	
1 dl	white wine	3½ fl oz
1 dl	pineapple juice	3½ fl oz

	1 teaspoon tomato ketchup	
	1 teaspoon mango chutney	
1 dl	dairy cream	3½ fl oz
	salt	

Garnish:

1 slice pineapple
2 slices Chinese gooseberry
2 slices mango
(fresh fruit if possible)

Brown the veal and onion very lightly in butter in a hot pan. Add the curry powder and coconut and continue frying for a short time. Remove from the pan and keep hot. Add the wine and pineapple juice to the pan to detach the sediment, bring to the boil and reduce by half, then add the chutney and return to the boil briefly. Mix well with the veal, add the cream, boil up for a moment and season lightly with salt. Transfer to warmed plates and garnish with the fruit which has been gently warmed. Serve with rice pilaf.
(Illustration, page 416)

(Felix Real, Liechtenstein)

Calf's foot with onions and chive sauce
Pieds de veau aux oignons sur sauce ciboulette
Gebackene Kälberfüsschen mit eingelegten Zwiebelchen und Schnittlauchsauce

2 portions   Cooking time: about 1 hour

	1 calf's foot	
	flavouring vegetables	
1 dl	corn oil	3½ fl oz
	white breadcrumbs	
	2 eggs	
	6 spring onions	
	oil	
	vinegar	

Blanch the calf's foot, then cook in salted water containing the vegetables until the skin comes away from the bones. Leave until cold, then bone and cut the meat into strips 1 cm (⅜ in) thick. Egg and crumb the meat, and deep-fry in hot corn oil until golden brown.

Blanch the onions, keeping them very firm, and marinate in a dressing of oil and vinegar seasoned with salt. For chive sauce recipe, see page 192.
(Illustration, page 769)

(Gerhard Gartner, Germany)

Quenelles of veal with Brie and vermouth sabayon
Quenelles de veau avec sabayon au brie et au vermouth

1 portion

60 g	3 veal quenelles each weighing	2 oz
	2 tablespoons leek julienne for nest	
	½ tablespoon pink peppercorns	
60 g	Brie and vermouth sabayon	2 oz
	(recipe, page 176)	
	1 sprig fresh watercress	

Veal quenelles: (8 portions)

400 g	fillet of veal	14 oz
60 g	fillet of pork	2 oz
	5 egg whites	
¾ l	dairy cream (35%)	1¼ pt
	a pinch of salt	
	a pinch of freshly ground pepper	
	a pinch of seasoning (commercial)	
115 g	butter	4 oz
1¹/₁₀ l	light veal stock	2 pt
225 g	poppy seed	8 oz

Leek nests: (8 portions)

	2 medium leeks (white and	
	light green parts)	
½ l	water	18 fl oz
80 g	butter	3 oz
	salt	
	pepper, freshly ground	

Arrange the leek julienne in nest fashion on a warmed plate. Spoon the sabayon into the centre of the nest and place the quenelles in it. Sprinkle with pink peppercorns and decorate with a sprig of watercress.

To make the quenelles, cut up the veal and pork, mince twice, using the finest cutter, then refrigerate for 1 hour. Place the meat in the mixer and run at maximum speed for 1 minute. Add the egg whites and seasonings and continue mixing at maximum speed for 1 minute. While the machine is still running, add the butter and cream, then mix for 5 seconds and switch off. Scrape down the sides of the bowl and run the mixer for a further 10 seconds. Remove the quenelle mixture from the bowl and cool for 30 minutes.

Bring the veal stock to the boil and turn down the heat to simmering point. Shape the mixture into quenelles with two tablespoons and poach in the stock for 12 minutes. Remove from the pan, roll in poppy seed and serve, allowing 3 quenelles per portion.

To prepare the leeks, cut them in half lengthwise and wash carefully. Cut away about 12–15 cm (5–6 in) of the root end as well as the dark green part at the other end. Remove the thick outer leaves. Cut the remainder into long strips and these into julienne strips 3 cm (1¼ in) long and about 2 mm (¹/₁₀ in) wide. Poach in water for 3 to 5 minutes, drain, toss in melted butter and season with salt and pepper.

(Edward Mathis, Canada)

Boiled veal Colmar style with spring vegetables and rice with currants

Veau bouilli à la colmarienne avec primeurs du pays et riz aux raisins de Corinthe
Gesottenes Kalbfleisch auf Colmarer Art mit Brechspargel, grünen Erbsen, Blumenkohlröschen und Rosinenreis

10 portions

1 kg 800	shoulder of veal, boned and rolled	4 lb
800 g	fresh calves' tongues	1 lb 12 oz
160 g	butter	5½ oz
⅓ l	white wine	12 fl oz
2 l	light bouillon	3½ pt
⅓ l	dairy cream	12 fl oz
80 g	flour butter	3 oz
250 g	small young peas	9 oz
500 g	asparagus	1 lb 2 oz
400 g	cauliflower florets	14 oz
	juice of 1 lemon	
	3 egg yolks	
45 g	white breadcrumbs	1½ oz
	a pinch of Cayenne pepper	

Rice with currants:

600 g	rice, boiled	1 lb 5 oz
	a pinch of saffron	
50 g	red peppers, finely diced	2 oz
110 g	currants, soaked	4 oz

Fry the veal and tongues lightly in 60 g (2 oz) hot butter, add the bouillon and a dash of white wine, cover and simmer gently until cooked. Prepare a white sauce with the stock remaining in the pan, the cream and the flour butter. Reduce well and strain. Thicken with the egg yolks which have been carefully blended with the rest of the wine and finish with lemon juice and a pinch of Cayenne pepper.

To serve, place a slice of veal weighing 80 g (3 oz) on each plate together with a 30 g (1 oz) slice of tongue. Surround with the vegetables which have been boiled, keeping them firm to the bite, and tossed in butter. Coat with the sauce. Mix 1 teaspoon buttered breadcrumbs, which have been browned, with chopped parsley and sprinkle on the vegetables.

Mix the rice, which has been boiled with a pinch of saffron and well seasoned, with the currants and the red pepper which has been lightly cooked in butter. Hand separately.

(Karl Brunnengräber, Germany)

Knuckle of veal with mushrooms
Jarret de veau aux champignons
Kalbshachse mit Champignons

10 portions

2 kg	knuckle of veal, boned	4 lb 8 oz
100 g	butter	3½ oz
200 g	mirepoix of leeks, celery, carrots and butter	7 oz
20 g	tomato purée	¾ oz
¼ l	white wine	9 fl oz
1 l	veal stock	1¾ pt
500 g	mushrooms	1 lb 2 oz
20 g	parsley, chopped	¾ oz
	salt	

Cut the meat into portions along the grain, allowing about 200 g (7 oz) per portion. Season with salt and brown on all sides in butter. Add the mirepoix and continue frying, then add the tomato purée and fry briefly. Stir in the wine, then the stock, and finish cooking in the oven. Towards the end of the cooking time the meat should become glazed due to the evaporation of the juices. Remove the meat and keep hot. Reduce the stock. Cut the meat into slices the thickness of one finger and dress on warmed plates. Cover with the reduced stock and the mushrooms which have been sautés separately and sprinkle with chopped parsley. Serve with risi-bisi and lettuce.

(Eduard Mayer, Austria)

Veal fillet with foie gras and truffle essence
Filets mignons de veau farcis de foie gras aux essences de truffes

4 portions

600–700 g	veal fillet	1 lb 5 oz– 1 lb 8 oz

30 g	butter	1 oz
120 g	fresh foie gras, poached	4 oz
	1 tablespoon Cognac	
	2 teaspoons truffle essence	
	8 tablespoons veal gravy	
	4 tablespoons dairy cream	
	salt, pepper	
	juice of half a lemon	

Cut the veal into slices 1 cm (⅜ in) thick, season with salt and pepper, and fry in butter in a thick-bottomed pan. Pour off the butter, stir in the veal gravy and truffle essence to detach the sediment, bring to the boil and reduce to the required consistency. Season with salt and pepper and add a few drops of lemon juice.

Slice the foie gras. Dress on plates alternately with the slices of veal, coat with sauce and serve at once.

(Illustration, page 236)

(Pierre Gleize, France)

Veal fillet Trois Frères

4 portions

600 g	veal fillet	1 lb 5 oz
	salt	
	pepper, freshly ground	
	sage, chopped	
2 dl	brown veal gravy	7 fl oz
150 g	butter	5 oz

Rice timbales:

200 g	rice	7 oz
50 g	onions	2 oz
4 dl	beef bouillon	14 fl oz
	2 eggs	
250 g	turnips	9 oz
150 g	red and green peppers, seeded	5 oz
250 g	celery	9 oz
½ l	veal stock	18 fl oz
	12 mushroom caps	

To make the rice timbales, prepare rice pilaf with the rice, onions, beef bouillon and a little butter. Allow to cool, then stir in the eggs. Fill into carefully buttered dariole moulds and bake for 12 to 15 minutes in an oven preheated to 190°C (375°F).

Trim the turnips to the shape of saucers and cook in a little salted water, keeping them firm to the bite. Pour off the water and toss the turnips in butter. Slice the peppers, season with salt and pepper and stew in butter. Blanch the celery and braise in veal stock.

Stew the mushroom caps gently in a little butter without adding liquid. Cut the veal into 12 thick slices. Season with salt and pepper, flavour with chopped sage and fry in butter until medium done. Add the gravy.

To serve, dress three slices of veal on a well-warmed plate, cover with the mushroom caps and garnish with the vegetables and an unmoulded rice timbale, which may be lightly browned under a salamander if desired.

(Germain Gretsch-Rösner, Luxembourg)

Veal fillet and calf's kidney Carmen
Filet et rognon de veau Carmen
Kalbsfilet und Kalbsnierchen Carmen mit Pistazienreis

10 portions   Cooking time: 30 minutes

35 g	10 slices calf's kidney each weighing	1¼ oz
90 g	10 medallions veal fillet each weighing	3¼ oz
200 g	butter	7 oz
¼ l	dry white wine	9 fl oz
	2 tablespoons oil	
3½ dl	sour cream	12 fl oz
100 g	paprika purée	3½ oz
100 g	bacon, cut into strips	3½ oz
350 g	red and yellow peppers, cut into strips	12 oz
40 g	pine kernels, roasted	1½ oz

Rice with pistachio nuts:

30 g	pistachio nuts	1 oz
200 g	rice, boiled	7 oz
30 g	Parmesan cheese, grated	1 oz

Cook the veal medallions gently in butter and the white wine. Fry the slices of kidney in butter. Make a thick sauce by carefully mixing the sour cream and paprika purée with the veal cooking juices. Fry the bacon. Stew the peppers.

To serve, dress the veal medallions on the kidney, coat with the sauce and cover with the bacon, peppers and pine kernels. Mix the rice with the pistachio nuts, work in a little butter and lightly fold in the cheese. Mould as desired and turn out on to the plates as a garnish.

(Karl Brunnengräber, Germany)

Fillet of veal with asparagus sauce

Filet de veau en sauce aux asperges
Kalbsfilet auf Spargelsauce

2 portions

400 g	fillet of veal	14 oz
	2 morels	

Roast the fillet of veal whole and keep hot. For asparagus sauce recipe see page 193. To serve, place the sauce on warmed plates and dress the sliced veal on top. Garnish each portion with a braised morel.

(Gerhard Gartner, Germany)

Veal fillet with scampi and Nantua sauce

Filet de veau aux crevettes géantes – sauce Nantua
Kalbsfiletspitzen mit Riesengarnelen in Nantuasauce mit jungen Kohlrabi und Morcheln

10 portions   Cooking time: 40 minutes

1 kg	veal fillet	2 lb 4 oz
	20 scampi tails	
200 g	butter	7 oz
	10 small kohlrabi globes	
400 g	morels	14 oz
400 g	fresh spinach	14 oz
	flour for coating	
	2 eggs	
½ l	Nantua sauce	18 fl oz
	salt, pepper	
50 g	shallots	2 oz
⅛ l	dairy cream	4 fl oz
	1 tablespoon Pernod	

Cut the veal into 20 slices, flatten, season with salt and pepper, then coat with flour and beaten egg. Fry in foaming hot butter until medium done. Place two slices on each plate and coat with Nantua sauce. Decorate each portion with two scampi tails and garnish with a stuffed kohlrabi globe and stewed morels (or chanterelles, flap mushrooms or field mushrooms, depending on the season).

To prepare the kohlrabi, hollow them out and cook in 60 g (2 oz) butter and the cream. Stuff with the spinach which has been coarsely chopped, cooked and flavoured with the Pernod. (Illustration, page 696)

(Karl Brunnengräber, Germany)

Veal medallions with mussels
Médaillons de filet de veau aux moules
Kalbsfilet mit Venusmuscheln

1 portion

160 g	veal fillet	5½ oz
1 dl	dry white wine	3½ fl oz
	1 tablespoon dairy cream	
½ l	mussels	1 pt
	juice of 1 lemon	
30 g	butter	1 oz
	salt, pepper	

Cut the veal into two medallions. Season with salt and freshly ground white pepper. Wash the mussels well. Cook them in white wine over gentle heat until they open, when they are ready to serve. Remove all but three from their shells.

Fry the veal medallions until medium done and keep hot. Pour off the butter, stir in the wine to detach the sediment, bring to the boil and reduce almost completely. Add the cream, then the mussels which were removed from their shells. Flavour with lemon juice and reduce to make a thick sauce, then strain. Dress the veal on a warmed plate, coat with the sauce and garnish with the three mussels left in their shells.
(Illustration, page 766)

(Gerhard Gartner, Germany)

Grilled calf's heart with garlic and paprika butter
Coeur de veau grillé au beurre de paprika
Kalbsherz vom Grill mit mildem Knoblauch und Paprikabutter

4 portions

	1 calf's heart	

Marinade:

	1 shallot, grated	
	juice of half a lemon	
	salt	
	pepper, freshly ground	
	olive oil	

Mild garlic:

	20 young cloves of garlic	
8 l	salted water	14 pt

15 g	butter	½ oz
	1 medium onion, very finely grated	

Mix the marinade ingredients together well. Trim the heart, removing all fat and sinews, slice, place in the marinade for 10 minutes, then grill.

Peel the garlic, place in a pan containing 2 l (3½ pt) lightly salted water and boil up. Repeat three times. Heat the butter in a copper pan, add the onion and brown slowly over low heat until the onion resembles breadcrumbs. Add the garlic, which has been squeezed dry, and fry well.

To serve, dress the slices of heart on warmed plates. Cover with the garlic/onion mixture and garnish with fondantes potatoes and paprika butter.
(Illustration, page 769)

(Gerhard Gartner, Germany)

Calf's brains with brown butter and lamb's lettuce
Cervelle de veau au beurre noisette avec salade de rampons
Kalbshirn mit brauner Butter mit Feldsalat

1 portion

120–140 g	calf's brains	4–5 oz
	1 dried morel	
2 dl	veal stock	7 fl oz
1 dl	white wine	3½ fl oz
	salt, commercial seasoning	
20 g	butter	¾ oz
70 g	lamb's lettuce, blanched	2½ oz
	2 medium potatoes	
	3–4 julienne strips red pepper	
	2 julienne strips parsley	
	1 teaspoon green peppercorns	

Blanch and skin the brains, then simmer slowly in veal stock for 8 to 10 minutes. Allow to cool, toss in brown butter and dress on the lamb's lettuce. Garnish with the green peppercorns and red pepper julienne. Serve with parsley potatoes and the morel which has been steeped in the white wine and a little veal stock, then gently cooked in veal stock. Pour brown butter over the brains just before serving.
(Illustration, page 941)

(Werner Dabernig, Austria)

Calf's brains with sage
Cervelle de veau au beurre et à la sauge
Cervella al burro e salvia

1 portion

120 g	calf's brains	4 oz
	butter	
	5–6 fresh sage leaves	
	1 egg yolk	
	flour, salt	

Trim the brains, cut into quarters, season with salt, coat with flour and beaten egg yolk and fry in butter. Add the sage leaves at the last minute to avoid burning them. Serve with parsley potatoes or mashed potatoes.
(Illustration, page 417)

(Giulio Casazza, Switzerland)

Calf's brains with vinaigrette and goat's beard
Cervelle de veau en vinaigrette sur barbe du prophète
Kalbshirn in feiner Vinaigrette auf Ziegenbart (Bart des Propheten)

4 portions

	1 set calf's brains	
100 g	goat's beard	3½ oz
	1 tablespoon preserved pink peppercorns	
	1 small bunch lemon balm	
1 dl	vinaigrette sauce, consisting of:	3½ fl oz
3 cl	nut oil	1 fl oz
3 cl	olive oil	1 fl oz
4 cl	honey vinegar	1½ fl oz
	salt	
	4 tablespoons brunoise of carrots, celery, leek	

Skin the brains under running water, remove the blood vessels and soak well in water. Place in cold water containing salt and vinegar, and boil up once. Allow to cool in the water, then remove and slice. Blanch the goat's beard in an ample amount of salted water and drain. Blanch the vegetable brunoise briefly and dress with the vinaigrette. Place the slices of brains on the goat's beard, surround with the brunoise and decorate with the pink peppercorns and the lemon balm. The goat's beard may be replaced, if desired, by very fine young French beans which have been blanched, keeping them firm to the bite.
(Illustration, page 768)

(Gerhard Gartner, Germany)

Calf's head alla cacciatora
Tête de veau chasseur
Testina di vitello alla cacciatora

	1 calf's head	
	1 large onion, cut in half	
	2 carrots, scraped	
	2 stalks celery	

Sauce:

50 g	streaky bacon, cut into thin julienne strips	2 oz
	1 medium onion	
	1 clove of garlic	
	zest of 1 lemon	
100 g	tomato purée	3½ oz
	oil and butter as required	
	1 tablespoon parsley, finely chopped	
	flour as required	
	salt	
	pepper, freshly ground	

Boil the head in lightly salted water containing the onion, celery and carrots, skimming from time to time. Lift out of the pan and remove the soft parts, then slice these thinly.

To make the sauce, chop the onion finely and cook gently without colouring in a mixture of equal amounts of oil and butter. Dust with flour, stir and slowly add calf's head stock. Stir in the tomato purée and continue cooking, then add the parsley together with the garlic which has been well crushed (or the garlic juice) and the bacon. Season with salt and pepper and cook for a further 20 minutes to make a fairly thick sauce.

Reheat the meat for a moment in the sauce, dress on individual plates and garnish with young peas and aubergine medallions (recipe, page 1008).
(Illustration, page 519)

(Franco Colombani, Italy)

Garnished veal cutlets
Côtelettes de veau garnies
Garnierte Kalbskoteletts

10 portions

180 g	10 veal cutlets each weighing	6 oz

	oil	
	salt, pepper	
100 g	mushrooms	3½ oz
50 g	butter	2 oz
200 g	rice	7 oz
	10 egg yolks	
10 g	Parmesan cheese, grated	⅓ oz

Season the cutlets with salt and pepper, fry on both sides in hot oil and transfer to a buttered pan. Slice the mushrooms and sauter in butter. Cook the rice.

Place a few mushrooms on each cutlet and cover with a spoonful of rice. Make a small hollow in the rice and carefully place a raw egg yolk in it. Sprinkle with Parmesan cheese and bake in an oven with good top heat until the egg yolk has set. Serve young peas as an accompaniment.

(Eduard Mayer, Austria)

Veal cutlet with lobster
Côtelette de veau homardine
Kalbskoteletts mit Hummer

2 portions

160 g	2 veal cutlets each weighing	5½ oz
400 g	1 lobster weighing	14 oz
	butter	
2 cl	Cognac	1 fl oz
5 cl	veal stock	2 fl oz
	3 tablespoons dairy cream	
	fresh dill leaves	
	fennel leaves	

Kill the lobster by leaving it in boiling water for about half a minute, then cut it in half. Sauter the cutlets in butter until medium done. Place the lobster in the butter remaining in the pan and sauter until glassy in appearance. If cooked beyond this point, the flesh will become tough. Remove the meat from the shell and keep hot. Crack the claws and carefully remove the meat.

Stir the Cognac and the veal stock into the sauté pan to detach the cooking juices, add the cream, reduce to the required consistency, strain and flavour with the dill and fennel leaves.

Slice the lobster meat. Divide three quarters of the sauce between two plates. Place a veal cutlet

on each plate and coat with the rest of the sauce. Arrange the lobster meat round the cutlets and cover these with the meat removed from the claws.
(Illustration, page 767)

(Gerhard Gartner, Germany)

Veal cutlet in paper
Côte de veau en papillote
Costoletta di vitello cartoccio

1 portion

160–180 g	1 veal cutlet weighing	5½–6 oz
3 cl	white wine	1 fl oz
	oil	
15 g	butter	½ oz
	3 mushroom caps, poached and thinly sliced	
	1 tablespoon calf's brains and sweetbreads, poached and finely cut	
	1 slice raw ham	
	2 tablespoons gravy	
	greaseproof paper	
	salt; pepper, freshly ground	

Flatten the cutlet a little, season with salt and pepper and brown in oil on both sides. Pour off the oil, add the butter, fry until cooked and stir in the wine. Add the mushroom caps, brains, sweetbreads and ham. Reduce until the wine has boiled away, then add the gravy.

Place the cutlet on a sheet of greaseproof paper. Cover first with the mushrooms, brains and sweetbreads, then with the slice of ham. Pour the gravy over. Fold over the paper to enclose the cutlet and seal the edges. Place in the oven or under a salamander to swell up the paper.

(Giulio Casazza, Switzerland)

Veal cutlet Jockey Club
Côte de veau Jockey Club

4 portions

200 g	4 veal cutlets each weighing	7 oz
	flour	
1 cl	oil	½ fl oz
20 g	butter	¾ oz

1½ dl	white wine	5 fl oz
2½ dl	brown veal stock	9 fl oz
	4 poached eggs	
	4 mushroom caps, turned and grooved	
	peppers cut into small oblongs	
	4 thin slices truffle	
	6 green asparagus tips, poached and	
	cut in half	
	salt	
	pepper, freshly ground	

Carefully trim the cutlets, season with salt and pepper, then flour them. Fry in oil and butter until brown on both sides, basting constantly. Remove from the pan and keep hot. Pour off the fat, detach the sediment with the wine and reduce. Add the stock and reduce to the desired consistency. Pass through a fine strainer and carefully season with salt and pepper. Poach the eggs meanwhile.

To serve, pour the sauce on to warmed plates and dress the cutlets on it. Garnish with the eggs, the asparagus which has been heated in butter, the mushroom caps, slices of truffle and pieces of sweet pepper.
(Illustration, page 241)

(Anton Mosimann, Great Britain)

Veal cutlet Pinzgau
Côtelette de veau Pinzgau
Kalbskotelett Pinzgauer Art

1 portion

120 g	1 veal cutlet weighing	4 oz
50 g	butter	2 oz
12 cl	white wine	4 fl oz
16 cl	brown veal stock	6 fl oz
	2 artichoke hearts	
	1 courgette	
	3 mushrooms	
	2 strips sweet pepper	
	2 potatoes	
	juice of half a lemon	
	salt, pepper	
	tarragon, chervil, marjoram	
	3 fresh tarragon leaves to decorate	

Trim and tie the cutlet. Season with salt and pepper. Melt the butter, brown the cutlet in it and cook slowly. Remove from the pan, detach the sediment with half the wine and add the veal stock.

Peel and precook the potatoes. Slice the artichoke hearts, courgette and mushrooms. Place the rest of the wine in a pan with a mixture of tarragon, chervil and marjoram, add the lemon juice, bring to the boil and reduce by half. Add to the veal stock, toss the vegetables and potatoes in this sauce and season with salt to taste. To serve, arrange the vegetables on a plate to make a base for the cutlet. Decorate with the tarragon leaves.

(Werner Dabernig, Austria)

Calf's liver with sultanas
Foie de veau aux raisins de Smyrne
Fegato di vitello con uva sultanina

1 portion

60 g	2 slices calf's liver each weighing	2 oz
	1 tablespoon sultanas	
	flour	
	butter	
	salt	

Lightly flour the liver and brown on both sides in butter. Add the sultanas which have been soaked overnight and well drained. Fry until cooked and serve with mashed potatoes.

(Giulio Casazza, Switzerland)

Veal chop with green tomatoes
Côte de veau aux tomates acerbes
Costoletta di vitello ai pomodori acerbi

1 portion   Cooking time: 20 minutes

250 g	1 veal chop weighing	9 oz
120 g	green tomatoes	4 oz
40 g	butter	1½ oz
4 cl	olive oil	1½ fl oz
1 dl	white wine (Vernaccia)	3½ fl oz
	salt	
	white pepper, freshly ground	

Wash the tomatoes under running water. Remove the stalk ends and dry with a cloth, then cut into quarters. Place in a small pan with the olive oil and season with salt and pepper. Season the chop on both sides with salt and pepper. Fry in 20 g (¾ oz) nut brown butter over moderate heat, allowing 6 to 8 minutes a side. Meanwhile cook the tomatoes separately over gentle heat for 8 to 10 minutes, when they should be lightly browned but still firm. Keep hot.

Pour off the butter in which the veal was cooked, stir in the wine to detach the sediment, bring to the boil, reduce by half, then finish the sauce with the rest of the butter and pass through a fine conical strainer. Pour the sauce on to a warmed plate, dress the veal chop on it and garnish with the tomatoes.
(Illustration, page 412)

(Daniel Drouadaine, Italy)

Fried calf's liver
Foie de veau frit
Gebackene Kalbsleber

10 portions

80 g	20 slices calf's liver each weighing	3 oz
	salt, pepper	
	marjoram	
150 g	flour	5 oz
	3 eggs	
200 g	white breadcrumbs	7 oz
	fat for deep-frying	

Snip the edges of the slices of liver, season with salt, pepper and marjoram, then flour, egg and crumb. Deep-fry at 180°C (355°F) until golden brown, drain and serve with mixed salad.

(Eduard Mayer, Austria)

Calf's liver Tyrolean fashion
Foie de veau à la tyrolienne
Kalbsleber auf Tiroler Art

8 portions

1 kg 200	calf's liver	2 lb 10 oz
4 cl	oil	1½ fl oz
	1 large onion	

80 g	butter	3 oz
	2 tablespoons flour	
¼ l	sour cream	9 fl oz
¼ l	brown stock	9 fl oz
	1 tablespoon capers, chopped	
	half a lemon (unsprayed)	
	salt, pepper	

Trim the liver, removing any coarse tubes, slice, season with salt and pepper, dust with flour on one side and quickly brown in hot oil, then remove from the pan and keep hot. Pour off the oil. Melt the butter in the pan, add the rest of the flour and the sour cream, then stir in the stock. Add the capers and the lemon zest which has been finely chopped. Boil up, reduce the heat, place the liver in the sauce and leave to stand for a few minutes without boiling. Serve with buttered potatoes and salad

(Eduard Mayer, Austria)

Calf's liver with walnuts and green almonds
Foie de veau aux noix et aux amandes vertes
Kalbsleberfilets mit Baumnüssen und grünen Mandeln, gedünsteter Staudensellerie

10 portions   Cooking time: 25 minutes

1 kg 300	calf's liver	2 lb 14 oz
200 g	bacon	7 oz
900 g	celery	2 lb
	15 green almonds	
250 g	walnuts, shelled and skinned	9 oz
½ l	thickened veal gravy	18 fl oz
200 g	butter	7 oz
	salt, pepper	
	flour	

Cut the liver into 10 slices. Flour lightly, fry in butter until medium done, then season with salt and pepper. Transfer to well warmed plates. Decorate with the walnuts which have been steeped in salted water for 12 hours before skinning. Garnish with the celery which has been stewed, including the young leaves, topped with strips of bacon and green almond halves, and with fried polenta triangles.
(Illustration, page 698)

(Karl Brunnengräber, Germany)

Calf's liver medallions with mustard cream sauce
Médaillons de foie de veau à la crème de moutarde
Kalbsleber-Medaillons auf Apfelscheiben mit Senfcreme, Magerspeckscheiben und gerösteten Senftrieben

10 portions   Cooking time: 30 minutes

70 g	20 calf's liver medallions each weighing	2½ oz
350 g	bacon	12 oz
120 g	butter	4 oz
	salt, pepper	
30 g	20 slices apple each weighing	1 oz
1 kg	broccoli	2 lb 4 oz
	flour for dusting	

Mustard cream sauce:

125 g	mild mustard	4½ oz
4 dl	dairy cream	14 fl oz
	3 egg yolks	
	juice of 2 lemons	
	salt, pepper	
5 cl	brandy	2 fl oz
	1 tablespoon chives, finely chopped	
	a pinch of sugar	

Season the liver with salt and pepper, flour, then fry until medium done. Sauter the apple slices in butter, place the liver on top, coat with mustard cream sauce and top with lightly fried bacon.

To make the sauce, mix the egg yolks with the mustard and beat with the brandy in a simmering bain-marie. Gradually add the cream and lemon juice, season with salt and pepper, add a pinch of sugar, then the chives, and continue beating until smooth and thick. This sauce should be kept hot in the bain-marie, but may on no account be allowed to boil.

To prepare fried mustard shoots for topping, sprinkle an appropriate amount of mustard seed on to a wet cloth, sprinkle with lukewarm water and cover with a second wet cloth. Leave at room temperature for two days, when the shoots will have grown. Fry these in butter and season lightly with salt and pepper before use. Arrange on top of bacon on liver medallions. Serve lightly cooked broccoli florets and buttered potatoes as accompaniments.
(Illustration, page 697)

(Karl Brunnengräber, Germany)

Veal medallions with Calvados
Médaillons de veau au Calvados
Kalbsmedaillons mit Calvados

5 portions

70 g	10 veal medallions (fillet) each weighing	2½ oz
100 g	butter	3½ oz
1 dl	Calvados	3½ fl oz

3 dl	dairy cream	10 fl oz
1 dl	veal stock	3½ fl oz
1 dl	white wine	3½ fl oz
	seasonings as desired	
	salt, pepper	

Season the veal with salt and pepper. Fry slowly on both sides over low heat, remove and dress on heated plates. Stir in the wine to detach the sediment; add the veal stock, cream and Calvados, together with seasoning. Reduce by half and pour over the veal medallions.

(Otto Ledermann, Switzerland)

Veal medallions with mushrooms
Médaillons de veau aux champignons
Borjuszelet Erdésznö módra

10 portions   Cooking time: 15–20 minutes

1 kg 600	fillet of veal	3 lb 8 oz
300 g	chicken livers	11 oz
50 g	salt	2 oz
200 g	flour	7 oz
300 g	lard	11 oz
100 g	butter	3½ oz
50 g	onions, finely chopped	2 oz
500 g	mushrooms, thinly sliced	1 lb 2 oz
3 g	black pepper, freshly ground	a good pinch
	parsley, finely chopped	
3 dl	sour cream	10 fl oz
2 dl	dairy cream	7 fl oz
1 dl	white wine	3½ fl oz
	lemon (for juice)	

Rice with ham:

| 600 g | rice, cooked | 1 lb 5 oz |
| 300 g | ham, finely cut | 11 oz |

Cut the veal into medallions, beat, trim, season with salt, flour and sauter in hot lard until half-cooked, then remove and place in a second pan. Fry the onions in the remaining lard until lightly coloured, add the mushrooms, salt, pepper and parsley, mix well and sauter.

Blanch the livers, cut into cubes, place on the veal, add the wine and cook gently under cover. Blend the sour and fresh cream well with the flour and add to the veal shortly before it is cooked. Flavour with lemon juice and finish cooking under cover, keeping the meat slightly pink inside.

Mix the rice and ham together. Dress the veal medallions on warmed plates and coat with the cooking juices which have been enriched with butter. Serve with the rice.

(Zsolt Körmendy, Hungary)

Veal medallions with figs and ginger sauce
Médaillons de veau aux figues en sauce au gingembre
Kalbsmedaillons mit Feigen in Ingwersauce, wilder Reis mit Pinienkernen

10 portions   Cooking time: 25 minutes

	20 veal medallions (cut from back)	
	salt, white pepper	
8 cl	oil	3 fl oz
¼ l	dry white wine	9 fl oz
3 dl	thick sour cream	10 fl oz
300 g	fresh figs	11 oz
	1 piece preserved ginger	
400 g	wild rice	14 oz
	flour	
	1 egg, beaten	
120 g	butter	4 oz

Season the medallions with salt and pepper, then flour them and dip in beaten egg. Fry on both sides in hot oil, keeping them juicy. Remove from the pan and keep hot. Stir in the wine to detach the sediment and bring to the boil. Add the sour cream and return to the boil. Add the figs which have been either left whole or cut in half, depending on size. Heat under cover. Dress the meat on individual plates and surround with the figs. Mix the sauce with the ginger which has been cut into strips and finish with knobs of butter.

Soak the wild rice in water for 2 hours, then cook for 40 minutes in double its volume (or a little more) salted water. Fill into a timbale mould, turn out on to a dish and sprinkle with pine kernels. Use as a garnish for the medallions, together with asparagus tips.
(Illustration, page 697)

(Karl Brunnengräber, Germany)

Veal medallions with ginger
Médaillons de veau au gingembre
Medaglioni di vitello allo zenzero

4 portions   Cooking time: 20 minutes

40 g	12 veal medallions each weighing	1½ oz
20 g	ginger	¾ oz
3 dl	plain white veal stock	10 fl oz

3 dl	clear brown veal stock	10 fl oz
2 dl	dairy cream	7 fl oz
40 g	butter, clarified	1½ oz
500 g	spinach	1 lb 2 oz
	24 button onions	
60 g	butter	2 oz
10 g	sugar	¼ oz
	coarse and fine salt	
	white pepper, freshly ground	

Peel the ginger and slice very thinly. Clean the spinach, cut off the stalks, wash under running water and drain. Blanch for about 2 minutes in 2 dl (7 fl oz) salted water containing 20 g (¾ oz) butter. Drain well, transfer to a fine sieve to cool, then squeeze dry. Wash the onions, place in a pan with 20 g (¾ oz) butter, a pinch of fine salt and the sugar, and cover with water. Cook over very gentle heat for 15 minutes, covering the pan with oiled paper. The onions should remain white. Allow to cool, hollow out and fill with the spinach. Melt 20 g (¾ oz) butter in a pan, arrange the onions in it side by side and pour in the brown veal stock. Cover with oiled paper.

Season the veal medallions with salt and pepper. Fry on both sides in the clarified butter in a copper pan for 8 to 10 minutes. Remove, pour off the butter, add the ginger and stir in 3 dl (10 fl oz) light veal stock. Reduce for 2 or 3 minutes, add the cream and pass through a strainer. Reheat the onions. Pour the sauce on to the plates, dress the medallions on top and surround with the onions.
(Illustration, page 412)

(Gualtiero Marchesi, Italy)

Veal medallions with morels and green sauce
Médaillons de veau aux morilles en sauce verte
Kalbsmedaillons mit Rundmorcheln in grüner Sauce

4 portions   Cooking time: about 30 minutes

	4 veal medallions (middle fillet cut)	
150 g	each weighing	5 oz
	4 morels	
2 cl	Madeira	1 fl oz
2 cl	white wine	1 fl oz
30–40 g	butter	1–1½ oz
	salt	

Green sauce:

	2 medium leeks
	1 bunch parsley

	1 cup spinach, blanched	
	1 bunch chives	
5 cl	white wine	2 fl oz
5 cl	dairy cream	2 fl oz
5 cl	chicken velouté	2 fl oz
	salt	
	lemon juice	

Season the veal with salt and fry in 20 g butter until medium done. Remove and keep hot.

Wash the morels thoroughly, place in the pan in which the veal was fried, add the Madeira and white wine and stand at the side of the stove until cooked. Reduce the stock and thicken with 10–20 g cold butter. To make the sauce, cut the leeks into small pieces and blanch. Wash the spinach well and blanch. Pour off the water and squeeze the vegetables dry. Place in the mixer with the parsley, chives, wine, cream and velouté. Mix at high speed and season with salt to taste. Flavour with lemon juice.

To serve, heat the sauce quickly, spoon into deep plates and dress the medallions on top. Cover with the morels and coat with the morel stock.
(Illustration, page 767)

(Gerhard Gartner, Germany)

Veal medallions Swedish style
Médaillons de veau à la suédoise

4 portions

	80 g	4 veal medallions each weighing	3 oz
	200 g	smoked ham, cut into 4 thin slices	7 oz
		salt, pepper	
		a little flour	
	50 g	butter	2 oz
		2 tablespoons oil	
Potatoes:			
	250 g	4 medium potatoes weighing a total of	9 oz
		1 tablespoon onion, finely chopped	
	3 dl	dairy cream	10 fl oz
		approx. 1 teaspoon flour butter	
		salt	
Peas:			
	300 g	young peas (fresh or frozen)	11 oz
	50 g	butter	2 oz
		1 tablespoon dill, finely cut	
		4 eggs	

Flatten the veal medallions lightly, season with salt and pepper, flour them and fry in brown butter and oil until golden. Quickly brown the ham without fat.

Dice the potatoes very finely, blanch, then briefly sauter with the onion. Add the cream, thicken with flour butter and season to taste. Blanch the peas and toss in the butter with the dill.

Fry the eggs, preferably in a special egg pan or a steel hoop to prevent the whites from spreading. Arrange the ham on warmed plates with the veal medallions on top. Cover each one with a fried egg and pour a little gravy round. Hand the potatoes and peas separately.

(Eric Carlström, Sweden)

Calf's liver medallions with herb and vinegar sauce and apple timbales
Kalbsleber-Medaillons in gekräutertem Sherryessig, Apfeltimbal

10 portions   Cooking time: 30 minutes

70 g	20 calf's liver medallions each weighing	2½ oz
1 dl	oil	3½ fl oz
	salt; pepper, freshly ground	

Apple timbales:

500 g	diced apples	1 lb 2 oz
	juice of 1 lemon	
	hot butter to colour	
50 g	rusks, finely crushed	2 oz
	1 egg	
	2 tablespoons dairy cream	

Herb and vinegar sauce:

½ l	Espagnole sauce	18 fl oz
150 g	shallots	5 oz
50 g	butter	2 oz
5 cl	sherry vinegar	2 fl oz
1½ dl	white wine	5 fl oz
100 g	herbs (parsley, chervil, tarragon, chives), chopped	3½ oz

To make the sauce, cook the shallots in the butter, mix with the remaining ingredients and reduce to a light coating consistency.

To make the timbales, sprinkle the diced apples with lemon juice (firm apples should be used). Fry in hot butter over high heat until coloured. Mix carefully with the rusk crumbs, the egg and the cream. Butter timbale moulds, fill with the apple mixture and cook in a bain-marie until set.

Fry the veal medallions in oil until medium done. Place on heated plates and pour the sauce over. Turn out an apple timbale on to each plate.

(Karl Brunnengräber, Germany)

Saltimbocca of calf's liver
Saltimbocca de foie de veau
Saltimbocca von Kalbsleber mit Roggennudeln, Austernpilzen und Tomaten

1 portion

150 g	calf's liver (end pieces)	5 oz
	sage leaves	
	2 thin slices smoked bacon	
60 g	butter	2 oz
	3 large mushrooms	
	1 teaspoon tomato purée	
	1 tablespoon tomato cullis	
	chives	
	1 portion rye noodles	

Gorgonzola cream:

20 g	Gorgonzola	¾ oz
	2 tablespoons dairy cream	

Cut the calf's liver into bite size pieces, cover with a sage leaf, wrap in the bacon and quickly brown in butter. Heat the rest of the butter in a second pan, quickly fry the mushrooms in it and season lightly with salt.

Cook the noodles *al dente,* drain and mix with the Gorgonzola cream. Heat the tomato purée and cullis briefly over low heat and season. Sprinkle the noodles with chopped chives before serving. To make the Gorgonzola cream, blend the cheese and cream together at the side of the stove.

(Gerhard Gartner, Germany)

Stuffed calf's liver slices with chestnut sauce and small onions
Tranches de foie de veau farcies, sauce aux marrons et aux petits oignons
Gefüllte Kalbsleberschnitte mit Maronen und kleinen Zwiebelchen in Marsala, Eierreisfladen

10 portions   Cooking time: 30 minutes

130 g	10 slices calf's liver each weighing	4½ oz
180 g	butter	6 oz

	30 small onions, blanched	
400 g	chestnuts, glazed	14 oz
½ l	thickened veal gravy	18 fl oz
⅛ l	Marsala	4 fl oz
⅛ l	white wine	4 fl oz

Forcemeat:

100 g	bacon, finely diced	3½ oz
60 g	shallots, finely cut	2 oz
250 g	mushrooms, diced	9 oz
	2 tablespoons parsley, chopped	
	1 tablespoon chives, chopped	
	2 eggs	
5 cl	sour cream	2 fl oz
	salt	
	pepper, freshly ground	
	mace, sage	

Rice cutlets:

20 tablespoons rice, cooked
10 eggs
salt
a pinch of Cayenne pepper

To make the forcemeat, fry the shallots with the bacon in 50 g (2 oz) butter until lightly coloured. Add the mushrooms, parsley and chives. Season with salt and pepper, and flavour with sage and mace. Cook until almost dry, remove from the heat and allow to cool, then fold in the sour cream and eggs.

The slices of liver should be 1 cm (⅜ in) thick. Cut a pocket on one side with a sharp knife and stuff with the forcemeat. Close the pocket with a small wooden skewer. Fry carefully on both sides in 50 g (2 oz) hot butter, stir in the white wine and cook for a few minutes. Remove the liver and keep hot. Reduce the stock and glaze the onions in it. Add the chestnuts, veal gravy and Marsala, and boil well. Pour over the liver to serve. Hand rice cutlets separately.

To make the cutlets, mix the rice with the beaten eggs, season with salt and Cayenne pepper, shape into small cutlets and fry in the rest of the butter.

(Karl Brunnengräber, Germany)

Calf's liver Soubise with lemon cream sauce
Foie de veau soubise, sauce crème au citron
Kalbsleberschnitten Soubise, Zitronensauce

10 portions

1 kg 400	calf's liver free from skin and tubes	3 lb

	salt	
	pepper, freshly ground	
	marjoram	
100 g	butter	3½ oz
	1 large clean pork caul	

Soubise sauce:

500 g	onions	1 lb 2 oz
80 g	butter	3 oz
¾ l	light veal or chicken stock	1¼ pt
100 g	rice	3½ oz
1 dl	dairy cream	3½ fl oz
	salt	
	pepper, freshly ground	

Lemon cream sauce:

70 g	butter	2½ oz
100 g	flour	3½ oz
¾ l	light veal or chicken stock	1¼ pt
	3 lemons	
	1 bouquet garni	
	3 egg yolks	
¼ l	dairy cream	9 fl oz
	salt	
	pepper, freshly ground	
	parsley, chopped	

To make the Soubise sauce, cut up the onions coarsely and blanch in boiling salted water to reduce their strong flavour. Cook gently with the rice in 40 g (1½ oz) butter without colouring, then stir in the stock and cook gently until very soft. Work to a purée in the mixer or rub through a sieve. Season with salt and pepper, mix well with the cream and finish with the remaining butter.

Slice the liver fairly thinly, season with a mixture of salt, pepper and marjoram, then brown in butter on one side only. Spread this side thickly with Soubise sauce. Wrap each slice separately in a piece of pork caul which has been cut to size. Fry on both sides in butter until cooked. To serve, coat with lemon cream sauce. Hand rice with paprika separately.

To make the lemon cream sauce, prepare a blond roux with the butter and flour, then add the stock to make a velouté, which should be left to simmer slowly with the bouquet garni and thinly pared lemon zest until cooked. Pass through a cloth, thicken with the cream and egg yolks, then add salt, pepper and a generous amount of lemon juice, and stir in chopped parsley to finish.

(Karl Brunnengräber, Germany)

Sweetbreads and goose liver with morels
Ris de veau et foie d'oie aux morilles
Kalbsmilch mit Gänseleber und Morcheln

6 portions

300 g	calves' sweetbreads	11 oz
	1 onion, stuck with a clove	
50 g	butter	2 oz
100 g	fresh morels or turban-tops	3½ oz
2 dl	veal stock	7 fl oz
	flour butter	
	Madeira	
	Cognac	
	salt	
	pepper, freshly ground	
150 g	fresh goose liver	5 oz
	2 egg yolks	
1 dl	dairy cream	3½ fl oz

Rinse the sweetbreads well under running water for several hours to whiten. Cook with the onion in salted water until medium done, skimming constantly. Remove the skin and gristle, then divide into segments.

Wash the morels well and sauter very carefully in the butter. Add the veal stock and the sweetbreads. Thicken slightly with flour butter. Flavour with Madeira and Cognac, and season with salt and pepper. Whisk the egg yolks with the cream and fold in at the side of the stove. At the last minute add the goose liver which has been well trimmed of blood vessels and sinews and cut into cubes. Do not continue cooking. Serve in bowls if possible. (Illustration, page 767)

(Gerhard Gartner, Germany)

Mignons of veal Forner's

1 portion

40 g	3 veal medallions (fillet) each weighing	1½ oz
	salt, pepper	
	flour	
	1 egg	
	cornflakes	
	almonds, blanched and flaked	

	butter	
5 cl	tomato-flavoured veal stock	2 fl oz
100 g	leaf spinach, cooked in butter	3½ oz
	2 tomatoes, skinned, seeded and finely diced	

Season and flour the medallions, dip in beaten egg, coat with a mixture of cornflakes and flaked almonds, press down well, and fry the medallions in clarified butter. Pour a thin layer of tomato-flavoured veal stock on to a hot plate. Place the golden brown medallions on top and garnish with the spinach and tomatoes.

(Jean Esslinger, France)

Mignons of veal with sorrel
Mignons de veau à l'oseille

4 portions

70 g	8 mignons of veal each weighing	2½ oz
2 dl	groundnut oil	7 fl oz
20 g	butter	¾ oz
4 cl	white veal stock	1½ fl oz
	salt	
	pepper, freshly ground	

Sauce:

10 g	butter	⅓ oz
2 g	shallots, finely chopped	1 small teaspoon
5 cl	white wine	2 fl oz
3 cl	Noilly Prat	1 fl oz
2 dl	white veal stock	7 fl oz
1½ dl	dairy cream	5 fl oz
60 g	butter to finish	2 oz
20 g	sorrel, cut into strips about 3 mm (⅛ in) wide	
	salt	
	pepper, freshly ground	

Season the veal with salt and pepper. Fry on both sides in groundnut oil and butter until light brown. Remove and keep hot. Pour off the fat and stir in the white veal stock to detach the sediment, bring to the boil and reduce by half.

To make the sauce, cook the shallots gently in butter without colouring, detach the sediment with white wine and Noilly Prat, and reduce. Add the white veal stock and reduce again, then add the cream, boil up and pass through a fine sieve. Add the cooking juices from the mignons of veal and carefully finish with butter. Lastly add the sorrel and season with salt and pepper.

To serve, pour the sauce on to warmed plates and place the veal on top. Serve spinach cooked in butter as an accompaniment.
(Illustration, page 241)

(Anton Mosimann, Great Britain)

Mignons of veal with chive sauce
Mignons de veau à la crème de ciboulette

4 portions

70 g	8 mignons of veal each weighing	2½ oz
	flour	
30 g	butter	1 oz
1 dl	white wine	3½ fl oz
1 dl	brown veal stock	3½ fl oz
20 g	chive purée	¾ oz
2 g	chives, finely cut	2 teaspoons
40 g	butter to finish sauce	1½ oz
	salt	
	pepper, freshly ground	
2 dl	dairy cream	7 fl oz

Garnish:

30 g	butter	1 oz
50 g	carrots, cut into strips	2 oz
50 g	courgettes, cut into strips	2 oz
50 g	celery, cut into strips	2 oz
50 g	fine French beans	2 oz
50 g	cauliflower florets	2 oz
50 g	sugar peas	2 oz
20 g	broad beans	¾ oz
	salt	
	pepper, freshly ground	

Trim the mignons of veal carefully, season with salt and pepper, and flour lightly. Fry on both sides in the butter until golden, keeping them juicy, then remove and keep hot. Pour off the rest of the butter, stir in the wine to detach the sediment, bring to the boil and reduce. Add the brown veal stock and cream, and reduce a little. Pass through a fine sieve. Add the chive purée and chives, and mix carefully. Finish with the butter which has been softened, season with salt and pepper, and pour on to warmed plates. Place the mignons of veal on the sauce and surround with the vegetables which have been blanched and stewed in butter.

To make the chive purée, chop 20 g (¾ oz) fresh chives as finely as possible with a sharp knife. Use at once.
(Illustration, page 241)

(Anton Mosimann, Great Britain)

Mignons of veal Wladimir

6 portions

1 kg 200	fillet of veal	2 lb 10 oz
80 g	black truffles, finely chopped	3 oz
¾ l	dairy cream	1¼ pt
¼ l	veal stock	9 fl oz
300 g	bacon for barding	11 oz
50 g	garlic, very finely chopped	2 oz
30 g	pine honey	1 oz
	salt	

Cut the veal into 12–18 medallions (at least 2 per portion). Season with salt, flatten a little and brown very briefly on both sides. Sandwich the medallions in threes with chopped truffles and wrap each set of three in a broad slice of bacon. Place in a sauté pan and roast in the oven at 180°C (355°F). Allow the bacon fat on both sides to melt for 3 minutes. Remove from the pan and pour off the melted fat, then unwrap the medallions and return to the pan without the bacon. Stir in the veal stock and ½ l (18 fl oz) cream and simmer over gentle heat for 5 minutes. Add the garlic, then the rest of the cream, reduce for 2 minutes and add the honey.

Transfer the meat to warmed plates and coat with the sauce which has been strained through a cloth. Serve French beans or broccoli as an accompaniment.
(Illustration, page 764)

(Wladimir Levyckyi, France)

Mignons of veal with onions on raw spinach
Mignons de veau aux oignons confits sur épinards crus

2 portions

200 g	fillet of veal	7 oz

150 g	button onions	5 oz
	4 spinach leaves	
1 dl	red wine	3½ fl oz
1 dl	veal stock	3½ fl oz
20 g	butter	¾ oz
5 cl	olive oil	2 fl oz
	1 small teaspoon sugar	
	salt, pepper	

Fry the onions over very low heat until very lightly coloured. When half cooked, add the sugar, together with salt and pepper to taste, and glaze lightly. Cut the veal into 4 mignons and fry in a little olive oil until medium done, then season with salt and pepper. Pour off the oil, stir in the wine to detach the sediment, then add the veal stock and reduce. Pass the sauce through a conical strainer and finish with butter. To serve, place 2 raw spinach leaves on each plate, arrange 2 mignons of veal on top and coat with sauce. Place the onions beside the meat. (Illustration, page 311)

(Roger Souvereyns, Belgium)

Mignons of veal First Lady
Mignons de veau First Lady
Kalbsmignons First Lady

4 portions

100 g	4 veal medallions (fillet) each weighing	3½ oz
40 g	butter	1½ oz
	12 asparagus tips	
	2 artichoke bottoms	
40 g	duck liver	1½ oz
1 dl	veal gravy	3½ fl oz
1 dl	dairy cream	3½ fl oz
	salt, coriander	
	flour	

Season the veal with salt and coriander, flour and slowly fry in butter on both sides until golden and medium done. Transfer to 4 heated plates and keep hot. Cut the asparagus tips into 2 cm (¾ in) lengths. If using raw asparagus, cook until nearly soft. Cook the artichoke bottoms until soft and cut each one into 8 segments. Place in the pan in which the veal medallions were fried, together with the asparagus and the duck liver. Cook gently for a short time without colouring, remove from the pan and place on top of the veal. Detach the cooking juices with the veal gravy and the cream, reduce by one third and pour over the meat. Serve rice pilaf as an accompaniment.
(Illustration, page 415)

(Felix Real, Liechtenstein)

Calf's lights and heart Viennese style
Coeur et mou de veau à la viennoise
Kalbslunge und—Herz auf Wiener Art

10 points

	1 calf's heart and lights	
200 g	root vegetables	7 oz
70 g	flour	2½ oz
80 g	fat	3 oz
¼ l	sour cream	9 fl oz
	2 tablespoons vinegar	
	bay leaf, peppercorns	
	thyme	
	onion, parsley	
	capers, anchovies	
	lemon zest, garlic	
	salt, pepper, marjoram	
	lemon juice, mustard	

Cook the heart and lights in salted water containing 1 tablespoon vinegar, the root vegetables, bay leaf, thyme and peppercorns, then slice very finely.

Make a brown roux with the flour and fat. Finely chop together the onion, parsley, capers, anchovies, lemon zest and garlic. Add to the roux, brown for a short time and stir in the rest of the vinegar. Add the stock from the heart and lights which has been strained, and boil well. Add the meat and continue cooking briefly. Finish with the sour cream, adding salt, pepper, marjoram, lemon juice and a little mustard. Serve with Austrian dumpling (recipe, page 1026).

(Eduard Mayer, Austria)

Calves' sweetbreads with three sauces
Délices de veau aux trois sauces

4 portions

400 g	calves' heart sweetbreads	14 oz
	1 calf's kidney	
200 g	veal fillet	7 oz
	16 asparagus spears	
2 dl	veal stock	7 fl oz
50 g	sorrel	2 oz
1 dl	dry sherry	3½ fl oz
5 cl	Noilly Prat	2 fl oz
1 dl	dairy cream	3½ fl oz

105 g	butter for sauces	3¾ oz
	2 egg yolks	
approx. 50 g	butter for frying	approx. 2 oz
	salt, pepper	

Soak and wash the sweetbreads well, divide into 4 portions, trim them, blanch for 4 minutes, then carefully remove the skin. Fry the sweetbreads in butter. Scrape the asparagus and blanch in salted water. (Heat if using canned asparagus.) Keep the meat and the asparagus hot.

Cut the veal fillet into 4 portions, fry in butter until medium done, season with salt and pepper, and keep hot. Detach the sediment with the Noilly Prat, add 1 dl veal stock, reduce, pour in the cream and reduce to the desired consistency. Cut the sorrel into very thin strips and add to the sauce.

Wash the kidney thoroughly, trim it and fry in its own fat until medium done (about 15 minutes). Place the sherry and the remaining veal stock in a separate pan and reduce until thick. Finish with 30 g (1 oz) butter and adjust the seasoning. Prepare Hollandaise sauce in the usual manner, using 2 egg yolks and 75 g (2¾ oz) butter.

To serve, place a portion of sweetbreads and 4 asparagus spears on each plate and coat with Hollandaise sauce; add a mignon of veal in sorrel sauce and a portion of kidney in sherry sauce. (Illustration, page 311)

(Illustration, page 311)

(Roger Souvereyns, Belgium)

Sweetbreads Zurich aristocrats' style
Ris de veau aristocratie zurichoise
Zürcher Aristokratengericht

100 portions

14 kg	calves' sweetbreads	31 lb
3 kg	mirepoix of carrots, celery, leeks, onions and parsley	6 lb 10 oz
2 l	white wine	3½ pt
2 l	veal stock	3½ pt
½ l	oil	18 fl oz
	peppercorns, cloves, bay leaves	
	salt	

Hollandaise sauce:

2 kg	butter	4 lb 8 oz
	18 egg yolks	
2 dl	vinegar	7 fl oz
2 dl	water	7 fl oz

100 g	shallots, chopped	3½ oz
2½ dl	whipped cream	9 fl oz
40 g	peppercorns, crushed	1½ oz
	salt, lemon juice	
	Cayenne pepper	

Spinach:

10 kg	leaf spinach, frozen	22 lb
30 g	garlic, finely chopped	1 oz
500 g	onions, finely chopped	1 lb 2 oz
8 dl	oil	28 fl oz
800 g	butter	1 lb 12 oz
	salt, pepper, nutmeg	

Tomatoes:

4 kg	tomatoes (small)	8 lb 12 oz
	salt, pepper	

Semolina gnocchi:

10 l	milk	17½ pt
2 kg	semolina	4 lb 8 oz
	16 egg yolks	
1 kg 200	butter	2 lb 10 oz
1 kg 200	cheese, grated	2 lb 10 oz
	salt, pepper, nutmeg	

Soak and wash the sweetbreads well. Blanch for 5 minutes in salted water containing the peppercorns, cloves and bay leaves. Brown the mirepoix in oil and place the sweetbreads on top. Add the wine and stock, and braise for 15 minutes. Slice before serving.

To make the Hollandaise sauce, place the vinegar in a pan with the shallots and peppercorns, reduce, add the water and whisk with the egg yolks in a bain-marie until thick and creamy. Draw aside and stir in the butter which has been melted. Add salt, lemon juice and Cayenne pepper to taste, then pass through a cloth. Fold in the whipped cream before using.

To prepare the spinach, lightly fry the onions and garlic in oil and butter without colouring, then add the spinach. Season with salt, pepper and nutmeg, and stew well without allowing the spinach to turn brown.

Cut the tomatoes in half and arrange on a roasting tray. Season with salt and pepper, and cook in the oven.

To make the gnocchi, place the milk in a pan with 800 g (1 lb 12 oz) butter and seasonings. Bring to the boil, add the semolina in a steady stream and cook over low heat for 15 minutes while stirring. Remove from the heat and stir in the egg yolks and 400 g (14 oz) grated cheese. Spread to a thickness of 2 cm (¾ in) on an oiled tray and allow to cool. Cut into crescents, sprinkle with cheese and melted butter, and brown in a hot oven.

To serve, place the spinach in the centre of each plate. Arrange three slices of sweetbread on top and coat with Hollandaise sauce. Glaze briefly under a salamander. Place a gnocchi crescent and half a tomato to the left and right of the spinach.

(Robert Haupt-Felber, Switzerland)

Sweetbreads with crayfish
Ris de veau aux écrevisses

6 portions

1 kg 500	calves' sweetbreads	3 lb 5 oz
2 kg	crayfish	4 lb 8 oz
100 g	chanterelles, finely diced	3½ oz
25 g	shallots, finely chopped	1 oz
¼ l	dairy cream	9 fl oz
	butter as required	
½ l	fish stock	18 fl oz
1 l	veal stock	1¾ pt
	mirepoix of	
150 g	onions	5 oz
150 g	carrots	5 oz
	court-bouillon (made with carrots, onions, salt, thyme, bay leaf, vinegar and water)	

Trim the sweetbreads and blanch in salted water. Brown the mirepoix in butter and place the sweetbreads on top. Add the fish and veal stock, and cook in the oven for 45 minutes. Remove the sweetbreads and pass the stock through a cloth. Stir in the cream and keep hot.

Cook the crayfish in the court-bouillon. Leave 6 of them whole. Carefully remove the tails of the remainder from the shells. Prepare a forcemeat with the creamy parts and the shallots and chanterelles which have been sautées in butter. Fill into 12 shells and place a crayfish tail on each. Dress the sweetbreads on warmed plates and decorate each with 2 stuffed shells and a whole crayfish. Place the rest of the tails in the stock which has been kept hot and hand separately. Garnish with suitable fresh vegetables in season.
(Illustration, page 764 – 2 portions)

(Wladimir Levyckyi, France)

Sweetbreads with shrimps
Ris de veau aux crevettes
Kalbsmilch in Sahne, mit Krebsen, Blattspinat und Karottenflan

10 portions   Cooking time: 35 minutes

1 kg 200	calves' sweetbreads	2 lb 10 oz
	salt, pepper	
	flour	
	2 eggs	
120 g	butter	4 oz
60 g	shallots, finely diced	2 oz
¼ l	sour cream	9 fl oz
⅛ l	sherry	4 fl oz
60 g	shrimp butter	2 oz
	20 shrimps	
800 g	spinach	1 lb 12 oz

Carrot moulds:

500 g	carrots (fresh)	1 lb 2 oz
60 g	shallots, finely cut	2 oz
	salt, pepper	
30 g	butter	1 oz
50 g	bacon, diced	2 oz
⅓ l	dairy cream	12 fl oz
	3 eggs	
	1 egg yolk	

Soak the sweetbreads (which should be quite fresh) in cold water until the water remains clear. Blanch them for 12 minutes, then remove the skin and gristly parts. Leave to cool under light pressure. When quite cold, cut into slices 2 cm (¾ in) thick. Season with salt and pepper, coat with flour and beaten egg, and fry in butter on both sides until cooked. Transfer to warmed plates, coat with sauce, decorate with 2 picked shrimps and garnish with a carrot mould and with spinach tossed in butter.

To make the sauce, cook the shallots in butter until lightly coloured, stir in the sherry, then add the sour cream and reduce to the required consistency. Finish with the shrimp butter.

To make the carrot moulds, cut up the carrots finely and season with salt and pepper. Fry the shallots and bacon in butter until transparent, add the carrots and cream, then reduce. Work to a purée in the mixer, then mix with the eggs and egg yolk. Fill into buttered dariole moulds and poach under cover over medium heat in a bain-marie.
(Illustration, page 696)

(Karl Brunnengräber, Germany)

Sweetbreads braised in Sauternes
Ris de veau braisé sauternes

6 portions

6 calves' heart sweetbreads

1 dl	oil	3½ fl oz
	mirepoix of	
500 g	carrots	1 lb 2 oz
200 g	onions	7 oz
	1 celeriac	
500 g	mushrooms	1 lb 2 oz
	1 clove of garlic, cut in half	
¾ l	Sauternes	1¼ pt
¾ l	veal stock	1¼ pt
	1 tablespoon foie gras mousse	
	bouquet garni (thyme, bay leaf, parsley)	

Garnish:

100 g	blanched julienne of celeriac	3½ oz
100 g	mushrooms	3½ oz
200 g	carrots	7 oz
	truffle liquor	
	salt, pepper	
	chervil	
	dairy cream as required	

Brown the mirepoix in 1 dl (3½ fl oz) oil. Trim the sweetbreads, but do not blanch. Place them on the mirepoix and allow to colour. Remove the fat, stir in ½ l (18 fl oz) Sauternes to detach the sediment, then add the veal stock, the bouquet garni and garlic. Cover and place in a preheated oven. Braise for 20 to 25 minutes, depending on size. Remove the pan from the oven, lift out the sweetbreads, skin carefully and keep hot. Pass the stock through a conical strainer and keep hot.

To make the sauce, add the stock to the rest of the Sauternes which has been warmed, reduce by three quarters, add the cream, blend together well, remove from the heat, add the foie gras mousse and truffle liquor, and adjust the seasoning. Place the sweetbreads on warmed plates, coat with the sauce and surround with the vegetable julienne. Sprinkle the meat with finely cut chervil.

(Jean Ramet, France)

Sauté sweetbreads with crab meat in avocado sauce
Ris de veau sauté avec crabe en sauce aux avocats
Gebakken zwezerik met avokado saus en crabe vlees

4 portions

| 1 kg 200 | calves' sweetbreads | 2 lb 10 oz |

	3 avocados	
100 g	shallots, finely cut	3½ oz
100 g	crab meat	3½ oz
50 g	butter	2 oz
1 l	bouillon	1¾ pt
2 cl	veal gravy	1 fl oz
2 cl	dairy cream	1 fl oz
2 cl	white wine	1 fl oz
	salt	
	pepper, freshly ground	
	flour	

Trim the sweetbreads carefully, soak well in cold water, blanch and slice. Season with salt and pepper, coat with flour and fry lightly in butter. Detach the sediment with the wine and cook slowly. Remove the sweetbreads from the pan, stir in the bouillon and veal gravy, reduce to the required consistency, and remove any fat.

Work the avocados to a purée in the mixer, add to the sauce and stir well. Cut up the crab meat. Sweat the shallots. Mix the crab meat, shallots and sauce together well, fold in the cream very carefully, and season to taste. To serve, coat the sweetbread slices with the sauce and hand fresh asparagus as an accompaniment.

(Bernard van Beurten, Netherlands)

Sweetbreads Vincent
Ris de veau Vincent

2 portions

180 g	2 calves' heart sweetbreads each weighing	6 oz
	6 lettuce leaves	
100 g	mushrooms	3½ oz
	1 tomato, skinned, seeded and finely diced	
	1 teaspoon herbs (chives, parsley, chervil, tarragon), finely chopped	
100 g	butter, melted	3½ oz
	3 egg yolks	
5 cl	dairy cream, whipped	2 fl oz
	juice of ¼ lemon	
	salt	
	pepper	

Soak the sweetbreads very well in cold water, blanch for 4 minutes and skin carefully. Fry in butter until medium done, then season with salt and pepper.

Dip the lettuce leaves quickly into hot water to soften them. Dice the mushrooms finely and sauter in butter, then season. Add the tomato and stir in the herbs to make a filling for the sweetbreads.

Whisk the egg yolks over very low heat until frothy. Slowly work in the butter. Flavour with lemon juice and carefully blend in the cream.

For each portion, spread out 3 lettuce leaves. Cut the sweetbreads in half, sandwich the halves together with the filling, wrap in the lettuce leaves and cook in the oven for 4 minutes. Place each portion in a buttered fireproof dish. Pour the sauce over and brown briefly in a very hot oven or under a salamander.
(Illustration, page 311)

(Roger Souvereyns, Belgium)

Calf's kidneys and sweetbreads on endives with white truffles
Rognons et ris de veau sur leur lit de chicorée aux truffes blanches

2 portions

	1 calf's kidney	
	1 calf's sweetbread (heart)	
	4 endives	
	1 tablespoon sherry vinegar	
10 g	white truffles	⅓ oz
	1 tablespoon olive oil	
	salt, pepper	

Thoroughly soak and wash the kidney and sweetbread. Blanch the sweetbread for 4 minutes, refresh in cold water, cut away the inedible parts and carefully pull off the skin. Remove up to about 80% of the fat from the kidney. Grill the sweetbread and kidney whole. The sweetbread should be well done and white inside, the kidney only medium done. Remove the remaining fat. Keep hot.

Using a sharp knife, cut a wedge out of the root end of the endives to remove the bitter flavour, then cut them into 3 cm (1¼ in) lengths. Sauter for a few minutes in the olive oil, season with salt and pepper, remove from the heat and add the vinegar, together with the white truffle cut into julienne strips. Divide the endives between 2 warmed plates, arranging them to make a flat bed for the sweetbread and kidney. Slice these and place the slices alternately on the endives to form a ring.
(Illustration, page 311)

(Roger Souvereyns, Belgium)

Sweetbreads and flap mushrooms with cress purée
Ris de veau et cèpes à la purée de cresson
Kalbsmilch und Steinpilzköpfe mit Kressepüree

10 portions   Cooking time: 35 minutes

1 kg 200	calves' sweetbreads	2 lb 10 oz
120 g	butter	4 oz
	salt, pepper	
½ l	dairy cream	18 fl oz
	2 tablespoons thick sour cream	
60 g	shallots, finely diced	2 oz
800 g	flap mushroom caps, fresh, dried or canned	1 lb 12 oz
90 g	fresh cress	3 oz
⅛ l	dry white wine	4 fl oz
	1 tablespoon lemon juice	

Remove the skin and blood vessels from the sweetbreads, then poach them. Carefully clean the flap mushroom caps, wash them, then cook gently in butter for about 3 minutes. Add the fresh and sour cream, together with the sweetbreads, cut into 20 slices, and simmer over low heat for 5 minutes. Transfer the sweetbreads to warmed plates. Briefly blanch the cress and rub through a fine sieve or work to a purée in the mixer.

Continue cooking the mushroom caps in the same stock, mix with the lemon juice and cress purée, remove from the heat, add the wine and mix with the shallots which have been gently cooked. Garnish each portion of sweetbreads with flap mushroom caps and a tomato-flavoured rice timbale, consisting of rice Creole mixed with tomato fondue and moulded.

(Karl Brunnengräber, Germany)

Calf's kidneys Charles
Rognons de veau Charles
Kalbsnieren Charles

4 portions

	2 calf's kidneys with little fat, each	
300 g	weighing approx.	11 oz
1 cl	oil	½ fl oz
	salt, nutmeg, flour	
80 g	onions, finely chopped	3 oz
40 g	butter	1½ oz
50 g	beef bone marrow, finely diced	2 oz
	1 tablespoon breadcrumbs	

1 teaspoon fresh dill, chopped

Wash the kidneys well and cut into slices 1 cm (⅜ in) thick. Season with salt and nutmeg, coat with flour and fry on both sides in oil until light golden and almost cooked. Transfer to a large gratinating dish and keep hot. Fry the onions lightly in butter until golden. Add the bone marrow, breadcrumbs and dill. Mix well and spread evenly on the slices of kidney, smooth down well and lightly brown under a salamander. Serve with Swiss potato cake ('rösti') and veal gravy mixed with English mustard.
(Illustration, page 416)

(Felix Real, Liechtenstein)

Calf's kidneys with Champagne mustard and shallots
Rognons de veau à la moutarde au champagne et aux échalotes
Kalbsnierchen in Champagnersenf mit glasierten Schalotten

4 portions

	2 calf's kidneys	
50 g	butter	2 oz
	1 tablespoon Champagne mustard	
1 dl	white wine	3½ fl oz
1 dl	dairy cream	3½ fl oz
1 dl	veal stock	3½ fl oz
	salt	
	pepper, freshly ground	
2 cl	Champagne marc brandy	1 fl oz

Glazed shallots:

	20 shallots	
	2 tablespoons sugar	
2 cl	wine vinegar	1 fl oz
1 dl	veal stock	3½ fl oz

Remove the fat from the kidneys and cut them into anatomical segments. Trim away the skin and vessels. Fry in 30 g (1 oz) butter until medium done, and keep hot.

Fry the mustard in the same pan over low heat for about 1 minute. Stir in the wine, then the cream. Add the veal stock and reduce until thick, then add the rest of the butter (cold) a little at a time. Season with salt and pepper, and flavour with Champagne marc brandy. Stir into the sauce the juices which have escaped from the kidneys.

Peel the shallots and fry lightly in a little butter. Sprinkle with the sugar and allow to caramelise a little. Stir in the vinegar, then the stock. Cook under cover, then uncover the pan and reduce the stock.

(Gerhard Gartner, Germany)

Flambé calf's kidneys
Rognons de veau flambés
Kalbsnieren, flambiert

2 portions

	2 calf's kidneys, sliced	
50 g	butter	2 oz
5 cl	olive oil	2 fl oz
50 g	shallots	2 oz
50 g	Meaux mustard (coarse)	2 oz
2 dl	thickened veal stock	7 fl oz
2 dl	dairy cream	7 fl oz
50 g	basil, sage, parsley, rosemary, finely chopped	2 oz
1 dl	Cognac	3½ fl oz
1 dl	dry white wine	3½ fl oz
	Cayenne pepper	

Sprinkle a plate with freshly ground pepper. Place the slices of kidney on it and season with more freshly ground pepper. Place the butter and oil in the flambé pan and melt the butter while tilting the pan from side to side to blend it with the oil as well as possible. When brown, add the kidneys and fry lightly on both sides. Pour off the surplus fat so that the sauce is not too fatty. Add the Cognac to the pan and ignite. Transfer the kidneys to a serving dish, cover and keep hot.

Place the shallots in the pan, cook gently in the pan juices without colouring, pour in the white wine, add the mixed herbs, stir and reduce slowly. Add the mustard and mix well. Pour in about 4 tablespoons veal stock, mix well, thicken with the cream and reduce. Add Cayenne to taste. Now season the kidneys with salt, dress on individual plates and carefully coat with the sauce.
(Techniques, page 110)

(Otto F. Müller, Switzerland)

Calf's kidney with raspberry vinegar
Rognons de veau au vinaigre de framboise
Kalbsniere mit Himbeeressig

1 portion

150 g	calf's kidney	5 oz

	1 small tomato	
	1 teaspoon shallot, finely chopped	
3 dl	raspberry vinegar	10 fl oz
2 dl	veal stock	7 fl oz
10 g	butter	⅓ oz
	salt	
	pepper, freshly ground	
	chives, chopped	
	1 bread croûton	
	oil as required	

Wash the kidney well, trim it and remove the fat, then cut into slices 5–7 mm (about ¼ in) thick. Skin, seed and finely dice the tomato. Season the kidney with freshly ground pepper, sauter in very hot oil, drain and keep hot.

Cook the shallot and tomato gently in the pan juices, stir in half the vinegar, bring to the boil, reduce completely, then pour in the veal stock, boil up for a few moments, season with salt and pepper, add the rest of the vinegar and finish the sauce with butter. Pour on to a warmed plate, add the slices of kidney, sprinkle with chives, and if desired, add 1 fried bread croûton. Serve with potatoes au gratin Dauphine style (gratin dauphinois).

(Roger Parrot, André Perret, Switzerland)

Calf's kidneys with tomatoes
Rognons de veau aux tomates
Rognone in umido

4 portions

500 g	calf's kidneys	1 lb 2 oz
400 g	ripe tomatoes *or*	14 oz
	canned peeled tomatoes	
	1 large onion, finely chopped	
1 dl	dry white wine	3½ fl oz
20 g	lard	¾ oz
	1 tablespoon parsley, finely chopped	
	salt	
	pepper, freshly ground	

Wash the kidneys thoroughly, trim, then slice very thinly. Place the slices in a pan and stand on the stove to drain out the water. Pour it off, transfer the kidneys to a sieve and leave to drain for about 20 minutes.

Fry the onion in the lard until golden brown, then add the tomatoes (diced if fresh, cut into pieces if canned). Stew for 15 minutes, then add the kidneys, turn, stir in the wine and cook over fairly low heat for 10 minutes. When cooked, season with salt and pepper. Serve sprinkled with chopped parsley.

(Franco Colombani, Italy)

Calf's kidneys with mustard sauce
Rognons de veau à la moutarde
Kalbsnieren in Senfsauce

10 portions

	3-4 calf's kidneys	
200 g	butter	7 oz
5 cl	Cognac	2 fl oz
50 g	mustard	2 oz
1 dl	white wine	3½ fl oz
200 g	flap mushrooms, finely cut	7 oz
5 g	basil, chopped	⅙ oz
5 g	garlic, crushed	⅙ oz
5 g	parsley, chopped	⅙ oz
20 g	onion, chopped	¾ oz
3 dl	dairy cream	10 fl oz
1 dl	veal stock	3½ fl oz
	10 slices white bread	
200 g	cress, chopped	7 oz
	seasonings as desired	

Trim the kidneys, but leave a little of their fat. Cut into slices 5 mm (¼ in) thick and season. Fry lightly on both sides in butter, pour in the Cognac and ignite. Remove from the pan and place on the slices of bread, which have been fried in butter, on a heated dish. Place the onion and garlic in the pan and cook in the pan juices until transparent. Add the flap mushrooms and the mustard. Cook gently for a short time, then stir in the wine to detach the sediment, add the veal stock and reduce by half. Stir in the cream and herbs, season to taste and continue cooking for a short time. Dress the kidneys and bread on individual plates and pour the sauce over.

(Otto Ledermann, Switzerland)

Calf's kidneys with wine vinegar sauce
Rognons de veau au vinaigre de vin

4 portions   Cooking time: about 15 minutes

	3 calf's kidneys with little fat,	
220 g	each weighing	8 oz

30 g	butter	1 oz
	3 shallots, finely chopped	
5 cl	red wine vinegar	2 fl oz
2 dl	red wine	7 fl oz
60 g	tomatoes, coarsely chopped	2 oz
3 dl	brown veal stock	10 fl oz
50 g	butter, soft, to finish sauce	2 oz
	salt	
	pepper, freshly ground	

Carefully trim the kidneys, removing any connective tissue. Season with salt and pepper and brown in a little butter. Cover the pan, place in a preheated oven and cook slowly and carefully for 12 to 15 minutes, basting constantly. Remove the kidneys and keep hot.

Discard the fat remaining in the pan, add a little fresh butter, allow to melt, then cook the shallots until lightly coloured. Detach the sediment with the vinegar and the wine, then reduce. Add the tomatoes, then the veal stock, and reduce to the desired consistency. Finish with the soft butter and season with salt and pepper.

To serve, pour the sauce on to well warmed plates and dress the kidneys, which have been sliced, on top. Serve with rice pilaf.

N.B. It is particularly important to reduce the vinegar/wine mixture very well.
(Illustration, page 240)

(Anton Mosimann, Great Britain)

Calf's kidney pans with onion sauce
Barquettes avec rognons de veau en sauce aux oignons
Korstdeeg pannetje met niertjes in uiensaus

4 portions

	4 short pastry cases	
	10 cm (4 in) in diameter with handles	
400 g	calf's kidneys, trimmed and sliced	14 oz
200 g	onions, finely cut	7 oz
20 g	Dutch mustard	¾ oz
¼ l	veal gravy	9 fl oz
	salt	
	pepper, freshly ground	
50 g	butter	2 oz
	herbs, finely chopped	

Season the kidneys with salt and pepper, and sauter in butter. Add the onions and brown well.

Add the mustard and gravy and cook for a few minutes. Fill into the pastry cases, which have been made to resemble frying pans, and sprinkle with herbs.

(Bernard van Beurten, Netherlands)

Cushion of veal Kalocsa
Noix de veau Kalocsa

5 portions

750 g	cushion of veal	1 lb 10 oz
400 g	fresh yellow peppers	14 oz
100 g	hot green peppers	3½ oz
200 g	ripe tomatoes, skinned and cut into wedges	7 oz
100 g	young onions	3½ oz
30 g	sweet Kalocsa paprika	1 oz
1 dl	oil	3½ oz
	salt, pepper	

Garnish:

1 kg	new potatoes	2 lb 4 oz
	butter	
	parsley, chopped	

Cut the veal into strips the thickness of the little finger. Cut the peppers and onions into strips of the same thickness as the meat. Fry the onions in oil until lightly coloured, add the meat and peppers, and sauter for 3 to 4 minutes. Add the tomatoes, sprinkle with the paprika and sauter for a few moments longer.

Serve on heated plates, surrounded with the potatoes, which have been peeled, boiled, tossed in butter and sprinkled with parsley. This dish should be prepared very quickly to prevent the meat becoming tough and the vegetables losing their fresh flavour.

(Gyula Gullner, Hungary)

Veal piccata Cavalieri
Piccata de veau Cavalieri

4 portions

30 g	12 veal escalopes each weighing	1 oz
	flour	
	2 eggs	

20 g	Parmesan cheese	¾ oz
5 cl	olive oil	2 fl oz
50 g	butter	2 oz
200 g	tomatoes, finely diced	7 oz
80 g	Mozzarella cheese	3 oz
5 cl	dairy cream	2 fl oz
150 g	fresh green noodles	5 oz
150 g	fresh white noodles	5 oz
3 dl	Madeira sauce (recipe, page 158) salt pepper, freshly ground	10 fl oz

Spinach noodles:

200 g	flour, sieved	7 oz
25 g	semolina	1 oz
1 cl	oil	½ fl oz
	1 egg	
3½ g	salt	a pinch
5 cl	water	2 fl oz
50 g	spinach, sieved	2 oz

Flatten the escalopes, season them with salt and pepper, flour them, coat with egg, then grated Parmesan cheese, and fry on both sides in butter and olive oil until golden.

Sauter the tomatoes in butter, and season with salt and pepper. Place on the meat, sprinkle with the cream and brown in a hot oven or under a salamander. Dress on a bed of noodles which have been cooked *al dente* and carefully seasoned. Serve with the Madeira sauce which has been enriched with butter. The noodles should preferably be freshly made.

To make spinach noodles, make a bay in the flour and semolina and place the water, salt, oil and egg in the centre. Gradually mix in the flour and semolina, drawing them in towards the centre. Add the finely sieved spinach and work to a firm, smooth dough. Let it rest for about an hour before use. If desired, the dough may be made in a mixer, as it should be of fairly tight consistency.
(Illustration, page 240)

(Anton Mosimann, Great Britain)

Sauté of veal Alpe Vicania
Sauté de veau Alpe Vicania
Spezzatino di vitello Alpe Vicania

30 portions   Cooking time: 1¾ hours in the oven

2 kg 500	shoulder of veal	5 lb 8 oz
2 kg 500	fillet of veal	5 lb 8 oz
1 kg	butter	2 lb 4 oz
1–1 kg 500	onions	2 lb 4 oz– 3 lb 4 oz
300 g	carrots	11 oz
500 g	celery	1 lb 2 oz
250 g	fresh flap mushrooms	9 oz
1 dl	white wine	3½ fl oz
3 dl	bouillon	10 fl oz
	parsley, finely chopped	
	pepper, freshly ground	
	salt	

Dice the veal and brown in a generous amount of butter. Cut up the vegetables finely and brown in the rest of the butter in a second pan, then add the contents of this pan to the meat. Cook slowly in the oven at 200°C (390°F) for 1¼ hours. Add the flap mushrooms which have been well washed, drained and, if desired, cut into pieces. Cook for a further 30 minutes, then season with salt, freshly ground pepper and sprinkle with white wine. Turn the meat repeatedly while cooking to keep it moist.

If desired, peas may be added to the meat instead of flap mushrooms. Sprinkle with chopped parsley and serve with polenta or mashed potatoes.

(Giovanni Albisetti, Switzerland)

Veal paupiettes Bari style
Paupiettes de veau à la Bari
Braciole alla barese

4 portions   Cooking time: 1½ hours

500 g	cushion of veal	1 lb 2 oz
100 g	bacon	3½ oz
100 g	Pecorino (goat cheese), grated	3½ oz
	parsley	
	tomato sauce	
5 cl	red wine	2 fl oz
	olive oil	
	salt and pepper, freshly ground	
	1 medium onion, sliced	

Cut the meat into 8 thin slices and flatten. Dice the bacon finely. Cover the meat with sprigs of parsley. Place a few bacon cubes and grated cheese in the centre, roll up and secure with toothpicks. Fry the onion gently until lightly coloured, then add the veal birds and brown.

Detach the sediment with the wine, add tomato sauce and braise over moderate heat for 1½ hours. The meat is ready for serving when a fork pierces the veal birds easily.

(Ristorante Vecchia Bari, Italy)

Veal paupiettes Bergamo style
Paupiettes de veau à la bergamasque
Fagottini alla bergamasca

6 portions

70–80 g	12 veal escalopes each weighing	2½–3 oz
150 g	ham, sliced	5 oz
100 g	Emmental or Gruyère cheese	3½ oz
50 g	parsley, finely chopped	2 oz
½ l	red wine	18 fl oz
	2 fresh ripe tomatoes, skinned, seeded and diced	
	OR 4 canned peeled tomatoes	
200 g	fresh flap mushrooms, thinly sliced	7 oz
¼ l	dairy cream	9 fl oz
	1 clove of garlic, finely chopped	
100 g	butter or margarine	3½ oz
	sage leaves	
	1 sprig rosemary	
	salt	
1 dl	oil	3½ fl oz
	flour	

Lightly brown half the garlic in 5 cl (2 fl oz) oil, add the parsley, stand over the heat for 1 minute, then stir in the flap mushrooms, add the cream, season with salt, and cook over low heat for about 20 minutes.

Flatten the escalopes well, beating them if necessary. Cover each one with a slice of ham of the same size, a finger of cheese and a little chopped garlic. Roll up, secure with a toothpick, and dust very lightly with flour. Brown for 5 minutes in the rest of the oil and 70 g (2½ oz) butter, then add the sage and rosemary, stir in the wine, and continue cooking slowly over low heat for 20 minutes.

Cook the tomatoes gently for 5 minutes in the rest of the butter in a separate pan, then add the veal birds with their stock and the flap mushroom sauce. Continue cooking over low heat for a further 5 minutes, then serve garnished with polenta or mashed potatoes.

(Gigi Milesi, Italy)

Veal olives La Cicogna
Paupiettes de veau La Cicogna
Uccelli impienuti La Cicogna

4 portions

	8 veal escalopes (cushion or	
50 g	fricandeau) each weighing	2 oz
	1 egg, beaten	
40 g	bacon	1½ oz
	2 tablespoons breadcrumbs	
40 g	calf's liver	1½ oz
40 g	ham	1½ oz
	1 teaspoon parsley, finely chopped	
	8 sage leaves	
	a pinch of grated nutmeg	
50 g	butter	2 oz
1 dl	white wine	3½ fl oz
	juniper berries, finely crushed	
	salt	
	pepper, freshly ground	
	flour	

Flatten the escalopes. Finely mince the liver, bacon and ham, or work to a purée in the mixer. Stir in the parsley and juniper berries, then add the breadcrumbs and egg. Season with nutmeg, salt and freshly ground pepper and mix thoroughly. Spread this filling on the escalopes, roll up, place a sage leaf on each, and secure with a toothpick or thin skewer. Dust very lightly with flour, brown in a little butter, stir in the wine, and braise under cover for 30 minutes. If the pan becomes too dry, add a little bouillon. Serve with polenta or mashed potatoes.

(Sergio Chiesa, Italy)

Veal paupiette Colonia
Paupiette de veau Colonia
Gefülltes Kalbsröllchen Colonia

1 portion

100 g	1 veal escalope weighing	3½ oz
40 g	spinach, blanched	1½ oz
	butter	
	1 egg, beaten	
	flour	

100 g	morels	3½ oz
20 g	shallots, finely chopped	¾ oz
	salt	
	chicken stock	
1 dl	dairy cream	3½ fl oz

Tomato butter: (10 portions)

	½ onion, finely cut	
	½ leek, finely cut	
	2 carrots, thinly sliced	
	4-5 fresh tomatoes	
	1 tablespoon concentrated tomato purée	
2 dl	bouillon	7 fl oz
200 g	butter	7 oz
	tarragon, finely chopped	
	lemon juice	
	parsley, finely chopped	

Brown the morels and shallots in fresh butter. Season with salt, dust lightly with flour, add a little chicken stock, then the cream, and allow to cool.

Flatten the escalope and season with salt on both sides. Cover the inside with the spinach and season. Place the cold morel filling on the spinach and roll up. Flour lightly, dip in lightly beaten egg and bake in butter in a medium oven for about 15 to 20 minutes. Serve coated with Hollandaise sauce and topped with a medallion of tomato butter.

To make the tomato butter, brown the onion, leek and carrots in a little butter. Skin, seed and finely dice the tomatoes, add to the pan, then stir in the tomato purée. Pour in the bouillon, reduce, then allow to cool. Pass through a fine sieve and blend well with 200 g (7 oz) butter. Add tarragon, parsley and lemon juice, and mix well again. Shape into a roll, wrap in aluminium foil and refrigerate until firm, then cut into medallions.

(Walter Haas, Germany)

Veal olives Trent style
Paupiettes de veau farcies à la trentoise
Involtini di vitello ripieni

4 portions

	8 veal escalopes (cushion or	
50 g	fricandeau) each weighing	2 oz
40 g	lean pork	1½ oz
40 g	veal	1½ oz
40 g	pork frying sausage	1½ oz
	1 egg, beaten	

	8 slices unsmoked bacon	
	1 teaspoon carrot, grated	
	1 teaspoon onion, very finely chopped	
	1 teaspoon celery, finely chopped	
	a little white breadcrumbs	
	5 sage leaves	
50 g	butter	2 oz
1 dl	white wine	3½ fl oz
3 cl	grappa (marc brandy)	1 fl oz
	salt and pepper	

Flatten the escalopes. Finely mince the veal, pork and sausage, or work in the processor. Place in a bowl with the vegetables, mix well, add the egg and breadcrumbs, season with salt and pepper and mix well again. Spread this filling on the escalopes, roll up and enclose each one in a slice of bacon, securing with a toothpick. Brown in butter with the sage leaves, detach the sediment with the wine, add the grappa, cover and braise over low heat. If the pan becomes too dry, add a little bouillon.

(Sergio Chiesa, Italy)

Piquant veal olive
Paupiette de veau piquante
Pikante Kalbsroulade

1 portion

120 g	1 veal escalope weighing	4 oz
30 g	spinach, blanched	1 oz
30 g	pie forcemeat	1 oz
	3 tablespoons cream sauce	
20 g	butter	¾ oz
	salt	

Forcemeat:

15 g	fresh pork fat	½ oz
10 g	lean pork	⅓ oz
5 g	foie gras trimmings	⅙ oz
	a pinch of spiced salt	

Harlequin rice:

boiled saffron rice mixed with finely
    diced ham, truffles and pistachio nuts

Beat the escalope well, spread with the forcemeat, cover with the spinach, roll up and tie. Season lightly with salt and brown quickly in butter, then cook slowly for about 15 minutes.

To make the forcemeat, chop the pork fat, pork and foie gras very finely, pass through a hair sieve and season. To serve, pour the cream sauce on to a plate, slice the veal roll and arrange on top, and garnish with harlequin rice and vegetables.

(Adolf Meindl, Austria)

Veal steak with paprika sauce
Steak de veau en sauce au paprika
Kalbsrückensteak in Paprikasauce

2 portions

	2 veal steaks (cut from the boned saddle)	
150 g	each weighing	5 oz
20 g	butter	¾ oz
	3 tablespoons red and green peppers, finely diced	
	1 tablespoon onion, chopped	
	1 tablespoon oil	
	1 teaspoon paprika	
1 dl	dairy cream	3½ fl oz
1 dl	clear gravy	3½ fl oz
	a little tarragon, chopped	
	salt, flour	

Season the veal with salt, flour it and fry slowly in butter until almost cooked, then transfer to hot plates. Cook the peppers and onion lightly in oil with the paprika, then stew over low heat for 10 minutes. Add the cream and gravy, reduce by half, add the tarragon and a little salt, and pour over the veal. Serve with *spätzle*.
(Illustration, page 416)

(Felix Real, Liechtenstein)

Veal steak with pear in Roquefort cream au gratin, fennel in red wine and spinach spätzle
Steak de veau avec poire au roquefort gratinée, fenouil au vin rouge et spaetzle
Kalbsrückensteak mit Birne und Roquefortcreme überbacken, Fenchel in Rotwein und Spinatspätzle

10 portions   Cooking time: 30 minutes

	10 veal steaks (cut from the saddle)	
130 g	each weighing	4½ oz

	salt	
	pepper	
	2 eggs	
200 g	butter	7 oz
	10 pear halves, poached	
	flour	

Roquefort cream:

2 dl	sour cream	7 fl oz
100 g	Gervais	3½ oz
	2 egg yolks	
200 g	Roquefort	7 oz
	a pinch of Cayenne pepper	

Fennel in red wine:

100 g	beef bone marrow	3½ oz
¼ l	red wine	9 fl oz
¼ l	gravy	9 fl oz
900 g	fennel, cleaned	2 lb

Spinach spätzle:

500 g	flour	1 lb 2 oz
	4 eggs	
150 g	spinach, cooked and finely sieved	5 oz
	mace	
	mineral water	
	salt	

Beat the veal steaks into shape with the ball of the thumb. Season them with salt and pepper, coat with flour, dip in beaten egg and fry in butter, keeping the meat juicy. Shortly before the steaks are cooked, add the pear halves which have been well drained, and heat them well. Place the steaks on warmed plates and arrange the pear halves on top.

To make the Roquefort cream, pass the Roquefort through a coarse sieve and mix well with the sour cream, egg yolks and Gervais to a spreading consistency. Season with Cayenne pepper. Mask the pear halves with this cream and brown under a salamander.

To prepare the fennel, cut in quarters and blanch in salted water. Transfer to a buttered fireproof dish and add the wine and gravy. Cover first with buttered paper, then with a lid, and braise in a hot oven. A few minutes before the fennel is cooked, remove the lid and paper and sprinkle with the bone marrow which has been diced or sliced. Glaze in the oven for a few minutes.

To make the spätzle, mix the flour well with the eggs and spinach, season with salt and mace, and add enough mineral water to make a firm dough. Shred the dough off the board into a pan of boiling salted water, or force into the water through a spätzle maker.

(Karl Brunnengräber, Germany)

Veal steaks with lemon sauce

Steak de veau à la sauce au citron
Kalbsrückensteak mit warmer Zitronenbutter

10 portions   Cooking time: 35 minutes

1 kg 200	saddle of veal, boned and trimmed	2 lb 10 oz
	3 eggs, beaten	
8 cl	oil	3 fl oz
180 g	butter	6 oz
2½ dl	thick sour cream	9 fl oz
⅛ l	white wine	4 fl oz
	salt, pepper	
	sugar	
	2–4 lemons (depending on size), unsprayed	
	2 tablespoons parsley, finely chopped	
	young vegetables in season	
	flour	

Pare the lemon zest very thinly and cut into thin julienne strips. Blanch the zest and the lemons briefly in boiling water and leave until quite cold. Cut 20 lemon segments, free from membranes. Collect the juice which escapes and set aside. Make syrup with a pinch of sugar and a little water, and pour over the lemon segments. Cut 10 veal steaks. Flatten them a little, coat with flour and dip in the beaten eggs. Fry on both sides in hot oil until medium done. Detach the sediment with the wine, add the sour cream and reduce to the required consistency. Enrich with fresh butter, flavour with the lemon juice and stir in the parsley.

Dress the steaks on warmed plates, place two warmed lemon segments on each, coat with lemon sauce and sprinkle with the lemon zest julienne. Serve with suitable young vegetables in season.

(Karl Brunnengräber, Germany)

Saltimbocca Monte Mario

Saltimbocca à la Monte Mario

4 portions

70 g	8 veal escalopes (cut from the under part of loin) each weighing	2½ oz
	8 sage leaves	
4 g	8 slices raw ham each weighing	⅙ oz

70 g	part of loin) each weighing	2½ oz
	8 sage leaves	
4 g	8 slices raw ham each weighing	⅙ oz
	flour	
40 g	butter	1½ oz
	salt	
	pepper, freshly ground	
20 g	butter (to sprinkle on steaks when serving)	¾ oz

Season the escalopes (which should be cut thinly) with salt and pepper. Place a sage leaf and a slice of raw ham on each and secure with a small wooden skewer. Flour lightly and fry on both sides in butter until golden.

To serve, dress on warmed plates and sprinkle with brown butter. Hand tomato noodles and Marsala sauce separately. To make tomato noodles, proceed as for spinach noodles (recipe, page 1029) using sieved tomatoes instead of spinach.

(Anton Mosimann, Great Britain)

Veal escalope Cordon bleu with cream sauce
Escalope de veau cordon bleu à la crème

4 portions

70–80 g	8 veal escalopes each weighing		2½–3 oz
	4 slices Ardennes ham (cooked),		
25 g	each weighing		1 oz
	8 slices Emmental cheese		
10–12 g	each weighing	approx.	½ oz
2 dl	dairy cream		7 fl oz
1 dl	meat glaze		3½ fl oz
	4 small tomatoes		
	2 small fennel		
500 g	potatoes		1 lb 2 oz
50 g	butter		2 oz
	salt		
	pepper, freshly ground		
	flour		
½ l	light veal stock		18 fl oz
	1 small Dutch cucumber		

Flatten the escalopes very well. Sandwich them in pairs with a slice of ham between two slices of Emmental, all cut to size. Press together well, season with salt and pepper, coat with flour and fry in butter, keeping the meat juicy. Pour off the butter remaining in the pan, detach the sediment with a little cream, then add the rest of the cream and the meat glaze, and stand over very low heat for a short time. Remove the escalopes and reduce the sauce.

Blanch the fennel and braise in the veal stock. Turn the cucumber and fry in butter. Skin and seed the tomatoes, and stew in butter. Boil the potatoes in their skins, then peel them, pour a little veal stock over and cook gently for a short time. To serve, dress the escalopes on plates, pour the sauce over and garnish with cucumber, tomato, potatoes and fennel.

(Germain Gertsch-Rösner, Luxembourg)

Veal escalopes Imperial style
Escalopes de veau à l'impériale
Kaiserschnitzel

8 portions

	8 veal escalopes (cut from top of leg)	
	salt	
100 g	flour (for coating)	3½ oz
15 cl	oil	5 fl oz
100 g	butter	3½ oz
½ l	veal stock or water	18 fl oz
½ l	sour cream	18 fl oz
80–90 g	flour (for sauce)	3 oz
	1 tablespoon capers, finely chopped	
	1 level tablespoon lemon zest, finely cut	

Snip the edges of the escalopes, flatten them and season with salt. Flour on one side only. Fry in hot oil, starting with the floured side, then turn. When cooked, remove from the pan and keep hot. Pour off the oil, add the butter, then the flour and then the sour cream, stir well, reduce and pour in the stock. Add the capers and lemon zest, and season with salt to taste. Heat the escalopes in this sauce without allowing it to boil. Serve with rice pilaf and salad.

(Eduard Mayer, Austria)

Veal escalopes Val Brembana
Escalopes de veau Vallée Brembana
Scaloppine della Val Brembana

4 portions

500 g	veal (cushion or fricandeau)	1 lb 2 oz
½ l	dairy cream	18 fl oz

	butter as required	
	olive oil as required	
200 g	fresh flap mushrooms	7 oz
5 cl	white wine	2 fl oz
	2 cloves of garlic	
	flour as required	
	salt, pepper	

Cut the meat into thin escalopes, season with salt and pepper, flour very lightly and brown on both sides in butter. Meanwhile fry the garlic in olive oil in a second pan until it takes on colour, then add the flap mushrooms which have been carefully cleaned, washed and sliced. Sauter the mushrooms with the garlic.

Stir the wine into the pan containing the escalopes, reduce completely, then place the flap mushrooms on the meat and continue cooking over low heat for about 20 minutes, depending on the thickness of the escalopes. Add the cream, boil up for a moment and dish. Serve with polenta.

(Ambrogio Cella, Italy)

Veal escalope Valsassina
Escalope de veau Valsassina
Scaloppina di vitello Valsassina

1 portion   Cooking time: 12–14 minutes

100 g	1 veal escalope (cushion) weighing	3½ oz
20 g	Gorgonzola	¾ oz
20 g	leaf spinach	¾ oz
2 cl	dairy cream	1 fl oz
55 g	butter	2 oz
	1 egg	
2 cl	water	1 fl oz
2 cl	groundnut oil	1 fl oz
30 g	bread (tin or sandwich loaf)	1 oz
3 cl	brown veal stock	1 fl oz

Garnish:

50 g	chanterelles	2 oz
10 g	butter	⅓ oz
	salt	
	white pepper, freshly ground	

Clean the spinach, stripping off the stalks and washing the leaves well. Stew it in 5 g (¼ oz) butter and allow to cool. Blend the Gorgonzola and cream together until smooth and of spreading consistency. Cut the crust off the bread and sieve the crumb. Beat the egg and oil together, add the water, and season with salt and pepper.

Cut the escalope evenly into two slices and flatten if necessary. Season on both sides with salt and pepper. Cover the slices with spinach leaves, spread with the Gorgonzola cream and fold over to make two 5 cm (2 in) squares.

Clean the chanterelles well, wash quickly under running water, drain and dry with a cloth. Cook the meat and the garnish at the same time, but separately. Fry the chanterelles gently in 10 g (⅓ oz) butter, cover and cook for 6 to 8 minutes. Heat 2 cl (1 fl oz) of the cooking juices with the brown veal stock and finish with 20 g (¾ oz) butter. Keep this sauce hot.

Heat 30 g (1 oz) butter in a small frying pan. Fry the two escalopes on both sides over low heat for 5 to 6 minutes, turning them once only, then keep hot. Pour the sauce on to a warmed plate, place the two escalopes on top and garnish with the chanterelles.

(Daniel Drouadaine, Italy)

Veal escalope Guildhall style
Escalope maison des corporations
Zunfthaus-Schnitzel

1 portion

180 g	1 veal escalope weighing	6 oz
	1 slice white bread	
	1 egg, poached for 3 minutes	
	Hollandaise sauce	
	gravy	

Fry the bread in butter until well browned, glaze the escalope and place it on top, cover with the poached egg and coat with Hollandaise sauce. Garnish with parsley and slices or wedges of lemon. Hand gravy separately.

(Otto Ledermann, Switzerland)

Veal rosettes Alfredo
Rosettes de veau Alfredo
Rosettine di vitello Alfredo

4 portions

60 g	8 veal escalopes each weighing	2 oz

150 g	ham, sliced	5 oz
150 g	pickled ox tongue, cooked	5 oz
40 g	dried flap mushrooms	1½ oz
	10 gherkins	
5 cl	Cognac	2 fl oz
5 cl	dry Marsala	2 fl oz
1 dl	demi-glace sauce	3½ fl oz
1 dl	dairy cream	3½ fl oz
20 g	parsley, finely chopped	¾ oz
	flour as required	
30 g	butter	1 oz

Trim the escalopes evenly. Cut into fine strips the ham, tongue and gherkins, and the flap mushrooms which have been soaked and squeezed dry. Season the escalopes with a little salt and dust very lightly with flour, then fry them in the butter. Add the ham, tongue, gherkins and flap mushrooms, pour in the Cognac and ignite. Add the Marsala, reduce by half, then add the demi-glace sauce. Bind with the cream and cook for 5 minutes over high heat. Transfer to warmed plates and sprinkle with parsley.

(Alfredo Sonzogni, Italy)

Piccata Pizzaiola
Piccata à la pizzaiola
Piccata alla pizzaiola

1 portion

40 g	3 veal escalopes each weighing	1½ oz
	¼ clove of garlic, crushed	
	1 tablespoon tomato, skinned, seeded and diced	
5 cl	white wine	2 fl oz
	1 tablespoon gravy	
	oregano, chopped	
	parsley, chopped	
	3 slices Mozzarella cheese	
15 g	butter	½ oz
	oil	
	flour	
	salt	
	pepper, freshly ground	

Flatten the escalopes lightly, season with salt and pepper and dust with a little flour. Brown them in a little oil, then pour off the oil, add the butter, then the garlic, and fry until the meat is cooked. Stir in the wine to detach the sediment, then add the gravy and the tomato.

Sprinkle with oregano and parsley. Transfer to an ovenproof dish, cover the meat with the slices of cheese and brown under a salamander.

(Giulio Casazza, Switzerland)

Veal piccata La Fenice
Piccata de veau La Fenice
Piccata di vitello La Fenice

1 portion   Cooking time: 8 minutes

90 g	cushion of veal	3 oz
60 g	courgettes (one only)	2 oz
40 g	flap mushrooms (one stalk)	1½ oz
25 g	butter	1 oz
	juice of half a lemon	
	salt	
	white pepper, freshly ground	

Cut a thin slice of cushion of veal, divide into 6 small escalopes and refrigerate. Cut the courgette into 2 x 3 cm (1¼ in) lengths, then cut these into strips 5 mm (¼ in) wide. Set aside. Carefully clean the flap mushroom stalk, rinse quickly, trim to a 3 cm (1¼ in) cube and cut evenly into strips. Set aside.

Heat 15 g (½ oz) butter in a sauté pan. Sprinkle the escalopes with salt and pepper, brown over high heat for 1 minute on each side, then remove and keep hot. Pour off the butter, add the courgette and cook gently over low heat for 3 to 4 minutes, then add the flap mushroom stalk, season with salt and pepper, and continue cooking. Finish with the lemon juice and thicken slightly with the remaining butter.

Place the garnish in the centre of a warmed plate, arrange the escalopes in a ring round it and pour a little of the sauce over.
(Illustration, page 412)

(Daniel Drouadaine, Italy)

Piccata with fresh artichokes
Piccata aux artichauts frais
Piccata con carciofi freschi

1 portion

	2 globe artichokes	
	lemon juice	
30 g	4 veal escalopes each weighing	1 oz

Yamazato Teppan menu (T. Nakanishi)

Cantonese cha shao barbecue roast pork, p. 983

Yamazato Sukiyaki menu (T. Nakanishi)

Peking lion's head meat balls, p. 887

693

5

◄ Small sweetbread soufflés with lemon sauce, p. 264
▼▼ Veal fillet with scampi and Nantua sauce, p. 636
▼ Sweetbreads with shrimps, p. 664

696

Veal medallions with figs and ginger sauce, p. 649 ►▲
Calf's liver medallions with mustard cream sauce, p. 646 ►▲▲
Mexican peppered steak, p. 526 ►▼
Stuffed belly of pork Danish style, p. 815 ►▼▼

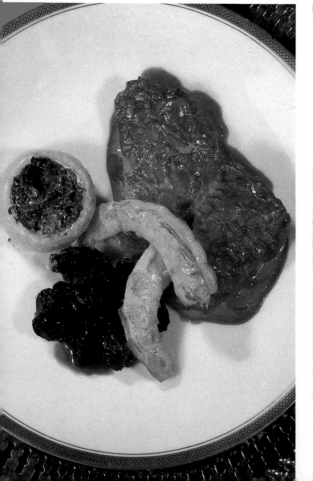

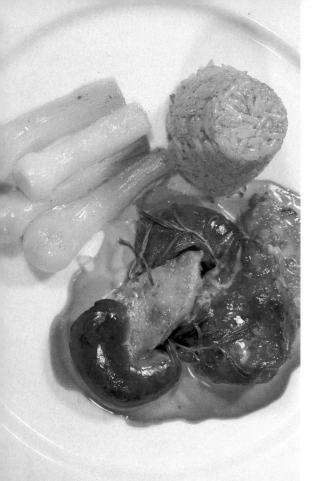

◄ Fricassée of lamb with rosemary cream sauce, p. 758
▼▼ Pork with horseradish Styrian fashion, p. 890
▼ Calf's liver with walnuts and green almonds, p. 646

698

3 cl	white wine	1 fl oz
	parsley, chopped	
	flour	
	butter	
	salt	

Trim the artichokes down to within about 3 cm (1¼ in) from the base, remove the hearts and cut into quarters. Slice each of these finely and blanch in salted water sharpened with a little lemon juice. Season the escalopes with salt, dust with flour, brown in butter, add the artichokes which have been drained, and continue cooking. Stir in the wine to detach the pan juices and add the parsley before serving.

(Giulio Casazza, Switzerland)

Veal piccata San Pellegrino
Piccata de veau San Pellegrino
Piccata di vitello San Pellegrino

4 portions

500 g	cushion of veal	1 lb 2 oz
¼ l	dairy cream	9 fl oz
1 dl	yoghourt	3½ fl oz
50 g	bacon	2 oz
5 cl	dry white wine	2 fl oz
	1 tablespoon parsley, chopped	
	oil as required	
	salt	
	flour	

Potatoes San Pellegrino:

800 g	potatoes	1 lb 12 oz
100 g	bacon	3½ oz
	1 tablespoon parsley, chopped	
	½ small onion, chopped	
	oil as required	
	salt	

Cut the veal into escalopes each weighing about 40 g (1½ oz). Beat them if necessary to flatten well, and dust lightly with flour. Finely dice the bacon and fry in a little oil until transparent, then add the escalopes, brown on both sides and detach the sediment with the wine. Reduce well, then add the cream and the yoghourt. Reduce over low heat for 10 minutes. Serve on warmed plates, sprinkling the piccata with parsley.

To prepare the potatoes, boil them in their skins, allow to cool, peel, slice and place in a vegetable dish. Dice the bacon finely and fry lightly in a little oil. Spoon the bacon and oil over the potatoes, season with salt, and sprinke with parsley and onion.

(Dino Oberti, Italy)

Stuffed veal medallions Ferdinand Hodler
Médaillons de veau farcis Ferdinand Hodler
Gefüllte Kalbsschnitzelchen Ferdinand Hodler

100 portions

8 kg	veal fillet, trimmed	17 lb 10 oz
2 kg	veal sausage meat	4 lb 8 oz
2 kg	raw ham	4 lb 8 oz
1 kg 500	mushrooms, cooked and finely chopped	3 lb 5 oz
1 kg	smoked bacon	2 lb 4 oz
1 l	oil	1¾ pt
150 g	parsley, finely chopped	5 oz
	salt, pepper	

Risotto with chanterelles:

6 kg	Italian Vialone rice	13 lb 4 oz
1 kg	onions, finely chopped	2 lb 4 oz
30 g	garlic, finely chopped	1 oz
1 l	oil	1¾ pt
1 kg	butter	2 lb 4 oz
10 g	saffron	⅓ oz
1 kg 500	Parmesan cheese	3 lb 5 oz
2 kg	chanterelles (canned)	4 lb 8 oz
5 l	bouillon	9 pt
1 l	white wine	1¾ pt

Julienne peppers:

4 kg	red and green peppers	8 lb 12 oz
2 l	thickened veal stock	3½ pt
	oil, butter	
	salt, pepper	

Cut the veal into 200 small escalopes and beat them carefully. Cover each one with a thin slice of raw ham. Make stuffing with the sausage meat mixed with the mushrooms and parsley, and place a teaspoonful in the centre of each escalope. Fold over and wrap in a thin slice of bacon. Season with salt and pepper, and fry on both sides in hot oil until golden brown.

To make the risotto, fry the rice lightly in hot oil without colouring, then add the onions and garlic and continue cooking. Add the bouillon which has been brought to the boil, then the saffron and half the wine. Simmer for about 15 minutes. Remove from the heat, add the rest of the wine and stand over low heat without boiling for 5 minutes. Fold in the butter and Parmesan, season to taste and stir in the chanterelles. The risotto should be firm to the bite and still somewhat moist.

To make the julienne, cut the peppers into thin strips and blanch them. Stew in a little oil and butter, and season with salt and pepper. To serve, dress the risotto in the centre of each plate. Place two stuffed escalopes on top and garnish with the julienne of peppers.

(Robert Haupt-Felber, Switzerland)

Veal steak Blatzheim
Steak de veau Blatzheim
Kalbssteak Blatzheim

1 portion

170 g	1 veal steak weighing		6 oz
	2 slices pickled tongue, the thickness of the back of a knife		

Stuffing:

	3 shallots, finely cut		
approx. 25 g	red peppers	approx.	1 oz
approx. 25 g	green peppers	approx.	1 oz
30 g	butter		1 oz
	a pinch of saffron		
	½ clove of garlic, grated		
	1 teaspoon parsley, finely chopped		
	1 egg		
50 g	Parmesan cheese		2 oz

Liver purée:

50 g	bacon or pork fat		2 oz
	1 small onion, finely chopped		
50–60 g	chicken liver		2 oz
	a dash of forcemeat flavouring		
	½ liqueur glass Madeira		

Soubise sauce:

20 g	butter		¾ oz
20 g	flour		¾ oz
approx. ⅛ l	milk	approx.	4 fl oz
	1 large onion		
	1 egg yolk		

Cook the shallots gently in butter until soft, together with the peppers which have been cut into fine julienne strips. Dust with a little saffron, and add the garlic and parsley.

Using a sharp knife, slit the veal steak lengthwise to open out. Spread with the stuffing, replace in position and secure with toothpicks. Dip in beaten egg, coat with grated Parmesan, and fry on both sides in clarified butter until golden. Place on a lightly buttered fireproof dish.

Sandwich the two slices of pickled tongue together with liver purée. Place on the veal steak, coat with 1 tablespoon Soubise sauce, then brown under a salamander.

To make the liver purée, render down the bacon or pork fat, add the onion together with the liver which has been thinly sliced, and brown lightly. Pass through a sieve, add the flavouring and mix with a little Madeira.

To make the sauce, prepare Béchamel sauce with the butter, flour and milk. Chop the onion very finely and cook gently until very soft. Add a few drops of bouillon and mix with the hot Béchamel sauce. Remove from the heat and bind with the egg yolk.

(Otto Brust, Germany)

Veal steak Galilee

8 portions   Cooking time: 15 minutes

180 g	8 veal steaks each weighing	6 oz
	8 slices smoked goose breast	
15 g	each weighing	½ oz
	1 onion, finely cut	
200 g	chicken livers, finely cut	7 oz
	2 clementines	
	salt	
	pepper, freshly ground	
1–2 dl	thickened veal gravy	3½–7 fl oz

Cut a pocket in the veal steaks with a sharp knife. Brown the chicken livers and onions in oil, place the mixture on the slices of smoked goose breast and roll up. Insert one of these rolls into the pockets cut in the steaks and close with a small wooden skewer. Season with salt and pepper and fry the steaks on both sides in oil.

Divide the clementines into segments and cook gently in the pan juices. Add the veal gravy and pour over the meat.

(Hermann Wohl, Israel)

Veal steak Gottfried Keller
Steak de veau Gottfried Keller
Kalbssteaks Gottfried Keller

6 portions

160 g	6 veal steaks each weighing	5½ oz
200 g	fresh mushrooms, cut in quarters	7 oz
600 g	spinach, blanched	1 lb 5 oz
500 g	potatoes, finely diced and fried	1 lb 2 oz
120 g	bacon, diced and fried	4 oz
100 g	bread (sandwich loaf), diced and fried	3½ oz
3 dl	thickened veal stock	10 fl oz
	3 eggs, hard-boiled	
150 g	butter	5 oz
1 cl	dairy cream	½ fl oz
	salt, pepper	
	flour	

Beat the veal steaks, season with salt and pepper, flour them and carefully fry for about 10 minutes in 80 g (3 oz) butter. Dress on the spinach which has been enriched with cream. Top with the diced potatoes, bread and bacon, and with the mushrooms which have been tossed in the rest of the butter. Garnish with the eggs, cut into quarters. Hand the veal stock separately.

(Willi Bartenbach, Switzerland)

Veal steak Oscar

4 portions

140 g	4 veal steaks each weighing	5 oz
	flour	
	2 eggs, beaten	
30 g	butter	1 oz
1 dl	dry white wine	3½ fl oz
2 dl	lobster sauce (recipe, page 178)	7 fl oz
1 cl	Cognac	½ fl oz
30 g	butter, softened (to finish sauce)	1 oz
	4 half lobster claws	
	4 thin truffle slices	
	salt	
	pepper, freshly ground	

Trim the veal steaks carefully, season with salt and pepper, then flour them. Coat with beaten egg. Fry on both sides in butter until golden, then remove and keep hot. Pour off the remaining butter, stir in the wine to detach the sediment, reduce, add the lobster sauce and boil up for a moment. Add the Cognac and strain the sauce. Carefully blend in the softened butter, and season to taste with salt and pepper.

To serve, pour the sauce on to warmed plates and dress the veal steaks on top. Garnish with the lobster claws, which have been heated, and the slices of truffle.
(Illustration, page 238)

(Anton Mosimann, Great Britain)

Veal steak with chive cream sauce
Pavé de veau à la crème de ciboulette

5 portions

1 kg	loin of veal, boned	2 lb 4 oz
70 g	butter	2½ oz
2 cl	oil	1 fl oz
50 g	chives, finely cut	2 oz
20 g	shallot, chopped	¾ oz
1 dl	chicken broth	3½ fl oz
1 dl	white wine	3½ fl oz
5 cl	Cognac	2 fl oz
6 dl	dairy cream	1 pt
	lemon juice	
	salt	
	pepper	

Cut the veal into 5 steaks. Fry on both sides over medium heat in the oil and 30 g (1 oz) butter, allowing 4 to 5 minutes a side. Remove from the pan and keep hot. Pour off the remaining fat. While the pan is still hot, add the shallot and chives, fry for a short time, then stir in the wine to detach the sediment and add first the Cognac, then the chicken broth. Reduce by three quarters and add the cream. Cook over gentle heat for 5 minutes.

Dip the steaks in the sauce to make them swell, remove and dress on warmed plates. Remove the sauce from the heat, adjust the seasoning, blend with the rest of the butter and sharpen with a few drops of lemon juice. Pass the sauce through a conical strainer and pour over the steaks. Sprinkle the sauce with finely cut chives. Serve with vegetables in season.
(Illustration, page 765)

(Jean-Paul Bossée-François, France)

Stuffed veal steak Max Dick
Steak de veau farci aux champignons Max Dick
Gefülltes Kalbssteak Max Dick

1 portion

110 g	1 veal steak weighing	4 oz
2½ dl	white wine	9 fl oz
50 g	butter	2 oz
	salt	
	pepper	

Stuffing:

1 tablespoon veal trimmings
1 tablespoon morels (dried or canned)
1 egg
salt, commercial seasoning
1 slice raw ham
1 Swiss chard leaf

Pepper ball:

	½ green pepper, seeded	
	½ red pepper, seeded	
1¼ dl	white wine	4 fl oz
	salt, pepper	
	3 mushrooms, turned and grooved	
	a little dill	
	1 tablespoon veal gravy	

Cut a pocket in the veal steak. Marinate in white wine for 3 to 4 hours. To make the stuffing, chop the veal trimmings very finely and mix well with the morels which have been soaked and cut up finely. Bind with the egg and season well.

Remove the meat from the marinade, stuff, and close the pocket with a small skewer. Season with salt and pepper, and fry slowly in butter for about 6 to 8 minutes. Allow to cool, then wrap the steak in the ham, then the Swiss chard. Fry again very slowly for 8 to 10 minutes. Blanch the red and green pepper in white wine for about 4 to 6 minutes. Skin, season and shape into a ball.

To serve, slice the veal stock and arrange on a plate. Garnish with the pepper ball and with the mushrooms which have been tossed in butter and decorated with dill. Pour the veal gravy over. If desired, hand boiled potatoes, tossed in butter, separately.
(Illustration, page 941)

(Werner Dabernig, Austria)

Minced veal steak with pear and Roquefort cream au gratin
Steak de veau avec poire au roquefort gratinée
Geschabtes Kalbssteak mit Birne und Roquefortcreme gratiniert

10 portions   Cooking time: 25 minutes

900 g	shoulder of veal, boned	2 lb
150 g	white bread	5 oz
	3 eggs	
	salt	
	pepper, freshly ground	
30 g	parsley, chopped	1 oz
50 g	ham, finely diced	2 oz
5 cl	dairy cream	2 fl oz
60 g	shallots, finely diced	2 oz
1 dl	oil	3½ fl oz
	20 pear halves, poached	
100 g	soft butter	3½ oz

Roquefort cream:

200 g	Roquefort	7 oz
2 dl	dairy cream (thick)	7 fl oz
	3 eggs	
100 g	Gervais	3½ oz
	a pinch of Cayenne pepper	
	lemon balm, chopped	

Mince the veal finely. Remove the crust from the bread, soak in milk and squeeze dry, then mix with the meat, eggs, parsley, shallots and ham until well blended. Season with salt and pepper, add the cream and butter, and work to a pliable consistency. Shape into flat oval cakes and fry on both sides in hot oil.

To serve, place the pear halves, which have been kept hot, on the steaks, coat with the Roquefort cream and brown in a hot oven. To make the Roquefort cream, pass the Roquefort through a sieve and mix well with the cream, eggs and Gervais to a spreading consistency. Season with Cayenne pepper and stir in the lemon balm.

(Karl Brunnengräber, Germany)

Triple grill of veal Brian
Trianon de veau grillé Brian

4 portions

50 g	4 slices calf's kidney each weighing	2 oz

50 g	4 veal medallions each weighing	2 oz
	4 slices poached calves' sweetbreads	
40 g	each weighing	1½ oz
2 cl	oil	1 fl oz
1½ dl	brown veal stock	5 fl oz
20 g	butter for sauce	¾ oz
	salt	
	pepper, freshly ground	

Carefully trim the slices of kidney and sweetbreads, and the veal medallions. Season with salt and pepper, and brush with oil. Grill carefully over high heat. Make a sauce with the veal stock, season carefully and finish with the butter.

To serve, pour the sauce on to warmed plates and dress the meat on top. Garnish with Anna potatoes and with okra which has been sauté in butter.
(Illustration, page 242)

(Anton Mosimann, Great Britain)

Lamb—Hot Main Dishes

Easter lamb with young vegetables
Agneau pascal aux primeurs

4–5 portions

	1 leg or shoulder of lamb	
	parsley, coarsely cut	
	salt, pepper	
	lemon juice	
	garlic (optional)	
	a little flour	
50 g	butter	2 oz
approx. 20 g	breadcrumbs	approx. ¾ oz
approx. 20 g	parsley, finely chopped	approx. ¾ oz

Accompaniments:

250 g	fresh morels or mushrooms	9 oz
300 g	young peas	11 oz
400 g	new potatoes	14 oz
	fresh salad, dressed with very little olive oil and lemon juice	

Bone the lamb, stuff with coarsely cut parsley and tie. Season by rubbing with salt, pepper, lemon juice and, if desired, a clove of garlic. Coat with flour and brown on all sides in lightly browned butter. Roast in a medium oven for about 25 minutes. Prick with a needle to test whether the meat is cooked. The meat juices should be slightly pink.

Remove from the oven, mix the breadcrumbs with the finely chopped parsley and spread thinly on the meat. Baste with the cooking butter, return to the oven and leave until golden brown. To serve, bring to the table before carving. Dish the accompaniments separately.

(Eric Carlström, Sweden)

Lamb curry

6 portions

1 kg 500	leg of lamb, trimmed of fat and boned	3 lb 5 oz

Sauce:

1 kg	onions, sliced	2 lb 4 oz
	½ tablespoon garlic, chopped	
	2 tablespoons ground ginger	
	1 teaspoon ground cinnamon	
½ l	dairy cream	18 fl oz
1 dl	meat glaze	3½ fl oz
	1 bay leaf	
	6 black peppercorns	
	salt	
	butter	
	oil	

Cut the meat into neat pieces and keep in a cool place. For the sauce, fry the onions in clear butter until golden, then add the cream, spices and meat glaze. Simmer slowly, strain and set aside in a cool place. Sauter the lamb in a little oil until golden brown. Pour the sauce over and simmer until the meat is cooked. Serve with pilaf rice.
(Illustration, page 695)

(Percy Sullivan, India)

Dzsigari
Abats d'agneau gratinés

10 portions   Cooking time: about 1 hour

2 kg	lamb's or calf's offal (lights, liver, heart, kidneys)	4 lb 8 oz
300 g	butter	11 oz
200 g	onions	7 oz
200 g	root vegetables	7 oz
	1 bunch parsley	
	1 bunch dill	
40 g	salt	1½ oz
10 g	black pepper, freshly ground	⅓ oz
1 g	ginger	a small pinch
1 g	tarragon	a small pinch
	15 eggs	
3 dl	sour cream	10 fl oz
	lemon juice	

Clean and trim the offal, wash well and blanch. Cook in an ample amount of lightly salted water. Remove each item from the pan when it is cooked and allow to cool. Chop or mince coarsely.

Chop the onions finely and fry in butter or oil until lightly coloured. Dice the root vegetables and add to the pan, pour in a little bone stock and simmer until cooked. Add the offal. Season with salt, pepper and grated ginger. Sprinkle with finely chopped parsley, dill and tarragon, and mix well. (In Georgia, additional seasoning is provided by a local plant called 'kinza'.)

Transfer to a fireproof dish, mix the eggs well with the sour cream, pour over and bake in the oven. Serve in the same dish, sprinkling with a little pepper and lemon juice to taste at the last minute.

(Zsolt Körmendy, Russia)

Lamb with dill
Ragoût d'agneau à l'aneth
Lamm i Dill

1 portion

250 g	breast of lamb	9 oz
	dill	
50 g	flour butter	2 oz
	salt	
	pepper, freshly ground	

Cut the lamb into cubes. Blanch, skim, season with salt and pepper, add sprigs of fresh dill and cook. Remove the meat, strain the stock, reduce and thicken with the flour butter. Mix with a generous amount of chopped dill. To serve, place the meat in a heated dish and pour the sauce over.

(Hroar Dege, Günther Rett, Norway)

Lamb with peas
Agneau aux petits pois
Intingolo di agnello con piselli

6 portions   Cooking time: about 2 hours

1 kg 500	leg of lamb, boned and cut in pieces	3 lb 5 oz
	3 tablespoons flour	
	4 tablespoons olive oil	
	salt	
600 g	young peas, frozen	1 lb 5 oz
	2 teaspoons meat extract	
	Parmesan, grated	

2 eggs, beaten
1 tablespoon parsley, chopped

Flour the meat, brown in oil, add the peas, together with 3 ladles water containing the dissolved meat extract, cover and braise. When the liquid is well reduced, remove from the heat, add the eggs, stir quickly, sprinkle with Parmesan and parsley, and serve.

(Salvatore Schifano, Italy)

Epigrammes of lamb René Carcan
Epigrammes d'agneau René Carcan
Epigramm von Lamm René Carcan

6 portions

1 kg 500	lean breast of lamb	3 lb 5 oz
	1 leek	
	1 onion	
	1 carrot	
	1 small celeriac	
	1 clove of garlic	
	1 bay leaf	
	2 cloves	
	black and white peppercorns	
	1 small sprig thyme	
	salt	
	1 dessertspoon English mustard	
	3 eggs, beaten	
250 g	breadcrumbs	9 oz
1 kg	white vegetable fat	2 lb 4 oz
OR 1 l	oil	1¾ pt

Béchamel sauce:

40 g	butter	1½ oz
50 g	flour	2 oz
½ l	milk	18 fl oz
	1 teaspoon English mustard	

Duchesse potatoes:

1 kg 500	potatoes	3 lb 5 oz
	salt, nutmeg	
20 g	butter	¾ oz
	3 egg yolks	
	1 egg, beaten	

Beans:

1 kg 500	young French beans	3 lb 5 oz
	butter	
	onion	
	pepper, freshly ground	
approx. 60 g	curled parsley	approx. 2 oz
	1 teaspoon dried savory	
	or a few small sprigs fresh savory	

Bone the lamb. Place in a shallow pan with the root vegetables, herbs and spices, and add sufficient water to cover. Cook for 1 hour and leave in the stock until lukewarm. Remove from the pan, place on a cloth and cut away any remaining gristle and bone. Cool completely overnight under light pressure.

Cut the meat into triangles with a 5 cm (2 in) base and 8 cm (3½ in) sides. Spread thinly with the mustard mixed to a paste with melted butter, egg and crumb, and fry in white vegetable fat or oil until golden.

Cook the beans in salted water, drain, toss in butter with the onion which has been finely chopped, add the savory leaves and season with freshly ground pepper.

Peel the potatoes and boil them in salted water. Drain, dry out very well and quickly press through a ricer. Season with salt and nutmeg, and mix with the butter and egg yolks. While still warm, pipe out in rosettes on to a buttered baking sheet, using a savoy bag and star tube. Brush with beaten egg and bake in a hot oven.

Make a Béchamel sauce with the butter, flour and milk, then mix with the mustard. Deep-fry the parsley very quickly. To serve, dress the beans pyramid fashion in the centre of a round or oval fireproof dish. Surround with the epigrammes of lamb and arrange the potatoes round them. Place small bunches of fried parsley between the meat and the potatoes. Hand the sauce separately.

(Otto Brust, Germany)

Fricassée of lamb with dill sauce
Fricassée d'agneau en sauce à l'aneth

4 portions

800 g	boneless lamb (neck and shoulder)	1 lb 12 oz
OR 1 kg 200	lamb on the bone (breast and shoulder)	2 lb 10 oz
	1 medium onion	
	1 carrot	
	salt, pepper	
	2 tablespoons butter	
	2 tablespoons flour	

	1 bunch dill	
	2 egg yolks	
1 dl	dairy cream	3½ fl oz
	a little vinegar and sugar	

Blanch the lamb. Place in a pan with the carrot, onion and seasoning, cover with water and simmer slowly under cover until tender, but do not overcook. Remove the bones (if present).

Prepare a blond roux with the butter and flour, blend in the lamb stock which has been strained, boil well and thicken with the egg yolk which has been blended with the cream.

Discard the dill flowers and stalks, cut the leaves very finely and add to the sauce. Finish with a little vinegar and sugar, then return to the boil. Pour the sauce over the meat to serve, and hand boiled new potatoes separately.

(Eric Carlström, Sweden)

Lamb in milk
Agneau au lait

12–14 portions   Cooking time: about 2–3 hours

1 house lamb
ewe's milk
salt

Clean and wash the lamb carefully, and rub salt into the flesh. Place in a large pan whole, pour in sufficient ewe's milk to cover, and cook. To serve, cut into portions and dress on a warmed dish. Serve with kajmak (recipe, page 147), ewe cheese and a salad of young onions.

(László Csizmadia, Yugoslavia)

Boned roast lamb
Agneau désossé rôti
Agnello disossato arrosto

6 portions

3 kg	a side of lamb weighing about	6½ lb
50 g	salt	2 oz
	3 cloves of garlic	
10 g	pepper	⅓ oz
	2 sprigs rosemary	
	¼ nutmeg, grated	

	a pinch of wild fennel seed	
2–3 dl	olive oil	7–10 fl oz

Pound together in a mortar the garlic, rosemary leaves, pepper, salt, nutmeg and fennel seed. Bone the lamb, remove as much fat as possible, and rub the meat well with the pounded seasonings. Roll up and tie securely. Place in a roasting dish and baste liberally with olive oil. Roast in an oven preheated to 250°C (480°F) for 1 hour, basting frequently. Serve with haricot beans Tuscan style (recipe, page 1009).

(Mario De Filippis, Italy)

Lamb with lemon
Agneau au citron
Angello al limone

4 portions

2 kg	boneless lamb (shoulder, breast, saddle)	4 lb 8 oz
	olive oil as required	
	4 eggs, beaten	
	juice of 2 lemons	
	salt	
	pepper, freshly ground	

Cut the meat in pieces, brown briefly in oil, season with salt and a little pepper, and cook under cover for about 15 to 30 minutes. Season the eggs with salt and pepper, mix with the lemon juice, and pour over the meat. Stand over low heat while turning the pieces of meat until the eggs have set. Serve hot.

(Salvatore Schifano, Italy)

Barbecued lamb
Agneau à la broche

	1 young lamb weighing about	
15 kg	(live weight)	33 lb
	salt	
3 dl	oil	10 fl oz

A mountain lamb should preferably be selected for this dish. The flesh has a much better flavour than that of a lowland lamb. Prepare the lamb, washing it thoroughly. Rub it carefully with salt inside and outside and fix on to a spit. Roast over the fire for about 2 hours, depending on size. Brush frequently with oil while roasting to produce a crisp golden crust.

(László Csizmadia, Yugoslavia)

Stuffed breast of lamb with sauerkraut Alsatian style
Poitrine d'agneau farcie avec choucroute à l'alsacienne
Gefüllte Lammbrust mit Elsässer Sauerkraut

10 portions

approx.

1 kg 500	breast of lamb with bones	approx.	3 lb 5 oz
300 g	fresh ox liver, finely chopped		11 oz
400 g	white bread		14 oz
	3 eggs		
	garlic		
	salt		
	marjoram		
	pepper, freshly ground		
	parsley, chopped		
	sauerkraut, cooked in white wine		
	(Alsatian style)		

Remove the flat bones from the lamb and slit in the centre of one side with a sharp knife to make a pocket.

To make the forcemeat, cut the crust off the bread and dice the crumb finely. Season the liver with salt, pepper, garlic and marjoram. Add a generous amount of parsley and the eggs, and mix very well. Fold in the diced bread. Stuff the lamb with this forcemeat and sew up the opening. Place in an oven preheated to 240°C (465°F). Roast for 1½ hours, reducing the heat to 200°C (390°F) after a time and basting frequently.

To serve, carve the lamb and dress on sauerkraut Alsatian style. Pour a little gravy over. Hand mashed potatoes separately.

(Otto Ledermann, Switzerland)

Stuffed breast of lamb housewife style
Poitrine d'agneau farcie bonne ménagère
Gefüllte Lammbrust Gute Hausfrau

6 portions   Cooking time: 1¼ hours

| 1 kg 200 | breast of lamb | 2 lb 10 oz |

Forcemeat:

240 g	lamb's liver	8 oz
180 g	breadcrumbs	6 oz
	2 eggs	
180 g	onions, cut into brunoise dice	6 oz
150 g	carrots, cut into julienne strips	5 oz
150 g	celery, cut into julienne strips	5 oz
120 g	leeks, cut into julienne strips	4 oz
30 g	flour	1 oz
6 dl	clear gravy	1 pt
750 g	potatoes	1 lb 10 oz
60 g	fine herbs	2 oz

Seasonings:

	marjoram, savory	
	salt	
	pepper, freshly ground	
	parsley	
	commercial seasoning	
	coriander, nutmeg	
120 g	vegetable fat	4 oz
60 g	butter	2 oz

To make the forcemeat, trim the liver of tubes and mince it. Add the eggs, onions and breadcrumbs, mix and flavour with herbs and spices. Bone the breast of lamb, cut a pocket with a sharp knife in the thick part, stuff with the forcemeat and sew up. Place in a medium oven and glaze slowly. Cut into 12 slices, allowing 2 per portion. Dress on a warmed dish, pour a little sauce over, cover with the vegetable julienne garnish, and serve with parsley potatoes.

To make the garnish, cook the vegetable julienne gently in fat, then add herbs, salt, pepper and commercial seasoning. Boil the potatoes and cook gently in butter, sprinkling them with parsley.

(Otto Ledermann, Switzerland)

Lamb fillets in foil with Provençal herbs
Filets d'agneau en papillote aux herbes de Provence
Lammfilet in Papierhülle mit provenzalischen Kräutern

10 portions

| 1 kg 400 | lamb fillets | 3 lb |

100 g	butter	3½ oz
	aluminium foil	

Marinade:

3 g	garlic	1 clove
10 g	onions	⅓ oz
10 g	parsley	⅓ oz
10 g	basil	⅓ oz
5 g	thyme	⅙ oz
10 g	chervil	⅓ oz
10 g	black pepper	⅓ oz
5 g	English mustard	⅙ oz
	white wine	
5 dl	oil	18 fl oz

Finely chop the garlic, onion, parsley, basil, thyme and chervil, and mix well. Blend the mustard powder to a paste with a little white wine, add pepper and a little oil, and mix with the herbs. Carefully rub this marinade into the lamb fillets and set aside for 4 hours or even overnight.

Brown the fillets in butter and wrap in foil. Cook for 10 minutes in an oven preheated to 240°C (465°F). The meat should be medium done. Serve at once, unwrapping the fillets, slicing them obliquely and dressing them on a warmed dish. Serve with French beans and potatoes au gratin Dauphine style (gratin dauphinois).

(Otto Ledermann, Switzerland)

Best end of lamb Sisteron
Carré d'agneau de Sisteron

2 portions

	8 lamb cutlets (best end) in one piece	
15 g	butter	½ oz
	½ teaspoon thyme flowers, powdered	
	2 tablespoons dry white wine	
	2 tablespoons lamb gravy	
	(recipe, page 121)	
	salt, pepper	

Trim the best end neatly, pull off the skin, remove the fat, chine, strip the ends of the bones

and shorten by sawing through. Spread the meat with butter, season with salt and pepper, and sprinkle lightly with the thyme. Roast in a hot oven for 8 to 10 minutes, basting frequently. Pour off the fat in the pan, stir in the wine and lamb gravy to detach the sediment, and boil up. If desired, commercial meat extract which has been diluted may be used instead of lamb gravy. Serve with potatoes au gratin Jabron style (recipe, page 1017).
(Illustration, page 256)

(Pierre Gleize, France)

Best end of lamb in a herb crust
Carré d'agneau en croûte de fines herbes
Lammkarree in Kräuterkruste

4 portions

800 g	best end of lamb	1 lb 12 oz
	salt, pepper	
	garlic	
2½ dl	lamb gravy	9 fl oz
5 g	tarragon	⅙ oz

Herb purée:

50 g	tarragon	2 oz
50 g	chervil	2 oz
50 g	parsley	2 oz
20 g	garlic	¾ oz
30 g	green peppercorns	1 oz
	4 tablespoons flour	
	1 egg white	

Roquefort tomatoes:

	2 tomatoes	
80 g	Roquefort cheese	3 oz
40 g	butter	1½ oz

Sweet corn fritters:

160 g	sweet corn (canned or frozen)	5½ oz
	4 tablespoons flour	
	4 tablespoons milk	
	1 egg	
	1 tablespoon parsley, chopped	
	a little salt	

Trim the best end, season with salt and pepper and rub with garlic. Brown briefly in oil and allow to cool. Work the herbs to a purée, season with salt and mix well with the egg white and flour. Rub this paste into the lamb and roast in a moderate oven for about 20 minutes.

Turn down the heat and leave to stand in the oven for a further 10 minutes to colour. Wash and skin the tomatoes, and cut them in half. Cover each half with a quarter of the Roquefort and butter, and brown under a salamander.

For the fritters, prepare a pancake batter with the flour, milk and egg. Add the parsley, sweet corn and salt, and mix well. Drop in spoonfuls into hot oil and shallow-fry on both sides until golden.

To serve, carve the lamb, dress the slices on a dish and coat with lamb gravy containing tarragon. Garnish with the tomatoes and the sweet corn fritters.
(Illustration, page 940)

(Adolf Meindl, Austria)

Best end of lamb Jären style
Carré d'agneau à la Jären
Lamme Carre fra Jären

6 portions   Cooking time: 25–30 minutes

1 kg 200	best end of lamb	2 lb 10 oz
	salt	
	pepper, freshly ground	
180 g	vegetable fat	6 oz
60 g	English mustard powder	2 oz
	fresh white breadcrumbs	
	butter as required	

Trim the lamb, season with salt and pepper, and brown well over high heat in the vegetable fat, then cool a little. Mix the butter and mustard powder to a paste of spreading consistency with white breadcrumbs. Spread thinly on the lamb and roast in an oven preheated to 220°C (430°F). Serve with vegetables in season.

(Hroar Dege, Günther Rett, Norway)

Lamb fillets with spinach sauce
Filets d'agneau – sauce aux épinards
Lamshaasjes met spinaziesaus

	4 lamb fillets	
100 g	butter	3½ oz

	pepper, freshly ground	
	salt	
1 kg	spinach	2 lb 4 oz
5 cl	veal gravy	2 fl oz
100 g	shallots, finely chopped	3½ oz
100 g	old Dutch cheese, grated	3½ oz
1 dl	dairy cream	3½ fl oz

Fry the lamb fillets until medium done. Carefully clean the spinach, blanch it, then chop finely. Cook gently in butter with the shallots, then add the veal gravy and the cream, and reduce to the desired consistency. Season with salt and pepper.

Cover the bottom of a fireproof dish with the sauce, dress the lamb fillets on top and sprinkle with the cheese. Brown for a few minutes in the oven or under a salamander.

(Bernard van Beurten, Netherlands)

Lamb fillets in puff pastry with grapes
Filets d'agneau en croûte aux raisins

6–8 portions

	4 lamb fillets (saddle)	
	larding bacon	
½ l	red wine	18 fl oz
	1 bouquet garni	
	1 carrot	
	2 cloves of garlic	
	oil and butter as required	
1 kg	puff pastry	2 lb 4 oz
	2 eggs	

Garnish:

black and white grapes, peeled

Lard the fillets and marinate in red wine for 24 hours. Brown them quickly in oil and butter, keeping them rare. Allow to cool.

Pin out the puff pastry, cut into rectangles and enclose each fillet in one of them. Brush with egg and bake for 15 minutes at 230°C (445°F).

To make the sauce, boil up the marinade with the vegetables, reduce, strain, and stir into the pan in which the meat was browned to detach the sediment. Add lamb gravy (recipe, page 121), reduce a little, enrich with butter and season with salt and pepper. Dress the fillets on a warmed dish and carve at the table. Hand the grapes and celeriac mousse (recipe, page 1014) separately.

(Emile Jung, France)

Knuckle of lamb Greek style
Jarret d'agneau à la grecque

4 portions   Cooking time: 1–1½ hours

1 kg	knuckle of lamb	2 lb 4 oz
	2 onions	
100 g	celery	3½ oz
5 dl	water	18 fl oz
	salt	
	3 tablespoons flour	
	a little cornflour	
	2 egg yolks	
	juice of 1 lemon	
	1 tablespoon butter	
	4 slices bread for toasting	
	1 tablespoon parsley, finely chopped	

Wash the knuckles well, blanching if necessary. Place in a pan with the water, celery, onions and salt to taste, and cook until the meat comes away from the bone. Pass the stock through a conical strainer and reduce to the amount of liquid required for the sauce. Blend the flour and cornflour with a little water and add to the reduced stock while boiling, then boil well and remove from the heat. Add the egg yolks which have been mixed with the lemon juice, finish with the butter and adjust the seasoning. Toast the bread and place on a serving dish. Dress the meat on top, coat with the sauce and sprinkle with the parsley.

(Emil Wälti, Greece)

Best end of lamb with green lemon sauce
Carré d'agneau au citron vert

4 portions

	4 best ends of lamb each comprising	
	3 cutlets	
	white wine as required	

Marinade:

16 cl	olive oil	6 fl oz

1 large onion, finely cut
1 small clove of garlic, crushed
juice of 1 lemon
1 sprig thyme
1 bay leaf
2 cloves
1 sprig parsley

Persillade:

4 tablespoons dried breadcrumbs
½ slice fresh white bread (tin loaf), sieved
4 tablespoons parsley, chopped
1 clove of garlic, grated
salt
pepper, freshly ground

Sauce:

2 dl	reduced lamb stock	7 fl oz
	4 slices green lemon, peeled	
	2 tablespoons dry white wine	
	butter as required	

Stuffed courgettes:

400 g	2 courgettes weighing	14 oz
600 g	tomatoes, skinned, seeded and finely cut	1 lb 5 oz
100 g	Gruyère cheese, grated	3½ oz
	1 clove of garlic	
	2 small shallots, finely cut	

Prepare the marinade. Leave the lamb in it for 2 days, then season with salt and pepper and brown on all sides in a very hot oven. Detach the pan juices with white wine and stand in a lukewarm place for 5 to 10 minutes.

Prepare the persillade, adding a little oil if necessary to bind. Spread on the lamb and return to the oven to brown the top. Dress the lamb on a warmed serving dish and carve at the table. Hand the sauce, the stuffed courgettes and Duchesse potatoes separately.

For the sauce, make stock with lamb bones and seasonings, strain and reduce well. Add the wine and enrich with butter. Lastly add the slices of green lemon, divided into segments.

To prepare the courgettes, cut them into 4 cm (1½ in) lengths and hollow out. Finely dice the courgette flesh and stew with the garlic juice, the shallots and the tomatoes. Season with salt and pepper. Cook the courgette shells gently in the oven, stuff with the cooked vegetable mixture, cover with the grated cheese and brown in the oven or under a salamander.

(François Kiener, France)

Leg of lamb Alberobello
Gigot d'agneau Alberobello
Cosciotto d'agnello Alberobello

8–10 portions   Cooking time: 40 minutes

1 kg 700	leg of lamb	3 lb 12 oz
350 g	yellow peppers	12 oz
350 g	red peppers	12 oz
350 g	aubergines	12 oz
250 g	white onions	9 oz
1 dl	groundnut oil	3½ fl oz
5 cl	olive oil	2 fl oz
2 dl	white wine	7 fl oz
3 dl	lamb stock	10 fl oz
	fresh thyme sprigs	
	salt	
	white pepper, freshly ground	

Remove the chump end bone, strip the knuckle end and shorten with a saw. Cut away any excess fat and trim the leg. Tie to keep in shape. Chop up the chump end bone and place on a roasting tray with the lamb trimmings and sprigs of thyme. Season the leg with salt and pepper, brush lightly with oil and place on the bed of bones and trimmings. Keep cool.

Peel the onions and cut into quarters. Cut off the stalk ends of the aubergines, wash and cut into pieces 3 cm (1¼ in) square and 5 mm (¼ in) thick. Cut off the stalk ends of the peppers, then cut the peppers into quarters, remove the pith and seeds, and rinse well under running water. Dry on a cloth and cut into 3 cm (1¼ in) squares. Arrange the vegetables on a second roasting tray, keeping them separate, and sprinkle with the olive oil.

Roast the lamb for 10 to 12 minutes in an oven preheated to 240°C (465°F), basting frequently. Turn the meat and reduce the oven temperature to 200°C (390°F). Continue roasting for 15 minutes, basting frequently. Place the vegetables in the oven and cook until the meat is done. Remove the meat and vegetables from the oven. Place the meat on a wire rack with a drip tray underneath to catch the meat juices.

Pour off the fat in the roasting tray, detach the sediment with the wine, add the lamb stock, reduce by half, season with salt and pepper, pass through a conical strainer and keep hot.

Cover the end of the leg bone with a frill, place on an oval dish, arrange the vegetables round the meat and decorate with sprigs of thyme. Hand the gravy separately.
(Illustration, page 413)

(Daniel Drouadaine, Italy)

Leg of lamb with borage
Gigot d'agneau à la bourrache
Cosciotto d'agnello alla borracina

6 portions   Cooking time: about 2 hours

2 kg	leg of lamb	4 lb 8 oz
100 g	white breadcrumbs	3½ oz
150 g	borage, finely chopped	5 oz
1 dl	white wine	3½ fl oz
	wine vinegar as required	
1 dl	olive oil	3½ fl oz
100 g	butter	3½ oz
	salt	
	pepper, freshly ground	

Trim the lamb of fat and sinew. Shorten the bone if necessary. Season with salt and pepper, place on a roasting tray with sprigs of rosemary and thyme, and roast at 200°C (390°F), sprinkling with vinegar from time to time. Detach the pan juices with the wine, bring to the boil and reduce.

Mix the breadcrumbs with the borage, and brown lightly in a separate pan. Carve the lamb, pour the sauce over and sprinkle with the borage and breadcrumbs.

(Mario Saporito, Italy)

Leg of lamb Grisons style
Gigot d'agneau à la grisonne
Lammkeule auf Bündner Art

10 portions   Cooking time: about 45 minutes

2 kg	leg of lamb	4 lb 8 oz
50 g	fat	2 oz
200 g	onions, thinly sliced	7 oz
	3 cloves of garlic, crushed	
1 kg 500	potatoes	3 lb 5 oz
600 g	carrots	1 lb 5 oz
400 g	celeriac	14 oz
	½ teaspoon thyme	
2 dl	white wine	7 fl oz
3 dl	brown stock	10 fl oz
	salt	
	pepper, freshly ground	

Carefully rub the lamb with salt, pepper and thyme. Brown in the fat and detach the sediment with the wine. Add the onions and garlic, cover tightly, place in a preheated oven and cook for about 45 minutes. Shortly before the meat is cooked, add the carrots, celeriac and potatoes which have been peeled and coarsely diced. Season with a little salt, add the brown stock and continue braising until cooked.

(Otto Ledermann, Switzerland)

Leg of lamb with eggs
Gigot d'agneau aux oeufs
Jagnjeća Kapama sa Jajima

6 portions   Cooking time: about 1½ hours

1 kg	leg of lamb	2 lb 4 oz
3 dl	oil	10 fl oz
500 g	spring onions *or* leeks	1 lb 2 oz
500 g	large onions	1 lb 2 oz
2½ dl	sour milk (recipe, page 147)	9 fl oz
	4 eggs	
100 g	flour	3½ oz
4 dl	water *or* bouillon	14 fl oz
	salt	
	pepper, freshly ground	

Cut the meat into 4–5 cm (about 2 in) pieces, season with salt, flour them and sauter in oil. Remove from the pan, add the large onions which have been thinly sliced and the spring onions or leeks which have been cut into strips. Cook gently in the oil remaining in the pan, add the meat and sauter for a further 15 minutes or so.

Transfer the meat and onions to a fireproof dish, add sufficient water or bouillon to cover, and season with salt and pepper. Place in a preheated oven and braise until the liquid has evaporated and the meat is cooked.

Beat the eggs, season with salt and pour over the meat. Brown in the oven, then serve in the same dish. Hand sour milk separately.

(László Csizmadia, Yugoslavia)

Leg of lamb with spinach
Gigot d'agneau aux épinards
Jagnjeća Jajina sa Spanaćem

6 portions   Cooking time: about 1½ hours

1 kg	leg of lamb	2 lb 4 oz
1½ dl	oil	5 fl oz
	1 tablespoon flour	
	2 small onions, finely cut	
2 dl	sour milk (recipe, page 147)	7 fl oz
1 kg	spinach	2 lb 4 oz
	salt	
	pepper, freshly ground	
7½ dl	water	1¼ pt

Wash the meat and simmer in the water until half cooked, then cut into 5–6 cm (about 2 in) pieces. Cook the onions gently in oil without colouring, and add the meat together with the spinach which has been washed and coarsely chopped. Dust with the flour and pour in the meat stock. Cover and cook in a moderate oven. Most of the liquid should have evaporated by the end of the cooking time. Serve with sour milk.

(László Csizmadia, Yugoslavia)

Leg of lamb with vegetable stuffing
Gigot d'agneau farci aux légumes
Pácolt báránycomb

5 portions

1 kg 250	leg of lamb	2 lb 12 oz
100 g	carrots, cut into julienne strips	3½ oz
100 g	parsley, finely chopped	3½ oz
50 g	onions, sliced	2 oz
20 g	black pepper, freshly ground	¾ oz
	1 bunch fresh tarragon	
	1 bay leaf	
3 dl	dry red wine	10 fl oz

Garnish:

(1)		5 tomatoes (firm)	
(2)	500 g	potatoes	1 lb 2 oz
	2 dl	sour cream	7 fl oz
		2 eggs	
	1 dl	oil	3½ fl oz
		salt, pepper	
		marjoram	
(3)	250 g	button onions	9 oz
	30 g	sugar	1 oz
	30 g	butter	1 oz

		salt, pepper	
(4)	250 g	fresh spinach	9 oz
	30 g	garlic butter	1 oz
		salt, pepper	

Carefully bone the lamb. Fill the cavity with a little more than half the carrot julienne and parsley and tie the leg to its original shape. Place in a braising pan together with the remaining carrots and parsley and the herbs; pour the wine over. Cover with the onions, dot with butter and braise in an oven preheated to 160°C (320°F), basting frequently. Add a little water if the pan becomes too dry.

To serve, carve the meat, dress on a warmed dish, pour the stock over and surround with the vegetables. For garnish (1) cut a cross in the top of the tomatoes, place them in a fireproof dish, lightly spread with butter, cover and cook in a fairly hot oven until soft, then season with salt and pepper.

For garnish (2) peel the potatoes and grate them very finely. Mix with the eggs and sour cream, and season with salt, pepper and marjoram. Shape into small cakes and fry in oil.

For garnish (3) brown the sugar in the butter, add the onions which have been peeled and washed, fry for a few minutes, then season with salt and pepper.

For garnish (4) remove the stalks from the spinach, clean it well, wash several times in an ample amount of water, blanch, drain, squeeze dry and reheat in garlic butter. Season to taste with salt and pepper.

(Gyula Gullner, Hungary)

Stuffed leg of lamb en croûte I
Gigot d'agneau farci en croûte
Gefüllte Lammkeule in der Kruste

6–8 portions

approx.			approx.	
	1 kg 500	leg of lamb, boned		3 lb 5 oz
		2 teaspoons salt/pepper mixture		
	5 cl	oil		2 fl oz

Stuffing:

		2 lamb's kidneys, finely diced		
	50 g	mushrooms, chopped		2 oz
		1 teaspoon truffle, chopped		
	50 g	foie gras parfait *or* liver sausage		2 oz
		Armagnac or brandy		
		salt, pepper, freshly ground		

Pastry:

2 dl	bouillon	7 fl oz
800 g	flour	1 lb 12 oz
100 g	butter	3½ oz
50 g	dripping	2 oz
approx. 1 dl	water (if required) approx.	3½ fl oz
	salt	
	2 tablespoons dairy cream	

Prepare the stuffing, insert into the boned leg of lamb, and tie in place. Season with salt and pepper, place in a braising pan with the oil and roast uncovered in a medium oven for about 1 hour. Allow to rest for 30 minutes.

Meanwhile prepare the pastry with the bouillon, butter, dripping, flour and salt. Depending on the type of flour, it may be necessary to add about 1 dl (3½ fl oz) water to make a soft dough. Chill, then roll out into an oval and wrap round the lamb. Brush with cream and bake in a hot oven for about 15 minutes or until the pastry is crisp.

(Emil Wälti, Switzerland)

Stuffed leg of lamb en croûte II
Gigot d'agneau farci en croûte
Gefüllte Lammkeule in der Teigkruste

10 portions

2 kg 500	leg of lamb	5 lb 8 oz

Stuffing:

280 g	lean lamb and pork fillet trimmings	10 oz
80 g	unsmoked pork fat or bacon	3 oz
20 g	flap mushroom duxelles	¾ oz
	1 egg, beaten	
	1 teaspoon shallot, finely chopped	
	1 tablespoon tarragon, finely chopped	
160 g	lamb's kidney, diced and sautés	5½ oz
120 g	mushrooms, diced and sautés	4 oz
	salt, pepper	

Sauce:

5 dl	lamb gravy (recipe, page 121)	18 fl oz
	2 tablespoons fresh tarragon, chopped	
	½ teaspoon potato flour	

Finely mince the meat trimmings and the pork fat or bacon, add the egg, shallot and tarragon, season with salt and pepper, and mix well. Stir in the kidneys and mushrooms and adjust the seasoning.

Remove the chump end bone from the leg of lamb, but leave the knuckle bone in place. Insert the stuffing into the pocket and sew up. Brown the meat all round for 20 minutes, then allow to cool and carefully remove the twine. When quite cold, wipe with a dry cloth to remove excess fat. Wrap in puff pastry, seal the edges with a little egg, then wash with egg and bake for 25 minutes in a medium oven. Serve with lamb gravy mixed with tarragon and thickened with very little potato flour.

(Roger Parrot, François Perret, Switzerland)

Stuffed leg of lamb en croûte III
Gigotin d'agneau farci en croûte

4 portions

1 kg 500	leg of lamb	3 lb 5 oz
½ l	lamb stock	18 fl oz
100 g	raw foie gras	3½ oz
350 g	puff pastry	12 oz
	lamb bones	
50 g	butter	2 oz
	2 shallots, finely cut	
	1 carrot, finely cut	
	1 stalk celery, finely cut	
	1 bay leaf	
	1 sprig thyme	
	2 egg yolks	
	salt, pepper	

Garnish:

	20 asparagus tips	
200 g	French beans *or* sugar peas	7 oz

Carefully bone the leg of lamb without damaging the flesh. Season inside with salt and pepper, stuff with the foie gras and tie. Fry in the butter until golden brown, then add the vegetables, bones, bay leaf and thyme. Remove the meat from the pan, stir in the lamb stock to detach the sediment, bring to the boil and reduce. Untie the meat. Pin out the pastry and wrap the meat in it. Brush with egg yolk and bake at 250°C (480°F) for 25 minutes.

For the sauce, pass the stock and vegetables through a conical strainer, enrich with butter and add finely chopped fresh herbs as desired (chives, parsley, tarragon, rosemary, sage, savory). Asparagus tips and French beans or sugar peas are especially suitable as accompaniments. (Illustration, page 307)

(Roger Souvereyns, Belgium)

Stuffed leg of lamb Sicilian fashion
Gigot d'agneau farci à la sicilienne
Cosciotto d'agnello ripieno

6 portions

1 kg– 1 kg 200	leg of lamb	2 lb 4 oz– 2 lb 10 oz
	4 cloves of garlic	
	2 sprigs rosemary	
50 g	butter	2 oz
	2 tablespoons oil	
	salt, pepper	
1 dl	white wine	3½ fl oz

Stuffing:

100 g	beef, finely minced	3½ oz
100 g	pork frying sausage, skinned	3½ oz
50–70 g	breadcrumbs	2–2½ oz
	milk as required	
	1 egg, beaten	
	1 tablespoon parsley, finely chopped	
20 g	butter	¾ oz
	1 clove of garlic, finely chopped	

To make the stuffing, fry the beef, sausage and garlic in the butter until lightly coloured, remove from the heat and allow to cool. Add the breadcrumbs which have been soaked in milk, together with the egg and the parsley. Mix until well blended, adding a little milk if too stiff.

Bone the leg, sprinkle a little salt and freshly ground pepper into the cavity, fill with the stuffing and sew up. Place in a roasting pan with the butter, oil and rosemary, and brown on all sides. Stir in the wine to detach the sediment, bring to the boil and reduce. Cover and cook for 1½ hours in an oven preheated to 200°C (390°F), turning the meat and basting occasionally. Carve the meat and serve on a warmed dish with the stock which has been strained.

(Salvatore Schifano, Italy)

Boiled stuffed leg of lamb Norwegian style
Gigot d'agneau farci à la norvégienne
Kokt fylt Lammelår med røtter

10 portions   Cooking time: 1½–2 hours

approx. 3 kg	leg of lamb	approx.	6 lb 10 oz
100 g	bacon		3½ oz
	4 bay leaves		
	2 tablespoons black peppercorns		
150 g	parsley, chopped		5 oz
500 g	parsley roots		1 lb 2 oz

500 g	carrots	1 lb 2 oz
500 g	leeks	1 lb 2 oz
	½ onion	
	parsley stalks	
	flour butter	
	salt	

Remove the bone from the lamb to leave a cavity through the middle. Prepare light forcemeat with the bacon and 200 g (7 oz) trimmings from the leg of lamb. Add half a tablespoon ground black pepper, 1 bay leaf and a quarter of the coarsely chopped parsley. Insert into the cavity in the leg and sew up securely. (If using commercial ready-made stuffing, add the same herbs and seasoning as above.) Wash the root vegetables carefully, trim and cut into small strips. Set aside the trimmings.

Place the lamb in a pan of boiling water containing 1 teaspoon salt per litre (1¾ pt) water, making sure that the meat is completely covered. Bring to the boil over high heat and skim. Add the vegetable trimmings, the onion, parsley stalks, leeks (tied in a bundle) and remaining herbs and seasoning. Simmer at 90°C (195°F) for 1½ to 2 hours.

Place the strips of vegetables in a pan, cover with a napkin or tammy cloth, pour in a little lamb stock and cook. Set aside about 5 dl (18 fl oz) of the lamb stock. Thicken the rest with flour butter and season to taste. Strain and mix with the rest of the chopped parsley.

Dress the leg on a heated dish. Carve at the table. Hand the vegetables and sauce separately, together with boiled potatoes or pilaf rice.

(Arvid Skogseth, Norway)

Boiled salt leg of lamb
Gigot d'agneau salé bouilli

4 portions   Cooking time: about 1½ hours

approx. 2 kg	leg of lamb, boned	approx.	4 lb 8 oz
	4 cloves of garlic		
	1 sprig thyme		
approx. 160 g	onions (two)	approx.	5½ oz
15 g	chives		½ oz
	1 clove		
	1 bay leaf		
	1 small bunch parsley *or* dill		
200 g	butter		7 oz
800 g	potatoes		1 lb 12 oz
	mirepoix of		
100 g	celery		3½ oz
	1 carrot		
	1 leek		

brine (18° Baumé)
stock or hot water

Place the lamb in brine and leave for two days. Remove and place in a pan of hot water or stock. Bring to the boil and skim. Add the garlic, onions, chives and mirepoix, and simmer over low heat for 1½ hours.

Cook the potatoes in their skins, peel and toss in 100 g (3½ oz) melted butter. Sprinkle with chopped parsley or dill.

Remove the lamb from the stock, slice and dress on a warmed dish. Melt the rest of the butter, and hand in a small dish. The potatoes are also handed separately. Cauliflower, asparagus, peas or carrots may be used as a garnish.

(Karl-Otto Schmidt, Denmark)

Lamb cutlets with chocolate
Côtelettes d'agneau au chocolat
Costillas de carnero con chocolate

6 portions

	18 lamb cutlets	
100 g	lard	3½ oz
300 g	button onions, peeled	11 oz
300 g	dried flap mushrooms	11 oz
1½ dl	white wine	5 fl oz
	5 tomatoes, skinned, seeded and diced	
80 g	chocolate, grated	3 oz
	1 cinnamon quill	
	1 sprig thyme	
	1 bay leaf	
	1 sprig oregano	
	salt	

Picada:

	2 cloves of garlic	
20 g	almonds	¾ oz
	2 macaroons (caraquinolis)	

Season the cutlets with salt, grill quickly and place in a fireproof cooking pot. Melt the lard and add while still warm, together with the onions, the flap mushrooms which have been soaked for a few hours, the herbs and spices and the tomatoes. Cover and cook over high heat for 10 minutes, then add the wine and reduce. Add the chocolate and the picada, made by pounding together the garlic, almonds and macaroons. Cover the cutlets with bouillon or water, then cover the pot with aluminium foil and cook for 45 to 50 minutes. When the cutlets are cooked and the sauce is reduced, remove the herbs and cinnamon and serve.

(Josep Lladonosa, Spain)

Crown of lamb roast
Couronne d'agneau rôtie

4 portions   Cooking time: about 45 minutes

	2 best ends of lamb (12 cutlets)	
	1 clove of garlic, peeled and crushed	
	½ teaspoon salt	
	½ teaspoon pepper	
	4 tablespoons oil	
	1 tablespoon dried rosemary leaves	
50 g	onions, peeled and chopped	2 oz
25 g	celery, chopped	1 oz
50 g	ham, diced	2 oz
	2 small carrots, scraped and chopped	
	1 sprig fresh thyme	
	1 bay leaf	
⅛ l	dry white wine	4 fl oz
⅛ l	brown stock	4 fl oz
	2 teaspoons cornflour	
	2 teaspoons water	

Remove the backbone from the best ends, cut off any excess fat and trim the cutlet bones neatly. Rub the meat with garlic, season with salt and pepper, brush with oil and sprinkle with rosemary. Tie the two joints together securely round an empty ½ kg (1 lb) can in the shape of a crown. Wrap the ends of the bones in foil to prevent burning. Place in a shallow roasting pan and roast for 30 minutes in an oven preheated to 205°C (400°F). Lower the oven temperature to 190°C (375°F) and roast for a further 15 minutes. Add the onions, celery, ham, carrots, thyme and bay leaf, and cook until the onions are brown. Transfer the crown to a warmed dish. Drain off the fat from the roasting pan and pour the drippings into a saucepan. Add the wine and brown stock and simmer for 5 minutes. Strain and return the gravy to the pan. Add the cornflour which has been blended with the water, bring to the boil and skim off the fat. Season to taste with salt and pepper and serve with the lamb.

(Hermann Rusch, USA)

Lamb's liver roll Serbian style
Roulade de foie d'agneau à la serbe
Sarma od Jagnjece Dzigerice

6 portions   Cooking time: about 1½ hours

750 g	lamb's liver	1 lb 10 oz
250 g	lamb's lights	9 oz
150 g	lard	5 oz
	3 eggs	
50 g	rice, cooked	2 oz
	3 onions	

2 dl	milk	7 fl oz
	parsley, finely chopped	
	salt	
	pepper, freshly ground	
	1 large lamb's caul	

Chop the onions finely and fry gently without colouring. Add the liver and lights which have been cooked and finely chopped. Remove from the heat and mix with the rice, one egg and parsley. Season with salt and pepper.

Grease a shallow fireproof dish and line with the caul so that the ends project above the top. Place the filling in the centre and fold the ends over to make a large roll (sarma). Bake in a moderate oven for about 1¼ hours or until golden. Beat the remaining eggs with the milk. Pour over the sarma evenly about 15 minutes before serving, and bake off.

To serve, slice the sarma and bring to the table in the same dish. Hand green or other salad separately.

(László Csizmadia, Yugoslavia)

Lamb medallions Clervaux
Médaillons d'agneau Clervaux

10 portions

	20 lamb medallions (cut from leg)	
80 g	each weighing	3 oz
50 g	butter	2 oz

Mushroom soubise sauce:

¾ l	milk	1¼ pt
250 g	onions, sliced	9 oz
125 g	rice	4½ oz
250 g	mushrooms, finely chopped	9 oz
⅛ l	dairy cream	4 fl oz
	4 egg yolks	
	nutmeg, bay leaf, cloves	
125 g	Parmesan, grated	4½ oz
	salt	
	pepper, freshly ground	

Season the meat with a little salt and pepper, and fry in the butter until medium done. For the sauce, boil the milk, add the onions and rice, and stir carefully. Add the seasonings and mix well. Cover and cook very gently in the oven until the milk has been almost completely absorbed. Pass through a sieve, mix with the mushrooms, and cook. Stir in the cream to bring to the required consistency, boil up briefly, remove from the heat and bind with the egg yolks.

Dress the medallions in a fireproof dish, pour the sauce over, sprinkle with the cheese and gratinate lightly. Serve with green bean seeds prepared with a little garlic, and with Dauphine potatoes.

(German Gertsch-Rösner, Luxembourg)

Lamb's kidneys with juniper and wild mint
Rognons d'agneau au genièvre et à la menthe sauvage

4 portions

	16 lamb's kidneys	
1 dl	dairy cream	3½ fl oz
1 dl	lamb gravy (recipe, page 121)	3½ fl oz
	1 teaspoon marc brandy	
	2 tablespoons dry white wine	
	6 fresh mint leaves	
15 g	butter	½ oz
	salt, pepper, freshly ground	
	juniper berries, freshly ground	
	juice of half a lemon	

Trim the kidneys of fat, sinew and gristle. Season with salt and with freshly ground pepper and juniper berries. Heat a thick-bottomed pan, melt the butter in it and fry the kidneys until medium done. Remove and keep hot. Pour off the butter and stir in the wine and the marc brandy to detach the pan juices. Add the cream, then stir in the lamb gravy. Reduce to the required consistency. Adjust the seasoning, sharpen with a little lemon juice and pour over the kidneys. Sprinkle with the finely cut mint. To make the garnish, cover an oblong of baked puff pastry with a layer of spinach which has been cooked in butter. Arrange turned carrots and fingers of white leek on top.
(Illustration, page 238)

(Pierre Gleize, France)

Lamb noisettes Brussels style
Noisettes d'agneau à la bruxelloise

6 portions

100 g	6 lamb noisettes each weighing	3½ oz
100 g	butter	3½ oz
100 g	cocks' combs	3½ oz
150 g	cocks' kidneys	5 oz
100 g	mushrooms, thinly sliced	3½ oz

	6 borders of Duchesse potato mixture	
1 dl	veal stock	3½ fl oz
1 dl	Madeira	3½ fl oz

Season the lamb, sauter in 50 g (2 oz) butter and keep hot. Pour off the butter, detach the sediment with the veal stock and set aside. Return to the boil just before serving and pour over the noisettes.

Soak the cocks' combs in cold water, then warm slightly to facilitate removal of the thin skin. Soak again to remove all blood, and cook until tender. Sauter in the rest of the butter together with the mushrooms and the cocks' kidneys which have been soaked in cold water. Detach the pan juices with the Madeira.

Dress the potato borders on a separate dish and fill the centre with the cocks' combs, kidneys and mushrooms.

(André Béghin, Belgium)

Lamb noisettes Henri Germanier
Noisettes d'agneau Henri Germanier
Lammnüsschen Henri Germanier

6 portions

50 g	18 lamb noisettes each weighing approx.	2 oz
	6 artichoke bottoms	
200 g	fresh mushrooms, cut into quarters	7 oz
500 g	potatoes	1 lb 2 oz
250 g	butter	9 oz
2 dl	veal stock	7 fl oz
5 cl	sherry	2 fl oz
10 g	tarragon, chopped	⅓ oz
	salt, pepper	

Season the lamb with salt and pepper and fry in 80–100 g (3–3½ oz) butter until medium done (about 6 minutes). Detach the sediment with sherry and veal stock. Add the tarragon and enrich the sauce with 50 g (2 oz) butter.

Peel the potatoes and trim them to the shape of cloves of garlic. Fry them in 50 g (2 oz) butter. Sauter the mushrooms in 50 g (2 oz) butter, season and add a few drops of lemon juice. Poach the artichoke bottoms and cut them into quarters, then mix with the potatoes and mushrooms. Dress in the centre of a round serving dish, surround with the lamb noisettes and coat these with a little stock. Sprinkle the whole dish with clarified butter. Hand the sauce separately.

(Willi Bartenbach, Switzerland)

Sauté lamb with fresh fennel
Sauté d'agneau au fenouil frais

6 portions

1 kg 100	leg of lamb, boned and trimmed	2 lb 8 oz
2½ dl	brown stock	9 fl oz
	2 fresh tomatoes, skinned, seeded and diced	
	2 tablespoons concentrated tomato purée	
	3 shallots	
1 dl	light stock	3½ fl oz
	1 teaspoon Ricard or Pernod	
	2 tablespoons caramel	
	2 tablespoons vinegar	
500 g	fennel	1 lb 2 oz
100 g	mushrooms	3½ oz
approx. 50 g	butter	approx. 2 oz
	salt	
	pepper, freshly ground	
	10 fresh tarragon leaves	

Garnish:

480 g	Soissons haricot beans	1 lb 1 oz
200 g	carrots	7 oz

Cut the fennel into 1 cm (⅜ in) cubes, wash, cook them in salted water, keeping them firm, and keep hot. Cut up the mushrooms, sauter them in butter, season with salt and pepper, and keep hot.

Fry the shallots in a little butter without colouring, detach the sediment with the brown and the light stock, then add the tomatoes and the tomato purée. Stir in the Ricard and the caramel which has been dissolved in the vinegar. Cook for about 15 minutes, then season with salt and pepper. Dice the meat coarsely and sauter in butter. Sauter the vegetables in butter separately.

To serve, dress the meat in a heated dish, add the mushrooms and the fennel which has been well drained, coat with the sauce which has been strained, and sprinkle with the tarragon leaves. Serve with Soissons haricot beans mixed with diced carrots.
(Illustration, page 169)

(Emile Jung, France)

Lamb pörkölt with red wine
Ragoût d'agneau au vin rouge
Barany pörkölt Vörösborban

10 portions   Cooking time: 40–50 minutes

2 kg 500	shoulder of lamb	5 lb 8 oz
300 g	lard	11 oz
400 g	onions	14 oz
20 g	garlic	¾ oz
40 g	paprika	1½ oz
40 g	salt	1½ oz
50 g	tomato purée	2 oz
300 g	yellow peppers	11 oz
150 g	tomatoes	5 oz
2 dl	red wine	7 fl oz

Bone the lamb and dice coarsely. Wash it and blanch carefully to remove its strong smell. Proceed as for veal pörkölt (recipe, page 596). Serve with *tarhonya* (recipe, page 1032) or *nockerln* (recipe, page 962).

(Zsolt Körmendy, Hungary)

Ragoût of lamb with endives and avgolemono
Ragoût d'agneau aux endives et avgolemono

4 portions

700–800 g	boneless shoulder of lamb	1 lb 8 oz– 1 lb 12 oz
	2 large onions, finely chopped	
1 dl	oil	3½ fl oz
	1 tablespoon flour	
2½ dl	water	9 fl oz
1 kg	endive or lettuce	2 lb 4 oz
	a little lemon juice	
	2 eggs	
	salt, pepper	

Cut the lamb into small cubes and brown in oil. Add the onions, cover and stew for about 30 minutes, stirring occasionally. Blend the flour with the water, pour over the meat, season with salt and pepper, and stew.

Meanwhile cut up the endive or lettuce coarsely, wash well and blanch. Drain well, then add to the meat. Cook under cover until the meat is tender (about 1 to 1½ hours in all), adding a little liquid if necessary.

Beat the eggs well, gradually add a few drops of lemon juice, blend with a little of the meat stock, and add to the meat. Heat to simmering point, but do not boil. Serve very hot. If the sauce is too thin, bind with cornflour; if too thick, add boiling milk.

(Emil Wälti, Greece)

Saddle of lamb Fontvieille
Selle d'agneau Fontvieille

6 portions

1 kg 600	saddle of lamb	3 lb 8 oz
200 g	shoulder of veal, trimmed	7 oz
3 dl	dairy cream (double)	10 fl oz
	2 lambs' brains	
10 g	parsley, finely chopped	⅓ oz
10 g	tarragon leaves, finely chopped	⅓ oz

Sauce:

1 dl	lamb gravy	3½ fl oz
5 cl	Madeira	2 fl oz
3 cl	wine vinegar	1 fl oz
	1 shallot, chopped	
	3 peppercorns, crushed	
	1 sprig tarragon	
40 g	butter	1½ oz

Garnish:

1 kg	French beans	2 lb 4 oz
	3 egg yolks	
8 cl	dairy cream	3 fl oz
	lemon juice	
	salt, pepper	
	cocotte potatoes	

Bone the saddle of lamb from the underside. Make a well reduced gravy with the bones (recipe, page 121). Mince the veal finely and prepare a mousse with the double cream, then mix with the herbs.

Poach the brains, allow to cool and drain well. Fill into a sausage casing with the mousse, roll in buttered aluminium foil, seal well and poach in the oven in a bain-marie for 20 minutes at 120°C (250°F). Cool, remove the foil and insert into the saddle of lamb in place of the backbone. Fold the flaps one over another, roll up to an oval shape and tie in place. Roast at about 200°C (390°F) for 30 minutes.

Blanch the beans in salted water, drain and arrange in layers in a lightly buttered fireproof dish. Whisk the egg yolks and cream together at the side of the stove as for sabayon, season with salt and freshly ground pepper, and sharpen with a few drops of lemon juice. Pour over the beans and glaze under a salamander.

For cocotte potatoes, peel the potatoes and trim them to the shape of large olives (a quarter the size of Château potatoes), then fry in clarified butter until golden.

To serve, cut the meat into 1 cm (⅜ in) thick slices. Hand the beans and potatoes separately. (Illustration, page 168)

(Emile Jung, France)

Roast saddle of lamb with parsley
Selle d'agneau rôtie persillée

4 portions

1 kg 200	saddle of lamb, trimmed	2 lb 10 oz
3 cl	olive oil	1 fl oz
30 g	butter	1 oz
	2 cloves of garlic, unpeeled	
	1 bouquet garni (thyme, parsley, bay leaf)	
3 dl	lamb stock	10 fl oz
	Dijon mustard	
20 g	parsley, chopped	¾ oz
	salt,	
	pepper, freshly ground	

Carefully trim the saddle of lamb and season with salt and pepper. Brown in hot oil for about 10 minutes, then pour off the oil. Add the butter, bouquet garni and garlic, and roast in a medium oven, basting frequently. The meat should remain pink inside when cooked. Remove the meat and keep hot. Detach the pan juices with lamb stock and reduce a little, then strain through a fine sieve and season to taste with salt and pepper.

Spread the saddle of lamb with a little Dijon mustard and coat with the chopped parsley. To serve, dress on a heated dish and pour the sauce round. Hand young carrots separately.

(Anton Mosimann, Great Britain)

Saddle of lamb with rosemary
Selle d'agneau au romarin
Rozmaringos báránygerinc

5 portions   Cooking time: about 1½ hours

1 kg 250	saddle of lamb	2 lb 12 oz
20 g	salt	¾ oz
20 g	rosemary	¾ oz
10 g	pepper, freshly ground	⅓ oz
10 g	garlic, crushed	⅓ oz
1 dl	demi-glace sauce	3½ fl oz
1 dl	dry red wine	3½ fl oz
1 dl	oil	3½ fl oz

Garnish:

(1)	1 kg	pumpkin	2 lb 4 oz
	50 g	butter	2 oz
(2)	300 g	broccoli	11 oz
	100 g	bacon, blanched and sliced	3½ oz

Freeze the lamb. While still frozen, saw evenly into 5 portions. Season with salt and pepper, rub with the garlic and sprinkle with the rosemary. Thaw the meat, then brown slowly in a little oil in a roasting pan. Add the wine and the demi-glace sauce and roast slowly for about 1½ hours, checking and basting constantly.

To serve, dress on a warmed dish and surround with the garnish. For garnish (1) slice and peel the pumpkin, place on a baking tray and bake until soft in an oven preheated to 130°C (265°F). For garnish (2) cook the broccoli slowly in salted water until soft. Remove and wrap the stalks in the bacon. Place on the baking tray with the pumpkin and leave in the oven until the bacon is light brown.
(Illustration, page 622)

(Gyula Gullner, Hungary)

Lamb fillets in herb forcemeat
Filets d'agneau en farce aux fines herbes
Lammrückenfilets in Kräuterfarce

8 portions

500 g	2 saddle fillets of lamb each weighing	1 lb 2 oz
	salt, pepper	
	oil or lard	

Forcemeat:

200 g	lamb	7 oz
200 g	fat neck of pork	7 oz
200 g	pig's liver	7 oz
1¼ dl	dairy cream	4 fl oz

2 eggs
1 clove of garlic, finely chopped
salt, pepper
lemon zest
fresh herbs, chopped
    (parsley, tarragon, marjoram, rosemary,
    basil)
1 pig's caul

Season the lamb fillets and stiffen in a hot pan while shaking backwards and forwards.

For the forcemeat, chop the lamb, pork and liver, but not too finely. Add the rest of the ingredients, including a liberal amount of herbs, and mix well. Spread out the caul and cover with a layer of forcemeat thick enough to enclose the lamb fillets. Place these in the forcemeat and fold the rest of the caul over the top several times. Brush a roasting pan with oil or lard (some lard will escape from the caul during cooking) and roast at about 200°C (390°F) for 18 minutes, when the meat should be medium done. Allow to rest for 5 minutes before carving.

Cut up the lamb bones and make gravy in the usual manner. Garnish with broccoli in brown butter, stewed courgettes, and fennel halves stuffed with finely diced tomatoes. Hand the gravy separately.
(Illustration, page 871)

(Helmuth Stadlbauer, Austria)

Saddle of lamb Françoise Deberdt
Selle d'agneau Françoise Deberdt
Lammsattel Françoise Deberdt

6 portions

approx. 3 kg	saddle of lamb	approx.	6 lb 10 oz
	white vegetable fat		
600 g	green beans		1 lb 5 oz
	salt		
	pepper, freshly ground		
	savory, finely chopped		
500 g	fresh flap mushrooms		1 lb 2 oz
250 g	onions, finely cut		9 oz
200 g	butter		7 oz
	Parmesan, grated		
	parsley, chopped		
½ l	milk		18 fl oz
	2 egg yolks		
	lemon juice		
50 g	flour		2 oz

a little curry powder
dry white wine as required

Trim the saddle of lamb carefully, fold the flaps under, season with salt and pepper, and roast in vegetable fat until medium done (about 35 minutes). Allow to cool a little.

Clean the flap mushrooms well, cut them up coarsely and cook gently in butter, seasoning with salt and pepper and sprinkling with a little lemon juice. Allow to cool and chop finely. Add chopped parsley and a little thick onion sauce, and mix to a smooth purée of spreading consistency.

Clean the beans carefully, cut them finely and cook gently in butter with a little chopped onion, savory, salt and pepper. When soft, pass through a sieve.

To make the onion sauce, prepare a roux with 30 g (1 oz) butter and 50 g (2 oz) flour. Blend in the milk, which should be boiling hot, cook for a few moments, remove from the heat and bind with the egg yolks. Add a little Parmesan, then the onions which have been cooked and sieved.

Cut off the saddle fillets carefully while still warm. Spread the carcase carefully with the flap mushroom purée and keep hot. Cut the fillets evenly into 18 to 20 small slices and spread each one with bean purée.

To serve, arrange the slices of fillet one overlapping another in a fireproof dish on either side of the saddle. Using a savoy bag and plain 5 mm (¼ in) tube, pipe a thin finger of onion sauce on to each slice. Sprinkle with a little Parmesan and melted butter, and brown quickly in a hot oven or under a salamander. The meat should remain pink. Serve with stewed fennel and onions, and with parsley potatoes. To make gravy, detach the lamb cooking juices with dry white wine and flavour with a little curry powder.

To prepare the fennel, wash and blanch briefly. Fry lightly in a little oil, season with salt and pepper, add a little lemon juice and bouillon, and stew until soft.

Cut a generous quantity of onions into strips, sauter in an equal mixture of oil and butter, sprinkle with saffron and a little white wine, and cook until soft. Slice the fennel, dress in a fireproof dish and cover with the onions.

(Otto Brust, Germany)

Saddle of lamb Massenet
Selle d'agneau Massenet

8 portions

1 saddle of lamb

	salt, pepper	
	1 clove of garlic	

Potato cake:

	10 large potatoes	
	salt, pepper	
50 g	butter/oil mixture	2 oz

Accompaniments:

	8 tomatoes, grilled	
	1 large can green beans	
	8 artichoke bottoms	
200 g	fresh mushrooms	7 oz
2 dl	dairy cream	7 fl oz
	1 teaspoon flour butter	
	salt, pepper	
	lemon juice	
4 dl	Béarnaise sauce	14 fl oz

Trim the saddle of lamb, removing the skin. Season with salt and pepper and rub with the garlic. Roast on a spit or in the oven for about 30 minutes, when the meat should be medium rare (it will be juicier if spit-roasted). When cooked, wrap the saddle in greaseproof paper and leave to rest in a warm place for at least an hour to keep the meat juicy.

Peel the potatoes, wash them, slice very thinly, and cut across into thin julienne strips. Squeeze well and dry with a cloth. Season with salt and pepper, and brown quickly in a little butter and oil in a wide pan. Heat a blini pan and press the potatoes into it firmly to a thickness of about 1 cm (⅜ in). When the underside is lightly browned, turn out on to a plate and slide back into the pan to cook the other side, pressing the edges down well.

Wash the mushrooms, cut into thin julienne strips, toss in flour butter and add the cream. Cook gently, add salt, pepper and a few drops of lemon juice and dress on the artichoke bottoms.

Carve the meat and sprinkle with gravy and a little brown butter. Hand the tomatoes, beans, artichoke bottoms and a light Béarnaise sauce separately.

(Eric Carlström, Sweden)

Saddle of lamb with Provençal herbs
Selle d'agneau aux herbes de Provence
Lammsattel mit provenzalischen Kräutern

10 portions

1 kg 800	saddle of lamb	4 lb

	oil	
	salt	
	herbs and spices as desired	
50 g	butter	2 oz

Marinade:

3 g	garlic	1 clove
10 g	onions	⅓ oz
10 g	parsley	⅓ oz
10 g	basil	⅓ oz
5 g	thyme	⅙ oz
10 g	chervil	⅓ oz
10 g	pepper	⅓ oz
5 g	English mustard (powdered)	⅙ oz
	white wine	
5 dl	oil	18 fl oz

Finely chop the garlic, onion, parsley, basil, thyme and chervil, and mix well. Blend the mustard powder to a paste with a little white wine, add pepper and a little oil, and mix with the herbs. Carefully rub this marinade into the saddle of lamb and set aside for 4 hours or even overnight.

Season the meat with salt. Pour the oil into a roasting tray and place the meat in it. Place in an oven preheated to 240°C (465°F), then reduce the heat to 200°C (390°F). Roast for about 20 minutes. The saddle fillets should be medium done (thermometer reading 50 to 55°C – 120 to 130°F).

(Otto Ledermann, Switzerland)

Saddle of lamb Schoenenbourg
Selle d'agneau Schoenenbourg

8 portions

	1 saddle of lamb	
1 kg	spinach	2 lb 4 oz
	1 clove of garlic	
200 g	foie gras mousse	7 oz
	1 tablespoon French mustard	
130 g	butter	4½ oz
	salt, pepper	

Carefully bone out the saddle from underneath and flatten out the loins and flaps. Season with salt and pepper. Chop up the carcase and prepare a well reduced stock with the bones.

Blanch the spinach in well salted water, refresh at once under running water, drain well, squeeze dry in a cloth and sauter in butter with the garlic which has been very finely cut (or the juice extracted from the clove of garlic). Allow to cool.

Fill the space between the loins from which the backbone was removed with the foie gras mousse. Cover the whole of the underside with spinach leaves, fold under the thin ends of the flaps, cover with aluminium foil and tie round at intervals of 4 cm (1½ in). Roast in a hot oven for 35 minutes. Place on an inverted soup plate and stand on a flat dish to collect the escaping meat juices. Mix these with the pan juices, mustard and butter to make a fine light sauce with the appearance and consistency of thickened gravy.

(François Kiener, France)

Shoulder of lamb canonical style
Epaule d'agneau à la mode des chanoines
Lammschulter Domherrenart

6 portions

1 kg 200	shoulder of lamb	2 lb 10 oz
	salt, pepper	
	thyme, marjoram, tarragon	
	2–3 cloves of garlic	
	1 bay leaf	
2½ dl	white wine	9 fl oz

Stuffing:

	lamb trimmings from shoulder	
	3 eggs	
120 g	spinach	4 oz
20 g	butter	¾ oz
	2–3 cloves of garlic	
	½ teaspoon fresh marjoram	
	½ teaspoon fresh thyme	
	½ teaspoon fresh tarragon	
	salt, pepper	

Vegetable garnish:

300 g	courgettes	11 oz
150 g	leeks (white part)	5 oz
100 g	mushrooms	3½ oz
150 g	carrots	5 oz
100 g	green, yellow and red peppers	3½ oz

| 50 g | butter | 2 oz |

Lyonnaise potatoes:

900 g	potatoes	2 lb
	3 medium onions, cut into rings	
60 g	butter	2 oz

Bone and trim the lamb, then slit to make a pocket. To make the stuffing, mince the trimmings finely, bind with the eggs, and add the herbs, finely chopped, and the juice extracted from the cloves of garlic. Mix well with the spinach which has been chopped and cooked in butter. Season to taste with salt and pepper. Insert into the pocket in the shoulder of lamb and sew up. Season with salt and pepper, and sprinkle with the thyme, marjoram and tarragon. Add the garlic, bay leaf, bones and sinews and braise in the oven for about 35 minutes. Remove the meat and keep hot. Detach the sediment with white wine and reduce a little, leaving the bones and sinews in the pan. Adjust the seasoning and pass through a hair sieve.

Slice the vegetables, which should be young, and cook slowly in butter, then season with salt and black pepper. Peel the potatoes, slice them, blanch briefly and place on a cloth. Brown the onion rings in butter, add the potatoes and sauter quickly.

To serve, carve the meat. Pour a little sauce on to a dish, dress the potatoes on it to make a base for the meat and arrange the meat on top. Garnish with the vegetables and hand the rest of the sauce separately. This dish is also suitable for individual plate service.

(Werner Dabernig, Austria)

Salt shoulder of lamb
Epaule d'agneau salée
Spraengt Lammebov

4 portions   Cooking time: about 1¼ hours

1 kg	shoulder of lamb, boned	2 lb 4 oz
100 g	parsley, coarsely chopped	3½ oz
2 l	brine (16° Baumé)	3½ pt
	8 juniper berries	
	10 white peppercorns	
	stock	
	mirepoix of	
	1 carrot	
	¼ celeriac	
	1 onion	
	1 leek	

Garnish:

800 g	vegetables in season (3 or 4 kinds)	1 lb 12 oz

Potatoes:

500 g	small potatoes, boiled in their skins and peeled	1 lb 2 oz
200 g	butter	7 oz
	1 small bunch parsley or dill	

Horseradish cream:

4 dl	dairy cream	14 fl oz
	juice of 1 lemon	
	a pinch of sugar	
80 g	horseradish, freshly grated	3 oz

Sprinkle the lamb on one side with the parsley. Roll up and tie. Place in the brine with the addition of the juniper berries and peppercorns, and leave to stand for 3 days. Place in a stew pan with the mirepoix, cover with stock and cook over low heat for 45 minutes, then leave to stand without boiling for a further 30 minutes. Whip the cream and mix with the horseradish, sugar and lemon juice. Place in a sauce boat, cover and refrigerate.

Cook the vegetables and keep hot. Toss the potatoes in melted butter and sprinkle with chopped parsley or dill. To serve, cut the lamb into slices about 1 cm (⅜ in) thick, dress on a warmed dish and surround with the vegetables. Hand the potatoes and horseradish cream separately.

Suitable vegetables include, in particular, carrots, asparagus, cauliflower, peas, green beans and Brussels sprouts. They should be selected to provide colour and variety. Broccoli, sweet corn, celery and fennel are also popular, and some of the classic vegetable dishes may also be used, such as cauliflower or asparagus Polonaise or Pompadour, and peas à la Française or Bonne Femme. This recipe is also suitable for duck, goose or pigeon.

(Karl-Otto Schmidt, Denmark)

Shoulder of lamb Chartreuse
Epaule d'agneau en chartreuse

8 portions

2 kg	shoulder of lamb, boned and trimmed	4 lb 8 oz
	2 carrots	
	1 onion, finely cut	
	2 cloves of garlic, very finely chopped	
	1 bouquet garni	
¾ l	white wine	1¼ pt
5 cl	olive oil	2 fl oz
	butter as required	
2 kg	white cabbage	4 lb 8 oz

Shred the cabbage. Fry the onion and garlic gently in a little butter without colouring. Add the cabbage, bouquet garni and wine, and cook gently until soft. Remove the bouquet garni, squeeze the cabbage dry, then leave to drain.

Cut the lamb into pieces and fry in the olive oil until golden. Butter a charlotte mould, line with the cabbage, fill with the meat and cover with the rest of the cabbage. Cook for 30 minutes in a bain-marie in an oven preheated to 220°C (430°F).

Meanwhile slice the carrots, trim with a fluted cutter, and blanch in salted water, then drain well. To serve, turn out on to a warmed dish and decorate with the carrots.
(Illustration, page 168)

(Emile Jung, France)

Shoulder of lamb with celery
Epaule d'agneau avec céleri

About 4 portions

> 1 shoulder of lamb
> salt
> pepper, freshly ground
> 1 medium celeriac
> 2 leeks (white part)
> celery
> parsley, finely chopped

Bone the lamb, tie securely and blanch briefly. Cut up the celeriac and leeks finely and place in a stew pan. Lay the meat on top, season with salt and freshly ground pepper, and pour in sufficient water or bouillon to cover. Place a piece of greaseproof paper over the top and cover tightly with a lid. Bring to the boil and simmer for about 1 hour, or until tender. Remove the paper, cover the meat thickly with finely cut celery, reduce a little and sprinkle with freshly chopped parsley. Serve boiled turned potatoes as an accompaniment.

(Eric Carlström, Sweden)

Shoulder of lamb with passion fruit
Epaule d'agneau aux fruits de la passion

4 portions

> 4 shoulders of lamb
> 4 grey shallots
> 2 leeks
> 4 cloves of garlic
> 2 tomatoes, skinned, seeded and
>   finely diced

200 g	green beans	7 oz
	1 courgette	
	4 passion fruit	
	8 tarragon leaves, chopped	
50 g	butter	2 oz
	olive oil	
	salt, pepper	

Cut the vegetables separately into brunoise dice. Brown the shallots in 5 cl (2 fl oz) olive oil, and add the brunoise of leeks, garlic, beans and courgette. After 10 minutes, add the passion fruit seeds and flesh together with the tomatoes. Boil up briefly, season, and blend in the butter to make a fairly thick sauce.

Rub the shoulders of lamb with salt and pepper. Fry for about 15 minutes in olive oil, or roast at about 250°C (480°F) for the same length of time. (The shoulders may be grilled if preferred). Cut the meat off the bone and slice thinly. To serve, pour the sauce into deep plates, place the meat on top and sprinkle with tarragon.
(Illustration, page 312)

(Roger Souvereyns, Belgium)

Stuffed shoulder of lamb Montparnasse
Epaule d'agneau farcie Montparnasse
Farceret, marineret Lammebov Montparnasse

6 portions   Cooking time: 1½ hours

2 kg 500	shoulder of lamb	5 lb 8 oz
1 l	water	1¾ pt
60 g	fat	2 oz
45 g	flour	1¾ oz

Marinade:

1 l	red wine	1¾ pt
	1 carrot, coarsely sliced	
	1 onion, coarsely sliced	
	½ celeriac, coarsely sliced	
	5 peppercorns	

Stuffing:

200 g	lean pork	7 oz
	1 onion, finely diced	
	2 eggs	
30 g	flour	1 oz
2 dl	dairy cream	7 fl oz
100 g	black olives, stoned and sliced	3½ oz
100 g	smoked ham, finely diced	3½ oz

sage leaves, finely chopped
thyme leaves, finely chopped

Garnish:

(1)		6 large potatoes	
		aluminium foil	
	150 g	butter	5 oz
(2)		2 lettuces	
	1½ dl	oil	5 fl oz
	5 cl	vinegar	2 fl oz
		salt	
		pepper, freshly ground	
(3)	1 kg	green beans	2 lb 4 oz

Mince the pork finely. Season with salt and pepper, add the eggs, flour and cream, and mix with the onion, olives, ham, sage and thyme. Bone the shoulder of lamb, spread the meat flat, cover with the stuffing, roll up and tie securely.

Prepare the marinade, place the lamb in it and leave for 6 hours. Remove, drain and carefully dry with a cloth. Brown the meat quickly with the bones removed from the shoulder. Add the remaining marinade and the water. Cover and braise in the oven. When the meat is cooked, remove and keep hot. Make a roux with the fat and flour, blend with the lamb stock, bring to the boil, season and strain.

Wash the potatoes carefully without peeling them. Wrap in foil and place on a baking sheet. Bake for about 1 hour, then cut a deep cross on top through the foil and open out. Place a knob of butter in the centre; the heat of the potato will melt it. Cook the green beans in salted water until tender.

To serve, slice the lamb, dress on a warmed dish and surround with the potatoes and beans. Dress the salad and hand separately.

(Eric Cederholm, Denmark)

Shoulder of lamb with onions and garlic
Epaule d'agneau à la confiture de racines

4 portions   Cooking time: 45 minutes

800 g	2 shoulders of lamb each weighing	1 lb 12 oz

Forcemeat:

	4 eggs, hard-boiled	
	2 egg yolks	
150 g	breadcrumbs	5 oz

approx. 5 cl	dairy cream	approx.	2 fl oz
100 g	parsley, chopped		3½ oz
	salt, pepper		
	thyme flowers (powdered)		

Garnish:

	16 button onions	
	16 shallots	
	32 cloves of garlic	
100 g	butter	3½ oz

To make the forcemeat, soak the breadcrumbs in the cream and mash with a fork. Mix with the hard-boiled eggs which have been finely chopped, the egg yolks and parsley, salt, pepper and thyme flowers to taste.

Trim the shoulders of lamb and slit to make a pocket in each. Stuff with the forcemeat, tie the shoulders to their original shape, and roast for 20 to 25 minutes in an oven preheated to 250°C (480°F). Add the onions and shallots and, 10 minutes later, the garlic. Shake occasionally to prevent sticking. After 45 minutes the meat and vegetables should be cooked.

Drain off the fat from the pan and detach the sediment with a glass of water. Remove from the oven. Add the butter and shake the pan to blend well.

Cut each shoulder lengthwise into two portions. Garnish with the onions and garlic. Reduce the sauce well and hand separately.
(Illustration, page 620)

(Jean Esslinger, France)

Leg of lamb pie
Pie de gigot d'agneau

6 portions

	1 small leg of lamb	
1 dl	meat stock	3½ fl oz
90 g	butter	3¼ oz
	2 onions, chopped	
	1 tablespoon flour	
	salt, pepper	
	2–3 tablespoons spring onion stalks, chopped	
	2 tablespoons parsley or dill, chopped	
250 g	white cheese	9 oz
250 g	short or puff pastry	9 oz

Bone the leg of lamb. Cut the meat into 3 cm (1¼ in) cubes, wash and soak in the stock. (The stock may be replaced by a bouillon cube dissolved in water.)

Meanwhile lightly brown the onions in 30 g (1 oz) butter. Add the meat which has been drained, dust lightly with flour, season with salt and pepper, and fry lightly, stirring occasionally. Add the stock and simmer under cover for about 30 minutes, or until the meat is tender and the liquid has been absorbed. Add a further 30 g (1 oz) butter and place the meat in a pie dish. Sprinkle with the spring onions and the parsley or dill. Cut the cheese into small pieces and scatter over the top. If the cheese is too dry, sprinkle with a little milk. Cover with pastry, press down well round the edges, brush with a mixture of egg and milk, and bake in a medium oven for about 35 minutes.

(Emil Wälti, Greece)

Lamb offal Ribetana
Abattis d'agneau Ribetana
Guisado de menudos de cordero Ribetana

6 portions

300 g	lamb's liver	11 oz
300 g	lamb's intestines and stomach	11 oz
300 g	lamb's heart	11 oz
1 dl	fresh coagulated blood	3½ fl oz
	3 onions	
	3 tomatoes, skinned and seeded	
	3 peppers	
	5 cloves of garlic	
3 dl	oil	10 fl oz
1 dl	white wine	3½ fl oz
1 dl	muscat wine	3½ fl oz
1 dl	aniseed liqueur	3½ fl oz
40 g	almonds, roasted	1½ oz
	2 macaroons (caraquinolis)	
	salt, pepper	

Slice the onions. Dice the peppers and tomatoes. Brown 3 cloves of garlic, onions and peppers in 1½ dl (5 fl oz) hot oil. When almost cooked, add the tomatoes, cook and remove from the heat.

Cut the offal into medium pieces, season with salt and pepper, and fry in the rest of the oil. Add to the pan containing the vegetables, then add the wine and liqueur, together with the coagulated blood which has been coarsely diced. Cook over high heat, adding a little water.

Prepare picada by pounding the two remaining cloves of garlic, the almonds and the macaroons in a mortar, add a little water and stir into the pan. Continue cooking over gentle heat for 20 to 25 minutes, or until the meat is cooked. Add salt if necessary. Hand aioli (garlic sauce) separately if desired.

(Josep Lladonosa, Spain)

Shish kebab Percy Sullivan

6 portions

1 kg 500	boned lamb, cut into 50 g (2 oz) pieces	3 lb 5 oz
	2 tablespoons olive oil	
	1 onion, grated	
	1 teaspoon garlic, chopped	
	1 tablespoon black pepper, freshly ground	
	1 teaspoon Jamaica pepper	
	salt	
	butter	

Garnish:

saffron pilaf
Madras curry sauce
1 tablespoon meat glaze
or duck glaze

Mix together the olive oil, onion, garlic, black and Jamaica pepper and salt to taste. Marinate the meat in this mixture, then skewer neatly. Grill first, then pan fry in butter. Serve with saffron pilaf and Madras curry sauce flavoured with meat or duck glaze.
(Illustration, page 695)

(Percy Sullivan, India)

Hot Lamb Dishes for Individual Plate Service

Fried lamb
Agneau frit
Gebackenes Lamm

10 portions

1 kg 500	boneless lamb (shoulder or leg)	3 lb 5 oz
150 g	flour	5 oz
	3 eggs, beaten	
200 g	breadcrumbs	7 oz
	salt	
	fat for deep-frying	
	1 large bunch parsley	

Cut the lamb into pieces, allowing two per portion. Season with salt, then flour, egg and crumb. Deep-fry at 180°C (355°F), drain well and serve with fried parsley and salad.

(Eduard Mayer, Austria)

Lamb with olives
Agneau aux olives
Agnello alle ulive

600 g	lamb (boned shoulder or other cut suitable for shallow-frying)	1 lb 5 oz
100 g	black olives	3½ oz
5 cl	olive oil	2 fl oz
	1 teaspoon oregano	
	juice of 1 lemon	
	salt	
	1 tablespoon flour	

Stone the olives and chop them coarsely. Cut the meat into cubes, flour, brown on all sides in hot oil over high heat, then season with salt. Drain off part of the oil, reduce the heat, stir in the lemon juice to detach the sediment, sprinkle the meat with the olives and oregano, and stir well. Serve hot.

(Franco Colombani, Italy)

Lamb fillet with rosemary
Filet d'agneau au romarin

4 portions

800 g	lamb fillet	1 lb 12 oz
	1 sprig rosemary	
250 g	brunoise of celery, carrots, onions, shallots	9 oz
	1 small teaspoon sugar	
	1 tablespoon white vinegar	
2 dl	lamb stock	7 fl oz
100 g	butter	3½ oz
	salt, pepper	

Roast the fillet in butter (whole) at 250°C (480°F) and season with salt and pepper. Add the brunoise and the rosemary, and roast for a further 3 minutes. Remove the meat and keep hot. Continue roasting the brunoise, add the sugar, stir in the vinegar to detach the sediment, add the stock, reduce and finish the sauce with the butter. Cut the meat into thin slices. Pass the sauce through a conical strainer and pour over. Decorate with rosemary.
(Illustration, page 313)

(Roger Souvereyns, Belgium)

Lamb fillet with candied garlic
Filet d'agneau aux gousses d'ail confites

4 portions

800 g	lamb fillet	1 lb 12 oz
	32 cloves of garlic	
	½ tablespoon ketchup	
2 dl	lamb stock	7 fl oz
1 dl	white vinegar	3½ fl oz
	1 teaspoon sugar	
50 g	butter	2 oz
	1 tablespoon Armagnac	
	salt, pepper	

Blanch the garlic four times, then allow to cool. Sauter in a little butter with the addition of salt and pepper and half the sugar. Cook gently over very low heat for a further 10 minutes, turning the garlic repeatedly, until well glazed.

Fry the lamb over fierce heat in 30 g (1 oz) butter until medium done. Pour off the butter, add the rest of the sugar, then stir in the vinegar to detach the sediment. Add the lamb stock, stir in the Armagnac and ketchup, reduce and pass through a conical strainer. Finish the sauce with the rest of the butter.

Carve the lamb, garnish with the garlic and surround with the sauce.
(Illustration, page 312)

(Roger Souvereyns, Belgium)

Lamb fillet Van Dijck
Filet d'agneau van Dijck

4 portions

200 g	lamb fillet	7 oz
	4 artichokes	
40 g	black truffles	1½ oz
200 g	mushrooms	7 oz
5 cl	dairy cream	2 fl oz
	1 tablespoon port	
30 g	butter	1 oz
	a pinch each of thyme, rosemary, savory, bay leaf	
	1 dessertspoon flour	
	juice of half a lemon	
	12 watercress leaves	
	salt	
	pepper	

Remove the leaves and chokes from the artichoke bottoms. Poach these for 25 minutes in water with the addition of salt, pepper and the lemon juice. Add the flour to the water when boiling to enhance the flavour and consistency of the artichokes.

Cut the mushrooms into very small dice and the truffles into julienne strips. Braise the mushrooms in the cream and port, and reduce until fairly thick while stirring, then stir in the truffles and a little truffle liquor.

Melt the butter in a sauté pan and add the herbs. Fry the lamb fillet whole in the hot butter until medium rare.

To serve, stuff the artichoke bottoms with the mushroom/truffle mixture. Cut the lamb into thin slices and arrange on top in the shape of a star. Decorate with three watercress leaves and a slice of truffle.
(Illustration, page 313)

(Roger Souvereyns, Belgium)

Fricassée of lamb with rosemary cream sauce
Fricassée d'agneau à la crème au romarin
Fricassée von Lamm in Rosmarinrahm mit Paprikareis und jungen Zwiebeln

10 portions   Cooking time: 35 minutes

70 g	10 lamb noisettes each weighing	2½ oz
	10 lamb's kidneys	
	20 slices lamb's brains, poached,	
25 g	each weighing	1 oz
125 g	butter	4½ oz
60 g	shallots, finely diced	2 oz
	salt, pepper	
	rosemary	
¼ l	sour cream	9 fl oz
½ l	veal gravy, slightly thickened	18 fl oz
100 g	spring onions	3½ oz

Paprika rice:

400 g	rice		14 oz
50 g	butter		2 oz
	1 medium onion, chopped		
approx. 8 dl	bouillon	approx.	1¼ pt
	1 teaspoon paprika		

Flatten the noisettes a little, season with salt and pepper, flour them and brown in butter. Core the kidneys, cutting them in half. Add to the lamb noisettes after a few minutes, together with the brains and shallots, cover and stew gently until cooked. Flavour the cooking liquid with rosemary, add the sour cream and veal gravy, and cook until well blended. Pass through a sieve and pour over the meat which has been dressed on warmed plates. Clean the onions, blanch them and stew in butter and a little bouillon. Add to the meat on the plates.

To make paprika rice, prepare rice pilaf in the usual manner. Fill into 10 small buttered timbale moulds and turn out on to the plates as an additional garnish.
(Illustration, page 698)

(Karl Brunnengräber, Germany)

Knuckle of lamb Galway
Jarret d'agneau Galway
Lammhachsen Galway

6 portions   Cooking time: 50 minutes

1 kg 800	knuckle of lamb (12 knuckles)	4 lb
	salt	

	pepper, freshly ground	
	garlic juice	
1 dl	oil	3½ fl oz
12 cl	white wine	4 fl oz
6 dl	demi-glace sauce	1 pt

Chasseur sauce:

60 g	smoked bacon, finely diced	2 oz
20 g	butter	¾ oz
60 g	onions, chopped	2 oz
300 g	mushrooms, canned	11 oz
300 g	tomatoes, skinned, seeded and finely diced	11 oz
30 g	parsley, chopped	1 oz
	salt; pepper, freshly ground	

Polenta:

150 g	coarse maize meal	5 oz
7 dl	water	1¼ pt
	salt; pepper, freshly ground	
	nutmeg	
60 g	butter	2 oz
30 g	parsley, chopped	1 oz

Wash the knuckles of lamb, clean the bones and dry with paper. Season with salt, pepper and garlic juice. Brown evenly all over in a little oil, then pour off the oil and detach the sediment with the wine. Add the demi-glace sauce and braise the knuckles for about 50 minutes, or until the meat is tender. Remove from the pan and keep hot. Reduce the cooking liquid by half.

To make the sauce, slowly fry the bacon and pour off the rendered fat. Set it aside. Add the butter to the pan, then the mushrooms which have been sliced and the onions. Cook gently, then add the tomatoes, then the lamb cooking liquid, boil up and season to taste.

To make the polenta, cook the maize meal in the usual manner and stir in the rendered bacon fat which was set aside. Season and fill into small enamelled cans. Refrigerate, then turn out and cut into slices 1½ cm (⅝ in) thick. Cut each of these in half and fry in butter until golden.

To serve, pour the sauce on to plates, place the knuckles of lamb in it and sprinkle with chopped parsley. Garnish with the polenta.

(Otto Ledermann, Switzerland)

Neck of lamb Maître Conrad
Cou d'agneau Maître Conrad
Lammhals Meister Conrad

6 portions   Cooking time: 1 hour

720 g	neck of lamb, boned	1 lb 9 oz
	salt	
	herbs and spices as desired	
5 cl	oil	2 fl oz

Forcemeat:

240 g	pork sausage meat	8 oz
5 cl	dairy cream	2 fl oz
10 g	butter	⅓ oz
40 g	onions, chopped	1½ oz
25 g	green pepper, canned	1 oz
60 g	red peppers, canned	2 oz
30 g	dried breadcrumbs	1 oz
20 g	parsley, chopped	¾ oz
	salt	

Sauce:

10 g	butter	⅓ oz
40 g	onions, chopped	1½ oz
25 g	green pepper, canned	1 oz
30 g	red pepper, canned	1 oz
150 g	tomatoes	5 oz
5 cl	white wine	2 fl oz
2 dl	demi-glace sauce	7 oz
5 cl	dairy cream	2 fl oz
2½ cl	brandy	1 fl oz

Garnish:

360 g	spinach noodles (recipe, page 675)	13 oz
30 g	butter	1 oz
	radicchio (wild chicory) salad	

To make the forcemeat, cook the onions, red pepper and green pepper gently in butter and allow to cool, then mix with the sausage meat, cream, parsley and breadcrumbs. Salt this forcemeat.

Beat the meat to flatten well, cover with the forcemeat, roll up and tie. Season with salt, add herbs and spices as desired, then carefully brown all over in oil. Add half the onions and tomatoes required for the sauce, cook gently, then stir in the wine to detach the sediment. Add the demi-glace sauce and braise the meat for 1 hour.

Cook the remaining onions and tomatoes gently in butter, together with the red pepper and the green pepper. Add the brandy and ignite. Set aside for decoration. Strain the lamb stock, stir in the cream, reduce a little if necessary, and season.

To serve, cut the meat into 12 slices. Pour a little sauce on to each plate, add 2 slices of meat and decorate with the vegetable mixture which has been set aside. Garnish with the noodles and hand the salad and sauce separately.

(Otto Ledermann, Switzerland)

Best end of lamb Harlequin
Carré d'agneau Arlequin
Carré d'agnello Arlecchino

4 portions   Cooking time: 15 minutes

	2 best ends of lamb each comprising	
500 g	6 cutlets and weighing	1 lb 2 oz
250 g	yellow sugar peas	9 oz
250 g	green sugar peas	9 oz
250 g	red peppers	9 oz
1 dl	sunflower oil	3½ fl oz
75 g	butter	2½ oz
2 dl	light stock	7 fl oz
10 g	fresh thyme	⅓ oz
10 g	fine salt	⅓ oz
10 g	white pepper, freshly ground	⅓ oz

Chine, trim and skin the best ends. Shorten the cutlet bones if desired. Remove some of the fat and score the remaining outside layer of fat evenly criss-cross fashion. Season with salt and pepper and set aside.

Wash the peppers, remove the stalk ends, cut in half, remove the seeds and white pith, then rinse under running water. Cut first into strips 2 cm (¾ in) wide, then into even-sized diamond shapes, and set aside.

Cook the three vegetables separately for 10 minutes in 25 g (1 oz) butter over low heat, covering each pan with greaseproof paper. Keep hot. Place the meat in a roasting tray, brush very lightly with oil, add the bones and thyme, and roast for 15 minutes in an oven preheated to 200°C (390°F). Remove the meat and keep hot. Drain off the fat, stir in the stock to detach the sediment, reduce by half, pass through a conical strainer and keep hot.

Cover the ends of the bones with cutlet frills. Arrange the cutlets crosswise on the plates with the vegetable garnish. Hand the gravy separately.
(Illustration, page 414)

(Gualtiero Marchesi, Italy)

Lamb cutlet Bolognese
Côtelette d'agneau à la bolognaise
Lammkotelett auf Bologneser Ragoût mit gedünsteten Gurken und Pistazienreis

10 portions   Cooking time: 35 minutes

120 g	10 lamb cutlets each weighing	4 oz
350 g	lamb, finely chopped	12 oz
200 g	butter	7 oz
400 g	tomatoes, chopped	14 oz
80 g	shallots, finely diced	3 oz
¼ l	red wine	9 fl oz
700 g	fresh cucumbers	1 lb 8 oz
400 g	rice	14 oz
80 g	pistachio nuts	3 oz
	salt, pepper	
	1 clove of garlic, grated	

Prepare a Bolognese sauce with the chopped lamb, the shallots, tomatoes and wine, keeping the ingredients firm enough to be recognisable when cooked. Season with salt and pepper, and add the garlic. Spoon on to warmed plates as a base for the lamb cutlets which have been fried until medium done. Surround with stewed cucumber and rice with pistachio nuts (rice pilaf mixed with chopped pistachios).

(Karl Brunnengräber, Germany)

Lamb chops with fresh tarragon
Côtes d'agneau à l'estragon frais

8 portions

	8 thick or 16 medium lamb chops		
1 dl	Vouvray		3½ fl oz
	2 tablespoons tarragon, very finely chopped		
approx. 100 g	butter	approx.	3½ oz
	4 tablespoons thickened veal stock		
	salt		
	pepper, freshly ground		

Garnish:

	8 artichoke bottoms, blanched	
400 g	mushroom duxelles	14 oz

Sautés mignons of rabbit with rosemary and chanterelles, p. 922

763

Crépines of veal and lobster with lobster sauce, p. 548

◄ Mignons of veal Wladimir, p. 659
◄◄ Tournedos with bone marrow, p. 448
◄◄◄ Sweetbreads with crayfish, p. 664

764

Veal steak with chive cream sauce, p. 704 ►▲
Mixed meat sauté with rosemary, p. 947 ►▲▲
Calf's and lamb's kidneys with shallots, p. 937 ►▼
Boiled beef Grand'mère Madeleine, p. 472 ►▼▼

7

9

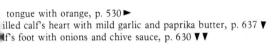

770 Tournedos and veal medallions Gumpoldskirchen, p. 947

Veal cutlets Saxonne, p. 568 ▲
Stewed oxtail Old Vienna, p. 455 ▼

Butter a sauté pan and brown the chops on both sides over high heat. Remove and keep hot. Detach the pan juices with the Vouvray, add half the tarragon and bind with the veal stock. Return the chops to the pan and heat gently. Transfer them to warmed plates. Remove the pan from the heat and stir in 1 tablespoon butter, then pour the sauce over the chops and sprinkle with the rest of the tarragon.

Meanwhile lightly brown the artichoke bottoms in butter with the addition of a little lemon juice. Fill with the hot duxelles and arrange on the plates with the meat.

(Patrick Klipfel, Armand Roth, France)

Lamb cutlets with tarragon sauce and green asparagus
Côtelettes d'agneau en sauce à l'estragon et aux asperges vertes

2 portions

70 g	4 lamb cutlets each weighing	2½ oz
25 g	butter	1 oz
	10 green asparagus tips	
	1 small teaspoon tarragon, finely chopped	
	10 tarragon leaves, blanched	
1 dl	port	3½ fl oz
25 g	butter for sauce	1 oz
	salt, pepper	

Trim the cutlets well, season with salt and pepper, and fry in butter, keeping them medium rare. Cook the asparagus until almost tender, then cut into 4 cm (1½ in) lengths. Dress on two plates with two lamb cutlets each and keep hot. Detach the pan juices with the port and reduce by half. Add the chopped tarragon and finish with the butter, then season lightly with salt and pour over the cutlets. Decorate with the tarragon leaves.
(Illustration, page 416)

(Felix Real, Liechtenstein)

Lamb cutlets Black Forest style
Côtelettes d'agneau Forêt noire
Lammkoteletts auf Schwarzwälder Art

10 portions   Cooking time: 20 minutes

3 kg	saddle of lamb	6 lb 10 oz
	salt	
	pepper, freshly ground	
	basil, thyme	

100 g	flour	3½ oz
1 dl	oil	3½ fl oz
1 dl	kirsch	3½ fl oz
1 l	cream sauce (recipe, page 172)	1¾ pt
1 dl	dairy cream, whipped	3½ fl oz
600 g	morello cherries, stoned	1 lb 5 oz
	parsley, chopped	
	lemon juice	
⅓ l	white wine	12 fl oz

Carefully skin and trim the saddle of lamb. Cut into 20 cutlets and scrape the cutlet bones. Season with salt, pepper, basil and a little thyme, flour lightly and fry until medium done, then add the kirsch and ignite. Transfer to a heated serving dish and cover with greaseproof paper or aluminium foil.

Stir the wine into the pan to detach the sediment, boil up, add the cream sauce and reduce to coating consistency. Strain and fold in the cherries. Add salt, pepper, a little lemon juice, chopped parsley and a few drops of kirsch. Just before serving, fold in the whipped cream and pour over the cutlets which have been dressed on warm plates. Serve with Anna potatoes or saffron noodles.

(Karl Brunnengräber, Germany)

Lamb cutlets on lemon balm and horseradish sabayon
Côtelettes d'agneau sur sabayon à la citronelle et au raifort
Lammkoteletts in Zitronenmelissen und Meerrettichsabayon

2 portions

	4 lamb cutlets	
	1 shallot	
	1 sprig rosemary	
	1 clove of garlic	
	lemon balm leaves and stalks	
	peppercorns, crushed	
4 cl	dry white wine	1½ fl oz
	2 egg yolks	
	a few drops sherry vinegar	
50 g	butter	2 oz
	1 teaspoon horseradish, grated	
	2 tablespoons dairy cream, whipped	
	1 tomato, skinned, seeded and diced	

Fry the cutlets in 35 g (1¼ oz) butter until medium done. Set aside in gentle heat under a salamander.

Place the shallot, rosemary, lemon balm stalks, garlic and peppercorns in a pan with the vinegar and wine. Bring to the boil, reduce a little and strain. Beat in the egg yolks over low heat and blend in butter to make a sabayon. Stir in the finely grated horseradish and finely chopped lemon balm leaves, setting aside 10 leaves for decoration. Finish with the whipped cream. Pour on to two plates.

Cut away the cutlet bones and slice the meat. Arrange on the plates, place the diced tomato in the centre and decorate with the lemon balm leaves.
(Illustration, page 766)

(Gerhard Gartner, Germany)

Mignons of lamb with port sauce
Mignons d'agneau au porto

4 portions

40 g	8 mignons of lamb each weighing	1½ oz
30 g	butter	1 oz
10 g	shallot, finely chopped	⅓ oz
5 cl	port	2 fl oz
2 dl	brown veal stock	7 fl oz
30 g	butter, softened (for sauce)	1 oz
	salt	
	pepper, freshly ground	

Trim the mignons and tie round carefully. Season with salt and pepper. Fry in hot butter until medium done on both sides. Add the shallot, cover and leave to stand over moderate heat for 2 to 3 minutes. Remove the meat and keep hot. Pour off the butter and stir in the port to detach the sediment. Add the stock and reduce, then pass through a fine strainer or a cloth. Blend in the softened butter and season with salt and pepper.

To serve, dress the mignons on heated plates and coat with the sauce. Garnish with rice oriental style and fresh broccoli.
(Illustration, page 240)

(Anton Mosimann, Great Britain)

Lamb's kidneys with Cognac
Rognons d'agneau au cognac

4 portions   Cooking time: about 20 minutes

8 lamb's kidneys

	3 teaspoons butter	
	¼ teaspoon salt	
	¼ teaspoon pepper	
	¼ teaspoon allspice	
	2 tablespoons flour	
	1 tablespoon onions, chopped	
⅛ l	dry white wine	4 fl oz
⅛ l	brown stock	4 fl oz
	½ tablespoon meat glaze	
	(recipe, page 122)	
8 cl	Cognac	3 fl oz
	hot cooked rice *or* buttered toast	

Preheat the oven to 175°C (350°F). Trim the fat from the kidneys, scald in boiling water for 3 minutes, then rinse in cold running water. Remove the skin, cut the kidneys into quarters, and remove the white veins and hard portions. Melt the butter in a sauté pan. Add the kidneys, salt, pepper and allspice. Sprinkle with half the flour. Sauter the kidneys until golden brown. Add the onion and sauter until transparent. Sprinkle with the remaining flour, mix well, add the wine, brown stock and meat glaze, and bring to the boil. Cover and cook in the oven for 10 minutes, then remove, add the Cognac, and season to taste with salt and pepper. Serve on rice or hot buttered toast. (N.B. The less lamb's kidneys are cooked, the more tender they are.)

(Hermann Rusch, USA)

Lamb's kidneys in bacon
Rognons d'agneau enrobés de lard fumé
Lammnierchen im Speckkleid

1 portion

	2 lamb's kidneys, cut in half	
	4 rashers smoked bacon	
	1 shallot, finely cut	
5 cl	dry red white	2 fl oz
10 g	butter	⅓ oz
	salt	
	pepper, freshly ground	
	1 sprig rosemary	

Garnish:

| | 2 carrots | |
| | 2 slices courgette | |

Wrap each half kidney in a rasher of smoked bacon, impale on a small skewer and cook in a hot oven until medium done. Remove and keep hot. Add the shallot to the pan, cook gently until transparent, stir in the wine, reduce almost completely, and blend in a knob of cold butter the size of a walnut. Add salt, pepper and rosemary to taste.

Remove the skewers. Strain the sauce over the kidneys. Garnish with the carrots which have been cooked until firm to the bite, and with the slices of courgette, also kept firm.

(Gerhard Gartner, Germany)

Lamb noisettes Alpes de Provence I
Noisettes d'agneau Alpes de Provence

1 portion

75 g	2 thick lamb noisettes each weighing	2½ oz
	1 teaspoon Beaumes de Venise muscat wine	
	1 pinch thyme, finely chopped	
	1 pinch rosemary, finely chopped	
	1 pinch bay leaf, finely chopped	
	1 pinch savory, finely chopped	
30 g	butter	1 oz
	2 tablespoons Bandol (red wine)	
	2 tablespoons lamb gravy (recipe, page 121)	
	2 rounds toast	
	salt, pepper	
	marc brandy	

Forcemeat:

50 g	pork fat or bacon, diced	2 oz
50 g	chicken liver	2 oz
	1 sprig thyme	
	¼ bay leaf	

Garnish:

	2 puff pastry rectangles
	1 tablespoon spinach
	double cream
	1 tablespoon turnip and carrot, finely cut
	butter

Cut the toast to the size of the lamb noisettes. Trim the noisettes and leave for at least 4 hours in a marinade of muscat wine, thyme, rosemary, bay leaf and savory. Fry in a heated pan in a little butter and keep hot. Stir in the Bandol to detach the sediment, add a drop of marc brandy, then the lamb gravy, and finish with a knob of butter. Cover the noisettes with the forcemeat, place them on the toast and coat with the sauce.

To make the forcemeat, brown the fat or bacon in a sauté pan, add the chicken liver, thyme and bay leaf, and season with salt and pepper. Fry until the liver is medium done. Remove the herbs. Work the liver and bacon to a very fine purée in the mixer or pass through a sieve.

For the garnish, prepare two thin rectangles of puff pastry and bake blind. Cover one with spinach bound with double cream, the other with finely cut turnips and carrots which have been blanched, then cooked in butter.

(Pierre Gleize, France)

Lamb noisettes Alpes de Provence II (modern recipe)
Noisettes d'agneau Alpes de Provence

1 portion

75 g	2 thick lamb noisettes each weighing	2½ oz
	1 teaspoon Beaumes de Venise muscat wine	
	1 pinch each thyme, rosemary, bay leaf, savory, finely chopped	
30 g	butter	1 oz
	2 tablespoons Bandol (red wine)	
	2 tablespoons lamb gravy (recipe, page 121)	
	salt	
	pepper, freshly ground	
	marc brandy	
Garnish:		
	2 tablespoons Soubise	
	1 tablespoon tomatoes, skinned, seeded and diced	
	1 puff pastry oval	

Trim the lamb noisettes and leave for at least 4 hours in a marinade of muscat wine, thyme, rosemary, bay leaf and savory. Fry in a heated pan in a little butter and keep hot. Make the sauce by stirring the Bandol into the pan to detach the sediment, adding a drop of marc brandy and the lamb gravy, and finishing with a knob of butter. Pour the sauce on to a warmed plate, place the lamb noisettes in the sauce and spoon the Soubise on to the plate next to them. Cover with the pastry oval and surround with the diced tomato. Sprinkle this with chopped parsley and decorate the pastry with a sprig of parsley.
(Illustration, page 236)

(Pierre Gleize, France)

Lamb noisettes with thyme butter on tomato fondue, flageolet beans
Noisettes d'agneau au beurre de thym sur fondue de tomates, flageolets
Lammnüsschen auf geschmolzenen Tomaten, mit Thymianbutter überglänzt, Flageolets

10 portions   Cooking time: 30 minutes

80 g	20 lamb noisettes each weighing	3 oz
	flour	
	salt	
	pepper, freshly ground	
8 cl	oil	3 fl oz
	2 cloves of garlic	
800 g	tomatoes	1 lb 12 oz
120 g	onions	4 oz
800 g	flageolet beans	1 lb 12 oz

Thyme butter:

200 g	butter	7 oz
	3 egg yolks, hard-boiled	
1 dl	dairy cream	3½ fl oz
	1 tablespoon thyme, chopped	
50 g	shallots, finely diced	2 oz
	salt	
	pepper, freshly ground	

Lightly flatten the noisettes with the ball of the thumb. Season with pepper and the garlic which has been crushed with salt. Flour lightly and sauter in oil on both sides until lightly browned and medium done.

Prepare tomato fondue with the tomatoes and onions. Place the lamb noisettes on top, cover with thyme butter and glaze under a salamander. Garnish with flageolet beans tossed in butter and Macaire potatoes.

To make thyme butter, cream the butter and mix with the egg yolks which have been sieved. Gradually blend with the cream, the thyme and the shallots which have been gently cooked. Season with salt and freshly ground pepper.

(Karl Brunnengräber, Germany)

Lamb noisettes with rhubarb and marjoram
Filet d'agneau à la rhubarbe et à la marjolaine
Nocette di agnello al rabarbaro e profumo di maggiorana

1 portion   Cooking time: 8–10 minutes

300 g	best end of lamb	11 oz
120 g	rhubarb	4 oz
40 g	butter	1½ oz
	1 sprig marjoram	
5 cl	water	2 fl oz
	salt	
	white pepper, freshly ground	

Cut off the best end fillet and divide it into 3 noisettes each weighing 50 g (2 oz). Cut the rhubarb into 4 cm (1½ in) lengths without peeling and place in a small pan with 20 g (¾ oz) butter, salt and pepper to taste.

Wash the marjoram, shake off the water and pick off the leaves. Season the lamb with salt and pepper, brown in a small sauté pan containing the rest of the butter, and continue cooking for 3 minutes on each side if required medium done, or 4 minutes if required well done. Meanwhile cook the rhubarb for 4 to 5 minutes. Set aside half the lengths of rhubarb, pass the rest through a fine sieve, and keep hot. Drain off the excess butter from the pan in which the meat was cooked, then add the marjoram leaves, stir in the water, reduce by two thirds and pass through a fine conical strainer. Adjust the seasoning.

Dress the sieved rhubarb on a warmed plate, place the lamb noisettes on top, surround with the strained stock and decorate with the lengths of rhubarb which have been set aside. (Illustration, page 413)

(Daniel Drouadaine, Italy)

Lamb noisettes Soubise
Noisettes d'agneau soubise
Lammnüsschen mit Zwiebelmus und Schinkenstreifen überbacken, in Genever-Rahm

10 portions   Cooking time: 25 minutes

1 kg 500	saddle of lamb	3 lb 5 oz
250 g	ham, cut into thin strips	9 oz
180 g	butter	6 oz
75 g	Parmesan cheese, grated	2½ oz
¼ l	veal gravy	9 fl oz
⅛ l	white wine	4 fl oz
	2 egg yolks	
6 cl	gin	2 fl oz
	garlic salt	
	pepper, freshly ground	

	1 tablespoon lemon juice	
	a pinch of Cayenne pepper	
	a pinch of sugar	
3½ dl	sour cream	12 fl oz
⅓ l	Hollandaise sauce	12 fl oz
	basil, chopped	

Soubise:

400 g		14 oz
300 g	onions, coarsely cut	11 oz
70 g	rice	2½ oz
5 cl	dairy cream	2 fl oz
⅓ l	light veal stock	12 fl oz

Cut 2 cm (¾ in) thick noisettes each weighing 60 g (2 oz) from the saddle, allowing two per portion. Trim them neatly, flatten a little, season with garlic salt and pepper, and fry in 90 g (3¼ oz) butter until medium done. To serve, cover each one with 1 teaspoon Soubise, coat with Hollandaise sauce, sprinkle with strips of ham and grated Parmesan, and brown under a salamander.

Detach the pan juices with the veal gravy, lemon juice and wine, mix with the sour cream and reduce until beginning to thicken. Bind with the egg yolks which have been mixed with the gin. Add the Cayenne pepper, sugar and basil. Pour round the noisettes which have been dressed on warmed plates, and garnish with stewed celery or French beans tossed in butter.

To make the Soubise, blanch the onions in boiling water, then cook gently with the rice in butter with the addition of the veal stock until very soft. Work to a purée in the mixer or pass through a sieve. Season with salt and pepper, and finish with the cream and a little butter.

(Karl Brunnengräber, Germany)

Lamb piccata with tomato and herb sauce and saffron rice timbale
Lamm-Piccata auf Tomatenkräutercreme, Safranreis-Timbal

10 portions   Cooking time: 25 minutes

1 kg 500	leg of lamb, boned	3 lb 5 oz
100 g	butter	3½ oz
60 g	flour	2 oz
	garlic salt	
	pepper, freshly ground	
	rosemary	
	3 eggs	

Sauce:

50 g	butter	2 oz
80 g	shallots, finely cut	3 oz
350 g	tomatoes, skinned, seeded and diced	12 oz
	2 tablespoons herbs, chopped	
	(parsley, basil, lemon balm)	
3 dl	dairy cream	10 fl oz
	salt	
	pepper, freshly ground	
300 g	bacon, cut into strips	11 oz
150 g	white bread, diced	5 oz

Saffron rice:

300 g	rice	11 oz
	a pinch of saffron	

Cut small escalopes each weighing 50 g (2 oz) from the boned leg of lamb, allowing three per portion. Flatten well and sprinkle with garlic salt, pepper and rosemary. Flour, dip in beaten egg, and fry in foaming butter until well browned, keeping the meat juicy.

To make the sauce, melt the rest of the butter, add the shallots and cook gently, add the tomatoes, herbs, cream, salt and pepper, and reduce until well thickened.

To serve, pour the sauce on to the plates and place the meat on it. Turn out a buttered saffron rice timbale next to the meat. Garnish with well fried strips of bacon and cubes (or strips) of white bread. Serve very hot.

(Karl Brunnengräber, Germany)

Navarin of lamb with yellow peppers and papaya
Navarin d'agneau au poivron jaune et papaya
Navarin d'agnello al peperone giallo e papaya

4 portions   Cooking time: 50 minutes

1 kg	shoulder of lamb	2 lb 4 oz
100 g	white onions	3½ oz
300 g	yellow peppers	11 oz
	1 papaya	
1 dl	groundnut oil	3½ fl oz
8 dl	light stock	1¼ pt
2 dl	dairy cream	7 fl oz
10 g	coarse salt	⅓ oz
	fine salt	
	white pepper, freshly ground	

Bone the lamb, remove the fat, trim and cut into about 60 g (2 oz) pieces, then refrigerate. Peel the onions, slice very finely and set aside. Cut the peppers in half lengthwise, remove the stalks, pith and seeds, rinse under running water, dry, cut into 2–3 cm (about 1 in) squares and set aside.

Peel the papaya, cut in half lengthwise and remove the seeds. Cut strips 3 cm (1¼ in) long and 5 mm (¼ in) wide. Cut the remaining flesh into slices 1 cm (⅜ in) thick.

Brown the lamb lightly in oil over high heat, then transfer to a conical strainer to drain off the excess oil. Add the peppers and the slices of papaya to the pan and cook gently for 5 minutes without colouring. Add the lamb and cover with the light stock which has been heated. Season with the coarse salt and two or three turns of the pepper mill. Bring to the boil and simmer very gently under cover for 35 to 40 minutes.

Remove the meat, add the cream, bring to the boil, reduce a little, and work in the processor or pass through a conical strainer to make a thick yellow sauce. Pour on to warmed plates, arrange the pieces of lamb symmetrically on top, and decorate with the strips of papaya.

(Daniel Drouadaine, Italy)

Shish kebab Caucasian
Brochette d'agneau à la caucasienne

6 portions

1 kg 500	boneless leg of lamb	3 lb 5 oz
⅛ l	red wine	4 fl oz
⅛ l	oil	4 fl oz
	1 tablespoon shallots, peeled and chopped	
	1 bay leaf	
	1 clove of garlic, peeled, crushed and chopped	
	2 tablespoons lemon juice	
	1 tablespoon dried thyme leaves	
	6 mushrooms, halved	
	2 tablespoons butter for mushrooms	
60 g	soft butter	2 oz
	12 2½ cm (1 in) squares green pepper, blanched	
	3 firm unpeeled tomatoes, cut into quarters	
	3 onions, peeled and quartered	
	2 tablespoons olive oil	

                    1 teaspoon dried tarragon leaves
                    salt and pepper to taste
                    saffron rice

Cut the lamb into 2½ cm (1 in) cubes and place in a deep bowl. Make a marinade with the wine, oil, shallots, bay leaf, garlic, lemon juice and thyme. Pour over the lamb, cover and refrigerate for 1½ hours. Drain the lamb thoroughly before cooking. Sauter the mushrooms in 2 tablespoons butter until lightly browned. Thread each of six skewers alternately with mushrooms, lamb cubes, green pepper, tomato and onion, pressed closely together. Brush with olive oil and arrange on a preheated grill 7½–10 cm (3–4 in) from the heat. Grill for about 8 minutes, turning occasionally to brown on all sides. Transfer to warmed plates. Mix together the soft butter and the tarragon. Spread the brochettes with the mixture and season with salt and pepper to taste. Serve with saffron rice.

                                        (Hermann Rusch, USA)

Grilled chump chop
Chump chop aux rognons grillé

4 portions

	4 chump chops with kidney	
320 g	each weighing	11 oz
2 cl	olive oil	1 fl oz
	salt; pepper, freshly ground	
	garden cress	

Season the chops carefully with salt and pepper, and sprinkle with olive oil. Grill over high heat until medium done. To serve, dress on warmed plates and decorate with a little garden cress. Garnish with young carrots and turnips.
(Illustration, page 242)

                                        (Anton Mosimann, Great Britain)

Grilled lamb brochettes
Brochettes d'agneau grillées
Souvlakia

4 portions

600–700 g	boneless leg of lamb	1 lb 5 oz– 1 lb 8 oz
	1 onion, finely chopped	

	2 tablespoons parsley, finely chopped	
	1 sprig oregano	
	1 tablespoon oil	
200 g	tomatoes	7 oz
	2–3 bay leaves	
	salt, pepper	

Greek salad:

	1 lettuce	
	2 tomatoes	
	1 onion	
	1 cucumber	
	1 sweet pepper, seeded	
	4 anchovy fillets	
	salt, pepper	
¼ dl	vinegar	1 fl oz
1 dl	oil	3½ fl oz

Cut the lamb into cubes weighing about 25 g (1 oz) and place in a bowl. Add the onion, parsley, oregano leaves, oil and pepper and mix well. Marinate the meat in the mixture for about 2 hours.

Wash the tomatoes, cut them in half, remove the seeds, then cut into quarters. Thread these on to metal or wooden skewers alternately with the meat and small pieces of bay leaf, allowing at least 6 cubes of meat per skewer. Season with salt and grill over a charcoal fire for about 15 minutes. Serve very hot on the skewers. (Thread the tomatoes on to the skewers starting on the skin side to keep them in place.)

To prepare the salad, wash the lettuce well, cut the tomatoes into quarters, the onion and cucumber into thin slices, and the pepper into strips. Mix all the ingredients together well, dress with oil, vinegar, salt and pepper, and garnish with the anchovy fillets.

(Emil Wälti, Greece)

Lamb brochettes Turkish fashion
Brochettes d'agneau à la turque
Hunkiav-Beyandi ('The Sultan loves me')

10 portions

1 kg 500	boneless leg of lamb, trimmed of skin and sinew	3 lb 5 oz
150 g	onions, finely chopped	5 oz
	2 cloves of garlic, grated	
	1 tablespoon herbs, finely chopped (sage, mint, parsley)	

	pepper, freshly ground	
1 dl	olive oil for marinade	3½ fl oz
	juice of 2 lemons	
500 g	mutton suet	1 lb 2 oz
	salt	
1 dl	olive oil for frying	3½ fl oz

Garnish:

1 kg 500	aubergines	3 lb 5 oz
150 g	onions, finely chopped	5 oz
5 cl	olive oil	2 fl oz
500 g	tomatoes, skinned, seeded and cut into pieces	1 lb 2 oz
	salt	
	pepper, freshly ground	
	bay leaf	

Cut the lamb into approximately 3 cm (1 in) cubes. Prepare a marinade with the onion, garlic, herbs, olive oil and lemon juice, and season liberally with freshly ground pepper. Add the lamb and marinate for about 6 hours, stirring and turning frequently. Blanch the aubergines for a minute or two in boiling water, remove, peel and slice thinly. Fry the onions gently in a little olive oil until transparent, then add the aubergines and tomatoes. Season with salt and pepper, add the bay leaf, and cook gently for about 15 minutes. Remove the bay leaf and add the marinade. Reduce the liquid completely over gentle heat and work to a purée.

Thread the lamb on to metal skewers alternately with thinly sliced suet. Fry quickly over high heat, keeping the meat juicy amd medium done. To serve, spoon the vegetable purée on to warmed plates and place the brochettes on top. Serve at once.

(Otto Ledermann, Turkey)

Lamb steak with stuffed morels and grapes
Steak d'agneau aux morilles farcies et aux raisins
Lammsteak mit gefüllten Morcheln und Trauben in Cordial Médoc

10 portions   Cooking time: 25 minutes

1 kg 500	leg of lamb (fillet end), boned	3 lb 5 oz
	2 tablespoons oil	
200 g	butter	7 oz
100 g	dried morels	3½ oz
or 500 g	fresh morels	1 lb 2 oz
	garlic salt	
⅛ l	red wine	4 fl oz
⅓ l	thickened veal gravy	12 fl oz

6 cl	Cordial Médoc	2 fl oz
400 g	grapes, skinned and seeded	14 oz
	a pinch of cinnamon	
	1 tablespoon brandy	
	pepper, freshly ground	
	lemon zest, grated	
	flour	

Stuffing:

150 g	boneless veal	5 oz
	1 egg yolk	
	1 tablespoon butter, melted	
	1 tablespoon herbs, finely chopped	
	(parsley, chervil, tarragon)	
⅛ l	dairy cream	4 fl oz

Cut the lamb evenly into 10 slices. Flatten them, season with garlic salt and pepper, sprinkle with grated lemon zest and the oil, and marinate under cover for 1 hour.

If using dried morels, wash them carefully and soak in lukewarm water. Finely mince the veal twice, then mix with the butter, egg yolk, herbs, cream, salt and pepper to make a firm stuffing. Using a savoy bag and plain tube, pipe into the morels. Cook for about 15 minutes in a little bouillon and keep hot.

Dry the slices of lamb gently with a cloth, flour lightly and fry in foaming butter until medium done. Drain off the butter, stir in the red wine and veal gravy, reduce a little, strain, blend in a few small knobs of butter and add the Cordial Médoc.

Place the lamb on warmed plates. Cover each slice with a few stuffed morels, coat with the sauce and garnish with the grapes which have been tossed in a little butter with the addition of the brandy and cinnamon. Serve with stewed leeks and Macaire potatoes.

(Karl Brunnengräber, Germany)

Blanquette of lamb with tarragon
Blanquette d'agneau à l'estragon
Tarkonyos barany

10 portions   Cooking time: 45–50 minutes

2 kg 500	shoulder of lamb	5 lb 8 oz
50 g	salt	2 oz
150 g	onions, peeled	5 oz
100 g	butter	3½ oz
100 g	lard	3½ oz
100 g	flour	3½ oz

3 dl	sour cream	10 fl oz
2 dl	fresh dairy cream	7 fl oz
	2 egg yolks	
50 g	tarragon	2 oz
5 cl	tarragon vinegar	2 fl oz
10 g	pepper, freshly ground	⅓ oz

Bone the lamb and dice the meat coarsely. Place in a pan of salted water with the onions, leaving these whole, and bring to the boil. Skim and cook until the meat is tender.

Make a blond roux with the flour and butter, stir in a little cold water, a little fresh cream and the sour cream, then the lamb stock from which the onions have been removed. Bring to the boil and add the tarragon, vinegar and pepper. Mix well and remove from the heat. Bind with the egg yolks and the rest of the fresh cream. Serve very hot with boiled rice.

(Zsolt Körmendy, Hungary)

Lamb's tongue Indian style
Langue d'agneau à l'indienne

2 portions

	2 lambs' tongues	
	1 apple	
	1 slice pineapple, cut up	
	2 shallots	
1 dl	lamb stock	3½ fl oz
5 cl	sour cream	2 fl oz
20 g	curry powder	¾ oz
	1 bouquet garni	
	salt, black peppercorns	
	Cayenne pepper	
5 cl	olive oil	2 fl oz
20 g	butter	¾ oz
	sugar	

Soak and wash the tongues, and cut off any gristle. Poach them in salted water with the addition of the bouquet garni and peppercorns. Skin and keep hot. Peel the shallots and slice thinly. Cut the apple in half, peel one half and dice finely. Cook gently in olive oil with the shallots, sprinkle with the curry powder, stir, detach the sediment with the lamb stock and add the sour cream. Reduce to the required consistency, add a little Cayenne pepper and pass through a conical strainer.

For the garnish, brown the remaining half apple and the pineapple in a little butter containing

a pinch of sugar. To serve, cut the tongues in half lengthwise, garnish with apple and pineapple, and coat with sauce. Serve with pilaf rice.
(Illustration, page 313)

(Roger Souvereyns, Belgium)

Mutton—Hot Main Dishes

The Barnsley chop

Barnsley chops are supposed to have made their appearance on the occasion of the market at the King's Head Hotel, Market Hill in 1849. The farmers who attended this event in the Yorkshire town of Barnsley used to patronise this hotel and were traditionally served this dish. When the new town hall was opened by His Royal Highness the Prince of Wales, Barnsley chops were provided for the official luncheon by Albert Hirst, purveyor of prime quality meat. The firm of Albert Hirst is still in existence in Barnsley.

4 portions   Cooking time: 1 hour

600 g	4 mutton chops each weighing (in one piece) salt, pepper	1¼ lb

Chine the chops and remove the skin. Trim well and cut along the rib bones, but leave these in place. Season with salt and pepper, brown for 15 minutes under the grill, then roast at 230°C (450°F) for 45 minutes. To serve, cut the meat off the bone in one piece, then cut into 6 slices and replace on the carcase. Serve with floury boiled potatoes.

(Victor Sassie, Great Britain)

Barnsley toad (mutton chops Barnsley style)
Recipe dating from 1850

4 portions

(A) *Batter:*

	2 eggs	
170 g	flour	6 oz
3 dl	milk	10 fl oz
5 cl	beer	2 fl oz
	½ teaspoon pepper	
	½ teaspoon salt	

(B)

approx. 600 g	2 mutton chops each weighing	approx.	1¼ lb
150 g	onions, finely chopped		5 oz
	1 dessertspoon mint, finely chopped		
	2 tablespoons Worcester sauce		

	2 tablespoons vinegar	
	2 teaspoons sugar	
	½ teaspoon salt	
	¼ teaspoon white pepper	
75 g	lard	2¾ oz

Beat the eggs. Sieve the flour into a bowl and mix well with the salt and pepper. Add the eggs and whisk well. Gradually whisk in the beer, then the milk, to make a smooth batter. Set aside. Remove the outer skin from the chops and cut the meat off the bone with a sharp knife. Trim away all gristle and fat, and cut the meat into 6 slices.

Fry the onions gently in 35 g (1¼ oz) lard until lightly coloured. Add the Worcester sauce, sugar, vinegar and mint, and stir over low heat for 2 minutes, when the mixture should be thick. Transfer to a deep fireproof dish and keep hot.

Season the meat with salt and pepper, and sear on both sides in 40g (1½ oz) hot lard. When well browned, transfer the meat and lard to the fireproof dish. Beat the batter again and pour over. Bake for 10 minutes at 240°C (465°F), then reduce the oven temperature to 190°C (375°F) and bake for a further 30 minutes, or until well risen and golden brown.

(Victor Sassie, Great Britain)

Mutton with broad beans
Mouton aux fèves
Castrato con fave verdi

6 portions

2 kg	mutton (shoulder or saddle)	4 lb 8 oz
2 kg	broad beans	4 lb 8 oz
	olive oil as required	
	salt, pepper	
	2 cloves of garlic, cut into small strips	
	2 tablepoons parsley, finely chopped	
	juice of 1 lemon	

Leave the meat for about 2 hours in salted water sharpened with the lemon juice, then rinse under cold running water and dry well. Insert the strips of garlic into the surface, together with pepper and the chopped parsley. Season with salt, place in a roasting tray with oil as required and roast in a medium oven. Shell the beans, place in a pan, season with salt and add a little oil. When the meat is well browned, add water or light stock to the roasting tray. Bring to the boil, add the beans and cook until the meat and beans are tender, adding water or stock if necessary to prevent sticking or burning.

(Salvatore Schifano, Italy)

Braised mutton with okra
Mouton braisé avec gombos marinés
Bamyes me arni

4 portions

800 g	mutton	1 lb 12 oz
800 g	young okra	1 lb 12 oz
	2 tablespoons tomato purée	
	2 tablespoons mutton fat or oil	
	salt	
4 dl	water	14 fl oz
2 dl	vinegar	7 fl oz

Cut off the okra stalks and wash the pods well. Mix 1 teaspoon salt thoroughly with the vinegar, pour over the okra and marinate for 30 minutes, stirring occasionally.

Melt the fat or oil in a braising pan. Add the meat which has been washed, dried and finely diced. Fry until golden, then add the tomato purée and fry well. Stir in the water and season with salt. Braise slowly for about 1½ hours, then adjust the seasoning. Draw the mutton to the centre of the pan and surround with the okra and marinade. Simmer very gently for 30 minutes, shaking the pan occasionally, but do not stir or the okra will break up. Serve with rice pilaf or boiled potatoes.

(Emil Wälti, Greece)

Leg of mutton Brno style
Gigot de mouton à la brunnoise
Skopová kýta po brněnsku

6 portions   Cooking time: about 1½ hours

1 kg	leg of mutton, boned	2 lb 4 oz
	3 cloves of garlic, crushed	
	salt	
80 g	lard	3 oz
	1 onion, finely cut	
	bouillon	
20 g	butter	¾ oz

Trim the meat of fat and rub all over with salt mixed with the crushed garlic, then tie. Melt the lard and cook the onion gently until transparent, add the meat and brown quickly all round. Add the mutton bones which have been chopped into small pieces. Roast at 230°C (445°F) until tender, basting occasionally and adding hot bouillon if necessary. Meat from an older animal will require preliminary braising under cover prior to roasting.

When the meat is tender, remove from the pan. Drain off the fat from the pan, add butter and salt, bring to the boil and strain. Carve the meat, dress on a warmed dish and pour a little stock over. Hand the rest of the gravy separately. Serve with boiled or fried potatoes and with spinach. Boned saddle or shoulder of mutton may be prepared in the same way.

(Vilèm Vrabec, Czechoslovakia)

Mutton with white cabbage
Ragoût de mouton à la norvégienne
Får i Kål

4 portions

750 g	mutton or lamb (breast or neck)	1 lb 10 oz
	sea salt	
	black peppercorns	
1 kg	white cabbage	2 lb 4 oz
3 dl	water	10 fl oz

Dice the meat coarsely. Cut the cabbage into small boat shapes. Arrange the meat and cabbage in alternate layers in a stew pan, sprinkling each layer with sea salt and freshly ground black pepper. Add the water and bring to the boil. Skim carefully, cover and cook slowly for about 1½ hours.

(Hroar Dege, Günther Rett, Norway)

Smoked mutton Montenegro style
Mouton fumé à la monténégroise
Paprikaš od Suvog Ovčijeg Mesa

6 portions   Cooking time: about 1½ hours

750 g	smoked mutton	1 lb 10 oz
OR 550 g	fresh breast of mutton	1 lb 3 oz
and 200 g	smoked neck of pork	7 oz
200 g	smoked bacon	7 oz
1 kg 500	white cabbage	3 lb 5 oz
750 g	potatoes	1 lb 10 oz
500 g	tomatoes	1 lb 2 oz
	2 onions	
	1 small red chilli pepper	
	salt	
	pepper, freshly ground	
	water	
	2 potatoes	

Wash the meat well in hot water and cut into cubes. Cut up the cabbage coarsely. Slice the onions and tomatoes thinly. Cut the bacon into 1 cm (⅜ in) cubes. Place all these ingredients in a stew pan, mix, add the chilli pepper and cover with water. Season with salt and cook for about 1 hour, or until the meat is tender, adding the potatoes, coarsely diced, shortly before the end of the cooking time. Season to taste with pepper before serving.

(László Csizmadia, Yugoslavia)

Mutton pilaf Montenegro fashion
Pilaw de mouton à la monténégroise
Pilav od Ovcentine

6 portions   Cooking time: 1½–1¾ hours

1 kg	shoulder of mutton, boned	2 lb 4 oz
	1 sheep's kidney	
⅛ l	oil	4 fl oz
250 g	onions, finely chopped	9 oz
125 g	rice	4½ oz
6 dl	water	1 pt
500 g	tomatoes, sliced	1 lb 2 oz
	2 green peppers, washed, seeded and cut into strips	
	parsley, finely chopped	
	pepper, freshly ground	
	salt	

Cut the meat and kidney into about 3 cm (1 in) cubes. Cook the onions gently in the oil without colouring, then add the meat and kidney and brown well. Season the peppers, tomatoes and parsley with salt and pepper, and mix with the meat. Pour in the water, cover and cook over low heat for 1 hour. Add the rice and cook for a further 20 minutes.

(László Csizmadia, Yugoslavia)

Ragoût of mutton with cheese
Ragoût de mouton au fromage
Youvetsi

6 portions

1 kg	shoulder of mutton	2 lb 4 oz

	2 teaspoons mutton fat or oil	
	1 onion, finely chopped	
500 g	tomatoes, skinned, seeded and diced	1 lb 2 oz
	1 tablespoon tomato purée	
5 dl	water	18 fl oz
4 dl	bouillon	14 fl oz
	salt	
	pepper	
100 g	grated cheese	3½ oz
	(Kasseri or Kefalotiri or, if not	
	available, Parmesan)	

Wash and dry the mutton and cut into pieces. Brown in mutton fat or oil, add the onion, tomatoes and tomato purée, and fry well. Season with salt and pepper, add the water and cook for about 1½ hours in a medium oven (175–180°C, about 350°F). Turn the meat occasionally and add bouillon and water if required. Adjust the seasoning, transfer to a fireproof dish or earthenware pot, sprinkle with the grated cheese and serve very hot. Hand boiled potatoes separately.

(Emil Wälti, Greece)

Shoulder of mutton Styrian style I
Epaule de mouton à la stirienne
Hammelschulter auf steirische Art

8 portions

2 kg	shoulder of mutton	4 lb 8 oz
	salt	
	6 peppercorns	
	1 teaspoon thyme	
⅛ l	vinegar	4 fl oz
60 g	onion	2 oz
80 g	celeriac	3 oz
80 g	parsley roots	3 oz
80 g	carrots	3 oz
80 g	swedes	3 oz
1 kg	potatoes, peeled and quartered	2 lb 4 oz
100 g	parsley, finely chopped	3½ oz

Remove the skin from the shoulder of mutton, bone it and cut the meat into fairly large cubes. Blanch them briefly, then cook until almost tender in salted water with the addition of the vinegar, peppercorns and thyme. Add the potatoes and the root vegetables which have been thinly sliced, and finish cooking. Sprinkle with the parsley to serve.

(Eduard Mayer, Austria)

Shoulder of mutton Styrian style II
Epaule de mouton à la stirienne
Hammelschulter auf steirische Art

6 portions

1 kg 200	boneless shoulder (or leg) of mutton	2 lb 10 oz
1 l	water or mutton stock	1¾ pt
2½ dl	dry white wine	9 fl oz
30 g	salt	1 oz
	3 tablespoons vinegar	
250 g	carrots	9 oz
250 g	celeriac	9 oz
200 g	onions	7 oz
200 g	leeks	7 oz
	bouquet garni of thyme, marjoram,	
	3 bay leaves, 1 clove of garlic,	
	4 cloves, 8 peppercorns	
	parsley, chopped	

Cut the mutton into cubes weighing about 40 g (1½ oz). Place the water or stock in a pan with the wine, bouquet garni, salt and vinegar, bring to the boil and add the meat. Simmer for about 1 hour, skimming off the fat frequently, then remove the bouquet garni, add the vegetables which have been cut into coarse strips and cook until tender. The liquid should be well reduced to give the dish a strong flavour. Sprinkle with a little parsley and serve with boiled potatoes flavoured with caraway seed, and with freshly grated horseradish.

(Johann Kögl, Austria)

Finnish Stew
Finsk fårestuing

4 portions

1 kg	breast of mutton	2 lb 4 oz
300 g	carrots	11 oz
200 g	leeks	7 oz
600 g	potatoes, peeled	1 lb 5 oz
	½ tablespoon salt	
	½ teaspoon pepper, freshly ground	

| approx. ½ l | light stock or water | approx. | 1 pt |
| | 2 tablespoons parsley, finely chopped | | |

Cut the mutton into 4–5 cm (about 2 in) cubes and season with salt and pepper. Leave to stand for 30 minutes, then place in a stew pan and cover with stock or water. Cover and cook gently for 45 minutes. Add the carrots, leeks and potatoes which have been sliced, and continue cooking until tender, adding stock or water if necessary.

(Otto Ramsbacher, Norway)

Mutton cutlets Udvarhelyi style
Côtelettes de mouton Udvarhelyi
Urüborda Udvarhelyi módra

10 portions   Cooking time: 15 minutes

100 g	20 mutton cutlets each weighing	3½ oz
40 g	salt	1½ oz
4 g	pepper, freshly ground	a good pinch
200 g	lard	7 oz
200 g	smoked bacon, finely diced	7 oz
800 g	tomatoes	1 lb 12 oz
1 kg	green beans, cooked	2 lb 4 oz
100 g	onions, finely chopped	3½ oz
1 g	garlic, crushed	half a clove
	parsley, chopped	

Brown the bacon, add the onions and cook gently until lightly coloured. Wash the tomatoes, cut into quarters, and add to the pan, together with the garlic, salt and pepper. Cover and cook gently until tender. Add the beans and sprinkle with parsley.

Season the cutlets with salt and pepper and fry in a second pan until medium done. Transfer to a serving dish, cover the meat with the tomatoes and beans, and pour the gravy over. Serve with French fried potatoes.

(Zsolt Körmendy, Hungary)

Sweet and sour leg of moorland mutton Roman style
Gigot de mouton lunébourgeois aigre-doux à la romaine
Heidschnuckenkeule süss-sauer auf römische Art

('Heidschnucke' is a breed of sheep found on Lüneburg Heath)

10 portions
Cooking time: 40–50 minutes per kg (20–25 minutes per lb)

2 kg 500–		
3 kg	2 legs of moorland mutton weighing	5½–6 lb
	salt	
	pepper, freshly ground	
	thyme, bay leaf	
	5 juniper berries	
	marjoram, sage	
	coarsely cut mirepoix of onions, carrots,	
	celery, parsley roots	
	red wine	
	castor sugar	
150 g	granulated sugar	5 oz
	wine vinegar	
2 l	Espagnole sauce	3½ pt
150 g	lard	5 oz
	Madeira	
150 g	plain chocolate couverture	5 oz
350 g	prunes, stoned and soaked in red wine	12 oz
	30 morello cherries	
	white wine	

Carefully skin the legs of mutton and trim in the same way as leg of lamb or venison. Remove the chump end bone, trim and bare the knuckle end and cut away the knuckle bone. Season with salt and pepper, and rub in a mixture of crushed thyme, bay leaf, juniper berries, marjoram and a little sage. Set aside for 2½ hours, then brown on all sides in a little lard, moisten a quarter of the way up with red wine, cover and braise in a medium oven. Baste frequently and add a little white wine from time to time to prevent excessive browning. When half cooked add the mirepoix. Shortly before the end of the cooking time, uncover the pan, increase the top heat, baste again, dust with a little castor sugar and leave in the oven to caramelise. Keep hot.

Boil the granulated sugar to the light caramel degree, pour in good wine vinegar and boil up to obtain the caramel. Add a little gravy if required, then stir in the Espagnole sauce, together with the mutton stock which has been strained. Reduce the sauce to the required consistency, adding a little flour butter if too thin, or Madeira if too thick. Remove any fat and pass through a cloth. Shortly before serving, add the prunes and cherries, then the couverture which has been dissolved in hot water.

To serve, carve the meat, dress on a dish and coat lightly with sauce. Mashed potatoes prepared with dairy cream or green noodles mixed with chanterelles make a suitable accompaniment. Hand the rest of the sauce separately.

(Karl Brunnengräber, Germany)

Braised shoulder of mutton Russian fashion
Daube de mouton à la russe
Kavardag

10 portions   Cooking time: about 2 hours

1 kg 500	shoulder of mutton, boned	3 lb 5 oz
2 dl	oil	7 fl oz
400 g	onions, finely cut	14 oz
40 g	salt	1½ oz
3 g	black pepper, freshly ground	⅛ oz
	1 bay leaf	
30 g	garlic, crushed	1 oz
	1 bunch parsley, chopped	
1 kg	aubergines, sliced	2 lb 4 oz
1 kg	potatoes, sliced	2 lb 4 oz
600 g	fresh tomatoes, cut into quarters	1 lb 5 oz
	vinegar	

Cut the mutton into 3½ cm (1½ in) cubes. Blanch in boiling water containing a little vinegar, rinse carefully and drain. Cook the onions gently in oil until lightly coloured, then add the meat, bay leaf and garlic. Pour in a little water, cover and cook slowly. When the meat is half cooked, add the potatoes, aubergines and tomatoes, together with chopped parsley. Pour in a little bone stock and finish cooking under cover in a medium oven. Serve in a warmed earthenware or fireproof dish, decorated with slices of tomato and sprinkled with parsley.

(Zsolt Körmendy, Russia)

Shoulder of mutton Mechlin style
Epaule de mouton à la malinoise

8 portions   Cooking time: about 1½-2 hours

approx. 2 kg 500	shoulder of mutton	approx.	5½ lb
	2 sheeps' tongues, blanched		
	8 small artichoke bottoms		
	8 heads chicory		
	12 small tomatoes		
	1 small celeriac, diced		
	4 shallots, chopped		
	3 cloves of garlic, chopped		
100 g	coriander		3½ oz
	4 sprigs thyme		

	2 bay leaves	
	2 good pinches powdered fennel	
	2 slices fat bacon	
200 g	Gruyère cheese, grated	7 oz
200 g	butter	7 oz
	1 bunch parsley	

Forcemeat:

300 g	shoulder trimmings	11 oz
200 g	pork	7 oz
200 g	streaky bacon	7 oz
	3 cloves of garlic, very finely chopped	
	2 shallots, finely chopped	
	2 tablespoons parsley, chopped	
5 cl	Pernod	2 fl oz
	1 egg, beaten	
	salt, pepper	
	a good pinch powdered fennel	

Bone out the shoulder of mutton and trim to yield about 300 g (11 oz) trimmings. Slit the meat to make a pocket. To prepare the forcemeat, mince the mutton trimmings, pork and streaky bacon, using the finest cutter, and place in a bowl. Add the shallots, garlic and parsley, together with salt, pepper and powdered fennel. Mix well, then add the Pernod and bind with the egg. Pass through the finest blade of the mincer again.

Stuff the shoulder with about three quarters of the forcemeat, tie securely and wrap in the fat bacon.

Line the bottom of a braising pan with 4 skinned, seeded and diced tomatoes, the celeriac, shallots, garlic, coriander, thyme, bay leaves and powdered fennel, and add the bones from the shoulder of mutton which have been chopped up. Lay the stuffed shoulder on the bed of vegetables, braise over low heat for 30 minutes, then add the tongues.

Turn the artichoke bottoms and blanch them in salted water. Using a sharp knife, cut a small cone out of the base of the chicory to reduce the bitter flavour, then braise. When partly cooked, cut in half, stuff with the rest of the forcemeat, and finish cooking in the oven.

Prepare the tomatoes Provençal style. Stuff the artichoke bottoms with a mixture of Gruyère cheese and finely chopped parsley, shallot and garlic, and brown in the oven or under a salamander. Keep the garnish hot until ready to serve.

Carve the shoulder of mutton and dress on a large warmed dish. Surround with the garnish. Slice the tongues and place a slice on each chicory half. Pass the braising stock through a conical strainer and remove the fat. Pour some of this gravy over the slices of mutton and hand the rest separately.

(André Béghin, Belgium)

Blanquette of mutton Emmental style
Blanquette de mouton à l'emmentaloise
Weissgericht von Hammel auf Emmentaler Art

10 portions   Cooking time: about 45 minutes

2 kg	boneless mutton (breast or shoulder)	4 lb 8 oz
7 dl	bouillon	1¼ pt
¼ l	white wine	9 fl oz
	seasonings as desired	
500 g	small onions	1 lb 2 oz
250 g	carrots	9 oz
100 g	celeriac, finely diced	3½ oz
100 g	turnips, finely diced	3½ oz
	¼ teaspoon saffron	
	½ teaspoon potato flour	
50 g	flour	2 oz
50 g	butter	2 oz

Cut the mutton into 50 g (2 oz) cubes and blanch, then drain and return to the pan. Add the bouillon, wine and seasonings and cook for 45 minutes, then add the vegetables and finish cooking.

Prepare flour butter with the flour, potato flour, saffron and butter, and blend with the cooking liquid to thicken. Boil up again for a moment. Serve with boiled potatoes and beetroot salad.

(Otto Ledermann, Switzerland)

Hot Mutton Dishes for Individual Plate Service

Turkish shish kebab
Shish-kebab à la turque

5 portions

900 g	leg of mutton, boned	2 lb
	1 large onion	
4 cl	olive oil	1½ fl oz
	juice of 2 lemons	
	1 tomato	
	1 sweet pepper	
5 cl	sour or fresh dairy cream	2 fl oz
	pepper, salt	

Trim the mutton and cut into 4 cm (1½ in) cubes. Cut the onion into quarters. Prepare a marinade with the olive oil and lemon juice. Marinate the meat and onion for several hours, then cut off the root end of the onion quarters and divide into pieces. Cut the tomato into ten pieces. Cut the pepper in half, remove the seeds and cut into ten pieces. Thread the meat on to wooden or metal skewers alternately with the pieces of tomato, pepper and onion. Brush with cream, season well and grill for as long as desired over a charcoal fire. If preferred, the kebabs may be seasoned after grilling. Serve with rice pilaf.

(Emil Wälti, Turkey)

Mutton cutlets in foil
Côtelettes de mouton en papillote
Hammelkoteletts in der Folie

4 portions

8 mutton cutlets
8 squares aluminium foil
fat for frying
1 cup mushrooms, finely cut
2 onions, finely cut
4 tomatoes, skinned, seeded and finely cut
1 bunch parsley, chopped

1 rasher streaky bacon, diced
2 tablespoons butter
salt
pepper, freshly ground

Beat the cutlets lightly and brown in fat on both sides for half a minute. Place each one on a square of foil, previously greased. Cook together the onions, tomatoes, parsley and bacon until soft and thick, making sure that all the liquid boils away. Place 1 tablespoon of the mixture on each cutlet, enclose in the foil and seal well at the top. Cook for 2 to 3 minutes in a preheated oven.

(Otto Ledermann, Switzerland)

Mutton cutlets with horseradish
Côtelettes de mouton au raifort
Hammelkoteletts mit Meerrettich

8 portions

	16 mutton cutlets	
	salt	
8 cl	oil	3 fl oz
150 g	carrots	5 oz
150 g	celeriac	5 oz
100 g	parsley roots	3½ oz
	1 tablespoon ground caraways	
1/8 l	white wine	4 fl oz
½ l	bouillon	18 fl oz
400 g	horseradish, finely grated	14 oz

Beat the cutlets lightly, season with salt and brown in oil. Add the vegetables which have been finely grated and the ground caraways, moisten with the wine, then add the bouillon and cook gently. Serve sprinkled with the horseradish, with fried potatoes as an accompaniment.

(Eduard Mayer, Austria)

Doner kebab
Brochettes de mouton à la turque
Döner Kebabi

1 kg	lean mutton, diced	2 lb 4 oz
	1 onion, grated	
	1 clove of garlic, crushed	

> pepper, freshly ground
> juice of 1 lemon
> 4 tablespoons olive oil
> almonds, flaked
> sour cream
> salt

Prepare a marinade with the onion, garlic, lemon juice and olive oil, and season liberally with freshly ground pepper. Add the meat and marinate for 8 to 10 hours. Thread the meat on to metal skewers and cook on a preheated grill over high heat for 4 minutes on each side. Season well with pepper and sprinkle with a little salt.

To serve, dress on well warmed plates on a bed of firm-grained saffron rice, sprinkle with flaked almonds and pour sour cream over. Hand tomatoes briefly cooked in the remaining marinade separately. Serve very hot.

This type of kebab has quite a different flavour from those originating from neighbouring countries.

(Otto Ledermann, Turkey)

Pork – Hot Main dishes

Sweet and sour pork

3–4 portions

1 kg 500	belly of pork	3 lb 5 oz
5 g	salt	⅙ oz
	1 egg	
50 g	cornflour	2 oz
100 g	self-raising flour	3½ oz
	oil for deep-frying	

Sauce and dressing:

	1 large onion	
	1 red pepper	
	1 green pepper	
	1 slice pineapple	
2 cl	oil	1 fl oz
3 cl	vinegar	1 fl oz
15 g	sugar	½ oz
10 g	cornflour	⅓ oz
2½ cl	water	1 fl oz
2½ cl	fresh orange juice	1 fl oz
15 g	tomato purée	½ oz
1½ cl	sherry	½ fl oz
5–6 g	lard	¼ oz

Remove the skin and half of the fat part of the pork. Cut the remainder into 2½ cm (1 in) cubes. Rub salt into the pork. Brush the pork with beaten egg, and dust and rub with a mixture of cornflour and self-raising flour. Cut the onion into thin slices, the peppers into strips, and the pineapple into small wedges. Mix together the remaining sauce ingredients until well blended.

Heat the oil in a deep-fryer until hot enough for a breadcrumb to sizzle when dropped into it. Shake the loose flour off the pork pieces and lower them into the oil. Deep-fry for 4 to 5 minutes, remove and drain.

Heat the lard in a frying pan and add the onion, peppers and pineapple. Stir over high heat for 2 minutes. Pour in the sauce mixture and continue stirring until the sauce thickens. Add the fried pork pieces and turn them quickly in the sauce with the other ingredients for 1 minute.

Serve in a deep serving dish. Alternatively, place the pieces of pork on a dish and pour the sauce and dressing over them.

(Kenneth Lo, China)

Szechuan twice-cooked pork

3–4 portions

1 kg	belly of pork	2 lb 4 oz

Sauce:

2 cl	soya sauce	1 fl oz
1½ cl	hoisin sauce	½ fl oz
15 g	tomato purée	½ oz
½ cl	chilli sauce	¼ fl oz
	3 stalks spring onion	
	3 cloves of garlic	
2 cl	oil	1 fl oz
15 g	black bean paste *or* salted black beans	½ oz
1 cl	sherry	½ fl oz

Cut the spring onion stalks into 4 cm (1½ in) lengths. Crush and chop the garlic coarsely. Place the pork in a large pan of boiling water and simmer for 35 minutes, then cut into thin bite-size pieces 5 x 3 cm (2 x 1¼ in), without removing the fat. Heat the oil in a large frying pan. Add the spring onions and garlic. Stir-fry for half a minute, then add the remaining sauce ingredients and stir for 1 minute, until well blended. Add the pieces of pork and turn them in the sauce over high heat for 3 minutes. Serve on a large well heated dish. This is a well known dish from West China and quite easy to prepare.
(Illustration, page 692)

(Kenneth Lo, China)

White-cooked pork
('White-cooking' in Chinese means cooking without soya sauce)

3–4 portions   Cooking time: 50 minutes

1 kg 500	belly of pork	3 lb 5 oz
2–3 g	mixed Chinese five spice powder	half a level teaspoon
	ginger	

Dip sauces:

(a)	1½ cl	soya sauce	½ fl oz
	5 g	soya paste	⅙ oz
	2 ml	chilli sauce	half a teaspoon
	3 ml	sesame oil	half a teaspoon
	2 g	garlic, chopped	half a teaspoon
(b)	1½ cl	soya sauce	½ fl oz
	5 ml	plum sauce	a teaspoon
	2 g	sugar	half a teaspoon
	5 ml	hoisin sauce	a teaspoon
(c)	1½ cl	vinegar	½ fl oz
	5 ml	sherry	a teaspoon
	10 g	root ginger, shredded	⅓ oz

Plunge the pork into a large pan of boiling water, boil vigorously for 10 minutes and drain. Transfer to a heavy pot or casserole, add 2 l (3½ pt) boiling water together with five spice powder and ginger, and simmer steadily over low heat for 50 minutes. Drain the pork and cut into thin bite-size pieces.

Prepare the dip sauces and pour into small saucer-size dishes. Place these at strategic points on the table so that the pork can conveniently be dipped into them.

(Kenneth Lo, China)

Quick stir-fried sliced pork with Chinese mushrooms and 'wood ears'

(Wood ears are a type of Chinese fungus which grows on tree trunks. When dried, they are blackish with uneven edges. They are soaked before use, and swell to about five times their original size, becoming brown and gelatinous. They should be well rinsed after soaking, to remove any adhering dirt. They are firm to the bite and have a delicate flavour. Larger ones may be cut up before soaking.)

3–4 portions

500 g	lean pork		1 lb 2 oz
	6–8 Chinese dried mushrooms		
4–5 g	dried wood ears	approx.	¼ oz
1½ cl	oil		½ fl oz
5 ml	sesame oil		a teaspoon
5 g	lard	approx.	¼ oz
	2 stalks spring onion		

1½ cl	soya sauce	½ fl oz
1 cl	hoisin sauce	½ fl oz
2 ml	chilli sauce	half a teaspoon
1 cl	rice wine or sherry	½ fl oz
1 cl	vinegar	½ fl oz

Soak the mushrooms in warm water for 30 minutes. Drain and cut each cap into four, discarding the stalks. Soak the wood ears in water for 20 minutes and drain. Cut the spring onions into 4 cm (1½ in) sections. Cut the pork into thin 4 x 2 cm (1½ x ¾ in) slices and rub with sesame oil.

Heat the oil in a frying pan. Add the pork and fry quickly over high heat for 1½ minutes, then remove and set aside. Add the lard, mushrooms, wood ears and spring onions to the pan. Stir over high heat for 2 minutes. Add the soya, hoisin and chilli sauces, vinegar and wine. Stir for half a minute, then return the pork to the pan and stir-fry for 1½ minutes. Transfer to a well heated dish and serve at once.

(Kenneth Lo, China)

Pork of 'original preciousness'

3–4 portions

Same ingredients and method as for red-cooked pork in pieces, with the addition of transparent pea starch noodles and celery as described below.

100 g	transparent pea starch noodles	3½ oz
100 g	celery	3½ oz

Soak the noodles in warm water for 10 minutes and drain. Clean the celery and cut slantwise into 3–4 cm (about 1½ in) sections. Line the bottom of a large deep fireproof dish with the noodles and celery. Pour the red-cooked pork with the gravy from the casserole on top. Place the dish in a steamer, covering the top with tin foil and steam vigorously for 15 minutes. Remove the foil and bring the dish to the table.

(Kenneth Lo, China)

Red-cooked pork in pieces
('Red-cooking' in Chinese means cooking with soya sauce)

3–4 portions   Cooking time: 1½ hours

1 kg	belly of pork	2 lb 4 oz
3 cl	soya sauce	1 fl oz

16 cl	water	6 fl oz
4 cl	red wine	1½ fl oz
5 g	sugar	⅙ oz
1 cl	oil	½ fl oz
5 g	anise	⅙ oz

Cut the pork through the skin into rectangular bite-size pieces approximately 4 x 6 cm (1½ x 2½ in). Heat the oil in a casserole and fry the pieces of pork over high heat for 6 to 7 minutes, turning them constantly. Add the soya sauce, water and remaining ingredients and turn the pork several times. Cover the casserole, stand it on an asbestos sheet over low heat, and cook steadily for 1½ hours, turning the pork every 30 minutes and adding a little water or wine when required. Serve in the casserole. This is an excellent dish for serving with rice and vegetables.

(Kenneth Lo, China)

Belly of pork rustic style
Poitrine de porc à la rustique
Pancetta di maiale alla rustica

15 portions   Cooking time: 1 hour

2 kg 500	belly of pork	5 lb 8 oz
	4 cloves of garlic	
	1 sprig rosemary	
	1 teaspoon fennel seeds	
	10 juniper berries	
	zest of 1 lemon	
	1 chilli pepper	
1 dl	white wine	3½ fl oz
100 g	ham, cooked	3½ oz
	salt	

Cut away the surplus fat from the meat, but leave the skin in place. Remove the rib bones without damaging the flesh. Cut the ham into strips. Pound the herbs and flavourings to a paste. Cut slits in the meat and insert the paste, finishing with the strips of ham. Season well all over with salt, place in an oiled roasting tray and roast for 1 hour at 180–220°C (355–430°F), turning the meat occasionally and moistening with white wine. Add bouillon if necessary. Serve hot with fried polenta slices or cold with salad.

(Franco Boffetti, Italy)

Roast pork Danish style
Carré de porc rôti à la danoise
Helstegt swinekam pa dånsk maner

4 portions   Cooking time: about 2 hours

1 kg	best end of pork	2 lb 4 oz
	2 cloves	
	1 bay leaf	
¼ l	brown stock (hot)	9 fl oz
¼ l	water	9 fl oz
	salt	
	pepper, freshly ground	
¼ l	dairy cream	9 fl oz
	flour butter as required	

Prunes:

200 g	prunes	7 oz
	1 vanilla pod	
50 g	sugar	2 oz
	1 slice lemon	
¼ l	water	9 fl oz

Brown potatoes:

1 kg	small even-size potatoes	2 lb 4 oz
100 g	unsalted butter	3½ oz
50 g	sugar	2 oz

Red cabbage Danish style:

1 kg	red cabbage	2 lb 4 oz
100 g	lard	3½ oz
¼ l	vinegar	9 fl oz
¼ l	water	9 fl oz
	2 tablespoons sugar	
	½ tablespoon white pepper, freshly ground	
3 dl	redcurrant juice	10 fl oz
	lemon juice	

Stuffed apples:

	2 large cooking apples	
100 g	redcurrant jelly	3½ oz
	1 teaspoon lemon juice	
¼ l	water	9 fl oz
150 g	sugar	5 oz

Chop the backbone off the joint of pork and place on a rack to keep dry. Using a sharp knife, score the skin evenly at intervals of 5 mm (¼ in). Season with salt and insert the cloves and bay leaf into one of the slits. Place the rack with the pork in a roasting tray and roast for about 1½ hours in an oven preheated to 225°C (435°F), taking great care to avoid contact between the meat and the cooking juices so that the crackling is very crisp. When the pork is cooked, remove and keep hot, but do not cover. Pour the brown stock into the roasting tray to detach the sediment, add the water and cook for about 20 minutes. Add the cream and thicken with flour butter (or roux). Season with salt and pepper and strain through a cloth.

To serve, remove the rib bones and carve the meat into slices 5 mm (¼ in) thick. Serve with brown potatoes, red cabbage Danish style, prunes and stuffed apple halves. To prepare the potatoes, boil them in their skins, then remove the skins and keep hot. Cook the sugar to light caramel in a heavy sauté pan. Carefully add the butter which has been melted and skimmed. Add the potatoes and toss over the heat until golden brown.

To prepare the red cabbage, remove the outer leaves, cut in half lengthwise, then cut away the stump and any thick leaf ribs. Wash and drain the leaves and cut them into julienne strips. Blanch briefly and drain. Heat the lard in a stew pan, add the red cabbage, then pour in the water and vinegar. Add the sugar, season with salt, cover and simmer over low heat until cooked. The liquid should have evaporated almost completely by the end of the cooking time. Add the redcurrant juice together with a little lemon juice and pepper to taste.

To prepare the prunes, soak them in cold water for 8 hours, then drain. Place in a pan with ¼ l (9 fl oz) fresh water, the sugar, lemon and vanilla, bring to the boil, then leave to stand in a warm place for 1 hour.

For the stuffed apples, prepare a syrup (18° Baumé) with the sugar and water. Add the lemon juice. Peel, halve and core the apples and poach at once in the syrup. Drain and stuff with the redcurrant jelly.

(Karl-Otto Schmidt, Denmark)

Mexican roast pork
Rôti de porc à la mexicaine
Adobo Mexicana

10 portions

2 kg	shoulder of pork	4 lb 8 oz
	4 tomatoes, coarsely cut	
200 g	onion rings	7 oz
	3–4 oranges	
	5 cloves of garlic, finely chopped	
	water	
	a little vinegar	
	salt, pepper	
	coriander, caraway	

Tie the shoulder of pork and place in the oven in a braising pan with a little water. When the water has evaporated, brown the meat well all over. Add the tomatoes, garlic (or juice), spices, seasoning and a little vinegar, and cook gently until tender.

Leave the onion rings in water. Slice the oranges. Garnish the meat with the onion rings and orange slices, and sprinkle with diced croûtons if desired. Pour the cooking liquid round the meat to serve.

(Emil Wälti, Mexico)

Roast pork Prague fashion
Rôti de porc à la pragueoise
Pražská vepřová pečeně

6 portions   Cooking time: 1½–2 hours

1 kg	pork (spare rib, fore loin or leg)	2 lb 4 oz
	salt	
2 g	caraway	half a teaspoon
50 g	lard	2 oz
	water or bouillon (for basting)	

Wash the meat. Remove part of the bone and chop up. Season the meat with salt and sprinkle with caraway. Place the lard, bones and meat trimmings in a roasting pan and lay the meat on top with the underside uppermost. Pour in a little water or bouillon and roast at 230–240°C (445–465°F) for 45 minutes to 1 hour on each side. Baste frequently and pour hot bouillon over if necessary. When the meat is cooked, remove from the pan. Drain off almost all the fat remaining in the pan, add a little bouillon, season with salt, boil for a few moments and strain. Carve the meat, dress on a heated dish and pour a little of the gravy over. Hand the rest separately. Suitable accompaniments include potato dumplings and various kinds of dumplings made with bread or flour. In Czechoslovakia boiled white cabbage is particularly popular with this dish.

(Vilèm Vrabec, Czechoslovakia)

Roast pork Prague fashion with crackling
Rôti de porc avec couenne à la pragueoise
Pražská veprová přečeně a kurčičkou

6 portions

Ingredients as for **Roast pork Prague fashion.**

To obtain crisp crackling, proceed as follows. Place the meat trimmings and bones in a roasting pan. Sprinkle the underside of the meat only (not the skin) with salt and caraway. Lay the meat on the bed of trimmings and bones with the skin side downwards so that the skin is not in contact with the bottom of the pan. Pour in a little bouillon and roast for about 45 minutes, or until the skin may be easily pierced with a fork.

Turn the joint over and score the skin criss-cross fashion without cutting the flesh. Dry the skin well with a cloth and season well with salt to obtain a layer of salt about 1 mm ($^1/_{20}$ in) thick. The more thickly the skin is covered with salt, the drier and crisper it becomes.

Continue roasting without basting the skin, otherwise the salt will be washed into the gravy, making the meat and gravy too salty, and the skin will remain tough. If the skin remains dry the salt will not penetrate the meat. Proceed as for *Roast pork Prague fashion*.

(Vilèm Vrabec, Czechoslovakia)

Roast pork Moravian style
Rôti de porc à la moravienne
Moravská vepřová prečeně

6 portions

Ingredients as for **Roast pork Prague fashion.**

Rub the pork thoroughly with crushed garlic, season with salt and roast in the same way as *Roast pork Prague fashion*. Bohemian bread or potato dumplings and spinach are particularly suitable as accompaniments.

(Vilèm Vrabec, Czechoslovakia)

Roast pork with cinnamon Vallée d'Auge
Rôti de porc à la cannelle vallée d'Auge
Zimt-Schweinebraten Vallée d'Auge mit glasierten Zwiebelchen und Apfelspalten

10 portions   Cooking time: 1½ hours

2 kg	spare rib of pork, boned	4 lb 8 oz
	2 cloves of garlic, cut into small strips	
	2 level teaspoons cinnamon	
	salt, pepper	

100 g	butter	3½ oz
	30 small onions, peeled	
	1 level teaspoon sugar	
	2 bay leaves	
2½ l	bouillon	4½ pt
4 cl	brandy	1½ fl oz
80 g	raisins	3 oz
	2 tablespoons rum	
	8 apples, cut into wedges	
	cornflour	

Carefully mix the cinnamon with salt and pepper. Rub into the pork well and insert the strips of garlic into the flesh. Brown all over in butter over moderate heat. Add the onions and allow to colour. Sprinkle with sugar and caramelise. Add the bay leaves. Moisten with the brandy and add the bouillon. Braise under cover for about 1 hour, then thicken the stock with a little cornflour.

Meanwhile macerate the raisins in the rum. Peel the apples, core them and cut into wedges. Brown them in butter in a sauté pan, then mix with the raisins. Transfer to a serving dish to make a base for the meat which has been sliced. Pour the sauce with the onions over the meat.

(Karl Brunnengräber, Germany)

Stuffed belly of pork Entlebuch
Poitrine de porc farcie Entlebuch
Gefüllte Schweinebrust Entlebuch

10 portions

800 g	belly of pork without skin, lightly salted	1 lb 12 oz
800 g	tin or sandwich loaf (white) or rolls	1 lb 12 oz
1 l	milk	1¾ pt
	5 eggs	
100 g	shallots, finely chopped	3½ oz
150 g	ham and ox tongue, diced	5 oz
100 g	butter	3½ oz
	pistachio nuts	
	herbs, chopped	
	salt	
	spices as desired	
	brown veal stock	
	mirepoix	

Plums in Burgundy:

1 kg	large plums	2 lb 4 oz

5 dl	red Burgundy	18 fl oz
100 g	sugar	3½ oz
	cinnamon	

Savoy potatoes:

2 kg	potatoes	4 lb 8 oz
2 l	bouillon	3½ pt
200 g	cheese, grated	7 oz
100 g	butter	3½ oz
	salt	
	spices as desired	

Slit the belly of pork on one side with a sharp knife to make a pocket. To make the stuffing, soak the bread or rolls in milk. Cook the shallots gently in butter without colouring, and add the diced ham and tongue. Squeeze the bread dry and mix carefully with the eggs, herbs, pistachios, shallots, ham and tongue. Season to taste. Fill into the pocket in the pork and sew up the opening carefully. Place on a heated roasting tray and brown, then add the mirepoix, continue browning and detach the sediment with brown veal stock. Roast in a moderate oven until golden, basting frequently. To serve, slice the meat and garnish with the plums which have been poached in the Burgundy, and with Savoy potatoes.

(Otto Ledermann, Switzerland)

Fillet of pork with parsley stuffing
Filet de porc farci au persil
Persille Filet

4 portions

600 g	fillet of pork	1 lb 5 oz
	1 bunch fresh parsley, finely chopped	
	salt	
	a good pinch pepper, freshly ground	
	2 heaped tablespoons butter	
2 dl	bouillon	7 fl oz
50 g	flour butter	2 oz
2 dl	dairy cream	7 fl oz
	prunes	
	stock syrup	
	a little lemon zest	

Trim the fillet of pork and make a deep lengthwise incision. Cream the butter carefully with the pepper, add the parsley, mix well and fill into the slit in the pork. Tie, season with salt and pepper, fry until well browned, stir in the bouillon to detach the pan juices, cover and braise on top of the stove for about 20 minutes. Remove the meat. Pour the cream into the pan, thicken with flour butter, reduce a little and adjust the seasoning.

Cut the meat into slices about 3 cm (1¼ in) thick and dress on a warmed dish. Pour the sauce over and serve with rice, peas cooked in butter, and stewed prunes. To prepare the prunes, soak them, then simmer in stock syrup with the addition of a little lemon zest.

(Hroar Dege, Günther Rett, Norway)

Pork fillets in raspberry vinegar and mustard seed sauce
Filet mignon de porc au vinaigre de framboise et aux graines de moutarde

4 portions

200 g	4 pork fillets each weighing	7 oz
15 g	butter	½ oz
	1 tablespoon mustard seed	
	1 tablespoon raspberry vinegar	
	2 tablespoons white wine	
	2 tablespoons pork gravy	
	1 tablespoon dairy cream	
	salt, pepper	

Garnish:

apple slices cooked in butter

Season the pork with salt and pepper. Roast in butter for 10 minutes in an oven preheated to 280°C (535°F). Remove the meat and keep hot. Pour off the butter, add the wine to the pan to detach the sediment, and reduce. Stir in the pork gravy, cream, vinegar and mustard seed, boil up for a moment and adjust the seasoning if necessary. Carve the fillets evenly, dish and coat with the sauce. Garnish with the apple slices.
(Illustration, page 237)

(Pierre Gleize, France)

Pork fillets with spinach and Gouda stuffing
Filet de porc farci avec épinards et fromage de Gouda
Varkenshaas met een vulling van spinazie en goudase kaas

4 portions

150 g	4 pork fillets each weighing	5 oz
20 g	flour	¾ oz

	salt	
	pepper, freshly ground	
100 g	Gouda cheese, finely diced	3½ oz
250 g	spinach	9 oz
	1 tablespoon parsley and chervil, chopped	
1 dl	veal gravy	3½ fl oz
1 dl	dairy cream	3½ fl oz
150 g	butter	5 oz
	2 egg whites	

Beans Dutch style:

400 g	green beans	14 oz
	1 medium onion, finely chopped	
50 g	butter, melted	2 oz

Run a tranchelard through the centre of the fillets and hollow out. Blanch the spinach and work to a purée in the mixer. Add the egg whites, cheese, salt and pepper. Fill into the pork fillets, season them with salt and pepper, flour them and brown in butter, then transfer to a warm oven and roast.

To make the sauce, mix the cream with the veal gravy, reduce to the required consistency, and stir in the herbs. Carve the fillets, dress on a dish and coat with the sauce. Serve with cucumber stuffed with mashed potato, and with cauliflower, carrots and green beans Dutch style. Cook the beans in salted water, keeping them firm to the bite. Pour off the water, add the butter and onion, and cook gently until the beans are soft.

(Bernard van Beurten, Netherlands)

Stuffed belly of pork Danish style
Poitrine de porcelet farcie à la danoise
Gefüllte Jungschweinebrust auf Dänische Art

10 portions   Cooking time: 1½ hours

2 kg 200	lean belly of pork (from a young animal)	5 lb
1 kg	apples, peeled and cored	2 lb 4 oz
100 g	raisins	3½ oz
	3 tablespoons rum	
	salt	
	pepper, freshly ground	
	marjoram	
	rosemary leaves	
	1 lemon	
250 g	white bread without crust	9 oz

	4 eggs, beaten	
	parsley, coarsely chopped	
½ l	cider	18 fl oz
1½ l	Espagnole sauce	2¾ pt
	1 onion, finely diced	
	butter, sugar as required	

Remove the rib bones from the belly of pork. Run the hand between the layers of connective tissue to open up a pocket; alternatively, slit lengthwise with a knife. Season on the outside and inside the pocket with salt, pepper and marjoram.

Sprinkle the apples with the lemon juice and mix with the raisins which have been moistened with the rum. Fry the onion in a little butter until lightly coloured, add the apples and raisins, sprinkle with a little salt and sugar, and set aside to cool.

Crumb the bread, mix with the eggs, then add parsley, rosemary leaves and the apple/raisin mixture. Fill into the pocket in the meat and sew up. Score the skin lightly and roast, basting at regular intervals. Pour in the cider, bring to the boil, and continue boiling until all the pan juices have been detached. Strain, mix with the Espagnole sauce, and boil. Hand this sauce separately.

(Karl Brunnengräber, Germany)

Belly of pork Pongau style
Poitrine de porc à la Pongau
Schweinebrust nach Pongauer Art

4 portions

800 g	belly of pork	1 lb 12 oz
6 cl	oil	2 fl oz
	salt, pepper	

Forcemeat:

200 g	shoulder of pork	7 oz
250 g	spinach, cooked	9 oz
	1 roll, soaked	
	salt, pepper	
	garlic	
	marjoram	

Stuffed cabbage leaves:

400 g	cabbage leaves, trimmed of stumps	14 oz
250 g	celeriac	9 oz
250 g	carrots	9 oz

100 g	smoked streaky bacon	3½ oz
2 dl	pork stock	7 fl oz
	salt, pepper	

Potato cakes:

400 g	potatoes	14 oz
	2 eggs	
	a little flour	
	salt, pepper	
	garlic	

Cut a pocket in the pork and score the skin. To make the forcemeat, chop the shoulder of pork very finely with the roll and the spinach. Add salt, pepper, garlic and marjoram, and fill into the pocket in the pork. Season the meat with salt and pepper. Heat 2 cl (1 fl oz) oil in a braising pan and place the pork in it with the skin uppermost. Braise in the oven for about 2 hours, basting frequently. Remove the meat and carve. Make gravy with the cooking liquid.

For the stuffed cabbage, blanch the cabbage leaves. Scrape the carrots, peel the celeriac and cut these vegetables into very thin strips. Dice the bacon finely and brown in 1 cl (½ fl oz) oil. Spread the cabbage leaves on a napkin, season with salt and pepper, sprinkle with the bacon and cover with the carrots and celeriac. Roll up tightly, tie and cook in well flavoured pork stock, keeping the cabbage firm. Remove and slice.

To make the potato cakes, peel the potatoes and grate finely. Squeeze out the moisture well and add salt, pepper and garlic. Mix with the eggs and flour. Shape into small flat cakes and fry on both sides in hot oil until golden brown.
(Illustration, page 870)

(Ewald Plachutta, Austria)

Pork fillet en croûte with horseradish sauce
Filet de porc en croûte – sauce au raifort

6 portions

1 kg	fillet of pork	2 lb 4 oz
	3 slices ham	
500 g	puff pastry	1 lb 2 oz
	1 egg yolk	

Marinade:

| ½ l | white wine | 18 fl oz |
| 100 g | carrots | 3½ oz |

50 g	onions	2 oz
	½ clove of garlic	
	1 clove	
	1 bay leaf	
	1 sprig thyme	
	parsley	

Sauce:

200 g	horseradish, grated	7 oz
1 dl	dairy cream (double)	3½ fl oz
	salt, pepper	
	nutmeg	
	vinegar	

Accompaniment:

gratin of potatoes and leeks
(recipe, page 1018)

Marinate the pork overnight, then drain well and wrap in the ham. Enclose in the pinned out puff pastry and brush with egg yolk. Bake for 45 minutes in an oven preheated to 200°C (390°F).

To make the sauce, whip the cream until it begins to thicken, stir in the horseradish, and add salt, pepper, nutmeg and a few drops of vinegar.
(Illustration, page 169)

(Emile Jung, France)

Fillet of pork Valle Maggia
Filet de porc Valle Maggia
Gefülltes Schweinefilet Valle Maggia

6 portions

	24 slices fillet of pork each	
30 g	weighing about	1 oz
40 g	dried flap mushrooms, soaked	1½ oz
150 g	pork sausage meat	5 oz
50 g	raw ham	2 oz
30 g	Parmesan cheese, grated	1 oz
20 g	shallot, finely chopped	¾ oz
80 g	butter	3 oz
	thyme, rosemary	
	pepper, salt	
	parsley, chopped	

Beat the slices of pork until very thin, season lightly and stuff with forcemeat. To make the forcemeat, chop the ham finely and fry gently in butter. Add the flap mushrooms, finely chopped, and the shallot. Season and flavour with the herbs. Mix with the sausage meat and Parmesan. Sandwich the slices of pork in pairs with the forcemeat and fry slowly in butter for about 10 minutes.

Serve with polenta, risotto or fresh noodles and a little fresh tomato sauce or thickened veal stock flavoured with a little Marsala.

(Willi Bartenbach, Switzerland)

Emincé of pork with vodka
Emincé de filet de porc au vodka
Geschnetzeltes Schweinefilet mit Wodka

10 portions   Cooking time: about 12 minutes

1 kg 500	pork fillets, trimmed	3 lb 5 oz
250 g	shallots, finely cut	9 oz
80 g	monosodium glutamate	3 oz
20 g	paprika	¾ oz
4 cl	vodka	1½ fl oz
1 dl	white wine	3½ fl oz
1 dl	white stock	3½ fl oz
1 l	Espagnole sauce	1¾ pt
70 g	butter	2½ oz
	juice of 1 lemon	
1 dl	oil	3½ fl oz
	parsley, chopped	

Slice the pork finely and sauter lightly in hot oil with the shallots. Season with the monosodium glutamate and paprika, add the vodka and ignite. Drain the meat on a sieve. Detach the pan juices with the wine and the stock, bring to the boil, reduce by half, add the Espagnole sauce and reduce to the desired consistency. Flavour the sauce with lemon juice and vodka and finish with fresh butter. Mix with the meat which has been kept hot and with freshly chopped parsley. Serve in a cocotte.

(Karl Brunnengräber, Germany)

Quick-fried diced pork cubes with prawns and cucumber

3–4 portions   Cooking time: 4½ minutes

250 g	fillet of pork	9 oz

250 g	large fresh prawns, shelled	9 oz
	1 15 cm (6 in) section of medium cucumber	
100 g	bamboo shoots	3½ oz
1½ cl	good stock	½ fl oz
1 cl	rice wine	½ fl oz
	1 egg white	
5 ml	soya sauce	a teaspoon
15 g	cornflour	½ oz
3 g	salt	half a teaspoon
4 g	sugar	a small teaspoon
2 cl	oil	1 fl oz

Cut the pork into small cubes the size of a lump of sugar. Wet them with beaten egg white, and dust and rub with cornflour. Cut the prawns into pieces of much the same size and rub them with salt. Cut the cucumber (unpeeled) and the bamboo shoots into pieces of the same size as the pork and prawns.

Heat the oil in a large frying pan, then add the pork and stir-fry over high heat for 1½ minutes. Add the prawns, bamboo shoots and cucumber. Continue to stir-fry over high heat for 1½ minutes. Add the sugar, stock, wine and soya sauce. Stir-fry for 1 more minute. Transfer to a heated dish and serve very hot. The heat is as much an integral part of the dish as any of the flavours.

(Illustration, page 693)

(Kenneth Lo, China)

Quick stir-fried diced cubes of pork

3–4 portions   Cooking time: about 3 minutes

500 g	fillet of pork	1 lb 2 oz
	½ egg white	
5 g	cornflour	⅙ oz
1½ cl	oil	½ fl oz

Sauce:

7 g	lard	¼ oz
10 g	salted yellow bean paste	⅓ oz
3 g	sugar	half a teaspoon
5 ml	hoisin sauce	a teaspoon

5 ml	rice wine or sherry	a teaspoon

Cut the pork into small cubes the size of a lump of sugar. Wet them with beaten egg white, and dust and rub with cornflour. Heat the oil in a frying pan, then add the pork and stir-fry quickly over high heat for 1½ minutes. Remove and set aside.

Add the lard to the pan. When it has melted completely, add the bean paste, hoisin sauce, sugar and wine. Stir and mix together into a glistening bubbling paste over low heat. Turn the heat high and return the pork cubes to the pan. Turn and mix with the bean paste over high heat for 1½ minutes only. Dress on a well heated dish and serve at once. The heat is as much an integral part of the dish as the majority of the ingredients.

(Kenneth Lo, China)

Shredded pork quick-fried with bamboo shoots and Szechuan hot pickles

3–4 portions   Cooking time: 6 minutes

500 g	lean pork	1 lb 2 oz
75 g	bamboo shoots	2½ oz
75 g	celery	2½ oz
50 g	Szechuan Hot Cha Tsai Pickles (available canned from Chinese food stores)	2 oz
	6 Chinese dried mushrooms	
	3 stalks spring onion	
1 cl	soya sauce	½ fl oz
1½ cl	good stock	½ fl oz
1½ cl	oil	½ fl oz
	a pinch of pepper	
5 g	lard	⅙ oz
5 ml	sesame oil	a teaspoon

Cut the pork, bamboo shoots, celery and pickles into matchstick strips or shreds. Cut the spring onions into 6 cm (2½ in) lengths. Soak the mushrooms for 30 minutes, discard the stalks and cut the caps into shreds.

Heat the oil in a large frying pan. Add the mushrooms and pork, and stir-fry them together over high heat for 2 minutes. Add all the other vegetables, together with the lard and the sesame oil. Stir-fry over high heat for 2 minutes. Add the soya sauce and stock, and continue to stir-fry for 2 minutes. Transfer to a heated dish and serve very hot as an accompaniment to rice.

(Illustration, page 693)

(Kenneth Lo, China)

Cantonese cha shao barbecue roast pork

3-4 portions   Cooking time: 12 minutes

1 kg	fillet of pork	2 lb 4 oz
2 cl	soya sauce	1 fl oz
1 cl	hoisin sauce	½ fl oz
5 g	bean curd 'cheese' (if available)	⅙ oz
5 g	sugar	⅙ oz
1 cl	sherry or red wine, or rice wine	½ fl oz
1 cl	sesame oil	½ fl oz

Trim the fillet of pork into regular-size strips. Mix all the other ingredients together to make a well blended sauce. Apply to the pork and rub in evenly. Leave to marinate for 1½ hours. Place the strips of marinated pork on a rack and roast for 12 minutes over a drip tray in an oven preheated to 240°C (465°F). Remove the strips of pork, which are now deep brown with an almost charred appearance because of the encrustation of the marinade. Place them on a chopping board and cut across into slices ¾–1 cm (about ⅜ in) thick. Serve hot or cold. (Illustration, page 691)

(Kenneth Lo, China)

Blackburn faggots or Mill workers' dinner

6 portions   Cooking time: 30-40 minutes

(1)	400 g	belly of pork	14 oz
	500 g	lean shoulder of pork	1 lb 2 oz
	250 g	pig's liver	9 oz
		1 pig's heart	
		1 pig's kidney	
	200 g	onions, chopped	7 oz
	250 g	fresh breadcrumbs	9 oz
		2 eggs	
	50 g	lard	2 oz
		1 heaped tablespoon parsley, chopped	
		1 teaspoon salt	
		1 teaspoon pepper	
(2)	1 kg	savoy cabbage	2 lb 4 oz
	500 g	potatoes	1 lb 2 oz
	200 g	onions, cut into thin half rings	7 oz

	½ teaspoon black pepper	
	1 teaspoon salt	
3 dl	bouillon	10 fl oz
50 g	flour	2 oz

Fry the chopped onions lightly and set aside until cold. Cut the pork and offal into cubes and mince in the following order: first the liver, then the kidney, heart, belly and shoulder. Place in a bowl and add the eggs, onions, breadcrumbs, parsley, salt and pepper. Mix well, divide into six portions and shape into six oval cakes.

Cut the savoy cabbage in half, remove the stumps and blanch for 2 minutes to reduce the strong smell. Pour off the water, cut the cabbage into quarters and each of these across into three pieces. Cut the potatoes into thick slices. Line the bottom of a baking dish with the halved onion rings and place the potatoes on top. Sprinkle with flour, then with pepper and salt. Arrange the pieces of cabbage on top, add the bouillon and place the faggots on the cabbage. Cover and cook for 30 to 40 minutes in an oven preheated to 230°C (450°F). Transfer to a heated dish and serve with the cabbage which has been mixed with the potatoes.

(Victor Sassie, Great Britain)

Pork and haricot bean croquettes
Fricadelles aux haricots blancs à la tchèque
Fazolové karbanátky s uzeným masem

6 portions   Cooking time: about 1¼ hours

450 g	haricot beans	1 lb
	1-2 eggs	
30 g	onion, finely cut	1 oz
10 g	parsley, finely cut	⅓ oz
50 g	butter	2 oz
250 g	cooked smoked shoulder of pork	9 oz
	salt	
1 g	pepper	a pinch

Coating:

80 g	flour	3 oz
	2 eggs	
120 g	breadcrumbs	4 oz
120 g	fat for frying	4 oz

Pick over the beans, soak them, then cook for about 1 hour, or until soft. Sieve them and mix well with the eggs, the onion which has been lightly fried, the parsley and the smoked pork which has been finely cut. Season with salt and pepper, shape into croquettes, dip these in flour, then egg and crumb them. Fry in hot fat for about 12 minutes, or until reddish brown. Serve with boiled potatoes, spinach or boiled sauerkraut.

(Vilèm Vrabec, Czechoslovakia)

Pig's trotters Mère-Royaume
Pieds de porc Mère-Royaume
Schweinefüsse Mère-Royaume

10 portions   Cooking time: 2½-3 hours

	15 pig's trotters	
1 dl	oil	3½ fl oz
	salt	
	pepper, freshly ground	
300 g	mirepoix	11 oz
	3 cloves of garlic	
1 l	white wine	1¾ pt
	(Genevois de Dardagny)	
5 dl	bouillon	18 fl oz
	bouquet garni of	
	1 sprig rosemary	
	thyme, tarragon	
	1 bay leaf	
60 g	hot mustard	2 oz
50 g	dried breadcrumbs	2 oz

Mushroom sauce:

500 g	mushrooms, coarsely cut	1 lb 2 oz
50 g	butter	2 oz
30 g	shallots	1 oz
500 g	tomatoes, finely diced	1 lb 2 oz
1 dl	Madeira	3½ fl oz
20 g	cornflour	¾ oz
	parsley, chopped	

Split the trotters in half lengthwise and season. Heat the oil in a frying pan and brown the trotters on both sides, then transfer them to a braising pan. Brown the mirepoix and the garlic in the oil remaining in the frying pan, detach the sediment with the wine and bouillon, then transfer to the braising pan and add the bouquet garni. Bring to the boil, cover tightly and braise slowly in an oven preheated to 180°C (355°F), adding bouillon if required. Remove the trotters when cooked, bone them and place in a fireproof dish. Spread with mustard, sprinkle with breadcrumbs and brown lightly in the oven.

For the sauce, cook the mushrooms, shallot and tomatoes gently in butter and mix with the braising stock which has been strained and thickened with cornflour. Add the Madeira, boil up and season to taste. Spoon the mushrooms from the sauce over the middle of the trotters and sprinkle with parsley. Hand the rest of the sauce separately.

(Otto Ledermann, Switzerland)

Pig's trotters Zeeland style
Pieds de porc à la zélandaise
Varkens pootjes uit zeeland

Cook the trotters in salted water and split in half lengthwise. Place them in a baking dish, pour a little bouillon over and sprinkle with brown sugar. Braise for 1 hour in an oven preheated to 150°C (300°F). Serve with white bread.

(Bernard van Beurten, Netherlands)

Sweet and sour pork trotters

3-4 portions   Cooking time: 2 hours

1 kg 500	pork trotters	3 lb 5 oz
3 cl	soya sauce	1 fl oz
3 cl	rice wine or sherry	1 fl oz
1 dl	water or stock	3½ fl oz
	2 large onions	

Sauce: see **Sweet and sour spare ribs,** page 855

Cut the onions into thin slices. Plunge the trotters into a pan of boiling water, boil for 15 minutes, then drain. Place the trotters and half the onion slices in a casserole. Add the soya sauce, the wine (or sherry) and the water or stock, and sprinkle with the rest of the onion slices. Bring the contents to the boil and turn them over a few times. Cover and cook for 2 hours in an oven preheated to 160°C (320°F), turning the contents every 30 minutes and adding a little stock or water if the contents become too dry. Lastly, place the casserole on top of the stove over low heat. Pour the prepared sweet and sour sauce over the trotters, turn these a few times in the sauce, and leave to cook very gently for 7 to 8 minutes. Serve in the casserole or transfer to a large serving dish or tureen.
(Illustration, page 692)

(Kenneth Lo, China)

Red-cooked leg of pork
('Red-cooking' in Chinese means cooking with soya sauce)

3-4 portions   Cooking time: 2¾ hours

1 kg 500– 2 kg 250	leg of pork (with skin)	3¼–5 lb
6 cl	soya sauce	2 fl oz
2 dl	water	7 fl oz
5 cl	red wine	2 fl oz
10 g	sugar	⅓ oz
	4–5 slices root ginger	

Heat 1½–2 l (2¾–3½ pt) water in a casserole to boiling point. Add the leg of pork and boil over high heat for 10 minutes. Drain off the water and add all the other ingredients. Turn the pork in the sauce several times. Transfer the casserole to an oven preheated to 180°C (355°F). Leave to cook for 45 minutes, then turn the pork and cook for a further 30 minutes at 160°C (320°F). Repeat three times, adding a little water or wine if the casserole becomes too dry. At the end of the cooking time the meat should be very tender, and the presence of the skin should make it very succulent. The meat may be sliced in the casserole at the table. Serve with rice or potatoes and a liberal amount of vegetables.

(Kenneth Lo, China)

Stewed knuckle of pork with sauerkraut
Jarret de porc en daube
Gedämpfte Schweinehachse mit Kraut

4 portions

1 kg 800– 2 kg	2 small fresh knuckles of pork (foreleg) weighing approx. salt, paprika 2 cloves of garlic	4–4½ lb
2 cl	oil	1 fl oz
100 g	onions, thinly sliced	3½ oz
40 g	smoked pork fat, diced	1½ oz
750 g	sauerkraut	1 lb 10 oz
150 g	apples	5 oz
150 g	carrots	5 oz
150 g	pickled cucumbers	5 oz
	1 pair Frankfurter sausages	
	1 small teaspoon caraways	
approx.	1 teaspoon sugar	
	8 juniper berries	

2½ dl	white wine	9 fl oz
1¼ dl	water	4 fl oz
20 g	4 rashers bacon each weighing about	¾ oz

Remove the skin from the knuckles of pork if desired. Rub them with salt, paprika and crushed garlic. Slice the apples, cucumbers and sausages thinly. Cut the carrots into small thin strips. Fry the onions and pork fat lightly in oil. Place the sauerkraut in a bowl with the apples, cucumbers, sausages and carrots. Add salt to taste, sugar and the caraways and juniper berries, and mix well. Line the bottom of a casserole with the fried onions and spread half the sauerkraut over them. Lay the knuckles of pork in the sauerkraut and cover with the remainder. Pour the wine and water over and place the bacon on top. Stew under cover in a preheated oven for about 2 hours. To serve, bone the knuckles, slice the meat and dish on top of the sauerkraut. Hand boiled potatoes separately.

(Ernst Faseth, Austria)

Red-cooked knuckle of pork with spinach
(Red-cooking in Chinese means cooking with soya sauce)

3-4 portions   Cooking time: 2½ hours

1 kg 500– 2 kg	knuckle end of pork	3¼– 4½ lb
4 cl	soya sauce	1½ fl oz
	3 slices root ginger	
6 cl	water	2 fl oz
5 g	sugar	⅙ oz
4 cl	sherry or red wine	1½ fl oz
350 g	fresh spinach	12 oz
	2 cloves of garlic	
3 g	salt	half a teaspoon
	1 medium onion	
2 cl	oil	1 fl oz

Scrub the knuckle clean. Plunge it into a pan of boiling water, boil vigorously for 10 minutes, then drain. Discard any tough and discoloured parts of the spinach. Wash, clean and drain thoroughly. Slice the onion thinly.

Place the knuckle lying down in a casserole. Add the soya sauce, root ginger, water, sugar and wine or sherry. Turn the knuckle in the sauce several times. Place the casserole in an oven preheated to 180°C (355°F) and cook for 30 minutes. Reduce the heat to 160°C (320°F), turn the knuckle and cook for 30 minutes. Repeat three times, adding a little water or wine if the casserole becomes too dry. When the pork is almost cooked, heat the oil in a large saucepan. Add the onion, garlic and spinach, and sprinkle with salt. Stir-fry over high heat for 4 to 5 minutes.

To serve, transfer the spinach to a large deep dish as a bed for the pork. Tip the contents of the casserole over the spinach. The contrast between the brown knuckle and the green glistening spinach makes the dish very attractive. The meat should be tender enough to be removed with a pair of chopsticks. The guests should be left to help themselves.

(Kenneth Lo, China)

Roast pork with apple and prune stuffing
Carré de porc farci aux pommes et aux pruneaux
Füldt svinekam med aebler og svesker

6 portions   Cooking time: 1¾ hours

1 kg 500	best end of pork	3 lb 5 oz
500 g	apples, peeled, cored and finely cut	1 lb 2 oz
225 g	prunes, soaked and stoned	8 oz
2 kg	red cabbage	4 lb 8 oz
½ l	vinegar	18 fl oz
1 l	water	1¾ pt
½ l	redcurrant juice	18 fl oz
75 g	sugar	2½ oz
	salt	
	pepper, freshly ground	

Sauce:

6 dl	water	1 pt
60 g	fat	2 oz
45 g	flour	1½ oz

Clean the red cabbage carefully, cut it into strips and place in a pan with the water, vinegar and sugar. Season with salt and pepper and cook gently for 1 hour. Add the redcurrant juice and cook for a further 30 minutes.

Chop the backbone off the pork and score the skin. Make a deep lengthwise incision on the underside and fill the resulting pocket with the prunes and apples. Season with salt and pepper and tie round carefully to keep the stuffing in place. Place in a roasting pan with the skin side downwards, add a little water and roast in a preheated oven for 30 minutes. Turn to bring the skin side uppermost and continue roasting, basting frequently. The skin should have formed dry, crisp crackling. Remove the meat. Add 6 dl (1 pt) water to the pan to detach the sediment and boil up. Make a roux with the fat and flour, blend in the gravy from the roasting pan, bring to the boil and strain.

Slice the meat and arrange on a heated serving dish. Pour the sauce over. Serve with boiled potatoes and the red cabbage.

(Eric Cederholm, Denmark)

Roast best end of pork with prunes Swedish style
Carré de porc à la suédoise

6 portions

approx. 2 kg	best end of pork	approx.	4 lb 8 oz
	salt, pepper		
	rosemary		
	1 long strip pork fat		
	12 prunes soaked in water and stoned		
	mirepoix of		
	1 onion		
	1 carrot		
	1 celeriac		
50 g	smoked bacon		2 oz
	a little thyme		
	prune stones, crushed		
	a little apple purée		
	a little lemon juice		

White cabbage:

2 kg	white cabbage, shredded	4 lb 8 oz
	salt, pepper	
3 dl	wine vinegar	10 fl oz
	1 onion, finely chopped	
	1 teaspoon caraway seeds	
100 g	lard	3½ oz
2 dl	bouillon	7 fl oz
	a little syrup	

Garnish:

	6 apples	
	6 large potatoes	
50 g	butter	2 oz

Chop the backbone off the pork. Rub with salt, pepper and rosemary. Embed prune halves in the strip of pork fat and draw through the middle of the joint. Roast for about 40 minutes in hot oil with the mirepoix and the prune stones, basting frequently and keeping the meat juicy. Make gravy with the pan juices, boil well and strain, then thicken. Flavour with a little apple purée and lemon juice.

Marinate the cabbage in the vinegar with the addition of salt and pepper. Cook the onion gently in the lard with the caraways, add the cabbage and pour in the bouillon. Cover tightly with greaseproof paper and cook until soft. Glaze with a little syrup. Peel the apples, cut in half, core and poach them, then stuff with prunes.

Carve the meat and dress on a serving dish. Garnish with the stuffed apples and fondantes potatoes. Hand the cabbage and gravy separately.

(Eric Carlström, Sweden)

Best end of pork with fig stuffing
Carré de porc farci aux figues
Schweinekarree mit Feigenfüllung

4 portions

700 g	best end of pork, boned	1 lb 8 oz
200 g	dried figs	7 oz
	½ red pepper, seeded	
3 cl	oil	1 fl oz
30 g	butter	1 oz
	salt	
2 dl	Samos (Greek dessert wine)	7 fl oz
100 g	mirepoix	3½ oz
200 g	pork bones, chopped	7 oz
2 dl	brown stock	7 fl oz

Potato roll:

500 g	potatoes (floury)	1 lb 2 oz
40 g	butter	1½ oz
	2 eggs	
50 g	semolina	2 oz
100 g	spinach, sieved and seasoned	3½ oz
	flour	
	salt	

Run a sharp knife through the centre of the boned best end and hollow out. Dice the red pepper coarsely, mix with the figs which have been cut up a little, and fill into the cavity in the pork. Line the bottom of a roasting pan with the bones. Season the meat, pour oil over, and place on the bones with the outside uppermost. Brown quickly in a hot oven, then reduce the heat and roast, basting frequently. After about 45 minutes, turn the meat and add the mirepoix. Roast for a further 45 minutes or so, then remove the meat and keep hot. Brown the bones and mirepoix well, drain off the fat, add the butter and cook until foaming, then add the wine and brown stock. Bring to the boil, cook for 20 minutes, then strain. Carve the meat and hand the sauce separately.

To make the potato roll, peel the potatoes, boil in salted water, sieve while still hot, and allow to cool. Mix with the eggs, semolina, butter, salt to taste and flour as required. Test the consistency before proceeding. Roll out into an oblong the thickness of one finger and spread thinly with the spinach. Roll up, wrap in a cloth and simmer in salted water for about 35 minutes. Remove from the cloth, slice and brush with melted butter.
(Illustration, page 869)

(Ewald Plachutta, Austria)

Pork chops Bácska style
Carré de porc à la batschka
Bácskai sertésborda

5 portions

1 kg	best end of pork, cut evenly into 10 chops	2 lb 4 oz
1 kg 500	white cabbage	3 lb 5 oz
200 g	lean smoked bacon	7 oz
200 g	onions, finely cut	7 oz
5 g	noble-sweet paprika	⅙ oz
100 g	tomatoes, cut in quarters	3½ oz
	1 bunch dill, coarsely chopped	
	1 green pepper, cut into rings	
4 dl	sour cream	14 fl oz
2 dl	oil	7 fl oz
	salt	
5 cl	water	2 fl oz

Flatten the chops, season with salt and fry quickly on both sides in a little oil over high heat until well browned. Dice the bacon finely and fry in oil in a stew pan. Add the onions and colour lightly. Sprinkle with the paprika, add 5 cl (2 fl oz) water and cover with the cabbage which has been well washed and cut into slices the thickness of one finger. Season with salt, place the pepper rings and tomato quarters on top, sprinkle with dill, cover and stew gently over low heat until the cabbage is cooked to a pulp. Place the chops on the cabbage and pour the sour cream over. Cook gently over low heat for a further 10 minutes to blend the aroma of the meat and cabbage. To serve, transfer the chops to a fireproof dish, cover with the cabbage and decorate with the pepper rings, tomato quarters and dill.

(Gyula Gullner, Hungary)

Best end of pork with fennel seeds
Carré de porc aux grains de fenouil
Carré di maiale ai semi di finocchi

4 portions   Cooking time: 50 minutes

1 kg	best end of pork	2 lb 4 oz
12 g	fennel seeds	½ oz

300 g	fennel stalks and trimmings	11 oz
2 dl	dry white wine	7 fl oz
2 dl	brown stock	7 fl oz
60 g	white onions	2 oz
100 g	fresh tomatoes	3½ oz

Garnish:

350 g	4 fennel weighing	12 oz
1½ dl	olive oil	5 fl oz
4 dl	water	14 fl oz
	salt, white pepper	

To prepare the meat, chop off the backbone, trim the chop bones well and tie into shape. Season liberally with salt and pepper a few hours in advance.

Peel and dice the onions. Wash and quarter the tomatoes. Trim the fennel of their tough outside covering, wash them and set aside. Preheat the oven to 200°C (390°F) and reduce the temperature to 180°C (355°F) after 15 minutes.

Chop up the bones and place them on a roasting tray. Place the joint on top, brush the meat with oil and brown on all sides in the oven. After about 20 minutes add the fennel stalks and trimmings which have been diced, together with the onions and tomatoes. Continue roasting, basting frequently.

Meanwhile cut the fennel in half lengthwise, make a slit in the centre, season with salt and pepper and place in a pan with the olive oil and water. Cook gently for about 15 minutes, then keep hot. Remove the meat from the oven after 50 minutes and keep hot. Drain off the fat from the roasting tray, detach the sediment with the wine, reduce and add the brown stock. Reduce again for 5 minutes, then strain, remove any remaining fat and keep hot. Brush the meat with a little oil, sprinkle with the fennel seeds and return to the oven to brown lightly.

Pour the gravy on to a warmed oval dish, place the meat in the centre, place cutlet frills on the ends of the bones and surround with the fennel.
(Ilustration, page 314)

(Gualtiero Marchesi, Italy)

Best end of pork Florentine fashion
Carré de porc à la florentine
Arista di maiale alla fiorentina

6 portions

| 1 kg 800 | best end of pork | 4 lb |

	2 cloves of garlic, cut into small strips	
	3 sprigs rosemary	
	2 cloves	
	salt	
	black peppercorns, crushed	
1 dl	olive oil	3½ fl oz

To prepare the joint, chop off the backbone and trim well. Make an incision along the back and insert the garlic, rosemary leaves and cloves. Rub the surface with salt and crushed peppercorns. Tie round so that the joint keeps its shape while roasting. Place in a roasting pan, baste with olive oil and roast for about 1¾ to 2 hours in an oven preheated to 180°C (355°F), basting and turning frequently.

To serve, untie, remove the bones and cut into slices 1–1½ cm (about ½ in) thick. In Tuscany the meat is served without gravy, garnished with lukewarm haricot beans sprinkled with olive oil. It may also be served cold.
(Illustration, page 516 – served cold)

(Franco Colombani, Italy)

Best end of pork Csaba
Carré de porc Csaba
Csabai sertéskaraj piros káposztával

5 portions

500 g	best end of pork	1 lb 2 oz
200 g	Csaba smoked (hard) sausage	7 oz
6 cl	oil	2 fl oz
200 g	onions	7 oz
1 kg	potatoes	2 lb 4 oz
	salt	

Garnish:

1 kg	red cabbage	2 lb 4 oz
1 dl	oil	3½ fl oz
100 g	onions, peeled and sliced	3½ oz
	vinegar	
	salt	
	caraway	
	a little sugar	

Make a lengthwise incision in the middle of the joint with a sharp knife and insert the sausage. Place in a roasting pan, season with salt and sprinkle with a little oil and water. Peel the onions, cut into wedges and add to the pan. Roast in an oven preheated to 150°C (300°F).

Boil the potatoes in their skins, then skin and slice them. Add to the meat when it is cooked and reheat.

Cut the red cabbage into thin strips. Heat the oil in a stew pan, add a little sugar and cook until golden, then add the onions, a little vinegar and the cabbage, and mix well. Season with salt and sprinkle with caraways. Cover and cook over high heat until the pan is dry. To serve, carve the meat, dress on a heated dish and surround with the potatoes and red cabbage. (Illustration, page 624)

(Gyula Gullner, Hungary)

Stuffed best end of pork
Carré de porc farci
Gefülltes Schweinekarree

4 portions

1 kg	best end of pork	2 lb 4 oz
	a little lard	
	a little water	
	salt	
	caraway	
	garlic	

Stuffing:

	4 stale rolls	
	2 eggs	
2½ dl	milk	9 fl oz
40 g	butter	1½ oz
30 g	onion	1 oz
	salt	
	nutmeg	

To prepare the joint, chop off the backbone and separate the rib bones from the meat at the top over a distance of about 4–5 cm (2 in). Make an incision starting from the backbone side. Open out the meat and flatten a little, spread with the stuffing, roll up, tie and sew up the sides.

To make the stuffing, cut the crusts off the rolls and dice these finely. Beat the eggs with the milk, salt and grated nutmeg, and pour over the rolls. Chop the onion finely, brown in butter and add to the rolls. Soak well, then mix thoroughly.

Rub the outside of the joint well with salt, caraway and garlic. Place in a braising pan on a bed of bones. Add a little fat and water and braise in the oven at 220°C (430°F) for about 1½

hours, basting frequently. When cooked, remove from the oven, strain off the gravy, carve the meat, dish and surround with the gravy.
(Illustration, page 874)

(Johann Kögl, Austria)

Smoked loin or best end of pork with mustard in foil
Echine ou carré de porc fumé à la moutarde en papillotte

6 portions

approx. 1 kg 200	smoked best end of pork	approx.	2 lb 10 oz
	butter or oil for foil		
	1 onion, finely cut		
	2 bay leaves		
	10 peppercorns, crushed		
	a little thyme		
5 dl	brown stock		18 fl oz
	arrowroot		
3 cl	Madeira		1 fl oz
	lemon juice		

Mustard crust:

	1 egg	
	½ tablespoon syrup *or* a little sugar	
	1 heaped tablespoon mustard	
	OR 1 teaspoon mustard powder	
	1 teaspoon potato flour	
	breadcrumbs	

Jerusalem artichokes:

400 g	Jerusalem artichokes	14 oz
50 g	butter	2 oz
3 dl	dairy cream	10 fl oz
	1 teaspoon flour butter	
	salt	

Potato croquettes:

500 g	potatoes	1 lb 2 oz
	4 egg yolks	
50 g	butter	2 oz
	salt, pepper, nutmeg	

The pork should be boneless, lightly pickled and smoked. Soak and blanch it to reduce the strong smoky taste. Butter or oil a double sheet of aluminium foil, sprinkle with the onion, bay leaves, crushed peppercorns and a little thyme, and place the meat on top. Fold the foil over to enclose the meat and seal tightly. Place on a rack and cook in the oven at 200°C (390°F) for about 30 minutes. Unwrap the meat and keep hot. Add the juices to strong brown stock, boil up, strain and, if necessary, thicken a little with arrowroot. Flavour with Madeira and a few drops of lemon juice.

To make the mustard crust, blend the egg with the syrup or a little sugar, add the mustard or mustard powder and potato flour and mix to a paste. Spread on the meat, sprinkle with bread-crumbs and press down lightly. Dry and brown in an open oven.

To prepare the Jerusalem artichokes, peel them and cook in lightly salted water. Slice, mix with butter/cream sauce and gratinate in the oven. For the croquettes, cook and sieve the potatoes, then mix them with the egg yolks, salt, pepper and a pinch of nutmeg. Shape into small balls and deep–fry in oil until golden.

To serve, carve the meat and dress on a warmed dish. Hand the sauce and accompaniments separately.

(Eric Carlström, Sweden)

Leg of pork
Cuisse de porc
Jungschweinkeule

10 portions

2 kg	leg of pork, boned	4 lb 8 oz
1 kg	pork bones, chopped up	2 lb 4 oz
	3 cloves of garlic	
10 g	caraway	⅓ oz
	salt	

Place the leg of pork in boiling water with the skin side downwards and boil for 10 minutes. Remove and score the skin criss-cross fashion with a sharp pointed knife at intervals of 1 cm (⅜ in). Place on a bed of bones in a roasting pan, sprinkle with salt and caraways and roast, basting from time to time with the meat juices. Shortly before the meat is cooked, add the garlic which has been finely crushed. The crackling should be very crisp and well browned. Remove the joint, keep hot and make a little gravy with the pan juices. Serve with dumplings and cabbage salad.

(Eduard Mayer, Austria)

Pickled leg of pork Hungarian fashion
Jambon frais mariné à la hongroise
Pácolt börös magyarosan

5 portions

1 kg	leg of pork, preferably from a young animal weighing about 60 kg (130 lb)	2 lb 4 oz

800 g	green peppers (sweet)	1 lb 12 oz
200 g	green chilli peppers	7 oz
400 g	ripe tomatoes	14 oz
200 g	young onions	7 oz
10 g	red paprika	1/3 oz
1 kg	potatoes	2 lb 4 oz
50 g	garlic, peeled	2 oz
	salt	
	butter	
	parsley	

Pickling brine:

3 l	cold water	5 pt
300 g	salt	11 oz
30 g	saltpetre	1 oz
10 g	allspice	1/3 oz
10 g	cloves	1/3 oz
10 g	mace	1/3 oz
20 g	peppercorns	3/4 oz

Bone the leg of pork and pickle for 3 weeks, making sure it is completely covered by the brine and leaving it in the refrigerator at a temperature of 5–10°C (40–50°F). Remove from the brine and tie to its original shape. Place in a pan of cold water, bring to the boil and cook for 2 to 3 hours, or until the skin is soft. Remove from the cooking liquid, score the skin to facilitate the escape of fat and insert the garlic into the slits. Roast in an oven preheated to 160°C (320°F), basting frequently, until the crackling is reddish–brown and crisp. Add the peppers, onions and tomatoes (whole) about 10 minutes before the end of the cooking time.

To serve, place the meat in the centre of a warmed dish. Skin the peppers and tomatoes and arrange round the meat. Mix the cooking juices with red paprika and pour a little over the meat and vegetables. Serve with the potatoes, which have been peeled, turned into barrel shapes, lightly blanched in salted water and coated with melted butter.
(Illustration, page 623)

(Gyula Gullner, Hungary)

Pickled leg of pork with bananas
Jambon frais mariné aux bananes
Pácolt börös malaccomb magyarosan

5 portions

1 kg 300	leg of pork, preferably from a young animal weighing about 65 kg (140 lb)	3 lb

1 kg	bananas	2 lb 4 oz
600 g	grapes	1 lb 5 oz
200 g	butter	7 oz
50 g	icing sugar	2 oz
10 g	cloves	⅓ oz

Pickling brine:

3 l	cold water	5 pt
300 g	salt	11 oz
30 g	saltpetre	1 oz
10 g	allspice	⅓ oz
10 g	mace	⅓ oz
20 g	peppercorns	¾ oz
10 g	cloves	⅓ oz

Bone the leg and pickle for 3 weeks, making sure it is completely covered by the brine and leaving it in the refrigerator at a temperature of 5–10°C (40–50°F). Remove from the brine and tie to its original shape. Place in a pan of cold water, bring to the boil and cook for 2 to 3 hours, or until the skin is soft. Remove from the cooking liquid, score the skin to facilitate the escape of fat and insert the cloves into the slits. Roast in an oven preheated to 160°C (320°F), basting frequently, until well browned.

Peel the bananas, dust with icing sugar, sprinkle with melted butter and grill under high heat until the sugar is well caramelised. Plunge the grapes into boiling water, skin them, cut in half, remove the seeds and heat in butter.

Carve the meat so that there is a piece of crackling attached to each slice, dress on a heated dish and arrange the bananas and grapes alternately round the edge.
(Illustration, page 623)

(Gyula Gullner, Hungary)

Pork cutlets with cabbage
Côtelettes de porc aux choux
Amagerkotelet

6 portions   Cooking time: 1¼ hours

200 g	6 pork cutlets each weighing	7 oz
2 kg	savoy cabbage	4 lb 8 oz
500 g	potatoes, peeled and sliced	1 lb 2 oz
300 g	onions, sliced	11 oz
1 kg 500	pork bones	3 lb 5 oz
2 l	water	3½ pt

salt
pepper, freshly ground

Brown the bones well in the oven, add the water and slowly reduce by half over low heat. Pass through a sieve. Line the bottom of a fireproof dish with the cabbage leaves. Cover with the potatoes and with the onions which have been lightly fried. Season with salt and freshly ground pepper.

Flatten the cutlets, season with salt and freshly ground pepper, and brown quickly for 1 minute on each side over high heat. Place them on the bed of vegetables in the fireproof dish, pour the bone stock over and cook under cover for 1 hour. Bring to the table in the cooking dish.

(Eric Cederholm, Denmark)

Ardennes pork chops
Côtes de porc à l'ardennaise

6 portions

200 g	6 pork chops each weighing	7 oz
	pepper, freshly ground	
	6 slices Ardennes ham (smoked)	
	flour as required	
200 g	fresh breadcrumbs	7 oz
600 g	potatoes, cut into	1 lb 5 oz
	1 cm (⅜ in) cubes	
170 g	butter	6 oz
250 g	bacon, blanched and diced	9 oz
	2 eggs	
100 g	button onions	3½ oz
5 cl	veal stock	2 fl oz
	1 tablespoon juniper berries, chopped	

Season the chops with pepper only and fry in 50 g (2 oz) butter until medium done. Wrap in the slices of ham, flour, egg and crumb and finish frying over gentle heat with the addition of 20 g (¾ oz) butter. Keep hot. Detach the sediment with the veal stock, add the juniper berries, boil up for a moment and keep hot.

For the garnish, fry the potatoes, bacon and onions in the rest of the butter over fairly low heat. Arrange the chops round the edge of a round serving dish, coat with the sauce and fill the centre with the garnish.

(André Béghin, Belgium)

Pork cutlets Bartok
Côtelettes de porc Bartok
Sertésborda Bartok módra

10 portions   Cooking time: 15-20 minutes

140 g	10 pork cutlets each weighing	5 oz
500 g	goose liver	1 lb 2 oz
	2 medium onions, finely cut	
40 g	fines herbes	1½ oz
300 g	lard	11 oz
50 g	salt	2 oz
100 g	flour	3½ oz
400 g	Parmesan cheese, grated	14 oz

Tokay sauce:

7 dl	Espagnole sauce	1¼ pt
3 dl	Tokay	10 fl oz
200 g	raisins	7 oz

Garnish:

5 portions buttered French beans
5 portions straw potatoes
10 medium tomatoes

Wash the goose liver well. Fry the onions in a little lard until lightly coloured, add the goose liver and cover with water. Poach, cool and cut into 10 slices. Slit the cutlets as far as the bone, but leave on the bone. Stuff each one with a slice of goose liver and secure the edges with toothpicks or small metal skewers. Season with salt, sprinkle with the herbs and cheese, and brown quickly under a salamander. Serve the cutlets on white roll croûtons with straw potatoes, French beans, grilled tomatoes and Tokay sauce.

(Zsolt Körmendy, Hungary)

Pork cutlets Cipriano
Côtelettes de porc Cipriano
Costolette di maiale Cipriano

6 portions   Cooking time: 10-15 minutes

260 g	6 pork cutlets each weighing	9 oz
200 g	butter	7 oz
	10 juniper berries, finely crushed	
	1 sprig rosemary	

	3 sage leaves	
30 g	parsley, chopped	1 oz
30 g	flour	1 oz
1 dl	red wine	3½ fl oz
2 dl	dairy cream	7 fl oz
	salt	
	pepper, freshly ground	

Slit open a pocket in one side of each chop. Cream 150 g (5 oz) butter in a bowl, add the juniper berries and the herbs which have been finely chopped, and mix to make a well blended herb butter. Fill into the pockets in the cutlets. Beat the edges of the cutlets lightly to seal and close the pocket securely with a toothpick. Season with salt and pepper, coat quickly with flour and fry on both sides in the rest of the butter. When the cutlets are cooked, pour off the butter, detach the sediment with the wine, and add the cream to finish the sauce. Remove the toothpicks, place the cutlets on a heated dish and coat with the sauce.

(Mario Saporito, Italy)

Foochow long-cooked pork chops

3-4 portions

180 g	5 or 6 pork chops each weighing	6 oz
2 cl	soya sauce	1 fl oz
10 g	anchovy	⅓ oz
5 ml	hoisin sauce	a teaspoon
5 cl	bone or meat stock	2 fl oz
2 cl	sherry or red wine	1 fl oz
	oil for deep-frying	
350 g	spring greens	12 oz
3 g	salt	half a teaspoon
1½ cl	oil	½ fl oz

Chop each pork chop through the bone into three pieces. Deep-fry in oil for 3 to 4 minutes and drain. Cut the spring greens into 3 cm (1 in) slices.

Place the chops in a casserole. Add the anchovy, soya sauce, hoisin sauce, stock and wine or sherry. Turn the chops in the mixture a few times. Cover and braise for 30 minutes in an oven preheated to 180°C (355°F). Reduce the heat to 160°C (320°F), turn the chops, return to the oven and cook for a further 30 minutes. Repeat once more.

Heat the oil in a large frying pan or saucepan. Add the spring greens and sprinkle with salt. Stir-fry for 2 minutes, then transfer to a deep fireproof dish to line the bottom. Place the pork chops with their gravy on this bed of greens, spreading them evenly. Cover the dish with foil, place in a steamer and steam for 15 minutes. Bring to the table and remove the foil. This is an excellent dish to serve with plain boiled rice.

(Kenneth Lo, China)

Pork cutlets Göcsej
Cotelettes de porc Göcsej
Göcseji Sertésborda

10 portions   Cooking time: 20–25 minutes

160 g	10 pork cutlets each weighing	5½ oz
200 g	lard	7 oz
200 g	smoked bacon, diced	7 oz
250 g	onions, finely chopped	9 oz
300 g	yellow peppers, seeded and cut into strips	11 oz
150 g	tomatoes, sliced	5 oz
30 g	paprika	1 oz
50 g	flour	2 oz
2 g	caraway seeds, finely chopped	half a teaspoon
20 g	garlic, crushed	¾ oz
50 g	salt	2 oz
300 g	mushrooms, diced	11 oz
600 g	green beans, parboiled in salted water	1 lb 5 oz

Tarhonya:

600 g	tarhonya	1 lb 5 oz
150 g	lard	5 oz
50 g	onions	2 oz
5 g	paprika	⅙ oz
30 g	salt	1 oz

Season the cutlets with salt, flour them, brown in hot lard and set aside. Add the bacon and onions to the pan, fry until lightly coloured, sprinkle with paprika, mix with the caraways and garlic, add water as required, season with salt, return the cutlets to the pan and cook gently under cover. Shortly before the end of the cooking time, add the beans, mushrooms, peppers and tomatoes.

To serve, dress the cutlets in the centre of a dish, cover with the stewed vegetables and pour the gravy over. Decorate with raw peppers which have been seeded and cut into rings, and with raw sliced tomatoes. Fry the tarhonya in lard until lightly browned, add the onions which have been finely chopped, sprinkle with paprika and add 12 dl (2 pt) hot water. Bring to the boil, cover and cook until soft.

(Zsolt Körmendy, Hungary)

Pork cutlets Hargita
Côtelettes de porc Hargita
Hargitai Sertésborda

10 portions   Cooking time: 50–60 minutes

600 g	shoulder or hand of pork, chopped or minced	1 lb 5 oz
140 g	10 pork cutlets each weighing	5 oz
300 g	lard	11 oz
500 g	Debrecen sausage (a fatty, paprika-flavoured lightly smoked sausage)	1 lb 2 oz
400 g	smoked bacon, finely diced	14 oz
200 g	onions, finely chopped	7 oz
2 kg	sauerkraut, washed	4 lb 8 oz
	10 large white cabbage leaves	
50 g	salt	2 oz
2 g	pepper, freshly ground	a good pinch
1 g	marjoram	a pinch
	dill, finely chopped	
150 g	flour	5 oz
1 l	sour cream	1¾ pt

Season the cutlets with salt, brown in hot lard and set aside. Fry the onions in lard until lightly coloured, add the minced or chopped pork, season and sauter. Allow to cool, then spread on the cutlets. Slice the sausage and place on top of the minced pork. Wrap the cutlets in the cabbage leaves and tie with twine.

Sauter the diced bacon in the lard remaining in the pan used to brown the cutlets. Add the sauerkraut, dill and salt, and cook gently. Add the cutlets, moisten with bone stock, cover and cook for about 1 hour, then remove the cutlets and set aside. Pour in the sour cream which has been blended with the flour, mix carefully and bring to the boil. Return the cutlets to the pan.

To serve, untie the cutlets and dish on a bed of sauerkraut. Pour sauerkraut liquor over and sprinkle with sour cream and dill.

(Zsolt Körmendy, Hungary)

Pork cutlets Kodaly
Côtelettes de porc Kodaly
Sertésborda Kodály módra

10 portions   Cooking time: 20–25 minutes

160 g	10 pork cutlets each weighing	5½ oz

60 g	salt	2 oz
300 g	lard	11 oz
200 g	onions, finely chopped	7 oz
30 g	paprika	1 oz
200 g	yellow peppers, seeded and cut into strips	7 oz
100 g	tomatoes, cut into quarters	3½ oz
½ l	sour cream	18 fl oz
2 dl	fresh dairy cream	7 fl oz
150 g	flour	5 oz
	dill	

Rice and goose liver timbale: 5 portions

600 g	salpicon of goose liver	1 lb 5 oz
150 g	salpicon of mushrooms	5 oz
300 g	rice	11 oz
150 g	lard	5 oz
50 g	onions, finely chopped	2 oz
20 g	salt	¾ oz
1 g	pepper, freshly ground	a pinch
5 g	marjoram	a teaspoon
200 g	peas, cooked	7 oz
	parsley	
100 g	Parmesan cheese, grated	3½ oz
2 dl	gravy	7 fl oz

Beat the cutlets to flatten, season with salt, flour them and brown in hot lard. Fry the onions until lightly coloured, sprinkle with paprika, add a little water and bring to the boil. Pour over the cutlets, add the peppers and tomatoes, cover and cook gently until tender. Blend together the sour and fresh cream and the flour. Pour over the cooked cutlets, add the dill and boil up. Transfer the cutlets to a serving dish and pour the sauce over. Serve with rice and goose liver timbale.

For the timbale, cook the rice, sauter the salpicons and onion in the lard and season with salt, pepper and marjoram. Carefully mix together the salpicons, rice, peas, Parmesan and gravy. If three or four persons only are to be served, fill the mixture into a pudding or savarin mould and turn out on the same dish as the cutlets. Alternatively, fill into small individual timbale moulds. If a larger number of guests are being served, hand separately in a large timbale mould.

(Zsolt Körmendy, Hungary)

Stuffed pork chops Hawaiian
Côtes de porc farcies à la hawaienne

6 portions

6 double pork chops, 2½ cm (1 in) thick

	6 tablespoons mushrooms, chopped	
	1 tablespoon onions, chopped	
	2 tablespoons fresh parsley, chopped	
	2 tablespoons fine dry breadcrumbs	
	1 teaspoon dried thyme leaves	
	1 egg, lightly beaten	
	¼ teaspoon salt	
	¼ teaspoon pepper	
40 g	flour	1½ oz
60 g	butter for chops	2 oz
	2 tablespoons butter for pineapple	
2 dl	dry white wine	7 fl oz
8 cl	pineapple juice	3 fl oz
⅛ l	brown sauce (demi-glace)	4 fl oz
	6 pineapple slices	

Preheat the oven to 190°C (375°F). Slit open a pocket next to the bone in each chop. Mix together the mushrooms, onions, parsley, breadcrumbs, thyme, egg, salt and pepper. Place 2 tablespoons of this filling in each pocket. Dip the chops in flour. Melt the 60 g (2 oz) butter in an ovenproof pan and slowly fry the chops on both sides until golden brown. Drain off half the butter and add the wine and the brown sauce. Cover and braise in the preheated oven for 30 minutes. Transfer the chops to a serving dish and keep hot. Add the pineapple juice to the pan and simmer over low heat for 20 minutes. Season to taste with salt and pepper. Melt the remaining 2 tablespoons butter in a second pan and lighly brown the pineapple slices. Place one on each chop and spoon the sauce over.

(Hermann Rusch, USA)

Pork cutlets San Fernando
Côtelettes de porc San Fernando
Schweinskoteletts San Fernando

4 portions

180 g	4 pork cutlets each weighing	6 oz
5 cl	olive oil	2 fl oz
6 cl	white wine	2 fl oz
	salt, pepper	
150 g	aubergines	5 oz

150 g	courgettes	5 oz
	2 tomatoes, skinned, seeded and cut into quarters	
100 g	mushrooms	3½ oz
	1 sweet pepper, seeded and diced	
100 g	onions, coarsely chopped	3½ oz
	12 stuffed olives, cut in half	
	3 cloves of garlic, crushed	
	1 teaspoon oregano	
	1 teaspoon basil	
	1 teaspoon parsley, chopped	

Sauce:

1¼ dl	yoghourt	4 fl oz
50 g	Parmesan, grated	2 oz
	2 egg yolks	

Trim the cutlets, scrape the bones clean and snip the edges lightly. Season with salt and pepper and fry in 2 cl (1 fl oz) olive oil on both sides for about 3 minutes. Transfer to a serving dish. Detach the pan juices with the white wine.

Peel the aubergines, wash the courgettes and dice. Brown the onions lightly in the rest of the olive oil. Add the aubergines, courgettes, tomatoes, mushrooms, sweet pepper, olives, garlic, basil and oregano. Season with salt and pepper, add the meat cooking juices and stew for about 5 minutes, then sprinkle with chopped parsley.

Mix the sauce ingredients together well. Cover the cutlets with the stewed vegetables, pour the sauce over and brown for about 15 minutes in a hot oven (220°C–430°F) or under a salamander.

(Franz Zodl, Austria)

Onion-smothered sliced liver

3–4 portions   Cooking time: 9½ minutes

750 g	pig's liver	1 lb 10 oz
	3 large onions	
2½ cl	oil	1 fl oz
3 g	salt	half a teaspoon

Sauce:

1½ cl	vinegar	½ fl oz

1 cl	soya sauce	½ fl oz
5 g	sugar	a teaspoon
1½ cl	meat stock	½ fl oz
1½ cl	rice wine or sherry	½ fl oz
	a pinch of pepper	

Cut the liver into thin 5 x 2 cm (2 x ¾ in) slice. Sprinkle with salt and rub with 4 ml (a teaspoon) oil. Slice the onions thinly. Heat three quarters of the oil in a frying pan. Add the sliced liver and spread the pieces evenly over the bottom of the pan. Fry over high heat for not more than 2 minutes, turning the slices a few times with a fish slice. Remove from the pan. Add the remaining oil and the onions and spread these over the bottom of the pan. Stir and turn them over high heat for 3 minutes. Add the sauce ingredients, stir and turn the onions in the sauce and cook over medium heat for 3 minutes. Turn the heat high and return the liver to the pan. Turn the liver in the bubbling sauce and mix with the onions, stirring and turning for no more than 1½ minutes. Serve very hot on a well warmed dish.
(Illustration, page 692)

(Kenneth Lo, China)

Ragoût of pig's liver Viennese style
Ragoût de foie de porc à la viennoise
Schweinelebertopf

8 portions

1 kg 200	pig's liver, diced	2 lb 10 oz
200 g	lard	7 oz
200 g	onions, finely cut	7 oz
½ l	stock or bouillon	18 fl oz
¼ l	red wine	9 fl oz
20 g	cornflour	¾ oz
	1 teaspoon marjoram	
	1 tablespoon paprika	
	4 pickled cucumbers in mustard sauce, diced	
	salt	

Fry the onions lightly in hot lard, add the liver and continue frying, season with salt, add the marjoram and paprika, then the stock or bouillon, and stew gently for about 10 minutes. Add the cucumbers and thicken with the cornflour which has been blended with the wine. Serve with mashed potatoes.

(Eduard Mayer, Austria)

Stuffed pig's stomach Alsatian fashion
Estomac de porc farci

About 10 portions

	1 pig's stomach		
750 g	neck of pork		1 lb 10 oz
approx. 400 g	pork fillet	approx.	14 oz
1 kg 500	potatoes, peeled and diced		3 lb 5 oz
100 g	butter		3½ oz
350 g	onions, coarsely chopped		12 oz
50 g	shallots, chopped		2 oz
	1 tablespoon parsley, chopped		
	1 teaspoon savory, chopped		
	2 eggs		
	salt, pepper		
	thyme, nutmeg		
	vinegar		

Wash the stomach thoroughly and soak for two days in salted water sharpened with vinegar. Turn inside out and scrape the inner wall well with a sharp knife, then wash again.

Blanch the potatoes. Cook the onions and shallots gently in butter until transparent and add the potatoes. Cook gently in the oven for 15 minutes without allowing the potatoes to colour or to break up.

Mince the neck of pork finely and mix with the fillet which has been cut into 5–6 mm (¼ in) cubes. Add the parsley, savory, eggs, salt, pepper, thyme and nutmeg and mix well. Lastly mix thoroughly with the potatoes, onions and shallots. Fill into the stomach and sew up. Prick the stomach a few times with a meat fork and place in a pan of water. Poach for 2½ hours at 80°C (175°F). When cooked, remove from the pan and allow to cool a little, then brown lightly in butter. Serve very hot and hand the gravy separately.

(Emil Wälti, France)

Stuffed pig's stomach with sauerkraut
Estomac de porc farci avec choucroute
Pfälzer Schweinemagen mit Sauerkraut

4 portions

	1 pig's stomach	
500 g	pork, chopped	1 lb 2 oz

2 onions, chopped
2 rolls, soaked and squeezed dry
3 eggs
parsley, chopped
salt, pepper
lemon zest
marjoram
potatoes, cooked
lard

Sauerkraut:

sauerkraut
onions
lard
sugar
juniper berries

Soak the stomach overnight and clean it very carefully. Prepare forcemeat with the pork, onions, rolls, eggs, parsley, potatoes, salt, pepper, lemon zest and marjoram. Fill into the stomach, sew up carefully, and poach slowly over low heat in lightly salted water. Remove, drain well, and brown all over in hot lard. Serve with sauerkraut which has been stewed in lard with onions, sugar and juniper berries.

(Otto Ledermann, Switzerland)

Chine of pork with broad beans
Echine de porc à la luxembourgeoise
Judd mat Gaardebounen

4 portions   Cooking time: 1–1¼ hours

800 g	smoked chine of pork	1 lb 12 oz
600 g	broad beans	1 lb 5 oz
50 g	butter	2 oz
50 g	flour	2 oz
75 g	smoked bacon	2½ oz
200 g	mirepoix	7 oz
75 g	onions	2½ oz
⅛ l	dairy cream	4 fl oz
	parsley, chopped	
	savory	
	pepper, freshly ground	
	bay leaf, cloves, marjoram	

Potatoes with diced bacon:

600 g	potatoes	1 lb 5 oz
75 g	fat bacon	2½ oz

If using chine of pork which was smoked some time previously and has become dry, soak it overnight in water. If freshly smoked, it may be used without soaking. Place the pork in a pan with the mirepoix, bay leaf, cloves, marjoram and pepper. Add sufficient water to cover well and cook for 1 to 1¼ hours.

Cook the broad beans in salted water with the addition of savory until soft. If using canned haricot beans instead, drain them carefully. Cut the smoked bacon into strips and chop the onions coarsely. Make a blond roux with the butter and flour, add the bacon and onions, and cook gently. Add the pork cooking liquid, together with savory leaves, and bring to the boil, then add the cream and parsley. Mix well and add the beans.

To serve, slice the pork and dress on a warmed dish. Serve with the beans and with potatoes which have been boiled and mixed with fried diced bacon.

(Germain Gretsch-Rösner, Luxembourg)

Braised pig's kidneys
Rognons de porc braisés
Vepřové ledvinky přírodní

6 portions   Cooking time: 4 minutes

900 g	pig's kidneys	2 lb
120 g	butter	4 oz
	2 onions, finely cut	
1 g	pepper	a pinch
	½ teaspoon ground caraways	
	salt	
	bouillon	

Cut the kidneys in half lengthwise, core them and remove the fat with a sharp knife, then wash well, dry and cut across into slices not more than 2 mm (¹/₁₀ in) thick. Cook the onions gently in the butter without colouring, add the caraways, pepper and kidneys, and fry quickly for 2 minutes, stirring from time to time. Do not fry longer than 2 minutes, or the kidneys will become tough and require more prolonged braising. Season with salt, add a little bouillon and braise briefly. Transfer the contents of the pan to a deep serving dish. A suitable accompaniment is well seasoned rice which has been cooked in bouillon.

(Vilèm Vrabec, Czechoslovakia)

Pig's kidneys and brains with marjoram
Rognons et cervelle de porc à la marjolaine
Schweineniere und Schweinshirn mit Majoran

8 portions

	8 pig's kidneys	
	4 pig's brains	
100 g	lard	3½ oz
100 g	onions, finely cut	3½ oz
	salt, pepper	
	1 teaspoon marjoram	

Cut the kidneys in half and core them. Soak for a short time in milk or in water containing a little vinegar. Remove, dry and slice thinly. Fry the onions in lard until lightly browned, then add the kidneys and fry quickly. Add the brains which have been skinned and chopped, and continue frying for a short time. Season with salt, pepper and marjoram, and serve very hot.

(Eduard Mayer, Austria)

Stuffed pig's ears
Oreilles de porc farcies
Gefüllte Schweinsohren

Cooking time: 2 hours

	2 pig's ears	

Forcemeat:

250 g	veal and pork	9 oz
50 g	bacon or pork fat	2 oz
	shallots	
	parsley	
	truffles	
	salt	
	nutmeg	
	pepper, freshly ground	
	2 eggs	
	dairy cream	
	bouillon	

Clean and wash the ears very thoroughly. Sew them together to make a pouch, leaving a small opening for stuffing.

Work the meat, bacon or pork fat, a little shallot, parsley and truffles together in the processor, season with salt, nutmeg and freshly ground pepper, and bind with the eggs and cream. Stuff the ears with this forcemeat and sew up the opening. Cook for about 2 hours in bouillon, remove and slice.

To serve, dress the slices on sauerkraut. Hand purée of peas or mashed potatoes separately.

(Otto Ledermann, Switzerland)

Pork paprikas with sauerkraut and sour cream
Ragoût de porc avec choucroute à la crème aigre
Paprikaš od Svinjskog Mesa sa Kiselim Kupusom

4 portions   Cooking time: about 1½ hours

1 kg	leg of pork	2 lb 4 oz
150 g	lard	5 oz
1 kg	sauerkraut, finely cut	2 lb 4 oz
¼ l	sour cream	9 fl oz
150 g	onions, finely chopped	5 oz
	pepper, freshly ground	
	salt	
30 g	paprika	1 oz

Fry 100 g (3½ oz) finely chopped onions in 75 g (2½ oz) lard without colouring. Add the sauerkraut and braise until soft, with the frequent addition of a little water.

Cut the meat into 2 cm (¾ in) cubes. Melt the rest of the lard in a second pan and gently fry the rest of the onions. Add the meat and cook for about 40 minutes, then add to the sauerkraut and mix well. Season with pepper and paprika, pour in a little water and add salt to taste. Cook for 20 minutes, adding half the sour cream towards the end of the cooking time. Remove from the heat and pour the rest of the sour cream over just before serving.

(László Csizmadia, Yugoslavia)

Brown sugar pork pudding

3–4 portions   Cooking time: 3 hours

1 kg 500	belly of pork	3 lb 5 oz
3 g	salt	half a teaspoon

½ g	black pepper	a pinch
2 cl	soya sauce	1 fl oz
5 ml	hoisin sauce	a teaspoon
	2 medium onions	
	4 cloves of garlic	
2 cl	rice wine or sherry	1 fl oz
20 g	brown sugar	¾ oz
1 cl	soya sauce	½ fl oz
500 g	sweet potatoes or yams	1 lb 2 oz

Cut the pork through the skin into lean and fat rectangular pieces about 4–5 cm (2 in) in length. Slice the onions thinly, then chop coarsely. Crush the garlic and chop finely. Add the onions and garlic to the pork, together with the salt, half the soya sauce, the hoisin sauce, the rice wine or sherry, and half the sugar. Work in with the fingers so that the pork is evenly seasoned. Marinate for 1 hour. Peel the sweet potatoes or yams and cut into 3 cm (1¼ in) wedges.

Line the bottom and sides of a basin with three quarters of the pork pieces, packing them in skin side down. Pack the yams or sweet potatoes into the well in the centre and place the remainder of the pork on top. Pour any residual marinade over and cover the top of the basin tightly with a lid or foil. Place the basin in a large saucepan one third full of boiling water. Return to the boil, then reduce to simmering point and simmer for 1½ hours, adding a little boiling water to the pan from time to time. Open the top, sprinkle with the rest of the sugar and soya sauce, close and simmer for a further 1½ hours.

To serve, turn out on to a deep dish. This is an interesting addition to the selection of dishes on a family dining table.

(Kenneth Lo, China)

Steamed pork pudding

3–4 portions   Cooking time: 2½–3 hours

1 kg 500	belly of pork	3 lb 5 oz
4 cl	soya sauce	1½ fl oz
2 cl	hoisin sauce	1 fl oz
	2 medium onions	
10 g	snow pickles (Chinese green pickles)	⅓ oz
150 g	turnips	5 oz
150 g	carrots	5 oz
10 g	lard	⅓ oz
1½ cl	sherry or red wine	½ fl oz
2 ml	chilli sauce	half a teaspoon
	3 medium yams or potatoes	

Cut the pork through the skin into large bite-size pieces. Cut the onions into thin slices, the yams or potatoes into 4–5 cm (2 in) wedges, and the carrots and turnips into pieces of similar size and shape. Blend together the soya, hoisin and chilli sauce and the sherry or wine, add to the pork and marinate for 1 hour.

Lard the bottom and sides of a large heatproof basin. Line with the pork pieces, placing those on the bottom skin side down and those round the sides skin side out. Add half the onions, then fill up first with the yams or potatoes, then with mixed turnips and carrots. Sprinkle the top with the rest of the onions and pour the residual marinade evenly over the contents. Seal the top of the basin with foil and place in a large saucepan one third full of water. Bring to the boil, cover with a lid, reduce the heat to simmering point, and simmer for 2½ to 3 hours, adding boiling water when required.

To serve, turn out on to a large deep dish and bring to the table. This is an inexpensive domestic dish useful for feeding a large family.

(Kenneth Lo, China)

Boiled lightly-pickled pork with kohlrabi
Côtes de porc aux choux-rave
Kokt lettsaltet Ribbeflesk

4 portions   Cooking time: 1 hour

1 kg	pork ribs, lightly pickled	2 lb 4 oz
	6 cloves	
	6 white peppercorns	
	1 onion	
	1 bay leaf	
	1 bunch parsley	

Wash the meat under running water, tie and place in a pan of cold water. Add the cloves, peppercorns, onion, bay leaf and parsley and bring to the boil, skimming well. Reduce the heat to simmering point and leave to stand over the heat for 1 hour. To serve, carve evenly, dress on a heated dish and serve with boiled kohlrabi.

(Hroar Dege, Günther Rett, Norway)

Red-cooked spare ribs

3–4 portions   Cooking time: 1¾ hours

| 1 kg 500 | pork spare ribs | 3 lb 5 oz |

3 cl	soya sauce	1 fl oz
5 ml	hoisin sauce	a teaspoon
	1 chicken stock cube	
5 cl	water or stock	2 fl oz
	2 medium onions	
	4 slices root ginger	
5 g	sugar	⅙ oz

Cut between the bones of the ribs to separate them. Slice the onions thinly and shred the ginger. Crumble the stock cube, add it to the water or stock, the soya sauce, hoisin sauce and sugar and mix well. Apply this marinade to the ribs and rub it in evenly.

Place the ribs in a casserole together with any residual marinade. Pour in stock to cover if necessary. Sprinkle the top with the ginger and onions. Cover and cook for 30 minutes in an oven preheated to 200°C (390°F). Reduce the temperature to 160°C (320°F) and simmer for 1 hour, turning the ribs every 20 minutes. Remove the lid, increase the temperature to 200°C (390°F) and return the ribs to the oven for 12 minutes to brown well. To serve, transfer to a well heated serving dish.

In Europe the ribs are eaten with the fingers. In China they are first chopped into 3 cm (1 in) lengths to be eaten with chopsticks. The meat is bitten off and the bone returned to the plate with the aid of the chopsticks.
(Illustration, page 693)

(Kenneth Lo, China)

Sweet and sour spare ribs

3–4 portions

This dish is a variation of **Red-cooked spare ribs** (recipe above). Proceed in the same manner, with the addition of sweet and sour sauce as described below.

3 cl	vinegar	1 fl oz
20 g	sugar	¾ oz
10 g	cornflour	⅓ oz
3 cl	water	1 fl oz
2 cl	orange juice	1 fl oz
5 ml	soya sauce	a teaspoon
2 cl	syrup from a can of pineapple	1 fl oz
	2 slices pineapple	
1 cl	oil for frying pineapple	½ fl oz

Cut each slice of pineapple into 8 wedges. Mix together all the other ingredients until well blended. Heat the pineapple by frying it in the oil, then add the sauce mixture and stir until the sauce thickens and becomes translucent. Pour the sauce evenly over the spare ribs on a serving dish.

This dish makes an attractive change from the other dishes, which are often dominated by the flavour of soya sauce.

(Kenneth Lo, China)

Ribs of pork with ginger
Côtes de porc au gingembre
Ribbestek uten svor

4 portions   Cooking time: 1½ hours

1 kg 500	ribs of pork, boned	3 lb 5 oz
	salt	
	pepper, freshly ground	
	1 teaspoon ground ginger	

Carefully mix the salt, pepper and ginger. Rub well into the meat and roll up with the fat outside. Tie with twine. Roast for 1½ hours in an oven preheated to 175°C (350°F) without adding fat, turning several times.

Carve and dress the meat on a warmed dish. Pour the gravy over. Serve with boiled potatoes and with red cabbage mixed with a little gravy and blackcurrant juice. This is a traditional Norwegian Christmas dish.

(Hroar Dege, Günther Rett, Norway)

Christmas pork
Côtes de porc de Noël
Jule-ribbe

6–8 portions   Cooking time: 1¼ hours

2 kg	ribs of pork		4 lb 8 oz
	2 teaspoons salt		
	1 teaspoon pepper, freshly ground		
	1 teaspoon caraway		
approx. 1 l	boiling water	approx.	1¾ pt

Saw or chop through the ribs at intervals of about 5 cm (2 in). Score the skin with a sharp knife. Rub with salt, pepper and caraway. Place in a roasting pan skin side down and roast in an oven preheated to 275°C (525°F). When well browned, pour a little boiling water into the pan. Halfway through the cooking time turn the meat and, if necessary, gradually add boiling water. Open the oven slightly for the last 10 minutes to make the crackling very crisp. This is a popular Christmas dish.

(Otto Ramsbacher, Norway)

Best end of pork in white wine
Carré de porc au vin blanc

10 portions

2 kg	best end of pork	4 lb 8 oz
500 g	mirepoix of carrots, celeriac, leeks, onions, parsley	1 lb 2 oz
1 l	dry white wine	1¾ pt
1 l	brown veal stock	1¾ pt
100 g	lard	3½ oz
	parsley, chopped	
	cornflour	
	salt	
	pepper, freshly ground	
	cloves	
	bay leaf, sage, thyme, marjoram	

Tie the pork to shape. Place in a roasting pan, add the mirepoix and fry in lard until golden. Add the seasonings and the wine, cover and cook for about 35 minutes in an oven preheated to 190–200°C (375–390°F). Remove and carve the meat. Strain the sauce and bind with a little cornflour.

Dress the slices of meat on a heated dish and pour the sauce over. Serve with Boulangère potatoes and fresh vegetables or mixed salad in a spicy dressing or braised red cabbage.

(Germain Gretsch-Rösner, Luxembourg)

Medallions of Prague ham spring style
Médaillons de jambon de Prague à la printanière
Prager Schinken auf Blätterteigböden auf Frühlingsart

3 portions

6 round slices Prague ham
8 cm (3½ in) across

	6 puff pastry rounds	
	8 cm (3½ in) across	
120 g	fresh mushrooms, finely chopped	4 oz
	1 tablespoon shallots, chopped	
120 g	Prague ham trimmings, finely chopped	4 oz
	1 tablespoon tomato purée	
	1 tablespoon parsley, chopped	
	salt	
	pepper, freshly ground	
	thyme	
	1 tablespoon thickened demi-glace sauce	
100 g	spinach, freshly cooked	3½ oz
100 g	asparagus tips, cooked	3½ oz
100 g	cauliflower florets, cooked	3½ oz
	6 tablespoons Parmesan cheese, grated	

Mornay sauce:

15 g	butter	½ oz
25 g	flour	1 oz
¼ l	boiling milk	9 fl oz
	1 egg yolk	
35 g	cheese	1¼ oz

Prepare a duxelles by cooking the shallots gently in butter, adding the mushrooms to colour lightly, then adding the trimmings from the slices of ham, the tomato purée, salt, pepper and a little thyme. Cook gently over low heat for 5 minutes, then mix with the parsley and the demi-glace sauce.

Warm the rounds of puff pastry, spread with the duxelles and place in a fireproof dish. Cover each one with a slice of ham. Garnish two of them with a ball of spinach the size of a pigeon egg, two others with asparagus tips, and the remaining two with cauliflower florets. Coat the vegetables with Mornay sauce very carefully, making sure not to cover the surrounding ham. Sprinkle with Parmesan and melted butter, and brown in a preheated oven. Serve with green salad.

To make Mornay sauce, prepare a roux with the butter and flour, blend in the boiling milk until smooth and bring to the boil. Stir in the cheese, remove from the heat and bind with the egg yolk.

(Otto Brust, Germany)

Ham en croûte
Jambon en croûte
Kenyérben sült sonka

10–12 portions   Cooking time: about 2 hours

3–4 kg	1 small smoked ham weighing	6½– 8¾ lb
2 kg	flour	4 lb 8 oz
25 g	yeast	1 oz
40 g	salt	1½ oz
	water	
500 g	potatoes, cooked and grated (optional)	1 lb 2 oz

Boil the ham on the bone with the skin and leave until cold.

Begin preparing the dough on the day before it is required. Sieve the flour and leave in a warm place in a wooden bowl. Disperse the yeast in a little water and leave to ferment on the flour overnight. If potatoes are used, they should be mixed with the flour. Next day add salt and sufficient water to make a pliable dough. After kneading, the dough should not stick to the fingers. Pin out the dough and wrap round the ham, which should be well chilled. (See Techniques, page 100)

Place the ham in a straw basket lined with a floured cloth, cover and prove in a warm place for 2 to 3 hours. Transfer to a baking sheet and place in a preheated oven. Bake for about 2 hours, or until crisp. Allow to dry for a short time after removing from the oven. Cut off the top of the crust to facilitate removal of the ham. Bone it carefully and carve, then replace the slices on the bone, return to the crust and replace the top crust. Serve with a liberal amount of grated horseradish.

(László Csizmadia, Hungary)

Sailors' ham
Matros Skinke

4 portions

2 kg	smoked, lightly salted knuckle of pork	4 lb 8 oz
1 kg	beetroots	2 lb 4 oz
	2 large onions	
	1 tablespoon caraway seeds	
	2 tablespoons sugar	
	1 tablespoon horseradish, grated	
	salt	
	6 cloves	
	2 bay leaves	
	vinegar	

Bone the pork, place in a pan, add water to cover, together with the onions, bay leaves and cloves, and cook until tender. Wash the beetroots and cook in salted water with the addition of the caraway seeds until soft. Grate them coarsely, add vinegar, the horseradish and a little salt, and leave until cold. Carve the meat and dress on a warmed dish. Serve with cold beetroot, boiled potatoes and purée of peas.

(Hroar Dege, Günther Rett, Norway)

Pickled leg of pork with cider vinegar sauce
Jambon braisé au vinaigre de cidre

20–30 portions

6 kg	fresh leg of pork	13 lb 4 oz
	10 apples	
1 l	cider	1¾ pt
2 dl	cider vinegar	7 fl oz
100 g	sugar	3½ oz
200 g	butter	7 oz
5 l	pickling brine	9 pt
	20 peppercorns, crushed	
	bouquet garni of leek, celery, shallot, onion, bay leaf, thyme, garlic	
	salt	

Leave the leg in the brine for 24 hours, then rinse under running water and blanch in boiling water. Place in a large pan of water with the addition of salt, the peppercorns and the flavouring herbs and vegetables. Cook for about 2 hours, skimming well, then drain. Reduce the cooking liquid well and add the cider. Roast the joint until golden brown in a little butter at 220°C (430°F), seasoning with salt if necessary. Test with a needle or skewer to determine when the meat is sufficiently cooked. Cover with the apples which have been peeled and thinly sliced, dust lightly with sugar and allow to caramelise in the oven.

Remove the joint. Detach the pan juices with the vinegar and add to the cooking liquid/cider mixture. Reduce a little, pass through a conical strainer and finish with butter.
(Illustration, page 312)

(Roger Souvereyns, Belgium)

Easter ham
Jambon de Pâques

Cooking time: 6½ hours

5 kg 500	1 country style ham weighing	12 lb
	water	
85 g	brown sugar	3 oz
	10 pineapple rings	
	10 prunes, stoned	

225 g	pine kernels	8 oz
2 dl	port	7 fl oz

Cover the ham with water in a roasting pan. Bake under cover for 6 hours in an oven preheated to 165°C (325°F). Drain off the water and rub the ham with brown sugar. Return to the oven until the sugar melts (a few minutes). Decorate with the pineapple and prunes fixed in place with toothpicks. Crush the pine kernels and mix with brown sugar. Sprinkle on the fruit. Sprinkle the port over the top and continue baking for 30 minutes. If a fully cooked (bone-in) ham is used, omit the water and bake uncovered for 4 hours.

(Hermann Rusch, USA)

Christmas ham Norwegian style
Jambon de Noël Larvik
Juleskinke fra Larvik

8 portions

2 kg 500–3 kg	lightly salted ham (raw)	5½–6½ lb

Paste:

1 kg 200	rye flour	2 lb 10 oz
4 dl	water	14 fl oz
	1 tablespoon ground ginger	
	2 tablespoons cloves, coarsely chopped	
	2 teaspoons basil	
	2 teaspoons rosemary	
	4 bay leaves	

Sauce:

	gravy	
	4 cloves	
	1 teaspoon ground ginger	
	Madeira	

Prepare a firm paste with the rye flour and water. Carefully remove the skin from the ham and cut away surplus fat. Rub the ham vigorously with the herbs and spices, wrap in the paste, place on the ham skin and bake for 2 hours in a preheated oven. The internal temperature of the ham while baking should be measured with a thermometer, which should give a reading of 77°C (170°F). Before serving, cut a hole in the paste so that the ham, baked to a golden colour, may be seen. Serve with sauerkraut, boiled potatoes with stewed apples and prunes, and the sauce, which should be well seasoned.

To make the sauce, remove the ham cooking juices from the paste, add the cloves and ginger, reduce, flavour with a little Madeira, and strain.

Aluminium foil may be used instead of flour and water paste, but the paste greatly improves the flavour. Christmas ham may be served hot or cold.

(Hroar Dege, Günther Rett, Norway)

Ham steak with walnut sauce
Steak de jambon avec sauce aux noix
Schinkensteak an Nuss-Sauce

4 portions

120 g	4 ham steaks each weighing	4 oz
	1 tablespoon butter	
	1 tablespoon flour	
80 g	sultanas, washed	3 oz
60 g	walnut pieces	2 oz
50 g	sugar	2 oz
2 dl	cider	7 fl oz
	1 tablespoon Calvados	
	1 teaspoon lemon juice	
	2 cloves	
	salt, pepper	

The ham steaks should be cut about 10–12 mm (½ in) thick. Arrange them one overlapping another in a buttered fireproof dish. Melt the remaining butter in a small pan, sprinkle in the flour and cook gently for a moment. Add the sugar, walnut pieces and sultanas, and brown lightly. Stir in the cider, add pepper, a little salt and the cloves, and cook gently for 5 minutes. Flavour with the Calvados and lemon juice, pour over the ham steaks and brown lightly for 15 minutes in a medium oven (170°C–340°F).

(Emil Wälti, Switzerland)

Escalopes of pork Coxydoise
Escalopes de porc à la coxydoise

4 portions

600 g	boneless pork (top of leg)	1 lb 5 oz

Forcemeat:

	5 eggs, beaten	
	5 shallots	
	2 cloves of garlic, peeled	
	1 tablespoon parsley, chopped	
300 g	fresh breadcrumbs	11 oz

150 g	butter	5 oz

Garnish:

	8 tomatoes (medium)	
700 g	mushrooms	1 lb 8 oz
	2 cloves of garlic, crushed	
	8 mushroom caps, turned and grooved	
1 kg	spinach, blanched	2 lb 4 oz

Sauce:

	2 shallots, finely chopped	
3 dl	white wine	10 fl oz
	2 tablespoons Dijon mustard	
3 dl	dairy cream	10 fl oz

Cut the pork evenly into 8 escalopes and beat until very thin. To make the forcemeat, chop the shallots and garlic very finely and mix with the parsley and eggs. Add the breadcrumbs, mix thoroughly and season. Place in the centre of half the escalopes, cover with the other half and tie securely to enclose the forcemeat. Fry in butter.

Hollow out the tomatoes and stuff with mushroom duxelles flavoured with garlic. Cook in the oven. Decorate each one with a mushroom cap. To make the sauce, cook the shallots lightly in the pan in which the escalopes were fried, detach the sediment with the wine, add the mustard and cream, and pass through a conical strainer.

Squeeze the spinach dry after blanching, cook in butter and pack into 8 small buttered timbale moulds. Turn out to serve. Garnish the escalopes with the tomatoes and spinach, and coat with the sauce.

(André Béghin, Belgium)

Escalopes of pork Kalman Mikszath
Escalopes de porc Kalman Mikszath
Sertészelet Kálmán Mikszáthl módra

(Kalman Mikszath was a famous Hungarian writer and gourmet.)

10 portions   Cooking time: 30 minutes

	10 escalopes of pork (cut from leg)	
160 g	each weighing	6 oz
80 g	OR 20 escalopes of pork each weighing	3 oz
200 g	lard	7 oz
OR 2 dl	oil	7 fl oz
100 g	flour	3½ oz
50 g	salt	2 oz

10 g	paprika	⅓ oz
150 g	onions, finely cut	5 oz
4 dl	sour cream	14 fl oz
200 g	green peppers, seeded and cut into strips	7 oz
200 g	tomatoes, cut into wedges	7 oz

Pancakes:

400 g	flour	14 oz
	4 egg yolks	
3 dl	milk	10 fl oz
OR 3 dl	dairy cream	10 fl oz
3 dl	soda water	10 fl oz
30 g	salt	1 oz
1 g	black pepper, freshly ground	a pinch
400 g	mushrooms, cut into fine julienne strips	14 oz
	½ bunch parsley, finely chopped	
200 g	lard	7 oz
OR 2 dl	oil	7 fl oz

Garnish:

	5 eggs, hard-boiled	
150 g	yellow peppers, seeded and cut into rings	5 oz
150 g	tomatoes, sliced	5 oz

Beat the escalopes lightly, season with salt, dust with a little flour, sauter in a little lard or oil until half cooked and remove. Add the onions to the pan and fry until lightly coloured. Sprinkle with paprika, pour in a little water and cook for a few seconds only. Add the escalopes, together with the tomatoes and peppers, and finish cooking over low heat. Transfer the meat to a fireproof dish. Blend the sour cream with the flour, add the meat stock, bring to the boil and strain.

To serve, pour the hot sauce over the meat. Cover with the pancakes and the hard-boiled eggs which have been sliced. Decorate with sliced tomatoes and pepper rings if desired. Finish off with a light sprinkling of sour cream.

To make the pancakes, prepare a batter with the milk (or cream which gives a finer flavour), flour, egg yolks and soda water and beat well. Season with salt and pepper. Sauter the mushrooms and parsley lightly in a little lard or oil and mix with the batter. Make 3–4 mm (about ⅛ in) thick pancakes in the usual manner, then cut them into noodles 1 cm (⅜ in) wide.

(Zsolt Körmendy, Hungary)

Escalope of pork Château de Gruyères
Escalope de porc Château de Gruyères
Schweineschnitzel Schloss Greyerz

10 portions

100 g	10 escalopes of pork each weighing	3½ oz
	salt	
	spices as desired	
50 g	flour	2 oz
100 g	butter or lard	3½ oz
OR 1 dl	oil	3½ fl oz

Mushroom ragoût:

500 g	woodland mushrooms in season	1 lb 2 oz
	OR canned chanterelles	
50 g	butter	2 oz
30 g	shallots, chopped	1 oz
2 dl	thickened with veal stock	7 fl oz
	salt	
	spices as desired	
	parsley, chopped	

Leeks in bacon:

1 kg 300	leeks (white)	3 lb
	bacon rinds	
2 dl	light stock	7 fl oz
	white mirepoix	
	salt	
	spices as desired	
250 g	bacon rashers	9 oz

Rissoles Château de Gruyères: recipe, page 299

Season and flour the escalopes. Fry gently until golden. To serve, dress on a heated dish and cover each one with about 50 g (2 oz) mushroom ragoût, prepared with the above ingredients. Cut the leeks into 8 cm (3½ in) lengths. Stew in the stock with the bacon rinds, mirepoix and seasonings. Remove and wrap in the bacon rashers. Prepare the rissoles and serve very hot.

(Otto Ledermann, Switzerland)

Escalope of pork with cabbage
Escalope de porc aux choux
Amagerkotelet

4 portions   Cooking time: about 35 minutes

180 g	4 slices neck of pork each weighing	6 oz
500 g	savoy or white cabbage,	1 lb 2 oz
	cleaned and blanched	
100 g	fresh butter	3½ oz
15 g	white peppercorns, freshly ground	½ oz

	salt	
	monosodium glutamate	
400 g	potatoes	14 oz
50 g	fine rye flour	2 oz
	1 carrot	
	½ celeriac	
	2 leeks	
	1 onion	
1 l	white veal stock	1¾ pt

Coat the pork with the rye flour and brown on both sides in fresh butter. Season with a little salt and monosodium glutamate. Line the bottom of a fireproof dish with a few of the cabbage leaves. Cover with a layer of potatoes which have been sliced 5 mm (¼ in) thick. Arrange the escalopes of pork on top side by side. Cover with another layer of cabbage leaves, then with more potato slices and finally with cabbage leaves. Season with the pepper, add the carrot, celeriac, leeks and onion, together with the veal stock, and cover with a lid or foil. Braise for 15 minutes in an oven preheated to 225°C (435°F). Uncover and leave in the oven for a further 20 minutes, or until the top is lightly browned.

(Karl-Otto Schmidt, Denmark)

Smoked belly of pork with white cabbage
Lard de poitrine fumé aux choux blancs
Fläsk med Brunkål

5 portions   Cooking time: 1¾ hours

1 kg 500	smoked belly of pork	3 lb 5 oz
2 kg	white cabbage, finely cut	4 lb 8 oz
	2 carrots, finely cut	
	½ celeriac, finely cut	
	1 large onion	
	2 cloves	
1 l	water	1¾ pt
75 g	lard	2½ oz
25 g	sugar	1 oz
	salt	
	pepper, freshly ground	
500 g	potatoes	1 lb 2 oz
	mustard	
	brown bread	

Melt the lard in a large pan. Add the sugar and cook to the caramel degree. Add the cabbage, the onion stuck with the cloves, the carrots and celeriac while stirring, then pour in the water. Add the pork and press well down into the vegetables. Season with salt and pepper, cover and

◄ Stuffed shoulder of pork autumn style, p. 388
▼◄ Stuffed saddle of lamb modern style, p. 378

869

Best end of pork with fig stuffing, p. 830 ▲►
Galantine of sucking pig Noblesse, p. 390 ▼

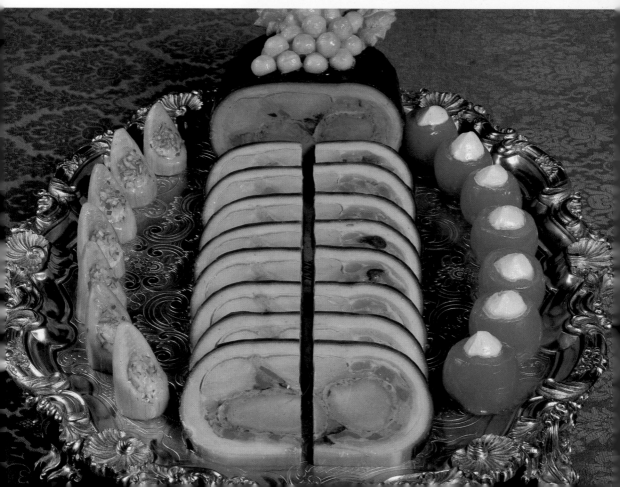

◄ Veal cutlets Denise, p. 565
▼▼ Sweetbread and kidney pie with saffron sauce, p. 265
▼ Belly of pork Pongau style, p. 816

870

Veal and kidney roast, p. 591 ►
Lamb fillets in herb forcemeat, p. 741 ►▼

'3

◄ Pork medallions in bacon, p. 897
▼▼ Savoury veal roll (Adolf Meindl)
▼ Stuffed best end of pork, p. 834

874

cook gently for 1¾ hours, then remove the meat and slice. Transfer the vegetables to a serving dish, arrange the slices of pork on top and surround with boiled potatoes. Serve with brown bread and mustard.

(Eric Cederholm, Denmark)

Pork steak Engadine style
Steak de porc à l'engadinoise
Schweinesteak auf Engadiner Art

10 portions

150 g	10 pork steaks each weighing	5 oz
	oil	
	spices as desired	
	salt	
¾ l	cream sauce	1¼ pt
50 g	red pepper	2 oz

Accompaniment: pizokels (speciality from Grisons)

2 kg	spätzle dough	4 lb 8 oz
1 kg	potatoes (raw), grated	2 lb 4 oz
300 g	streaky bacon, cut into strips	11 oz
	butter	
	spices as desired	
	salt	

Garnish:

1 kg 500	quinces	3 lb 5 oz
100 g	sugar	3½ oz
50 g	honey	2 oz
	lemon zest	
2 kg	Brussels sprouts	4 lb 8 oz
100 g	butter	3½ oz
50 g	shallots, finely chopped	2 oz

Season the steaks and fry on both sides in hot oil until medium done. Coat with cream sauce and sprinkle with the red pepper.

To make pizokels, season the spätzle dough and the potatoes well and mix together carefully. Prepare coarse spätzle and poach in salted water, then drain and toss in hot butter. Garnish with strips of crisply fried bacon.

Slice the quinces, stew them with the sugar, mix with the honey and lemon zest, and use as a garnish together with the sprouts.

(Otto Ledermann, Switzerland)

Pork steak with olives
Steaks de porc aux olives
Bistecche di maiale con olive

6 portions

1 kg	boneless loin of pork, trimmed	2 lb 4 oz
500 g	peeled tomatoes, canned	1 lb 2 oz
OR 800 g	fresh tomatoes	1 lb 12 oz
	20 black olives, stoned if possible	
	20 green olives, stoned if possible	
	½ teaspoon fennel seeds	
	2 cloves of garlic	
¼ l	olive oil	9 fl oz
	bouillon as required	
	salt, pepper	

Cut the pork into 6 slices. Fry the cloves of garlic in oil until lightly coloured, add the meat, fry on both sides until browned, add the fennel seeds and season with salt and pepper. Crush the tomatoes and add, together with a little bouillon if necessary. Add the olives and braise over low heat for about 20 minutes, turning the meat from time to time. Serve with mashed potatoes.

(Mario De Filippis, Italy)

Pork and beans Austrian style
Cassoulet à l'autrichienne
Schweineschulter mit Bohnen

4 portions

600 g	lean shoulder of pork (with skin if possible)	1 lb 5 oz
6 cl	oil	2 fl oz
250 g	haricot beans, soaked overnight and drained	9 oz
	1 tablespoon tomato purée	
	OR 1 fresh tomato, diced	
	bouquet garni of bay leaf, thyme, peppercorns, allspice, savory	
	salt	
	1 small teaspoon paprika	

	1 small teaspoon caraway	
	3 cloves of garlic	
	1 onion, finely chopped	
	1 teaspoon flour	
1¼ dl	white wine	4 fl oz
approx. 1 l	water	approx. 1¾ pt
150 g	carrots	5 oz
150 g	fresh young onions	5 oz
	4 mushrooms	
	parsley, chopped	

Remove the skin from the pork just before it is required. Cut the meat into fairly small cubes. Season with salt, paprika, caraway and garlic, then mix with the chopped onion and the flour. Heat the oil in a frying pan and brown the meat quickly. Transfer to a fireproof dish and mix with the tomato purée or fresh tomato and with the beans. Detach the pan juices with the wine and pour over the meat. Add the water and bring to the boil on the stove. Add the bouquet garni and cook slowly in the oven under cover for 1½ to 2 hours.

Meanwhile scrape the carrots and cut them into strips. Peel the young onions and quarter the mushrooms. Brown all these together in oil, then add salt and parsley. Transfer to the fireproof dish containing the meat and beans towards the end of the cooking time, and finish cooking. Serve in a deep serving dish.

(Ernst Faseth, Austria)

Tyrolean sliced pork
Emincé de porc rôti à la tyrolienne
Tiroler Röstfleisch

8 portions

800 g	shoulder of pork, very thinly sliced	1 lb 12 oz
60 g	lard for frying meat and onions	2 oz
80 g	onions, finely cut	3 oz
	salt, pepper	
	a little bouillon or water	
2 kg	potatoes	4 lb 8 oz
80 g	lard for potatoes	3 oz
	salt, marjoram	

Fry the onions in hot lard until golden, add the meat, season with salt and pepper, moisten with a little bouillon or water, and cook gently until tender. Boil the potatoes in their skins, then remove the skins and slice them. Brown in lard and season with salt. Add the meat and flavour with marjoram to serve. (Beef or the remains of a joint may be used instead of pork.)

(Eduard Mayer, Austria)

Csechochbili
Porc en daube à la russe

10 portions   Cooking time: about 1 hour

1 kg 600	shoulder of pork, boned	3 lb 8 oz
300 g	lard	11 oz
OR 3 dl	oil	10 fl oz
200 g	onions, freshly cut	7 oz
100 g	tomato purée	3½ oz
250 g	fresh tomatoes, skinned and cut into wedges	9 oz
10 g	garlic, crushed	⅓ oz
40 g	salt	1½ oz
3 g	black pepper, freshly ground	half a teaspoon
	1 bay leaf	
	1 lemon	
50 g	flour	2 oz
	1 bunch celery leaves	
2 dl	white wine	7 fl oz
	bone stock	

Curd cheese szirnyki:

1 kg	curd cheese	2 lb 4 oz
1 kg	potatoes	2 lb 4 oz
200 g	lard	7 oz
OR 2 dl	oil	7 fl oz
200 g	flour	7 oz
	3 eggs	
40 g	salt	1½ oz

Cut the meat into 2½ cm (1 in) cubes. Wash well, drain and dry with a cloth. Flour lightly and season with salt and pepper. Brown the meat in a little lard or oil in a sauté pan, then transfer to a stew pan, pour in sufficient bone stock to cover and stew under cover. Brown the onions and tomato purée for a few minutes. Add to the meat, together with the garlic, bay leaf and a little lemon zest. Season with salt and pepper if necessary, mix well and continue stewing. Shortly before the meat is cooked, add the celery leaves, finely chopped, together with the tomatoes and wine. Sharpen with lemon juice.

To serve, transfer the contents of the pan to a fireproof dish. Decorate with tomato wedges and sprinkle with finely chopped celery leaves. Garnish with curd cheese szirnyki.

To make the szirnyki, boil the potatoes in their skins, then skin them, cut into small pieces, mix with the curd cheese and sieve. Mix with the eggs and flour, season with salt and knead well. Pin out on a floured board to the thickness of one finger, cut into ovals, flour them and fry on both sides in a little hot lard until well browned. If desired, the mixture may be flavoured with a little chopped dill.

Szirnyki with sour cream may be served on their own as a separate dish. Csechochbili may be made with chicken intead of pork. The remaining ingredients and method are the same.

(Zsolt Körmendy, Russia)

Goulash gipsy style
Goulash tzigane
Szegediner Gulyas (Zigeunergulasch)

10 portions

1 kg 500	boneless shoulder of pork	3 lb 5 oz
500 g	onions, finely chopped	1 lb 2 oz
50 g	lard	2 oz
OR 5 cl	oil	2 fl oz
	1 tablespoon noble-sweet paprika	
	1 tablespoon caraway	
	salt	
	3 large potatoes, peeled	
1 kg	sauerkraut	2 lb 4 oz
¼ l	sour cream	9 fl oz

Fry the onions in lard or oil until lightly browned, add the paprika and at once stir in a little water. Add the meat which has been diced and seasoned with salt, together with the sauerkraut and caraway. Stew until almost tender. Thicken with the potatoes which have been finely grated and finish cooking. Serve with boiled potatoes.

(Eduard Mayer, Austria)

Sauerkraut garnished Alsatian fashion
Choucroute garnie à l'alsacienne

5 or more portions

800 g	pickled loin of pork	1 lb 12 oz
400 g	smoked belly of pork	14 oz
	5 Strasbourg sausages	
	5 liver quenelles (recipe, page 135)	
600 g	smoked shoulder of pork	1 lb 5 oz
	1 pickled knuckle of pork	
1 kg 500	sauerkraut	3 lb 5 oz

100 g	goose fat (or lard if not available)	3½ oz
100 g	onions, sliced	3½ oz
	bouquet garni of	
	2 cloves	
	2 cloves of garlic	
	1 bay leaf	
	4 juniper berries	
2 dl	white wine	7 fl oz
1 kg	potatoes, peeled	2 lb 4 oz
	salt, pepper	

First wash the sauerkraut in cold water, then in hot, and squeeze dry. Cook the onions gently in the lard or goose fat until transparent, add the sauerkraut and mix well with the aid of two forks. Add the wine and sufficient water to cover the sauerkraut halfway. Add the bouquet garni, season with salt and pepper, and cover the pan with greaseproof paper. Cover tightly with a lid and cook for 1 hour. Mix again, add the loin and belly of pork, and continue cooking over low heat for about 2 to 2½ hours. Add the shoulder of pork about 45 minutes before the end of the cooking time; 15 minutes later, place the potatoes on the sauerkraut, and finish cooking.

Remove the bouquet garni. Remove the potatoes and meat and keep hot. Stir the sauerkraut well to disperse the fat evenly through it and transfer to a serving dish, keeping it very hot. Carve the meat and place on the sauerkraut, together with the knuckle of pork which has been cooked separately and the quenelles and sausages which have been heated. Surround with the potatoes.

(Emil Wälti, France)

Hungarian pork platter
Charcutailles Csarda
Hazi sült kolbasz

10 portions

	4 portions liver sausage (recipe, page 885)	
	4 portions black pudding (recipe, page 883)	
	3 portions frying sausage (recipe, page 883)	
100 g	10 pork chops each weighing	3½ oz
150 g	lard	5 oz
	5 portions braised white cabbage (recipe, page 1015)	
	5 portions fried potatoes with onions (recipe, page 1021)	

Cook the liver sausage, black pudding and frying sausage separately. Flatten the chops a little, season them and sauter in lard. To serve, place the potatoes in the centre of a warmed flat dish to form a base for the meat and sausage. Slice the sausage and arrange neatly on top, together with the chops. Surround the potatoes with the cabbage.

If preferred, the potatoes and cabbage may be replaced by cabbage strudel (recipe, page 272). Leave the strudel to rest for 5 to 10 minutes after removing from the oven, then slice evenly at a slight angle. Arrange the slices on a dish with the sliced sausage and the chops.

(Zsolt Körmendy, Hungary)

Barbecued pork vinegrower style
Porc sauté à la vigneronne
Vinogradski Ćevap

6 portions   Cooking time: about 10 minutes

1 kg	leg of pork, boned	2 lb 4 oz
500 g	onions	1 lb 2 oz
	salt	
	pepper, freshly ground	
	oil	

Cut the meat into slices 2 cm (¾ in) thick and 5 cm (2 in) square. Slice the onions, place in a saucepan with the meat and shake the pan to mix well. Set aside for 2 to 3 hours.

Take out the pieces of meat one by one, remove any pieces of onion adhering to them, brush with oil, impale on a skewer and cook over a glowing fire. To test whether the meat is sufficiently cooked, prick with a fork; the escaping juice should be colourless.

When cooked, return the meat to the pan of onions, mix, cover with a lid and shake thoroughly.

(László Csizmadia, Yugoslavia)

Sucking pig with curd cheese
Cochon de lait au sérac
Falsomagro di porchetta di latte

6 portions

1 kg	belly of sucking pig (with skin)	2 lb 4 oz
400 g	veal	14 oz
	3 eggs, hard-boiled and cut in half lengthwise	
	2 eggs (raw)	
	2 tablespoons dry breadcrumbs	

150 g	fresh curd cheese	5 oz
	5 slices cooked ham	
	3 button onions, finely chopped and	
	lightly fried	
	2 tablespoons mint, chopped	
	2 tablespoons parsley, chopped	
	10 pistachio nuts	
50 g	Parmesan, grated	2 oz
1 dl	white wine	3½ fl oz
	salt, pepper	
	1 onion, chopped	
1 kg	peeled tomatoes, canned	2 lb 4 oz
OR 250 g	tomato purée	9 oz
	water as required	

Singe the belly of sucking pig and the skin, then wash in hot water and scrape the skin with a knife to clean it. Rinse under cold running water. Mince the veal, using the finest cutter, mix well with the Parmesan, breadcrumbs, mint and raw eggs, and season with salt and pepper. Spread on to the underside of the meat and cover with the hard-boiled eggs, the ham, button onions, pistachio nuts and curd cheese. Roll up carefully and tie securely. Prick the skin with a thick needle. Brown the meat in a little fat, detach the sediment with the wine, add the chopped onion and the parsley, then the canned tomatoes with their juice or the tomato purée and as much water as required. Cook over low heat for at least 2 hours, turning the meat roll several times and adding water if any of the stock boils away. When cooked, slice the meat and coat with stock.

(Salvatore Schifano, Italy)

Black pudding
Boudin noir
Bloedworst

Cooking time: 2 hours

1 l	pig's blood	1¾ pt
500 g	pork fat or fat bacon	1 lb 2 oz
500 g	rye flour	1 lb 2 oz
30 g	salt	1 oz
3 g	pepper, freshly ground	half a teaspoon
	cloves	
	herbs, chopped	

Dice the pork fat or bacon finely and blanch. Pass the blood through a fine strainer and mix thoroughly with the flour, pork fat or bacon, salt, pepper, cloves and herbs. Fill into pig's intestines which have been thoroughly cleaned, but do not pack tightly. Poach for 2 hours.

(Bernard van Beurten, Netherlands)

Fried black pudding with apples
Boudin noir sauté aux pommes
Gebakken bloedworst met appel

Cut the black pudding into slices 1 cm (⅜ in) thick, flour them and fry slowly in butter. Cut the apples into slices of the same thickness, fry in butter and place on the slices of black pudding. Serve with mashed potatoes and braised red cabbage.

(Bernard van Beurten, Netherlands)

Hungarian frying sausage
Saucisse à rôtir hongroise
Hazi vegyes disznotoros

10 portions   Cooking time of finished sausage: 15 to 20 minutes

1 kg 800	pork (neck, shoulder, belly or other trimmings)	4 lb
40 g	salt	1½ oz
20 g	red paprika	¾ oz
10 g	white pepper, freshly ground	⅓ oz
20 g	garlic	¾ oz
1 g	ground cloves	a pinch
3 m	pig's small intestines	3½ yd
	lard	

Trim the meat, removing any sinew or skin, and cut into pieces, then mince, using the medium cutter. Grate the garlic and soak in tepid water.

Place the meat in a bowl and season with salt, pepper, cloves and red paprika. Pour off the water in which the garlic has been soaked, squeeze out the garlic juice and add to the meat, then mix carefully. Soak the intestines (whether salted or fresh) in tepid water, changing the water several times, and wash thoroughly. Leave in water for 1 to 2 hours, or until they are to be filled, first rinsing inside several times.

Fill the sausage mixture into the prepared intestines, but do not pack too tightly, or the sausages will be liable to burst while cooking. Indent the filled casing with the hand at intervals of 25–30 cm (10–12 in) and twist 2 or 3 times at each indentation to divide up evenly. Tie a knot in the casing at each end to keep the filling in place. Rinse well in clean water and drain. Hang up in the refrigerator to stiffen and dry a little.

To prepare for cooking and serving, prick at intervals of 4–5 cm (about 2 in) with a sharp-pronged fork or a needle; this will prevent bursting while cooking. Either bake in a medium oven or fry in a little hot lard. When well browned on one side, carefully roll over with the aid of a fork and brown on the other side. The sausages should not be allowed to become dry, but should remain succulent inside.

(Zsolt Körmendy, Hungary)

Hungarian black pudding
Boudin hongrois
Véreshurka

10 portions   Cooking time of finished sausage: 15 to 20 minutes

1 l 2 dl	pig's blood	2 pt
300 g	pork back fat	11 oz
600 g	neck of pork	1 lb 5 oz
	4 stale rolls	
250 g	lard	9 oz
250 g	onions, finely cut	9 oz
50 g	salt	2 oz
10 g	black pepper, freshly ground	$\frac{1}{3}$ oz
1 g	ground cloves	a pinch
2 g	powdered marjoram	a good pinch
2½ m	pig's large intestines	3 yd

Wash the back fat and neck of pork well. Place in a pan with sufficient water to cover well, and cook steadily until tender. Remove the fat before it becomes too soft, cool and dice finely. Cook the onions gently in lard until lightly coloured. Dice the rolls finely and evenly, place on a baking sheet and brown lightly in the oven.

When the pork is tender, remove from the pan, cut into fairly large strips, then mince and place in a large bowl. Add the pork fat, the diced rolls, the onions and the blood. Season with salt and pepper, add the cloves and marjoram, moisten with a little bouillon, and mix carefully. The mixture should be firm.

To prepare and fill the casings and to cook the sausage, proceed as for liver sausage (recipe, page 885). Remove the skewers before serving, and slice the sausage evenly at a slight angle.

(Zsolt Körmendy, Hungary)

Pork sausages cacciatora
Saucisses à rôtir chasseur
Salsicce alla cacciatora

5 portions

1 kg 500	pork sausages	3 lb 5 oz
5 cl	olive oil	2 fl oz
	2 cloves of garlic	
	3 sage leaves	

	salt	
1 kg	peeled tomatoes (canned) in their juice	2 lb 4 oz
	water	

Fry the garlic and sage gently in the olive oil until lightly coloured. Add the tomatoes and juice. Cook for about 20 minutes over fairly low heat. Add the sausages, which should be covered by the tomato juice. If it has become too thick, add water. Season very lightly with salt and cook slowly over low heat for at least 30 minutes (depending on the thickness of the sausages). Serve with mashed potatoes.

(Mario De Filippis, Italy)

Hungarian liver sausage
Saucisse de foie hongroise
Majashurka

10 portions   Cooking time of finished sausage: 15 to 20 minutes

1 kg 200	pig's lights	2 lb 10 oz
500 g	pig's liver	1 lb 2 oz
300 g	pork back fat	11 oz
200 g	rice	7 oz
250 g	lard	9 oz
250 g	onions, finely cut	9 oz
50 g	salt	2 oz
10 g	black pepper, freshly ground	1/3 oz
1 g	ground cloves	a pinch
1 g	powdered marjoram	a pinch
10 g	red paprika	1/3 oz
2½ m	pig's large intestines	3 yd

Clean the intestines, rinse them well several times in tepid water, then leave in tepid water until they have completely lost their smell. Wash the lights carefully and place in a pan with the back fat and sufficient water to cover well. Cook, then remove from the liquid, leave until cold and mince, using the medium cutter.

Wash the rice carefully in a liberal amount of water, drain and cook in the stock from the lights, keeping the grains firm to the bite. Cook the onions gently in lard until lightly coloured.

Mince the liver (raw), using the finest cutter. Place in a large bowl with the lights and back fat, and add the rice and onions. Season with salt, pepper and red paprika, add the marjoram and cloves, moisten with a little fat bouillon, and mix carefully. The mixture should be of medium consistency; if it is too stiff, add a little bouillon, taking care not to make it too soft, which could cause it to escape from the casings.

Cut the intestines into 20–25 cm (8–10 in) lengths and insert a 4 cm (1½ in) wooden skewer at one end to secure. After filling, secure the other end with a wooden skewer in the same way. Do not pack too tightly, or the sausages will be liable to burst while cooking. Boil the sausages in their own cooking liquid (used for the lights and back fat), first bringing it to the boil, then adding the sausages and cooking them over medium heat until they rise to the surface. If necessary, add water to the pan.

After boiling, remove the sausages and place them in a liberal amount of cold water, taking care not to damage them. Leave in the water until they have stiffened a little, then drain, transfer to a board and set aside in a cool, airy place until cold. If they are not intended for immediate use, the sausages may be stored in a refrigerator for up to 24 hours.

To prepare the sausages for serving, arrange them on a baking sheet at intervals of 4–5 cm (about 2 in). Prick with a fork or needle, brush with melted lard, and bake in a moderate oven until well browned on one side, then carefully turn with the aid of a fork and brown well on the other side. Before serving, remove the skewers and slice evenly at a slight angle.

Black pudding and liver sausage should always be prepared at the same time. The method of filling, cooking and serving is the same.

(Zsolt Körmendy, Hungary)

Smoked sausage Gelderland
Saucisse fumée à la façon de Gueldre
Fijne gelderse rookworst

5 kg	lean dry pork	11 lb
3 kg 500	pork fat or fat bacon	7 lb 11 oz
	pepper	

Chill the meat and fat well, then cut into pieces. Season carefully with pepper and mince, using the 3 mm (⅛ in) cutter. Fill into casings which have been thoroughly cleaned and dried at 15°C (60°F) for 24 hours, then smoke at 18°C (65°F) for 24 hours. This sausage is boiled before serving. Favourite accompaniments are typical Dutch vegetable dishes, including boerenkool (cabbage) or sauerkraut.

(Bernard van Beurten, Netherlands)

Austrian brawn
Fromage de tête a l'autrichienne
Mühlviertler Leberschädel

6–8 portions

750 g	pig's head	1 lb 10 oz

250 g	stewing beef	9 oz
	flavouring vegetables	
	salt, pepper	
	bay leaf	
5 dl	water	18 fl oz
250 g	pig's liver	9 oz
100 g	ox liver	3½ oz
150 g	onions, finely chopped	5 oz
	1 tablespoon oil	
	2 cloves of garlic	
	1 egg	
	1 roll (stale)	
40 g	breadcrumbs	1½ oz
1¼ dl	bouillon	4 fl oz
	1 small teaspoon marjoram	
	1 small teaspoon thyme	
	2 teaspoons parsley	

Cook the pig's head and beef in the water with the addition of the flavouring vegetables, salt, pepper and bay leaf for 30 minutes in a pressure cooker. Place the head in cold water and bone it. Soak the roll in water and squeeze dry. Finely chop the meat, liver, roll and garlic, and mix with half the onions. Brown the rest of the onions lightly in oil, then add to the chopped meat mixture together with the breadcrumbs, herbs, salt, pepper and the bouillon. Mix thoroughly.

Grease a round fireproof mould, sprinkle with breadcrumbs and fill with the meat mixture. (In the original recipe, the mould is lined with a pig's caul instead of breadcrumbs.) Bake for about 40 minutes in a preheated oven with good centre heat. Allow to cool a little before cutting into portions and dressing on a serving dish.

Suitable accompaniments are mashed potatoes, boiled sauerkraut or raw sauerkraut salad. The brawn may be served cold with salad or pickles.

(Ernst Faseth, Austria)

Peking lion's head meat balls

3–4 portions   Cooking time: 2 hours

500 g	lean pork	1 lb 2 oz
250 g	fat pork	9 oz
10 g	salt	⅓ oz
20 g	cornflour	¾ oz
	1 egg, beaten	

	3 water chestnuts, coarsely chopped	
3 cl	soya sauce	1 fl oz
	oil for deep-frying	
	2 slices root ginger, shredded	
	3 stalks spring onion	
	4 medium tomatoes	
4 dl	chicken stock	14 fl oz
4 cl	vinegar	1½ fl oz
10 g	sugar	⅓ oz
1 cl	sesame oil	½ fl oz

Mince the lean and fat pork. Mix with the salt, half the soya sauce, the egg and the water chestnuts. Form the mixture into 4 large meat balls. Deep-fry these in hot oil 2 at a time for 6 to 7 minutes. Cut the spring onions into 4 cm (1½ in) lengths and the tomatoes into wedges.

Place the meat balls in a casserole. Pour in the chicken stock and vinegar, and add the sugar and the rest of the soya sauce. Sprinkle with the ginger and the spring onions. Bring to the boil on top of the stove, then cook for 1½ hours in an oven preheated to 160°C (320°F), turning the meat balls twice. Remove the ginger and spring onions with a pair of chopsticks, and sprinkle the top of the meat balls with sesame oil, then return the casserole to the oven and cook for a further 30 minutes at the same temperature.

To serve, drain the meat balls and arrange them in a deep dish pyramid fashion, with one on top of the other three. Surround with the tomato wedges. Reduce the cooking liquid by half over high heat, then pour over the meat balls. These large meat balls are divided up into small portions at the table.
(Illustration, page 691)

(Kenneth Lo, China)

Hot Pork Dishes for Individual Plate Service

Sauerkraut garnished Austrian style
Choucroute garnie à l'autrichienne
Bauernschmaus

8 portions

100 g	8 slices roast loin of pork each weighing about	3½ oz
80 g	8 slices cooked ham or other smoked meat each weighing about	3 oz
	4 pairs Frankfurter sausages	
	or 8 frying sausages	
1 kg	sauerkraut	2 lb 4 oz
	8 bread dumplings	

Cook the sauerkraut and place it in the centre of the plates. Surround with the meat and sausages, and garnish with the dumplings. Pour a little gravy round the edge. This dish is always served on individual plates.

(Eduard Mayer, Austria)

Moravian sparrows
Moineaux à la moravienne
Moravští vrabci

6 portions   Cooking time: 1–1½ hours

500 g	boneless shoulder of pork	1 lb 2 oz
500 g	boneless belly of pork	1 lb 2 oz
	salt	
	1 teaspoon caraway	
100 g	onions, finely chopped	3½ oz
	2 cloves of garlic, crushed	
60 g	fat	2 oz
	meat stock or bouillon cube and water	

Rinse the meat and cut into oblong pieces weighing about 40 g (1½ oz). Season with salt.

Heat the fat, brown the meat quickly all over, sprinkle with the caraway, add the garlic, onions and a little stock or bouillon, and roast at 240°C (465°F) until tender, basting frequently and adding stock or bouillon if necessary.

Remove the meat, drain off almost all the fat from the pan, add a little stock or bouillon, butter and salt, boil up briefly and strain. Transfer the meat to warmed plates and pour the gravy over. Serve with bread or potato dumplings and with braised white cabbage.

(Vilèm Vrabec, Czechoslovakia)

Pork with horseradish Styrian fashion
Porc au raifort à la styrienne
Steyrisches Krenfleisch

10 portions   Cooking time: about 1½ hours

1 kg 500	lean belly of pork	3 lb 5 oz
1 kg 500	shoulder of pork	3 lb 5 oz
	1 bouquet garni	
300 g	onions	11 oz
300 g	celeriac	11 oz
300 g	carrots	11 oz
200 g	parsley roots	7 oz
	cornflour	
	salt, pepper	
250 g	horseradish, grated	9 oz
	parsley, freshly chopped	
15 g	peppercorns, coarsely crushed	½ oz
	water	
	wine vinegar	
	1 bay leaf	

Place the pork in a pan of water without removing the skin. Add salt, the peppercorns, the bay leaf, bouquet garni and a little vinegar, bring to the boil and cook over moderate heat until just tender.

Cut the vegetables into julienne strips. Cook gently for a short time in a little of the pork stock, then add sufficient stock to cover and finish cooking, but do not overcook. Season with salt to taste, sharpen with a little vinegar if desired, and thicken a little with cornflour.

To serve, slice the meat, arrange on warm plates and pour the vegetable stock with the

julienne over. Sprinkle with parsley and a liberal amount of horseradish.
(Illustration, page 698)

(Karl Brunnengräber, Germany)

Pork fillet Dijon style
Filets mignons de porc à la dijonnaise

4 portions

150 g	4 pork fillets each weighing	5 oz
30 g	butter	1 oz
	1 tablespoon oil	

Sauce:

¼ l	dairy cream	9 fl oz
	2 tablespoons strong Dijon mustard	
	1 tablespoon shallots, very finely chopped	
	4 gherkins, finely cut	
	1 tablespoon wine vinegar	
	salt	
	pepper, freshly ground	

Fry the pork fillets on both sides in the oil and butter for a total of 8 to 9 minutes, turning them after half the cooking time. Season lightly with salt, remove from the pan, drain and set aside on a warmed metal dish. Pour off the fat remaining in the pan.

To make the sauce, place the cream in a bowl and mix well with the mustard, gherkins, shallots and vinegar. Transfer to the pan in which the meat was fried. Bring to the boil and cook for 2 minutes while stirring with a wooden spatula.

Dress the fillets on warmed plates, coat with the sauce and garnish with gratinated or Duchesse potatoes.

(Patrick Klipfel, Armand Roth, France)

Pork fillet in foil
Filet de porc en papillotte
Vepřová panenská pečená v alobalu

2 portions   Cooking time: 30 minutes

125 g	2 pork fillets each weighing	4½ oz

	½ red pepper, cut into strips	
	1 pickled cucumber, cut into strips	
	salt	
	a good pinch of pepper	
50 g	butter	2 oz
250 g	green beans, frozen or canned	9 oz
	2 firm tomatoes	
	aluminium foil	

Remove the skin from the fillets. Insert the strips of red pepper and cucumber into the surface of the meat, season with salt and pepper and place on greased foil. Season the beans with salt. Cut a slit in the top of the tomatoes and season with salt. Place the beans and tomatoes on foil. Seal the foil well and cook in the oven at 250°C (480°F) for about 20 to 25 minutes. Open the foil and place on plates to serve. Garnish with boiled potatoes and demi-glace sauce.

(Vilèm Vrabec, Czechoslovakia)

Pork fillet with ginger and coriander
Filet de porc au gingembre et au coriandre

4 portions

800 g	pork fillet	1 lb 12 oz
2 dl	veal stock	7 fl oz
	1 tablespoon vinegar	
	1 tablespoon Armagnac	
	1 tablespoon ketchup	
	1 teaspoon sugar	
20 g	butter	¾ oz
	10 coriander seeds, crushed	
	12 mint leaves	
	1 fresh ginger root	
1 dl	Sauternes	3½ fl oz
	juice of half a lemon	
	a little sugar to sweeten Sauternes	
	salt, pepper	

Peel the ginger root and cut into fine julienne strips. Poach for 5 minutes in the Sauternes which has been sharpened with the lemon juice and slightly sweetened.

Season the pork fillet with salt and pepper. Fry in butter over very low heat until medium done (about 10 minutes). Pour off the remaining butter. Add the sugar which has been lightly caramelised and stir in first the Armagnac, then the vinegar to dissolve the sugar. Add the veal stock and ketchup and reduce to the required consistency. Pass through a conical strainer and enrich with butter. Add the corianders.

Slice the meat. Pour the sauce on to the plates and arrange the slices of meat in a circle in the centre. Place a mint leaf on each slice and decorate with the ginger julienne.
(Illustration, page 314)

(Roger Souvereyns, Belgium)

Pork fillet with wild garlic
Filet de porc à l'ail sauvage

4 portions

150 g	4 pork fillets each weighing		5 oz
160 g	wild garlic		5½ oz
1 l	milk		1¾ pt
1 dl	dairy cream		3½ fl oz
100 g	butter		3½ oz
20 g	flour		¾ oz
500–600 g	potatoes	approx.	1¼ lb
1 dl	gravy		3½ fl oz
	salt		
	pepper, freshly ground		
	marjoram		
	nutmeg		
	chives		

Trim the fillets well and season with pepper and marjoram. Brown lightly in butter, season with a little salt, and fry until medium done. Peel the garlic, blanch in a liberal amount of water, then drain. Cook until soft in milk with the addition of a little salt, then pour off the milk.

Make a roux with the flour and an equal amount of butter. Blend in ¼ l (9 fl oz) milk, season with pepper, nutmeg and salt, and add the cream. Mix the garlic with this sauce and add finely chopped chives. Boil the potatoes in their skins in salted water. Skin and slice them, then fry in butter and sprinkle with a little coarse salt to enhance their flavour.

To serve, slice the meat and dress on warmed plates. Garnish with the wild garlic sauce and the fried potatoes.

(Germain Gretsch-Rösner, Luxembourg)

Pork fillet Lueger
Filet de porc Lueger
Schweinefilet Lueger

8 portions

180 g	8 pork fillets each weighing	6 oz
8 cl	oil	3 fl oz
40 g	breadcrumbs	1½ oz
	maître d'hôtel butter	
	salt, pepper	

Slit the fillets lengthwise, open out, flatten well and season with salt and pepper. Dip in oil, coat with breadcrumbs and grill. Dress on plates and garnish with maître d'hôtel butter. Hand French fried potatoes and Béarnaise sauce separately.

(Eduard Mayer, Austria)

Pork fillet with Poivrade sauce
Filet de porc en sanglier

2 portions

200 g	pork fillet	7 oz
2 dl	veal stock	7 fl oz
100 g	butter	3½ oz
30 g	redcurrant jelly	1 oz
2 cl	Cognac	1 fl oz
2 cl	wine vinegar	1 fl oz
	1 tablespoon groundnut oil	
	6 peppercorns, crushed	

Marinade:

	½ medium onion	
	1 clove of garlic	
	1 carrot	
	2 sprigs thyme	
	1 bay leaf	
	6 juniper berries	
½ l	red wine (Burgundy)	18 fl oz

Trim the pork carefully and marinate for 12 hours.

To make the sauce, brown the pork trimmings and the marinade vegetables in the groundnut oil, detach the sediment with the vinegar and the remaining marinade, bring to the boil, reduce and skim. Add the crushed peppercorns about 10 minutes before passing through a conical strainer. Keep hot.

Dry the meat and brown lightly in butter in a sauté pan. Transfer to a medium oven and roast for 12 minutes, then remove and keep hot. Pour off the butter, stir in the Cognac to detach the sediment, reduce, add the sauce which has been kept hot, bring to the boil and add the red-currant jelly. Remove from the heat, finish with butter and pour over the meat which has been cut on the slant into fine strips, reserving some of the sauce to hand separately. Garnish with poached apple halves stuffed with cranberries, and with celeriac mousse (recipe, page 1014).

(Jean Schillinger, France)

Pork medallions with caraway
Filet de porc au cumin
Medaillons von Schweinefilet in Kümmel, gedünstete Champignons mit Blattspinat

10 portions   Cooking time: 30 minutes

1 kg 200	pork fillet, well trimmed	2 lb 10 oz
	salt	
	pepper, freshly ground	
	flour	
	1 egg, beaten	
6 cl	oil	2 fl oz
80 g	butter	3 oz
2 ml	brandy	half a teaspoon
	1 tablespoon Pernod	
60 g	shallots, diced	2 oz
	1 teaspoon caraway seeds, finely chopped	
	2 tablespoons kümmel	
30 g	parsley, chopped	1 oz
½ l	thickened veal gravy	18 fl oz
700 g	small fresh mushrooms (caps only)	1 lb 8 oz
200 g	fresh spinach, blanched	7 oz

Cut the pork into 30 medallions. Flatten, season with pepper and salt, coat with flour, then with beaten egg, and sauter in the oil. Remove the meat and set aside. Drain off the oil and add the butter to the pan. Add the shallots and caraways, pour in the veal gravy and cook for 8 minutes. Add the brandy, Pernod, kümmel and parsley. To serve, dress the meat on plates and coat with the sauce. Garnish with the mushroom caps which have been cooked in butter and tossed with the spinach.

(Karl Brunnengräber, Germany)

Pork medallions with mustard sauce
Médaillons de porc en sauce à la moutarde
Medaillons von Schweinefilet in Senfsauce

2 portions

60 g	4 pork fillet medallions each weighing	2 oz
20 g	butter	¾ oz
	salt	
	flour	
1 dl	white wine	3½ fl oz
1 dl	dairy cream	3½ fl oz
	1 small teaspoon mustard seed, soaked in hot water for 10 minutes	
	1 small teaspoon hot mustard (Thomy yellow mustard)	
	1 tablespoon hard-boiled egg, chopped	

Season the pork with salt, flour it and fry in butter. Dress on warmed plates. Detach the sediment with the wine and cream. Add the mustard seed and reduce by half. Add the mustard, bring to the boil and pour over the medallions. Sprinkle with the chopped egg. Serve with rice pilaf and spinach. (As the pan sediment and the mustard contain salt, care should be taken when adjusting the seasoning.)

(Felix Real, Liechtenstein)

Pork medallions with port sauce
Médaillons de filet de porc à la sauce au porto
Medaillons von Schweinefilet in Portweinjus, mit Rhabarber und jungen Karotten

10 portions   Cooking time: 25 minutes

900 g	pork fillet	2 lb
150 g	butter	5 oz
	salt	
	pepper, freshly ground	
	flour	
750 g	rhubarb, cut into short pieces	1 lb 10 oz
1 dl	white wine	3½ fl oz

Port sauce:

2 tablespoons shallots, finely diced
1 teaspoon thyme, chopped
juice of 3 oranges

	zest of 1 orange, finely cut	
	juice of 1 lemon	
1½ dl	port	5 fl oz
	1 level tablespoon cornflour	
or 40 g	flour butter	1½ oz
	a pinch of Cayenne pepper	
½ l	veal gravy	18 fl oz

Cut the pork into 10 medallions. Flatten them, season with salt and pepper, flour them lightly and sauter in butter.

To make the sauce, place the port in a pan with the shallots and thyme, and reduce a little. Add the orange and lemon juice and the orange zest, and cook for 5 minutes. Thicken with the cornflour or flour butter. Stir the veal gravy into the pan in which the medallions were fried, boil up to detach the sediment, and add to the port sauce.

Cook the rhubarb in the white wine with a little butter and a pinch of salt and sugar, but do not overcook. Season with freshly ground pepper. To serve, dress the pork medallions on plates, coat with the sauce and garnish with the rhubarb and glazed young carrots.

(Karl Brunnengräber, Germany)

Pork medallions in bacon
Médaillons de porc en chemise
Medaillons von Schweinefilet im Speckhemd

4 portions

60 g	8 pork medallions each weighing	2 oz
15 g	8 rashers streaky bacon each weighing	½ oz
60 g	onions, finely chopped	2 oz
120 g	fresh mushrooms, thinly sliced	4 oz
20 g	parsley, chopped	¾ oz
40 g	butter	1½ oz
1 dl	veal or pork gravy	3½ fl oz
	salt, pepper	

The medallions should be lean and cut to the thickness of one finger. Beat them lightly, season with salt and pepper and fry or grill quickly until medium done. Brown the onions lightly in butter. Add the mushrooms and parsley, and continue frying for a short time. Season with salt and pepper and spread evenly on to the medallions. Wrap each one in a rasher of bacon and fry in a little butter. Detach the pan juices with the veal or pork gravy and strain over the medallions. Serve with carrot purée (recipe, page 1011), braised leeks and parsley or Château potatoes.
(Illustration, page 874)

(Johann Kögl, Austria)

Pork medallions with Tokay and walnut sauce on apple potato cake
Médaillons de filet de porc en sauce au tokay sur roesti aux pommes
Medaillons von Schweinefilet mit Tokayer-Walnuss-Sauce auf Apfelrösti

10 portions   Cooking time: 25 minutes

1 kg 400	pork fillet	3 lb
	salt, pepper	
100 g	butter	3½ oz
	flour	

Apple potato cake:

300 g	potatoes, baked in their skins	11 oz
400 g	firm apples, peeled and cored	14 oz
100 g	butter	3½ oz
	3 tablespoons oil	
	1 tablespoon white breadcrumbs	
	1 teaspoon noble-sweet paprika	

Tokay and walnut sauce:

80 g	shallots, finely cut	3 oz
⅛ l	veal gravy	4 fl oz
	1 tablespoon basil and lemon balm, chopped	
200 g	grapes	7 oz
	juice of half a lemon	
2 dl	Tokay	7 fl oz
	flour butter	
2 ml	brandy	half a teaspoon
	a pinch of Cayenne pepper	
200 g	walnuts, chopped	7 oz

Cut 20 medallions out of the fillet, flatten them, season with a little salt and pepper, and dust with flour. Fry in the butter, keeping them juicy, and keep hot. To serve, arrange the medallions on the apple potato cake and coat with the sauce.

To make the potato cake, peel the potatoes when cold and grate them coarsely together with the apples. Mix with the paprika, the breadcrumbs and a little salt. Fry in a mixture of hot oil and butter in the same way as Swiss potato cake (recipe, page 1017). To serve, fold over like an omelette and use as a base for the medallions.

To make the sauce, express the juice from the grapes and add to the pan in which the medallions were fried, together with the veal gravy. Boil up to detach the sediment, strain into a saucepan, add the shallots and reduce by a third. Add the Tokay and the walnuts and bring to the boil. Blend with a little flour butter to the desired consistency. Flavour with the Cayenne pepper, herbs and lemon juice.

(Karl Brunnengräber, Germany)

Pork medallions gipsy fashion
Médaillons de porc à la tzigane

4 portions   Cooking time: 25 minutes

80 g	4 pork medallions each weighing	3 oz
150 g	butter	5 oz
25 g	flour	1 oz
100 g	onions, finely chopped	3½ oz
100 g	noble-sweet paprika	3½ oz
	1 green pepper, seeded, trimmed of pith and cut into strips	
	4 tomatoes, skinned, seeded and finely cut	
400 g	melon, seeded and diced	14 oz
15 g	tomato purée	½ oz
½ l	white wine	18 fl oz
¼ l	dairy cream	9 fl oz

Rice pilaf:

200 g	rice	7 oz
	1 onion, chopped	
4 dl	water	14 fl oz
25 g	butter	1 oz
	salt	

Trim the medallions, which should be cut from the fillet, flatten them a little, season with salt and pepper, and dust with flour. Fry in 150 g (5 oz) butter, remove and keep hot. Add the onions to the pan, fry until lightly coloured, then sprinkle with paprika. Add the tomato purée, tomatoes, melon and green pepper. Pour in the wine, bring to the boil, reduce and finish with the cream. To serve, place the medallions on warmed plates and cover with the sauce. Garnish with the rice.

To prepare the rice, cook the onion gently in the butter without colouring, add the rice and mix carefully. Pour in the water, cover and cook over low heat. Remove from the heat, fold in the 25 g (1 oz) butter and season with salt.

(Eric Cederholm, Denmark)

Pork cutlets Old Graz
Côtelettes de porc Vieux Graz
Schweinekoteletts alt Graz

4 portions

160 g	4 pork cutlets each weighing	5½ oz
4 cl	oil	1½ fl oz
2 g	paprika	a good pinch

2 g	caraway	a good pinch
	salt	
100 g	2 ripe apples, each weighing	3½ oz
	4 pickled plums	

Sauce:

	2 tablespoons onions, chopped	
	2 cloves of garlic, crushed	
	1 teaspoon flour	
	1 teaspoon tomato purée	
1¼ dl	rosé wine	4 fl oz
2½ dl	bouillon	9 fl oz
50 g	gherkins, finely chopped	2 oz
	salt, sugar, mustard	

Accompaniment: country style potatoes

500 g	potatoes, cooked and diced	1 lb 2 oz
40 g	butter	1½ oz
	4 tablespoons onions, chopped	
40 g	bacon, diced	1½ oz
80 g	flap mushrooms or cultivated mushrooms, diced	3 oz
	1 teaspoon parsley, chopped	
	salt	

Beat the cutlets, season and fry on both sides in oil. Peel the apples, cut them in half and core them. Make a series of cuts into, but not right through, the apples very close together to leave thin slices attached at the base. Fry with the cutlets.

To make the sauce, lightly fry the onions and garlic in the pan used for the cutlets. Dust with flour and add the tomato purée. Stir in the wine, then add the bouillon, together with salt, sugar, mustard and the gherkins. For the accompaniment, fry the onions and bacon lightly in the butter. Add the potatoes and mushrooms, fry well, season and sprinkle with the parsley.

Place the cutlets on a serving dish or on warm plates and pour a little sauce over. Flatten the apples into fan shapes and place on top. Decorate with the pickled plums, fixing in position with a small skewer. Hand the rest of the sauce and the potatoes separately.

(Ernst Faseth, Austria)

Curried pork cutlets
Côtelettes de porc au curry
Karry Koteletter

4 portions

200 g	4 pork cutlets each weighing	7 oz

	salt	
	pepper, freshly ground	
	2 tablespoons vegetable fat	
	2 teaspoons curry powder	
5 cl	port	2 fl oz
2 dl	dairy cream	7 fl oz
	½ level teaspoon mustard	
	1 cucumber, thinly sliced	
1 dl	bouillon	3½ fl oz

Season the cutlets with salt and pepper. Fry slowly in the fat, remove and keep hot. Stir the curry powder and mustard into the pan, add the bouillon, port and cream, and stir well. Add the cucumber and leave to stand over the heat for a short time. Place the cutlets on warmed plates and pour the sauce over. Garnish with Brussels sprouts and cranberries.

(Hroar Dege, Günther Rett, Norway)

Pork chop Frivolité
Côte de porc Frivolité

4 portions

200 g	4 pork chops each weighing	7 oz
2 cl	oil	1 fl oz
	flour	
1 dl	white wine	3½ fl oz
2 dl	brown veal stock	7 fl oz
1½ dl	dairy cream	5 fl oz
30 g	butter, softened	1 oz
	salt	
	pepper, freshly ground	

Garnish:

50 g	carrots, cut into strips	2 oz
50 g	courgettes, cut into strips	2 oz
50 g	celery, cut into strips	2 oz
40 g	sugar peas	1½ oz
40 g	cauliflower florets	1½ oz
	salt	
	pepper, freshly ground	

Trim the chops carefully, season with salt and pepper, and flour lightly. Heat the oil a little and fry the chops in it, then remove and keep hot. Drain off the oil, pour in the wine to detach the sediment, reduce a little and add the veal stock. Boil up well and add the cream, then reduce to the required consistency and pass through a fine strainer. Carefully blend in the butter and season with salt and pepper.

To serve, pour the sauce on to heated plates, place the chops on top and garnish with the vegetables which have been blanched, tossed in butter and carefully seasoned, and with Williams potatoes.
(Illustration, page 242)

(Anton Mosimann, Great Britain)

Pork chop Heidebitt with stuffed potatoes
Côte de porc Heidebitt – pommes de terre farcies

2 portions

230 g	2 pork chops each weighing	8 oz
1 dl	veal stock	3½ fl oz
1 dl	sour cream	3½ fl oz
30 g	fresh chanterelles	1 oz
30 g	fresh flap mushrooms, cut in pieces	1 oz
	1 potato	
	chives, finely cut	
50 g	butter	2 oz
	salt, pepper	
	Heidebitt*	

Boil the potato in its skin in salted water. Fry the chops in 30 g (1 oz) butter over low heat until medium done (6 minutes). Season with salt and pepper. Pour off the butter, add Heidebitt* and ignite. Remove the chops and keep hot. Detach the sediment with the veal stock, add the sour cream, reduce to the required consistency, adjust the seasoning and pass through a conical strainer. Sauter the chanterelles in the rest of the butter, then add the flap mushrooms, cook gently, season with salt and pepper, add the chives and stir well.

Cut the potato in half while still hot. Scoop out the pulp, mix with the mushrooms and replace in the potato skins. To serve, place a chop on each plate, coat with sauce and garnish with the potato halves. (*Instead of Heidebitt, the author recommends a mixture of two thirds Curaçao triple sec and one third gin.)

(Roger Souvereyns, Belgium)

Breaded pork chop with sage
Côte de porc panée parfumée à la sauge

1 portion

200 g	1 pork chop weighing	7 oz

1 tomato
3 potatoes
1 tablespoon parsley, finely chopped
butter
powdered sage
1 egg, beaten
dry breadcrumbs
salt, pepper
3 tablespoons light stock

Season the chop with salt and pepper, sprinkle with sage and leave to stand, then egg and crumb. Fry lightly on both sides in clarified butter over low heat for 5 minutes, then transfer to an oven heated to 180°C (355°F) and cook for a further 10 minutes. Cut a cross in the top of the tomato and place in the oven at the same time. Peel and boil the potatoes, toss them in butter and sprinkle with parsley. Pour the stock on to a warmed plate and place the chop, tomato and potatoes on top.

(Jean Esslinger, France)

Pork cutlet with flap mushrooms
Côtelettes de porc aux cèpes
Braciola di maiale con funghi

6 portions

200 g	6 pork cutlets each weighing	7 oz
60 g	dried flap mushrooms	2 oz
	1 clove of garlic	
	¼ medium onion, cut in pieces	
	6 tablespoons olive oil	
	salt, pepper	
	lettuce leaves	

Soak the flap mushrooms in water, then squeeze dry. Brown the onion and garlic lightly in the oil, add the flap mushrooms and cook over low heat for 15 minutes, then work to a fine purée in the mixer and keep hot in a bain-marie.

Flatten the cutlets and grill over fierce heat for 10 minutes, then reduce the heat and continue grilling for a further 5 to 8 minutes, turning the cutlets frequently to cook evenly on both sides. Season with salt and pepper. Spread the cutlets with the mushroom purée and dress on warmed plates, surrounding the meat with lettuce leaves.

(Mario Saporito, Italy)

Pork cutlet gipsy baron style
Côtelette de porc baron tzigane
Schweinskotelett Zigeunerbaron

10 portions

1 kg 800	best end pork	4 lb
150 g	lard	5 oz
	3 somewhat tart apples	
	10 rashers bacon	
300 g	onions, finely cut	11 oz
	salt, pepper	
	a little flour	

Rice with wine:

500 g	rice	1 lb 2 oz
50 g	butter	2 oz
¼ l	wine	9 fl oz
¼ l	water	9 fl oz
	1 small onion	
	2 cloves	
	salt, pepper	

Divide the best end into 10 cutlets, season with salt and pepper, flour on one side, then fry on both sides in hot lard until well browned. Transfer to heated plates.

Slice the apples and fry them. Fry the onions. Snip the edges of the bacon rashers comb fashion and brown quickly. Cover the cutlets with the apple slices, sprinkle with the onions, garnish with the bacon and surround with the pan juices.

Cook the rice gently in the wine and water with the addition of the butter, salt and the onion stuck with the cloves. When cooked, remove the onion and season with pepper to taste. Hand a salad of sweet peppers separately.

(Eduard Mayer, Austria)

Ragoût of pork exotic style
Ragoût de porc exotique
Schweineragout auf exotische Art

6 portions   Cooking time: about 50 minutes

810 g	pork	1 lb 12 oz
2½ cl	olive oil	1 fl oz

90 g	onions, chopped	3¼ oz
5 g	ground corianders	⅙ oz
2 g	ground caraways	half a teaspoon
2 g	ground ginger	half a teaspoon
2 g	ground cardamoms	half a teaspoon
1 g	garlic powder	a good pinch
2 g	ground turmeric	half a teaspoon
1 g	pepper, freshly ground	a good pinch
	salt, Cayenne pepper	
4½ dl	meat stock or bouillon	15 fl oz
2 dl	plain yoghourt	7 fl oz
150 g	red, green and yellow peppers	5 oz
600 g	courgettes and tomatoes	1 lb 5 oz
	lemon juice	

Spätzle:

2 dl	water or milk	7 fl oz
5 cl	oil	2 fl oz
	5 eggs	
500 g	flour	1 lb 2 oz
	salt	
	nutmeg	
60 g	butter for frying	2 oz

Cut the pork into about 45 g (1½ oz) pieces. Heat the oil and gently cook the onions, add the spices and seasoning, continue cooking briefly, then add the pork and cook briefly again. Pour in the stock or bouillon and braise under cover over medium heat for about 50 minutes, or until the sauce is of the desired consistency. Add the yoghourt and lemon juice to taste.

Prepare the spätzle dough, pass through a spätzle strainer into boiling water, cook and strain. Fry in butter until golden and check the seasoning. Cook the courgettes and tomatoes together in butter. Cook the peppers in butter.

To serve, dress the ragoût on individual plates, add the spätzle and the courgette/tomato mixture, place the peppers on top of the meat and bring to the table very hot. The spätzle may be replaced by boiled rice with fruit (pineapple, bananas, peaches or dessert cherries).

(Otto Ledermann, Switzerland)

Pig's liver Agrigento fashion
Foie de porc à la mode d'Agrigente
Fegato di maiale all'agrigentina

6 portions

1 kg	pig's liver	2 lb 4 oz

100 g	ewe cheese, sliced	3½ oz
	2 cloves of garlic, chopped	
	2 tablespoons parsley, chopped	
	salt, pepper	
	1 pig's caul	
	oil as required	

Slice the liver, then cut into squares. Season with salt and pepper, sprinkle with the parsley and garlic, and cover with the slices of cheese. Wrap each slice of liver separately in a piece of caul and fry in oil for 15 minutes. Dress on warmed plates and garnish with spinach.

(Salvatore Schifano, Italy)

Grilled pig's kidney on mushroom purée
Rognon de porc grillé sur purée de champignons
Gegrillte Schweineniere auf Champignonpüree

2 portions

	1 pig's kidney	
30 g	butter	1 oz
	2 shallots	
100 g	field mushrooms (*not* cultivated mushrooms)	3½ oz
5 cl	veal stock	2 fl oz
5 cl	dairy cream	2 fl oz
	lemon juice	
	salt	
	pepper, freshly ground	

Trim the fat from the kidney, cut away the veins and hard portions, score the surface criss-cross fashion, wash thoroughly and dry. Coat with oil and grill. Do not season until after grilling, or the juices will escape while cooking. After seasoning with salt and pepper, keep hot.

Cook the shallots gently in a copper pan until transparent, then add the mushrooms, the veal stock and the cream. Cover and cook for 3 minutes, then work to a purée in the mixer. Season with salt and pepper, and add lemon juice to taste. Spoon the mushroom purée on to plates and place the kidney on top.
(Illustration, page 768)

(Gerhard Gartner, Germany)

Marinated pork gamekeeper style
Civet de porc à la garde-chasse
Schweinepfeffer auf Wildhüter Art

10 portions   Cooking time: about 1 hour

2 kg 200	boneless pork (neck or shoulder)	5 lb

Marinade:

1 l	red wine	1¾ pt
1 dl	red wine vinegar	3½ fl oz
1 l	bouillon	1¾ pt
	mirepoix of carrots, celeriac and onions, coarsely cut	
	1 clove of garlic	
	2 cloves	
	1 bay leaf	
	8 juniper berries, crushed	
	thyme	
	a few young fir shoots	
1 dl	oil	3½ fl oz
80 g	flour	3 oz
150 g	lean bacon, diced	5 oz
250 g	button onions	9 oz
300 g	chanterelles *or* flap mushrooms	11 oz
2 dl	pig's blood	7 fl oz
	⅓ tumbler gin	
2 dl	dairy cream	7 fl oz
	sliced white bread for croûtons	
	parsley, chopped	
1 l	bouillon	1¾ pt
	salt, pepper	

Cut the meat into 40 g (1½ oz) cubes, mix with the mirepoix and place in an earthenware pot. Cover with the rest of the marinade ingredients and weight with a board or plate of suitable size. Leave in a cool place for 8 to 10 days, then strain and set aside the contents of the strainer (i.e. the meat and mirepoix). Boil up the marinade for a few moments to coagulate the proteins in it. Strain through a cloth to remove these unwanted particles from the sauce.

Heat the oil in a sauté pan and brown the meat and mirepoix lightly. Transfer to a braising pan, dust with flour and place in the oven uncovered for a few minutes. Season with salt, detach the sediment with the marinade, add the bouillon, cover and braise in the oven until the meat is tender. Transfer to a second pan with a fork and keep hot in a bain-marie. Reduce the cooking liquid a little if necessary. Season with salt and pepper.

Place the pig's blood in a bowl and mix with the cream and gin. Blend with the cooking liquid from the meat, but do not boil. Strain this sauce over the meat and mix very carefully.

Peel and glaze the button onions. Blanch the bacon and fry lightly, then add the mushrooms and onions to the pan and cook gently. Cut the bread into small triangles and fry in butter. To serve, cover each portion of meat with mushrooms and onions, surround with fried croûtons and sprinkle with parsley. Serve with small potato dumplings or spätzle.

(Karl Brunnengräber, Germany)

Mexican ragoût of pork
Ragoût de porc à la mexicaine
Mancha manteles de cerdo

10 portions

1 kg 800	shoulder of pork	4 lb
2 dl	oil	7 fl oz
20 g	onion, chopped	¾ oz
	6 cloves of garlic, chopped	
1 kg	tomatoes, cut into quarters	2 lb 4 oz
3 dl	white wine	10 fl oz
1 l	brown veal stock	1¾ pt
	salt, pepper	
	chilli powder	
	ground cinnamon	
1 dl	redcurrant jelly	3½ fl oz
	5 slices pineapple	
	3–4 apples, cooked	

Cut the pork into 3 cm (1¼ in) cubes and sauter in oil. Pour off the oil, add the onion, garlic and tomatoes, and stew. Stir in the wine, continue stewing, then add the veal stock, together with the seasonings, and stew until tender. Remove the meat, strain the sauce, finish with the redcurrant jelly, adjust the seasoning, and pour over the meat. Cut the pineapple slices and the apples into quarters and use as a garnish. Hand plain boiled rice separately.

(Emil Wälti, Mexico)

Ragoût of pork Trogen style
Ragoût de porc à la Trogen
Trogener Schweineragout

4 portions

700 g	shoulder of pork	1 lb 8 oz

5 cl	oil	2 fl oz
150 g	onions, finely chopped	5 oz
	1 tablespoon flour	
2½ dl	cider	9 fl oz
100 g	sweet peppers, finely diced	3½ oz
	salt, pepper	
	1 teaspoon paprika	
	1 bay leaf	
2½ dl	demi-glace sauce	9 fl oz
600 g	potatoes	1 lb 5 oz

Cut the pork into 3 cm (1¼ in) cubes and brown in hot oil. Add the onions and cook gently until transparent, dust with flour and fry lightly. Stir in the cider, reduce a little, then add the demi-glace sauce. Add the peppers, season with salt, pepper and paprika and add the bay leaf. Cover and stew gently for about 1 hour. Dice the potatoes and add to the meat, together with a little water or bouillon if required. When the potatoes are cooked, adjust the seasoning and consistency. Serve with mashed potatoes.

(Emil Wälti, Switzerland)

Pork rolls Swabian fashion
Paupiettes de porc à la souabe
Schwäbische Schweinsröllchen mit Sauerkraut

8 portions   Cooking time: about 2 hours

150 g	8 slices boned neck of pork each weighing	5 oz
50 g	8 slices ham each weighing	2 oz
	8 tablespoons sauerkraut	
150 g	lard	5 oz
500 g	mirepoix of celeriac, carrots and	1 lb 2 oz
	parsley roots	
	peppercorns, crushed	
	juniper berries, crushed	
	½ bay leaf	
7 dl	dry white wine (Riesling if possible)	1¼ pt
½ l	dairy cream	18 fl oz
	2 sweet peppers	
	½ cup flour butter	
	oil	

Seed the peppers, cut them into strips, fry lightly in a little oil and set aside.

Flatten the meat. Cover first with the ham, then with sauerkraut, roll up and tie. Brown in lard and set aside. Add the mirepoix to the pan, together with the peppercorns, juniper berries and bay leaf. Fry until brown, constantly moistening with wine until half of it has been added. Return the meat to the pan, stir in the rest of the wine, add the cream and cook until tender. Bind the sauce with flour butter, add the peppers and boil up. Serve with spätzle.

(Gerhard Gartner, Germany)

Stuffed ham slices
Tranches de jambon farcies
Gefüllte Schinkenscheiben

10 portions

600 g	ham, cut into 20 slices	1 lb 5 oz

Stuffing:

1 kg	chicken livers	2 lb 4 oz
250 g	unsmoked fat bacon	9 oz
30 g	shallots, cut into pieces	1 oz
150 g	apples, cut into pieces	5 oz
1 dl	Cognac and Madeira	3½ fl oz
	3 egg yolks	
	salt	
	pepper, freshly ground	
	thyme, marjoram	
	nutmeg, basil	
1 l	bouillon	1¾ pt
4 dl	Madeira sauce	14 fl oz

Clean the livers carefully, removing any gall and green parts. Dice the bacon, brown lightly and remove from the pan. Add the livers to the pan and brown lightly, then add the shallots and apples and cook gently for a few moments. Detach the sediment with the Cognac and Madeira, transfer to a mortar, add all the seasonings and pound finely. Mix carefully with the egg yolks and spread to a thickness of 2 mm ($^1/_{10}$ in) on half the slices of ham. Cover with the rest of the slices, fix in place and poach in a little stock. Dress on warmed plates and coat with Madeira sauce. Garnish with rice with diced tomatoes and green beans.

(Otto Ledermann, Switzerland)

Escalope of pork with sauerkraut stuffing
Escalopes de porc farcies à la choucroute
Schweinerückenschnitzel mit Weinkraut gefüllt, glasierte Maronen und Anna-Kartoffeln

10 portions   Cooking time: 25 minutes

140 g	10 escalopes of pork each weighing	5 oz

600 g	sauerkraut	1 lb 5 oz
200 g	butter	7 oz
	1 tablespoon honey	
⅛ l	white wine	4 fl oz
	salt	
	pepper, freshly ground	
⅓ l	brown veal stock	12 fl oz
	1 tablespoon lemon juice	
	1 teaspoon lemon zest, grated	
100 g	shallots, finely cut	3½ oz
4 dl	dairy cream	14 fl oz

Glazed chestnuts:

1 kg	chestnuts	2 lb 4 oz
100 g	sugar	3½ oz
	1 tablespoon butter	
⅓ l	Espagnole sauce	12 fl oz
	1 cup veal gravy	

Beat each escalope with the ball of the thumb and slit on one side with a sharp knife to make a pocket. Cook the sauerkraut under cover in the wine with the addition of the honey and a little butter, then allow to cool. Fill into the pockets in the escalopes. Season with salt and pepper and brown all over in butter. Add the shallots, lemon juice, zest and veal stock, cover and cook until tender. Transfer the meat to warmed plates. Pour the cream into the pan and reduce the sauce to coating consistency. Pour without straining over the meat which has been garnished with glazed chestnuts.

To prepare the chestnuts, shell them, blanch in boiling water and remove the skins. Lightly caramelise the sugar in the butter, and pour in the veal gravy and Espagnole sauce. Add the chestnuts and braise until soft. Remove them from the pan and keep hot. Reduce the stock by a third and toss the chestnuts in it. If desired, chestnuts prepared in this way may be covered with greaseproof paper and stored.

(Karl Brunnengräber, Germany)

Shoulder of pork with horseradish
Epaule de porc au raifort
Schweineschulter mit Meerrettich

8 portions

1 kg 500	shoulder of pork	3 lb 5 oz
2 l	water	3½ pt
¼ l	vinegar	9 fl oz

80 g	carrots	3 oz
80 g	parsley roots	3 oz
80 g	celeriac	3 oz
60 g	onions, sliced	2 oz
	10 peppercorns	
	salt	
1 kg	potatoes	2 lb 4 oz
150 g	horseradish, finely grated	5 oz

Cut the root vegetables into thin strips. Cook the meat in salted water until almost tender. Add the vegetable julienne, onions, vinegar and peppercorns, and finish cooking.

Peel and quarter the potatoes. Boil them in salted water. Carve the meat, place on warmed plates and add the vegetable julienne and potatoes. Sprinkle the vegetables with the horseradish.
(Illustration, page 942)

(Eduard Mayer, Austria)

Pork steak with prunes
Steak de porc aux pruneaux

4 portions

	4 pork steaks (cut from the loin)	
170 g	each weighing	6 oz
	flour	
2 cl	olive oil	1 fl oz
20 g	butter	¾ oz
1 dl	white wine	3½ fl oz
1½ dl	brown veal stock	5 fl oz
30 g	butter, softened (for sauce)	1 oz
	salt	
	pepper, freshly ground	

Garnish:

20 g	butter	¾ oz
50 g	carrots, cut into fine strips	2 oz
50 g	turnips, cut into fine strips	2 oz
50 g	courgettes, cut into strips	2 oz
	8 small prunes, stoned	
	parsley, chopped	

Season the pork with salt and pepper and flour lightly. Fry on both sides in hot oil and butter, basting constantly and keeping the meat juicy. Remove and keep hot. Drain off the fat remaining in the pan, detach the sediment with the wine and reduce a little. Add the veal stock and reduce to the desired consistency. Finish carefully with the soft butter, pass through a fine strainer and season with salt and pepper.

Blanch the carrots, turnips, courgettes and prunes. Cut the prunes in half. Carefully glaze the vegetables and prunes in butter. To serve, pour the sauce on to warmed plates, dress the meat on top and cover with the vegetable garnish and the prunes. Sprinkle with freshly chopped parsley.

(Anton Mosimann, Great Britain)

Skewered pork rolls
Paupiettes de porc en brochettes
Spanische Reiter

10 portions   Cooking time: 30 minutes

1 kg 200	boneless leg or loin of pork	2 lb 10 oz
200 g	lean bacon, cut into strips	7 oz
150 g	onions, cut into strips	5 oz
100 g	pickled cucumbers in mustard sauce, cut into strips	3½ oz
1 dl	oil	3½ fl oz
	garlic salt	
	1 tablespoon parsley, chopped	
	1 teaspoon rosemary, chopped	
	a pinch of Cayenne pepper	

Rice with tomatoes:

	1 tablespoon shallots, finely cut	
300 g	tomatoes, skinned, seeded and coarsely chopped	11 oz
	1 tablespoon tomato purée	
	1 teaspoon noble-sweet paprika	
80 g	butter	3 oz
500 g	rice	1 lb 2 oz
1½ l	light veal stock	2¾ pt

Shallot cream sauce:

200 g	shallots, cut into quarters	7 oz
50 g	maître d'hôtel butter	2 oz
3 dl	dairy cream	10 fl oz
5 cl	tarragon vinegar	2 fl oz

juice of 1 lemon

1 l	tomato sauce	1¾ pt

Cut the meat into 30 slices (allowing 3 per portion). Flatten well, season with garlic salt and a little Cayenne pepper, cover with strips of bacon, pickled cucumber and onion, roll up and thread in threes on to small skewers. Coat with oil and grill.

To prepare the rice, fry the shallots gently in butter until lightly coloured, add the tomato purée and tomatoes, and fry for a short time. Add the rice, mix well and add the stock which has been brought to the boil. Return to the boil, cover and cook in the oven for 15 to 18 minutes. Serve the brochettes on a bed of rice and hand shallot cream sauce separately.

To make the sauce, cook the shallots gently in melted maître d'hôtel butter without colouring. When transparent, add the vinegar to detach the sediment, then pour in the tomato sauce and cream, and reduce to a creamy sauce of thick coating consistency. Add a pinch of Cayenne pepper, sharpen with the lemon juice, and serve without straining.

(Karl Brunnengräber, Germany)

Kid—Hot Main Dishes

These recipes appear in the original continental edition and are suitable for the preparation of young lamb in the U.K.

Kid old Basel style
Cabri frit vieux Bâle
Zicklein auf Alt-Basler Art

10 portions

1 kg 500	kid (boned neck, shoulder or breast)	3 lb 5 oz
2 l	well seasoned light veal stock	3½ pt

Batter:

350 g	flour, sieved	12 oz
5 cl	oil	2 fl oz
3 dl	beer	10 fl oz
1 dl	water	3½ fl oz
	salt	
	nutmeg	
	3 egg whites, whipped to a snow	
	oil for frying	
6 dl	fresh tomato sauce	1 pt

Cut the meat into neat 40 g (1½ oz) pieces and boil in the veal stock for about 30 minutes, then allow to cool in the stock. Prepare frying batter with the ingredients indicated above. Remove the pieces of meat from the stock and coat with the batter, then deep-fry in oil heated to 170°C (340°F) until crisp. Serve very hot. Hand tomato sauce and mixed salad separately. Alternatively, the boiled meat may be marinated for 2 hours in a mixture of mustard and chopped herbs, then crumbed and fried.

(Otto Ledermann, Switzerland)

Kid Cécile
Cabri Cécile

8 portions

	1 kid	
100 g	butter (for meat)	3½ oz

	2 tablespoons oil (for meat)	
30 g	butter (for vegetables)	1 oz
	1 tablespoon oil (for vegetables)	
250 g	carrots, thinly sliced	9 oz
250 g	onions, thinly sliced	9 oz
	3 tablespoons flour, sieved	
5 cl	dry white wine	2 fl oz
½ l	veal stock	18 fl oz
	1 bouquet garni	
	1 tablespoon fine herbs	
	1 clove of garlic, crushed (or juice)	

Garnish:

12 button onions, glazed
6 tomatoes, skinned, seeded and diced
12 mushroom caps, turned and grooved
8 heart-shaped croûtons

Cut the kid into pieces weighing about 50 g (2 oz). Brown lightly all over in the oil mixed with the butter over medium heat, then remove from the pan and keep hot. Add the butter and oil for the vegetables to the fat already in the pan. When the butter has melted, add the vegetables which have been mixed together, and stir-fry. Return the meat to the pan, heat it and dust with the flour. Mix well, allow to colour lightly, then stir in the wine followed by the veal stock. Add the garlic and bouquet garni when the stock has come to the boil. Cover and continue cooking over moderate heat for 40 minutes.

Transfer the meat to the centre of a deep serving dish. Surround with the vegetables. Reduce the sauce and strain over the meat and vegetables, sprinkling these with chopped fresh herbs.

(Patrick Klipfel, Armand Roth, France)

Fricassée of kid spring style
Fricassée de cabri à la printanière

8 portions   Cooking time: 1½ hours

	1 saddle, shoulder and neck of kid	
	salt, nutmeg	
	pepper, freshly ground	
100 g	flour	3½ oz
100 g	butter	3½ oz
100 g	lard	3½ oz
2 dl	white wine (Riesling)	7 fl oz
2½ dl	dairy cream	9 fl oz
	4 egg yolks	
50 g	chives, blanched	2 oz

	4 potatoes, thinly sliced	
	8 wild leeks, sliced	
2 l	light stock	3½ pt

Cut the meat in pieces, flour it and brown lightly in the butter and lard. Detach the sediment with the wine, add the stock and bring to the boil. Add the leeks and potatoes, together with salt and freshly ground pepper, and cook over low heat until the meat is tender. Remove it from the pan, place in a deep dish which has been well warmed, cover and keep hot.

Pass the stock through a conical strainer, thicken with the egg yolks and stir in the cream. Add freshly grated nutmeg and two or three turns of the pepper mill. Pour over the meat and decorate with the chives. Serve with coarse bread, thickly sliced and toasted, or with mashed potatoes.
(Illustration, page 620)

(Jean Esslinger, France)

Roast kid
Cabri au four
Capretto al forno

6 portions

3 kg 200–			
2 kg 300	half a kid weighing	approx.	7 lb 4 oz
750 g	potatoes, peeled and sliced		1 lb 10 oz
	1 tablespoon parsley, finely chopped		
	1 teaspoon basil, finely chopped		
	1 teaspoon mint, finely chopped		
	2 cloves of garlic, chopped		
50 g	fresh cheese		2 oz
50 g	butter		2 oz
	3 sprigs rosemary		
	salt, pepper		
	6 peeled tomatoes (canned) (optional)		

Cut up the kid coarsely, rinse under running water and dry well. Mix together the chopped herbs, garlic and fresh cheese, and season with salt and freshly ground pepper. Score the pieces of meat with a sharp knife and fill the slits with the mixture and small pieces of butter. Arrange the potato slices in an oiled fireproof dish, place the meat and the rosemary on top, and season with salt and pepper. Add the tomatoes if desired. Roast for about 2¼ hours in an oven preheated to 190–200°C (375–390°F).

(Salvatore Schifano, Italy)

Kid with prunes
Cabri aux pruneaux

8 portions

2 kg 500	kid	5 lb 8 oz
1 dl	Cognac	3½ fl oz
	1 onion, finely diced	
	1 carrot, finely diced	
	1 small bouquet garni	
	water or light stock as required	
150 g	unsmoked bacon, diced	5 oz
60 g	tomato purée	2 oz
¾ l	red wine	1¼ pt
	32 prunes, stoned	
	salt, pepper	

Cut up the kid, season with salt and pepper, and marinate in the Cognac overnight.

Soak the prunes overnight before stoning. Brown the bacon and meat lightly together. Detach the sediment with the marinade, then add the diced vegetables, the bouquet garni and the tomato purée. Stir in the wine, add water or, preferably, light stock and cook slowly under cover for 1¼ hours. Remove the meat and keep hot.

Reduce the sauce if necessary. Add the prunes, reheat and adjust the seasoning. Place the meat in a warm deep serving dish and coat with the sauce. Decorate the top with the prunes.

(Emile Jung, France)

Kid piacentina style
Cabri à la plaisantine
Capretto alla piacentina

1 kg	kid (forequarters)	2 lb 4 oz
50 g	butter	2 oz
50 g	bacon, finely cut	2 oz
5 cl	olive oil	2 fl oz
1 dl	dry white wine	3½ fl oz
	1 onion, chopped	
2 dl	bouillon	7 fl oz
	2 cloves of garlic (juice only)	
	1 tablespoon parsley, chopped	
	1 tablespoon tomato purée	
	salt	

pepper, freshly ground

Cut the meat in pieces. Cook the onion gently in the butter and oil without colouring, add the meat and brown on all sides. Detach the sediment with the wine, add the tomato purée which has been blended with the bouillon, and season with salt and pepper. Add the garlic, parsley and bacon, cover and cook slowly until the meat is tender and the stock well reduced.

(Franco Colombani, Italy)

Sicilian stuffed kid
Cabri farci à la sicilienne
Capretto farcito alla siciliana

6 portions
Cooking time: about 2¼ hours, depending on the quality of the meat

3 kg 200– 3 kg 400	half a kid weighing about	7–7½ lb
	3 small onions	
	3 cloves of garlic	
	2 tablespoons parsley	
	10 mint leaves	
100 g	fresh cheese	3½ oz
5 cl	olive oil	2 fl oz
	1 lemon	
	salt, pepper	

Chop the parsley, mint, onions and garlic very finely, mix well and work into the cheese. Cut up the meat coarsely and score to make wide slits. Fill these with the herb/cheese mixture. Arrange in a fireproof dish, season with salt, brush with oil and roast in an oven preheated to 200°C (390°F), basting with a mixture of oil and lemon juice from time to time.

(Salvatore Schifano, Italy)

Rabbit—Hot Main Dishes

Rabbit Alpe Vicania
Lapin Alpe Vicania
Coniglio Alpe Vicania

4–6 portions

1 kg 500–		
1 kg 800	rabbit	3¼–4 lb
350 g	butter	12 oz
	2 onions	
	2 carrots	
150 g	celery	5 oz
	2 sprigs rosemary	
	8–10 sage leaves, chopped	
	2 bay leaves	
1 dl	bouillon	3½ fl oz
1 dl	white wine	3½ fl oz
	salt and pepper	

Joint the rabbit and brown in butter. Cup up the vegetables finely, brown in butter in a second pan and add to the meat together with the butter. Pour in the bouillon, add the sage, the rosemary sprigs and the bay leaves, season with salt and pepper, and cook slowly in the oven at about 200°C (390°F). Add the wine towards the end of the cooking time. Turn the pieces of rabbit occasionally to keep them moist. Adjust the seasoning before service. (Illustration, page 946)

(Giovanni Albisetti, Switzerland)

Rabbit Ligurian style
Lapin à la ligurienne
Coniglio alla ligure

4 portions   Cooking time: 1¼–1½ hours

1 kg 600–		3½–
2 kg	rabbit	4½ lb
1½ dl	olive oil	5 fl oz
	3 cloves of garlic	
2–3 dl	white wine	7–10 fl oz

3 peeled tomatoes, canned
20 black olives
2 sprigs rosemary
salt, pepper

Joint the rabbit, wash well, place in a pan and stand over the heat to draw the water from the meat. Remove the meat and dry well. Heat the oil in a pan, add the rosemary and fry briefly to flavour the oil. Add the meat, season and brown well. Stir in the wine, cover and cook slowly over low heat, moistening with bouillon if the pan becomes dry. When the meat is half cooked, add the tomatoes and olives.
(Illustration, page 519)

(Franco Colombani, Italy)

Rabbit with plums or prunes
Lapin aux prunes de Dro'
Coniglio con le susine di Dro'

4 portions

1 kg 500	rabbit	3 lb 5 oz
1 l	red wine (Pinot)	1¾ pt
5 cl	red wine vinegar	2 fl oz
300 g	plums or prunes	11 oz
100 g	flour	3½ oz
	2 carrots, sliced	
	1 onion, cut into pieces	
	1 bouquet garni of rosemary, thyme, sage, bay leaf	
	4 cloves of garlic	
1 l	bouillon	1¾ pt
80 g	butter	3 oz
	salt, pepper	

If no plums are available, soak the prunes for at least 12 hours before use.

Prepare a marinade with the wine, vinegar, carrots, onion, garlic and bouquet garni. Joint the rabbit and marinate for 24 hours. Remove, dry each piece well, flour and brown well on all sides in butter. Moisten with half the marinade, add the bouillon, season with salt and pepper, and braise.

Add the prunes and the bouquet garni from the marinade. Cook slowly over low heat for 1 hour, turning the meat from time to time. Add a little flaked butter. Transfer the meat to a warm dish and strain the cooking liquid over.

(Sergio Chiesa, Italy)

Rabbit with hyssop
Lapereau à l'hysope

6 portions

1 kg 500	rabbit	3 lb 5 oz
	4 sprigs hyssop	
	½ lemon	
100 g	carrots	3½ oz
100 g	leeks	3½ oz
50 g	celery	2 oz
	1 clove garlic	
	2 tablespoons cream	
½ l	champagne	18 fl oz
	butter as required	

Stock:

	1 sprig thyme	
	3 sprigs hyssop	
	1 bay leaf	
	2 sprigs savory	
	1 tablespoon olive oil	
½ l	water	18 fl oz
1 dl	champagne	3½ fl oz
	salt, pepper	

Prepare good stock in the usual manner with the above ingredients and the fore part of the rabbit. Reduce to ½ l (18 fl oz). Dice the carrots, leeks and celery. Joint the hind part of the rabbit, season and brown lightly in butter under cover, then set aside. Add the diced vegetables to the pan, cook gently without colouring, then add the crushed clove of garlic, the lemon which has been peeled and sliced, and the hyssop. Continue browning in the oven for a short time, then add the rabbit stock and the champagne. Cook for 10 minutes. Remove the meat. Pass the stock and vegetables through a conical strainer or work to a fine purée in the mixer. Remove any fat and thicken if desired. Add the cream and adjust the seasoning. Pour over the rabbit.
(Illustration, page 237)

(Pierre Gleize, France)

Sautés mignons of rabbit with rosemary and chanterelles
Mignons de lapereaux sautés au romarin et aux girolles

8 portions

1 kg 500	4 rabbits each weighing	3 lb 5 oz

	groundnut oil as required	
Sauce:		
	2 sprigs fresh parsley	
	1 onion, finely chopped	
	3 shallots, finely chopped	
	3 tablespoons flour	
3½ dl	dry white wine	12 fl oz
1 l	chicken stock	1¾ pt
¼ l	dairy cream	9 fl oz
	salt	
	pepper, freshly ground	
Garnish:		
1 kg	chanterelles	2 lb 4 oz
	3 tablespoons groundnut oil	
	3 tablespoons butter	
	1 clove of garlic	
	1 shallot, finely chopped	
	1 tablespoon parsley, finely chopped	

Use only the back fillets of the rabbits. The rest of the meat may best be used for rabbit or game terrines.

Fry the fillets in the oil over high heat until golden brown, then remove, drain and pour off the oil. Return the meat to the pan with the onion and shallots, cook gently until lightly coloured, then detach the sediment with the wine and add the chicken stock which has been heated. Bring to the boil, add the rosemary, season with salt and pepper, cover and braise for about 5 minutes.

Remove the meat from the stock, place on a warm dish, cover and keep hot. Strain the stock, remove the fat and reheat. Stir in the cream, add salt and pepper if required, boil up for a moment, beat well and thicken with butter to the required consistency.

Clean and wash the chanterelles well, blanch briefly, then dry. While the meat is cooking, sauter the chanterelles in oil and butter, add the crushed clove of garlic and the shallots, and cook until soft and lightly browned.

To serve, cut each fillet on the slant into 4 slices, arrange in the centre of a warm dish and surround with the chanterelles. Sprinkle these with the parsley and coat the meat with sauce. (Illustration, page 763)

(Patrick Klipfel, Armand Roth, France)

Fricassée of rabbit with chives and green pepper
Fricassée de lapin à la ciboulette et au poivre vert
Kaninchenfrikassee mit Schnittlauch und grünem Pfeffer

10 portions   Cooking time: 10–15 minutes

2 kg 500	rabbit	5 lb 8 oz
60 g	butter	2 oz
80 g	shallots	3 oz
	1 small sprig thyme	
	2 cloves of garlic	
	spices as desired	
	salt	
	pepper, freshly ground	
	flour	

Sauce:

150 g	chives, finely cut	5 oz
70 g	shallots, chopped	2½ oz
3 dl	dry white wine	10 fl oz
3 dl	dairy cream	10 fl oz
250 g	butter	9 oz
15 g	green pepper	½ oz
40 g	mustard	1½ oz
8 cl	tarragon vinegar	3 fl oz

Remove the liver and kidneys from the rabbit. Cut off the legs and divide into two or three pieces. Cut off the shoulders and divide in half. Cut away the thorax with scissors and chop off the head and neck. (These parts may be used for soup or rabbit stock.) Using a sharp, pointed knife, carefully skin the saddle and cut this into pieces 4 cm (1½ in) wide. Season the pieces of meat with salt and pepper, flour lightly and remove any surplus flour.

Peel the shallots. Heat 60 g (2 oz) butter in a thick-bottomed pan until foaming and add the shallots, the garlic (unpeeled) which has been lightly crushed, the thyme and the meat. Fry slowly over gentle heat until medium done (about 15 minutes), or roast in a moderate oven for the same length of time. Remove the saddle meat after 10 minutes, as this requires less cooking. The meat should be lightly browned only. Transfer the meat to a dish and keep hot in a preheated oven.

Pour off the butter remaining in the pan, add a little water and reduce almost completely. Scrape off the sediment and pass through a conical strainer to be used for the sauce. Prepare the sauce while the meat is cooking. Wrap the finely chopped shallots in a cloth and wash under running water, then squeeze dry. Place in a pan with the wine, vinegar and meat sediment, and reduce until thick. Work in the butter and cream a little at a time, then add the mustard, the green peppercorns which have been well rinsed, and the chives. The sauce should be highly seasoned; adjust if necessary. Pour over the meat and serve at once.

(Otto Ledermann, Switzerland)

Ragoût of rabbit Ticino fashion
Lapin sauté à la tessinoise

10 portions

4 kg	rabbit	8 lb 12 oz

	oil	
1½ l	brown veal stock	2¾ pt
½ l	red wine	18 fl oz
600 g	tomatoes	1 lb 5 oz
600 g	onions, chopped	1 lb 5 oz
500 g	flap mushrooms, fresh or frozen	1 lb 2 oz
500 g	chanterelles, fresh or frozen	1 lb 2 oz
	herbs (parsley, chives chopped)	
	salt	
	spices as desired	
	garlic	
100 g	butter	3½ oz

Polenta:

1 kg	coarse maize meal	2 lb 4 oz
3 l	water	5 pt
50 g	butter	2 oz
50 g	onions	2 oz
	salt	
200 g	cheese	7 oz
800 g	tomatoes, skinned, seeded and diced	1 lb 12 oz
50 g	butter	2 oz

Mixed salad Greek style:

1 kg	carrots	2 lb 4 oz
1 kg	celeriac	2 lb 4 oz
1 kg	turnip tops	2 lb 4 oz
1 kg	turnips	2 lb 4 oz
4 dl	oil	14 fl oz
2 dl	vinegar	7 fl oz
	salt	
	spices as desired	
	herbs	

Cut the rabbits into even size pieces, season and fry on all sides in hot oil until golden. Cook the onions gently without colouring, add the tomatoes and stir in the wine and stock. Cover and braise until the meat is tender. Strain the sauce, season to taste and pour over the meat. To serve, cover with the mushrooms which have been fried, and sprinkle with the herbs.

Serve polenta, garnished with diced tomatoes, and mixed salad Greek style as accompaniments. To prepare the salad, cut the vegetables into small thin strips and dress Greek style.

(Otto Ledermann, Switzerland)

Saddle of rabbit with herbs
Râble de lapin aux herbettes

2 portions

	1 saddle of rabbit with liver	
3 cl	port	1 fl oz
60 g	butter	2 oz
	1 tablespoon groundnut oil	
5 cl	rabbit glaze	2 fl oz
1 dl	dairy cream	3½ fl oz
	fresh savoury, sage, rosemary	
	salt, pepper	
	red Burgunday	
	veal stock	

Insert savory, sage and rosemary leaves into the flesh right along the saddle, then season with salt and pepper. Heat the oil with 20 g (¾ oz) butter, add the saddle without the liver and fry on all sides until golden brown. Cover the pan and continue cooking for 10 to 15 minutes over medium heat to keep the meat tender. Transfer the meat to a serving dish and keep hot.

Reduce the pan juices well, drain off the fat, moisten with the port, reduce a little, add the rabbit glaze, then the cream, and reduce until thick. Remove from the heat and work in the rest of the butter. Add a little finely chopped savory, sage and rosemary, adjust the seasoning and pour over the meat which has been carved. Add the rabbit liver which has been fried in a little butter. Serve with home made noodles or maize cakes.

Brown the rabbit bones in fat with a mirepoix, add seasoning and herbs (savory and rosemary), continue browning, moisten with red Burgundy and a little veal stock if necessary, reduce well until very thick, pass through a conical strainer and reduce again until syrupy. Place in a small jar or pot and leave to set like jelly. Store in a cool place.

(Jean Schillinger, France)

Hot Rabbit Dishes for Individual Plate Service

Rabbit Agrigento style
Lapin à la mode d'Agrigente
Coniglio tirato

6 portions

approx. 1 kg 500	rabbit	approx.	3¼ lb
	6 cloves of garlic		
	1 tablespoon oregano		
1–2 dl	olive oil		3½–7 fl oz
5 cl	wine vinegar		2 fl oz
	salt		

Joint the rabbit, wash and dry well. Place in a pan without oil, season with salt and dry over gentle heat. Add the oil, brown the meat quickly, add the garlic, moisten with the vinegar, cover and continue cooking, turning the meat occasionally. Sprinkle with oregano and turn again. Dress on plates and serve with mashed potatoes, vegetable purée or vegetables in season.

(Salvatore Schifano, Italy)

Rabbit with basil
Lapereau au basilic
Jong konijn met basilicum

2 portions

	1 young rabbit	
5 dl	Beaujolais	18 fl oz
2 dl	dairy cream	7 fl oz
	1 bouquet garni	
	4 sprigs basil	
	salt	
	pepper, freshly ground	
	butter	

Cut off the rabbit legs and fillets. Prepare stock with the rest of the meat and the wine, and simmer over low heat for 2 hours. Season and strain. Cook the legs gently in the stock for 1 hour, then remove and keep hot. Add the cream to the stock, together with 6–8 basil leaves, and bring to the boil. Meanwhile sauter the fillets in butter, slice on the slant and dress on warmed plates. Place a leg on each plate. Strain the sauce over the meat and decorate the plates with a few basil leaves.

(Paul Fagel, Netherlands)

Leg of rabbit with old marc
Cuisse de lapin au vieux marc
Kaninchenkeule mit altem Marc

100 portions

17 kg	rabbit legs	37½ lb

Marinade:

½ l	oil	18 fl oz
500 g	onions, diced	1 lb 2 oz
500 g	carrots, diced	1 lb 2 oz
300 g	celery, diced	11 oz
330 g	salt	12 oz
100 g	commercial seasoning	3½ oz
100 g	cloves, thyme, marjoram, sage, juniper berries	
10 g	pepper, freshly ground	⅓ oz
1 l	marc brandy	1¾ pt
500 g	butter	1 lb 2 oz
10 l	cream sauce	17½ pt
2 kg	white grapes	4 lb 8 oz
7 kg	noodles	15 lb 8 oz
330 g	salt	12 oz

Prepare the marinade and lay the rabbit legs in it for 3 days. Remove and roast slowly in the butter, basting frequently. Add the marinade which has been clarified. Remove the meat and add the cream sauce to the pan juices. Reduce to the required consistency, adjust the seasoning and add the grapes. To serve, place the rabbit legs on plates and coat with the sauce. Garnish with noodles.

(Otto Ledermann, Switzerland)

Rabbit leg with juniper berries and fresh noodles
Cuisse de lapin aux baies de genièvre et aux nouilles fraîches
Coscia di coniglio alle bacche di ginepro – tagliatelle fresche

1 portion   Cooking time: 40 minutes

140 g	rabbit leg	5 oz

1½ dl	Cognac	5 fl oz
	10–12 juniper berries	
10 g	butter	⅓ oz
5 cl	rabbit stock	2 fl oz
5 cl	dairy cream	2 fl oz

Garnish:

25 g	fresh noodles	1 oz
5 g	butter	⅙ oz
5 dl	water	18 fl oz
	coarse and fine salt	
	white pepper, freshly ground	

Leave the rabbit leg in the Cognac with the addition of the juniper berries for 24 hours. Drain well, dry with a cloth and season with salt and pepper. Colour lightly on all sides for 5 minutes in the butter over fairly low heat, then transfer to an oven preheated to 180°C (355°F) and cook for 25 to 30 minutes. Remove and keep hot. Meanwhile, cook the noodles and prepare the sauce. Boil the noodles in salted water, keeping them firm to the bite, drain well and mix with butter and freshly ground pepper.

Drain off the butter remaining in the pan used to cook the rabbit leg, detach the sediment with the Cognac from the marinade, ignite, reduce by two thirds, pass through a conical strainer, add the juniper berries, rabbit stock and cream, and adjust the seasoning. Pour on to a warm plate, and place the rabbit and noodles on top.
(Illustration, page 414)

(Daniel Drouadaine, Italy)

Rabbit in tomato and white wine sauce
Lapin en sauce à la tomate et au vin blanc
Coniglio al sugo

6 portions

1 kg 500	rabbit	3 lb 5 oz
	2 bay leaves	
	salt	
1 kg	tomatoes	2 lb 4 oz
2 dl	olive oil	7 fl oz
1 dl	white wine	3½ fl oz
	1 chilli pepper	

Prepare tomato sauce in the usual manner, adding the chilli pepper. Joint the rabbit and blanch in acidulated water. Dry, then brown on all sides in olive oil with the addition of the bay leaves. Add the tomato sauce and braise. Shortly before the meat is cooked, add the wine and reduce well. Adjust the seasoning.

(Salvatore Schifano, Italy)

Ragoût of rabbit Val Verzasca
Ragoût de lapin Val Verzasca
Stufato di coniglio Valle Verzasca

100 portions   Cooking time: 40 minutes

22 kg	rabbit (saddle and legs of fresh rabbits only)	48 lb
1 kg	carrots	2 lb 4 oz
1 kg	celery	2 lb 4 oz
2 kg	onions, chopped	4 lb 8 oz
50 g	garlic	2 oz
4 l	red wine (Barbera or Valpolicella)	7 pt
5 l	thickened veal stock (brown)	9 pt
300 g	dried flap mushrooms	11 oz
1 l	oil	1¾ pt
10 g	fresh sage	⅓ oz
10 g	fresh rosemary	⅓ oz
800 g	tomato purée	1 lb 12 oz
	salt, pepper	

Polenta:

2 kg 500	medium maize meal	5 lb 8 oz
2 kg 500	coarse maize meal	5 lb 8 oz
20 l	water	35 pt
1 kg	butter	2 lb 4 oz
1 kg	Parmesan cheese	2 lb 4 oz
	salt, nutmeg	

Tomatoes:

5 kg	tomatoes (50)	11 lb
1 kg 500	Mozzarella cheese	3 lb 5 oz
	salt, pepper	
	oregano	

Luganighe:

4 kg	luganighe (Ticino sausages) (50)	8 lb 12 oz

Season the rabbit with salt and pepper and brown well on all sides in hot oil. Dice the carrots and celery finely and add, together with the onions and garlic. Continue frying for a short time, then add the sage, rosemary and tomato purée, and cook well. Pour in the wine, bring to the boil and reduce by half. Add the veal stock and cook until the meat is tender, adding the flap mushrooms (which have been soaked) for the last 10 minutes. Season well.

To make the polenta, bring the water to the boil with the addition of salt, nutmeg and the butter. Add the semolina in a steady stream and cook slowly over low heat for 1 hour, then fold in the Parmesan. Wash the tomatoes, cut them in half and arrange on a baking tray. Season with salt and pepper and cover with a piece of Mozzarella. Sprinkle the cheese with a little oregano and bake in the oven. Blanch the sausages well and allow to cool. Grill well on a hot grill and cut in half.

To serve, place half a tomato on each plate with a ball of polenta on either side. Dress the ragoût next to it and garnish with half a sausage.

(Robert Haupt-Felber, Switzerland)

Hot Main Mixed Meat Dishes

Bernese platter
Plat bernois
Berner Platte

10 portions

800 g	beef for boiling	1 lb 12 oz
600 g	salt or smoked fat pork	1 lb 5 oz
600 g	salt or smoked fore loin of pork	1 lb 5 oz
400 g	pickled ox or pig's tongue	14 oz
400 g	Bernese tongue sausage	14 oz
	10 marrow bones	
300 g	flavouring vegetables and herbs	11 oz
2 kg	sauerkraut	4 lb 8 oz

Boil the beef for 2 to 2½ hours and remove from the pan. Prepare strong clear soup with the stock, to be served at the beginning of the meal with bone marrow and croûtons.

Boil the tongue until tender. Cook the pork and sausage with the sauerkraut. Transfer the sauerkraut to a deep serving dish. Slice the meat and sausage and arrange attractively on the sauerkraut. Hand boiled potatoes separately.

(Otto Ledermann, Switzerland)

Meat in sour milk Metohija style
Poêlée à la Kosovo–Metohija
Metohijska Tava

6 portions   Cooking time: 1½–2 hours

1 kg	boneless veal or lamb	2 lb 4 oz
4½ dl	sour ewe's milk	15 fl oz
	(recipe, page 147)	
	4 eggs, well beaten	
2 dl	oil	7 fl oz
50 g	kajmak (recipe, page 147)	2 oz
	½ glass water	
	dill, chopped	
	salt	

Roast the meat in a little oil for about 1 hour, then cut into pieces and transfer to a fairly large shallow pan. Mix the sour milk well with the water, eggs and dill and pour over the meat. Season with salt. Melt the kajmak and pour over. Bake for about 15 minutes. To serve, place the meat in the centre of a heated dish and pour the curdled milk round. Hand baked new potatoes separately.

(László Csizmadia, Yugoslavia)

Cotechino Bergamo fashion
Cotechino alla bergamasca

400 g	veal (shoulder or breast) in one piece	14 oz
300 g	fresh cotechino (Italian pork sausage)	11 oz

Beat the veal well to flatten. Remove the sausage meat from its casing, lay it on the meat, roll up tightly and sew up to secure. Place in boiling water and simmer over gentle heat for 2½ hours.

Serve hot, cut into slices, with spinach or mashed potatoes. To serve cold, cut into slices and glaze with white wine aspic if desired.

(Guido Belotti, Enzo Ronzoni, Carlo Calvetti, Italy)

Duvec
Gratin à la serbe

6 portions   Cooking time: about 2 hours

1 kg	mutton, cut into small pieces	2 lb 4 oz
OR 500 g	pork, cut into small pieces	1 lb 2 oz
and 500 g	beef, cut into small pieces	1 lb 2 oz
1½ dl	oil (olive or other)	5 fl oz
60 g	rice	2 oz
1 kg 500	tomatoes, sliced	3 lb 5 oz
1 kg 750	onions, sliced	3 lb 14 oz
	1 aubergine, finely diced	
	5 fleshy green peppers, finely diced	
	2 courgettes, finely diced	
	1 bunch parsley, finely chopped	
	¼ bunch celery leaves, finely chopped	
	salt	
	pepper, freshly ground	

Place the onions, aubergine, peppers, courgettes, parsley and celery leaves in a bowl, season carefully with salt and pepper and pour the oil over. Leave to marinate for a time.

Place half the tomato slices in a fireproof dish, cover with half the marinated vegetables, then the meat (raw), then the rest of the vegetables. Sprinkle with the rice (raw) and cover the top with the rest of the tomato slices. Pour in 2 glasses water and the oil from the marinade. Bake in a slow oven for about 2 hours. Add a few tomato slices while baking. Bring to the table in the same dish.

(László Csizmadia, Yugoslavia)

Three fillets Villa Recreatio
Les trois filets Villa Recreatio
Tre filetti Villa Recreatio

1 portion

30 g	1 beef medallion (fillet), weighing about	1 oz
30 g	1 veal medallion (fillet), weighing about	1 oz
30 g	1 pork medallion (fillet), weighing about	1 oz
	1 slice calf's kidney	
3 cl	Madeira	1 fl oz
	1 tablespoon meat glaze	
	flour	
15 g	butter	½ oz
	oil	
	salt	
	pepper, freshly ground	

Season the meat. Lightly flour the veal, pork and kidney and briefly brown in oil. Pour off the oil, add the butter and the beef, and fry until the meat is cooked. Remove from the pan and keep hot under cover. Detach the sediment with the Madeira, add the meat glaze and enrich the sauce with butter. Pour over the meat and serve at once. A suitable accompaniment is amandines potatoes (potato balls with almonds).

(Giulio Casazza, Switzerland)

Meat loaf Stefanie
Hachis rôti Stefani
Stefaniebraten

10 portions

800 g	beef	1 lb 12 oz

600 g	pork	1 lb 5 oz
600 g	veal	1 lb 5 oz
	4 rolls, soaked in water	
	2 eggs, beaten	
	1 large onion, finely cut and fried	
50 g	parsley, finely chopped	2 oz
	2 cloves of garlic, finely chopped	
	a little caraway and marjoram	
	salt	
	4 eggs, hard-boiled	
	2 pairs Frankfurter sausages	
	1 pig's caul	
5 cl	oil	2 fl oz

Mince the meat with the rolls, onion, parsley, garlic, caraway and marjoram. Bind with the beaten eggs and season with salt. Place on a moistened board and shape into an oblong 50 x 30 cm (20 x 12 in). Place the Frankfurters and the hard-boiled eggs on top and enclose these in the minced meat mixture to form a roll. Wrap in the caul which has been well soaked and washed. Roast in the oil in a braising pan for about 45 minutes. Serve with mashed potatoes and salad.

(Eduard Mayer, Austria)

Meat balls with peas
Bitoks aux petits pois
Albondigas con guisantes

6 portions

600 g	lean pork	1 lb 5 oz
600 g	lean veal	1 lb 5 oz
200 g	bacon or pork fat	7 oz
	2 eggs, beaten	
3 dl	oil	10 fl oz
	2 onions, chopped	
	6 ripe tomatoes, skinned, seeded and cut in pieces	
	3 cloves of garlic	
	parsley	
50 g	dry breadcrumbs	2 oz
100 g	flour	3½ oz
1 dl	white wine	3½ fl oz
	salt	
	ground cinnamon	
500 g	peas	1 lb 2 oz

Picada:

	saffron	
50 g	almonds	2 oz
	3 bitter macaroons (caraquinolis)	

Mince the meat and bacon and place in a bowl. Chop the parsley and garlic very finely and add to the meat together with the eggs. Mix thoroughly and add the breadcrumbs. Season with salt and cinnamon. Shape into small balls, flour them and fry in hot oil. Remove and keep hot. While the oil is still hot, cook the onions gently in the same pan without colouring, add the tomatoes, season with salt, and cook over gentle heat, stirring repeatedly, until the liquid has almost boiled away. Moisten with the wine, reduce well, add a little water and boil up for a few moments. Pour over the meat balls, add the peas which have been cooked, and flavour with picada.

To make picada, pound the macaroons, saffron and almonds to a fine paste in a china mortar and blend with a little water.

(Josep Lladonosa, Spain)

Mexican meat balls
Boulettes de viande à la mexicaine
Albondigas a la mexicana

10 portions

750 g	shoulder of veal	1 lb 10 oz
750 g	shoulder of pork	1 lb 10 oz
200 g	onions, finely chopped	7 oz
100 g	olives, stoned	3½ oz
	4 eggs, beaten	
	2 eggs, hard-boiled and chopped	
3 cl	oil	1 fl oz
OR 30 g	butter	1 oz
	bouillon	
	salt, pepper	

Mexican rice:

600 g	pilaf rice	1 lb 5 oz
50 g	lard	2 oz
500 g	peas	1 lb 2 oz
200 g	onions, chopped	7 oz
50 g	tomato purée	2 oz
	bouillon as required	
	salt, pepper, paprika	
200 g	frying sausage	7 oz

3 eggs, hard-boiled
1 tablespoon parsley, finely chopped
2 tablespoons cheese, grated

Tomato sauce:

| 1 kg | tomatoes, skinned, seeded and finely chopped | 2 lb 4 oz |

2 cloves of garlic, crushed
coriander, chilli powder to taste
a little flour if required

Mince the meat finely. Cook the onions gently in oil or butter until transparent and add to the meat together with the olives which have been finely chopped, the eggs, salt and pepper, working the ingredients together until smooth. Shape into balls, allow to rest a little, then poach in bouillon. Suitable accompaniments include Mexican rice with piquant tomato sauce.

To prepare the rice, place in boiling water, leave for 15 minutes, drain and rinse in cold running water until no longer starchy. Slice the sausage, fry lightly in the lard and keep hot. Add the rice to the pan and fry until golden, pouring off any surplus lard. Add the onions and cook gently without colouring. Add the tomato purée, moisten with bouillon, season with salt, pepper and paprika and cook until rather soft. Stir in the peas which have been cooked. To serve, sprinkle the rice with the grated cheese, cover with the slices of sausage and the eggs which have been sliced, and sprinkle with parsley.

To make the sauce, mix the tomatoes well with the garlic, season with coriander and chilli powder, and dust with a little flour, if required, to make a paste. Add to tomato sauce made in the usual manner.

(Emil Wälti, Mexico)

Calf's and lamb's kidneys with shallots
Rognons de veau et d'agneau aux échalottes

6 portions

	3 calf's kidneys, soaked and trimmed	
	6 lamb's kidneys	
70 g	butter	2½ oz
2 dl	reduced veal stock	7 fl oz
3 cl	Cognac	1 fl oz
5 cl	white wine	2 fl oz
30 g	shallots, finely chopped	1 oz
100 g	young shallots, whole	3½ oz
10 g	sugar	⅓ oz

salt
pepper, freshly ground

Peel the whole young shallots and arrange them in a small stew pan. Cover with water and add a pinch of salt, the sugar and 20 g (¾ oz) butter. Cook over low heat until all the water has boiled away. Shake the pan to roll the shallots in the syrupy pan juices until evenly coloured.

Slit the lamb's kidneys lengthwise. Remove the skin and fatty cores. Dice the prepared calf's kidneys coarsely, removing all fat and sinew. Season with salt and freshly ground pepper. Heat 30 g (1 oz) butter in a sauté pan and brown the kidneys lightly. Sauter quickly over high heat to keep them tender, then transfer to warmed plates and keep hot.

Fry the chopped shallots in the same pan until lightly coloured. Moisten with white wine, then with Cognac. Reduce by half and add the veal stock. Boil for 2 minutes. Remove from the heat and blend in 20 g (¾ oz) butter to thicken the sauce. Add salt and pepper to taste. Pass through a small conical strainer and pour over the kidneys. Garnish with the shallots and with vegetables in season.
(Illustration, page 765)

(Jean-Paul Bossée-Francois, France)

Lamb and veal brochettes Greek style
Brochettes d'agneau et de veau à la grecque
Souvlakia

4 portions

750 g	lamb (leg), veal (loin or cushion) and/or lean pork (fillet)	1 lb 10 oz
	1 tablespoon oil	
	2 tablespoons onion, chopped	
	2 tablespoons parsley, chopped	
	2 small tomatoes, each cut into 8 wedges	
	1 teaspoon oregano	
	4 bay leaves, cut in half	
	salt and pepper to taste	

Cut the meat into walnut-size pieces. Prepare a marinade with the onion, parsley, oil, salt and pepper and lay the meat in it. When well marinated, thread on to metal or wooden skewers about 8 cm (3½ in) long, alternating the pieces of meat with tomato wedges and half bay leaves. (Impale the tomato wedges skin side first to keep them in place.) Fry or grill for about 15 minutes and sprinkle with finely chopped oregano. Serve very hot. Hand green salad with sliced tomatoes separately.

(Emil Wälti, Greece)

Fillet of beef Charlois, p. 414 ► ▲
Stuffed pickled saddle of lamb, p. 380 ►

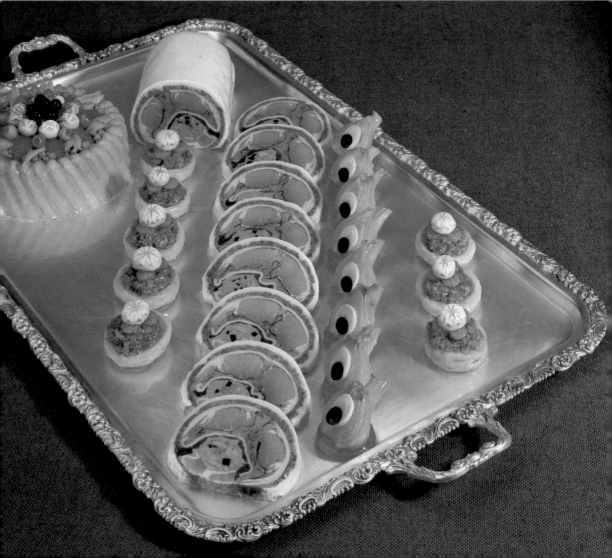

941

◄ Shoulder of pork with horseradish, p. 911
▼▼ Plated pork in aspic, p. 331
▼ Stuffed calf's kidney on Swiss chard, p. 590

942

Smoked ox tongue modern style, p. 382 ►
Lamb pâté Verecke, p. 992 ►▼

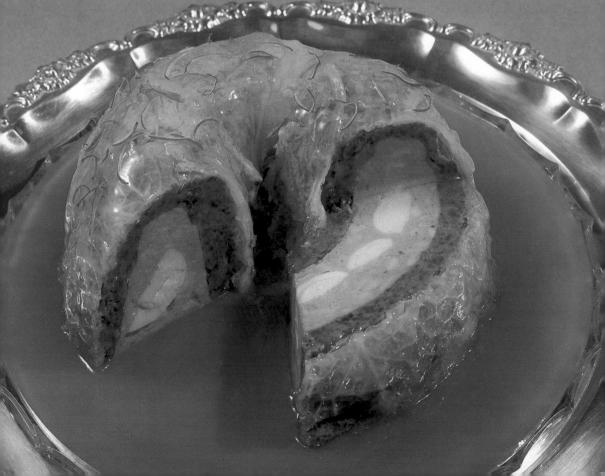

945

Mixed meat sauté with rosemary
L'assiette des quatre viandes au romarin

4 portions

50 g	4 veal medallions each weighing	2 oz
	4 lamb cutlets	
50 g	4 small tournedos each weighing	2 oz
	4 guinea fowl breasts	
20 g	fresh rosemary	¾ oz
180 g	butter	6 oz
20 g	shallots, chopped	¾ oz
3 dl	white wine	10 fl oz
2 dl	reduced veal stock	7 fl oz
2 cl	oil	1 fl oz
5 cl	sherry	2 fl oz
	salt	
	pepper, freshly ground	

Season the meat and guinea fowl. Heat the oil in a large sauté pan together with 30 g (1 oz) butter until nut brown. Depending on the nature of the meat, fry on each side for 2 to 3 minutes. Keep hot. Pour off the fat. Add the shallots, rosemary, wine and sherry to the pan. Reduce by three quarters, then add the veal stock and reduce by half to a syrupy consistency. Remove the pan from the heat and whisk the rest of the butter into the sauce. Adjust the seasoning and pass through a fine conical strainer. Blend in the juices which have escaped from the meat while kept hot.

Arrange the meat and guinea fowl on warmed plates and coat with sauce. Hand vegetables in season as an accompaniment.
(Illustration, page 765)

(Jean-Paul Bossée-François, France)

Tournedos and veal medallions Gumpoldskirchen
Tournedos et médaillons de veau Gumpoldskirchen
Lendenschnitten und Kalbsmedaillons Gumpoldskirchen

4 portions

90 g	4 tournedos each weighing	3¼ oz
90 g	4 veal medallions each weighing	3¼ oz
40 g	8 slices foie gras each weighing	1½ oz
30 g	butter	1 oz
30 g	fat	1 oz
	salt, pepper	

◄ Rabbit Alpe Vicania, p. 918

                2 eggs, beaten
                dry breadcrumbs

Sauce:

40 g	flour	1½ oz
40 g	butter	1½ oz
6 cl	white wine	2 fl oz
2½ dl	veal stock	9 fl oz
	2 egg yolks	
	salt, lemon juice	

Garnish:

200 g	grapes	7 oz
30 g	butter	1 oz
6 cl	white wine	2 fl oz
1¼ dl	demi-glace	4 fl oz

Season the meat. Fry in butter on both sides for about 2 minutes and place on a rack. Season the foie gras and place in the butter for about 1 minute, then place on top of the meat and allow to cool. Egg and crumb. Deep-fry for about 5 minutes in hot fat at about 160°C (320°F), coat with the sauce, garnish with the grapes and serve at once.

To prepare the sauce, make a white roux with the butter and flour, blend in the wine, then the stock, and simmer for about 5 minutes. Add salt and lemon juice to taste and thicken with the egg yolks. Use very hot.

For the garnish, peel the grapes, cut them in half, seed them and toss in butter. Stir in the wine, reduce a little and thicken with the demi-glace. Serve Dauphine or Duchesse potatoes as an accompaniment.
(Illustration, page 770)

                                        (Franz Zodl, Austria)

Pljeskavica
Steaks hachés à la serbe

4 portions

350 g	pork	12 oz
350 g	veal	12 oz
200 g	onions, finely chopped	7 oz
	salt	
	pepper, freshly ground	
	small green chilli peppers	
	(optional)	

Mince the meat and season with salt and pepper. Mix with the onions and, if desired, with small green chillis, finely chopped. Knead well and allow to rest for 3 hours. Form into flat, round cakes and grill over high heat on a grid greased with bacon fat. Cover the centre of a dish with finely cut raw onions and surround with the minced steaks. Serve very hot.

(László Csizmadia, Yugoslavia)

Razňjici
Brochettes à la serbe

6 portions   Cooking time: about 10 minutes

500 g	veal	1 lb 2 oz
500 g	pork	1 lb 2 oz
250 g	onions	9 oz
	salt	
	pepper, freshly ground	

Cut the meat into about 3 cm (1¼ in) cubes. Thread on to metal skewers 15 cm (6 in) long, alternating the veal and pork and allowing 2 skewers per portion each containing 6 meat cubes. Grill over high heat on a grid greased with bacon fat. Season with salt and pepper and dress on a warm dish. Serve with finely cut raw onions.

(László Csizmadia, Yugoslavia)

Emincé of fillet of beef with sausages and marrons glacés
Emincé de filet de boeuf aux marrons glacés
Geschnetzelte Rinderfiletspitzen mit kleinen Schweinebratwürsten und glasierten Maronen

10 portions   Cooking time: 25 minutes

1 kg 300	fillet of beef	3 lb
	20 small pork sausages	
	1 clove of garlic	
	salt	
	pepper, freshly ground	
¾ l	Espagnole sauce	1¼ pt
¼ l	dairy cream	9 fl oz
600 g	marrons glacés	1 lb 5 oz
	20 Duchesse potato cases	
	parsley, chopped	
200 g	onions, finely diced	7 oz
	Calvados	

Using a savoy bag fitted with plain tube No. 8, pipe 20 small cases of Duchesse potato mixture on to a greased baking sheet. Brush with egg yolk and bake in a hot oven.

Slice the beef very thinly, season with salt and freshly ground pepper and brown quickly in hot clarified butter. Add the onions and the garlic and brown very lightly. Remove the meat from the pan. Add a dash of Calvados to the pan and ignite. Pour in the cream and the Espagnole sauce and cook for a few minutes. Remove this sauce from the heat, add the parsley and toss the meat in it.

To serve, place the potato cases on a dish. Fill them with the meat and decorate with fried pork sausages and marrons glacés, allowing 2 potato cases per portion.

(Karl Brunnengräber)

Serbian stuffed sauerkraut
Feuilles de chou fermenté farcies
Kiselog Kupusa (Sarma)

6 portions   Cooking time: 3½–4½ hours

500 g	pork	1 lb 2 oz
250 g	beef	9 oz
200 g	smoked pork ribs	7 oz
150 g	smoked bacon, thinly sliced	5 oz
1¼ l	water	2 pt
	1 tablespoon flour	
2 kg	cabbage (whole), fermented in salt	4 lb 8 oz
30 g	rice, washed	1 oz
	1 egg	
150 g	lard	5 oz
	1 small onion	
	parsley, chopped	
	1 teaspoon paprika	
	salt, pepper	

Remove the cabbage leaves singly and cut away the thick ribs. Wash them very carefully, changing the water several times.

To make the stuffing, cook the onion gently in 100 g (3½ oz) lard. Trim the fresh pork and the beef, and mince finely, then mix with the rice and sauter with the onion until golden brown. Season with salt and pepper. Add the egg and chopped parsley, and mix well.

Line the bottom of a 3 l (5 pt) stew pan with a few cabbage leaves. Place a spoonful of stuffing in the centre of each of the remaining leaves, roll up and secure to keep the stuffing in place. Arrange in the pan in rows. Wash the smoked pork in hot water and cut into pieces. Place these between the cabbage rolls, together with the bacon. Add the water (cold), cover and cook over low heat for 3 to 4 hours. Make a roux with the rest of the lard and the flour, season with the paprika and add to the stuffed cabbage. Cook for a further 30 minutes.

(László Csizmadia, Yugoslavia)

Scottiglia La Pergola

4 portions

1 kg	lean veal, chicken, rabbit, pork, guinea fowl and pigeon, cut into small pieces	2 lb 4 oz
500 g	fresh tomatoes, sieved	1 lb 2 oz
1 dl	olive oil	3½ fl oz
	1 clove of garlic	
	1 onion	
	10 basil leaves	
	bouillon as required	
1 dl	white or red wine	3½ fl oz
	4–8 slices household bread, depending on size	
	salt, pepper	
	1 bunch parsley	

Chop the onion, garlic, parsley and basil finely. Fry the garlic lightly in the oil and add the onion and herbs. When lightly coloured, add the pieces of meat, rabbit and poultry, brown lightly, then stir in the wine, bring to the boil and reduce well. Add the tomatoes, mix well, season with salt and pepper, and cook until the tomato juice has thickened. Add bouillon as required and continue cooking. Brown the bread in the oven. While still hot, rub with a clove of garlic and place on plates. Cover with the meat and serve hot.

(La Pergola, Italy)

Scottiglia Tuscan style
Scottiglia alla toscana

10 portions

350 g	beef	12 oz
650 g	chicken	1 lb 7 oz
400 g	pork	14 oz
500 g	guinea fowl	1 lb 2 oz
400 g	lamb	14 oz
600 g	rabbit	1 lb 5 oz

450 g	turkey	1 lb
500 g	duck	1 lb 2 oz
500 g	goose	1 lb 2 oz
650 g	hare	1 lb 7 oz
	2 stalks celery	
150 g	carrots	5 oz
	1 onion	
	2 tablespoons parsley	
	2 cloves of garlic	
	2 bay leaves	
	5 basil leaves	
	a pinch of ground ginger	
	1 sprig rosemary	
1 l	dry white wine	1¾ pt
1 kg	peeled tomatoes, canned	2 lb 4 oz
	bread, sliced	

Cut up the celery, carrots, onion, parsley, garlic, bay leaves, rosemary and basil, and pound in a mortar, then mix with the ginger. Cut the meat, poultry, rabbit, and hare into fairly large pieces. Brown in a double bottomed pan over fierce heat without adding any fat, turning the contents of the pan constantly to avoid sticking or excessive browning. Sprinkle with the pounded vegetables and herbs, mix well, cover and leave to stand over the heat. When the contents of the pan are half cooked, moisten with the wine, stir well, cover and reduce well over gentle heat. Add the tomatoes in their juice and finish cooking. Toast the bread and place on plates or in fireproof earthenware bowls while still hot. Soak in a little stock, cover with the scottiglia, and serve hot.

(Mario De Filippis, Italy)

Swedish pan
Poêlée à la suédoise

4 portions

60–80 g	4 small veal fillets each weighing	2–3 oz
60–80 g	4 small pork fillets each weighing	2–3 oz
	4 slices calf's kidney, cut lengthwise	
	salt, pepper	
	a little flour	
	oil	
	2 medium onions, blanched	
	8 medium potatoes, blanched	
	1 small bouquet garni	
	2 bay leaves	
	1 teaspoon allspice	

2 dl	bouillon	7 fl oz
	1 glass of beer or white wine	
	parsley, finely chopped	

Skin and trim the kidney, then season and flour, together with the meat. Heat oil in a shallow pan and cook the meat and kidney gently without colouring. Place the onions, herbs and spices on the meat and add the bouillon. Cover with buttered paper, then cover the pan and cook. After 10 minutes, add the potatoes and the beer or wine. The liquid should just cover the contents of the pan. Cover tightly and cook slowly for a further 20 minutes or so. The meat should be kept firm. When cooked, remove the herbs and spices, sprinkle with chopped parsley and serve very hot.

(Eric Carlström, Sweden)

Pot-au-Feu Des Isles

15 portions

2 kg	leg of lamb	4 lb 8 oz
	3 knuckles of veal	
approx. 5–6 kg	kid or rabbit	approx. 11–13 lb
1 kg 500	fillet of beef	3 lb 5 oz
2½ dl	dairy cream	9 fl oz

Flavouring ingredients:

	2 onions	
	2 carrots	
	¼ medium celeriac	
	1 bouquet garni	
	1 clove of garlic	
2 g	saffron (whole)	half a small teaspoon
	salt, peppercorns	

Vegetable garnish:

15 small turnips
15 pieces celeriac, turned
15 pieces cucumber, turned
15 carrots, turned
15 young green cabbage leaves
10 tablespoons rice, blanched
butter as required
Gruyère cheese, grated, as required

Place the meat in a large pot with water and the flavouring ingredients. Bring to the boil and cook, skimming regularly. The knuckles of veal and the kid should be very well done and require more prolonged cooking than the lamb or beef. Keep the meat hot in part of the broth. Reduce the rest fairly well and thicken with the cream.

Blanch the turned vegetables and the cabbage leaves separately. Drain well. Mix the rice with butter and Gruyère cheese. Spread out the cabbage leaves, spoon rice on to each one and roll into a ball. Carve the meat. Pour the sauce on to the plates, place the meat on top and surround with the vegetables.
(Illustration, page 167)

(Emile Jung, France)

Zurich councillors' dish
Poêlée des conseillers zurichois
Zürcher Ratsherrentopf

4 portions

150 g	veal fillet, cut into 4 medallions	5 oz
150 g	calf's liver, cut into 4 slices	5 oz
150 g	fillet of beef, cut into 4 slices	5 oz
150 g	calf's sweetbreads, blanched and cut into 4 slices	5 oz
150 g	calf's kidneys, trimmed and cut into 4 slices	5 oz
	oil	
80 g	bacon (4 rashers)	3 oz
500 g	peas, fresh or frozen	1 lb 2 oz
300 g	carrots	11 oz
200 g	mushrooms	7 oz
30 g	shallots, chopped	1 oz
40 g	butter	1½ oz
1 kg	potatoes	2 lb 4 oz
1 dl	thickened veal stock	3½ fl oz
	salt	
	spices as desired	

Grill or fry all the meat in oil on both sides. Season with salt and freshly ground pepper or with spiced salt. Fry the bacon until crisp. Clean and wash the mushrooms carefully. Slice them, cook gently in butter with the shallots, and season.

Prepare noisette potatoes. Cook the carrots and peas. To serve, place the peas and carrots in a pot, cover with a layer of mushrooms, then a layer of potatoes, then the portions of meat and offal arranged one overlapping another, and finish with the bacon. Hand gravy or demi-glace sauce separately.

(Otto Ledermann, Switzerland)

Ćulbastija
Tchoulbastija

6 portions   Cooking time: 12–14 minutes

1 kg	pork (top of leg)	2 lb 4 oz
	OR beef (sirloin)	
250 g	onions	9 oz
	1 tablespoon salt	
	pepper, freshly ground	

A cut from a young animal should be used if possible. Leave the meat on ice for 24 hours, then cut into 6 slices and beat well. Grill, turning frequently. Season with salt and pepper and dress on a well heated dish. Sprinkle with finely cut raw onions and serve at once. Hand green chilli peppers separately.

(László Csizmadia, Yugoslavia)

Tongue and brains with spring vegetables
Langues et cervelles aux primeurs

4 portions

	2 lamb's tongues	
	2 pig's tongues	
	1 calf's tongue	
	2 calf's brains	
200 g	spring onions	7 oz
	2 leeks	
	4 turnips	
½ l	tongue stock	18 fl oz
100 g	cream cheese	3½ oz
	1 bunch chives, finely cut	
	2 tablespoons sour cream	
	1 bouquet garni	
	3 bay leaves	
	30 juniper berries	
	3 cloves of garlic	
	black pepper, crushed	
	coarse salt	
	vinegar	

Wash the tongues well and place in a pan of water containing salt, pepper, the bouquet garni, bay leaves, juniper berries and garlic. Bring to the boil and cook until tender. The cooking time will vary according to the type of tongue. Remove the tongues and keep hot. Skim the fat off the stock. Blanch the vegetables in the stock or separately.

Rinse the brains well, remove the skin and blood vessels and wash again thoroughly. Cook separately in salted water with the addition of a dash of vinegar, keeping the water at simmering point.

Reduce the tongue stock to ½ l (18 fl oz). Mix with the cream cheese, sour cream and chives.

Skin the tongues carefully and cut into portions. Arrange on a large serving dish with the brains and vegetables. Hand the sauce separately.
(Illustration, page 308)

(Roger Souvereyns, Belgium)

Hot-Pots

Alsatian hot-pot I
Baeckeofe à l'alsacienne

4–6 portions

500 g	boneless shoulder of lamb	1 lb 2 oz
500 g	neck of pork or brisket of beef, boned	1 lb 2 oz
	2 large onions, sliced	
	2 cloves of garlic	
	1 bouquet garni (bay leaf, thyme)	
1 kg 200	potatoes	2 lb 10 oz
	pepper, salt	
	parsley, chopped	
5 dl	white wine	18 fl oz

Cut the meat into slices or neat pieces and marinate for 1 day in the wine with the addition of the onions, garlic, bouquet garni and pepper. Peel the potatoes, slice them and place half the slices in a cast iron braising pan. Place the meat and onions on top and cover with the rest of the potatoes. Strain the marinade over and season with salt. Cover tightly and braise in the oven for 2 to 2½ hours. Sprinkle with chopped parsley before serving.

(Emil Wälti, France)

Alsatian hot-pot II
Baeckeofe à l'alsacienne

6 portions   Cooking time: ¾–1 hour

500 g	neck of pork, boned	1 lb 2 oz
500 g	brisket of beef	1 lb 2 oz
300 g	onions	11 oz
	1 clove of garlic	
1 kg	potatoes, peeled	2 lb 4 oz
½ l	dry white wine (Edelzwicker)	18 fl oz
	salt	
	pepper, freshly ground	
	1 bay leaf	
	thyme	
50 g	lard	2 oz

| 50 g | butter | 2 oz |

Cut the meat into 3 cm (1¼ in) cubes and marinate overnight in the wine. Next day, cut the onions into strips and the potatoes into fairly thick slices. Grease a fireproof earthenware casserole with the lard. Pound the garlic with salt. Place in a bowl with the meat, onions, potatoes, herbs, pepper and butter, mix well and transfer to the casserole. Pour the wine over, cover tightly and cook in a preheated oven. Serve with green salad.

(Otto Brust, France)

Biksemad
Poêlée familiale danoise

4 portions

400 g	boiled or roast beef, pork, lamb or veal	14 oz
200 g	onions	7 oz
500 g	firm potatoes, boiled	1 lb 2 oz
100 g	butter	3½ oz
	salt	
	pepper, freshly ground	
	1 tablespoon soya sauce	
	4 eggs	

Cut the meat, potatoes and onions evenly into 1½ cm (about ½ in) cubes. Heat half the butter in a sauté pan. Add the meat and potatoes, and sauter. Melt the rest of the butter in a second pan and sauter the onions until crisp. Mix the meat, potatoes and onions together in a frying pan, add the soya sauce and season with salt and pepper. Fry the eggs in the same pan.

To serve, place the meat, potatoes and onions in a heated cocotte or earthenware dish and cover with the fried eggs. Hand gherkins and brown or rye bread (not white bread) separately.

(Karl-Otto Schmidt, Denmark)

Pontesel stew
Poêlée de Pontesel
Tonco de Pontesel

200 g	boneless knuckle of veal	7 oz
130 g	pork	4½ oz
130 g	beef	4½ oz
30 g	salami	1 oz
30 g	fat bacon	1 oz

30 g	flour	1 oz
170 g	Lucanica (fresh pork sausage)	6 oz
½ l	dry white wine	18 fl oz
	1 clove of garlic	
	1 sprig rosemary	
	1 bay leaf	
	1 sprig thyme	
	bouillon as required	
10 g	butter	⅓ oz

Dice the bacon and salami finely, and the meat coarsely. Fry the garlic, bacon and salami in the butter without colouring, add the herbs, fry lightly, then add the meat and sauter. Depending on the thickness of the cubes of meat, continue cooking for about 30 minutes, then stir in the wine, add the flour, brown lightly and mix with the meat to thicken the stock. Cook for about 1½ hours over fairly low heat without covering the pan, adding hot bouillon as required. Slice the pork sausage and cook separately in a little meat stock. Transfer the meat stew and sausage to a fireproof dish, dot with butter and brown at 220°C (430°F). Serve with polenta. This is a typical dish from Trento.

(Sergio Chiesa, Italy)

Valais stew
Potée à la valaisanne
Eintopf auf Walliser Art

10 portions   Cooking time: about 1 hour

600 g	smoked fat pork	1 lb 5 oz
600 g	salt fat pork	1 lb 5 oz
600 g	Valais smoked sausage	1 lb 5 oz
300 g	carrots	11 oz
150 g	turnips	5 oz
150 g	celeriac or celery	5 oz
500 g	savoy cabbage	1 lb 2 oz
100 g	butterfat (10%)	3½ oz
300 g	dried pears, smoked	11 oz
2 dl	white wine (Fendant)	7 fl oz
800 g	potatoes, diced	1 lb 12 oz
	salt	
	pepper, freshly ground	

Cut the vegetables evenly into large cubes or strips. Heat the butterfat and stew the vegetables in it. Add the pears which have been well drained, the pork, wine and about 2 dl (7 fl oz) water. Season, cover the pan tightly and simmer for 40 minutes. Place the potatoes and sausage on top of the other ingredients and cook over low heat for a further 20 minutes.

Transfer the vegetables to a shallow dish. Slice the pork and sausage and place on top.

(Otto Ledermann, Switzerland)

Housewife's hot-pot
Pot-au-feu à la ménagère

6 portions

approx. 1 kg 200	chuck steak, trimmed of sinew	approx.	2 lb 10 oz
	salt		
	1 bouquet garni		
	peppercorns, cloves		
	1 bay leaf		

Garnish:

12 small onions
2 medium onions
4 turnips
6 large potatoes

Cut the meat into 5 cm (2 in) cubes and blanch them. Add sufficient cold water to cover. Season with salt, add the herbs and spices, cover tightly and cook. When the meat is half cooked, remove the herbs and spices, add the vegetable garnish and cook slowly until tender. Before serving, thicken a little with a grated raw potato. To serve, transfer to a deep dish or to small individual dishes. Hand small bowls of grated horseradish, capers, chopped parsley and finely cut chives as accompaniments.

(Eric Carlström, Sweden)

Suffolk stew

8 portions   Cooking time: about 2 hours

	24 lean lamb cutlets from the best end,		
75–80 g	each weighing	approx.	3 oz
250 g	carrots		9 oz
250 g	turnips		9 oz
250 g	swedes		9 oz
125 g	onions		4½ oz
125 g	leeks		4½ oz
95 g	barley		3¼ oz
95 g	lentils		3¼ oz

2¼ l	lamb stock	4 pt
	salt, pepper	

Wash the lentils well and soak in water for 24 hours, then drain. Clean the vegetables and cut into 2½ cm (1 in) cubes. Season the lamb cutlets with salt and pepper and place them in a large earthenware pot. Cover with the lentils, barley and vegetables. Add the lamb stock. Cover tightly and cook for 2 hours. Check that all the ingredients are well cooked; if not, continue cooking for a short time. Check the seasoning. Serve hot with pickled red cabbage.

(Samuel J. Chalmers, Great Britain)

Turlou
Potée turque dite 'turlou'

5 portions

	shoulder of mutton, boned	
750 g	*or* stewing veal	1 lb 10 oz
50 g	butterfat	2 oz
or 5 cl	oil	2 fl oz
100 g	onions, chopped	3½ oz
200 g	fresh beans	7 oz
400 g	courgettes	14 oz
400 g	tomatoes	14 oz
200 g	okra, fresh or canned	7 oz
200 g	green peppers	7 oz
400 g	potatoes	14 oz
	salt, pepper	
approx. 5 dl	water	approx. 18 fl oz

Cut the meat into pieces and brown lightly in hot butterfat or oil. Add the onions, cook gently and pour in the water. Transfer to a pan with a well-fitting lid (or a steamer) and cook gently for about 20 to 30 minutes, depending on the type and quality of meat used.

Meanwhile, prepare the vegetables. Cut the beans into short sections; peel the courgettes, remove the seeds and fibres, and cut into 3–4 cm (1½ in) cubes; skin, seed and quarter the tomatoes; cut the okra in half and remove the ends; cut the green peppers in half, seed and dice them; peel the potatoes and cut into about 4 cm (1½ in) cubes.

Place the vegetables on top of the meat, season with salt and pepper, and add a little liquid if necessary. Cover and finish cooking. Almost all the liquid should have boiled away. Serve in the cooking pot if possible, otherwise transfer carefully to a suitable dish.

(Emil Wälti, Turkey)

Southern Norwegian stew
Poêlée à la norvégienne
Sörlands Byssemat

4 portions

1 kg	brisket of beef, pickled and smoked	2 lb 4 oz
approx. 1 l	good stock approx.	1¾ pt

Barley pudding:

400 g	barley	14 oz
½ l	water	18 fl oz
½ l	good stock	18 fl oz
50 g	butter	2 oz
	2 large onions	
	salt, pepper	
	thyme	
	2 eggs, beaten	
	dry breadcrumbs	

Boil the meat in the stock, allow to cool, then slice. Blanch the barley briefly in boiling water. Pour off the water and cook the barley in the stock until soft (about 30 minutes). Chop the onions finely and toss quickly in butter. Season with salt, pepper and a little thyme and add the eggs. Mix all the ingredients well with the barley and fill into a buttered fireproof mould which has been sprinkled with breadcrumbs. Dot with butter and brown lightly in a preheated oven. Serve with red cabbage salad and coleslaw.

(Hroar Dege, Günther Rett, Norway)

Stuffed cabbage Koloszvar style
Chou farci à la Koloszvar
Koloszvári töltött káposzta

5 portions
Cooking time: about 2 hours

250 g	shoulder of pork, minced	9 oz
60 g	5 pork chops each weighing	2 oz
300 g	sausages	11 oz
50 g	smoked pork fat	2 oz
500 g	sauerkraut	1 lb 2 oz
	5 cabbage leaves, fermented in salt	
100 g	rice	3½ oz
	2 eggs	
	2 medium onions	
	2 cloves of garlic	

	1 bunch dill	
	1 bay leaf	
5 g	caraway	⅙ oz
3 dl	sour cream	10 fl oz
10 g	noble-sweet paprika	⅓ oz
	salt, pepper	
	oil	
	1 green pepper, finely diced	
	1 tomato, finely diced	

Melt 25 g (1 oz) finely diced pork fat and fry a finely cut onion in it until lightly coloured. Mix well with the minced shoulder of pork, the rice, eggs, salt and pepper. Divide into 5 equal parts and enclose in the 5 cabbage leaves.

Cut up the rest of the pork fat finely and fry in a little oil in an ovenproof dish. Cover with the second onion, finely cut, then with the sauerkraut, and arrange the stuffed cabbage leaves on top. Add sufficient water to cover well. Season with salt and sprinkle with the bay leaf and caraway, finely chopped dill, and the green pepper and tomato. Cook under cover for about 2 hours in an oven preheated to 140°C (285°F), then remove, pour the sour cream over and bring to the boil.

Beat the pork chops, season with salt, and fry quickly in a little oil over high heat. Fry the sausages. Place the chops and sausages on the cabbage, decorate with rings of green pepper and sliced tomatoes, and sprinkle with chopped dill. Bring to the table in the cooking dish.

(Gyula Gullner, Hungary)

Olla podrida

5–6 portions

500 g	beef for boiling	1 lb 2 oz
250 g	veal	9 oz
	1 small chicken	
	1 young pigeon or partridge	
80 g	raw ham	3 oz
50 g	carrots	2 oz
50 g	celeriac	2 oz
30 g	parsnip	1 oz
	1 parsley root	
50 g	onions, finely chopped	2 oz
50 g	kohlrabi	2 oz
	1 clove of garlic, finely chopped	
50 g	chick peas	2 oz
75 g	chorizo	2½ oz
	salt, spices	

2 l	water	3½ pt

Boil the meat and poultry together in the water, skimming occasionally and removing each item as soon as it is cooked. Season. Dice the raw ham and place in a pan with the onions and garlic. Cook gently for a few moments, then add the vegetables which have been thinly sliced and continue cooking briefly. Add the meat and poultry stock and cook until soft. Cook the chick peas separately and add to the vegetables.

Carve the meat and cut up the poultry. Pass the remaining stock through a cloth and return to the pan or pour into a serving dish. Keep the meat and poultry hot in the stock. Heat the chorizo, slice and add to the meat. Check the seasoning.

The stock may be served with the meat, or separately as soup. Favourite accompaniments are white radishes, small red radishes, cucumber salad, or rolled anchovy fillets with butter.

(Emil Wälti, Spain)

French pot-au-feu
Pot-au-feu à la française

5 portions

1 kg	beef (top rib or flat ribs)	2 lb 4 oz
500 g	beef bones	1 lb 2 oz
250 g	celeriac	9 oz
150 g	carrots	5 oz
150 g	leeks (white part)	5 oz
50 g	parsley roots	2 oz
	5 beef marrow bones, cut up	
	1 onion stuck with a clove	
	salt, pepper	

Blanch the beef bones, pour off the water, cover the bones with cold water again and cook for 1 hour over low heat. Add the meat and continue cooking for 1 hour, then add the vegetables which have been cleaned, season with salt and pepper, and cook slowly, skimming repeatedly to obtain clear broth. The soup is served very hot with toast. Carve the meat and arrange on a heated dish surrounded with the vegetables. Serve very hot. Hand pickled gherkins and various kinds of mustard separately.

(Emil Wälti, France)

Hot-pot Colmar style
Potée colmarienne

4–5 portions

	2 salted knuckles of pork	1½ lb

600–700 g	smoked shoulder of pork	1¼– 1½ lb
1 kg 250	turnips fermented in salt	2 lb 12 oz
100 g	onions, sliced	3½ oz
	2 cloves of garlic	
100 g	lard	3½ oz
2 dl	white wine	7 fl oz
1 kg	potatoes	2 lb 4 oz

Wash the turnips first in cold, then in warm water and squeeze dry. Cook the onions gently in the lard until transparent, using a pan with a well-fitting lid. Add the turnips, garlic and meat. Pour in the wine and an equal amount of water, and bring to the boil. Cover tightly and cook (in the oven if desired) for about 1½ hours, depending on the size of the pieces of pork and the type of pan used. Cook the potatoes separately. Carve the meat and dish in the same way as pork and sauerkraut Alsatian style. Serve very hot.

(Emil Wälti, France)

Norwegian sailors' beef
Poêlée des marins norvégiens
Sjömannsbiff

4 portions

500 g	rump steak	1 lb 2 oz
	salt, white pepper	
	3 large onions	
	8 large potatoes, sliced	
5 dl	beer	18 fl oz
5 dl	bouillon	18 fl oz
	parsley, chopped	

Slice the steak thinly and brown lightly on both sides. Remove from the pan, season with salt and pepper, and place in a casserole in alternate layers with the potatoes and the onions which have been lightly stewed. Pour the juices from the pan in which the meat was browned into the casserole, together with the beer and bouillon. Cook in a slow oven for about 35 to 40 minutes. Garnish with chopped parsley and serve with cucumber salad.

(Hroar Dege, Günther Rett, Norway)

Danish sailor's beef stew
Poêlée du marin danois
Skipper Lobescoves

1 portion   Cooking time: 1½ hours

| 150 g | pickled beef (brisket or shoulder cut) | 5 oz |

200 g	potatoes, peeled	7 oz
100 g	onions	3½ oz
50 g	butter	2 oz
20 g	chives, finely chopped	¾ oz
¼ l	bouillon	9 fl oz
	½ bay leaf	
	white pepper, freshly ground	

Cut the beef into 1½ cm (½ in) cubes, blanch and refresh well. Simmer over low heat in the bouillon for 40 minutes. Cut the potatoes and onions into cubes of the same size as the meat, add to the pan and cook for a further 50 minutes, then season with pepper to taste.

Serve very hot in a cocotte. Hand small balls of butter, finely chopped chives and brown bread separately. The usual beverage is beer, or sometimes aquavit.

(Karl-Otto Schmidt, Denmark)

Pig's trotters with pea soup
Pieds de porc en potage St. Germain
Vepřové nožičky s hrachovou polévkou

6 portions   Cooking time: 2 hours

	6 pickled pig's trotters	
300 g	peas (green)	11 oz
	2 medium leeks	
	1 small celeriac	
	5 carrots	
60 g	fat	2 oz
	3 potatoes	
	salt	
	soup seasoning	
2½ l	bone stock	4½ pt

Clean the trotters, wash them well, place in a pan of hot water, bring to the boil and cook until tender (about 1½ to 2 hours). If they are very salty, soak them for 1 to 2 hours before use. Pick over the peas well and soak overnight in a generous amount of water. Clean the fresh vegetables and dice or slice. Cook gently in hot fat for 10 minutes, then add the peas which have been well drained, pour in the stock and cook for 1 hour. Add the potatoes and cook for a further hour or so, or until the peas and potatoes are soft enough to thicken the soup. If not thick enough, bind with roux. Season with salt and a little soup seasoning.

Serve with the hot pig's trotters and bread. The recommended beverage is beer.

(Vilèm Vrabec, Czechoslovakia)

Vaudois hot-pot
Papet vaudois

10 portions

800 g	Vaudois cabbage sausages (saucisses aux choux)	1 lb 12 oz
800 g	Vaudois liver sausages (saucisses au foie)	1 lb 12 oz
2 kg	leeks (white)	4 lb 8 oz
200 g	onions, finely cut	7 oz
100 g	butterfat (10%)	3½ oz
	salt	
	pepper, freshly ground	
	nutmeg	
5 dl	light stock	18 fl oz
2 dl	white wine	7 fl oz
1 kg	potatoes	2 lb 4 oz
1 dl	dairy cream	3½ fl oz

Wash the leeks carefully and cut into sections about 5 cm (2 in) long. Cook the onions in the butterfat until lightly coloured, add the leeks which have been well drained, and stew. Season with salt, pepper and nutmeg, then stir in the stock. Cover tightly and cook for 15 minutes. Add the potatoes which have been diced or sliced, place the sausages on top and simmer gently for at least 20 minutes. Remove the sausages and thicken the leek/potato mixture with cream. Check the seasoning.

To serve, place the vegetables in a deep dish, cut the sausages in thick slices and arrange on top. Serve at once.

(Otto Ledermann, Switzerland)

Bosnian meat and cabbage stew
Poêlée aux choux à la bosnienne
Bosanska Kalja od Kupusa

8–10 portions   Cooking time: 2–3 hours

1 kg	mutton (best end) *or* pork (ribs)	2 lb 4 oz
2 kg	white cabbage	4 lb 8 oz
200 g	lard	7 oz
	4–5 cloves of garlic, chopped	
	1 onion, finely cut	

	3–4 fresh tomatoes	
or 100 g	tomato purée	3½ oz
	1 tablespoon flour	
	red paprika	
	salt	
	pepper, freshly ground	
	water or bouillon	

Cut the meat into 5 cm (2 in) cubes and brown in 100 g (3½ oz) lard. Add the onions and continue frying.

Remove the outer cabbage leaves and cut up the cabbage coarsely. Depending on quality, the cabbage may be blanched for a short time if necessary. Grease a stew pan with the rest of the lard and line the bottom with cabbage leaves. Cover with a layer of meat, then alternately with cabbage and meat until used up. Season with salt. Slice the tomatoes and place on top. Add the garlic, pepper and a sprinkling of paprika. Cover and stew over low heat for 2 to 3 hours, adding a little water or bouillon from time to time if required. Do not stir on any account, but merely shake the pan.

(László Csizmadia, Yugoslavia)

Cold Main Dishes

Beef

Cold tossed boiled beef

3–4 portions   Cooking time: 45 minutes

1 kg	beef (topside or rump)	2 lb 4 oz

Dressing:

3 cl	soya sauce	1 fl oz
1½ cl	hoisin sauce	½ fl oz
1 cl	chilli sauce	½ fl oz
1½ cl	sesame oil	½ fl oz
2½ cl	vinegar	1 fl oz
1 cl	rice wine or dry sherry	½ fl oz
	3 cloves of garlic	
	2 stalks spring onion	
5 g	sugar	⅙ oz

Chop the spring onion finely. Crush the garlic and chop finely. Mix with the other ingredients for the dressing. Place the beef in a pan of boiling water, return to the boil, then simmer for 45 minutes. Drain and cut into very thin 5–6 cm (about 2 in) rectangular pieces. Arrange the slices of meat on a serving dish and pour the dressing over.
(Illustration, page 694)

(Kenneth Lo, China)

Cold boiled beef Vital
Boeuf bouilli froid Vital
Rindfleisch Vital

4 portions

800 g	beef (silverside)	1 lb 12 oz
100 g	celeriac	3½ oz
100 g	carrots	3½ oz
50 g	swedes	2 oz
50 g	onions	2 oz
	2 cloves of garlic	
	1 bay leaf	
	peppercorns	
	salt	

Marinade:

150 g	low fat curd cheese	5 oz
1¼ dl	sour cream or yoghourt	4 fl oz
	1 clove of garlic, crushed	
	1 teaspoon fresh parsley, chopped	
	1 teaspoon fresh tarragon, chopped	
	1 teaspoon fresh chervil, chopped	
	a good pinch of ground ginger	
	tabasco or pepper	
	salt	

Garnish:

2 sweet peppers (red and green)	
2 eggs, hard-boiled and chopped	
1 bunch chives, finely cut	

Cook the meat slowly for about 2 hours with the vegetables and seasonings in just enough water to cover. Remove the meat and place in water containing a little vinegar until cold, then carve. Mix together the ingredients for the marinade and pour over the meat. Seed the peppers and cut finely. Arrange the slices of meat on a serving dish one overlapping another, with the marinade poured over. Sprinkle with the peppers, chopped egg and chives.

(Ernst Faseth, Austria)

Beef daube in aspic with leeks in nut oil vinaigrette
Daube de boeuf en gelée – poireaux à l'huile de noix

10 portions

1 kg 500	leg of beef, boned	3 lb 5 oz
	1 calf's foot	
1 l	red wine	1¾ pt
250 g	carrots	9 oz
75 g	onions	2½ oz
	1 clove of garlic	
	1 large bouquet garni	
	10 sheets gelatine	
8 cl	wine vinegar	3 fl oz
150 g	goose or duck liver, cooked	5 oz
1 kg	thin leeks	2 lb 4 oz
	oil as required	
2½ dl	vinaigrette sauce made with walnut oil	9 fl oz
100 g	French beans	3½ oz
	small peas as required	
	salt, pepper	

Prepare a marinade with the wine, the onions and 150 g (5 oz) carrots cut into strips, the clove of garlic and the bouquet garni. Lay the meat in it for 24 hours. Brown the meat and the calf's foot on all sides in oil in a braising pan. Pour in the marinade and the vinegar, season with salt and pepper, add water if required, and braise under cover in the oven for about 2½ hours.

When the meat is cooked, cut it into cubes. Pass the cooking stock through a cloth and add the sheets of gelatine which have been soaked. Dice the liver. Arrange the meat and liver in layers in a deep dish. When the stock is cold, pour it over slowly. Refrigerate until set. Cut the beans and the remaining carrots into strips of equal length. Arrange in a mosaic pattern on top of the dish, decorate with peas, and brush lightly with aspic jelly. Cut the leeks into 12 cm (5 in) lengths and blanch.

To serve, cut a slice of beef in aspic and place on each plate with a leek. Pour vinaigrette over. (Illustration, page 165)

(Emile Jung, France)

Lancashire potted beef

6–8 portions   Cooking time: 4 hours

1 kg	shin of beef	2 lb 4 oz
	3 calf's feet	
	1 level teaspoon black pepper	
	2 level teaspoons salt	
	10 black peppercorns	
	8 allspice berries	
	1 bay leaf	
	1 small bunch parsley	
	1 onion	

Place the meat, calf's feet, bay leaf, allspice, onion, parsley and peppercorns in a pan. Add about 2 l (3½ pt) cold water to cover. Bring to the boil, then simmer over low heat for 2 hours. Remove the beef and calf's feet. Strain the cooking liquid into a saucepan, add the calf's feet and simmer for a further 2 hours. Shred the beef and set aside under cover.

Remove the calf's feet from the pan, cut the meat off the bone and shred. Boil the cooking liquid over high heat to reduce to ½ l (18 fl oz). Add the shredded meat. Season with salt and pepper and reduce until the liquid barely covers the meat. Fill into a wetted mould, cool and refrigerate overnight.

Before serving, wrap the mould briefly in a cloth dipped in hot water to facilitate unmoulding. Turn out on to a dish, cut into thick slices and serve with pickled walnuts.

(Victor Sassie, Great Britain)

Veal

Veal with tuna sauce
Noix de veau au thon
Vitello tonnato

1 kg	cushion of veal	2 lb 4 oz
	1 calf's foot	
	2 bay leaves	
2 l	stock flavoured with carrots, onions and celery	3½ pt
5 cl	white wine vinegar	2 fl oz
	1 lemon, sliced	
	2 cloves of garlic	
	1 onion, cut into quarters	
5 cl	oil	2 fl oz
	1 tablespoon flour	
250 g	tuna, canned	9 oz
	3 tablespoons capers	

Wrap the veal in greaseproof paper and tie in the same way as a galantine. Cook in the stock with the calf's foot until tender, then leave in the stock for 12 hours. Set aside the stock. Heat the oil in a saucepan and fry the garlic and onion until golden brown. Remove from the heat, dust with the flour and moisten with a little vinegar. Pour in the stock, mash the tuna and add, return to the heat, bring to the boil, reduce until thick, then pass through a conical strainer, adjust the seasoning and leave until cold. Slice the veal, coat with the sauce and decorate with capers.
(Illustration, page 516)

(Franco Colombani, Italy)

Calf's feet in aspic
Pieds de veau en aspic
Regel kruscha

10 portions

1 kg 500	calf's feet	3 lb 5 oz
	3 eggs, hard-boiled and sliced	
	mirepoix	
	4 cloves of garlic	
	bay leaves	
	cloves	
	salt	

> white pepper, freshly ground
> parsley, chopped
> sliced lemon *or* vinaigrette sauce

Have the calf's feet blanched, cleaned and sawn through several times by the butcher. Place them in a pressure cooker or steamer with 2 l (3½ pt) water and cook for 50 minutes. Add the mirepoix and seasonings, and cook uncovered for a further 10 minutes. Remove the calf's feet from the cooking liquid and bone them. Chop the meat coarsely. Pass the cooking liquid through a strainer. Set aside about 1 dl (3½ fl oz) to line the mould, mix the rest with the meat and season well. Mask the mould with the cooking liquid which has been kept back when it is half-set, and decorate with the slices of egg. Fill the mould with the meat and cooking liquid. Place in the refrigerator overnight to set. Serve with chopped parsley and slices of lemon or vinaigrette sauce.

(Hermann Wohl, Israel)

Cold calf's brains Dijon style
Cervelle de veau aux moutardes de Dijon
Kaltes Kalbshirn nach der Art von Dijon

4 portions

200 g	calf's brains	7 oz
3 cl	oil	1 fl oz
80 g	onions, finely chopped	3 oz
10 g	parsley, finely chopped	⅓ oz
	1 egg	
200 g	spinach	7 oz
	salt, white pepper	
	red wine vinegar, lemon juice	
	olive oil	

Sauce:

2 tablespoons mayonnaise
1 tablespoon sour cream
1 tablespoon Pommery mustard
a little Maille mustard
a little Noilly Prat
lemon juice
white pepper, freshly ground

Wash the brains, remove the skin, chop them and cook gently in hot oil in a braising pan for a short time together with 60 g (2 oz) finely chopped onion. Season with salt and pepper, then fry well. Bind with the egg and stir in the parsley. Allow to cool, then shape into small balls each weighing about 40 g (1½ oz).

Wash the spinach and blanch in salted water, then refresh in cold water and squeeze dry. Cut up a little and lay in a marinade consisting of red wine vinegar, lemon juice, olive oil, salt and pepper, and the rest of the onions. Shape the spinach into small loaves and place the brains on top. Mix the ingredients for the sauce until well blended, check the seasoning and pour over the brains.

(Ewald Plachutta, Austria)

Lamb

Best end of lamb Bombay
Carré d'agneau Bombay

6 portions

	best end of lamb (12 cutlets)	
250 g	rice	9 oz
	2 cloves of garlic	
	a pinch of saffron	
1 kg	small peas, frozen	2 lb 4 oz
approx. 350 g	sweet corn, canned	approx. 12 oz
	or 2 corn cobs	
	6 pineapple slices, cut in half	
500 g	vegetable salad, canned	1 lb 2 oz
	3 cucumbers, blanched	
	6 carrots, blanched	
	6 medium tomatoes	
500 g	asparagus, blanched	1 lb 2 oz
	1 green leek	
	salt, pepper	
	powdered rosemary	
	powdered thyme	
	bay leaves	
	6 slices truffle	
approx. 2 dl	aspic mayonnaise	approx. 7 fl oz
½ l	aspic jelly	18 fl oz

Carefully remove excess fat from the cutlet bones and trim neatly. Roll the best end round a 500 g (1 lb) can, tie in place and wrap the bones in aluminium foil to protect them from the heat. Season the cutlets with salt and pepper, flavour with rosemary and thyme, and rub with garlic. Roast in a moderate oven for 20 minutes, then allow to cool. Place on a large round dish and remove the foil and twine.

Meanwhile prepare pilaf rice with saffron. Cook the peas in boiling salted water, keeping them green. Allow to cool, then mix with the rice and add the sweet corn. Place the half pineapple slices in between the cutlets. Fill the centre of the crown with the rice. Cut the tomatoes in half, scoop out the seeds and invert on a metal rack to drain. Season and stuff with the vegetable salad which has been mixed with aspic mayonnaise. Decorate with a slice of truffle.

Arrange the asparagus in bundles. Tie with a thin strip of poached leek. Cut the cucumbers evenly into short sections, hollow out and cut round the top zig-zag fashion. Fill with small carrot balls. Arrange the various items of vegetable garnish alternately round the crown of lamb and brush with aspic jelly if desired. Place a cutlet frill on each cutlet bone if desired.

(André Béghin, Belgium)

Jellied lamb
Daube d'agneau en gelée

6 portions

1 kg 200	leg or shoulder of lamb	2 lb 10 oz
	4 lamb's trotters	
	or 1 calf's foot	
	2 onions	
	4–5 carrots	
7 dl	white wine	1¼ pt
2½ dl	bouillon	9 fl oz
15 g	salt	½ oz
	a pinch of pepper	
	3–4 tablespoons olive oil	
	3–4 cloves of garlic	
	1 clove	
	1 bouquet garni of	
	1 stalk celery, thyme, chervil, savory,	
	rosemary	

Bone the lamb and remove all the fat. Blanch and singe the lamb's trotters or calf's foot. Cut the lamb into 4 or 5 pieces and brown well on all sides in olive oil in an earthenware pot. Remove and keep hot. Place the carrots, onions and garlic in the pot and fry until lightly coloured, then pour off the oil. Return the meat to the pot and add the trotters or calf's foot. Heat the wine and add, together with the hot bouillon. Cover and simmer over low heat for 1½ hours. When the lamb and vegetables are cooked, remove them from the pot and continue cooking the trotters or calf's foot until tender.

Pass the cooking liquid through a cloth, place in a saucepan, carefully remove the fat and season to taste. When cold, the liquid should set hard. Test by pouring a few drops into a saucer, and refrigerate. Mask a terrine or suitable mould with a little of the liquid jelly and place in the refrigerator to set. Bone the trotters or calf's foot and cut up the meat. Fill the mould with alternate layers of meat and vegetables to make an attractive pattern when sliced. Pour the jelly over and refrigerate until set.

To serve, dip the mould in hot water for a moment, dry and turn out on to a dish. Serve with the following sauce. Chop fresh thyme and savory leaves very finely, add freshly chopped parsley, place the garlic in a china mortar after blanching it twice, pound very finely, add olive oil, continue pounding and mix with the herbs to make a fairly thick sauce.
(Illustration, page 170)

(Pierre Gleize, France)

Pork

Czechoslovak brawn
Fromage de tête à la tchèque
Tlačenka

10–12 portions	Cooking time: about 2½–3 hours	
2 kg	pig's head, yielding about	4 lb 8 oz
1 kg	meat without bone	2 lb 4 oz
	1 pig's tongue and heart	
400 g	pork rinds	14 oz
	water	
	salt	
3 g	ground pepper	half a teaspoon
4 g	powdered marjoram	a small teaspoon
	3 allspice berries, ground	
	1 pig's stomach *or* large sausage casing	

Wash the pork rinds, head, heart and tongue. Cook in salted water until fairly soft. Bone the head and skin the tongue. When cold, cut all the meat into 3 cm (1¼ in) cubes. Mince the rinds and place in a bowl together with the meat. Strain the cooking liquid and pour sufficient into the bowl to bind the mixture. Add the seasonings and fill into the stomach which has been thoroughly washed and tied on one side with twine. Do not fill completely to prevent bursting while cooking. Tie the opening securely and simmer in hot water for about 1¼ hours.

Remove the brawn carefully from the stock, place between two boards under pressure, and refrigerate for a few hours. To serve, slice, garnish with onion rings, and pour vinegar and oil over.

(Vilèm Vrabec, Czechoslovakia)

Brawn with juniper
Hure de porc au genièvre

    1 pig's head, lightly salted
    1 calf's foot
    flavouring ingredients:
      2 carrots
      2 leeks

	1 knob of garlic	
	parsley	
	20 juniper berries, crushed	
	1 bay loaf	
	2 cloves	
	water	
	6 gherkins, very finely diced	
	5 juniper berries, crushed	
100 g	parsley, finely chopped	3½ oz
	1 teaspoon powdered sage	
	a pinch of nutmeg	

Cook the pig's head and the calf's foot in water with the flavouring ingredients. Allow the meat to cool, then remove from the bone and dice coarsely. Add the gherkins, the 5 juniper berries, the parsley, sage and nutmeg, and mix thoroughly.

Check the seasoning of the cooking liquid, adjust if necessary, pour over the meat mixture and fill into a suitable mould. Place in a warm oven for 30 minutes, remove and allow to set. Slice and serve with gherkins, pearl onions, radishes or salad as desired.

(Jean Esslinger, France)

Tuscan sausage
Saucisson à la toscane
Sopressata casalinga

15 portions

3 kg 500	pig's head, tongue, lights, kidneys, pork rinds, ham trimmings	7 lb 12 oz
	juice of 1 lemon	
	salt, pepper	
	1 pinch each of ground corianders, cinnamon, fennel seeds	
	2 cloves of garlic, very finely chopped	
50 g	pine kernels	2 oz
50 g	pistachio nuts	2 oz
	1 orange (juice and zest)	

Cook the meat and offal in water sharpened with lemon juice, skimming repeatedly. Allow to cool and pour off the cooking liquid. Remove the bones and gristle, cut up the meat and offal coarsely, mix well and add the seasonings, garlic, pine kernels, pistachios and orange zest and juice. Mix well again, adding salt and pepper if required. Fill into a special porous linen or cloth bag, tie and weight until all the liquid has been expressed, then refrigerate. Remove the bag and slice the sausage as desired. In Tuscany this sausage is served with 'crostini casalinghi' (Tuscan toast).

(Mario De Filippis, Italy)

Parsley ham Burgundy style I
Jambon persillé à la bourguignonne

10–12 portions

2 kg	ham (or pickled shoulder of pork)	4 lb 8 oz
	1 calf's foot	
	1 bouquet garni of	
	leek, thyme, bay leaf, parsley	
	1 onion	
	2 cloves	
	3 carrots	
	10 peppercorns	
7 dl	white Burgundy (Aligoté)	1¼ pt
150 g	parsley, chopped	5 oz

Wash the ham or pork well and leave in cold water overnight. Cut the calf's foot in half, place in a pan of unsalted water with the bouquet garni, the onion which has been stuck with the cloves, the carrots, peppercorns, wine and pork or ham. Cook for 2½ hours, skimming frequently, especially at the beginning. Allow to cool in the cooking liquid.

Sprinkle the inside of a salad bowl with chopped parsley. Cut up the ham coarsely and arrange the pieces in the bowl, sprinkling with parsley in between. Adjust the seasoning of the cooking liquid, strain through a cloth and pour slowly over the ham until the top is covered to a depth of about 3 cm (1¼ in). Refrigerate until set, and leave overnight. To serve, turn out of the bowl and slice. Hand gherkins separately.
(Illustration, page 164).

(Emile Jung, France)

Parsley ham Burgundy style II
Jambon persillé à la bourguignonne

About 20 portions   Cooking time: about 3 hours in all

	1 medium ham	
	2 calf's feet	
400 g	pork rinds (raw)	14 oz
600 g	knuckle of veal	1 lb 5 oz

	1 teaspoon chervil	
	1 teaspoon tarragon	
	1 teaspoon parsley	
	1 teaspoon thyme	
	1 teaspoon celery leaves	
	12 peppercorns	
	1 bay leaf	
	2 bottles Meursault or white Burgundy	
5 cl	tarragon vinegar	2 fl oz
200 g	parsley (for aspic)	7 oz
	2 shallots	

Soak the ham in cold water overnight, then pour off the water. Place the ham, knuckle of veal, calf's feet and pork rinds in a pan of cold water to cover well, bring to the boil and cook for 20 to 30 minutes. Remove the rinds, continue cooking for 15 minutes, then remove from the heat and drain. Trim and bone the ham. Cut the ham and knuckle of veal into large cubes, place in a pan with the calf's feet, herbs, peppercorns and bay leaf, and add the wine to cover the meat completely. If required, pour in more wine or water. Bring to the boil on top of the stove, then transfer to a hot oven and simmer, but do not boil, until cooked.

Strain the cooking liquid through a cloth and set aside. Pick out the meat and transfer to a bowl. Chop the shallots and parsley very finely and add to the cooking liquid when it begins to set. Stir in the vinegar. Mash the meat with a fork and pour the cooking liquid over. Fill into terrines or china dishes and refrigerate until set. Serve in the dish, or turn out and slice.

(Emil Wälti, France)

Alsatian brawn
Tête de porc en gelée à l'alsacienne

5–6 portions

	1 pig's trotter	
	1 calf's foot	
	½ pig's head	
500 g	neck of pork	1 lb 2 oz
250 g	leeks	9 oz
100 g	onions	3½ oz
	2 cloves of garlic	
	1 bouquet garni	
	salt, pepper	
	nutmeg	

Wash the meat well, cut up the head, and place in a pan of water to cover. Cook for about 2½ hours. Remove the meat, cut it off the bone, trim off any gristle, and allow to cool.

Wash the leeks well, mince with the onions and garlic, using the medium cutter, add to the liquid in which the meat was cooked, and cook for about 5 minutes, or until soft.

Mince the meat and add to the vegetables in the pan. Bring to the boil and season with salt, pepper and nutmeg. Reduce the liquid a little if necessary, then fill into brawn moulds and refrigerate until set. Serve with vinaigrette sauce.

(Emil Wälti, France)

Brabant brawn
Fromage de tête à la brabançonne
Hoofdkaas (Brabant)

	1 pig's head	
600 g	lean pork	1 lb 5 oz
	salt	
	pepper, freshly ground	
	nutmeg, grated	
3 dl	vinegar	10 fl oz

Wash the head and the meat carefully and cook in salted water. Remove the meat from the bones, mince and season. Allow the cooking liquid to cool, then place a little of it in a pan with the vinegar and the meat, boil again and fill into a brawn mould. Chill thoroughly, turn out and slice to serve.

(Bernard van Beurten, Netherlands)

Utrecht liver sausage
Saucisse de foie de porc à la façon de Utrecht
Leverworst (Utrecht)

1 kg 500	pig's liver	3 lb 5 oz
1 kg	neck of pork	2 lb 4 oz
600 g	pork fat or fat bacon	1 lb 5 oz
30 g	salt	1 oz
5 g	cloves, finely crushed	⅙ oz
10 g	pepper, freshly ground	⅓ oz
1 dl	bouillon	3½ fl oz

Poach the liver and the neck of pork in water for 10 minutes, then mince twice, using the finest cutter. Add the salt, pepper and cloves. Mix well with the bouillon until smooth.

Cut the rind off the pork fat or bacon, dice and carefully mix with the minced meat and liver. Fill into a prepared sausage casing, tie off and poach over low heat, then allow to cool. When quite cold, slice and serve.

(Bernard van Beurten, Netherlands)

Roast pork Danish style
See *Hot main dishes—pork*, page 808

Cantonese cha shao barbecue roast pork
See *Hot main dishes—pork*, page 821

Best end of pork Florentine style
See *Hot main dishes—pork*, page 832

Hot Pies, Pâtés and Terrines

Old-fashioned sweetbread pie
Pâté chaud de ris de veau à l'ancienne

10 portions

Sweetbreads:

2 kg	calves' sweetbreads	4 lb 8 oz
400 g	mushrooms	14 oz
20 g	butter	¾ oz
	2 large truffles	
100 g	pistachio nuts	3½ oz

Forcemeat:

250 g	lean pork	9 oz
500 g	fresh pork fat	1 lb 2 oz
	2 eggs, beaten	
4 g	salt	a small teaspoon
1½ dl	Cognac	5 fl oz
2 dl	dairy cream	7 fl oz
	Cayenne pepper	

Pie pastry:

500 g	flour	1 lb 2 oz
300 g	butter	11 oz
	3 eggs	
1½ dl	water	5 fl oz
50 g	sugar	2 oz
10 g	salt	⅓ oz

Sauce:

2 dl	velouté (recipe, page 162)	7 fl oz

Prepare the pastry in the usual manner, using only 1 egg. Mould into a ball, wrap in a cloth and allow to rest in a cold place for at least 2 hours. The remaining eggs are required for brushing the pastry.

Mince the pork and fat finely, place in a large china mortar and pound well with the eggs to make a very fine forcemeat. Stand the mortar on ice, fold in the cream and add the seasoning and Cognac.

Wash the sweetbreads thoroughly, trim them, blanch for 3 to 4 minutes and refresh in cold water. Remove all the hard, inedible parts. Place between 2 boards for a few hours under light pressure to compress the fibres and prevent shrinking during cooking. Cut into escalopes 1 cm (3/8 in) thick.

Fry the mushrooms gently in the butter until lightly coloured, allow to cool, then slice coarsely. Slice the truffles. Prepare the pistachios.

Grease a 30 x 10 cm (12 x 4 in) hinged pie mould well. Pin out the pastry 5 mm (1/4 in) thick, flour lightly and mark out the base of the mould 4 times. Cut off one of the 4 pieces and set aside to make a lid. Flour the mould and line with the pastry, which should project 1 cm (3/8 in) beyond the top of the mould. Press well against the inside of the mould.

Cover the bottom of the pastry with a 2 cm (3/4 in) layer of forcemeat, then place a layer of escalopes of sweetbreads on top, then a layer of sliced mushrooms, then a layer of sliced truffles and cover with forcemeat. Repeat in the same order, finishing with a layer of forcemeat, and smooth the top. Fold the projecting pastry inwards and moisten with beaten egg. Cover with the pastry lid and press down well. Seal and decorate the edge with the help of pastry pincers. If desired, pastry motifs may be added for final decoration, the underside being moistened to fix in position. Cut a 2 cm (3/4 in) hole in the centre of the lid and insert a small steam vent made of oiled parchment paper. Egg wash the pastry. Bake in a medium oven for 1 3/4 hours, then leave to stand for 15 minutes at the side of the oven or stove. Open the hinges, carefully remove the pie and dress on a napkin. Remove the vent and carefully pour the velouté through the hole. Decorate with small bunches of parsley and serve at once.

(André Béghin, Belgium)

Danish liver pâté
Dansk Leverpastej

5–6 portions   Cooking time: 1 hour 50 minutes

500 g	pig's liver	1 lb 2 oz
250 g	fresh pork fat	9 oz
	2 medium onions	
	4 anchovy fillets	
30 g	flour	1 oz
1/4 l	dairy cream	9 fl oz
	approx. 1/2 teaspoon thyme	
	approx. 1/2 teaspoon marjoram	
	2 eggs	
	salt	

	pepper, freshly ground	
50 g	butter	2 oz
200 g	mushrooms	7 oz
	4 tomatoes	
	cress	
	5–6 rashers bacon	

Cut the pork fat and the onions into 2 or 3 cm (about 1 in) pieces and blanch. Cut the pig's liver into larger pieces or strips. Mince the liver, pork fat, onions and anchovy fillets three or four times, using the finest cutter. Add the eggs and flour and mix until well blended, then add the cream and mix again.

Grease a cake tin or mould carefully, fill with the mixture and bake for 50 minutes in an oven preheated to 180°C (355°F), then leave to stand for about 1 hour in a warm place.

Remove the pâté from the tin, cut into slices 1–1½ cm (about ½ in) thick, and place on plates. Allow 1 slice per portion as an hors d'oeuvre, or 2 as a light luncheon dish. Garnish each portion with fried mushrooms, fried tomatoes and a fried rasher of bacon. Decorate with a little cress.

The pâté may form part of a buffet or smørrebrød. In this case it is presented whole on a serving dish. It may be served hot or cold.

(Karl-Otto Schmidt, Denmark)

Lamb pie
Agneau en pie

6 portions

1 kg 200	leg or shoulder of lamb, trimmed		2 lb 10 oz
2 dl	lamb gravy		7 fl oz
approx. 300 g	half puff pastry	approx.	11 oz

Ratatouille:

1 onion
1 medium courgette
1 aubergine
4 tomatoes, skinned and seeded
2 cloves of garlic
salt, pepper
2 tablespoons olive oil

To prepare the ratatouille, dice the courgette, aubergine and tomatoes. Slice the onion and garlic very thinly and cook gently in the oil without colouring, then add the diced vegetables, season with salt and cook until soft. Cut the meat into small pieces, brown in oil, add the lamb gravy and reduce well.

Place the ratatouille at the bottom of a pie dish and cover with the meat in its stock. Place a half puff pastry lid on top, press down well and bake for 35 minutes in an oven preheated to 220°C (430°F).

(Emile Jung, France)

'Umble pie

6 portions   Cooking time: 2 hours 20 minutes

Pastry:

250 g	flour	9 oz
200 g	margarine mixed with lard	7 oz
	½ teaspoon salt	
	¼ teaspoon pepper	
	5 tablespoons cold water	

Filling:

225 g	ox kidney	8 oz
200 g	lambs' sweetbreads	7 oz
120 g	streaky bacon	4 oz
	1 sheep's head	
	1 sheep's tongue	
	1 sheep's heart	
225 g	rump steak	8 oz
200 g	onions, chopped	7 oz
250 g	potatoes	9 oz
150 g	carrots	5 oz
	1 tablespoon parsley, chopped	
	½ teaspoon dried mixed herbs	
	1 heaped teaspoon salt	
	1 level teaspoon white pepper	

To make the pastry, place the flour and salt in a bowl and mix well. Rub in the margarine and lard with the fingertips until the mixture resembles fine breadcrumbs. Add the water and mix with a spatula or knife to a soft paste of rolling consistency. Place on a floured board, dust with flour and cover with a cloth. Set aside in a cool place until required.

To prepare the filling, wash the sweetbreads, tongue, head and heart well, place in a pan with 1 l (1¾ pt) water, bring to the boil and simmer for 5 minutes. Remove the sweetbreads and set aside. Simmer the rest of the contents of the pan for a further 30 minutes, then remove the tongue, skin it while still hot and place with the sweetbreads. Simmer the head and heart for a further 15 minutes and remove. Cut all the meat off the head and place with the tongue and sweetbreads. Return the bones to the pan. Boil over high heat to reduce the stock to ½ l (18 fl oz).

Cut the kidney, steak and bacon into 2 cm (¾ in) cubes. Cut the onions into half rings, the potatoes into 3 cm (1 in) cubes and the carrots into 1 cm (½ in) cubes.

Brown the bacon and onions lightly for 5 minutes in a large saucepan, add the kidney and steak and fry for a further 5 minutes. Pour in the reduced stock and add the salt, pepper and herbs.

Cut the tongue into six pieces. Cut the heart into three slices and each of these in half, making six half slices in all. Cut the meat from the head into uneven pieces. Add all these ingredients to the saucepan and simmer for 40 minutes. Dust the meat with flour and mix carefully with a wooden spoon.

Cut the sweetbreads into 3 cm (1 in) pieces and add to the saucepan. Transfer the contents to a deep pie dish. Add the potatoes and carrots. Moisten the edge with water, cover with the rolled out pastry, press down well and pinch up. Make a cut across the centre for the escape of steam. Bake for 20 minutes at 230°C (450°F), then reduce the oven temperature to 180°C (350°F) and bake for a further 20 minutes.

(Victor Sassie, Great Britain)

Terrine of sweetbreads and fillet of veal Grubbenvorst
Terrine de ris de veau et filet de veau à la Grubbenvorst
Terrine van kalfszwezerik en-haas Grubbenvorst

4 portions   Cooking time: 40 minutes

	2 calves' sweetbreads	
180 g	fillet of veal	6 oz
	oregano	
	salt	
	pepper, freshly ground	
30 g	butter	1 oz
	fresh asparagus	
	white breadcrumbs	
10 g	parsley, chopped	⅓ oz
50 g	hard, dry Dutch cheese, grated	2 oz

Slice the sweetbreads thinly, season with salt and pepper, and flavour with oregano. Slice the fillet of veal thinly, and season and flavour in the same manner. Clean the asparagus thoroughly and cut into even lengths.

Butter a terrine carefully and fill as follows:
   1st layer–sliced sweetbreads

Prepare pastry with the flour, butter, lard, water, salt and nutmeg, knead well and allow to rest. Brown the onions and the frying veal lightly in a buttered sauté pan, then moisten with the brandy. Set aside to cool.

Pass the shoulder of pork and veal, the pork fat and the fried veal through the finest blade of the mincer several times, then through a hair sieve. Stir in the cream. Add the cubes of veal and tongue together with the pistachio nuts and mix well, then add the seasonings.

Pin out two thirds of the pastry into an oblong about ½ cm (¼ in) thick and trim the edges. Line a buttered pie mould 40 cm (16 in) long with the pastry, which should project 1 cm (⅜ in) above the edge of the mould. Press firmly against the sides and into the corners. Prick, then half fill with forcemeat. Place two 2 cm (¾ in) sections of foie gras parfait on top and press down lightly. Fill up the mould with the rest of the forcemeat. Egg wash the projecting pastry, place the prepared pastry lid on top and seal well with the help of broad pincers. Cut 1 cm (⅜ in) holes in the top for the escape of steam, one of them in the centre, the others 10 cm (4 in) from the outer edges. Carefully egg wash the lid and decorate with pastry motifs. Insert tubes of tin foil into the holes as vents. Bake for 1¼ hours in an oven preheated to 180°C (355°F). Remove and leave until quite cold.

Make the jelly and pour into the pie through the vents to fill the spaces left between the pastry and the forcemeat after baking. Allow to set before slicing. Garnish if desired with a lightly stewed apple ring covered with foie gras purée, small pieces of truffle, quarter strawberries and pistachios. Other types of garnish may, of course, be used.

(Erwin Frohmann, Bernd Moos, Werner Schall,
Rudolf Achenbach Delicatessen, Germany)

Hungarian pork pâté
Pâté de porc à la hongroise
Magyaros huspástétom

10 portions   Cooking time: about 1½ hours

1 kg	shoulder of pork	2 lb 4 oz
430 g	shoulder of sucking pig	1 lb
430 g	leg of sucking pig	1 lb
50 g	noble-sweet paprika	2 oz
12 g	pepper, freshly ground	½ oz
	3 egg whites	
	1 clove of garlic, crushed	
350 g	smoked pork fat, finely diced	12 oz
25 g	salt	1 oz
	12 stale rolls	

Mince the meat finely. Soak the rolls in water, squeeze dry and crumble with the fingers. Mix well with the meat, garlic, pork fat and egg whites. Season with salt, pepper and paprika. Work well in the processor or with the hands until the mixture is well blended and holds together. Wrap in double cellophane, tie at both ends, mould to an oblong shape and tie round several times in both directions with twine. Place in boiling water, return to the boil, then poach at 90°C (195°F) for 1½ hours. Remove and cool between two boards under light pressure to make the pâté more compact and facilitate slicing. Refrigerate until required. Serve with various salads or cold sauces.

(László Csizmadia, Hungary)

Sweetbread pie
Pâté de ris de veau
Pâté van kalfszwezerik

400 g	shoulder of veal	14 oz
200 g	calf's liver	7 oz
400 g	calves' sweetbreads, blanched and sliced	14 oz
	3 walnut-size pieces truffle	
2 dl	dairy cream	7 fl oz
	4 egg yolks	
100 g	veal suet	3½ oz
250 g	pork fat or fat bacon, sliced	9 oz
	Cognac (to taste)	
500 g	pie pastry	1 lb 2 oz
½ l	veal jelly	18 fl oz

To make the forcemeat, mince the veal, liver and suet, using the finest cutter. Stir in the cream and egg yolks, together with seasonings, mix well and work in the processor until finely blended. Slice the truffle thinly and mix with the forcemeat.

Pin out two thirds of the pastry, trim the edges neatly and line a buttered pie mould. The pastry should project about 1 cm (⅜ in) above the edge. Cover the bottom and sides with slices of pork fat or bacon and fill the mould in the following order: a layer of forcemeat, then sliced sweetbreads, then another layer of forcemeat, and so on, finishing with forcemeat.

Place prepared pastry lid on top, make a hole for the escape of steam, egg wash, bake in a well heated oven. Remove, leave until cold, and pour cold veal jelly into the pie through the hole. (Illustration, page 944)

(Bernard van Beurten, Netherlands)

Lamb pâté Verecke
Pâté d'agneau Verecke
Vereckei Báránypástétom

10 portions

1 kg	shoulder of lamb	2 lb 4 oz
3 g	saltpetre	1/8 oz
15 g	salt	1/2 oz
6 g	black pepper	1/4 oz
2 g	powdered rosemary	half a small teaspoon
150 g	smoked pork fat, chopped	5 oz
	6 eggs, hard-boiled	
400 g	mushroom purée	14 oz
2 dl	aspic jelly	7 fl oz
300 g	savoy cabbage leaves, blanched	11 oz
	2 radishes	
	1 teaspoon caraways, finely ground	

Carefully oil a ring mould. Mix the pork fat with the lamb which has been chopped, treated with saltpetre for its effect on the colour, and left to stand for 72 hours in a cold place. Season with salt, black pepper and rosemary.

Cut off the base of the eggs, then cut each egg in half lengthwise. Line the mould with meat, arrange the half eggs on it with the cut surface facing inwards, and cover with the rest of the meat. Place a sheet of fireproof glass or metal on top and weight or clamp in position. Cook in the oven at 75–80°C (about 170°F), allowing 30 minutes per kg meat (15 minutes per lb). Remove the mould from the oven. Leave under pressure and stand in cold water reaching three quarters of the way up. When cool, refrigerate under pressure for a few hours to set.

Remove the weight and turn out the pâté on to a marble or glass slab. Mix the mushroom purée with the half set aspic. Spread over the pâté, sprinkle with the caraways and cover completely with the savoy cabbage leaves which have been well drained and flavoured with garlic juice. Brush the whole surface with aspic and sprinkle with very finely cut radish peel.

The pâté may be dressed on a dish lined with tomato aspic (see illustration). (Illustration, page 943)

(Josef Csanyi, Hungary)

Hungarian ham pie
Pâté de jambon à la hongroise
Sonkapástétom

10 portions

Pastry:

500 g	flour	1 lb 2 oz
125 g	lard	4½ oz
2 dl	lukewarm water	7 fl oz
	1 egg	
	1 teaspoon salt	

Forcemeat:

500 g	shoulder of pork	1 lb 2 oz
500 g	fresh pork fat	1 lb 2 oz
	2 eggs	
300 g	lean cooked ham	11 oz
5 cl	Cognac	2 fl oz
250 g	salt pork fat, sliced	9 oz
	2 pinches of pepper, freshly ground	
	salt	

Warm the lard to about 40°C (105°F). Make a bay in the flour. Place the lard, egg, salt and water in the centre. Mix to a smooth, well blended, pliable paste. Mould into a ball and wrap in a floured cloth. Allow to rest for 24 hours.

Pass the pork and fresh pork fat through the fine blade of the mincer several times, then through a sieve. Mix well with the eggs and with the ham, half of it finely diced and the other half shredded. Season with salt and pepper, flavour with the Cognac and mix thoroughly.

Grease a pie mould very lightly and line with the pastry which has been thinly rolled out, setting aside enough to make a lid. Cover the pastry with slices of salt pork fat. Fill with the forcemeat, press down well and cover the top with the remaining slices of salt pork fat. Egg wash the edges of the pastry lightly and place the pastry lid on top. Seal well with pincers and egg wash. Cut two or three holes for the escape of steam and insert small tubes of greased paper as vents. Bake in an oven preheated to about 180°C (355°F).

Allow to cool, then pour in cold liquid jelly through the holes to fill up. When set, slice 1 cm (⅜ in) thick with a thin, sharp knife. Serve with various salads and, if desired, cold sauces.

(László Csizmadia, Hungary)

Basel Christmas pie
Pâté de Noël à la bâloise
Basler Weihnachtspàstete

10 portions as hors d'oeuvre, 6 portions as main dish   Cooking time: 1¼ hours

300 g	leg of pork or veal, thinly sliced	11 oz
	3 tablespoons Cognac or Armagnac	
	pepper, freshly ground	
	1 teaspoon salt	
	1 clove of garlic	
	a small pinch of marjoram	

	a small pinch of thyme	
	1 bunch parsley, chopped	
200 g	fresh mushrooms	7 oz
	1 tablespoon onion, chopped	
	1 tablespoon fat for frying	
100 g	pickled ox tongue, diced	3½ oz
100 g	cooked ham, diced	3½ oz
	1 tablespoon pistachio nuts	
	or gherkins, diced	
	1 tablespoon morels *or* craterelles	
	or truffles, finely cut	
150 g	veal sausage meat	5 oz
	1–2 tablespoons cornflour	
	a small pinch of forcemeat flavouring	
	egg white	
	egg yolk	
750 g	short or pie pastry	1 lb 10 oz
	dry breadcrumbs	

Mix together the Cognac or Armagnac, salt, a little pepper, forcemeat flavouring, garlic, marjoram, thyme and parsley. Add the pork or veal and mix carefully. Leave to stand for 1 hour.

Wash the fresh mushrooms thoroughly, dry them and cut in quarters. Fry the onion gently in the fat until lightly coloured, add the mushrooms and a little forcemeat flavouring, and cook until the pan is dry. Add the mushrooms to the meat. Add the diced tongue and ham, the pistachios or gherkins, the morels, craterelles or truffles, the sausage meat and cornflour. Mix well and knead until the mixture holds together well.

Grease a 24–26 cm (10 in) pie tin well and sprinkle with dry breadcrumbs. Pin out two thirds of the pastry and line the tin, leaving 1 cm (⅜ in) of the pastry to project above the edge. Prick with a fork. Fill carefully with the forcemeat.

Pin out the rest of the pastry to make a lid, allowing for a 1 cm (⅜ in) projection all round. Brush the edges of the lid and the pastry in the tin with egg white, press together, then press on to the edge of the tin. Mix the rest of the egg white with egg yolk and brush the top. Decorate as desired with pastry trimmings.

Bake for 40 minutes in an oven preheated to 180 or 190°C (355 to 375°F). Mark a 2 cm (¾ in) ring in the centre of the lid with a pastry cutter. Remove from the oven and cut out to leave a hole for the escape of steam. Return to the oven and bake for a further 20 minutes.

Cool the pie on a wire rack. When cold, pour in jelly through the hole to fill up to the lid. Refrigerate. If desired, the jelly may be flavoured with Madeira or Cognac. Make a pie a few days in advance to enhance the flavour. Store in the refrigerator. If the pie is to be served hot, omit the jelly.

(Otto Ledermann, Switzerland)

Terrine of sweetbreads with truffle cream
Terrine de ris de veau à la crème de truffes

6 portions

800 g	calves' sweetbreads	1 lb 12 oz
2 dl	white wine (e.g. Cassis, Pouilly)	7 fl oz
2 dl	veal stock	7 fl oz
100 g	carrots, finely diced	3½ oz
100 g	leeks, finely diced	3½ oz
30 g	celery, finely diced	1 oz
	½ clove of garlic	
	1 sprig thyme	
	½ bay leaf	
50 g	butter	2 oz
	1 tablespoon olive oil	
	flour	

Forcemeat:

200 g	veal	7 oz
200 g	pork fat	7 oz
100 g	sweetbread trimmings	3½ oz
	1 egg	
8 g	salt	¼ oz
1 g	pepper	a good pinch
	sweetbread stock	

Sauce:

5 dl	dairy cream	18 fl oz
30 g	black truffles, finely chopped	1 oz
	salt	
	pepper	
	lemon juice	

Wash the sweetbreads for 6 hours under a thin stream of water, then blanch briefly, cool well, trim and remove any inedible parts. Season with salt and pepper and dust with flour. Fry on all sides for 8 minutes in olive oil and butter to colour lightly, remove from the heat and keep hot. Add the diced vegetables, the clove of garlic, the sprig of thyme and the bay leaf to the pan and cook gently for 5 minutes.

Place the sweetbreads on top, add the wine and veal stock, and stew for 10 minutes. Remove the sweetbreads. Drain off the fat from the pan, reduce the stock, pass through a conical strainer and allow to cool. Use this stock in preparing the forcemeat.

To make the forcemeat, cut the meat into small cubes and work to a fine purée in the mixer with the other ingredients. Line a terrine with a little forcemeat, place the sweetbreads on it, cover well with forcemeat and poach in a medium oven in a bain-marie for 40 minutes. Allow to cool, then refrigerate overnight to set. Store in a cool place.

To make the sauce, whip the cream carefully until fairly thick, add the truffles, season with salt and pepper, and finish with a few drops of lemon juice.
(Illustration, page 170)

(Pierre Gleize, France)

Terrine of veal Hungarian fashion
Terrine de veau à la hongroise
Borjuhuspástétom

4 portions

300 g	fillet of veal	11 oz
300 g	shoulder of veal	11 oz
300 g	smoked pickled loin of pork (raw)	11 oz
2 dl	dairy cream	7 fl oz
	1 egg	
	1 teaspoon nutmeg, grated	
20 g	salt	¾ oz
	2 pinches pepper, freshly ground	
300 g	salt pork fat or streaky bacon, sliced	11 oz
1 dl	Cognac	3½ fl oz
100 g	flour	3½ oz

Pass the shoulder of veal and half the loin of pork through the finest blade of the mincer several times, then through a sieve. Cut the rest of the loin of pork and the fillet of veal into strips 1 cm (⅜ in) thick. Pour 5 cl (2 fl oz) over them, add salt, pepper and nutmeg, and stand aside to marinate.

Remove the meat from the marinade. Mix the marinade well with the minced meat and add salt, pepper and nutmeg.

Line the bottom and sides of a fireproof dish with the thinly sliced pork fat or bacon, reserving sufficient to cover the top. Fill the dish with alternate layers of minced meat and marinated strips of meat, starting with minced meat. Cover with the remaining slices of pork fat or bacon, then place a lid on top and seal the edge with flour and water paste. Stand the terrine in a roasting tin containing 4–5 cm (about 2 in) water and cook in a well heated oven for 1 to 1½ hours. Remove from the oven, cover the terrine with a small board, stand a 1 kg (2 lb) weight on top and allow to cool. Place in the refrigerator until well chilled. To serve, turn out on to a dish. Hand a variety of salads separately.

(László Csizmadia, Hungary)

Terrine of lamb, veal and pork
Marbré aux trois parfums

20 portions

	1 knuckle of veal	
	1 knuckle of pork	
	1 shoulder of lamb, trimmed of fat	
7 dl	Riesling	1¼ pt
1 dl	oil	3½ fl oz
2 l	water	3½ pt
	1 red pepper, finely cut	
	1 green pepper, finely cut	
100 g	pistachio nuts	3½ oz
	3 leeks	
	3 carrots	
	1 stalk savory	
	1 stalk celery	
	3 onions	
	10 cloves of garlic	
	salt	

Special vinaigrette sauce:

1 dl	vinegar	3½ fl oz
4 dl	oil	14 fl oz
	1 tablespoon mustard	
	1 tablespoon chives, very finely chopped	
	2 tomatoes, skinned, seeded and very finely chopped	
	salt	
	pepper	

Bone the meat, cut it into fairly large cubes and brown in oil in a large cocotte. Pour off the oil, add the flavouring vegetables and garlic, season with salt, pour in the wine, cover and stew over low heat for 30 minutes. Add the water and continue cooking. When the meat is cooked, remove from the stock, cool, then dice finely. While the stock is still hot, drain off the fat and strain.

Place the meat in a saucepan with the pistachios and peppers. Mix well, add the stock and boil up briefly. Transfer to a wetted terrine and allow to set. Turn out, slice and serve with special vinaigrette.

To prepare the vinaigrette, blend the vinegar, oil, mustard, salt and pepper together well, then add the chives and tomatoes. Make the terrine on the day before it is required.

(Jean Esslinger, France)

Week-end terrine
Terrine de fin de semaine
Wochenendterrine

15–20 portions	Cooking time: 1½ hours	
750 g	veal sausage meat	1 lb 10 oz
1 dl	dairy cream	3½ fl oz
30 g	20 slices cooked ham each weighing	1 oz
	4 eggs, hard-boiled	
5 dl	meat aspic jelly	18 fl oz
40 g	16 veal medallions each weighing	1½ oz
30 g	shallots, finely chopped	1 oz
	salt	
	forcemeat flavouring	
	parsley, finely chopped	

Mix a little cream and water with the sausage meat to soften. (If desired, 6 raw veal frying sausages without their casings may be used as sausage meat.) Line the bottom of a terrine with sausage meat and fill alternately with slices of ham, veal medallions and slices of egg, sprinkling each layer with a little shallot, parsley and forcemeat flavouring. Cover with the rest of the sausage meat, then with a tight-fitting lid. Poach for 15 minutes in a bain-marie on top of the stove, then transfer to a preheated medium oven and poach for a further 1¼ hours.

Allow to cool in the bain-marie, but replace the lid of the terrine with a board of suitable size and stand a 1 kg (2 lb) weight on top to compress the filling. When quite cold, carefully remove the fat which has risen to the surface, cream it and replace. Pour in cold liquid meat aspic jelly and refrigerate until set. (If desired, well beaten pork fillets may be used instead of veal medallions.)

(Otto Ledermann, Switzerland)

Danish liver pâté
See *Hot pies, pâtés and terrines,* page 985

Ham and herb pie Gelderland
Pâté de jambon de Gelderland avec épices vertes
Gelderse ham pâté met groene kruiden

600 g	Gelderland (cooked) ham	1 lb 5 oz
600 g	neck of pork	1 lb 5 oz

500 g	spinach	1 lb 2 oz
	3 eggs	
10 g	parsley, chopped	⅓ oz
10 g	chives, chopped	⅓ oz
10 g	tarragon, chopped	⅓ oz
¼ l	dairy cream	9 fl oz
	salt	
	pepper, freshly ground	
250 g	fresh pork fat, sliced	9 oz
500 g	pie pastry	1 lb 2 oz
½ l	aspic jelly	18 fl oz

Cut the pork in pieces and season with salt and pepper, then mince finely. Blanch the spinach and dry well. Mix with the parsley, chives and tarragon, and mince finely. Mix with the pork and the cream until well blended.

Line a buttered pie mould with pie pastry, then with slices of pork fat. Cut the ham into strips of the same length as the mould. Fill the mould in layers, each one consisting of strips of ham separated by strips of pork/spinach forcemeat to produce a chessboard pattern. Cover the filling with strips of pork fat, place a pastry lid on top and press down well. Cut a hole in the centre for the escape of steam. Bake in a medium oven. When the pie is quite cold, pour in the jelly through the hole.
(Illustration, page 944)

(Bernard van Beurten, Netherlands)

Terrine Restaurant au Crocodile

10 portions

300 g	chicken breast	11 oz
200 g	shoulder of veal	7 oz
100 g	neck of pork	3½ oz
400 g	pork fat	14 oz
100 g	chicken liver	3½ oz
50 g	pistachio nuts	2 oz
2 dl	dairy cream	7 fl oz
150 g	foie gras, diced	5 oz
300 g	salt pork fat, sliced	11 oz
40 g	shallots, finely cut	1½ oz
100 g	truffles, cut into pieces	3½ oz
1 dl	Cognac	3½ fl oz
	a pinch of fresh thyme	
	salt, pepper	

The day before the terrine is required, finely dice the chicken breast, 100 g (3½ oz) shoulder of veal and the neck of pork. Season with 8 g (¼ oz) salt, sprinkle with 4 cl (1½ fl oz) Cognac and marinate.

Next day, prepare gratin forcemeat. Fry the chicken liver lightly in a sauté pan with 100g (3½ oz) pork fat, add the shallots and thyme, pour in the rest of the Cognac and ignite, then allow to cool. Mince this forcemeat finely with the remaining pork fat and mix well.

Prepare a mousse with the rest of the veal which has been finely minced, the cream and the truffles. Mix with the foie gras and shape into a sausage of the same length as the terrine on buttered aluminium foil. Wrap in the foil, poach, cool and unwrap.

Mix the marinated cubes of chicken breast, veal and pork with the gratin forcemeat and add the pistachios.

Line the terrine with slices of salt pork fat, half fill with forcemeat, place the mousse/foie gras sausage on top, cover with the rest of the forcemeat, then with slices of salt pork fat, and close tightly with a lid. Poach in a bain-marie in the oven at 80°C (175°F) for 1 hour 20 minutes. (Illustration, page 163)

(Emile Jung, France)

Accompaniments

Cold Garnishes

Marinated courgettes
Courgettes marinées
Zucchine marinate

1 kg	courgettes	2 lb 4 oz
1 dl	sunflower or corn oil	3½ fl oz
	2 anchovy fillets	
	OR 1 tablespoon anchovy paste	
1 dl	white vinegar	3½ fl oz

Cut the courgettes into slices 5 mm (¼ in) thick without peeling. If using anchovy fillets, mash them finely with a fork. Warm the oil and mix thoroughly with the anchovy fillets or paste, add the courgettes and colour lightly for 3 minutes on each side. Remove from the heat and add the vinegar. Leave until cold, then fill into a glass jar with a lid and place in the refrigerator. Use for decoration or as a garnish instead of gherkins.

(Paolo Teverini, Italy)

Guacamole
Recipe, page 449
(*Tournedos Mexican style*, E. Wälti, Mexico)

Piquant courgettes
Courgettes blanchies et relevées
Zucchine scottate piccanti

Wash, dry and slice the courgettes. Fry anchovy fillets lightly in oil and remove. Cook the courgettes in the same oil, keeping them firm and turning them carefully from time to time with a wooden spoon. Season with salt. Fill into a glass jar, add vinegar, close tightly and store in a cool place. Use as a garnish for cold roasts, boiled meat, ham, etc.

(Franco Colombani, Italy)

Preserved peppers with horseradish
Poivrons au raifort

	10–12 fleshy yellow or green peppers	
150 g	horseradish, coarsley grated	5 oz
	bay leaves	
5–8 cl	20% vinegar or wine vinegar	2–3 fl oz

Cut the peppers in half, remove the seeds and bake lightly in the oven for about 20 to 30 minutes, then skin them. Sprinkle inside with salt and place in a bowl. Leave to stand for 12 hours to draw out the liquid. Fill up a glass jar with alternate layers of peppers and horseradish, placing a bay leaf between the layers. Do not fill higher than 5 cm (2 in) from the top. Add the vinegar and the sweet pepper liquid, cover the jar with a small plate and leave to ferment for 7–10 days, depending on the room temperature. Season with salt, add a little vinegar, together with finely cut onions if desired. Pour in oil to a depth of the thickness of two fingers, seal tightly and set aside for at least 1 to 2 weeks, or until required.

Before serving, rinse the peppers under running water in a vegetable drainer. Transfer to a bowl and pour oil over.

(László Csizmadia, Yugoslavia)

Pickled tomatoes
Recipe, page 499
(*Braised beef bourgeois,* E. Carlström, Sweden)

Green tomatoes in oil
Tomates acerbes (vertes) sous huile
Conserva di pomodori acerbi

600 g	green, unripe tomatoes	1 lb 5 oz
600 g	red, green and yellow peppers	1 lb 5 oz
	2 onions	
75 g	salt	2½ oz
	white wine vinegar as required	

olive or corn oil as required

Cut the tomatoes and peppers into quarters, seed them, then cut into strips 1 cm (⅜ in) wide. Slice the onions finely. Place in an earthenware dish, season with salt, and leave to stand for 24 hours, mixing from time to time. Collect the water which has been drawn from the vegetables and add an equal amount of wine vinegar. Pour over the vegetables and marinate for 24 hours, then remove, drain well and dry with a fine cloth. Fill into glass jars, add oil to fill up and seal tightly. Keep in a cool place (e.g. a cellar).

(Franco Colombani, Italy)

Hot Garnishes—Vegetables

Serbian ajvar
Srpski Ajvar

4 portions   Cooking time: 30–40 minutes

> 2 large aubergines
> 6 large round red peppers
> pepper, freshly ground
> salt
> 2 cloves of garlic, chopped (optional)
> oil
> lemon juice or vinegar

Cut the aubergines and peppers in half and bake in the oven for 30 to 40 minutes. Skin and seed them while still hot, then chop or mince finely. Season with salt and pepper, and add the garlic (optional). Sharpen with vinegar or lemon juice and add as much oil as the mixture will absorb. Mix thoroughly. To serve, transfer to a glass bowl and decorate with parsley.

(László Csizmadia, Yugoslavia)

Stuffed artichokes
See *Hot hors d'oeuvre,* page 235

Spinach
Recipe, page 662
(*Sweetbreads Zurich aristocrats' style,* R. Haupt-Felber, Switzerland)

Fried aubergine sticks
Bâtonnets d'aubergines frits
Bastoncini di melanzane fritti

Peel the aubergines, cut them into cylinders, then into strips as for Pont-Neuf potatoes. Flour them, dip in beaten egg mixed with a few drops of oil, then coat with breadcrumbs. Deep-fry in hot fat and drain.

(Franco Colombani, Italy)

Aubergine medallions
Médaillons d'aubergines
Medaglioni di melanzane

1 tablespoon basil, chopped
1 tablespoon parsley, chopped
1 clove of garlic
olive oil as required

Express the garlic juice and mix with the basil, parsley and olive oil to a paste of spreading consistency. Season the unpeeled aubergines with salt, sprinkle with a little oil and spread with the paste. Place on an oiled baking sheet and cook in the oven. Serve as a garnish for grills, roast sirloin and fillet of beef.

(Franco Colombani, Italy)

French bean gratin I
Recipe, page 739
(*Saddle of lamb Fontvieille,* E. Jung, France)

French bean gratin II
Gratin de haricots verts
Rakott Zöldbab

4 portions   Cooking time: 50–60 minutes

800 g	French beans	1 lb 12 oz
50 g	butter	2 oz
2 dl	sour cream	7 fl oz
	2 egg yolks	
	salt	
	a pinch of nutmeg	
80 g	Parmesan cheese, grated	3 oz

Cook the beans in salted water, drain and dry with a clean cloth. Place in a buttered fireproof dish. Mix the sour cream with the egg yolks, add the nutmeg and a little salt, and pour over the beans. Dot with butter, sprinkle with the grated cheese and brown in a well heated oven. This dish is a suitable accompaniment for grilled or fried veal or pork fillets, roast veal, etc.

(László Csizmadia, Hungary)

French beans with chanterelles
Recipe, page 525
(*Tournedos with garlic and orange,* K. Brunnengräber, Germany)

Haricot beans Tuscan style
Haricots blancs à la toscane
Fagioli all'uccelletto

6 portions

1 kg	haricot beans	2 lb 4 oz
2½ l	water	4½ pt
	10 sage leaves	
	6 cloves of garlic	
approx. 1 dl	olive oil	approx. 3½ fl oz
600 g	peeled tomatoes, canned, with juice	1 lb 5 oz

Soak the beans, then cook in salted water with the addition of 3 cloves of garlic and 5 sage leaves. Pour off the water, but set aside a little of it. Drain the beans well. Heat the oil in an earthenware or fireproof pot with the addition of the garlic which has been finely cut and the sage leaves.

When the garlic is lightly coloured, add the beans, season with salt and freshly ground pepper, and mix carefully. Cook over gentle heat for 20 minutes.

Strain the tomatoes with their juice over the beans and add a little warm water if required. Cover and cook for a further 20 minutes over very low heat, carefully stirring in a little of the cooking water from the beans from time to time. The beans should remain whole, and the sauce should be smooth and creamy.

(Mario De Filippis, Italy)

Endive with scrambled egg
Recipe, page 568
(*Veal cutlets Saxonne,* F. Zodl, Austria)

Stewed fennel
Recipe, page 742
(*Saddle of lamb Françoise Deberdt,* O. Brust, Germany)

Fennel in red wine
Recipe, page 682
(*Veal steak with pear in Roquefort cream au gratin,* K. Brunnengräber, Germany)

Vegetable dumplings
Quenelles de légumes
Knedle od Povrća

8–10 portions   Cooking time: 40–50 minutes

600 g	mixed vegetables:	1 lb 5 oz
	carrots	
	savoy cabbage	
	kohlrabi	
	cauliflower	
	potatoes	
	mushrooms	
200 g	butter	7 oz
50 g	dry breadcrumbs	2 oz
	2 rolls	
	2 eggs	
1 dl	milk	3½ fl oz
250 g	flour	9 oz
	bouillon or water	
	salt	
	pepper, freshly ground	

Chop the vegetables finely and cook gently in 100 g (3½ oz) butter, adding a little water occasionally if required. Dice the rolls and fry in a little butter. Mix with the cooked vegetables.

Whisk the eggs, flour and milk together in a bowl to make a very thick batter. Add the vegetables and diced rolls, and season with salt and pepper. Shape into small balls, repeatedly flouring the hands or dipping them in cold water. Cook the dumplings in salted water, drain well and arrange on a serving dish. Sprinkle with breadcrumbs fried in butter.

(László Csizmadia, Yugoslavia)

Vegetable pudding
Pouding de légumes
Sformato di verdura

500 g	spinach, blanched and sieved	1 lb 2 oz
500 g	Swiss chard, blanched and sieved	1 lb 2 oz
100 g	Parmesan cheese, grated	3½ oz
100 g	butter	3½ oz

Béchamel sauce:

80 g	butter	3 oz
100 g	flour	3½ oz
1 dl	milk	3½ fl oz

Place the vegetables in a pan over low heat and stir in the butter, then the Parmesan. Beat in the Béchamel sauce, which should be very thick and firm, adding only a little at a time and taking care to avoid the formation of lumps.

Butter a fireproof mould or individual dariole moulds thoroughly, dust with dry breadcrumbs and fill with the vegetable mixture. Cook in a bain-marie in an oven preheated to about 250°C (480°F) for 40 minutes.

(Mario De Filippis, Italy)

Carrot moulds
Recipe, page 664
(*Sweetbreads with shrimps,* K. Brunnengräber, Germany)

Carrot purée
Purée de carottes
Karottenmus

4 portions

300 g	young carrots	11 oz
30 g	butter	1 oz
¼ l	mineral water	9 fl oz
8 g	salt	¼ oz
4 g	granulated sugar	⅛ oz
2 cl	dairy cream	1 fl oz

Scrape and slice the carrots. Melt the butter in a pan and fry the carrots lightly without browning. Stir in the mineral water, season with salt and sugar, and cook gently for about 10 minutes. When the liquid has boiled away, work the carrots to a purée with the cream in a mixer. Adjust the seasoning. Keep hot. The purée may be shaped into small dumplings with the help of 2 tablespoons.

(Johann Kögl, Austria)

Stuffed cabbage leaves
Recipe page 457
(*Stewed oxtail Lorraine,* K. Brunnengräber, Germany)

Cabbage balls
Recipe page 495
(*Braised beef Viennese style*, F. Zodl, Austria)

Stuffed kohlrabi
Recipe page 565
(*Veal cutlets Denise*, E. Plachutta, Austria)

Cabbage strudel
See *Hot hors d'oeuvre*, page 272

Stuffed courgettes I
Courgettes farcies

1 kg	courgettes	2 lb 4 oz
	filling as for stuffed peppers	
	dill, finely chopped	

Peel the courgettes and cut off the tip. Hollow out with a small spoon. Stuff in the same way as stuffed peppers. Add a little dill to the sauce. Serve with sour milk (recipe, page 147).

(László Csizmadia, Yugoslavia)

Stuffed courgettes II
Recipe page 721
(*Best end of lamb with green lemon sauce*, F. Kiener, France)

Peppers Italian style
Poivrons doux à l'italienne
Peperonata

4–6 portions

1 kg	red, yellow and green peppers	2 lb 4 oz
	1 medium onion	

	1 clove of garlic, crushed	
500 g	peeled tomatoes, canned	1 lb 2 oz
	or fresh tomatoes, skinned and diced	
1 dl	olive oil	3½ fl oz
	salt	

Peel and slice the onion. Cut the peppers in quarters and seed them, then cut into strips. Cook the onion gently in the olive oil until transparent, add the peppers, cook lightly and add the garlic. When the peppers are half cooked, add the canned tomatoes which have been coarsely cut or the finely diced fresh ones. Continue cooking over medium heat, stirring from time to time to avoid sticking. Season with salt. Cook until the pan is almost dry. Adjust the seasoning. Serve hot or cold.

(Franco Colombani, Italy)

Julienne of peppers
Recipe page 612
(*Stuffed escalope of veal*, Ferdinand Hodler, R. Haupt-Felber, Switzerland)

Ratatouille I
Recipe page 986
(*Lamb pie*, E. Jung, France)

Ratatouille II

10 portions

1 kg	courgettes	2 lb 4 oz
50 g	onions, finely cut	2 oz
500 g	tomatoes, skinned, seeded and coarsely diced	1 lb 2 oz
500 g	red, green and yellow peppers, seeded and cut into strips	1 lb 2 oz
500 g	aubergines, sliced	1 lb 2 oz
2 dl	oil	7 fl oz
	parsley	
	oregano	
	salt	

Cook the onions gently in the oil without colouring, add the tomatoes, then the aubergines and peppers. Season with salt, add the herbs and cook until all the liquid has boiled away.

(Otto Ledermann, Switzerland)

Roquefort tomatoes
Recipe page 718
(*Best end of lamb in a herb crust,* A. Meindl, Austria)

Red cabbage Danish style
Recipe page 808
(*Roast pork Danish style,* K. O. Schmidt, Denmark)

Baked tomatoes with Mozzarella
Recipe page 930
(*Ragoût of rabbit Val Verzasca,* R. Haupt-Felber, Switzerland)

White cabbage Norwegian style
Chou blanc à la norvégienne
Norsk surkål

4–6 portions

750 g	white cabbage, shredded	1 lb 10 oz
	1–2 tablespoons lard	
	1–2 cooking apples	
	approx. 2 teaspoons salt	
	approx. 2 teaspoons caraway	
	1½ tablespoons flour	
½ l	light stock or water	18 fl oz
	½ tablespoon vinegar	
	½ tablespoon sugar	
	1–2 tablespoons redcurrant juice *or* jelly	

Blanch the cabbage in boiling water and drain. Peel, core and slice the apples. Mix them carefully with the cabbage and season with salt. Add the caraway. Fill into a stew pan layer by layer, sprinkling each one with flour. Pour in cold stock or water, cover and cook slowly over low heat. When the cabbage is cooked, add the vinegar, sugar, redcurrant juice or jelly, and lard, and return to the boil. This is a popular Christmas dish in Norway.

(Otto Ramsbacher, Norway)

Celeriac mousse
Mousse de céleri-rave

1 kg	celeriac	2 lb 4 oz
300 g	potatoes	11 oz
50 g	rice	2 oz
100 g	onions, thinly sliced	3½ oz
1½ l	milk	2¾ pt
	salt	
	nutmeg	
50–100 g	butter (as desired)	2–3½ oz

Peel the celeriac and cut into pieces. Peel and dice the potatoes. Cook the celeriac, potatoes, onions and rice in the milk with the addition of salt. Pass through a sieve, add salt and nutmeg to taste, and finish with butter.

(Emile Jung, France)

Braised cabbage
Chou braisé
Párolt káposzta

10 portions   Cooking time: about 25–30 minutes

3 kg	white cabbage	6 lb 10 oz
150 g	lard	5 oz
100 g	onions, sliced	3½ oz
5 cl	white wine vinegar	2 fl oz
30 g	salt	1 oz
80 g	sugar	3 oz
2 g	caraway	half a small teaspoon

Clean the cabbage carefully and shred or cut into fine julienne strips. Sprinkle with a little salt and set aside for 30 minutes.

Cook the sugar to light caramel in the lard, add the onions, mix quickly and sprinkle with caraways. Squeeze the cabbage dry, add the onions, mix and sharpen with a little vinegar. Cook gently, stirring constantly, until the cabbage is pulpy, then continue cooking under cover over medium heat until quite soft.

If desired, white wine may be used instead of vinegar. If red cabbage is used instead of white, it is prepared with red wine vinegar or red wine.

(Zsolt Körmendy, Hungary)

Courgette purée
Purée de courgettes
Purea di zucchine

courgettes
water
salt
butter

Slice the courgettes without peeling, blanch in salted water, pour off the water, drain well and sieve. Melt butter in a sauté pan. Add the courgettes and stir until the pan is dry. Enrich with butter.

(Franco Colombani, Italy)

Potatoes

Swiss rösti potatoes (potato cake)
Rösti

Boil the potatoes in their skins and leave until quite cold. Skin them and grate or flake coarsely. Fry lightly in butter or lard, if possible in a cast iron pan. First turn briefly with a fork, then press down lightly with a palette knife, keeping the potatoes away from the side of the pan. When brown underneath, turn the potato cake over (with the help of a large lid), and brown the other side in hot butter or lard. Turn out on to a round dish.

Apple potato cake
Recipe page 898
(*Pork medallions with Tokay and walnut sauce on apple potato cake,* K. Brunnengräber, Germany)

Potatoes au gratin Jabron style
Gratin du Jabron

2 portions

300 g	potatoes	11 oz
80 g	butter	3 oz
5 dl	dairy cream	18 fl oz
	½ clove of garlic, very finely chopped	
	1 tablespoon Gruyère cheese, grated	
	salt, pepper	

Peel and wash the potatoes, slice them fairly thickly, sauter briefly in butter over low heat, and season with salt and pepper. Transfer to a buttered shallow fireproof dish and mix with the garlic and cheese. Pour the cream over and brown in the oven at 200°C (390°F) for 10 minutes.

(Pierre Gleize, France)

Brown potatoes
Recipe page 808
(*Roast pork Danish style,* K. O. Schmidt, Denmark)

Duchesse potatoes
Recipe page 711
(*Epigrammes of lamb René Carcan*, O. Brust, Germany)

Gratin of potatoes and leeks
Gratin de pommes de terre et de poireaux

6 portions

1 kg	potatoes	2 lb 4 oz
	2 medium leeks	
	1 egg	
2 dl	milk	7 fl oz
2 dl	dairy cream	7 fl oz
	salt	
	butter	

Peel the potatoes and slice thinly. Cut the leeks into 1 cm (⅜ in) slices, mix with the potatoes, season with salt and place in a buttered fireproof dish. Mix together the milk, cream and egg, and pour into the dish. Poach in a bain-marie in the oven for 40 minutes, then brown the top. Serve hot or cold.

(Emile Jung, France)

Potato dumplings
I. recipe page 354
(*Potato dumpling soup Nyirség style*, Z. Körmendy, Hungary)
II. recipe page 461
(*Ragoût of oxtail Palatinate style*, K. Brunnengräber, Germany)

Bohemian potato dumplings
Quenelles de pommes de terre à la bohémienne
České bramborové knedlíky

6 portions   Cooking time: 10 minutes

900 g	potatoes (floury if possible)		2 lb
40 g	butter		1½ oz
approx. 10 g	salt	approx.	⅓ oz
	2 eggs		

| 120 g | flour | 4 oz |
| 120 g | fine semolina | 4 oz |

Boil the potatoes either peeled or unpeeled in salted water, then pour off the water and dry them over the heat or skin them. Pass through a sieve or ricer while still hot and mix at once with the butter, semolina and flour. Add the eggs and salt and knead quickly. Shape into a roll on a floured board. Cut up evenly and form each piece into a round dumpling 4 cm (1½ in) across. Place at once in boiling salted water and cook slowly over moderate heat for 10 minutes, using a skimmer to detach any dumplings sticking to the bottom of the pan. When cooked, lift out carefully with the skimmer and transfer to a hot dish. Brush with melted butter and keep hot.

It is essential to use the dough immediately, as it becomes sticky and loses its firmness if allowed to stand for some time. The dumplings should be cooked in sufficient water to keep them moving without sticking; the best utensil is a large wide saucepan.

The boiled potatoes may be used cold; in this case they are grated or minced. The dumplings are somewhat drier and more brittle. Potato dumplings are mainly served with roast pork, minced meat loaf and similar dishes.

(Vilèm Vrabec, Czechoslovakia)

Swiss potato gratin
Gratin aux pommes de terre
Kartoffelkugel

10 portions   Cooking time: about 2 hours

2 kg	potatoes	4 lb 8 oz
	6 eggs	
100 g	onions	3½ oz
	salt	
	pepper, freshly ground	
	commercial seasoning	
50 g	margarine	2 oz

Mince the potatoes and onions finely, then carefully squeeze dry. Fold in the eggs and add the seasonings. Carefully grease aluminium moulds with margarine, fill with the mixture and bake in an oven preheated to 200°C (390°F) for about 2 hours, or until the top is well browned. Slice and serve hot on heated plates.

(Gérard van Dijk, Switzerland)

Potato pancakes
Recipe page 565
(*Veal cutlets Denise,* E. Plachutta, Austria)

Potato cakes I
Galettes de pommes de terre
Kartoffelpuffer

4–6 portions

1 kg 600	potatoes	3 lb 8 oz
	½ onion, grated	
	2 eggs, beaten	
	salt	
	pepper, freshly ground	
	lard	

Peel the potatoes. Grate half of them finely, drain in a conical strainer and squeeze dry. Grate the remainder coarsely, drain and dry in the same manner. Mix together, add the onion and eggs, and season with salt and pepper. Form into medallions and deep-fry in hot lard until golden brown.

By mixing together finely and coarsely grated potatoes, improved cohesion is achieved.

(Gerhard Gartner, Germany)

Potato cakes II
Recipe page 816
(*Belly of pork Pongau style,* E. Plachutta, Austria)

Potato roll
Recipe page 830
(*Best end of pork with fig stuffing,* E. Plachutta, Austria)

Mint mousseline potatoes
Recipe page 513
(*Tournedos Bercy with mint mousseline potatoes,* K. Brunnengräber, Germany)

Fried potatoes with onions
Pommes de terre aux oignons rôties
Hagymás törtburgonya

10 portions

3 kg	potatoes	6 lb 10 oz
100 g	lard	3½ oz
150 g	onions	5 oz
30 g	salt	1 oz

Boil the potatoes in their skins. Grate them coarsely or slice or flake with a small knife. Cut the onions finely and fry gently in lard until lightly coloured. Add the potatoes and mix well. Season with salt and fry on one side until browned. To serve, turn out on to a warmed dish so that the browned side is uppermost.

(Zsolt Körmendy, Hungary)

Miscellaneous

Stuffed apples
Recipe page 808
(*Roast pork Danish style*, K. O. Schmidt, Denmark)

Apple timbales
Recipe page 652
(*Calf's liver medallions with herb and vinegar sauce and apple timbales*, K. Brunnengräber, Germany)

Prunes
Recipe page 808
(*Roast pork Danish style*, K. O. Schmidt, Denmark)

Lokshen pudding
Vermicelles au four
Lokschenkugel

500 g	vermicelli	1 lb 2 oz
	4 eggs	
150 g	sugar	5 oz
10 g	cinnamon	1/3 oz
200 g	margarine	7 oz
100 g	seedless raisins	3½ oz
	salt	
	breadcrumbs	
	oil	

Cook the vermicelli in a large pan of salted water, refresh under cold running water and drain. Beat the eggs with the sugar, cinnamon and salt, and add the vermicelli. Melt the margarine and add, then stir in the raisins.

Carefully oil an aluminium mould and sprinkle with breadcrumbs. Fill with the pudding mixture and sprinkle the top with breadcrumbs. Bake for 1 hour in an oven preheated to 200°C

(390°F). Slice and serve hot on dessert plates. This pudding may be used as a garnish for any hot kosher dish.

(Gérard van Dijk, Switzerland)

Serbian maize bread
Pain de maîs à la serbe
Srpska Proja

10 portions   Cooking time: 50–60 minutes

600 g	maize meal, sieved	1 lb 5 oz
180 g	lard	6 oz
	5 eggs	
½ l	cold milk	18 fl oz
	a pinch of salt	

Carefully mix the maize meal, lard and eggs with 3 dl (10 fl oz) milk, season with salt and beat for 15 minutes. Add the remaining milk and mix thoroughly again. Fill into a well greased round or rectangular cake tin and bake in a preheated medium oven for 50 to 60 minutes. The finished loaf should be crusty.

This bread is served warm with Serbian cheese or kajmak (recipe, page 147) as an hors d'oeuvre. It is also eaten instead of ordinary bread with various sauerkraut dishes, especially stuffed sauerkraut Serbian style.

In former times, Serbian villagers ate maize bread, baked without eggs and spread with lard, instead of bread made from wheat flour.

(László Csizmadia, Yugoslavia)

Glazed chestnuts
Recipe page 910
(*Escalope of pork with sauerkraut stuffing*, K. Brunnengräber, Germany)

Cottage cheese dumplings
Recipe page 463
(*Ragoût of beef Erdberg style*, E. Faseth, Austria)

Matzo dumplings

Yield – 70 dumplings   Cooking time: 30 minutes

500 g	matzo meal	1 lb 2 oz
	12 eggs	
500 g	vegetable fat, melted	1 lb 2 oz
½ l	water	18 fl oz
	salt	
	commercial seasoning	
	pepper	

Beat the eggs well, then beat in the fat, water and matzo meal. Season and leave to stand for 30 minutes. Wet the hands and shape into balls 2 cm (¾ in) across. Drop them at once into boiling water and poach under cover for 30 minutes.

(Gérard van Dijk, Switzerland)

Parmesan pancakes
Crêpes au parmesan
Kleine Pfannkuchen mit Parmesan

Yield – approx. 30 pancakes

½ l	milk	18 fl oz
½ l	dairy cream	18 fl oz
100 g	butter, melted	3½ oz
40 g	yeast	1½ oz
	salt	
	sugar	
	2 tablespoons Parmesan, grated	
225 g	flour	8 oz
	7 eggs	

Blend the flour and milk together, add the yeast and allow to stand at room temperature for 1 hour. Add the eggs and the remaining ingredients in any order, and mix well. Cook on one side in a wrought iron pancake pan until lightly coloured, then turn and cook in the oven.

(Gerhard Gartner, Germany)

Galuska
Spätzlis ou petits gnocchis à la hongroise

6 portions   Cooking time: 15–18 minutes

500 g	flour	1 lb 2 oz

	6 eggs	
	salt	
1 dl	water	3½ fl oz

Prepare a dough with the eggs, flour, water and salt. Knead until bubbles form. Force with the hand through a special spätzle maker, or place on a board, hold it over boiling water with the left hand and pull off small pieces with the help of a knife. Keep the water boiling while the galuska are cooking. Remove them from the pan with a skimmer when they rise to the surface. Do not cook too many at once to avoid overcooking them by leaving them too long in the water. When cooked, refresh in cold water, drain and toss in hot lard or butter. Season with salt before serving.

(László Csizmadia, Hungary)

Bohemian bread dumplings
Quenelles à la bohémienne
České houskové knedlíky

6 portions   Cooking time: 25 minutes

400 g	flour		14 oz
or 200 g	flour		7 oz
and 200 g	semolina		7 oz
10–20 g	butter	about	½ oz
	3 rolls		
or 150 g	white bread		5 oz
	1 egg		
	or 2 egg yolks		
approx. 5 g	salt	approx.	⅙ oz
¼ l	milk, scalded and cooled		9 fl oz
or ¼ l	soda water		9 fl oz
3 g	baking powder (optional)		½ a rounded teaspoon

Remove the crusts from the rolls, dice them finely, fry in hot butter and leave until cold. Sieve the flour into a bowl, add the eggs (or yolks) which have been beaten with the milk, season with salt and beat with a spoon to a smooth, shiny batter which does not stick to the spoon. Add the diced rolls and mix well. Sprinkle the top with a little flour, cover the bowl with a cloth, and rest for 30 minutes. This procedure gives the dumplings a particularly good flavour.

Transfer to a floured board and shape into two oblong rolls. Plunge these into boiling salted water and simmer for 25 minutes, turning them frequently with a large spoon. When cooked, remove from the pan and cut at once into slices 1 cm (⅜ in) thick. It is best to use a fairly large wide pan for these dumplings.

If the dumplings are made with soda water, it is added to the flour separately from the eggs, and the batter is not left to rest after adding the rolls, but shaped and cooked at once. If baking powder is used, it is first well mixed with the flour. If a resting period is desired, the baking powder is mixed with a little flour only, and added afterwards.

The dumplings make a particularly suitable accompaniment for all kinds of fried and roast pork, as well as many other meat dishes.

(Vilèm Vrabec, Czechoslovakia)

Austrian dumpling
Serviettenknödel

10 portions

	10 day-old rolls, diced	
	4 eggs	
¼ l	milk	9 fl oz
50 g	butter	2 oz
	parsley, chopped	
	salt	
	nutmeg	

Mix the eggs, milk, salt, nutmeg and parsley well and pour over the diced rolls. Roll in a buttered napkin, tie up and boil in salted water or steam for about 30 minutes. Remove from the napkin and cut into slices the thickness of one finger.

(Eduard Mayer, Austria)

Spinach spätzle
I. recipe page 608
(*Veal steak Klöntal style*, W. Bartenbach, Switzerland)

II. recipe page 682
(*Veal steak with pear in Roquefort cream au gratin*, K. Brunnengräber, Germany)

Cereals and Pasta

Rice cutlets
Recipe page 653
(*Stuffed calf's liver slices with chestnut sauce and small onions*, K. Brunnengräber, Germany)

Farfel

10 portions   Cooking time: about 2 hours

1 kg	flour	2 lb 4 oz
	8 eggs	
10 g	salt	⅓ oz
100 g	margarine	3½ oz
100 g	onions, finely cut	3½ oz
	salt	
	pepper, freshly ground	
	commercial seasoning	

Mix the flour and salt together well. Stir in the eggs and continue stirring until all the flour has been worked in and has formed pearl-size lumps. Transfer to a metal tray and air-dry for 24 hours, then grate coarsely.

Heat the margarine in a pan, add the onions and cook gently without colouring, then add the grated dough (farfel) and continue cooking briefly. Pour in about 2 l (3½ pt) water, bring to the boil and cook for about 2 hours, stirring constantly. If the farfel becomes too dry, add a little water. Season with salt, pepper and commercial seasoning.

(Gérard van Dijk, Switzerland)

Rice and goose liver timbale
Recipe page 844
(*Pork cutlets Kodaly*, Z. Körmendy, Hungary)

Semolina gnocchi
Recipe page 662
(*Sweetbreads Zurich aristocrats' style*, R. Haupt-Felber, Switzerland)

Gnocchi Roman style
I. recipe page 537
(*Stuffed breast of veal Alsatian style,* J. Esslinger, France)

II. recipe page 617
(*Veal ragoût Viennese style,* E. Faseth, Austria)

Semolina dumplings
Recipe page 495
(*Braised beef Viennese style,* F. Zodl, Austria)

Sweet corn fritters
Recipe page 718
(*Best end of lamb in a herb crust,* A. Meindl, Austria)

Maize cakes
Galettes de maîs
Maisplätzchen

2½ dl	milk	9 fl oz
2½ dl	water	9 fl oz
180 g	coarse maize meal	6 oz
70 g	butter	2½ oz
	2 egg yolks	
	salt	
	nutmeg	
	Parmesan cheese, grated	

Place the milk and water in a pan with 40 g (1½ oz) butter and bring to the boil. Add salt and nutmeg and pour in the maize meal in a steady stream while stirring. Add the egg yolks and Parmesan and mix well. Spread on a metal tray and leave until cold. Cut into rounds and fry in the rest of the butter until golden.

(Ewald Plachutta, Austria)

Nockerln
Recipe page 962
(*Veal cutlets Bakony style,* Z. Körmendy, Hungary)

Noodles Alsatian style
Nouilles à l'alsacienne

500 g	fine white flour, sieved	1 lb 2 oz
10 g	salt	⅓ oz
	8 eggs	
	1 teaspoon wine vinegar	
	butter	

Beat the eggs in a large bowl, add the salt and vinegar, then the flour a little at a time. Work to a smooth dough, wrap in a white cloth and allow to rest for about 1 hour. Divide the dough into pieces the size of a duck's egg. Pin each one out 2 mm (¹/₁₀ in) thick on a floured board. Air-dry the dough, either on a clothes line or flat, in which case it should be turned frequently.

After 20 minutes, dust lightly with flour and roll each sheet of dough up separately. Cut into strips 2 mm (¹/₁₀ in) thick. Spread out thinly on a board. Set aside some of the noodles for frying. Drop the rest into a pan containing 2 l (3½ pt) boiling salted water. Remove from the heat and leave to stand for 8 minutes. Drain well, dish, pour melted butter over, turn and decorate with a handful of noodles fried in butter.

(Patrick Klipfel, Armand Roth, France)

Fresh noodles
Nouilles aux oeufs
Tagliatelle fresche

6–10 portions, depending on use

1 kg	flour	2 lb 4 oz
	4 eggs	
3 dl	water	10 fl oz

Work the ingredients to a pliable dough, pin out very thinly on a floured board and cut into narrow strips. Shape into nests and dry.

(Ivo Balestra, Switzerland)

Spinach noodles I
Nouilles vertes
Tagliatelle verdi

6–10 portions, depending on use

1 kg	flour	2 lb 4 oz
	4 eggs	
100 g	spinach, blanched	3½ oz
2 dl	water	7 fl oz

Work the spinach to a very fine purée in the mixer. Add to the remaining ingredients and work to a pliable dough. Roll out on a floured board and cut into narrow strips. Shape into nests and dry.

(Ivo Balestra, Switzerland)

Spinach noodles II
Recipe page 675
(*Veal piccata Cavalieri,* A. Mosimann, Great Britain)

Tomato noodles
Nouilles à la tomate
Tagliatelle al pomodoro

6–10 portions, depending on use

1 kg	flour	2 lb 4 oz
	4 eggs	
200 g	tomatoes, skinned and seeded	7 oz
	1 tablespoon tomato purée	
2 dl	water	7 fl oz

Blanch the tomatoes and work to a purée in the mixer. Add to the remaining ingredients and work to a pliable dough. Roll out on a floured board and cut into narrow strips. Shape into nests and dry.

(Ivo Balestra, Switzerland)

Rice pilaf
I. recipe page 604
(*Veal quenelles with rice pilaf,* O. Brust, Germany)
II. recipe page 899
(*Pork medallions gipsy fashion,* E. Cederholm, Denmark)
III. recipe page 598
(*Skewered beef olives Hôtel des Bergues,* O. Ledermann, Switzerland)

Polenta
Recipe page 930
(*Ragoût of rabbit Val Verzasca,* R. Haupt-Felber, Switzerland)

Chanterelle risotto
Risotto aux girolles
Risotto con gallinacci

800 g	Italian Vialone rice	1 lb 12 oz
60 g	onions, finely chopped	2 oz
	1 clove of garlic, finely chopped	
1 dl	oil	3½ fl oz
100 g	butter	3½ oz
250 g	chanterelles, canned	9 oz
1½–2 l	bouillon	2¾–3½ pt
1 dl	white wine	3½ fl oz

Cook the onions and garlic gently in the oil and half the butter without colouring, then add the rice and cook gently while stirring. Moisten with the wine and stir in the hot bouillon a little at a time. Cook the rice 'al dente' (keeping it firm to the bite), stirring very frequently. Towards the end of the cooking time, add the chanterelles which have been warmed in the canning liquid and well drained. Finish with the rest of the butter. The grains of rice should be separate and the risotto should be slightly liquid. Chanterelles have a very fine aroma; consequently, the risotto should be served without cheese. If desired, mix with 1 tablespoon chopped parsley before serving.

(Italy)

Tarhonya

4 portions   Cooking time: 20–25 minutes

180 g	tarhonya	6 oz
70 g	lard	2½ oz
	1 small onion, finely chopped	
	½ bunch parsley, finely chopped	
	salt	
9 dl	water	1½ pt

Cook the onion and parsley gently in hot lard. Add the tarhonya and brown very lightly in the same way as rice. Stir in the water, season with salt and cook over gentle heat for 15 minutes. Serve very hot, mixed with a little hot lard if desired.

(László Csizmadia, Hungary)

INDEX—NATIONAL DISHES

GERMANY

INDEX

Page numbers in **bold** refer to illustrations.